Lawyer's Lawyer

John W. Davis striding across the plaza of the Supreme
Court Building after arguing the steel seizure case of 1952

Lawyer's Lawyer

THE LIFE OF JOHN W. DAVIS

《 《《 《   》 》》》

William H. Harbaugh

NEW YORK   OXFORD UNIVERSITY PRESS
1973

FOR WAYNE

PREFACE

This book could not have been written without the cooperation of John W. Davis' daughter, Julia Davis Healy. In 1958 Mrs. Healy made her father's personal and miscellaneous legal papers available to me, on the understanding that I would write a full-scale, documented biography. With the same tolerance and generosity which characterized her father's personal relations, she emphasized that she would retain no right to censor. Three years later she gave the entire collection of papers to Yale University. Her sole restriction was that no one could publish material from them without my consent until this biography was published. That restriction was removed a decade ago, when I realized that other writing and professional obligations were preventing me from devoting my full energies to the manuscript. Mrs. Healy has not seen my final draft, and she is not responsible for any inclusions, exclusions, or interpretations.

I am also heavily indebted to three men who were John W. Davis' partners: Ralph M. Carson, Porter R. Chandler, and George A. Brownell. They supplied a fund of anecdotes, clarified many technical points, and made numerous constructive suggestions. They also corrected many errors. Throughout, they adhered scrupulously to the American Bar Association's Code of Professional Responsibility on the confidentiality of relations between client and counsel. They did not agree with many of my interpretations and emphases in the draft that they read, and I suspect that they will disagree with many aspects of this published version. They did not see the final draft, and neither they nor any other members of John W. Davis' firm, now Davis Polk & Wardwell, are responsible for Mr. Davis' biography as I have written it.

A grant I received from the Davis estate in 1958 enabled me to organize John W. Davis' papers and conduct interviews with dozens of his old friends, colleagues, and acquaintances. An appointment as Senior Fellow at the Yale Law School in 1960–61 gave me an opportunity to audit various courses and read some law. Subsequent grants

from the American Philosophical Society, the American Council of
Learned Societies, and the research committees of Bucknell University and the University of Virginia relieved me of summer teaching
duties on four occasions. A Sesquicentennial Fellowship at the University of Virginia in 1971–72 freed me from all teaching and colle-
giate responsibilities for a semester.

My former secretary at Bucknell, Mrs. Mary Farley, was most
helpful in transcribing my first draft. Three fine typists in the University of Virginia's Center for Advanced Studies—Shirley J. Sands,
Patricia B. Crow, and Maebelle L. Morris—and a superb grammar-
ian, Frances S. Lackey, met my final deadlines with skill and equa-
nimity. I have also benefited greatly from the research assistance of
a number of able students: Robert Pringle, Michael Ebner, Jack T.
Camp, Darden Asbury Pyron, Robert A. Murdock, Mark Edelman,
and J. Brent Tarter. Mr. Murdock and another assistant, Frank
Roche of the University of Virginia Law School, were especially helpful in legal research at an intermediate stage. This past year Mr.
Tarter has investigated numerous problems with scholarly imagination. He has also suggested stylistic changes, caught countless errors in
the galleys, and compiled the index.

The scope of this work has made my professional debts even greater
than normal. Many friends and colleagues in history, law, and other
disciplines at the University of Virginia and elsewhere have made
helpful suggestions on selected chapters. Among them are David
Burner, Paul T. David, Robert Dawidoff, Charles Dew, David H.
Flaherty, David Grimsted, R. Justus Hanks, Julian N. Hartt, August Meier, Willie Lee Rose, Elliott Rudwick, Roy Schotland, David
Underdown, Preston Warren, J. Harvie Wilkinson III, and Calvin
Woodard. Several seminar students and honors candidates have also
made contributions, as cited in the notes.

My mentor, Arthur S. Link, who has provided wise counsel for
twenty-five years, read all the chapters on the Wilson period with his
usual acumen. Professor Wythe Holt of the University of Alabama
School of Law made a great many perceptive comments on my treatment of Davis as a lawyer. Professor Richard Lowitt of the University of Kentucky shared his extraordinary knowledge of twentieth-
century political history. William W. Abbot, my friend and department
chairman at the University of Virginia, read the entire manuscript
with insight and sensitivity at a critical juncture. More generally,
my luncheon sessions with Dumas Malone, that Jeffersonian gentleman and master biographer, have exposed me to a rare and ripened
historical wisdom.

I am pleased to acknowledge the permission given by a number of individuals, institutions, and commercial organizations to publish photographs: Washington and Lee University for the photograph of the Colonnade and for the portraits of John W. Brockenbrough, James A. Quarles, Charles A. Graves, and John Randolph Tucker; the Clarksburg Public Library for the picture of John Jay Jackson: G. Wayne Smith for that of Nathan Goff, Jr.; and the Library of Congress for those of the Supreme Court in 1916, of John W. Davis as Solicitor General, and of Robert M. La Follette. United Press International furnished the photographs of John G. Johnson, of Davis denouncing the Ku Klux Klan in 1924, of Davis conferring with Ferdinand Pecora, and of Davis and Thurgood Marshall, as well as the group photograph of Rosika Schwimmer, Douglas C. Macintosh, and Marie A. Bland and that of J. Lindsay Almond, Davis, and T. Justin Moore. The frontispiece, a photograph of Davis striding across the plaza of the Supreme Court Building, is also published by permission of United Press International.

Wide World Photographs gave me permission to publish the following: Davis and Charles W. Bryan; Pecora, Carter Glass, and J. P. Morgan; Theodore Kiendl and Davis; and James F. Byrnes and Davis. The individual pictures of Charles Evans Hughes, Philip B. Perlman, Alger Hiss, Davis before the House committee, and J. Robert Oppenheimer are also from Wide World. The photograph of Calvin Coolidge is reproduced by permission of Underwood and Underwood. That of Felix Frankfurter is from the Law School Collection of Harvard University. Those of Davis and his wife attending a polo match, of Davis and Morgan conferring, of the Davises and J. P. Morgan aboard the *Corsair,* and of Davis and Isador Kresel are Acme photographs. All others are from private collections. Copies of all these photographs, and several which have not been published, have been deposited in the Sterling Library of Yale University.

I should like further to thank Byron Hollinshead and Sheldon Meyer of the Oxford University Press. They understood me and what I was trying to do—to describe Davis the man, and to put Davis the political figure and Davis the practicing attorney into both historical context and historical perspective. In addition, Mr. Meyer assigned the manuscript to an exceptionally capable editor, Caroline Taylor. She has made editing an informative, stimulating, and congenial experience.

Finally, it is my pleasant duty to acknowledge the contributions of my personal staff: Lyn Hartridge, William Talbot, and Henry Richmond. They borrowed (permanently) scores of my pens and pencils;

they claimed proprietary rights to my scissors, Scotch tape, and best bond paper; they broke my typewriter three, and probably four, times; they compelled me—always at the moment of an intellectual breakthrough—to play ping-pong or pass the football (Ricky's friends Charlie McClellan and Rufus Davis are implicated in this); they made me their chauffeur on instant demand; and, more recently, the oldest, and first named above, subjected me to those very large sounds which she and her circle denominate as music. Had they not done these things, I can almost truthfully say, the manuscript would have been completed six months earlier. But to what consequence?

To their mother, who helped much at the beginning and again at the end, I dedicate this book.

W.H.H.

Chaplin, Conn.
July 1973

CONTENTS

We reach a different plane of social and moral values when we pass to the privileges and immunities that have been taken over from the . . . federal bill of rights and brought within the Fourteenth Amendment. . . . [N]either liberty nor justice would exist if they were sacrificed. . . . This is true . . . of freedom of thought and speech. Of that freedom one may say that it is the matrix, the indispensable condition, of nearly every other form of freedom.

BENJAMIN CARDOZO

Human rights and rights of property are not different or antagonistic but parts of one and the same thing going to make up the bundle of rights which constitute American liberty. History furnishes no instance where the right of man to acquire and hold property has been taken away without the complete destruction of liberty in all its forms.

JOHN W. DAVIS

Prologue

At 12:24 Monday afternoon, May 12, 1952, a stately, white-haired gentleman of seventy-nine years rose from the counsel table and began his one hundred and thirty-ninth oral argument in the United States Supreme Court. A man of somewhat more than moderate height, he had a fair, almost pink, complexion and a pleasantly forceful expression. He wore a dark sack coat and matching vest, morning trousers of subdued grays, a starched white shirt, and a striped black and gray four-in-hand. From his upper pocket protruded a three-pointed white handkerchief. A plain gold watch chain was stretched across his vest, adding to the aura of simple elegance and quiet authority.

By then John W. Davis was a living legend among lawyers. He had already made more oral arguments in the Supreme Court than any lawyer since the age of Daniel Webster, and this, his next to last, was to be his greatest. Davis had first come into prominence as a Congressman from West Virginia in 1912, when his colleagues pronounced him the ablest lawyer in the House of Representatives. He was so esteemed as an advocate that, during his five years as Solicitor General of the United States from 1913 to 1918, every member of the Supreme Court expressed the wish that President Woodrow Wilson would appoint him to the high tribunal. Eventually, Oliver Wendell Holmes, William Howard Taft, Learned Hand, and Hugo Black would term him one of the most persuasive advocates they had ever heard.

As Ambassador to the Court of St. James's at the end of World War I, Davis earned the near universal affection of British leaders, including King George V. In 1924 he won the Democratic presidential nomination on the one hundred and third ballot of the long fratricidal convention in Madison Square Garden. Following his defeat by Calvin

Coolidge that November, he faded into political obscurity, to re-
emerge briefly a decade later as one of the organizers of the anti-New
Deal Liberty League. Meanwhile, he became head of an eminent Wall
Street law firm and counsel to the J P Morgan Co. and several of the
most powerful corporations in the nation. He sat by Morgan's side
during the sensational Pecora investigation of 1933, and in the middle
and late 1930's he argued several test cases of important New Deal
laws.

Davis also took a number of public interest cases without fee. He
served as counsel to the Rev. Dr. Douglas C. Macintosh, the Yale theologian and selective conscientious objector. And he was of counsel to
Dr. J. Robert Oppenheimer in his appeal to the Atomic Energy Commission for restoration of his security clearance. He was also involved
indirectly in the Alger Hiss affair. In addition, he defended several
members of the bench and bar on misconduct charges of one sort or
another. He closed out his career in the Supreme Court as counsel for
the state of South Carolina in 1954 in an epic duel with Thurgood
Marshall of the National Association for the Advancement of Colored
People in the school segregation suit.

As Davis opened his oral argument in May of 1952, in a chamber
overcrowded with high government officials, labor union leaders, and
corporate executives, he prepared to assert that President Harry S
Truman had flagrantly violated the Constitution of the United States
and had imperiled the freedom of the American people by seizing the
steel industry to avert a strike five weeks earlier.

« BOOK I »

The Growth of a Lawyer

CHAPTER 1

Origins

Let it be written among the laws of the Persians and the Medes, that it be not altered.

ESTHER I:19

« I »

John William Davis was descended from Caleb Davis, a clockmaker who lived in the Shenandoah Valley and was probably born near Annapolis, Maryland, in 1767. The line was predominantly Scots-Irish, though the name is Welsh. In 1816 Caleb's oldest son, John, settled in Clarksburg, Virginia, a picturesquely sited village of six or seven hundred inhabitants some 150 miles west of the Blue Ridge. It lay in a cup 1100 feet above sea level, at the confluence of Elk Creek and the West Fork of the Monongahela River, in what is now the north central part of West Virginia.[1]

Clarksburg's leading citizens were always oriented outward, first toward Pittsburgh and the Ohio River towns, later toward Baltimore as well. They seem to have been as informed and national in outlook as most Northern villagers, and after the Baltimore & Ohio Railroad came through in 1856, they read the metropolitan newspapers on the day of publication. The inner community was Presbyterian in tone. The substantial classes were thrifty, ambitious, and moralistic in the Calvinist manner, and only their graciousness and softness of speech distinguished them from small-town Yankees. Travelers found the men kind and hospitable, the ladies refined and educated. A young French visitor recorded his impressions in 1846:

The denizens of Clarksburg are chiefly of Old Virginia descent, and constitute a somewhat exclusive conservative set with all the traditions and social prejudices, pertaining to an ancient moss grown aristocratic town. . . . With very few exceptions there was but very little actual wealth to back up their pretensions, which were by common consent founded upon antiquity of pedigree and superior culture and manners. The language was uniformly correct, their conversation refined and their hospitality generous within their means.[2]

Clarksburg had been named for George Rogers Clark following permanent settlement in 1773. It soon became the seat of Harrison County. Bishop Francis Asbury, the indefatigable Methodist Episcopal circuit rider, preached there to a crowd of seven hundred in 1788, and in 1790 the Baptists put up the town's first church. But when Randolph Academy, a branch of the College of William and Mary and the first chartered institution of learning west of the Alleghenies, opened its doors in 1795, its master was a Presbyterian clergyman. The village soon became a collecting point for cattle, which were driven west to the Ohio River. Furs and skins were also prepared for pack-shipment east, and cornmeal and whiskey were floated down the Monongahela to Pittsburgh.[3]

Caleb Davis' son John established a saddle and harness business with his younger brother, Rezin, in 1819. Six years later he married Eliza Arnold Steen, the schoolteacher daughter of Scots-Irish immigrants. A tall, raw-boned man with huge hands, bushy eyebrows, and a shock of straight upright hair which eventually whitened, John Davis was powerful in physique, stern of countenance, and pronounced in conviction. He served several terms as a justice of the peace and one as county sheriff. He was an exacting businessman, respected for his fairness. As a ruling Presbyterian elder, he disdained the emotionalism of the Baptists and Methodists. "You say . . . the North Church has a great revival," he wrote his son in 1854; "they have had a meeting in progress for several weeks, and have made a great noise, and I hope they have done some good, yet I fear that the passions and not the heart has been affected."[4]

« II »

John Davis' firstborn son, John James, later the father of John William, had no disposition to enter the saddler's trade or any other; from his youth he was enamored of words, logic, and forensics. Soon after his seventeenth birthday in 1852 he began to read law in the office of George H. Lee, former judge of the Supreme Court of Appeals of Virginia and one of a half-dozen gifted men who gave regional distinction to Clarksburg's bar. In 1854 he entered the Lexington Law School, forerunner of the Washington and Lee School of Law.[5]

The school's founder and only instructor was United States District Judge J. W. Brockenbrough. A genial, kindly man with a quick and hearty laugh, Judge Brockenbrough had studied in Winchester under Judge Henry St. George Tucker, son of the annotator of Blackstone's *Commentaries*. In 1837 he himself edited two volumes of John Marshall's circuit decisions. Twelve years later he established the Lexington Law School, in the persuasion that "every man is under a high moral obligation to render himself useful . . . in the sphere, be it humble or exalted, which Providence has allotted to him."[6]

Judge Brockenbrough divided his score or so of students into two classes and assigned them the standard treatises of the day.* He eschewed formal lecturing because it was "quite idle to expect that the student should comprehend and digest a long lecture from merely having it read from the professor's chair." Instead, he quizzed rigorously, explicated obscure passages, and gave updated illustrations of the treatises' abstract propositions. He also tried to imbue his students with his own ideals as they had come down through the Tuckers from Thomas Jefferson's teacher, George Wythe:

> I trust, gentlemen, that in selecting the law as your profession, you have been influenced by other and higher considerations than that it may secure you mere social position, or even that the bar is the avenue to political and judicial honors. I hope you have consulted both your taste and genius in resolving to dedicate your talents to the cultivation of a science which is beset with more difficulties, both of theory and practice, than any other. . . .
> . . . I never knew a successful lawyer who did not love his profession with an ardent, enthusiastic love.

Yet he knew that idealism was not enough: "The cause is ended, the victory is won! Clients now pour in upon you, who before had none.

---

* Stephen's and Tucker's *Blackstone;* Starkie and Greenleaf on evidence; Stephen, Chitty, Mitford, and Gould on pleading; Lube on equity pleading; Lomax's digest of real property, and the same author's work on executors and administrators. He also used Conkling's book on the civil, criminal, and admiralty jurisdiction of the federal courts, and, when it became available, Mathews' *Digest of the Statute Law of Virginia.*

. . . Your reputation is now established . . . and the voice of hissing envy shall not retard your onward march." [7]

John J. Davis carried through life a respect and affection for Judge Brockenbrough such as he felt for few other men. From Brockenbrough he acquired a belief in natural law, a reverence for the Constitution, and a conviction that property rights were sacrosanct—principles which girded his own long and brilliant career at the bar.

Shortly before his twentieth birthday in 1855, Davis opened a law office in Clarksburg. A gangling young man more than six feet in height, he weighed less than 130 pounds and had a long somber face which he later covered with a patriarchal beard. From his youth he fretted constantly about his health. "Far from well, far from well" was his reply to the most routine inquiries about his well-being. As his son remarked, "he's the hardest human being . . . to tell how he really is. When mortal agony and cut finger evoke the same expression the patient might as well be dumb so far as any light he throws upon his condition is concerned." [8]

John J. Davis was so self-conscious that he kept the blinds drawn when he first went into practice. He was uncomfortable in almost any society, but he lavished affection upon animals. At home he was unpredictable. "We never knew what mood [he] . . . would bring home to dinner," his granddaughter recalled, "but the chances were against it being a bright one." When not eating in silence, he would provoke his wife to argument with a disputatious, but always impersonal, remark; only late in life did he show a jovial side. Like many men of strong passions, however, he inspired affection. "Father has his foibles, which anyone can see," his son also wrote, "but I admire and love him more than any man I know." [9]

In the courtroom or on the platform John J.'s driving compulsion to win or convert transformed him. He larded his speeches with adverbs, adjectives, and obscure classical allusions, yet his logic flowed clearly from his fixed assumptions; even his most emotion-ridden passages supported his main line of argument. He was unmatched in Harrison County for ease of delivery and flow of words, and he shunned the devices of the studied speaker. He would reach his main point quickly, then sustain it for an hour or more through force of conviction and power of rhetoric. In many a doubtful case his vivid word pictures moved juries to tears and won a favorable verdict. [10]

A merciless debater, John J. paid no reverence to age and gave no quarter to youth. More than once he addressed a cantankerous judge

as "Your worship," and in one unforgettable scene he was threatened
with contempt in a federal court. Lowering his voice near the end of his
summation, he pointed his long, thin forefinger at the prosecution's
phalanx of witnesses and said that it was "hard for one man to contend with the world"; swinging the finger around until it was aimed at
the prosecutor, he added, "the flesh"; then, shaking it menacingly at
the judge, he hissed, "and the devil." [11]

John J. seems never to have doubted the soundness of his reasoning
or the righteousness of his cause. "I have never known any man who
was more insistent on making up his own mind and really less inclined to yield to the opinions of others," his son reflected years later.
John J. regarded himself as a Jeffersonian, and in a literal sense he
was; but, in the manner of states' rightists then and since, he ripped
the great Virginian's strictures against federal power from their historical context and transformed them into philosophic absolutes. No speculation on the organic nature of law, no musings on the changing needs
of each generation, ever shook John J.'s belief in immutable principles. The Jefferson who wrote that "laws and institutions must go
hand in hand with the progress of the human mind" and that each
generation "has a right" to amend the Constitution as "new discoveries
are made" and "new truths disclosed" was alien to his mind. A Calvinist to the marrow, John J. was closer to Calhoun than to Jefferson in
spirit. He kept the gloomy South Carolinian's portrait in his library,
and he freely conceded that if only Calhoun had not challenged the
Ark of the Covenant itself, he, rather than the optimistic Monticello
philosopher, would have been his beau ideal.[12]

« III »

John J. Davis first rose to prominence as a twenty-five-year-old dele-
gate-elect to the Virginia General Assembly during the bitter debate
over secession in the winter of 1860–61. From the onset of the crisis he
condemned the doctrines of William L. Yancey and Jefferson Davis as
"heresy," and no sooner had South Carolina fixed upon its fateful
course than he wrote his fiancée, Anna Kennedy of Baltimore, that
"men in their rage threaten to pull down the temple of Liberty and
trample Freedom under their feet." He predicted that Virginia would
hold a secessionist convention dominated by "spies" who would use all
means, "fair or foul, to inflame the public mind . . . [and] excite and
arouse the worst and most depraved portion of the population, like

the Yancey vigilance committee." And he urged publicly that a convention be held "for the purpose of adopting proper measures for forming a new State in the Union" if Virginia seceded.[13]

Young Davis prayed that extreme action would be unnecessary. "I yield to no one . . . in devotion to the South. I love the sunny clime, its people and its customs and institutions, and it is because I *do* love these and believe that their preservation depends upon the unity of the government and federal protection, that I am for maintaining that government." He insisted, nevertheless, that if Virginia seceded, economics would dictate the separation of the northwestern counties from the Old Dominion. "It will be our only hope of safety," he wrote just before Virginia ratified the ordinance of secession. "We have no intercourse with the East. Our commerce & trade is all with Maryland & Pennsylvania. Cut us off from them and we are a ruined people." [14]

John J.'s pro-slavery views almost made him oppose the New State Movement. "The Northern fanatics seem bent on destroying . . . slavery. I look upon secession and abolition as twin brothers." Only, he confessed, because he was "bound and biased" by the will of his constituents did he finally support creation of a new state.[15]

As a member of the new West Virginia House of Delegates, Davis declaimed against bills to confiscate rebel property, impose test oaths, and free the slaves gradually. The radicals, he complained, "have never told us what disposition they intend to make of the negroes after they are free." He spoke three hours against censuring State Senator John S. Carlile of Clarksburg for his refusal to support West Virginia's petition for statehood. And he cried "dictation" when the West Virginia Constitutional Convention adopted an emancipation clause under pressure from Congress. He was snubbed by old friends. He lost most of his clients. He was denounced in the press. He was twice threatened physically.[16] Nothing, it seemed, could stop him from speaking out.

In 1863 Davis was forced out of politics temporarily because of his opposition to the New State Movement. In 1870, he returned to the House of Delegates where he opposed ratification of the Fifteenth (suffrage) Amendment because it would "by one stroke make the negroes our equals." Nominated for Congress that summer, he announced that he stood for "the white man's party . . . [and] a white man's government, instituted by white men for the benefit of white men." His views contrasted sharply with those of his opponent, Nathan Goff, Jr., Union war hero and scion of a well-to-do Clarksburg merchant family. "I am for the Fifteenth Amendment," Goff declared, as he and Davis stumped the district together. "It is part of the constitution of the land. . . . I respect every word of that sacred instrument. . . . I believe that all men should be free and independent. . . . The accident of birth, of fortune, of race, or color . . . should add nothing to or take nothing from the right . . . of franchise." [17]

Neither Goff's appeal for human equality nor the Republican press' plea to Union veterans to vote as they shot availed. Davis won by a heavy majority, and he took to Washington the struggle for white supremacy, states' rights, and an unamendable fundamental law.[18]

On March 23, 1872, in a speech worthy of Calhoun, Davis asserted in the House that the Fourteenth and Fifteenth amendments had been fraudulently adopted and that they subverted the Constitution because they usurped the inviolable rights of the states. He conceded that the voluntary absence of the seceding states at the time of the Thirteenth's ratification put that Amendment in a somewhat different light, but he charged that it too encroached upon the rights of the people. Slaves were property, and Congress had no power "even under the guise of amendments" to allow three-fourths of the states "to deprive the citizens of either a single State or one fourth of the States of any species of property whatever." [19]

Davis also denounced a bill to guarantee Negroes equal rights in inns, public conveyances, theaters, and other public places. "This feeble attempt to evade nature's law and crush out by legislation prejudices implanted by the Deity in the breast of the white man can only result in injury to both." He would place no obstacles in the way of the blacks' advancement; on the contrary, he wished them Godspeed. But he felt duty-bound both to affirm his belief "in the superiority" of his own race and to denounce attempts "to degrade it by a forced equality and an involuntary association with an inferior race . . . as impious and wicked." [20]

Meanwhile, Davis' refusal to support the regular Democrats' endorsement of the Republican candidate, Horace Greeley, for the Presidency in 1872 compelled him to stand for re-election as an Independent Democrat. He won comfortably, then lost his seat in 1874 as a result of his vote for the so-called "Salary Grab" bill to increase Congressmen's salaries from $5000 to $7500. Six years later he made an abortive bid for the United States Senate.[21]

By 1880 the North's acquiescence in the South's repression of the black man had settled the race issue for John J. Davis; for the next thirty years he vented his spleen on big business and its spokesmen in the Republican party. He charged them with creating an aristocracy of wealth more despotic than any in the Old World. He repeatedly quoted Jefferson's maxim, "that government is best which governs least." He endorsed the agrarian Democrats' effort to shift the tax burden: "What is wrong with this income tax? Ask . . . any Republican gathering, and . . . they all begin to croak at once, like frogs in a swamp." He even broke with "McKinley's Aid Society," as he labeled the conservative Cleveland wing of the Democratic party, in 1896. The gold standard, declared Davis, was imposed by "the compact forces of the organized, unscrupulous and desperate money power"; government by injunction was a device "to suppress" labor's right to combine against the great corporations for its own protection.[22]

John J. Davis lacked both the will to forgive and the capacity to forget. His problem, mused his son, was that he never understood the difference between dissent and apostasy. In his old age he consoled himself in the realization that even his enemies regarded him as incorruptible and that bench and bar alike recognized his preeminence in court. "I remember the feeling of apprehension . . . when I found myself aligned against him," remarked one of his adversaries. "What tremendous force and ability and persuasive powers were his!" Davis also found satisfaction in the conviction that law was a profession, not a business, and in the untold hours he had spent defending farmers, laborers, and Negroes for petty fees. Among his papers is a moving tribute by a young newspaper publisher from a neighboring town:

> In order that you might keep in close touch with the great throbbing heart of the common people you have withheld your valued professional services from the great corporations and those interests that prey upon the masses. . . . Of course it is a lawyer's privilege to hire himself out to any dirty corporation or thieving combine that will offer him a tempting salary; but he cannot avail himself of that privilege and expect to retain the confidence and respect of his fellow men.[23]

« IV »

For more than half a century John J. Davis was married to a woman his opposite in all but strength of character. He first met Anna Kennedy, the daughter of a Baltimore lumber merchant of Scots-Irish and English Quaker stock, in 1858. She had just been graduated from the Baltimore Women's College, the second institution in the nation to confer degrees on women. A short, plump girl with an attractive face framed by brown curls that tumbled to her shoulders, she could be gay and gregarious, but she was also tough-minded, strong-willed, and self-possessed. Her son remembered her as the "most commanding person" he ever knew, her granddaughter, as "the mistress of herself."

Through life John J. fought unsuccessfully to convert Anna to his own point of view. "Em," he would say to his oldest daughter, "your mother is mulish; she is *mulish,* Em!" In time she became more liberal than her husband. ("I tell you Anna," he often said in his old age, "read the history of the Roman Empire. We are taking the same path. Plain living and high thinking are no more.") For years, indeed, Anna taught free-thinking classes on the exegesis of the Bible, while still dutifully attending the little Presbyterian church that John J. served as guiding elder. "I haven't believed in . . . [the Virgin birth] since I was able to think for myself," she once confided to her granddaughter. "Christ's place in history and the value of his teaching are not dependent on a physical miracle." She refused to let her son be christened.

John J. Davis and Anna Kennedy were married in Baltimore in the summer of 1862. They returned to Clarksburg on the last train to get through before Jackson's cavalry tore up the B. & O. lines, and they moved in with his parents, who both died within five years. Following his service in Congress, John J. built his own house on a two-acre, maple-shaded slope on Lee Street, near the center of town. An imposing yet pleasing yellow brick structure of sixteen rooms, it had a mansard roof of heavy slate, numerous dormers, four great chimneys, and just enough scroll work to embellish. The house overlooked both the county courthouse on the next block and John J.'s second-story office across the street from it.

Anna Kennedy Davis never assumed the social leadership that could have been hers. She was consumptive during the early years of their marriage and suffered from neuralgia through the middle and later years. She also bore six children within a decade and a half and always had less help than she needed. Although she gave up painting and music soon after marriage, she read voraciously—Greek drama, Shakespeare, and even the philosophy of history. In her late middle age she spent a year studying Hebrew with a rabbi, she mastered Dante in the original in her seventieth year, and she began to learn Spanish shortly before her death at seventy-six. Her granddaughter's clearest recollection of her was "with a big book in a big chair, her back against one arm, her small feet dangling over the other." A half-century after her death she was still remembered as the driving force behind Clarksburg's most vital intellectual group, The Tuesday Club, which she helped found in 1888. She often gave scholarly papers based on fifteen or twenty volumes sent out by the Peabody Institute in Baltimore, and to the end of her life she opened the packages as a child opens a box of candy.

Anna was reading Gibbon's *Decline and Fall of the Roman Empire* on April 13, 1873, Jefferson's birthday, when she went into labor for the fifth time. She put down the volume and gave birth to her first and only son, John William. "He is," said her sister in presenting him, "a noble Roman." [24]

« CHAPTER 2 »

Roots of Conviction

[The] lawyer has been always the sentinel on the watchtower of liberty. In all times and all countries has he stood forth in defense of his nation, her laws and liberties, not, it may be, under a shower of leaden death, but often with the frown of a revengeful and angry tyrant bent upon him.
Fellow-classmates of 1895, shall we . . . prove unworthy?

JOHN W. DAVIS
LAW CLASS ORATION, WASHINGTON AND LEE, 1895

« I »

"John W. Davis had a noble face even when small," his Sunday School teacher recalled. He used better English, kept himself cleaner, and was more dignified than most youngsters. He was also extraordinarily well-mannered. As a sister explained, "we gave him an overdose of care." He had little interest in athletics, but loved books and music. For years he played mainly with his younger sister Estelle and older sister Nan, the two most contentious, dominating, and imaginative of the Davis children. The few boys who knew John liked him, for his reserve, considerateness, and lack of aggressiveness were quietly appealing. He had one black friend, "Billy Coon," whom he played with only in sight of the house. He rarely disobeyed his parents, though he sometimes raided a peach orchard or slipped across town to watch hogs be butchered. His favorite recreation, aside from reading, was fishing.[1]

Davis' only unpleasant memory of childhood was of the regimen on Sundays. Promptly after Sunday School he attended a two-hour church service marked by several short prayers, a medium prayer, and one long prayer wherein the minister "gave the Lord a full recital of all the important news on local and world wide fronts, with thanks where thanks were appropriate, and advice as to suitable divine action where the facts were otherwise." An hour-long sermon closed the service. Following a dinner of roast beef, the children were marshaled into the library to memorize scriptural passages. Afterwards they read something uplifting, novels, toys, and games being forbidden on Sunday. Late in the afternoon John accompanied his father on a half-mile walk to the family plot in the Odd Fellows Cemetery. Afterwards, fortified by a cold supper of leftovers, everyone went back to church for the evening service. It featured more music and less praying. Home again, the children listened to their father discuss the state of the denomination with a visiting churchman. Then came family prayers and bed. Young John protested in the only way he dared: he slept through parts of the services and refused to witness for Christ.

If young John rejected his father's theology, he accepted much of his legal and political philosophy. As a boy he spent many hours observing John J. wage his epic battles in the courtroom and on the stump. "I am making this speech for my son," the senior Davis would often begin, "in order that he may be grounded in the fundamental principles of government and may be able to carry the light." To the end of his life John W. considered himself a Jeffersonian Democrat and a natural rights lawyer in his father's tradition.

John W. was more like his mother in temperament and style, though he lacked her tendency to dominate. Both were embarrassed by displays of affection, both wrote matter-of-fact letters, both disciplined themselves stringently and bottled up their emotions. He never accepted her politics—she stood staunchly for pacifism, woman suffrage, and social reform in her maturity—but the consciousness of her feelings always weighed heavily upon him.

Anna Kennedy Davis taught her son to read before he memorized the alphabet, then put him on the sets of Carlyle, Macaulay, Parkman, Dickens, Poe, Scott, and Shakespeare that lined the library walls. Study hours were regular, and when she made an assignment, John did it. "The oracle had spoken." He could lie, sit, or sprawl, but if his attention flagged for an instant, he was reprimanded. "I *knew* I must be attentive. I *knew* I must follow what she said. I *knew* that it wasn't worthwhile to file a petition for a re-hearing. That case was closed."

His mother also made him learn by rote and write with dispassion. One of his most vivid memories was of his parents arguing over an early composition. "You are cutting the soul out of it!" John J. protested. "You're ruining that boy. He gives you something, and you pare it down until there's nothing but the bare bones." Tersely, Anna replied: "I want to make him positive—brief—concise." She viewed her son realistically. "I do not think John is brilliant," she said the year of his graduation from college, "but I am sure he will work as hard as any man alive."

A few months after his tenth birthday, John was enrolled in a class for older students preparing to take the state teacher's examination. He did so well that it was suggested that he take the certifying examinations. Two years later he and three or four other boys entered the Clarksburg Female Seminary, a private boarding and day school of about sixty-five girls. John's grades ranged from 94 in Latin and 99 in Arithmetic to 100 in Neatness; moreover, the "Charge, Chester, charge" elocution teacher taught him to breathe properly. Yet the total experience was unsatisfactory, and he regretted through life his failure to attend public school. "I felt out of step with my fellows," he explained.

In September 1887 John was sent to Pantops Academy, a preparatory school for boys outside Charlottesville, Virginia. He was even more string-like in appearance than his father, and he was soon dubbed "Bones," a nickname he carried through college. A few days after his arrival, several boys accosted him and he was forced to engage in the only fight of his youth. Although pummeled severely, he emerged the moral victor on discovery that his adversary was both older and experienced as a boxer. Soon afterward he had his first communion with Thomas Jefferson. He and a friend scrambled up Monticello Mountain, which lay about a mile south of Pantops, paid a caretaker ten cents for a peek through the door of the house, then walked down to the cemetery, where John slipped through the iron rail fence and picked some acorns off Jefferson's grave.

John adjusted rather easily to the separation from his family. "A good many of the boys are the home-sickest fellows you ever saw," he reported. "I am home-sick very little till it comes to the singing in the evening. That kind of unsettles a fellow." He drove himself unmercifully, and though he failed to win the Gold Medal his first year, he won it in the second with grades of 90 or above in all subjects except trigonometry. He also participated in debate. ("Our subject for next time is 'Whether ancient or modern warfare is most destructive.' Do not like it much.") Meanwhile he began to feel somewhat at ease with girls. By the end of his second year he was writing that he intended to make the acquaintance of some Clarksburg girls that summer. But when one of the few he did take out suggested that he call her Nina instead of Miss Nina, he abruptly turned his buggy around and drove her home.

By his sixteenth year, John was ready to enter college. He preferred the University of Virginia, but his parents disapproved because of its reputation for dissipation. His mother's choice was Princeton, his father's Hampden-Sydney, a small institution tightly controlled by the Presbyterian Synod of Virginia. They compromised on Washington and Lee, and John was enrolled as a sophomore in the fall of 1889.[2]

Washington and Lee was in straitened circumstances at the time. By grace of Robert E. Lee's presidency from 1865 to 1870 it still had an aura of romance, but the General's son and successor, Custis Lee, had given virtually no leadership during a tenure that was to last until 1897. Enrollment was down to 200, the curriculum was obsolete, and the faculty was ill prepared to take the institution into the modern era. Five years after Davis' graduation, Lee's replacement, the distinguished tariff reformer William L. Wilson, dilated on the institution's problems. One function of a university, he pointed out, "is to generate and develop the desire and the power of independent, original research"; another is to enrich men so that "they can decide on this or that economic doctrine, as it may advance or impair the general welfare." Unfortunately, Washington and Lee shared the South's "lack of . . . historical, economic . . . and political studies, such as now form so large a part of the course offered in the great universities and colleges of other parts of the country." [3]

In the privacy of his diary, Wilson was more blunt. "The School has a bad case of dry rot," he wrote. Nominally secular, it was Presbyterian in most essentials. "They claim that they try only to choose the best man, but it always turns out that 'the best man' is a Presbyterian." Yet the trouble ran deeper; the real difficulty said Wilson, Scots-Irish himself, was that Scots-Irishmen lacked "progressiveness and spirit." [4]

Nevertheless, there were some good teachers, a few superior minds, and many exemplary personalities among the dozen or so gentleman scholars who comprised the Washington and Lee faculty in Davis' time. Most were too imbued with the received principles of the past to be responsive to the creative findings of the present, but they did strengthen their students' power to memorize and to reason from fixed assumptions. They also nurtured their character and polished their manners, for relations between faculty and students were close and the gentleman's code inviolable. "Of what I carried away," Davis reflected, "the personality of the old faculty is of greater value . . . than any book learning they were able to drill into me." French had been taught as a dead language. He had been out of his depth in Latin, his major, and had never understood quantity or scansion. Mathematics had been a nearly total loss. "I never knew what the calculus was about or why I was doing what I did."

By diligent and systematic study, however, Davis won honors in English and geology, placed in the lower part of the first quarter of his class in several other subjects, and made the middle in mathematics. His physics professor felt that he was not unusually bright, but stood far above his peers in some subjects and was eminently fitted for the law. Dr. James A. Quarles, a philosophy professor and Presbyterian minister, was more enthusiastic: "Davis has a mind of unusual power, which he has cultivated with judgment and success." [5]

Dr. Quarles' class in logic and rhetoric was young Davis' one stimulating course. Quarles was a rigorous analyst and a forceful moralist whose forte was precise exposition of the mathematical relationships of the various branches of logic. His method, Davis often said afterwards, was the basis of his work at the bar. Yet Quarles, too, had his limitations. "I cannot recall," Davis also said, "that any student was ever willing to take his life in his hands by challenging the evidences of Christianity which Dr. Quarles expounded." [6]

Outside the classroom, John's life was full and pleasant. He joined Phi Kappa Psi, dabbled in intramural sports, and sang first bass in the glee club and Presbyterian choir. He also "took calico," as attending mixed parties was called. Forced to husband his energy on being found to be diabetic, he accepted office only when it was thrust upon him. At first he boarded in the home of a retired Presbyterian clergyman, but when one of his classmates appeared for grace with a blackened face, he and the others were asked to leave. He then took a room in the house of his venerable professor of Greek, James J. White, who had commanded the college company in the First Battle of Bull Run. An ineffectual teacher, Dr. White was beloved for his integrity, gentleness, and dignity; the memory of his character was "a mainstay" to Davis through life. [7]

« II »

Davis would have entered law school in 1892 had funds remained from his father's sale of a farm three years earlier. Instead, he agreed to serve as tutor to the nine children and six nephews and nieces of Major Edward H. McDonald of Charles Town, West Virginia. The salary was $300 and board for nine months. A warm but imperious man, McDonald was a short, wiry ex-cavalryman who had served under Ashby and Stuart and had been wounded at Appomattox. After the war he practiced law in Louisville for twenty-five years. "Media," as his farm was called, was the inheritance of his wife, the sweet, gentle daughter of an Episcopal clergyman. She was the "most saintly" person Davis ever knew. The main house was one of those formless yet dignified places that dot the Maryland, Virginia, and West Virginia countrysides. It was built around a two-story log cabin, and its several additions included one of limestone and another of vertical slats in the Gothic manner. The wing John was quartered in lacked an inside staircase to the second floor. The house stood on a spacious knoll surrounded by magnificent virgin oaks and looked out to the east on a series of undulating fields framed by the distant Blue Ridge.[8]

Major McDonald drove his sons so relentlessly that Davis felt obliged to work just as hard himself. His students ranged from six to twenty in age, and each weekday morning for five hours unrelieved by any recess he drilled them in a log cabin behind the main house. At the end he would be drained, the class on the verge of rebellion. Every afternoon and most evenings went into preparation of the next day's classes in rhetoric, geography, Latin, arithmetic, algebra, botany, natural history, and elementary reading. "No," John wrote, "I am not one of the born teachers; I lack patience & tack [sic], & among other things, devotion to the cause." By winter's end he was deep in depression. The class seemed not to have progressed. Diabetes was sapping his strength. And the isolation was almost unbearable. "I need the society of other people as much as anyone I know," he lamented. By spring, however, he was in love with the McDonalds' second daughter.

Julia McDonald was nineteen years old, alternately gay and introspective, lighthearted and serious-minded. She sang so much that her father called her "Birdie," yet she took her religion so seriously that she felt guilty about dancing. Her figure, said John, was the "finest" he had ever seen. Her own description was more modest: "A girl of about 5.5 in height weight 120 lbs.," she noted in her diary, "have mud color hair, blue-eyes, with a scar on left cheek left by a burn received New Years eve 1876 or 7 and with enough good looks to keep from being 'hideously ugly.' "[9]

It had taken months for John to overcome his own reserve and to penetrate Julia's. She responded blithely to his teasing: "You are such an absurd man. I expect to get *fat* laughing at your nonsense some day." But only after they spent several afternoons in the spring, collecting specimens for his botany lessons, did they begin to breach their shyness. Then, following a round of dances and parties, they came to a vague understanding: they would become serious when John, then only twenty, had begun to establish himself. "I shall not commit myself on paper now," Julia said in her diary just after he left Media, "but I think some day, when I have more time—I may write a little romance entitled 'One Winter.' "

« III »

Young Davis returned home in uncertainty in June 1893. Clarksburg was feeling the full force of the depression brought on by the financial panic that spring, and his father had hardly enough cash to run the household. John was on the point of arranging to return to Media when the senior Davis suggested that he read law in his office.

For fourteen months young John copied documents in a neat, legible hand, attended court with his father, and read cases and commentaries in his spare time. He also took depositions and performed other routine tasks. Through it all John J. remained uncommunicative. He put an old copy of Blackstone in his son's hands the first day and said: "Now read that. Then I'll talk to you about it." He never did discuss it, however, and John W. read it through without knowing which commentaries were out of date.[10]

The apprenticeship strengthened John's resolve to become an attorney. He could have continued to read law until ready for the bar examination, a procedure most young men were still following, but his passion for excellence dictated a year of formal study. So he appealed to his father: "If you will go on my note of $300, I will enter law school at once and graduate in a year." [11]

In the fall of 1894, just forty years after John J. Davis had begun study under Judge Brockenbrough, young John registered at the Washington and Lee School of Law. He was one of the two members of his class who held a bachelor's degree. The school's fifty or sixty students outstripped its meager facilities, a lecture room and a musty library, but its two-man faculty, Dean John Randolph Tucker and Professor Charles A. Graves, brilliantly upheld the tradition of narrow excellence set by Brockenbrough. They also maintained the line back to

George Wythe, for Tucker was the grandson of the annotator of Black-stone's *Commentaries* and Graves had been Brockenbrough's student.

Tucker had taught at Lexington until the mid-1870's, then spent twelve years in Congress and several years in private practice before re-turning to teaching. In 1892–93, he was honored with the presidency of the American Bar Association. A handsome, demonstrative man whose zest for life and generosity of spirit uplifted almost everyone he touched, he was alternately profound and playful, metaphysical and anecdotal. As Davis wrote, "he filled the dullest student with a percep-tion of the majesty of the law, the dignity of the profession . . . and a sense of the eternal verities by which all law is underlaid." In 1856, when called upon to take a case for the Commonwealth, Tucker had refused to set a fee: "The State has a claim to my services . . . [and] I cannot weigh my sense of duty in the scales of Mammon." Three de-cades later he represented the Haymarket Anarchists in an appeal to the Supreme Court. "I do not defend anarchy," he explained to critics, "I defend the constitution." [12]

Dean Tucker's passion was constitutional law. A strict construction-ist, he idolized Jefferson and Calhoun and was unshakeably committed to the reserved powers of the states. "There is no school in the country . . . that teaches the States' rights doctrine in its purity [as] he does here," one of his students reported. Like the senior Davis and Judge Brockenbrough, Tucker believed that man was endowed by nature with a right to liberty and property and that the two were inseparable. On natural law, English history, and the Bill of Rights, Tucker took fire, carrying his students on in a flow of exalted reasoning. He deemed both Constitution and statutes to be fixed in meaning, and his impassioned attacks on change by judicial interpretation often drew bursts of applause. "Law," he insisted in words that Davis never forgot and never doubted, "is a rule of conduct prescribed by the supreme legislative power in the state enjoining what is right and prohibiting what is wrong." * Tucker opposed all forms of paternalism, including the tariff and railroad subsidies, and he stood with Grover Cleveland for what conservatives of the era thought was a sound and stable cur-rency. Davis felt that Tucker's lectures on constitutional and natural law were unexcelled, but that he was neither methodical nor thorough on technical matters such as negotiable instruments. [13]

Professor Graves was a dispassionate, meticulous man who lacked

---

* This is almost a direct quotation from Blackstone.

Tucker's generalizing bent and had never practiced nor participated
in affairs of moment. He loved the academic life in all its aspects, and
during Tucker's long absences in the 1870's and 1880's he had carried
the law school alone. "Prof. Graves is a trifle dry when he lectures &
has nothing of Mr. Tucker's ornateness of style," John confided to his
father, "but his head is as clear as a bell & he is undoubtedly a splendid teacher." As he grew older, Davis' feeling for Graves became almost reverential:

> He was, in my judgment, an educational genius; and I question
> whether any teacher in the history of this country has ever possessed a
> greater power to impart knowledge and awaken the minds committed
> to his charge. One who sat under him could not escape him, but was
> forced to learn. . . . If to achieve success in the calling one has chosen
> is to be great, that adjective cannot be denied to Mr. Graves. I think of
> him constantly with reverent affection, and I realize that I owe to him
> a debt beyond my power to repay.[14]

Neither Tucker nor Graves used the pure case method, which had
been introduced at Harvard in 1871 by Christopher C. Langdell. "I
will not be understood to decry case-learning," Tucker declared; "but
it should aid, not supplant; stimulate, not suppress, the intense work of
the native intellect." Graves was more appreciative of the method's
pedagogical value, for he believed with Langdell that the real authority of law was to be found in the principles underlying reported decisions. But he also agreed with Theodore W. Dwight of Columbia, who
felt that the method was not wholly suited to the "great and important class of men of average ability" which "exists and always will exist
in the profession." * He therefore combined formal lectures with oral
quizzes on treatise assignments and cases which he himself had culled
from the reports.[15]

Although Davis considered Graves' approach to be more sound than
Tucker's, he realized that both men gave their students a great fund of
unclassified, and often unrelated, knowledge. "They could make it
very clear to the student that he didn't know what he was talking
about. . . . I would hesitate to say that they were capable of drawing
from a student an answer he didn't know he had."

The larger strengths and weaknesses of both the treatise and case

---

* Although three-quarters of the law students at Harvard in the mid-1890's
were college graduates, fewer than half those at Columbia held undergraduate degrees. The percentage was far lower for the nation at large.

methods were really quite similar. James Bryce observed in his *American Commonwealth* that the "extraordinary excellence" of many American law schools often produced a level of attainment higher than that of the barristers and solicitors of London. But the British commentator was also struck by the greater resistance to change in procedure and substantive law engendered by the American system's heavy emphasis on both case law and constitutional fundamentals: "Thus one finds the same dislike to theory, the same attachment to old forms, the same unwillingness to be committed to any broad principle which distinguished the orthodox type of English lawyers sixty years ago." Woodrow Wilson was even more critical. In the 1880's he complained of law's "narrowing" influence and "its power to make a man . . . like a *needle,* a thing of one eye and one point"; and a decade and a half later he was still decrying law's separation from the dynamic force of politics, morality, and industry:

> Austin [the English positivist] has done us the great disservice of putting his analysis of law into such terms as to create the very general impression among lawyers who do not think, but swallow formulas, that law is somehow made independently of the bulk of the community, and that it is their business to accept it and apply it as it is without troubling themselves to look beyond the statute or decision in which it is embodied.[16]

Many active practitioners also perceived the conservative character of legal education and practice in the United States. Newton D. Baker, who was a class ahead of Davis at Washington and Lee, later lamented the tendency of lawyers to become "experts in technical business." Even Elihu Root, one of the master technicians of the age, was troubled enough to comment privately. "The pure lawyer," said Root in 1906, "seldom concerns himself about the broad aspects of public policy. . . . Lawyers are almost always conservative. Through insisting upon the maintenance of legal rules, they become instinctively opposed to change." [17]

Indubitably, the conservatism in the upper reaches of the bar was more reflective of the influence of powerful clients than of the inhibiting character of legal education. As a leader of the Chicago bar explained, "the more important and able the lawyer, the more he is in touch with the most important business interests of the community, and the more . . . he cannot propose or advocate any reform of an extensive character which will not be unwelcome to some particular client's interest." Yet the most casual acquaintance with the minds of men like Judge Brockenbrough, Dean Tucker, and the senior Davis, all of whom had their counterparts in the North, confirms Bryce's conclusion that their "habits of legal thought" figured large. Certainly Davis' passing remarks indicate that the whole educational milieu was well ordered to inculcate the view, as Holmes disdainfully put it, that the law "contained only the axioms and corollaries of a book of mathematics." There was historical exposition, but virtually no historical analysis of the sort Holmes had written into his epochal *Common Law* more than a decade earlier; nor was there any intimation that the law could or should be different. "The professors . . . were more concerned that you should learn what the law was," Davis recalled with approval, "than that you should be invited to speculate on what the law *ought* to be." [18]

The students attended classes dutifully, rarely challenged their professor's basic assumptions, and lived in fearful anticipation of their first day in court. They bypassed most of the outside reading—Davis described the pitifully small library as "covered with the dust of the ages"—and they displayed a greater sense of immediate utility than did the liberal arts students. "They were all eager to get what they could, and to incidentally pass their examinations. But I don't recall that there was very much philosophizing." [19]

After he went into practice, of course, Davis invariably invoked the most modern judicial construction when his client's interest demanded it and the authority seemed binding. Yet in his policy pronouncements as a leader of the bar he always emphasized that the lawyer's proper role was that of the highly skilled technician. Unlike the architect, engineer, or artist, he asserted, "the lawyer as a lawyer does not build or erect or paint anything. He does not create. All he does is lubricate the wheels of society by implementing the rules of conduct by which the organized life of men must be carried on." [20]

At that time, Washington and Lee was one of the eight law schools in the nation that allowed students to complete their course work in one year, and Davis, like most of his classmates, chose that option. Ordinarily he studied until eleven at night. Sometimes he sparred a little before supper or swung dumbbells before breakfast, but his academic routine was so grueling that he refused to join the Presbyterian choir even as a paid member. "I am socially a hermit, a dweller in caves." Formal debate, in which he excelled, was his one diversion.

The pace soon told. Worn down by nervous dyspepsia, Davis gave up hope of leading his class. "A double-course man has no right to cherish such dreams, the handicap is too great." By his first examination he was even doubting that a degree was worth the effort. On earning the fifth highest grade in one of Graves' courses, however, the dyspepsia went away. He accepted the presidency of the glee club and accompanied it to Louisville during the Christmas holidays. He also "took a little calico."

Not even the loss of his remaining $150 in a bank failure that winter depressed Davis unduly; he told his father that he could probably pass the bar examination that summer anyway. Pleased when he was ordered to stay in school, he grumbled only about the volume and complexity of the material he had to master. Meanwhile he was elected Law Class Orator.[21]

Davis' commencement oration that June was a ringing call for the rule of law. Of all the factors that promote human advancement, he declared, civil law was paramount. "Never has there been either progress or liberty of which organic and fixed law was not the cause or inseparable companion." With a fervor reminiscent of his father's, he asserted that justice had been betrayed in every quarter, including the courts. He closed with an appeal to his classmates to uphold the lawyer's historic role as "the sentinel on the watch-tower of liberty" and to preach "the doctrine of Reverence for the Law." [22]

CHAPTER 3

Professorship and Marriage

*To be eminent in my profession, make a good living and have a good
wife to share it and encourage me—those are my dearest dreams and
ambitions.*

JOHN W. DAVIS, 1898

« I »

Davis had acquired two of the three signatures necessary for a license
before leaving Lexington. The first judge questioned him perfunctorily, and the second remarked gruffly that he was too busy to examine
him. John was so confident that the third would sign out of courtesy
that he did not even glance at his course notes before presenting himself. To his surprise and dismay, the judge quizzed him sharply and
exposed him mercilessly. "Of course, it didn't make any real difference," John reflected, "but I should have liked to have done better for
the honor of the name." [1]

Another surprise followed. Davis told his father that he was going to
put an announcement in the newspaper. "Wait, and I'll write it for
you," John J. said. He then typed out a notice:

JOHN J. DAVIS   JOHN W. DAVIS

DAVIS AND DAVIS

ATTORNEYS AT LAW

CLARKSBURG, W. VA.[2]

Young Davis' first three cases ended ignominiously. He was wondering how to handle a Negro client, whose minister had absconded with
$22.00, when a farmer walked into the office.

"John," he asked, "have you ever had a case?"

"No."

"Want one?"

"Yes."

The farmer, who was in connivance with the senior Davis, then asked him to prosecute a neighbor for stealing an old turkey hen and twenty-nine chickens. The hearing was set for a country store across the district line, ostensibly to accommodate all parties. Shortly before it came up, the defendant alleged want of jurisdiction and secured a rule from the Circuit Court to show cause why a writ of prohibition should not be issued. John thought that a writ of prohibition "had something to do with alcohol." All his father would do was point to a thick volume on a shelf. From eight o'clock that night until one a.m. young John read intently. Then, early in the morning, he rode ten miles to the country store and filed answer, only to have his opponent demur. The circuit judge, another of John J.'s friends, ruled that the justice of the peace lacked authority to try a case outside his magisterial district. Afterward, the judge complimented John effusively on his presentation, then struck him lightly on the head with his mallet —a "gracing," as Francis Bacon termed it.

The second case involved a cow that had been killed by a B.&O. train. "She was a good cow," Davis recollected, "and her genealogy was greatly improved by this unfortunate accident. . . . I sued for the owner of the cow. I proved her unfortunate death as the corpus delicti. I proved her impeccable pedigree and her great utility. The jury . . . found in my favor, and I took judgment to the amount set in my summons." Again, the other side appealed. "What in the world is wrong with this?" the young lawyer asked himself. The circuit judge explained: He had failed to ask the jury to assess damages. "I thought if they were for me," Davis said, "they must be for me back, down, and across."

The third defeat was the client's fault. He had purchased a horse on a note for $130 but had refused to pay because the horse had a curb, or swelling. After putting on the stand a veterinarian who swore that the horse "had the curb to end all curbs," Davis rested his case. To his dismay, the opposing counsel then introduced a letter written by John's client some weeks after the sale. The letter praised the horse unreservedly, adding that a mate would make the pair be worth $500. As the jury found for the claimant, John turned to his client and exclaimed: "I don't see why you wrote that damnfool letter." [3]

Tired and discouraged, John arrived home late, scraped the mud off his horse, and went to the library where his father was reading beside his coal fire. "I'm going to quit this business," he said, as tears began to form. "I don't like it. I want to be in some business that isn't a fight all the time. I'll never make a lawyer." He was still talking when old John J. sprang to his feet and gave him "the damndest" lecture he had ever received.[4]

Thereafter John's fortunes slowly rose, and by the end of the year he had taken in $492 in fees. He accepted most cases as they came in, though he sometimes asked for five dollars in advance. He took depositions, searched titles, collected debts, and drew up wills and contracts. Occasionally his resources failed him. As he confided to Julia McDonald at one point, "You would have been amused . . . if you could have seen my efforts to wriggle out when a worthy fellow citizen asked my professional advice on a matter I knew nothing . . . about. I hunted through every book I could lay my hands on, but had to 'squeal' finally and turn him over to the senior member of the firm." [5]

At times precise knowledge made considerable difference in trying a case, and often it made no difference whatever; it depended on the justice of the peace. Most were untrained and uninformed, but some meted out a crude justice more effective for its disregard of technicalities; others were open to persuasion, usually by the attorney who spoke last. "It was purely catch-as-catch-can." Davis recalled. The younger members of the bar used "to rassle each other around" in those courts, and "if you didn't know any [law] you had to make it up to fit the case." [6]

Even when suing for recovery of a pig, Davis invested himself totally. And though he came in time to accept defeat gracefully, he was veritably obsessed with winning. As he often said, it was "the *gaudium certaminis*—the love of battle, the joy of battle" that made trial work absorbing.[7]

Near the end of his first year of practice, just as his self-confidence was beginning to develop, Davis was offered an assistant professorship of law at Washington and Lee at a salary of $1000. In urging him to accept, Dean Tucker emphasized the "prestige" of the position and his promise as a teacher, Professor Graves the warmth of his recommendations. Both men offered the use of their lectures and course materials. John was sorely tempted, for he was nostalgic even then about the university—the stately red brick buildings with their great columned

porches, the Georgian, Federal, and Greek Revival town houses, the
genteel townspeople, and the aura of culture that gave Lexington a
local reputation as the Athens of western Virginia.[8]

Davis' mother had always wanted her son to become a college professor, but at least one Davis bridled at the prospect—Rezin, brother
of John J., ex-Confederate cavalryman, and Louisville, Kentucky, attorney. "If you love the strife of battle and can bear the wear & tear of
the law with its trials & disappointments," he warned his nephew,
"then dont take the place." A professorship would afford ease and
comfort; but it would also "leave dormant many a faculty & stunt
many an energy that the struggle & battle of independent self reliant
effort would develop." Young John should realize that the Davis blood
was essentially "a warring blood and the quiet & languor of peace does
not contribute to its enjoyment." [9]

John agreed in principle. But he also realized that nine months'
teaching would wipe out his indebtedness and enhance his reputation.
After deliberating as long as he decently could, he accepted for one
year, to a chorus of congratulations from his classmates.[10]

« II »

Gripped by "acute stage fright" and convinced that "no heretic ever
dreaded the stake more," Davis appeared for his first class in mid-September 1896. He was twenty-three years old, five feet, eleven inches
tall, and weighed about 128 pounds. His complexion was sallow. A
broad, high brow set off a long triangular face, a rather small nose,
and reflective eyes of pale blue. He carried himself with uncommon
grace, and his natural dignity conveyed an impression of maturity unusual for one so young. He began his lecture haltingly, but was soon
speaking in deep, resonant cadences. Only his speed of delivery hinted
at his inner tension. Finishing fifteen minutes early, he snapped his
notebook shut and dismissed the class. "Davis is one of the brightest
young men I ever met," wrote one of the students in his diary.[11]

As the weeks passed, the strain increased. He had three separate
courses each quarter, and he complained constantly that he was always
half-prepared. "I am ploughing in stiff soil now with contracts," he
wrote in November. "I unloaded a lecture on conditions & warranties
which has been weighing on my mind like a bad dinner for three
days," he reported in December. "My head wouldn't work & I had to

be content with a very weak quiz & the reading of some cases to tide over the emergency." So it went, month after month.[12]

The burden became even heavier when Dean Tucker fell ill that winter and Davis took over half his courses. "It's the old story about praising a fool horse until he kills himself." Distressed by his ignorance in federal procedure, he implored his father to recommend a book by return mail. By spring, however, he was conceding that the year had brought "more learning . . . more experience, more . . . self-control, and more determination to follow Shakespeare's advice when he says— 'Cease to lament for that thou canst not help. . . .' " [13]

Davis' year in practice reinforced his view that he should prepare his students for the bar, not government or politics; his one political allusion of record was an affirmation of Grover Cleveland's maxim, "Public office is a public trust." Only in equity pleading did he grapple with the theoretical, and then simply because he had assigned Christopher C. Langdell's pioneering *Summary of Law of Contracts and Equity Pleading* at Professor Graves' suggestion. The work, he said, was a fine piece of logic; but it was excessively abstruse and metaphysical. "To inflict such a work on a class who . . . are trying to make their bread & meat is an absolute imposition. I am keeping a mighty stiff upper lip on the subject, & am trying to load them with Mr. Tucker's notes & lectures by myself." [14]

Davis' examinations were patterned on those he himself had taken as a student. One part called for definitions, the other for the application of laws and rules of procedure to hypothetical situations. The phraseology was clear and precise; and although the questions were moderately analytical, they reflected the prevailing view that law was a science, not a speculative discipline, and as such had no causal connection with social change; in eighty questions on seven courses, the word "why" appeared only twice.[15]

Meanwhile, Dean Tucker died. Called to his bedside the afternoon of his death, Davis entered the room as Tucker was lowering a cup from his lips. "I see they are still trying to poison you," he remarked. "Oh, no John, we mustn't call a good whiskey poison," the Dean replied with a last flash of gaiety. A few moments later Tucker professed his complete devotion to the Christian faith in phrases of majestic eloquence.[16]

Dean Tucker's death brought pressure on Davis to continue at Washington and Lee at a higher salary and rank. He wavered briefly, partly in anticipation that Custis Lee's retirement would give the university new life. But he finally concluded that he preferred the "rough & tumble" of private practice to the "daily grind" of teaching and that he owed it to his father to return to Clarksburg.[17]

He never regretted the decision. Yet neither did he ever question the value of the experience: "That one year of teaching was perhaps the most profitable single year I ever spent. A professor has the profound satisfaction of watching the seed he sows . . . bear fruit in other men's lives. A practitioner has the joy of combat, not to be separated . . . from the wounds." [18]

« III »

Nineteen months earlier John and Julia McDonald had fallen out over his insistence on a more definite commitment. Unable to bear the separation, she had soon beseeched him to write candidly. "I feel so wretched, if it is a misunderstanding, why not correct it?" Her self-knowledge, she assured him, was now much clearer. Yet a visit by John in the summer of 1896 had failed to recapture the old intimacy, and when he walked his bicycle up the oak-lined lane at Media on his way home from Washington and Lee a year later, Julia greeted him apprehensively.

For several days their conversation was guarded, even forced. Then, late one evening, John showed her a commendation from the trustees, took her in his arms, and poured out his feelings. "I surrendered, weakened, ignominiously if you will," he said. "Dream patient Julia," she wrote in her diary, "he loves me yet." Furthermore, she had won him on her own terms. "I can truthfully say, I *did not* seek but *was* sought." She had only one regret:

He has never professed religion and seems very indifferent which distresses me greatly & I don't know what to do for him but pray & try to lead a consistent life myself. . . . Still with all his faults I love him still —and he is working now for the "accomplishments of very dear ambitions" he says.

Six months later he gave her a diamond ring.

For the next eighteen months John and Julia exchanged letters almost daily. He was often self-deprecatory. He wrote that it was hard for him to think of others or put himself out to please them, but that Julia was "so good and unselfish" that she would always be ministering to the wants of others. He also fretted over his incapacity to express his love. "I know what I have felt only when some chance remark from a friend or some book gives it expression for me." Julia replied in kind. "I have always said that I was no good as a love maker, but I do believe I will be a success as a wife."

At times the tension was considerable. "I have never been able to be half as nice to people that I have looked forward to seeing for months & years even as I wanted to," Julia explained following a quarrel. Once, after John admitted to his mother that he had been at fault in a dispute, Mrs. Davis admonished him in words that cast a sharp light on her own relations with his father. "Ah, it is all very well to fix up lovers' tiffs, but every quarrel you have after you are married will chip just so much off your life and happiness. Don't have them."

John's wry humor cut deeper than he realized, and his cavalier attitude toward organized religion heightened the strain. He said that he was "better physically, mentally, yes & morally" for missing church and taking a thirteen-mile bicycle ride. He described how he had run into a "hornet's nest" at dinner by asking in feigned innocence if Calvin had ordered the burning of Servetus. He ridiculed the clergy mercilessly. "Do they really think . . . that they are speaking as God's selected messengers, moved and directed by him?" he wrote after listening to a Baptist evangelist. "The Lord deliver us from preachers as a class. I wonder sometimes if Christianity isn't after all just another one of the world's religions, destined to decay & give place to something else just as Buddhism & Judaism & others have done." [19]

The most amusing thrust followed his attendance at an Episcopal service on Julia's request:

> They have vested choir you know, & *process* & *recess* around the little 8 x 10 room as if it was a cathedral—but I could go that; they rise when the plates with 6 nickels on each are handed to the preacher and the choir triumphantly announces to the Lord that all that money is his—I can stand that; but this time they got mixed up in the prayers & where I had always heard the congregation make a response to the preacher the choir droned it out in a melancholy chant that had about as much music & certainly no more devotion in it than the howling of an Indian Medicine Man.

He added that he said to himself, "do those people really believe in the Trinity? I believe in God, the Father Almighty, maker of Heaven & Earth—but the rest of my creed is badly mixed." [20]

More commonly, he was tender and considerate. "I wish I could be

more of a believer in what is so holy & sacred & so dear to you. I want
the truth if I can find it, and you must help me if I ever reach the
light." She should not fear that he would compel her to abandon her
church. "You are worried, are you, dearest, at the idea of giving up the
service you have been taught to love? I don't think I ever asked that of
you, did I?" As for himself, he preferred the Presbyterian form of worship, but doubted that he would ever join any church.

John's unorthodoxy broadened Julia a little. She continued to pray
that he would be converted, and she insisted that they plan to study
the Bible together every Sunday. But she also conceded, after reading
George Eliot, that Eliot's insights into human nature had enriched her
greatly.

The severest strain was over the wedding date. "I don't merely *want*
you, I *need* you," John told her. He insisted, nevertheless, that they
wait until he could support them comfortably. "I don't think I have
'very extravagant ideas,' Dear, but I do like to be *easy* in mind &
body." Not until Major McDonald warned Julia more than a year
later that John would probably not save much until he was married
did she reject John's plan to wait until they could build a house. "Remember, my love, you are a *rising* young man . . . plenty of good people have lived happily on $700 a year & less."

By then Davis was the most prominent, the most popular, and the
busiest young lawyer in Harrison County. He had taken in $1240.20 in
cash during the preceding nine months, and he had $600 in the bank;
in addition, a railroad company owed him more than $1100, and he
was about to receive a retainer of $150 a month. Even his own family
began to lose patience. His mother suggested that he and Julia board
at home indefinitely, and his father offered to give them a building
lot. If John intended to wait two or three more years, he should break
the engagement, John J. said in the fall of 1898. "When I got married,
I hardly had enough to pay the wedding fee." Six months later John
J. told his son that no young man in the state had begun practice with
more advantages.[21]

John was not quite persuaded. "One of the things I dread worst in
poverty," he explained to Julia, "is the effect on my temper; I want to
be pleasant around home, especially around my dearest wife if I can,
but . . . when I am worked a little too hard or feel utterly busted financially, I get as peevish & fretful as a dyspeptic rhinoceros."

Finally, in March 1899, John arranged to borrow $2000 to build a
house and tentatively set the wedding for June. No sooner had he

done so than he began to back off, ostensibly because of pending law
suits. Shortly, however, he fixed the date at June 20, early enough to
free the McDonalds for haying. "My guess," said Julia, "is that we
were both scared to death."

A few weeks later Washington and Lee asked Davis to replace Professor Graves, who had accepted a chair at the University of Virginia.
"So, sweetheart, there you are—$3000 a year & a house—congenial
friends, freedom from business or financial cares, three months vacation each year, a trip to Europe next summer." Against all that was
the exhilaration of active practice and the "millions in it." Was there
any comparison? Julia agreed that there was not. Teaching, she told
him, would not lessen his labors materially; he was bound either to
work or to study. To his mother's regret, John declined the offer.[22]

« IV »

Early in the evening of June 20, 1899, six years after they had come
to their first informal understanding, John William Davis and Julia
McDonald were married beneath the oaks on Media's spacious lawn
before two hundred guests. He was twenty-six; she was twenty-five.
Wearing a gown of Paris muslin over white satin which she had made
herself, Julia walked down an aisle of daisy chains and myrtle wreaths
to a sylvan chancel covered with country flowers. An Episcopal priest
pronounced them man and wife. They took a late train to Washington, where John forgot to write his bride's name on the hotel register
and was asked to identify "the lady." On their return to Clarksburg
they moved in with the Davises.[23]

"I've lived more . . . than in all the rest of my life," John confided
to Julia while she was visiting Media in August. "We have thrown
over as much reserve & are as close in mind & heart as if we had been
married for years." Julia agreed. "I can't tell you how much I appreciate the sacrifices you are always making for me. . . . All the love &
devotion of my life are small compensation, but I give you it all. . . .
I have been thinking all the morning, with heartfelt gratitude to my
Heavenly Father for giving me such a . . . considerate, thoughtful loving indulgent & patient husband. . . . Oh! how our lives have grown
together."

Julia's warmth and enthusiasm brought gaiety and spontaneity into
the Davis household. Laughter punctuated the meals, and the entire
family often gathered in the library after supper to hear John and

Julia sing or play duets on the violin and piano. Yet Julia longed to be her own mistress, and she urged John to rent a little flat even if they had to take in roomers. His family objected so strenuously, however, that they stayed on.

For all her new happiness, Julia missed Media, "beloved place, beloved people." Her life at home, wrote her father, was a sweet memory. "I called you Birdie because your infant life was as bright and songful as a woodland bird. . . . You were a precious charge. . . . I was never lonesome in my life before." The old major closed abruptly: "your marriage to a devoted faithful husband I regard as our chief blessing."

That autumn Julia became pregnant. She feared for the unborn baby, dreaming that "just as the little thing was winding itself around our hearts, it died." In mid-July, several weeks late, she went into labor. The family doctor was indisposed, so they called in another physician, who arrived half-drunk. He handled the delivery briskly, but failed to sterilize his instruments. At first both Julia and the baby, a robust girl whom they named Anna Kennedy, did well. But soon Julia came down with puerperal fever. For three weeks, with her husband holding her hand and singing softly night after night, she struggled for life. "Don't cry, John, she murmured, "I'm going to fight it out." Gradually her strength ebbed until, sensing that she was dying, she pointedly told John's oldest sister that it was not right for a man to live alone. Late Sunday night, August 17, 1900, she died.

Mrs. McDonald gave young Davis the most solace in the bitter aftermath. He envied her the strength of her religious convictions, and he prayed that he would win the fight for faith. "What a bitter struggle that is," he confided to her. He also drew some comfort from the Stoic philosophers, especially Epictetus. Yet he could not really believe that all would ever be well. "How good it is that we cannot read what the years have in store, otherwise our joys would grow stale by anticipation & we should be crushed between the weight of past & future sorrows like wheat between the millstones." He worked, he said, because occupation was his best refuge, but the ambition and stimulus were gone.

Not even the baby eased his grief. He renamed her Julia at his mother's suggestion, and he tried in his unaggressive way to get close to her. "God only knows how much the preservation & continuance of her life mean to me." But his work seemed always to intrude. His mother and sisters brought the child up, and he became almost a stranger to her. "Of all her train I am least to her liking. I long for the day when there will be something I can do for her." In time, he bought her a pony, sent her to private schools, and encouraged her to spend summers with the McDonalds at Media. But he never gave her what she craved. Long afterward, Julia described their relationship:

> His hours grew longer, his trips more frequent, his return to the office after dinner invariable. He was always kindly, often abstracted, but I knew then, and I know still, that looking at me hurt his heart. . . .
> What I wanted from him was his time, and he had little to spare.

Davis' stringent self-control deprived him of the comfort that confidences afford. "I am sure," he said, "that the chief duty which grief owes the world is silence." Two years passed before he attended a social function, and then it was to be best man in a wedding. Night after night he dreamed of Julia, though always of her last four weeks rather than of "the days of golden happiness that preceded them." He dreaded travel because his recollections then took undisputed possession of his mind. He even thought of Julia while reading speeches. Eventually the anguish passed, but the sense of loss never did. As Mrs. McDonald observed in wishing him happiness on his thirtieth birthday in April 1903, "the word seems like a mockery, when I recall your countenance, so full of patient, silent sorrow—a sorrow which we have shared together, but which has lost so much of its bitterness to me, looked at through the eyes of Faith."

A full decade after Julia's death the memories still hurt. Time had changed many things, Davis confided to Mrs. McDonald, but there were some which it was powerless to alter. "Every now and then . . . I am seized by a paroxysm of regret—each one more & not less bitter than the last. Every visit I have made to Media was a pleasure, & yet . . . there have been times when the rush of memories proved too strong for me & drove me back to work sooner than I might have gone otherwise." Every Easter for almost half a century he had Julia's sister place flowers over "the dear dust that slumbers in Zion Churchyard— my only way of bearing testimony to the great hope that alone makes life supportable. Resurgam!" [24]

« CHAPTER 4 »

The Making of a Lawyer

This I am willing to vouch: Whatever professional success I have had is due primarily to the training I got in the rough and tumble of the Clarksburg bar. It was sometimes rough and, as I look back, I did a good deal of tumbling, but it was a healthy discipline for all of that.
                                                    JOHN W. DAVIS, 1955

« I »

West Virginia was in the midst of a spectacular economic boom when young Davis returned from his professorship at Washington and Lee in 1897. Production of coal had doubled since 1890 and would multiply fourfold again by 1912. The oil and natural gas industries were expanding even more rapidly. In Clarksburg four banks, three newspapers, two telephone exchanges, and twenty passenger trains a day serviced the 5000 residents. Every contractor was booked ahead, and not a single house was listed for rent. Electric power and gas and water mains had already been installed, and a horse-drawn trolley line would go into operation in 1900. Dozens of new plants were under construction, especially in chemicals and blown glass; and four brickyards, three planing mills, and three machine shops were accepting more orders than they could handle. On Saturday afternoons scores of Belgians, Italians, and Poles rubbed shoulders with the descendants of the Irish railroad workers who had been brought in by the Baltimore & Ohio Railroad in the 1850's. Some five or six hundred Negroes, whom the local press referred to as "darkies," "black boys," or "colored," added to the mixture.[1]

Still, much of the old flavor lingered. The red brick Victorian courthouse remained the focal point of community life. Hitching posts lined the streets, and all males were bound by masculine honor to join the fire bucket brigade. Friction between town and country people was slight, and, though the heavy-drinking Irish supplied the margin for repeal of the Prohibition ordinance in 1899, the oil riggers alone were raucous. Serious crime continued to be the virtual monopoly of the old-stock whites in the backcountry: "Dastardly Deed," "The Most Horrible Murder," "Rape Charged," "A Terrible Crime," "Bloody Tragedy," and "Another Brutal Crime." [2]

Most of the new capital came from out of state, and much of the profit went back to the source. Assuredly, native lawyers, doctors, and merchants participated in the development, and by the turn of the century many West Virginians had acquired considerable wealth. Nevertheless, the state was little more than a fiefdom of Northern interests. In one county Northern agents acquired the rights to the choicest timber and mineral lands for as little as $2.00 an acre by telling the ignorant, impoverished mountaineers "they would never be of any possible use to them"; even in Harrison County, subsoil leases went for $5.00.[3]

Leading West Virginia developers such as Johnson Newlon Camden, politician, mine owner, and one-time lobbyist for Standard Oil, commonly thwarted fair assessment of mineral lands. "When you double taxable values," Camden explained, "you double the limits at which towns and counties can increase their indebtedness and you know they always manage to tax to the limit." By capitalizing on the provincialism of the backcountrymen, many of whom were scarcely literate, Camden and dozens of other promoters starved the state and county governments of revenue for public services, including schools.[4]

The short-term result was affluence for native promoters and the professional men and merchants who serviced them. Yet, even during the halcyon years, the wealth was ill-distributed. In 1897 the average annual wage of miners in West Virginia was $275, the lowest in the industry except for the Pittsburgh area, where southeastern Europeans made up the bulk of the labor force. Only schoolteachers were worse off. At the peak of the boom in 1910 their average monthly salary for a six-month term was $36.70.[5]

The long-term result was economic and cultural disaster. By mid-twentieth century the rich hardwood forests were gone, the oil and natural gas reserves depleted, and the richest coal veins nearly exhausted. "It was a beautiful countryside with great, rolling hills," Davis lamented in 1954. "Now . . . they are doing what they call strip mining. . . . You have a very gaping, sore scar all along the hills, which, being of the older generation, I bitterly resent." But the worst legacy was an inferior educational system.[6]

« II »

John W., as young Davis was known in Clarksburg, was just beginning to master the routine aspects of practice in the summer of 1897 when he was thrust into one of the most dramatic cases of his early career. Low-cost coal from West Virginia's rich bituminous veins had set back the United Mine Workers' efforts to raise wages in western Pennsylvania, Ohio, Indiana, and Illinois, where the union was strong but the deposits thin; and on July 4 the union president, M. D. Ratchford, called an industry-wide strike. UMW leaders demanded higher wages, honest weighing of tonnage, better working conditions, and, most important, recognition of their locals in West Virginia.[7]

Success required a solid front, for the operators' private armies had already converted some sections of the state into semi-feudal baronies. Ratchford persuaded President Samuel Gompers of the American Federation of Labor to support the walkout, and on July 27 the front-line leadership of the labor movement descended on West Virginia to hear Gompers address a throng of 17,000 in Wheeling. By then about 5000 of the state's 23,000 miners had struck; Vice President John Mitchell of the UMW had been forced to flee a company town and swim across an icy stream amidst a hail of bullets; and the legendary organizer, Mrs. Mary H. "Mother" Jones, a great-souled Irish immigrant whose intensity was said to be something one could almost feel physically, had been jailed and enjoined not to agitate.[8]

One of the mines struck by the UMW was a property in Fairmont, a mining town about twenty-five miles northwest of Clarksburg, owned by Johnson Camden. On Camden's complaint, a Marion County judge issued such a sweeping injunction against Eugene V. Debs that West Virginia's scholarly governor, George W. Atkinson, was prompted to affirm labor's abstract rights. The state constitution, said Atkinson, guaranteed the right to assemble, organize, and use moral suasion; only trespass and intimidation were prohibited.[9]

The injunction was never enforced, and the organizing activity continued. For several days spirited groups of strikers marched up and down the county roads near Fairmont, camping in the fields at night about twenty miles from Clarksburg. Then, on Monday, August 16, banners flying and a small band blaring, about 200 men marched to Fairmont, where two mines were still operating. At 4:00 a.m. Tuesday they set off again. They halted outside the entrance of one of the properties, spread themselves along the county road at five-foot intervals, and stood in silent contempt as 150 non-strikers, many with eyes averted, entered the mines. Late that afternoon federal marshals served an *ex parte* injunction.[10]

The injunction had been issued in Clarksburg by United States District Judge John Jay Jackson, a stern, gruff, and strong-willed man whose obsession with order and property rights had earned him the sobriquet "The Iron Judge"; now, far into the evening of his career, he was fixed on a course that would make him go down as "The Injunction Judge." As Davis remarked years later, "the first thing the coal companies would do in the case of a strike was rush over to John Jackson and get an injunction *ex parte*. That injunction would enjoin them from doing pretty nearly everything except carry food home for their babies." [11]

Back at the mines the strikers received Judge Jackson's injunction in high good humor: "We will take the consequences." "We're used to papers like that." "I'll eat mine for breakfast." The injunction said nothing about the county roads, so they struck up their makeshift band and resumed marching. Counsel for the operators then wired Jackson for a more precise order. At eight o'clock the next morning federal marshals arrived with a clarification, really an amplification, which prohibited "marching to and fro through the company's property." Protesting that their right to use the county roads through the property was inalienable, the strikers defied the order. Twenty-seven were then arrested and dispatched to Clarksburg, where the senior Davis agreed to represent them.[12]

Late that afternoon John J. Davis sent young John W. to court to move for a continuance because he had a trial elsewhere the next day. Judge Nathan Goff, Jr., John J.'s onetime political rival, denied the motion, and Davis assigned the case to his son. John W. was terrified. He knew nothing about the newly developing law of labor injunctions, and he would be opposed by two experienced counsel: A. B. Fleming, a former Governor and Circuit Court judge, and W. W. Meredith, also an ex-judge. He implored his father to let him off, but John J. refused. In near panic, John W. began preparation after supper. He stopped at 2:30 a.m. to sleep three hours in his chair, and at nine that morning he persuaded the miners to hire an older lawyer,

Winfield Scott, to assist him. Then, "scared to death," he walked across the street to the courthouse. Every seat was taken, the aisles were jammed with standees, and a sizeable crowd milled about the doors and spilled down the wide steps.[13]

To everyone's surprise, Davis opened by asserting that a writ of attachment was required in each case. Following an animated discussion, Judge Goff overruled Davis' motion to dismiss. A writ, said the judge, had been necessary "anciently," but the rule now was that a court could enforce its orders in contempt proceedings without one. The question was whether the miners had violated the order of the District Court, and on this the evidence would be heard.[14]

Davis knew at once that all he could hope for was a light sentence. Spelled intermittently by Scott, who "was about three sheets in the wind," he matched wits with Fleming and Meredith for two full days. The phrases "natural rights," "free speech," and the "liberty of citizens" came repeatedly to his lips, and by Friday afternoon he had convinced the court that the strikers had refrained from taunts or threats and had sincerely believed they had a "right" to demonstrate on the county roads. In an eloquent closing statement, he charged that the injunction violated both the state and federal constitutions:

> These men had simply marched along the public highway, peaceably and quietly; they had made no threat and offered no abuse. They had not disturbed a blade of grass on the property of the company, nor offered violence to any of its employers, but even their silence had been charged against them. . . . The right of free speech has often been assailed but never before the right of free silence. The construction of the order is still in the breast of the court, and while the court must enforce the law, until it did so, counsel could not believe that the law would ever authorize an injunction prohibiting any man or body of men from passing up and down the public highway when they did so in peace and order. If the law has gone this far then our constitutions and bills of right will soon become mere shadows from which all substance has departed.[15]

Although Judge Goff's solicitude for property rights would eventually rank him with Judge Jackson as an enemy of labor, he was more committed than his colleague to freedom of speech in the abstract; apparently Davis' Jeffersonian rhetoric had touched his conscience. Before a full, tense court Saturday morning, Goff declared defensively that all he had to find was that the strikers had violated Jackson's order. Then, in a long, modern-sounding "balancing" digression, he dismissed Davis' contention that the strikers' constitutional rights had been violated. The organizer had spoken "to his heart's content" in hamlets, at crossroads, on street corners, and in public buildings with a freedom "gratifying to all true lovers of republican government." * Goff conceded, however, that the testimony Davis had drawn out in cross-examination indicated that the miners had truly believed that they had a right to march on the public highway. Their disobedience was without "malice" and warranted the lightest possible punishment: three days in jail.[16]

Even the union construed the light sentences as a moral victory. Davis was told that his future was assured, that he would soon outgrow Clarksburg, and that the miners would support him for Congress. Dismissing the praise as "blarney," he insisted that he had done nothing extraordinary:

> Here I am in the office of an old lawyer to whom such a case would naturally come & one who is ready & anxious to step aside & leave me to win whatever glory I may in one of the most important & celebrated trials they've had here in years. . . . I could never have forgiven myself if I had not swallowed my fears & waded in.[17]

Davis never again represented labor in an important matter. Yet the memory of the miners' case influenced him profoundly as a member of Congress fifteen years later.[18]

« III »

Davis' realization that recognition was the surest way to new business weighed heavily upon him during those years. Though he found it "agony on the half shell" to "hippodrome around with a lot of people . . . whom you would not walk across the street to speak to," he put himself forward discreetly. He helped organize a lodge of Elks and threw himself into the Masons "on account of the opportunity it gives a man—and especially a young man—to extend his acquaintance." He asked Judge Jackson to appoint him referee in bankruptcy when a new federal law mandated a 1 per cent commission for referees. He agreed to stand for the city attorneyship partly because it offered "a certain amount of advertising." And he told Julia again and again that he was "after every dollar in sight." He also did many other

* This was a misstatement of fact. Goff professed to describe conditions in all West Virginia, but he actually described only the situation in the Fairmont region, if that. Witness the attack on John Mitchell by company guards elsewhere.

things which confirm the observation of the historian Hurst, that the
average lawyer's "urge to get on" often conflicted with his vaguely defined aspirations to serve the commonwealth. When asked, for example, to serve as a special judge in a disputed election in near-by Wes-
ton, Davis pleaded lack of time because he knew that he would be
called a traitor if he decided one way and a coward if he decided the
other.

> I would run those risks & do any amount of work on the *chance* of
> gaining prestige by it. But a man don't like to go gunning for enemies
> unless he is paid—& well for it.[19]

It was the compromises that Davis refused to make which set him
off from his peers and earned him a reputation for independence and
integrity. He invoked the wrath of a group of schoolteachers by refusing to endorse woman suffrage. When he stood for the city attorneyship he refused to campaign because "there are still times when the office should seek the man." And he invariably impressed opposing
counsel with his fairness. Neither would he try to ingratiate himself at
social events, although largely because of self-consciousness. "I wonder
sometimes," he wrote after an especially awkward evening, "if I talk as
well—or rather as easily—as I used to." The trouble, he concluded, was
that he thought too much about himself. Only with the young lawyers
and merchants in his circle was he outgoing. "In his cups," recalled
one who knew him well, ". . . he was delightfully friendly and interesting, gracious and happy, and with all his natural dignity and most
careful discipline of his language and conduct, he at times . . . became
exuberant even to that blissful, but often repentant state called
joviality." [20]

Davis became an adept speech-maker. Every year, "quaking" in his
shoes and "feeling queezy" in his stomach, he made at least a half-
dozen addresses, sometimes because he could not decline gracefully,
more often because he was reluctant "to lose any opportunity" to advance himself. An invitation to address the State Bankers' Association
was welcome because "the bankers are—in a business way at least—
'good people,' & it is good to know & be known of them." But a request to speak to a Negro Sunday school convention on the advancement of the Negro race had no appeal whatever; he could see with
"prophetic vision" that he would be "too much rushed" when the time
came. Although he complained that his speeches were unsatisfactory,
his dignity, clarity, and straightforwardness induced respect and con-

veyed conviction; within two or three years he was one of the most sought-after speakers in the area.[21]

The speech that gave Davis the most anguish—a Memorial Day address in 1898—brought him the warmest tributes. All through the winter of 1898 he had brooded over the impending war with Spain. "I belong to the peace party," he wrote privately; "if there is to be a war, it will be due to the Republican demagogues." The notion that the Spanish had destroyed the *Maine* with a bomb or torpedo was absurd.[22]

Resignedly, Davis had accepted the resort to war in April. "If we have to fight—let's give them thunder. . . . We must all be *pro patria.*" Under no circumstances, however, would he volunteer. "I don't *believe* I'm a coward, although no man knows until he is tried; but I couldn't go into the fight now with a bit of heart." McKinley's war message "was a pretty fair sample of the art of saying nothing in words." War would increase the national debt and transform the United States into a colonial and military power. "Oh! for a President big enough to deal with the situation, instead of a human fishing worm." [23]

Forced to suppress most of these thoughts in his Memorial Day address on the courthouse steps, Davis called the roll of heroes and rationalized the new cause: "Today it is no longer brother against brother, nor American against American, but humanity against cruelty and liberty against despotism." But then, in a long fervent peroration, he urged the nation to honor its pledge not to make the conflict a war of conquest:

> There are many who say that we want all the territory we can get, and who think the time is ripe for us to enter upon a colonial policy, forgetting that in union only is there strength, that liberty is best preserved in small areas, and that men, not acres, make a country great.[24]

« IV »

Most of Davis' days were routine, and many were sheer drudgery. At times the work load was almost unbearable. Would it not be better, he often mused, to be a professor than "to be fighting for existence . . . without enough respite for one well-considered thought?" Always the answer was negative: "I wouldn't give one day like this for a dozen droned away in a sleepy classroom." Sometimes he was on his feet

three or four days in a row searching titles. He spent three nights su-
pervising the auction of a bankrupt grocery firm's stock for a $200
commission. ("I'd rather peddle law.") And several times he rode deep
into the country through driving rain or piercing wind to see a client,
only to learn that the client had gone to Clarksburg by a different
route. No less frustrating was the tendency of judges to hold cases over
until the next term without giving prior notice.[25]

Life on circuit was often grueling. In Parkersburg the hotel was a
"vile, ill-smelling place, with the dirtiest dining room." In New Martinsville the proprietor went down the hall at 6:30 every morning,
beating a tattoo on the doors. Everywhere the cooking was "villainous"
and the bedbugs abundant. Only the camaraderie made the life tolerable. As one of the circuit judges remarked near the end of a term:

> Now, gentlemen, we have been having a fine time eating and drinking
> and joking together, but there's got to be a change. Tomorrow is deci-
> sion day, and somebody is going to be beat and he is going to be beat
> bad.[26]

Davis' unfailing courtesy and unusual combination of warmth and
reserve drew people to him wherever he went; even casual acquaintances wanted to confide in him and win his good opinion. As a result,
he was often overburdened. "Why don't the general public learn to
. . . be sociable at the proper times?" he grumbled after a seven-hour
seige in his office by an out-of-town acquaintance. The worst nui-
sances, however, were garrulous clients—the kind who "sit by your
side for hours and dwell away about their cases until you feel like resigning them & their oft repeated story to the bottomless pit." In des-
peration, he resorted to locking his office door.[27]

Eighteen months after his brilliant performance in the miners' trial,
Davis still wondered if he would ever go into court without being
wracked by tension. Like most effective advocates, he immersed himself in a case so deeply that he usually identified with his client.
(Rarely, however, did he lose awareness of his opponent's points of
merit.) For all his outward calm, his "blood" was often up; and nothing gratified him more than to be told, as he frequently was, that he
"just 'tore that case all to pieces.' "[28]

Night after night Davis toiled until ten or eleven o'clock and sometimes even later; day after day he complained that he was never fully
prepared. The county Circuit Court met only two or three times a
year for sessions of not more than a month, so he had to be ready to

rush cases through "or be cussed" by his clients. More exasperating still, given his forensic ability, the judge he appeared before most often regarded oral argument as sheer waste and nodded approvingly when cases were submitted on briefs.[29]

Davis' compulsion for thorough preparation made him intolerant of sloppiness. "For ignorance a man might forgive himself," he said on entering a case that previous counsel had botched, "but for carelessness, never." The two or three cases he himself lost on procedural errors depressed him deeply. "I am in despair," he wrote in the summer of 1898. "I have been slowly forced to the conclusion that the other fellow is right & . . . for the second time in my professional experience I must go out of court on a question other than the merits." Shamefacedly, he told his client that he would not bill him.[30]

Davis' idealism went beyond his compulsion for technical perfection. Once he left court fuming and returned in contrition. "I went back to the office to look up cases to prove you were wrong," he told the judge. "I found you were right." On another occasion he dropped everything to ride three miles into the country to draw up a will for a sick widow. On countless other occasions he passed over substantial fees by advising clients to settle out of court. "Let it alone," he would say; "you haven't a case." [31]

Davis was keenly sensitive to the attorney's role as conciliator. As he once remarked after resolving a domestic quarrel, the lawyer was obligated to prevent strife when possible, and the man who appreciated the real height of the profession had as many opportunities to do good as a clergyman. Unfortunately, many lawyers failed to fulfill the ideal. "The profession is so loaded with these miserable shysters & strife-scarers (who are the buzzards & carrier birds of the community) that one has often to blush for the name of lawyer." [32]

Davis never expressed himself on withholding evidence from opposing counsel. The practice was common at the time, and it was rationalized informally on the notion that the attorney's sole obligation was to his client and that justice was the judge's responsibility. In a notable commentary on appellate techniques in 1940, Davis urged "the telling of the worst as well as the best." But the real thrust of that statement was tactical: failure to concede what had been brought out in a lower court would backfire if opposing counsel were competent. With that exception, Davis' legal papers and private letters are barren of comment on the problem. All that is certain is that he and another lawyer once withheld chance knowledge of an impending special term of court in order to hold down their opponent's time for preparation.[33]

During these years West Virginia law broadly favored the railroads and extractive industries that Davis came increasingly to represent. This slowly forced him to inure himself to the injustices wrought against individuals. "It was my duty," he reflected a half-century later, "to find out what the law was, and tell my client what rule of life to follow. That was my job. If the rules changed, well and good." It was hard, even so, to suppress his compassion. In 1898 he represented a railroad against an old family-friend who sued to prevent tracks from being laid six feet from his kitchen door. "Poor old fellow," Davis wrote, "it's a hard sort of law at the best that a railroad corporation can carve right through [anyone's] property. . . . I confess I can't make any very vigorous showing." Some months later his feelings were "harrowed" when a coal company insisted that he force the sale of a widow's property under the terms of an earlier, and unfavorable, agreement. Davis' sensitivity and fairness usually enabled him to escape ill will. Nevertheless, he brooded: "The lawyer must steel himself like the surgeon to think only of the subject before him & not of the pain his knife may cause. . . . He spends his life making enemies in other people's quarrels." [34]

« V »

Davis' practice was never more varied than between 1897 and 1902. His reputation as a craftsman drew more and more of the new corporate business, yet the small clients his father had always served continued to come in. Much of John W.'s time went into real estate, rights of way, mechanics' liens, dower rights, partnership agreements, and articles of incorporation. But he also handled a little liquor business:

> I have had two very loquacious and unprofitable clients. One was a "speak-easy-keeper" who has just been indicted for unlawful retailing. . . . The other was a brick-mason who is about to turn "speakeasy" keeper, & wanted to know how he could put his property beyond the reach of prospective fines. . . . I advised both repentant sinner & intended transgressor to the best of my ability & bade them depart in peace.[35]

Fees remained low and difficult to collect until well into the new century. He would feel better, Davis remarked after a woman stopped by with two cakes, some maple syrup, and an invitation to supper, if

she would only pay him the $25 she owed him for losing her suit.
Small cases often took as much time as the big ones, and by the end of
his first year of practice Davis was rejecting some of the least profitable. He was also turning down a few for personal reasons. He refused
to handle a matter for a lawyer whom he had virtually charged with
perjury some time earlier. He also declined to represent a woman
whose husband had deserted her. "I've no doubt she tells the truth
when she says that 'Ed as a lover and Ed as a husband are two different things.' Still . . . I shan't take her case and wouldn't for a whole
house and lot." [36]

At first he took many criminal cases: "A man murdered another
out at Wilsonburg two days ago, & takes refuge with us. Another
man has embezzled to the amount of some $2,000 & has shown similar
discretion in his choice of counsel. . . . Oh, it's a gay trade, this of
ministering to other men's miseries." Davis defended a railroad contractor arrested for carrying a pistol. He represented a white youth
who shot "a darkey here some days since—not fatally, unfortunately
for the good of the community but fortunately for my client." He
cleared "the meanest man in Harrison County" of a charge that he set
fire to a coal bank. And he won an acquittal for a postal clerk accused
of opening mail. He disliked the work, however, and he eventually refused to handle criminal cases.[37]

Years later Davis liked to romanticize these cases. A special favorite
was that of four brothers indicted for robbing a post office. "All four,"
he recalled, "were loud in their protestations of innocence, and the
chief witness to their alibi was their venerable father who was by way
of being a local preacher in Webster County. He was ready to swear
them out of it, but when I told him that the Government had suggested a plea of guilty by two and the release of two others, the old
man said, 'Who do they want to plead guilty?' I said: 'Phil and John.'
'Well,' said he . . . 'They's the very fellows that done it.' " [38]

Meanwhile Davis' part-time services to the West Virginia Short Line
Railroad involved him in one of the most bitter disputes of the period. For several years a Clarksburg entrepreneur named Colonel
T. M. Jackson had envisioned tapping a rich coal, oil, and timber area to
the west with a new railroad from Clarksburg to New Martinsville, on
the Ohio River. He won the backing of a group of Standard Oil men,
working through the Guaranty Trust Company of New York, and persuaded the city council to approve a right-of-way through town. Later,
another local group formed a corporation to build a bridge across Elk

Creek to connect to a new B. & O. depot. The resultant decline in the value of property Jackson owned near the old B. & O. station embittered him; he also resented the council's refusal to condemn certain properties for his own station and, especially, its issuance of a new order to run his tracks under the proposed bridge. Apparently Davis advised him that the original order was legally binding; in any event, the Colonel decided to challenge the second order.[39]

Late one night in mid-November 1897, Jackson brought a huge gang of workmen into town. He ordered them to "die in the ditch" fighting anyone who interfered, and at one a.m. they began to lay track. By daybreak they had put down a quarter of a mile. It went straight down the middle of a street, ran perilously close to a new school, and passed over the approach to the bridge at ground level. "We are now trying by injunction etc to hold it down," Davis wrote privately that morning. "Don't think that as a grasping corporation our people are overriding the rights of citizens. We claim that everything so far has been only what we had a right to do." [40]

For two and a half weeks Davis worked feverishly to outmaneuver the city council's special attorney. Once he stayed up all night, relieved only by an hour's nap in his chair. But then, just before the trial date, Jackson's New York backers learned of his tactics and urged him to compromise. Reluctantly, the Colonel agreed to move the Short Line's tracks to the side of the street and to run them beneath the bridge. In return, the city council condemned the properties of the site of Jackson's proposed station.[41]

Davis viewed the entire matter procedurally. Maintaining that he and his client had won every legal point, he lamented only that they had "got less than we were fighting for." None of his comments mentioned the substantive issue—the right of a community to assure public safety, keep its streets passable, and give reasonable protection to private property. As the Clarksburg *Telegram* observed editorially, "The Council [has] taken a broad view . . . and [has] impartially considered all the interests of the public, as well as the conflicting claims of the corporations." [42]

The aftermath of the affair cast a long shadow on Davis' relations with his father. Colonel Jackson had planned to make John J. the Short Line's chief counsel, but the Standard Oil people insisted on selecting a man of their own. To pacify the senior Davis, they turned over their local business to him. With characteristic contempt, John J. assigned it to his son. The business brought in $25 for each land con-

demnation case, and John W. sometimes earned as much as $175 in a
day. Within a year and a half the Short Line made him regular counsel at $150 a month.[43]

The senior Davis said nothing at the time, yet his worst moods coin-
cided with his son's deepest involvement with the railroad. Early in
the new century, his resentment surged to the surface when the despised Baltimore & Ohio bought out the Short Line and appointed
John W. local counsel. Exclaiming that "this office has always stood
for the little man," John J. brought suit for an old friend whose cow
had been killed on the B. & O. tracks.[44]

By then relations between father and son had changed subtly but
importantly. At first John W. had leaned heavily on John J.—
"unconsciously in great measure, for I know that strength doesn't
come from depending on others." Gradually, however, John J. came to
defer to his son's judgment on many important matters. He also let
him manage the firm. John W. handled collections and correspondence, took most of the depositions, and did the burden of the research. The arrangement pleased young John: "I love method & order,
he detests both; I like accurate book-keeping . . . [but] he is satisfied
with a memorandum or more often carries his accounts in his head."

John J. was so gratified to be relieved of office chores that he suggested that John W.'s share of the profits be increased from a third to
a half. (John W. refused for several years.) Yet he also brooded over his
own declining status. He became so morose at one point that he
hardly worked at all for two full weeks. Finally, late one night, he lost
his self-control: he complained that he had become a "back number,"
that he had to leave the office to avoid thinking of himself, and that
prospective clients walked out when John W. was unavailable.

John W. treated his father with such solicitude, recalled a lawyer
who knew them both, that "it was a wonderful thing to see." Nevertheless, he failed to stay the older man's painful withdrawal. By 1899,
John J.'s sixty-third year, John J. was turning over to his son cases
that he had accepted himself. Everything was becoming more and
more distasteful to him, and his lifelong tendency to procrastinate was
growing worse.

One of the roots of the problem was young John's attractiveness to
clients. Osman E. Swartz, who entered the firm a few years later, felt
that John W.'s tact was superior to any he ever knew. Even the strong
ego so evident in his letters was suppressed in public. His wit never
cut, and his confidence, which fed on one success after another, never

verged on cockiness. Free of cant, he was studious, hardworking, and knowledgeable without being ponderous. By 1900 scores of men long repelled by John J.'s "orneriness" were pouring into the office; and by the middle of the decade judges and lawyers who held that the father had the more penetrating mind were also holding that the son was the more effective advocate.[45]

CHAPTER 5

Politics and Law
1898 ~ 1910

*John Davis was commanding in appearance, was impressive, forceful
and convincing in arguments, and was free of partisan or personal attitudes or expressions. . . . His bearing was uniformly serious and dignified, his manner courteous, his arguments logical, his diction exact,
almost to perfection, and he scrupulously never violated his unvaried
duty to the court and the respect due adversary counsel. . . . His serene confidence and innate dignity created respect and compelled conviction.*

CHARLES B. JOHNSON TO THE
WEST VIRGINIA BAR ASSOCIATION

« I »

Politics was Davis' one interest outside the law, but his interest in it
was marginal; the only office he ever actively sought was a federal
judgeship. His first political venture had come in the summer of 1898,
the year before his marriage. Party leaders believed that he could become the first Democrat to represent Harrison County in the House of
Delegates in fourteen years, and they threatened for weeks to draft
him. Although he realized that a term in the legislature would enhance his reputation, he feared that the five-week session would hurt
him financially. "Lord save us from our friends," he complained,
". . . I have been besought, berated, bedevilled until I am on the verge
of tears." [1]

As attorney for the county, Davis was attempting at the time to prevent a railroad that had failed to fulfill its contract from collecting
$150,000 in county bonds. He became the logical candidate for dele-

gate when the Republicans nominated a young man, Richard
Lowndes, who was identified with the railroad through his family.[2]

Within hours of Lowndes' nomination an emissary from a group of
Republicans, all heavy taxpayers, came to Davis. The emissary swore
the twenty-five-year-old lawyer to secrecy, then promised Republican
support if he accepted the Democratic nomination: he would not have
to spend a cent of his own money on the campaign. Davis realized that
the Republican dissidents merely wanted to use him as "the cat's paw
to pull out their chestnuts," and on that account and others he decided not to run. At the Democratic convention that August he buttonholed delegates in the lobby, protested from the floor, and begged
for release after he was nominated by acclamation. But in the end he
submitted. "It is an embarrassing thing to refuse the call of one's
party," he explained privately, "& unwise if any future party favors are
to be hoped for." [3]

Almost everything about the campaign repelled Davis: "I haven't
the face to rush up & shake hands with men I never did more than
bow to before"; "I hate to fawn around people for a purpose anyhow";
"if I were a miner and a candidate made me crawl out . . . just to
shake hands with him, I'd be tempted to give that candidate a good
cussing rather than a vote." The blacks, especially, irritated him.
Asked to pay five dollars a head for their votes, he gave them a "frosty
face" and a dime or quarter. With the Irish, however, he struck a rapport. He professed to have no confidence in their word, but he liked
their "care-free Blarney-ing spirit." [4]

During the campaign that fall Davis assailed tax favors to railroads,
called for a reduction in spending, and promised to vote against assumption of West Virginia's share of the pre-Civil War Virginia debt.
He also hammered hard on the bond issue while his backers flooded
the county with circulars:

Voters of
Harrison County!
**Beware of Voting for any
man who is in Favor of
Making Harrison County Pay
$*150,000*
RAILROAD BONDS [5]**

Davis drew far larger crowds than his opponent. (He discreetly discouraged his father from appearing with him.) And even the militantly Republican *Telegram* conceded that his morals, ability, and so-

cial standing were impeccable. The fundamental issue, it insisted, was control of the state legislature. The new legislature was to elect a United States Senator, and selection of a Democrat would put the tariff on coal, lumber, and wool in jeopardy. Nevertheless, some four hundred anti-bond-issue Republicans crossed over on election day to give Davis a substantial victory. John W. Davis, said his opponent's wife, had fought "a clean fight." [6]

« II »

The turnover in the House of Delegates that year was unusually high and the average age of its members extraordinarily low. Only nine delegates were lawyers—the same number as were physicians—and almost half were farmers. Six educators, five clergymen, three journalists, a publisher, a handful of businessmen, and a carpenter, a brick mason, and a traveling salesman rounded out the lot. In these circumstances, Davis was touted for the speakership and the chairmanship of the judiciary committee even before he arrived in Charleston. After weighing the pros and cons, he decided that the speaker's control of patronage would make too many enemies. "There is no financial gain in the thing & I am not going to become a politician, so I hope only to get . . . as much reputation as I can & not spoil my chances for running for whatever I *may* want in the future." [7]

Within forty-eight hours of being named floor leader and head of the judiciary committee, Davis was catapulted to prominence. In a speech variously described as "magnetic," "terse," and "forcible," he persuaded the more responsible Republicans to support his motion to refer a dispute over the election certificates of two of their delegates to the committee on privileges and elections. A day or two later he made the headlines again with a one-sentence response to the state Attorney General's expostulation that he would ride through Charleston "in blood to his bridle bits" before he would allow the Democrats to dominate the legislature and choose the United States Senator. Said Davis:

> West Virginia can survive the election of another Republican Senator, but it cannot survive the destruction of orderly government which would attend a reign of riot and bloodshed. [8]

The six other lawyers on the judiciary committee deferred almost totally to Davis. "Really, I am amused to see the importance that some of them attach to my opinion on legal questions," he reported; they had made him "a sort of general 'bill-doctor.' " Night after night he persuaded them to kill ill-considered bills; day after day new ones were dropped into the hopper. Only because his colleagues were "pretty kind" in sustaining his opinions was the situation bearable. Meanwhile he remained silent on the floor unless a measure offended his moral, social, or fiscal sensibilities.[9]

Yet he did interject himself with unwonted abruptness in one serio-comic incident. Murderers were still hanged publicly in West Virginia at that time, and one of the delegates introduced a bill to make all executions private. The wording had escaped Davis' attention, and he was dozing in his seat on the final reading when he heard the clerk intone: "all convicts confined in the State Penitentiary shall suffer death in private within the walls of the prison." Davis bolted up, rushed to the author's seat, and insisted that he withdraw the bill; there was no time, he said, to explain why. Afterwards he inserted a clarifying phrase: "all convicts . . . *under sentence of death*." [10]

By the end of the session Davis had revealed himself as a mild reformer on some matters and a staunch conservative on others. He pushed a bill to publish a revised edition of the West Virginia Code. At the instance of his sister Nan, he drove through a measure authorizing local school boards to establish kindergartens. (It did not provide for funding.) He also presented a petition by the United Mine Workers for legislation to strengthen inspection of mines, prohibit employment of boys in pits, and outlaw the importation of strikebreakers. In addition, he spoke briefly for bills to ban child labor in dangerous enterprises and to require factories to install women's rest rooms, fire escapes, and guard rails around dangerous machinery.[11]

More indicative of Davis' real concerns was his attitude toward appropriations. He supported a resolution disclaiming West Virginia's obligation to assume part of the old Virginia debt. He put through an amendment to reduce the appropriation for salaries at the struggling little state university at Morgantown from $32,500 to $28,500. (Others wanted an even larger reduction.) And he helped bury a bill embodying Governor Atkinson's request for $60,000 to construct a building to house the Supreme Court of Appeals, the State Library, and the State Historical Society. The extravagance, he said privately, "galled me . . . no little." [12]

Davis also fought a bill to create a state board empowered to place abandoned, neglected, or cruelly treated children in approved institutions. He regarded the proposal as an "iniquitous" usurpation of the rights of parents, and he deplored in particular the circumstances of its passage. "The personality of a woman [lobbyist] . . . carried it through over my vigorous opposition & the good judgment of one-half the men that voted for her." He added:

> If I wanted to put a measure through—no matter how silly or outrageous—I would simply get a handsome woman—with a sort of cheerful ring in her voice—to come down here & lobby for it. . . . How a man can let his gallantry or his sentiment run away with his better judgment in matters of this sort is more than I can see.

To forestall a similar stampede on woman suffrage, he arranged to table a resolution inviting a prominent Charleston suffragette to address the House.[13]

Meanwhile, Davis fought a lonely battle against an incorporation measure and a fire insurance bill. The former came down from the Senate to informal promises of support by two-thirds of the House. It was designed to allow out-of-state businesses to incorporate in West Virginia even if they did not operate in the state, and it was supported by the majority for its revenue-producing features. Indignant that West Virginia should create trusts "too bad to be kept at home, but not too bad to . . . fatten on the people of other states & bring in tribute of their ill gotten gains," Davis succeeded in burying the bill.[14]

The fire insurance bill was a populist measure which even Davis' father approved. It made companies liable for the face amount of the policy in cases of total destruction regardless of the actual amount of the loss; and as Davis cogently argued in a long speech on the floor, it constituted an open invitation to arson. "I concede that it is a popular bill," he explained to John J., "but I believe a vicious one." He then summarized his speech:

> In the first place, fire insurance is a contract of strict indemnity & not of speculation. . . . When a man takes out a $2000 policy on his house he does not pay to get $2000 when his house burns, but to get the *amount of his loss* not to exceed $2000—Secondly—if he & the company are unable to agree on the value, nearly every policy contains an equitable arbitration clause, & failing in that the courts are always open to him with every chance & every prejudice of the jury in his favor. Thirdly—statistics show that wherever such laws have gone into force . . . the ratio of fires has largely increased, in some cases over 20%. . . . A man gets over-insured—he knows that by this law investigation into the true amount of his loss is precluded. . . . Fourth—premium rates have largely increased . . . & in the long run, not the insurance co., but the policy-holders pay the losses. In other words, I

am taxed higher on my honest policy, in order that my dishonest neighbor may be reimbursed for his arson.[15]

Nevertheless, the measure rolled through both houses; and though Governor Atkinson pronounced it "wrong and unjust" in a long, thoughtful statement which echoed Davis' arguments, he declined to veto it.[16]

Davis' forthright stand on the incorporation and fire insurance bills added to his reputation as the ablest and most respected young member of the legislature. When he left Charleston in February 1899, he did so to predictions that he would someday become governor. As a veteran observer of the capital scene wrote old John J., "he is indeed a worthy son." [17]

« III »

For more than a decade Davis insisted that, though it was the duty of every man to express his political opinions, he was not obligated to run for office. He served a term or two as chairman of the local Democratic organization around the turn of the century, and he helped found a Democratic daily, the Clarksburg *Exponent,* a few years later. He also attended the Democratic National Convention of 1904 as a delegate, supporting the gold standard candidate, Judge Alton B. Parker of New York. But he steadfastly rejected all pleas to stand for Congress or the governorship.[18]

The perennial presidential candidacy of William Jennings Bryan gave Davis his severest trial. He deplored the Great Commoner's views on free silver, his increasing emphasis on federal regulation, and, above all, his evangelical style; yet he shared Bryan's antimonopolism. In a series of speeches during the campaign of 1900, Davis charged that almost all trusts convert consumers into slaves of the market, thwart the rise of new industry, and resort to extremes to escape disclosure and investigation. He held that Standard Oil, in particular, was an incubus on Harrison County because of its power to raise or lower the price of crude oil at will. He also charged that the Federal Steel Company had closed many of its shops and thrown thousands of men out of employment in order to maintain prices by limiting production. "Yet gentlemen tell us there are no trusts. Is it possible that they are hiding in this matter behind a legal quibble—lawyers are sometimes accused of splitting hairs, but it is a dangerous business for statesmen." [19]

Davis' strident antimonopolism failed to drive the trusts from his own door. As Louis D. Brandeis observed at about that time, business hired the best lawyers, and "the leaders of the Bar, without any pre-conceived intention on their part . . . have, with rare exceptions, been ranged on the side of the corporations." Davis continued, of course, to take some public interest cases. In 1902, for example, he and his father represented the city of Clarksburg in an action which broke a local electric power monopoly. Yet the firm's rural and small business clients tended to be handled more and more by the senior Davis and the junior partners, Osman Swartz and Bryan Templeman. After John W. became counsel to the B. & O., the suits against railroads upon which his father had built so much of the practice virtually stopped.[20]

Davis' corporate retainers inevitably imposed subtle restraints on his freedom of action. Two cases, one involving the B. & O., the other the United Mine Workers, are sharply illustrative. The tremendous expansion of coal production during these years created a serious shortage of coal cars. Great trunk lines like the B. & O. allocated a fixed number of cars to the independent lines that serviced the mines, and the independents in turn assigned a quota to each mine, for potential output far exceeded haulage facilities. Small mining companies complained bitterly that the allotments favored the big companies, particularly those owned by the railroads; they also charged that the practice of supplying additional cars on contract discriminated against small companies, most of which lacked the financial resources to engage a specified number of cars in advance. In 1903 the president of one of these small companies, Kingswood Coal, asked Davis to file suit against "the jerkwater" line that serviced his mine. Before taking the case, Davis asked the B. & O.'s general counsel, Hugh Bond, if this would embarrass the B. & O. "Certainly not," Bond said, "we have nothing to do with that."[21]

After entering the case, Davis learned that the principal witness for the defendant would be the B. & O. official in charge of allocating cars to coal companies; more embarrassing still, he uncovered evidence linking the B. & O. to Kingswood's shortage. Concluding that the B. & O. would have to "take care of itself," Davis grilled the line's official so relentlessly when he took the stand that the B. & O.'s allocation system was exposed in all its most discriminatory aspects. "I had to go through him . . . ," Davis recalled. "I had to do it, but I was fouling my own nest." It was very "painful" to the B. & O.[22]

In a decision that created a minor sensation throughout the state, the court found for Kingswood Coal. The small independents, said

Davis, thought "there was 'a god in Israel' in some court," and they
soon asked him to challenge the Chesapeake & Ohio on the same
counts. Once again he asked Bond if he could take the case. This time
the B. & O. general counsel replied that "there ought to be a limit to
the fool questions that could be presented to a court." Davis then rejected the case.[23]

In the UMW matter, Davis opposed some of the same union organizers he had defended in 1897. Early in the spring of 1902 UMW officials asked the operators to discuss a new wage scale. The operators
refused, and on June 7 about 80 per cent of the state's miners struck,
while a horde of organizers, including Mother Jones, descended on the
state. Two weeks later a bill of complaint was filed in the name of the
Guaranty Trust Company of New York. Guaranty Trust was the mort-
gagee of the Clarksburg Fuel Company, one of Davis' regular clients.
Non-resident "agitators," the complaint alleged, had entered a conspiracy to foment a strike and had tried to incite the hatred and animosity
of the miners against the operators of the Clarksburg and Fairmont
coal companies. Judge Jackson forthwith ordered the organizers not to
intimidate, march, or assemble near the Fuel Company's property.[24]

The organizers promptly defied the injunction by holding a meeting
about a thousand feet from the Clarksburg company's property line.
Mother Jones and six men were then arrested for contempt and tried
by Judge Jackson without a jury. "The Constitution," declared Jackson in sentencing the males to sixty to ninety days in jail, "don't guarantee rights to the citizens to go into the domain of another state and
incite the people to violence." He then banished Mother Jones from
the state with the admonition that she forego labor agitation for charity work such as "the Allwise Being intended her sex should
pursue." [25]

Davis entered the case about two weeks later, when the organizers
contended on appeal that Judge Jackson had lacked jurisdiction because the Guaranty Trust Company had sought diverse citizenship as a
pretext to get the case into a federal court. In a hearing before Judge
Goff, union lawyers insisted that the Clarksburg Fuel Company should
have been made a party and that the case should have gone to a state
court. Both the United States Attorney and counsel for Guaranty vigorously challenged these contentions, and Davis, acting for Clarksburg
Fuel, summed up their arguments so dispassionately that even the
miners' attorneys complimented him on his fairness. Judge Goff then
rejected the appeal.[26]

« IV »

During Davis' decade and a half of practice in West Virginia, he was probably admired most for his all-round craftsmanship. Before he was thirty, clients were signing documents he drafted without reading them. ("If he drew them up, that's good enough for me.") And by his mid-thirties he was the recognized leader of the younger bar. He was never regarded as the most learned or brilliant lawyer in the area; others, including his father, had specific faculties superior to his. But no one else possessed his combination of gifts. As a Clarksburg colleague said in summing up his qualities, his ability to impart his thoughts to others in simple, lucid language was truly extraordinary:

> He was intellectual without the flaw of austerity . . . much less disparagement of the opinions of the lesser endowed; he was dignified without loss of friendly interest; he was scholarly without the fault of pretention; he enjoyed success but demanded immunity from praise. He was never abstruse, never deceptive, and never employed argument to cloud or confuse an issue. He was always direct and explicit. Integrity was a naturally dominant element of his character.[27]

Davis himself never analyzed the reasons for his success so directly. But as his later advice to fledgling lawyers suggests, he attributed much of it to the remarkable memory which his mother's rote assignments had done so much to develop. "Force it . . . , lean on it, refuse it artificial aid, and sooner or later it will answer your call." Davis' deep, sonorous voice was also a powerful asset, especially in jury trials; regardless, almost, of what he said, his words carried authority. In addition, he was a superb cross-examiner. It was hard work. As he said at the time, a day on the stand against a shrewd, sharp witness imposed the severest strain that he knew. But it was also rewarding. "If there is anything pleasanter than to see your adversary's own witness 'fall down on him,' I don't know what it is." [28]

Davis professed no general rule for calling a witness. He realized that juries frequently treated the failure of witnesses to take the stand as a confession of guilt; he also knew that a vulnerable witness could confuse rather than clarify the facts. So he relied on his instincts. "There is a sixth sense—I don't know what it is—by which you can feel the temper of people around you." A hostile witness should not be pushed to the point that the jury became sympathetic. "You say to yourself . . . I'd like to ask him that one more question, but I'm not sure that response would be right. Do I dare risk it?' " Sometimes he took the chance and won, sometimes he lost. But usually he sensed when to stop. He relished the memory of a case in which his client, a lawyer, sat at his elbow and urged him on. "Ask him this," the client whispered. "I think not," Davis replied. "I'd like you to ask him." In exasperation, Davis put the question and lost the case on the spot. "I hope," he said, turning to the lawyer-client, "you've learned not to ask the one question too many." [29] A judge who had heard both John W. and his father try many cases compared their techniques:

> If John J. Davis thought a witness were lying it would arouse all of the innate hostility and belligerence in his nature, and on cross-examination he would tear into him. Usually he would get the truth, but would anger the witness. John W. Davis . . . would set his trap, lead the witness into it, and get the truth in half the time and with half the effort; and without arousing any antagonism. He would also sit down and figure out the case in advance, so that . . . he would know about what the other lawyer had up his sleeve. I seldom knew him to be caught unawares. John J. Davis was so partisan in his mental processes he could only see one side of the case, and would frequently be embarassed by some development he had not anticipated.[30]

Davis' outward dispassion was more a function of his extraordinary powers of self-discipline than of lack of emotion. He struggled for many years to master his temper, and several times during his early manhood he lost his self-control. In 1898 he struck an opposing counsel in court, and was held in contempt. ("Scratch the skin of civilized man," he ruefully remarked afterwards, "and you'll find the savage.") In 1900 he threw an inkwell at another attorney, again in court. And in 1903 he had an angry encounter in the middle of town with the fiercely Republican editor of the *Telegram,* Wilbur Morrison, who had charged the senior Davis with distributing liquor in one of his campaigns for Congress in the 1870's. Old John J. proposed to lash him with a dog whip, Clarksburg's ultimate weapon of contempt. But before he could act, young John strode to the *Telegram*'s office with a buggy whip. When Morrison came out he exclaimed, "Wilbur, you dirty dog," then chased him up the street, flailing furiously all the while. Afterwards, to avoid a heavy fine by a Republican justice of the peace on Morrison's complaint, he had his junior partner, Osman Swartz, swear out a warrant before a Democratic justice of the peace. He fined him $5.00.[31]

Three years after the whipping incident, Davis was elected president of the West Virginia Bar Association. He was thirty-three years old at the time, and had been secretary for several years. He had also served, or would serve, on the committees on legal education, legal reform, and judicial administration. Although the association was primarily a social organization, a sometimes weighty intellectual fare was sandwiched between the "chicken à la lawyer" and "sweetbreads à la Warm Springs" at its three-day annual meetings. Some of the talks were anecdotal or "off the top of the head," and an occasional speaker complained that too many books on the law were being written or that too much education was dangerous. But most of the formal papers and addresses were thoughtful, and many were quite scholarly. With the notable exception of the revolution in substantive due process,* they treated most of the important questions of the times. On procedural and administrative matters such as standards of admission and reorganization of the state court system, they were consistently reformist. But on the relationship between law and social change they revealed a sharp and continuous division.[32]

Davis rarely spoke in the discussions, and his few extant letters contain no references to the Association's intellectual activities or to his own reading in jurisprudence. All that remains is a 1907 letter to Major McDonald in which he lamented his lack of time to improve himself along general lines. Nevertheless, the Association's proceedings cast considerable light on the intellectual milieu in which Davis functioned.[33]

Two papers in particular bore on matters that were later to involve Davis deeply when he was in Congress. The first enumerated many of the long-standing abuses of the injunction in labor disputes. The second, a learned statement of the case for workmen's compensation, neatly juxtaposed the prevailing notion that the fellow-servant doctrine † was "the best law to govern the relationship of employer and employee that has ever been devised by human ingenuity" with Henry Asquith's contrary view: "The idea originated with Lord Abinger, of the Chief Justice's Bench, Baron Alderson watered it, and the devil gave it increase." [34]

* During the last quarter of the nineteenth century, the Supreme Court extended to corporations privileges that effectively shielded them from much regulation by both state and federal government. This was accomplished through judicial construction of the due process clause of the Fourteenth Amendment, the original purpose of which was to guarantee civil liberties to former slaves.

† The fellow-servant rule absolved the employer from liability when an injury was caused by the negligent act of another fellow servant (worker).

Other papers supported the legal formalism on which Davis had been nurtured. One asserted that the police power was fostering "a low standard of private morality" through poor debtors' laws, stay laws, homestead exemptions, and the issuance of free school books. Another argued that to change a rule of property by judicial construction was to trespass on the legislative sphere. A third proposed that *stare decisis* be incorporated into statutory law in order to prevent the overturn of established precedents.[35]

These doctrines were frequently and forcefully challenged. As early as 1889 a Wheeling judge criticized *stare decisis* and the profession's disposition to put its faith in unchanging principles. The rules, he declared, must be "just in themselves, just, not in any abstract sense, but just, as being in accordance with the common sentiment of mankind." Two decades later another judge quoted Cicero—*"tempora mutantur et mutamus in illis"*—in support of the view that "changed conditions often will justify change of decision." A few years before that a Martinsburg attorney categorically asserted that the general submission of lawyers to commercialism was "demoralizing" the profession.[36]

Davis' own presidential address, "The Growth of the Commerce Clause," was one of the fullest philosophical statements he ever made. A superb exercise in logic, it revealed his consuming concern for the preservation of individual liberties, state and local rights, and constitutional principles. It also posed the central dilemma of his political-legal thought—how to reconcile the felt needs of a changing social and economic polity with an immutable fundamental law. "I fancy," he said, "that every member of this Association sympathises heartily in the end sought by . . . [federal regulatory laws]. But let us not deceive ourselves as to the meaning of the methods employed. The steady expansion of the Federal power inevitably means by just so much the diminution of the power of the States. And let us remember further in the language of Marshall that—'Questions of power do not depend on the degree to which it may be exercised. If it may be exercised at all, it must be exercised at the will of those in whose hands it is placed.' "[37]

Davis used the Employers' Liability Act of 1906 as an illustration. At one stroke, he declared,

> the Act abolishes the doctrine of fellow-servants, destroys contributory negligence as a defense, restores the doctrine of comparative negligence long since repudiated by the courts, prescribes the respective provinces

of judge and jury, nullifies contracts between the carrier and the employee, removes all limit on the amount of the recovery, fixes the statute of limitations at one year and permits recovery in case of death only for the widow, children, parents or next of kin. . . .

"How can this be said to be a regulation of commerce?" [38]

He also commented indirectly on Senator Albert J. Beveridge's charge that child labor in America, including that in the West Virginia glass industry, was "as brutal and horrible in its inhumanity as anything the pen of Dickens ever painted." Davis himself was much too kindly, of course, to condone child labor *per se.* Yet his abhorrence of federal power was so great, his view of society so formalistic, that he could not face the realities behind Beveridge's call for a federal solution. ("If one State passes good laws and enforces them, and another State does not," said the Indianan, "then the business men in the former State are at a . . . disadvantage.") Davis dilated, accordingly, on the counter truth: "If Congress can prohibit the transportation of the product of child labor, it can also prohibit the transportation of goods manufactured by 'scab' labor . . . and thus close the door of the factory to every workman who does not have a union card." [39]

Davis concluded with a sharp thrust at President Theodore Roosevelt, who had long railed against a static conception of law. "I do not need to remind you," he warned in a classic restatement of the conservative position, "that dissatisfaction with a law—either organic or statutory—does not justify disobedience; that contempt for the higher laws in high places must bring contempt for lesser laws among the lowly; and that constitutional distortion is as much a crime as constitutional destruction." [40]

« V »

All through these years Davis' financial situation steadily improved. He helped form a half dozen gas and oil companies, and he invested heavily in established oil and gas companies, in Clarksburg's leading bank, and in a fire insurance company. Occasionally he miscalculated. Once he and two friends built a small plant to produce liquid coffee, but they lost everything when their process proved deficient. On the whole, however, the returns were good. He began to take trips each summer—to New England, the Jersey shore, Quebec, and once to Europe. He also gave considerable attention to clothes, dressing fashionably, but conservatively. "I never saw him when he wasn't well turned out," a close friend recalled. On the whole, however, his expenses were minimal until Julia reached her teens and he sent her to boarding school. The firm's seven rooms on the third floor of the new Goff Building rented at $93 a month, secretarial help could not have run more than $200, and board at home was minimal. By 1910 he was taking in close to the $10,000 in fees he had set as his goal, and by 1911 his investments totalled $83,093.[41]

Meanwhile, pressure mounted for Davis to run for high state or national office. It was almost the Democrats' supreme duty to nominate him for governor, the Greenbrier *Independent* declared in 1908. "He is in the prime of a vigorous manhood, is a leader at a bar famed for its learning and ability, and is forceful, earnest, honest and fearless." Although Davis decried the agitation, party leaders decided in 1910 to nominate him for Congress in the First District. Rising prices, charges of corruption against state Republicans, and general dissatisfaction with President William Howard Taft augured a Democratic year, and the leaders went to Davis because "he's the best man we've got and the only one we can elect." [42]

Davis pleaded financial insecurity. "I agree heartily with what you say about . . . money," he wrote an editor who had implied that he worried too much about his income; nevertheless, it would be a "great sacrifice" to run, and he preferred to wait until his own and his dependents' future would not be imperiled. But, as he admitted to his mother, the trouble ran deeper:

> When I am honest with myself, I know that . . . down in my soul, about this as about most things, I don't really care a rap, one way or the other. A real, genuine, unmixed impulse, if it were even to climb the outside of the Washington monument, would be a positive relief." [43]

On his arrival in Wheeling the night before the district convention opened in mid-July 1910, Davis told reporters that he would not accept the nomination under any circumstances. But his Clarksburg neighbor, Dr. J. W. Johnston, plied the newsmen with so much liquor, that they failed to file the story for the morning papers. Another friend withheld two telegrams old John J. had sent, ordering his son not to yield, while party leaders showed him pledges of support by prominent Republicans. At four a.m. Davis gave in.[44]

A tense moment followed during the nominating speech late that morning, when Davis grew visibly restless. Fearful that he would announce his withdrawal, someone moved his nomination by acclamation. Four men then dragged him to the platform. "Now damn you, accept this nomination!" one of them exclaimed. Afterwards, the reluctant candidate returned home to an enthusiastic welcome by his townspeople and a bitter reprimand from his father. Old John J. called Dr. Johnston a "katydid," charged another local leader with making a poor politician out of a good lawyer, and threatened to turn John out of the house. Only the warm testimonials to his son finally reconciled him.[45]

As the campaign unfolded, it became apparent that Republican business leaders were more concerned with tariff protection than with the party livery of the candidates. Sensing that Davis was likely to win, their editorial spokesmen waged a subtle campaign to convert him to protectionism. Davis' business connections were mainly with tariff-protected industries, the Charleston *Star* observed; surely he, along with most other West Virginia Democrats, would rank as a moderate protectionist. To their bitter surprise, Davis scored the G.O.P.'s tariff policy in every speech of the campaign. The climax came in Wheeling where a crowd of 500 roared approval of his assertion that the Republicans had enriched "the few at the expense of the many, and had enhanced the swollen profits of those already rich, beyond the dreams of avarice." [46]

Between attacks on the tariff, Davis commended his party perfunctorily for pioneering in the regulation of railroads, anti-trust legislation, direct election of Senators, and the graduated income tax. Only against the increased cost of government necessitated by new schools, highways, hospitals, mental and penal institutions, courthouses, research stations, and other social services did he speak with real force. "I protest again," he repeatedly declared, ". . . the wild reign of extravagance in the disbursement of the people's money." [47]

That November Davis became the first Democrat to represent the First Congressional District since 1894. He had won by 20,370 votes to 16,962. "I am not vain enough to accept the result as . . . a personal triumph," Davis announced. "The very size of the majority shows that there has been . . . a great uprising against boss rule, machine domination and the disregard of the plain principle of morality in politics." As the Democratic sweep all over the North suggests, the statement was broadly accurate. Yet personality and reputation had also figured large. "It is no disgrace," said the Republican candidate, Charles E. Carrigan, "to be beaten by a man like John W. Davis." [48]

BOOK II

The Private Man in Public Life

« CHAPTER 6 »

The Ablest Lawyer
in Congress

*The reforms embodied in this bill are wise and consonant with the
promise of Magna Charta, that justice shall be denied or delayed to no
man and that the administration of justice shall not be so cumbrous,
dilatory, and . . . expensive that it shall be obtainable only by the
rich.*

JOHN W. DAVIS ON A
JUDICIAL PROCEDURE MEASURE, APRIL 26, 1912

« I »

Never, said Speaker of the House Champ Clark in the summer of
1913, did he recall a young Congressman earning so great a reputation in so short a time as had John W. Davis of West Virginia.[1] Reports of Davis' skill as a lawyer had preceded him to Washington, and
on taking his seat in the Sixty-second Congress in March 1911, he was
assigned to the judiciary committee because Chairman Henry D. Clayton of Alabama needed an able draftsman. This assignment, rare for a
freshman, carried unusual opportunity, for every bill to change an existing law came before the committee. Davis first won the notice of the
House, however, with a speech on a Democratic bill to revise the wool
schedules of the Payne-Aldrich Tariff of 1909. Wool growers in his
own district strongly opposed the measure.[2]

In mid-June of 1911, his head filled with statistics gleaned from the
writings of academic authorities, Davis rose to charge that protection
of the wool-growing industry was economically indefensible. He
pointed out that Ohio and West Virginia growers had failed to expand production despite a long succession of tariffs. He charged that a

"co-conspiracy" of manufacturers and a handful of specialized sheep breeders had protected manufacturers alone. And he noted that sheep raising was profitable only where grazing land was plentiful, as in Australia and Argentina. Heads of families employed in the industry in the United States averaged only $400 a year. "What becomes of all the talk about the 'American standard of living,' " he asked, "when a man is [forced] . . . to live and raise a family on a paltry wage of $10.49 per week?" Patently, the Payne-Aldrich wool schedule had been framed "not to raise money for the general welfare but to put profits into the pockets of a special class." [3]

Nine months later Davis framed a bill to prevent the abuse of the injunction as he had so often observed it abused in West Virginia. In every presidential campaign since 1896, the Democrats had written anti-injunction planks into their platforms, and, on six separate occasions between 1905 and 1909, Theodore Roosevelt had urged Congress to act. Twelve times during William Howard Taft's first two years in office remedial bills had died in Congress. But not until March 1912 did Clayton, a bumbling, imperious man who swam with the strongest currents, appoint Davis to a subcommittee to draw up a new bill.[4]

Davis believed that the issuance of injunctions should be limited as a matter of equity. But he was unwilling, as he phrased it, "to go . . . [labor's] length and pull down the pillars of the temple." For several days running he worked on his bill until midnight, then tossed sleepless afterwards. At length he hammered out a moderate draft which the full committee accepted with only slight modification. The measure forbade federal judges to grant injunctions in labor disputes unless they were necessary to prevent irreparable injury to property or to a property right. It specifically protected the right to boycott as well as the right to persuade others to boycott, although it did not use that term. It prohibited the issuance of injunctions to stop peaceable assembly, the "recommending, advising or persuading" of workers to strike, and several other actions that Judges Jackson and Goff had enjoined routinely. It also tightened the conditions under which necessary injunctions were to be issued.[5]

Piqued by Clayton's insistence that the measure be brought out under his (Clayton's) name, Davis refused to volunteer to write the report. "I hate to see the bill massacred by the sort of report . . . [Clayton] is likely to make," he wrote his father in March, "but I feel that I have contributed all the ideas I care to for other men's use." He would hold his "thunder" temporarily. Not until mid-May did he defend the measure on the floor.[6]

Davis began by reminding the Republicans of Roosevelt's six injunction messages. He then challenged Republican assertions that the injunction had not been misused. He listed five glaring abuses:

> The issuance of injunctions without notice.
> The issuance of injunctions without bond.
> The issuance of injunctions without detail.
> The issuance of injunctions without parties.
> And, in trade disputes particularly, the issuance of injunctions against certain well-established and indisputable rights.[7]

To allay fears that the bill would prevent the government from acting in crises like the Pullman Strike of 1894, Davis noted that in the Pullman matter the *Debs* injunction had been brought by the United States in its own name and did not involve employer-employee relations. He made it clear, however, that his bill would have prevented the sweeping injunction against "all other persons whomsoever" which was actually issued. He further attacked the notion that the courts' recognition of the right to strike and picket made legislation unnecessary. The answer, he said, was to be found in numerous decisions to the contrary. Thus, in *Atchison, Topeka & Santa Fe v. Gee,* the presiding judge had actually declared that "there is and can be no such thing as peaceful picketing any more than there can be chaste vulgarity or peaceful mobbing or lawful lynching." Davis also denied that the measure was a form of "class legislation." Employers' liability acts, workmen's compensation bills, and eight-hour laws, he asserted, were all of a piece:

> It is no objection to any law that it is intended to right the wrongs of any class, race, or section of society, so only it gives no more than equal and exact justice. Class legislation, in the vicious sense of the word, means special privilege, and special privilege only.[8]

Davis concluded with a blistering attack on Theodore Roosevelt and the recall of judicial decisions. "There were some," he said, "who wanted to rush headlong after so-called remedies which . . . will only aggravate the disease they are supposed to cure." Among them was a "distinguished ex-President—eager as always to be newer than the newest, more original than the most original, and more progressive than the most advanced." In an apparent effort "to out-Herod Herod," Roosevelt had proposed that certain types of decisions be revised by popular vote. This assault on the heart of the legal system should be beaten back, for "a judge cowed into impotence or tempted to excess by dependence upon the constant favor of the appointing power or the continued smile of public approval is of all men most pitiable and dangerous." [9]

Davis' speech, wrote Felix Frankfurter, was the "ablest" of the entire debate. Shortly after Davis finished, the anti-injunction bill rolled through the House 243 to 31, as Samuel Gompers beamed approval from the gallery. The Senate then pigeonholed it. Eighteen months later, substantially in the form Davis had framed it, the measure became part of the Clayton Antitrust Act.[10]

Meanwhile, the West Virginia Congressman applied himself to a bill to require jury trials in contempt cases. Its history and its fate paralleled that of the anti-injunction measure. Fifty-three times between 1897 and 1909 jury bills had been introduced, and fifty-three times they had died in committee. Ten new measures, including one loosely drawn by Clayton, were dropped into the hopper in the first session of the Sixty-second Congress under heavy pressure from the American Federation of Labor. Two compelling concerns animated the A. F. of L.: the judge who granted an injunction also tried those charged with violating it, and juries in mining and industrial communities were likely to be less anti-labor than were federal judges.[11]

Davis had no desire to supplant biased judges with biased juries. Yet he knew Jackson's and Goff's frame of reference too well to deny that the judiciary was broadly predisposed toward property. He therefore rephrased Clayton's bill in accordance with Article III of the Constitution. Despite rumblings from the Republican minority, the full committee accepted his phraseology, and the bill was reported out in Clayton's name.[12]

Reluctant to appear overly aggressive, Davis inserted his prepared remarks in the *Congressional Record* instead of delivering them on the floor. As Frankfurter and James M. Landis later observed, he demonstrated the "utter barrenness" of his opponents' contentions. He first noted that the history of the power of courts to punish for contempt was one of progressive restriction. He then denied that Congress lacked authority over District Courts. Were such a proposition maintained, he pointed out, all court reforms would have to come from within; repeatedly, however, the Supreme Court had ruled that inferior courts were the creatures of Congress. "No words of mine can add either force or clearness to these expositions of the law"; manifestly, the legislative power that creates a court may define the acts constituting contempt and prescribe the manner of their trial and punishment.[13]

« II »

The heaviest of Davis' congressional burdens was boredom. Once, he and a colleague, Martin Littleton of New York, walked out of the chamber in disgust. "I can't stand this thing," Littleton said, as they waited for a drink at the Congress Hotel. "I'm used to trying cases, and when a case is tried, it's tried, and that's the end of it. Here, no matter . . . how hard you work, some damned fool who has never thought about it will throw a monkey wrench into your position." The West Virginian agreed emphatically. Weeks, months, a year, slipped by without accomplishment: "Endless *cunctation*—active obstruction, sometimes, more often mere passive inertia—until I wish myself at something else." [14]

Davis complained especially of the hypocrisy of Southern Democrats. As he confided to his father, of the sixty-six members of the caucus who voted for a freewheeling investigation of the money trust early in 1912, less than a third really favored the resolution. "The rest were simply demagoging." Hardly less annoying were the little compromises necessary to his own survival. Davis introduced twenty-nine pension or relief bills for constituents in his first session. He sent out 8000 franked copies of his tariff speech. (He told his mother that he was "a pious fraud.") He arranged for the construction of a public building in his district. He even accompanied a delegation to Trenton in January 1913 to urge President-elect Woodrow Wilson to appoint Clayton Attorney General. Clayton, he confided to his father, was an execrable lawyer; but at least he was preferable to Louis D. Brandeis. Ideally, Wilson should select the best lawyer available *"red hot* from the bar." [15]

Patronage also wore Davis down. He had six calls from job-seekers the day he took his seat, and he was so harassed at the time of Wilson's inauguration that he stayed away from his office for days. "You never saw such a torrent of people, except if you had been down there and seen Eisenhower come in," he said forty years later. He claimed that he made at least nine enemies for every available position, and

that he did not always make a friend of the man he appointed.
"You're either a prince because you got him a job or awful because
you haven't. And if you're a prince, he's not very grateful to you because he got it on his own merits, see? It's terrible, really terrible." [16]

Davis' practical strain often tempered his idealism. Yet, except when
bound by the caucus, his attitude toward legislation usually reflected
three criteria: Was a bill constitutional? Did it serve his own conception of the general welfare? Was it moderate rather than radical? If a
bill failed to meet any of these criteria, he worked within committee to
change it. More than once he opposed the interests of former clients,
including the B. & O., and more often than not he gave professional
lobbyists no satisfaction whatever. Usually his facility for listening pa-
tiently and disagreeing graciously spared him ill will. But the strain
was nonetheless intense:

> When I get through explaining to Moundsville, New Martinsville,
> Wellsburg, Fairmont, Salem & Clarksburg why they can't have public
> buildings; to the Tin Plate people why their tariff was reduced beyond
> what they recommend; to the W.C.T.U. why it is sometimes necessary
> to consider the constitution of the U.S. before enacting laws; to the la-
> borites, why the Wilson Anti-injunction bill is impossible; to the jin-
> goes, why I voted against battle-ships last night; & to Mr. W. J. Bryan
> why I think Bob Henry's so-called "Money-trust" resolution is the rank-
> est piece of demagogy ever gotten up for individual exploitation and
> advertisement—when, as I say, these tasks are finished I shall be ready
> for a nice long rest in the seclusion of private life.[17]

Meanwhile, two election bills put Davis' strict constructionism on severe trial. The first test came on a motion to give federal courts jurisdiction over violations of a proposed law requiring compulsory publicity of campaign contributions in both primary and regular elections.
The motion was doubly offensive to the South, for it flouted the
Southern conception of state's rights and opened the all-white Democratic primary to eventual challenge. Southern leaders made it a caucus issue, and Davis dutifully voted to strike it out when it reached the
floor of the House. The Senate then restored the crucial provision, and
Davis, almost alone among Southerners, voted for the conference version.[18]

The second test of Davis' intellectual honesty came over a Southern
effort to frame the Seventeenth Amendment for direct election of Senators so as to vitiate Congress' right to regulate federal elections under
Article I and the Fifteenth Amendment. The House wording reaf-

firmed that part of Article I which empowered the states to prescribe
the "Times, Places and Manner" of federal elections, but it omitted all
reference to the clause authorizing Congress to "make or alter such
Regulations." It also failed to mention the Fifteenth Amendment's assertion that "Congress shall have power to enforce . . . [the Amendment's guarantee of voting rights] by appropriate legislation." [19]

Some Republican Senators opposed the House provision because
they believed in full Negro suffrage as a matter of right. But others, including Elihu Root of New York and George Sutherland of Utah,
wanted only to provoke Southerners into rejecting the Seventeenth
Amendment outright. They insisted on reaffirming Congress' constitutional authority over elections. This sparked an acrimonious debate in
the House, which was still considering its own emasculating language.
"You southern Democrats," declared Minority Leader James R. Mann
of Illinois, "believe . . . that this may be construed as a partial repeal
of the fifteenth amendment, and whether it so operates as a matter of
theoretical law, you know that you intend that it shall operate so in
fact." Most Southerners, he concluded, not only wished "to reduce . . .
[Negroes] to a condition of practical serfdom and servitude," they
wanted Northerners "to condone and approve" their action.[20]

Mann's rhetoric failed to shake Davis' commitment to the caucus.
Late in June 1911, he joined almost every other Democrat in the
House in voting against the Senate construction. By 1912, when the
measure came up again, Majority Leader Oscar W. Underwood of Alabama was striving to acquire a national image in order to advance his
presidential aspirations, so he decided not to bind the caucus. This allowed Davis to stand on his own constitutional scruples. In a break
with James F. Byrnes, Martin Dies, Sr., and eighty-six other Southern
Democrats, he voted against a new motion to deny Congress' constitutional right to regulate elections and prohibit the use of federal marshals at the polls. He then supported a compromise which made no
reference to regulation of elections.[21]

A disingenuously framed liquor-control measure—the Webb-Kenyon bill—subsequently forced Davis into a new wrestle with his conscience. By early 1913, Prohibition was the law in one form or another
in thirty-one states, and the movement for a federal law had gathered
irreversible momentum. Few members of Congress wanted national
legislation, but fewer still had the courage to defy the Anti-Saloon
League and its zealous supporters in the evangelical churches. After
stalling as long as they could, the Democratic leaders decided to pass

the bill immediately; Taft, rather than Woodrow Wilson, would then have to bear the onus of a veto.[22]

Davis soon concluded that the Webb-Kenyon Bill was improperly framed, had been submitted in bad faith, and was of dubious constitutionality. On its face, it banned shipment of alcoholic beverages into states where their sale was illegal; but in the absence of a penalty clause, the ban was a pure sham. Sensing the mood of the House, Davis concluded that the most he could hope for was an honestly framed measure. He therefore prevailed on the subcommittee to add a penalty clause and to affirm the right to ship liquor for sacramental and personal use.[23]

These amendments embroiled Davis in the most bitter controversy of his congressional career. First, West Virginia prohibitionists sent him an insulting telegram demanding that he support the unamended version. Next, the Reverend E. D. Dinwiddie, the Anti-Saloon League's "goggle-eyed, weasel-faced" lobbyist, as Davis angrily described him, attacked the amendments in a circular broadside. Finally, the bill's supporters spread a rumor that the amendments were dishonestly conceived.[24]

On February 8, 1913, Davis took the floor to charge Dinwiddie with "double-dealing" and "intellectual dishonesty." He noted that the Anti-Saloon League had earlier conceded the constitutional right of a citizen to have alcohol shipped to him from another state, but that Dinwiddie now insisted that Davis' amendment guaranteeing that right was against "the real policy and underlying principle" of the bill and would "shackle and hobble the States." Davis also maintained that the penalty clause was absolutely necessary:

> Has it ever been seriously suggested before . . . that we may create a crime but not punish it; that we shall have the will to denounce an offence but not the courage to punish the offender? . . . What a potent evasion of responsibility. What cowardice to say that Congress has the constitutional right to forbid a thing but not the constitutional courage to attach a penalty to its prohibition.[25]

Twice the House interrupted the speech with applause. Yet no appeal to logic, conscience, or the Constitution could break the Democrats' resolve to pay lip-service to the Prohibition lobby and give political aid to the incoming Wilson administration. The penalty amendment was rejected by 214 to 79, and the personal and sacramental use amendment went down by a voice vote. Davis then voted to pass the Webb-Kenyon bill as a whole.[26]

Afterwards he confided to his father that the measure was constitutional only by a course of reason not far removed from casuistry, and that he should have opposed the entire bill. There was one consolation: "I had the satisfaction of taking a fall out of Bro. Dinwiddie." Three weeks later, in the worst compromise of his congressional career, he voted to override President Taft's veto.[27]

By then Davis was engrossed in a struggle within the judiciary committee for a workmen's compensation bill. For two decades reformers had been arguing that accidents involving machinery that had not even been in existence when the fellow-servant and contributory negligence rules were written into the common law made those doctrines anachronistic. In 1902 President Roosevelt had taken up the cause, and in 1906 Congress had passed a weak measure covering workers in interstate commerce. This Act overturned the fellow-servant rule, but it failed to make compensation automatic. The Supreme Court struck it down the next year.[28]

Even before the Court's action, Roosevelt had urged Congress to put all federal employees under an automatic compensation system. Declaring it an outrage that the entire cost of an accident should fall on the helpless man and his family, he charged that in no other industrialized nation "could such an injustice occur." Congress then re-enacted the 1906 law so as to meet the Court's objections, but it rejected automatic compensation. As a self-styled Jeffersonian Democrat, Senator Joseph W. Bailey of Texas, explained, "every man takes the consequences of his own folly." [29]

The facts mocked Bailey's rhetoric. Although the overwhelming majority of industrial accident victims were not to blame for their injuries and deaths, the common law right to sue afforded scant relief to them or their families. Not only did workers lack the resources to employ able lawyers, the courts hewed so closely to the fellow-servant and contributory negligence doctrines that adequate compensation was hardly ever awarded; the widow who received as much as $300 could consider herself blessed. So scandalous was the situation that even the American Bar Association drew up a model bill. Meanwhile, a federal commission riddled the notion that the common law was less susceptible to adaptation than the Constitution itself:

> To say that . . . we are bound to forever perpetuate such of its principles as we have once accepted as suited to our institutions is to deny . . . a "flexibility and capacity for growth and adaptation" which was "the peculiar boast and excellence" of the system in the home of its origin. . . .[30]

Davis, it will be recalled, had opposed automatic compensation in his presidential address to the West Virginia Bar Association in 1906. "I don't know that I ever encountered the question of my being unhappy with the 'master and servant doctrine,'" he later reflected, "I never conceived at that time that it was my duty to reform the law." By the spring of 1912, however, he had changed his views. Over the opposition of three Southern colleagues, he fought hard within committee to win approval of an automatic compensation measure. Clayton was inclined to have it reported out in his own name, but at the last moment, said Davis, "he got cold feet at the thought of some of his railroad men down home" and asked Davis to revise a report prepared by a Georgia colleague.[31]

Davis' two-page report was the most advanced document he had written to that time. In a radical departure from the restrictive language of his address of 1906, he argued that the measure was defensible as a regulation of commerce. He further defended it on grounds of humanitarianism and of economic expediency. Existing laws, he noted, brought recovery in only a small percentage of cases, resulted in enormous waste, and fostered strife and bitterness between employer and employee. Automatic compensation, he pointed out, would give the entire sum to those entitled to it. Furthermore, the railroad operators' hidden costs would go down, even though their direct costs would rise.[32]

After winning a fifteen-to-five endorsement in committee, Davis reported the bill out twice, first in February 1913 and then in the special session of the Sixty-third Congress. No action was taken under Taft, and Wilson was too preoccupied by tariff, banking, and antitrust legislation to give the measure priority; moreover, he was unsympathetic to further expansion of federal power at that time. Not until 1916 did the progressives persuade him to support automatic compensation.[33]

« III »

By the time of Wilson's inauguration in March 1913, Davis had probably moved as close to the mainstream of twentieth-century progressivism as he would ever come. Variously defined as a quest for order, a drive for efficiency and bureaucratization, an upper middle class effort to regain status, and a sophisticated effort to create a corporate state, the progressive movement was all of that and considerably more. However materialistic the interest groups which formed its parts, its central thrust was toward the creation of a more equitable, enlightened, and productive society through positive governmental action—and this regardless of the controls it imposed upon men and their institutions or the violence it did to liberal abstractions.[34]

In 1910, Davis had been essentially a nineteenth-century liberal. By the time he came up for re-election in 1912, however, he had been forced to reexamine some of his fundamental assumptions. He remained unalterably opposed to the recall of judicial decisions, but he was of mixed mind about direct primaries and the popular election of Senators. He shared Wilson's prejudice against woman suffrage, and he supported the literacy test as a means of restricting immigration from eastern and southern Europe. Yet he voted for the creation of a children's bureau and seems to have sympathized with the principle of the income tax amendment. He doubted that more stringent regulation of railroads was in order, and he was undecided on antitrust legislation. "There is still debate & difference," he explained to his father, "not only as to the cure, but . . . even as to the existence of the disease." [35]

Fortunately, Davis' views on most of these issues had little effect on his constituents' attitude toward him; they esteemed him for his personality and character, not for his progressivism or lack of it. Everywhere he went during his campaign for re-election in the autumn of 1912 warm and responsive audiences greeted him. "Oh! how those people clapped and yelled," twelve-year-old Julia reported. "A gentleman called Mr. Graccelli presented Daddy, of the kindness of his heart personally with $100 for his campaign." The Democratic press was no less enthusiastic:

DAVIS MAKES VOTES IN GREATEST SPEECH OF 1912 CAMPAIGN
CARROLL CLUB THRONGED WITH ENTHUSIASTIC
ADMIRERS OF THE BRILLIANT FIRST DISTRICT CONGRESSMAN
A VERY STRONG SPEECH BY CONGRESSMAN DAVIS.[36]

Nevertheless, Davis' forthright stand on the tariff gave his opponent, George A. Laughlin, a debating point. The district employed more than six thousand tin plate workers and had two of the largest potteries in the world, as well as the largest carbon plant in existence. Relentlessly, Laughlin played on the fears of the factory workers. If President Taft had signed the Underwood bill as voted for by Davis, Laughlin told them again and again, the local tin mill would have been compelled to shut down. As the president of the La Belle Iron Works said, "He never heard of so gross a case of neglect of constituents' welfare as . . . John Davis is guilty of. Why, it's preposterous. I understand that Mr. Davis is for free trade in everything, but that shouldn't prevent his exercising a little common sense." [37]

Davis invariably replied that wages in tariff-protected industries were appallingly low, that manufacturers kept them low by importing cheap labor, and that business' spokesmen in Congress had opposed Democratic measures to uplift workingmen. In contrast to the Republicans' "pretense" of protection to the American workingman, he asserted, the Democrats had passed bills to create a Department of Labor, extend the eight-hour law, protect seamen from involuntary servitude, broaden the authority of the Bureau of Mines, and regulate the issuance of injunctions. They had also declared for the graduated income tax and imposed a corporation tax while increasing pensions to veterans, supporting federal aid to highways, and extending aid to agricultural, mechanical, and industrial education. Nor was that all they had done. They had served the district directly with a $3,400,000 appropriation for improving navigation on the Ohio River.[38]

Had Theodore Roosevelt's Progressive party made it a three-way race by nominating a congressional candidate of its own, Davis would have won in a landslide. Instead, the Progressives endorsed his Republican opponent. This put Davis at a tremendous disadvantage, for the combined presidential vote of Taft and Roosevelt ran almost 7000 above Wilson's. Nevertheless, Davis' extraordinary personal popularity enabled him to slip in by 148 votes.[39]

« IV »

Meanwhile, Davis' desire to marry the daughter of his father's foremost rival at the bar, Ellen Graham Bassell, was severely straining his relations with his parents. Nell, as Ellen was called, was the oldest of five sisters famed locally for their beauty and spirit; as a young man, John had been both charmed and distracted by her and her sisters. "They aspire to lead the fast set here," he had confided to Julia on the eve of their wedding in 1899, "and I think would rather be called 'swagger' than any other adjective in the dictionary." Nell eventually married a Clarksburg man who became an adulterer and a drug addict. In time they separated, and, shortly before his death, she divorced him.[40]

Davis became seriously interested in Nell Bassell in 1907 or 1908, and by 1910 he wanted to marry her. His family urged him to give her up, ostensibly because of the divorce, but really because they regarded her as deficient in character. John pleaded with his mother: "She is not the basely artful and designing creature you believe her, but only a woman who has both loved and suffered much. I do not believe that you or Father or I are capable of either so greatly." Four times within the year he broke with Nell, and four times he went back to her. "I blame myself . . . for worrying you," he wrote his mother, "while . . . you reproach me and I reproach myself when I deny you the confidences you have the right to demand. To whom may one go if not to his mother when in trouble?" The family's bitterness, he said, outran his wildest expectations:

> You think that if I marry Nell Bassell I shall be unhappy. *You may be right.* I know that if I do not I shall be of all men most miserable. . . . I must discharge this load of raging discontent before I can do my full duty to my child, to you, or—in the descending scale—to my country or my clients. . . . It may be that I was not predestined to domestic peace or happiness—some people are not, & when I think of the suffering I have brought on others, I can well believe that I am not only bewitched myself, but have the evil eye beside." [41]

In April 1911, shortly after his thirty-eighth birthday, John set a wedding date and had announcements printed. His sister Lillie spoke up for Nell. "After all," she said to her mother, "the question resolves itself chiefly into 'what will people say?' She is older and wiser than she once was. . . . If she were a man, her regrets & present good behavior would be sufficient to secure forgiveness, & she might marry whom she would, and no comments be made." Mrs. Davis refused, nevertheless, to consent, and John sorrowfully broke the engagement. [42]

For months John pleaded with his mother. "I realize the damage done a woman's reputation by mere discussion," he wrote. "And yet is it courage or cowardliness, discretion or poltroonery, for a man to deny to a woman he loves under such circumstances the protection of his name? . . . And, Mother, one thing more, the *curse* of our household & our family—each & all of us—has been & is that we have kept our feelings and affections in 'cold storage.' " [43]

For almost a year Davis suffered alone in his suite in the Hotel Portland in Washington. Finally, concluding that the decision should be his own, he married Nell in the rectory of the Episcopal Church in Clarksburg in a small private ceremony on January 2, 1912. Emma and Lillie treated Nell civilly, and Mrs. Davis maintained a cordial correspondence with her over the years. She also assured Mrs. McDonald, who had favored the marriage, that Nell was very sensible and tactful and that John's life would be less empty. She added that neither Nell nor anyone else could ever fill "our dear Julia's place in his heart." [44]

Nell had been moved by the Davises' reluctant acquiescence. "Emma's presence at the rectory last night and your note were the crowning touches of happiness," she told Mrs. Davis. "The anguish and bitterness of the past were swept away by an avalanche of hope and promise for the future and my cup was indeed full." John, too, refused to let the past cloud the present. Fifteen months later, on his fortieth birthday, he wrote his mother:

> To have you say that . . . you are still proud of me, is praise enough. If ever any man was the work of another's hand, I am of yours, and the mental habits you rubbed into me in my first ten years of life, went too deep for alteration. In temperament and disposition too, we are entirely too much alike for either of us to criticize the other safely. [45]

A classic Anglo-American beauty with golden hair, blue eyes, and perfect, if severely chiseled, features, Nell was a master of feminine arts. She once told young Julia, "John didn't marry me; I married him. A smart woman can get any man she likes. It is better to lie a little than to suffer much." She was astute but unlearned, having given up school in the seventh grade following a severe case of scarlet fever; and, though she was sophisticated about political personalities, she had little interest in issues or ideas. Outwardly, her life merged with her husband's. She entertained his relatives, reported his achievements to his mother, and cultivated those who might help advance him. Men were captivated by her beauty and graciousness, women by her poise and sense of position. A few thought her cold, frivolous, or contriving, and some found her intimidating. In the view of most, however, she "graced" her husband's table and aided his career substantially. [46]

Inevitably, Nell brought new tensions into Davis' life: "A man in your position ought to have a better car . . . somebody between me and the stove . . . a parlor maid to do the things for your clothes I have been doing . . . a mending woman to make things last longer." He submitted, for he wanted her to be happy. [47]

Nell perceived the inviolable nature of her husband's relations with the McDonalds, and she never intruded. She also tried to win young Julia's affection. "I wanted to be so much to you," she tearfully exclaimed when her stepdaughter agreed to call her Mother. Yet she

could not conceal her relief over John's decision to have Julia continue school in Clarksburg and spend summers at Media. "I was the
living representative of a past which she wished to expunge," Julia reflected. "She could not bear to leave the two of us alone together." [48]

Despite the tensions, the marriage revived Davis' spirits. Within a
week he was assuring his mother that he was going to be happier than
he had been in years, and in truth he was. Nell rekindled his old love
of music and drama, interested him in antiques, and encouraged his
desire for luxury. Most important of all, she forced him to overcome
his shyness. In the end, she even won over old John J. Shortly before
his death he told her that he was glad he had lived long enough to realize what "a noble woman you are." [49]

« V »

Back in Congress following his marriage, Davis played an important
role in two rare proceedings, the impeachment trial of a federal judge
and a contempt action against a prominent Washingtonian. On July
11 1912, Robert W. Archbald, formerly United States District Judge in
Pennsylvania and, since February 1911, a Circuit Judge assigned to the
United States Commerce Court, was impeached for using his position
to advance his business interests. As his trial revealed, the sixty-three-
year-old Judge had made contracts at advantageous prices for the purchase of coal banks owned by railroads which were litigants before the
Commerce Court. These transactions were under cover, in the name of
third parties. He had also secretly advised a railroad attorney how to
rectify his pleadings.[50]

For some time proponents of the recall of judges had been contending that impeachment was hopelessly unwieldy. Only five federal
judges had been impeached since 1789 (ten others had resigned after
inquiries or hearings had begun), and only two had been found guilty
and removed from office. Many conservatives viewed Archbald's trial
as an opportunity to sap the strength of the recall movement by dem-
onstrating the efficacy of impeachment. As a West Virginia coal operator wrote Davis, "the prompt and emphatic action of your committee
. . . will have a wonderful effect. . . . Many people had reached the
conclusion that there was no possible relief . . . except through the
recall." [51]

Davis shared those sentiments. Nonetheless, he was determined to
maintain an open mind and to give Archbald a fair hearing when he

was brought before the judiciary committee in May 1912. Appalled by Clayton's tendency to prosecute rather than interrogate, he pronounced the chairman's examination of the principal witness the first day the worst butchery he had ever witnessed; a green boy fresh out of law school could have done better, he said to his wife.[52]

Davis' pleas that each witness be examined by a single member had little effect on Clayton and the others. "They are so all dead anxious to get their names in the papers . . . ," the West Virginian wrote in disgust, "that every examination is shot all to pieces by interruptions until the proceeding becomes almost farcical." By then Davis had privately concluded that, although Archbald had not indulged in direct corruption, he had exhibited an improper degree of intimacy with railroad officials and had accepted financial favors. After trying in vain to persuade the committee to drop five articles pertaining to Archbald's District Court judgeship, he supported impeachment on thirteen separate charges.[53]

The trial before the full Senate held little appeal for Davis, despite his appointment as one of seven House managers (prosecutors); throughout, he suffered the professional's agony over the amateur's performance. He thought for a while that he would take no part at all, yet he kept abreast and, in late December, drafted a summary argument. At the last minute he decided not to give it orally because of his irritation at Clayton's assignment of four and a half of the seven hours for argument to himself (Clayton) and the senior Republican manager. Instead, he put his argument in the *Congressional Record*, where it was widely read and complimented.[54]

Davis believed that a man could not be impeached in one office for offenses committed in another, so he addressed only the charges against Archbald's conduct on the Commerce Court. A judge, he insisted, must be like Caesar's wife. "More cannot be expected of him, but nothing less should be permitted." Conceding that Archbald's actions were not punishable under the common statute law, he held that the case turned on whether the constitutional provision that judges shall hold their offices during good behavior really meant "so long as they are guilty of no indictable crime." He concluded that Alexander Hamilton's statements in the sixty-fourth, seventy-eighth, and seventy-ninth *Federalist Papers* indicated that it did not. He further concluded that the record of previous impeachments showed that the word "misdemeanor" has always been treated as having a meaning of its own in parliamentary law, and that impeachment proceedings had been based repeatedly upon offenses not indictable as crimes. Patently, Archbald was guilty: "No man can justly be considered fit for public office . . . who does not realize the double duty resting upon him—first, to administer his trust with unflinching honesty, &, second, . . . to so conduct himself that public confidence in his honesty shall remain unshaken." [55]

The Senate's decision to limit its finding of guilt to Archbald's conduct on the Commerce Court gratified Davis. He was also satisfied that the Judge's removal would prove salutary. Nevertheless he pitied him, then and later. "I don't think," he mused forty years afterwards, "that the poor devil had the slightest conception that he had done anything out of the way." [56]

Compliments on Davis' Archbald summation were still coming in when a contempt action was taken against Charles C. Glover, a well-known Washington banker and social leader. Late in the third session of the Sixty-second Congress, Representative Thetus W. Sims of Tennessee had made a vitriolic attack on a bill for the purchase of a large tract of land owned by Glover. Glover brooded over Sims' remarks for weeks until, one day, he noticed the Congressman walking through Farragut Square alone. The banker stopped his car and accosted him. "I want to tell you to your face that you are a contemptible liar," he exclaimed, "yes, a miserable contemptible liar. Furthermore, I mean to show you just what I think of you." He then struck Sims on the jaw.[57]

A few days later, Speaker Champ Clark appointed Davis chairman of a five-man committee to investigate. The committee found no questions of fact, for Glover admitted everything. But no one was certain of the law. What were the privileges of the House? Were any to be inferred beyond those expressly stated in the Constitution? Did the privilege against being "called in question" extend to a personal or corporal as well as juridical immunity? If privilege had been broken, what procedure was to be followed for trial of the offender? And what punishment might be inflicted? Davis asked his father for advice, noting that the case would be closely watched and that his report would have to stand a test of both law and common sense.[58]

On April 26, 1912, Davis reported that an assault upon a member of the House for words spoken in debate constituted contempt of the House in which that member was then sitting, even if the words had been spoken in a prior Congress. He recommended that Glover be arrested, brought before the House, and given counsel if he so desired. Then, in a speech which several colleagues pronounced the best they

ever heard on a constitutional question, Davis defended the report. Asserting that a Congressman's freedom of speech was inviolable, he insisted that he could not be challenged in any other place for a speech
made in Congress:

> These two great immunities are the defense and support of every leg-
> islative body. They are indispensable to the proper exercise of its func-
> tions and, even if not provided by the express language of the Consti-
> tution, the very necessity of the case and the whole history of
> parliamentary government would have justified the conclusion that
> they had been conferred by implication. How vital the makers of the
> Constitution deemed this freedom of speech becomes at once apparent
> when we consider the sweeping language in which it is conferred.
>   In the first place, the express language of the Constitution is that
> Senators and Representatives shall not be questioned in any other
> place, thus making the immunity absolutely unrestricted in point of
> space, whether it be a court, a similar assembly, a popular gathering, a
> public highway, or a private chamber.
>   In the second place, this immunity is left absolutely unrestricted in
> point of time. No attempt is made to set a period beyond which a
> member shall be no longer protected; but from the moment when
> words are spoken on this floor to the very day of his death, there is ex-
> tended over him at all times the shield of the Constitution.[59]

The House approved the report decisively following a five-hour debate. Glover was then arrested, brought into the well of the chamber,
and rebuked by Speaker Clark.[60]

Davis' brilliant performances in the Archbald and Glover cases attracted the interest of Attorney General James C. McReynolds, who
was then searching for a Solicitor General. As it happened, McReynolds already possessed a thick file of recommendations on Davis.
They had been inspired by Davis' campaign, earlier in the year, to win
appointment as Judge Nathan Goff's successor on the United States
Court of Appeals in the Fourth Circuit. (Goff had been elected to the
United States Senate.)

Indeed, Davis had been so "hell-bent" to go on the bench that he
had openly sought preferment for the only time in his life. "I have
asked myself," he wrote his father, ". . . if my desire for the place was
merely an ambition for high office; and while it is always easy to convince one's self in favor of one's ambitions, I do feel a genuine conviction that in this office as perhaps in no other I can be of real service."
Not even the reduction in salary, from $7500 to $7000, mattered much.
"If I can do the work . . . well, it will bring to me and mine more

than money can buy." Besides, he expected his gas interests to bring in
not less than $10,000 per year for at least ten years.[61]

Nell felt differently. She wrote Mrs. Davis that she inclined to approve because of John's great desire for the appointment, but that she
would like him to resume his practice and save some money before
trying to realize his life's ambition. Then, after assuring Mrs. Davis
that she would not stand in his way, she remarked that "he is young to
take the veil and it is a life of renunciation." She added that Richmond was a small town where nothing but ancestors counted and
bridge was the principal form of entertainment.[62]

Davis himself did all that he "decently" could to influence the President. He asked Goff to recommend him, solicited support from prominent West Virginians, and mobilized his many friends in Washington.
But his real strength was his reputation as a man of character and as
the ablest lawyer in Congress. "If the Almighty every created a finer
man than John W. Davis, I never knew him," recalled the 1920 Democratic presidential candidate James M. Cox, then a colleague in the
House. "He captivated the members of both branches by his dignity of
manner, his intellectual courage, and the penetrative qualities of his
mind." Hardly had Davis disclosed his ambition, in fact, than the judiciary committee unanimously endorsed a resolution supporting his
candidacy. Before long, virtually every county bar association in West
Virginia, the entire state delegation in both houses of Congress, and
the two District judges in West Virginia had endorsed him. "We are
Republicans from the word 'Go,'" the Grafton *Daily Sentinel* announced, "but when we have to have Democrats . . . we want to get
the best they have, and that party doesn't contain any better." [63]

President Wilson was impressed but unmoved. "I fear," he told
Henry Clayton, "that it is too late . . . as I have committed, no not
committed, for I do not commit myself, but have aroused expectations
that another man would be appointed." Soon afterwards he nominated
an old friend, Justice Charles A. Woods of the Supreme Court of
South Carolina. (Shortly after Woods was confirmed, Nell sat next to
the President at a dinner party. Wilson talked of his pleasure in recently appointing a South Carolina friend to a judgeship. "I have
heard of Judge Woods," Nell responded. The President paused momentarily, then exclaimed: "Oh my God!" They laughed together.) [64]

While the Senate held up Woods' confirmation, the House judiciary
committee tried to create a place for Davis by drafting a bill to add a

judgeship in the Fourth District. But Minority Leader Mann refused unanimous consent to bring it up. "Killing that bill was a great personal service," Davis wrote Cox three decades later. "I'd have gone on that bench just as sure as God made little apples. . . . It cured me." [65]

Less than two months after the judgeship bill died, the President nominated Davis Solicitor General of the United States. On hearing the news, Champ Clark left the Speaker's chair and walked over to Davis' desk.

"You gonna take that job upstreet?" he asked in his Missouri drawl.

"I think I will, Mr. Speaker," Davis replied.

"Great mistake. Great mistake. You ought to stay in the House."

Perhaps so, Davis mused afterwards, "but when you've dropped from a 3000 plurality to 148, staying in the House didn't look so hot." [66]

On August 1, 1913, Davis dissolved his law partnership and drew up secret articles of agreement with Osman Swartz and Bryan Templeman. They provided that, if his father's share of the new firm's earnings ever fell below $4000, he would make up the difference without the senior Davis' knowledge. [67]

CHAPTER 7

Solicitor General of the United States 1913-1915

I think the office of the Solicitor General is the most attractive office within the gift of the government for the man who loves the practice of law.

JOHN W. DAVIS

Davis became the government's chief appellate trial lawyer at a critical juncture in the history of the Supreme Court. During his five years as Solicitor General many of the most controversial actions of the Roosevelt, Taft, and Wilson administrations were challenged in the Court, and in the more important cases he made the oral arguments himself. He defended federal regulation of private oil lines, argued the right of the Executive to protect federal lands, and called for the dissolution of the mammoth International Harvester and United States Steel Corporations. He supported regulation of child labor under the commerce clause, and he defended legislation President Wilson drove through Congress to avert a nationwide railroad strike on the eve of America's entrance into World War I. Then, after war came, he argued the constitutionality of the draft. Meanwhile, in two civil rights cases of moment, he charged that Oklahoma's "grandfather clause" deprived Negroes of their right to vote and that Alabama's convict lease system forced them into peonage.

Davis often entertained private doubts about the measures he was constrained to defend. As he confided to his father, "I should like to get some constitutional question which I could feel free from doubt."

Yet never, not even when broad extensions of federal power were at issue, did his personal views intrude. At least once, in fact, he made the oral argument himself after an assistant confessed that he could not in conscience argue the government's side. "For what purpose," Davis asked in an address in 1915, "can the Government ever approach its courts save that the law may be declared and enforced; and when this has been done what does it care for the terms plaintiff and defendant, or winner or loser?" The policy behind legislation, he said and believed, was not the concern of the Solicitor General. If he won, he had the satisfaction all lawyers feel in victory. But if he lost, he took comfort in the maxim: "Whenever the case is decided right the government wins." Indubitably, as one of his subordinates put it, "While John W. Davis was Solicitor General, the government was his client. That's all." [1]

« I »

Davis awaited his first oral argument in the fall of 1913 in unrelieved anxiety. Sixteen cases inherited from the Roosevelt and Taft administrations had been advanced for early hearing in the October Term, and he had reserved the toughest ones for himself. He wondered why he had left Clarksburg. "This is cold water, and I'm going in before the ice cracks." [2]

The new Solicitor General was much better prepared than he would admit. Although he had never made an oral argument in the Supreme Court, he had appeared often before the West Virginia Supreme Court of Appeals. He was already a master of appellate techniques, and rarely, after his first few cases, did he have to put more than an outline and a few quotations on paper. "I skeletonize my argument . . . but to write it out and read it to the court, or to memorize it, that I couldn't do. All the life would be gone." [3]

As the men who drafted most of Davis' briefs emphasized, almost all his arguments were creative performances; though grounded on the briefs, they stood alone. Invariably he began with an inclusive, but succinct, statement of the facts:

> You see, there you are, sitting on the bench as a court of appeal.
> There's a man standing up before you . . . calling on you to do something. What's the first thing you want to know? "What's this all about?
> How did this question come here?" . . . I've seen lawyers start . . .
> right into the law of the case. . . . That isn't what you want to know.

. . . What is the question? How did it arise? What happened? When you've got on to that, well, then you're ready to take up what's the rule of law that ought to control this. If you go to an appellate court and don't give them the facts you might just as well sit down.[4]

Davis never let his attachment to *stare decisis* or his abhorrence of judge-made law weaken his argument. He preferred, of course, to stand on the wording of the relevant statute or the latest judicial ruling. But he realized that considerations of law and policy were often intermingled; and when interpretations and the exact boundaries of *stare decisis* were in doubt, he readily invoked semantics, legislative history, or public policy—usually all three.[5]

One of Davis' most distinctive characteristics was his ability to interject an element of intellectual tension into an essentially abstract matter. This, even more than his graceful flow of language, enlisted the bench's attention. As he once explained, "I may not strike people as one who enjoys battle, but with the different kinds of battle come different kinds of joy. No exhilaration in the world exceeds that of being clearly seized of your case, convinced that you've got an answer for all your adversary's propositions, and then to stand up and let him have it." All these qualities came out in Davis' first case as Solicitor General.[6]

The Hepburn Act of 1906 had put oil pipelines held to be common carriers under regulation by the Interstate Commerce Commission. The act failed to mention lines owned by subsidiaries of unregulated companies, however, and when the ICC ordered several Standard Oil-owned pipeline companies that transported oil exclusively to parent refineries to file rate schedules, they appealed to the Commerce Court. "To make the owners of private pipe lines common carriers," declared their principal counsel, John G. Milburn, was to subject private property to a public use; this was a "taking" of property in violation of the due process clause of the Fifth Amendment. The Commerce Court had accepted Milburn's reasoning unqualifiedly, adding that the government had no right to achieve antitrust objectives under the "guise" of regulation.[7]

On first reading the record, Davis leaned so far toward the Commerce Court's holding that he called the case "a tight squeak." But two Assistant Attorneys General, Blackburn Esterline and Thurlow Gordon, insisted that Standard's requirement that all oil shipped over the pipe companies' lines be sold to their parent refineries encouraged monopoly by forcing small independent producers to conform or go out of business. "The refinery," said Esterline in a memorandum to Davis, "is the real party in interest and is getting the benefit of the cheap transportation to the exclusion of other purchasers and refiners of crude oil"; the entire process "is a sham." [8]

Thus persuaded, Davis approved a forceful brief which argued that Congress had included private lines in the Hepburn Act by implication. The brief also cut to the core of the economic issue, declaring that the Act's real purpose was to preserve competition, and that the ICC was therefore obligated to regulate "private" lines: Possession of exclusive pipelines through auxiliaries "enables the Standard to absolutely control the price of crude petroleum and to determine . . . the prices which its competitors in a given locality shall pay. . . . *More than anything else, the pipe line has contributed to the monopoly of the Standard Oil Company.*" [9]

Meanwhile, Davis continued to fret over his impending debut. "No schoolboy ever dreaded his commencement day oration more," he confided to his mother in mid-September. "I have a positively smothering sense of my own inadequacy . . . closely bordering on panic." One of his greatest deficiencies, he added to his father, was "a lack of knowledge of the philosophy of the law." [10]

Sustained by the realization that he had always surmounted his fears, yet so nervous that he made his wife stay at home, Davis seated himself at the counsel table in the Supreme Court chamber just before noon on October 15, 1913. The instant he rose to his feet the words began to pour our rapidly and lucidly. Within moments Chief Justice Edward D. White, whose great frame had been hunched over the bench, heaved an audible sigh of relief. The new Solicitor General, he said to himself, was fully capable of representing the government's interests. Glancing infrequently at his notes, Davis asserted that, although the pipeline clause had been enacted to free the nation from the oil monopoly, the dissolution of Standard Oil in 1911 had failed to prevent the rise of new monopolies based on control of pipelines by successor companies. Patently, the real test was the companies' actions, not their rhetoric. [11]

Davis knew at once that he would never again lack confidence, never again stand in "awesome dread" of Supreme Court Justices:

> For men are men, and judges are judges, wherever you find them. It was after all the feeling that so many people were watching me to take my measure that gave me the "nervous deets." [12]

Eight months later the Court sustained the government, eight to one, with Oliver Wendell Holmes writing the majority opinion. The pipeline companies, declared the Justice, were "common carriers now in everything but form" and thus fell automatically under the purview of the Interstate Commerce Commission. To Davis' surprise, the opinion ignored his central contention—that the companies were in violation of the antitrust laws.[13]

Shortly after the ruling, Davis dropped by Holmes' house to wish him a pleasant vacation. What, the Justice asked, did he think of his opinion in the *Pipe Line* cases? Brashly, Davis replied that he was gratified by the outcome but surprised by the justification. "Well," responded Holmes, "that's the way it is. I circulate an opinion to my brethren. One of them pulls out a plum here, another a plum there and they send me back a mass of shapeless dough." Not until Holmes' papers were opened after his death did the reasons for his "question-begging" opinion, as Felix Frankfurter termed it, come out. Holmes' first draft had supported Davis' contention that the pipeline provision was a lawful regulation of monopoly under the commcerce clause. But, so Frankfurter reported, "the boys wouldn't stand for it." Anxious to prevent the case from going over to the next term, Holmes had them put together an opinion acceptable to the majority. "I regard this as inadequate reasoning," he said in a marginal note, "and am compelled to strike out what I had thought the real argument. . . . See first draft." [14]

« II »

The day after the *Pipe Line* hearing Davis argued two civil rights cases, *Guinn v. United States* and *United States v. Mosley*. In each he defended federal authority over the power of the states; and in the first, and more important, he was opposed by former Senator Joseph W. Bailey of Texas, the doctrinaire states' rightist who had opposed workmen's compensation. Davis pegged his argument in *Guinn* on the Fifteenth Amendment (the suffrage amendment which his father had so vehemently insisted was void), and the case itself proved a benchmark in the Negroes' struggle for civil rights which Davis himself was to end his career by opposing. At almost that very instant, moreover, officials in other departments were aborting civil rights. Negroes were refused appointment to positions they had once filled; governmental cafeterias were peremptorily segregated; and the desks of Negro civil service employees were screened off—all this, so President Wilson explained, because he "honestly thought segregation to be in the interest of the colored people." [15]

The issue in *Guinn* was the grandfather clause in the Oklahoma constitution. The clause exempted from the literacy test all potential voters whose ancestors had been eligible to vote in any state or foreign nation prior to January 2, 1866, and its inevitable effect, as Davis contended, was to disfranchise most illiterate Negroes and virtually no illiterate white men. Several other Southern states had similar clauses, and in 1904 the United States Supreme Court had refused to overturn the Alabama provision on the grounds that it had no authority either "to compel . . . registrars to enroll . . . negroes" or to "undertake the task of enforcing political rights." Then, just a few months before Davis' oral argument, the highest court in Oklahoma had affirmed the constitutionality of that state's grandfather clause.[16]

The case grew out of the arrest of two Oklahoma election officials for refusing to allow a group of blacks to vote in the congressional elections of 1910. The District Court declared the grandfather clause invalid at their trial, and the jury found the officials guilty. The Circuit Court then certified that it could not dispose of the appeal until the Supreme Court ruled on the constitutionality of the disputed clause.[17]

Although Davis never spoke or wrote of blacks with the vehemence of his father, he privately questioned the wisdom of Negro suffrage; at the time of his oral argument, in fact, his wife remarked sardonically that he "was in danger of winning." Yet he had never agreed with his father that the Fifteenth Amendment should be disregarded because the South had been coerced into ratifying it. As his earlier break with his Southern colleagues on the policing of federal elections indicates, he believed fervently that evasion of the clear intent of the Constitution was intolerable. Now, in preparing *Guinn,* he suppressed his racial prejudices completely.[18]

Presumably because the tendency of appellate courts to decide on the narrowest possible ground made it unwise to hazard too much, Davis based his brief solely on the explicit provisions of the Fifteenth Amendment rather than on the more far-reaching "equal protection" clause of the Fourteenth.* Nevertheless, he cordially accepted an *amicus*

* The applicable provisions in the Fourteenth Amendment are: "No State shall make or enforce any law which shall abridge the privileges or immunities of citizens of the United States . . . or deny to any person within its ju-

curiae brief, grounded in part on the Fourteenth Amendment, for the National Association for the Advancement of Colored People. It was written by Moorfield Storey of Boston, a past president of the American Bar Association, who was then president of the NAACP. Among other things, Storey emphasized that Justice Joseph B. Bradley had stated in 1880 that the Amendment contained "a necessary implication of a positive immunity" which exempted Negroes from "legal discriminations implying inferiority in civil society." [19]

Davis was so sure of his ground that he deemed his defense impregnable. His brief asserted that the Fifteenth Amendment extended the protection of the Constitution to "the humblest member" of the Negro race and contended that any law to the contrary, no matter how adroitly disguised, was invalid. "To sustain a suffrage amendment such as the present, it must appear not that under certain conditions some of every race may be admitted to the suffrage, but that under no condition will any member of any race be excluded *for racial reasons.* In each and every line and syllable, in meaning as well as in phrase, in fulfillment as well as in promise, the races must stand side by side." [20]

"I was very proud of John," Davis' wife wrote his mother, immediately after the oral argument. "Your heart would have swelled too had you heard & seen him; for it is his manner upon the floor . . . that is so delightful—his dignity, calm & deferential bearing. . . . Bailey is persuasive & leans over his desk entreating the Court as it were, to see the question his way—he gets warm physically." But her husband, she noted, moved quietly and slowly to his place, then spoke so rapidly and distinctly that he conveyed the impression that unnecessary entreaty was futile and an imposition on the Justices' time. "As you know, he lacks neither words nor ideas & he had the knowledge of the Law at his command.[21]

She did not add that Davis had deflected Bailey's effort to draw him into a discussion of the Fourteenth Amendment. He would let that point rest, he had replied to the Texan, with what the NAACP had said in its brief. The tactic was probably sound, given the conservative composition of the bench; not until the 1930's did the Court begin to construe the Fourteenth Amendment broadly in civil rights cases. Fur-

risdiction the equal protection of the laws" (Section 1). The Fifteenth Amendment says: "The right of citizens of the United States to vote shall not be denied or abridged by the United States or by any State on account of race, color, or previous condition of servitude." A second section explicitly empowers Congress to enforce this provision.

thermore, Storey's brief provided ample rationale had the majority wanted to rest on the equal protection clause.[22]

Davis' judgment was vindicated when Chief Justice White failed to mention the Fourteenth Amendment when he declared, for a unanimous Court, that the grandfather clause violated the Fifteenth. "We have difficulty in finding words to more clearly demonstrate the conviction we entertain," the former Confederate soldier and Louisiana planter averred, that the grandfather clause "has the characteristics which the Government attributes to it." Never before had the United States Supreme Court ruled a state law unconstitutional as in violation of the Fifteenth Amendment.[23]

Another felicitous comment on Davis' argument, this one by Holmes, marked the second Oklahoma case, *United States v. Mosley.* In 1912 a group of Oklahoma election officials were indicted under Section 19 of the United States Criminal Code for failing to report the congressional returns in eleven precincts where Negroes had voted. The District Court sustained their demurrer, and the case went up to the Supreme Court on a writ of error filed by Homer N. Boardman, the same conscientious United States Attorney who had pressed suit in the *Guinn* case.[24]

The defense centered on two propositions: the right of suffrage did not include the right to have one's ballot counted; and Section 19 was derived from the Enforcement Act of 1870, which had been aimed at the physical excesses of the Ku Klux Klan, and was meant to apply only to forcible prevention of voting. In language that clearly bore his stylistic imprint, Davis' brief riddled both contentions: "A right to vote entails of necessity the right to have that vote recorded; otherwise the vote is no vote at all, but simply so much waste paper. A constitutional guaranty of such significance . . . should not be frittered away by a process of hair-splitting definition." As for Section 19, it did not follow that because the peril of "the forcible invasion of the rights of colored citizens at the polls . . . is happily past, application should be restricted to the rights of the negro voter." Methods change as conditions change, and "if the utter violation of a right guaranteed by the Constitution does not injure or oppress unless accompanied by a blow over the head, the protection afforded by the statute is largely illusory." [25]

Holmes agreed so emphatically with Davis' first point that in his majority opinion he dismissed the defense's argument with a few sweeping sentences. The only things that required discussion, he said, were Section 6 of the Enforcement Act of 1870 and Section 19 of the United States Criminal Code, and not even they required much discussion, for "just as the Fourteenth Amendment, to use the happy analogy suggested by the Solicitor General, was adopted with a view to the protection of the colored race but has been found to be equally important in its application to the rights of all, Paragraph [Section] 6 had a general scope and used general words that have become the most important now that the Ku Klux have passed away." [26]

If the Oklahoma cases illuminated some of the means used to deprive Negroes of the suffrage, the Alabama peonage cases exposed the inhumanity that blacks were powerless to combat because of their inability to vote. For three decades Alabama had been evading the Thirteenth Amendment's proscription of involuntary servitude by permitting sureties to pay the fines of Negroes convicted of petty crimes and to work them on their plantations under court-approved contracts. The blacks were invariably bound for periods in excess of their jail terms, and they were frequently charged with fresh offenses, found guilty, and subjected to new, and longer, contracts before the first ones had expired. An appeal for relief by one of the victims says all that need be said:

> I hope if your please that you will do something to stop those Monroe County Officers from putting me in jail and taking away every thing that I have on earth, for nothing, when in the first place I live in Conecuh County, in the second place I am over fifty years old, they have already collected from me 85, 60 and still claim that I owe them $42.50, is there anything that you can do as an officer to stope them from treating me that way. have I no rights that the courts will respect. I appeal to you as an officer of the law to do something to keep these men from putting me in jail for nothing except what they call failure to work the road, they have already kept me in jail five months for this so called offence, of not working the roads one day, in Monroe County when I live in Conecuh, and I am over fifty years old.[27]

At the instance of United States Attorney William H. Armbrecht, another of those obscure public servants who made the federal government a dynamic agency of reform during the Progressive era, several peonage suits were filed in the spring of 1911. Armbrecht expected a slashing counterattack by Alabama leaders. Instead, the influential Mobile *Register* expressed gratification over extension of "the protecting arm of the federal law"; more important, the State Attorney General agreed to cooperate in two test cases. These found their way to the Supreme Court by March 1914, and, at the request of Armbrecht's successor, Davis moved that they be advanced.[28]

There is no record of Davis' oral argument in the peonage cases, but if it followed his brief, it was succinct, learned, and sardonic. "Once bound to this wheel," he wrote of the practice of rearresting the Negro and then renegotiating his contract, "there is no escape, and the life of the Father of the Marshalsea was not more devoid of hope." Those who kept a man in such condition, whether by threats or by process of law, were guilty under the Peonage Act of 1867, and the Alabama statute authorizing such action was "obnoxious" to the Thirteenth Amendment.[29]

Davis also attacked the provision in the Alabama law that resulted in one defendant's being hired out four times as long as the state could have imprisoned him and another almost five times as long. "So far from the statute which permits such things being a humane law, which allows the convict to choose his own master, it would seem rather to be a most ingenious engine of oppression. If the Constitution did not stand in its path, *reason and public policy* should [emphasis added]." [30]

Justice William R. Day and most of the Court saw the cases in the same light. In a majority opinion that closely paralleled Davis' reasoning, Day ruled that the Alabama peonage system violated both the Thirteenth Amendment and the statutes designed to implement its proscription of involuntary servitude.[31]

« III »

Meanwhile, Davis dutifully defended the expansion of federal power in several other spheres. He had little heart for *Henry v. Henkel,* which involved a stockbroker's refusal to reveal the names of his customers. As he said privately, "I turn . . . to an effort to punish a poor devil for failing to answer all the impertinent questions asked him by the Pujo Money Trust Committee." Only at the urgent request of the head of the ICC, moreover, did he act against the Louisville & Nashville Railroad for refusing to produce all its interoffice communications on the ICC's order. The suit that gave him the most agony, however, was *United States v. Midwest Oil Company.* A case of far-reaching implications for both the conservation movement and the expansion of Executive authority, it grew out of President Taft's bungling effort to raise a legal umbrella over the land-withdrawal policy dramatized by Roosevelt.[32]

Soon after Taft's inauguration in March 1909, government scientists warned of the need to prevent private companies from usurping federal oil lands. Although Taft believed that Roosevelt had exercised the power to withdraw public lands from private entry "beyond legal limitations," he reluctantly withdrew a vast acreage in California and Wyoming on September 27, 1909. Three and a half months later, the conscience-stricken President asked Congress to ratify his withdrawal order by expressly authorizing Executive withdrawals. A majority of the Senate Committee on Public Lands thought the practice too well established to require such action, but they humored Taft by reporting out a bill. It was passed and signed in late June 1910. It sanctioned future withdrawals, but neither validated nor invalidated previous withdrawals. Taft then withdrew the California and Wyoming lands a second time.[33]

Some months before the bill was passed, oilmen had begun to sink a well in Wyoming on a section withdrawn under the order of September 27, 1909. By December 1911, when the government finally demanded that the Midwest Oil Company vacate the lands they had thus occupied, government property worth perhaps $100,000,000 was at stake. Western lawyers condemned the government's action as *ex post facto,* and the Midwest Company refused to suspend operations. Assistant Attorney General Ernest Knaebel then filed suit in the District Court in Wyoming, where a sympathetic, Western-born judge ruled against the government.[34]

Davis had never displayed any interest in conservation up to this time; moreover, he was distressed by the apparently tenuous quality of the government's case. "It's a pretty close question," he confided to his father, in a letter that virtually endorsed the oil company's position. Nevertheless, he recognized that the government's interest was so great that it deserved the most forceful representation possible, and he resolutely decided to participate himself.[35]

In due course, Davis signed a persuasive brief drawn up by Knaebel. It asserted that legislative consent could be inferred from the indirect approval or even the mere acquiescence of Congress, and it emphasized that the public lands were national property held in trust for all the people. "Did the Constitution mean to lock up the power over public property so exclusively in Congress that the Executive head of the Nation could not touch it, use it, or deal with it in any way, even for its protection, unless he could point to some statutory authorization?" Such a view was absurd, the brief added, in words that echoed Roosevelt's most impassioned declarations. The public lands constantly demand protection against trespass, spoliation, and fire. "Protection implies action, and action can only come from the Executive." The President must act in emergencies, even without specific statutory authority; and if he abused this power, the remedy should be legislative, rather than judicial:

> But in so far as this reservation may properly be the subject of judicial scrutiny, it should be viewed . . . with due regard to its immense public importance, liberal presumptions should be allowed in favor of governmental convenience and in support of governmental action, and strict constructions should be avoided.[36]

Knaebel was so consumed by the case when he opened oral argument in mid-January of 1914 that Davis let him use all but ten minutes of his own time. "When the bell rang," the Solicitor General wrote home that night, "I was still floundering around in the year 1856. I felt that I had made an ass of myself to attempt it at all." Subsequently, the Court divided four to four in conference and called for reargument. Davis then took a full hour, and reported himself "better satisfied." [37]

Nine months after the second argument, Justice Joseph R. Lamar, a Georgia Democrat, upheld the government's side for a five-to-three majority in a landmark decision. His opinion put the Court's stamp of approval on both the conservation program inspired by Roosevelt and the enlarged conception of the public interest embodied in the progressive movement as a whole. More specifically, it emphasized that two hundred prior withdrawal orders obligated the judiciary to give weight "to the usage itself,—even when the validity of the practice is the subject of investigation." The decision, said former Attorney General Thomas W. Gregory two decades later, was "one of the greatest victories won by the Department of Justice in the last 20 years." [38]

In a long, biting dissent, Justice Day, a McKinley Republican, took strong exception. Original grants of authority ought not to be amplified by judicial decisions. The Constitution gave Congress control of public lands; and that fact, coupled with Congress' refusal to expressly sanction withdrawals prior to the act of June 1910, made the government's case untenable.[39]

After reading his opinion, Day scrawled a note in pencil and sent it down to Davis: "And you, a Jeffersonian Democrat, have done this thing!" The Solicitor General smiled wryly. "I should have answered Day," he wrote that night, "that my lapse from virtue was due to the duty of defending Republican presidents." [40]

« IV »

Within a month after his first argument, Davis knew that he was making an extraordinary impression on bench and bar alike. Friends told his wife that opposing counsel were saying that they would now have to prepare their cases with exceptional care. Attorney General James C. McReynolds reported that every member of the Court was delighted with her husband. And Justice Charles Evans Hughes remarked that it was "an intellectual treat" to hear the new Solicitor General argue. The Chief Justice himself told Davis that he was the greatest comfort the Court had had in his twenty-one years on the bench. Justice Lamar added a novel twist. "John W. Davis has such a perfect flow of language," he confided to a friend, "that we don't ask questions when we should." [41]

Even the pages were enamored of Davis. "All four of us loved him," one of them recalled. "There were old colored people who had been around the Court for years. They also loved him. He had great dignity, yet he was invariably kind and approachable. Everyone was always rooting for Mr. Davis." On Saturdays the pages would sit in an outer room while the Justices conferred with the door open. "I've heard Holmes, and old Judge Day, and the others say, 'He's so clear; he presented that well.' One didn't hear that about the others." [42]

Something of Davis' own techniques may be inferred from his private comments on other lawyers. "I disappointed myself as usual," he wrote after an especially frustrating afternoon; yet his adversary had been even more lackluster. "[He] knew . . . only what he read in the brief his colleagues had written [and] made much of his argument with his nose between the leaves of his brief. . . . There is little difference in lawyers save in industry; a great name is a poor substitute for the latter." Another letter described an opponent who "roared as if he were addressing an audience of ten thousand people or wanted to shatter the sky-lights." [43]

Davis never changed briefs radically if they had the substance that he wanted. Neither was he a "comma chaser." "One felt, consequently, that he wasn't standing over one." But he did insist that briefs be clear, concise, logical, and accurate, and if they were not, he sent them back or revised them himself. As he complained after a midnight siege with an appallingly bad draft that had been submitted by a lawyer from another department: "A typical sentence— 'Appellant *concludes* in his petition *by way of an attempted allegation* that by reason of the discontinuance of said contract he was damaged as follows.' " What, he asked, should be done with thirty pages of such English, given the sensibilities of its author and his own regard for the mother-tongue and the good opinion of the Court? It required all his self-control not to tear up such a document.[44]

Sometimes he had to give offense. Once he rewrote a bad brief completely. Its author then blamed "the absence of some of his pet (& most absurd) ideas" on one of the senior men. Gently, Davis told him that he had rewritten the brief himself. "I would have gone into detail," he wrote to his father, "but remembered your favorite motto that it is 'a waste of lather to shave an ass.' " On another occasion he said of a finished brief: "I think that's a very good argument. I have only one objection to it. I argued exactly the contrary in a case six weeks ago and they haven't decided it. I don't think it would look just right if two briefs came from the Department of Justice on different sides of the same question." Garrulousness or lack of focus in conference also tried Davis' patience. He rarely cut anyone off, but he sometimes indicated annoyance by a humorous thrust. "Now, gentlemen," he once said at the end of a long, rambling discussion, "if one of you will loan me a pipeload of tobacco, both of your lengthy arguments will be forgiven." [45]

Such incidents were unusual. The progressive movement drew many of the finest young minds in the nation to Washington, and the Assistant Attorneys General assigned to Davis were exceptionally able and intelligent. None equalled him in general excellence, but many were more imaginative than he. In case after case they urged their sociologically founded or broad constructionist views upon him; and, though he continued to have reservations, they gave him the support he needed to resolve his doubts in the government's interest.[46]

The most mature of the half-dozen men who worked closely with Davis was William Wallace, Jr., ten years his senior. A New Freedom Democrat and a strong proponent of *stare decisis,* he had his chief's unqualified respect. When Wallace resigned in 1917, Davis felt as though he had "lost a leg." But his special favorite was G. Carroll

Todd, a thirty-five-year-old Virginia gentleman who headed the Antitrust Division. To most of the antitrust suits of the era Todd brought acute intelligence, absolute dedication, and a sure instinct for the essentials. "I genuinely loved Todd," said Davis, years later; "he had one of the clearest and most honest minds I ever encountered." [47]

Davis also relied heavily, though with less enthusiasm, on Blackburn Esterline, a Taft appointee and a rather eccentric bachelor. Esterline was an authority on interstate commerce, but he larded his arguments with unnecessary detail and was always darkly suspicious of the opposition. No less emotional and much more likable was Huston Thompson, a Pennsylvania Democrat who put into public service the same fiery energy that he had put into football at Princeton. Thompson admired Davis profoundly, but thought his oral arguments too cold. "John," he once burst out, "why don't you be more assertive, more passionate!" Davis mused a moment, then, in obvious strain, related how he had been held in contempt for throwing an inkwell in court at Clarksburg. "All my life," he added, "I've been trying to suppress my passions." [48]

Three other men, Ernest Knaebel, Thurlow Gordon, and Robert Szold, helped ease the Solicitor General's burden. Knaebel was a resourceful, public-spirited Republican who had trained at Yale. He had organized the Public Lands Division, and he was esteemed by Davis as one of the finest legal minds he ever knew. Gordon and Szold were *Law Review* men from Harvard. Both were broad constructionists, and both were moderately attuned to the sociological jurisprudence of Roscoe Pound. Gordon was a specialist in antitrust law and the author of the briefs in the *Pipe Line* cases and several other major suits. (His brief in the *Reading Railroad* case, said Davis, was the best "for sustained continuity" submitted during his five years as Solicitor General.) Davis leaned even more heavily on Szold, his young personal assistant. A charming, high-minded Jew of Polish extraction whom Davis described as "brilliant," Szold was fervently devoted to the public interest. He was the principal author of the briefs in about a fourth of the cases Davis argued as Solicitor General.[49]

All these men had an almost reverential feeling for Davis. "He never made an enemy I know of," Thompson said. "I never heard him criticize a man. He could get along with anyone." "Nobody," Szold observed, "could have treated me better. He was witty, pleasant, and unfailingly courteous. He would go to see the Attorney General and wait on others to go through first. He always had time for small,

kindly things." Davis was a little reserved with outsiders, Gordon recalled, but not with members of the department. "He was just a lovely
man." Above all else, said John Lord O'Brian, who joined the group
in 1917, "John W. Davis had the gift of graciousness." [50]

Everyone deemed the Solicitor General a "lawyer's lawyer." There
was nothing superficial about his work, Szold emphasized. "He didn't
have the knowledge of Brandeis or the profundity of Hughes. Yet he
went to the core, laid aside the chaff. By sheer ability and character he
became a great, perhaps the greatest, Solicitor General." One of his
distinctions, O'Brian pointed out, was his fine, discriminating knowledge of the law. This, together with his power of close reasoning,
made him a born advocate. "He let the facts take him where they
would." Furthermore, he gave such distinction to the Solicitor General's office that it became more important to lawyers during his tenure
than the attorney generalship was. Everything was on a high level—
his preparation, his oral argument, his personal relations. "The whole
atmosphere," said Szold, "was of lofty dedication to the public welfare.
In this milieu, John W. Davis towered as the supreme consummate
lawyer." [51]

Normally, Davis consulted with the Assistant Attorneys General on
matters involving their special competence and with the Attorney General on questions of moment. But he also made many decisions on his
own and many others in the Attorney General's name. By custom long
established, it was the Solicitor General who decided which cases
should be appealed and who should argue them. Under a directive issued by McReynolds shortly after Davis took office, he also approved
all papers, motions, and briefs submitted to the Circuit Courts of Appeal as well as to the Supreme Court. He usually based his decision to
appeal on the legitimacy of the case. But in some instances he appealed because the government's interest was so grave that it would
have been unthinkable not to pursue it. In others he gave in to pressure from interested departments. In a few cases he even deferred to
the overly zealous views of his assistants. On one notable "Opinion
Day" when the Court handed down seven decisions in the government's favor and three against it, all three losses were cases the Solicitor General had thought inadvisable to appeal. Always, however, he
took defeat with urbanity; and almost always he justified the more political appeals by observing that even an adverse decision was in the
public interest. Only in his private letters did he reveal the intensity of
his desire to win.[52]

The day-to-day demands were stimulating in their variety and frustrating in their immediacy. The job, Davis said, reminded him of fighting a prairie fire. "You keep it down if you never relax, but you cannot afford to give it even a day's start." One morning the Attorney General might walk up unannounced from his office in the room below Davis' in a converted house on K Street, North West, and ask whether he should advise the President to sign or veto a particular bill. An hour—sometimes a whole day and an evening—was then lost studying the bill. The next day a Congressman might seek the Solicitor General's opinion on the constitutionality of a proposed bill. The following day Davis might be required to go out of town to file a motion. And so it went. "I have been steadily at work every day, and have been bringing my portfolio home at night full of papers." "I had a call to go to the White House." "I contemplated a clear field . . . but on motion of sundry adversaries the Court has advanced several cases." [53]

Experience relieved the tension, but not the work load. "Since I reached my office yesterday morning," Davis wrote in the spring of 1915, "I have passed upon or considered the appeal taken to the Sup. Ct. by Davis Lamar, 'The Wolf of Wall Street,' convicted for impersonating [Representative A. Mitchell] Palmer; the appeal of certain Russian immigrants from an order deporting them from Portland, Oregon; the decision of a judge in Milwaukee that marriage wipes out the offense in white slave cases; . . . an application to revoke an order suspending sentence—this being an invasion of the pardoning power; a *certiorari* in the anti-trust prosecution against the Dayton Cash Register Co.; and the intervention, at the instance of the Navy Department, in a suit involving patents of wireless apparatus; etc., etc." He had also spent part of an afternoon at the Court waiting for decisions in two minor cases. Yet he enjoyed the burden hardly less than the challenge. "Thank God," he confided to his mother, "for a life filled with work and responsibilities; I have moments when I allow myself the luxury of grunting and bemoaning, but down in my soul I know it is all play-acting." [54]

« V »

Davis' relations with Attorneys General McReynolds and Gregory were especially good. To many acquaintances and some intimates, McReynolds was a curt and crotchety bachelor, narrow in intellect,

mean in spirit, and vindictive in deed. He was the scourge of the
pages, to whom he was "nice on Sunday at the house, but not during
the week"; and after he and Louis D. Brandeis became colleagues on
the Supreme Court, he took primitive pleasure in flaunting a strain of
anti-Semitism. But partly because Davis' dignity and charm seem to
have had the same elevating effect on McReynolds as they did on most
other men, and also, apparently, because the two had substantially the
same outlook toward the law, there was never any friction between
them. No one, said Davis, ever had a more considerate, cooperative,
and encouraging chief. "He was intensely interested in the work and
problems of all of his subordinates, prompt with approval where approval was warranted and candid in criticism where criticism was deserved; ready to take full responsibility for any ultimate decisions and
firm in his support of those who acted under him." McReynolds, in
Davis' view, was a grossly misunderstood man. He believed fiercely in
the Constitution as he understood it, and it was difficult for him to
avoid disliking those who believed differently. "What was sometimes
charged to him as prejudice against this person or that was more often
I think the outcome of his intensity of conviction." [55]

Davis' opinion of Gregory, who became Attorney General when
McReynolds went on the Supreme Court in 1914, was more qualified.
He had been bruised by Gregory's appointment. The new Attorney
General, he wrote his father at the time, was an agreeable man who
ranked as a good lawyer in Texas and had performed capably in the
New Haven Railroad merger case. Yet he could not help weighing
Gregory's qualifications against his own. Rejecting suggestions that he
resign in protest ("I could not with dignity quit on the instant & pro-
claim myself piqued & chagrined"), he resolved to make the best of it.
It was well that he did, for he grew to like Gregory immensely. Their
relations, he recalled long afterwards, were both friendly and intimate.
"If it were not so, the office would be almost impossible in
administration." [56]

Davis' association with the entire Court was on the same plane. As
he once said, the Solicitor General lived in great intimacy with the
Court "if they have any confidence in him and like him"; and, as he
did not say, the Court did have confidence in him and did like him.
The result, so at least one commentator inferred, was a subtle bias in
Davis' favor:

> When he appeared in the Supreme Court chamber every interested
> observer used to be reminded . . . of doting grandfathers enjoying the
> performance of a precocious and favorite grandson. The Court fairly

hovered over Mr. Davis in its solicitude, particularly Chief Justice White. The Court can be most unapproachable and aloof in its demeanor toward the bar. . . . But it never heckled its fair-haired boy.[57]

The Solicitor General's special favorite was Justice William R. Day, whom he regarded as one of the wisest men he ever knew. "If I were in trouble myself and wanted advice from anybody, I would to go Day, yet nobody knows much about Day." Davis also admired Justice Willis Van Devanter, a close friend and occasional Sunday morning golf partner. All his colleagues, Davis recalled, "said that Van Devanter was the most valuable man in the conference room—which, of course, is the place where he ought to be valuable." He himself liked what he called Van Devanter's "Doric" writing style; "he aimed to be a judge and not a litterateur." He was also partial to Van Devanter's legal philosophy—his reluctance to overturn prior decisions and his insistence that constitutional grants, limitations, and prohibitions were "very real and sacred things." [58]

The Solicitor General also enjoyed the company of Justice Joseph R. Lamar—"one of the sweetest, kindliest gentlemen" he ever knew. He regarded him as an excellent lawyer, but thought that he "agonized" too much and attended too many dinners for his own good. Davis was less intimate with Justices Joseph McKenna and Mahlon Pitney; neither his letters nor his Oral Memoir more than mention the former, and his only reference to the latter was anecdotal: "Pitney was always eager to get at the argument and always started questioning the lawyer almost as soon as he got underway. In one case he started . . . questioning the lawyer almost as soon as the lawyer had said the opening sentences. White turned to Holmes and said, 'I want to hear the argument.' Holmes said, 'So do I, damn him!' That was heard across the bench." [59]

Of the three most renowned members of the Court, Chief Justice White, Justice Hughes, and Justice Holmes, Davis was close only to White. The two often took long walks together, and though the Chief Justice talked sparingly of himself, he once stopped suddenly, planted his huge feet on the sidewalk and said, "You know, Mr. Davis, I'm not an educated man. Everything I get I've got to get through my ears. If you say that something happened in 1898, and the next time you say it happened in 1888, why Sir, it's just as if you'd stuck a knife in me. . . . On Friday night in my study I say out loud what the cases are that are coming up the next day [for conference]. If I can't look at the back of the record or brief and do that, I know I'm not ready for it." [60]

As a devout Roman Catholic, White was perplexed by Holmes' relativism. "You know, Mr. Davis," he exclaimed in another scene which Davis never forgot, "I am one of these men who thinks that somewhere, sometime I must give an account of the deeds done in the body." But, he continued, his heavy jowls shaking and his resonant voice rising to a crescendo, "My brother Holmes don't believe in anything: If you say to him, this is right and that is wrong, he will say, 'Now you are using terms that I don't know anything about.' " [61]

The old Chief Justice came close to being a hero to the Solicitor General. Davis rarely used superlatives in later life—the mountains, he explained, "flatten out as you get to them." Nevertheless, his Oral Memoir glistens with an affection and admiration for White such as he expressed for few other men. He conceded that White could be martinet-like and that his reasoning was sometimes obscure: "He wasn't happy until he had produced a paradox. If he produced a paradox, that showed that that wouldn't wash. But as he got older his opinions got quite muddy, and his style was not as good as when he first went on the bench." Davis also admitted that the Chief Justice was more impressive verbally than on paper. "When he sat in the middle of the bench he never had a note. And when he would rip out his opinions, it sounded like Jove was being heard from." He further conceded that Hughes had a better trained and more scholarly mind than White did. But partly because he felt that Hughes tended to reach his conclusion and then reason to it, and largely because he believed that White approached greatness in character, he rated White above Hughes.[62]

The belief in absolutes that Davis had acquired from his father and his mentors at Washington and Lee made it almost inevitable that he would share White's judgment of Holmes. Assuredly, he found the great Justice a fascinating, if disconcertingly self-centered, personality; he also agreed that he was "a great and distinguished figure." He felt strongly, however, that Holmes' impact upon constitutional law was baneful in two respects: "The first was his literary style and his fondness for epigrams. . . . This many lesser men on our bench have attempted to imitate with results that have not always been commendable. . . . The first requirement of any judicial opinion is utter clarity. . . . The other . . . is that in the philosophy of Holmes there was little room for absolutes in the law. My thinking is that the law is underlaid by absolutes or it is not law at all." [63]

CHAPTER 8

Davis, the Law, and World War I

John W. Davis has been more feared by certain prominent attorneys who have opposed the government in various suits than any other man in the Department of Justice.
"CHICAGO JOURNAL," SEPTEMBER 27, 1918

« I »

Early in January 1917, Davis defended the most controversial enactment of the Wilson era—the Adamson eight-hour law for railroad workers—under the sharpest questioning he had yet faced. A thinly disguised wage-regulation measure passed under the threat of a nation-wide strike in September 1916, it had been one of the central issues of the presidential campaign of that year. Six times before Congress passed the Adamson bill in September, President Wilson had implored the railroad presidents to accept the eight-hour principle, and six times he had been rebuffed. "I pray God to forgive you," he exclaimed as he walked out of one White House conference. "I never can." Society, he pointed out in a public letter, had come to sanction the eight-hour day; and even where the actual work exceeded eight hours (as in many railroad operations), eight hours should be adopted as the basis for wages. Wilson had then gone to Congress.[1]

"Cities will be cut off from their food supplies," the President warned a joint session on August 29, "the whole commerce of the Nation will be paralyzed, men of every sort and occupation will be thrown out of employment, countless thousands will in all likelihood be brought . . . to the very point of starvation." It was imperative that

Congress write the eight-hour prinçiple into law. It should also empower the President to seize the railroad industry and to draft managers and workers into the military service if necessary.[2]

A few days later Administration leaders drove an eight-hour bill through both houses, as Republicans shouted "craven submission" at the Democratic majority. The new law raised the effective wage rate by establishing eight hours as the base and providing for overtime. It did not give the President power of seizure.[3]

The Atchison, Topeka & Santa Fe immediately announced that it would not comply with the Adamson Act until the Supreme Court had ruled on its constitutionality. Other lines made similar announcements, and the small Missouri, Oklahoma & Gulf Railroad, already in federal receivership, was finally given the "honor" of testing the statute for the industry as a whole. A Western District Court promptly declared the Act unconstitutional in order to get it before the Supreme Court with all dispatch, and early in December Davis moved that *Wilson v. New*, as the suit was named, be advanced. Meanwhile he worked overtime on a seizure bill for the President.[4]

At three p.m. on January 8, the Solicitor General opened his argument in a tense chamber crowded with railroad executives, union presidents, government officials, and leaders of the bar. Opposing counsel included Walker D. Hines, general counsel of the Santa Fe, and, especially, John G. Johnson of Philadelphia. Johnson was the most renowned "business lawyer" of the era. Only Davis, in the view of many observers who heard both men argue in their prime, would equal or surpass him at the appellate bar. The last of the great independents, he took few retainers and sat on no corporate boards. His railroad clients normally awaited their turn in his anteroom, and he once refused to board a special train sent down to Philadelphia by J. P. Morgan to take him to an important conference. "I'm busy," he said; "those fellows in New York think I can run over whenever they wiggle a finger!" He often charged $10 for a judgment on another lawyer's opinion, and when corporations tried to pay on their customary scale, he sometimes returned as much as $25,000. Brilliant and supple, Johnson was as wise in the ways of men as he was informed in the nuances of the law; he had no scruples whatever about playing on the emotions and political prejudices of the bench, and like Davis, he had a facility for discerning the essential point. Even more than Davis, he often rested an argument after a few salient remarks. In a career that stretched back more than half a century, Johnson had argued more cases before the Supreme Court than any man then living. This, his seventy-first, was his last.[5]

Davis planned at first to stand on Congress' established right to regulate interstate commerce and fix hours of labor in hazardous industries. At least one Justice was known to have been shocked by the circumstances of the Adamson Act's passage, and it was believed that the measure offended the political principles of a majority of the others. As Szold suggested in a memorandum, Davis should stress those considerations that would allow the Court to sustain the Act on the narrowest possible ground. This Davis did brilliantly until the bench forced him onto the broad ground he had hoped to skirt.[6]

Davis began with a powerful exposition of Congress' authority under the commerce clause. Even the railroads' chief spokesman, he said, had testified that the Adamson Act was not primarily a wage-regulation measure. (Here he passed over the numerous assertions by Congressmen, including Oscar W. Underwood, who had driven the bill through the House, that it was designed to regulate wages and that Congress should admit it.) To say that wage regulation was Congress' basic purpose, declared the Solicitor General, was to reach "the heights of imagination." [7]

Several Justices seemed unpersuaded. "My view is continually running across the line of your argument," the Chief Justice said. "Do you claim the same power in fixing wages as in fixing rates?" "We do," Davis replied. "I do not follow that argument," White responded; "the subject is regulation of service." Refusing to fall back, Davis insisted that regulation of wages was tied into Congress' power to regulate other aspects of commerce. "That is most vital of all. If employees are underpaid and discontented, the safety of commerce in charge of the employees is affected. Wages also have a direct relation to rates, investment and expense of service." [8]

To this the Chief Justice retorted that Davis went far beyond considerations of public safety. McReynolds and Day then took up White's line of reasoning. Did the Solicitor General believe, McReynolds asked, that Congress could prescribe what railroads should pay for locomotives and land? "I am not sure that Congress has not that power," Davis replied. "All authority is dependent upon its reasonable and not arbitrary use." Was it not true, interjected Day, that Congress' power was limited by the constitutional prohibition of confiscation? Responding that Congress was empowered to regulate issues of railroad stocks and bonds, Davis added that the Court should not be concerned with the wisdom of the measure. "It may be that Congress did not please the railroads, the employees, or the public, but the body that made the law should amend it, and the judiciary must not usurp that function." [9]

Hines opened for the railroads by contending that Congress' failure to limit the actual working day to eight hours proved that the Adamson Act was essentially a wage-regulation measure. This prompted Justice Brandeis to imply that he was inclined to justify the measure for precisely that reason. "Shouldn't this Court take judicial notice of the fact that there has been a great increase in the cost of living? . . . Isn't it a historical fact that in . . . reducing the hours of labor many of the states began in fixing . . . a standard day and later in the progress of legislation there came an actual prohibition of more?" Hines lamely replied that wages had not been increased much, then fell back on the contentions of his brief—that the Act was an "arbitrary" intrusion on private contracts, affected commerce only remotely, and had no more than an "incidental" relationship to the public interest.[10]

Johnson closed for the railroads with a biting discourse on policy. The Adamson Act, said the Philadelphian, flouted the public interest and was an impracticable means of establishing the eight-hour day. Congress had acted under duress and might just as well have bought off "a gang of highwaymen with a bribe." The unions, at least, had been honest enough "not to pretend that they were protecting the public"; they simply stood upon "their own selfish ends." [11]

The Chief Justice had let Johnson speak without interruption, probably in deference to his age and reputation. He regarded his remarks as so irrelevant, however, that he cut off Davis' special assistant, Frank Hagerman, when he tried to answer them. "What has this got to do with the law question?" White asked. The Chief Justice then joined the laughter when Hagerman assured Hines, Johnson, and their battery of assistants that the Railroads need not fear the United States because, as Billy Sunday had said, " 'While the light still burns the vilest sinner may return.' " [12]

Despite the claims that Day's and McReynolds' questioning had forced him to advance, Davis was told at every hand that he had defended the government's interests masterfully. His argument, said Senator J. Hamilton Lewis of Illinois, was "one of the most lucid, forceful and irrefutable" he had ever heard on a constitutional question. Davis' own commentary was more modest: "I only know that I have rarely argued a case of which I felt myself more the master." [13]

Two months later the Chief Justice held, for a badly divided Court, that Congress' right to regulate hours was unchallengeable. Both the government and the railroads "are right and in a sense . . . wrong," he said. The former's assertion that the Adamson Act was not a wage-regulation measure and the latter's contention that it was solely such a measure were not mutually exclusive. The commerce clause empowered Congress to do that which was essential to maintain operations, including the establishment of a legislative standard of wages. White then amplified Davis' warning against judicial usurpation, declaring that the "very highest of judicial duties is to give effect to the legislative will and . . . to scrupulously abstain from permitting subjects which are exclusively within the field of legislative discretion to influence our opinion or to control [our] judgment." [14]

Four members of the Court took vigorous exception, with Day and Pitney writing separate dissents. "I cannot agree," said Day, "that constitutional rights may be sacrificed because of public necessity, nor taken away because of emergencies." He added a novel twist: Congress had violated the due process clause of the Fifth Amendment by failing to deliberate and investigate before legislating. Pitney was especially scornful of Davis' sociology: "The suggestion that an increase in the wages of trainmen will increase their contentment, encourage prompt and efficient service, and thus facilitate the movement of commerce is altogether fanciful." [15]

The majority opinion gratified Davis at the time. Three decades later, however, he was to conclude that Day, not the Chief Justice, had been right. "Nobody can tell how far the emergency doctrine will carry us," he wrote in reaction to the New Deal in 1938. "It is pretty heretical, [and] . . . perhaps the Adamson case . . . was its fountainhead." [16]

« II »

On the eve of the Adamson decision, Davis had argued the second of the two great antitrust suits of his solicitor generalship, *United States v. United States Steel Corporation*. In no case, aside from the *International Harvester* suit, which preceded it by two years, was he more personally committed to the government's position, and in none did he invest himself more totally. Both involved a clear application of his antimonopoly principles; both saw him advance the controversial thesis that *potential* power warranted dissolution.

Davis had contended in *Harvester* that the company's good conduct in the past offered no assurance that it would not abuse its vast power in the future. "Its attorneys forget," he reminded the Court, "that the Sherman Law was passed because kings were being set up to rule the country's commerce." Unless the liberty to combine was checked, liberty itself would be imperiled; and in that event, the government would be forced to rely on the Federal Trade Commission instead of the courts.[17]

The Court had failed to rule on the potential power thesis in *Harvester*, for the Harvester combine had agreed to dissolve by consent. Possibly it would have viewed the thesis favorably in *U.S. Steel* had Davis argued that case in the spring of 1916. But Brandeis had not yet been confirmed; and whether because Davis felt that Brandeis would be sympathetic or because he simply wanted a full bench, he refused to move for advancement. When the hearing was finally held, late in the winter of 1917, war was imminent and the need to mobilize industry urgent.[18]

For almost a month Davis pored over the fifty-seven-volume record: "I have read . . . until my eyes feel and look like burnt holes in a blanket." "I . . . began work a little after eight in the morning and stopped at midnight. . . . How's that for the defender of the eight-hour law?" "Hang the Sherman law—its framers, evaders, interpreters, all . . . save its toiling defenders, of whom I am humbly which." [19]

The Solicitor General insisted both in his brief and in oral argument that potential power was more crucial than past conduct. "The Government brings this suit," he said to the Court in closing on March 13, "in the belief that . . . restraint is undue . . . when combining competitors possess a preponderant or dominant share of the [market]." But even if that were not true, he added, the corporation's past conduct was more than enough warrant for a dissolution order. J. P. Morgan and the other organizers had had but two purposes in forming the company: "to escape the disadvantages of competition and to secure the profits of stock promotion." [20]

Davis then dismissed as irrelevant the defense's portrayal of U. S. Steel Chairman Elbert H. Gary as an altruist; the government was "trying to dissolve" the corporation, not Gary, he sardonically observed. He added that the establishment of a pension program * did not blot from his memory the $56 million profits of the promoters; the

---

* The pension program's coverage was grossly inadequate. In 1923, moreover, Gary would resist President Harding's and Secretary of Commerce Hoover's pressure to eliminate the company's twelve-hour day.

managers alone knew how much their liberality was "induced by the
menace of the Sherman law." As for the plea that the law should be
invoked against future violations, that would be analogous to suspending sentence in a criminal case. The notion that the corporation's disintegration would impair the war effort was hardly less defensible:
"That entirely misstates this case. This is not an attack on the steel
industry in any sense. Units will remain. This suit is aimed to restore
healthful competition in the steel industry under which it can best
flourish." [21]

Tired and drained, Davis again knew only that he had done his
best. "Thank heaven, we finished the Steel Case today . . . ," he wrote
his mother that night. "I spoke with ease to myself; whether with conviction to the court, we must no doubt wait weary months to know." [22]

The months stretched into three years. The Chief Justice ordered a
rehearing in June 1917, but the Treasury Department feared that a
dissolution order would disrupt the War Bond market by setting off a
mad scramble for new capital. Attorney General Gregory then arranged an indefinite postponement. Davis was no longer Solicitor General when final judgment was rendered in March 1920, and it was well
that he was not. Justice McKenna's opinion, for a four-to-three majority, rejected all his main theses.[23]

The government's case, declared McKenna, was based on the alleged
power for evil rather than actual evil. This assumed that the Supreme
Court was "expected to enforce abstractions" and overlooked the fact
that it must adhere to the law—a law which did not make "mere size"
or "unexerted" power an offense. The government's contention that
past conduct alone justified a dissolution order was also beside the
point: "Whatever there was of evil effect was discontinued before this
suit was brought and this, we think, determines the decree." [24]

A vehement dissent by Justice Day echoed Davis' original contention, that the corporation had been formed in violation of the Sherman Act and that it had continued to violate it for a full decade. "I
know of no public policy which sanctions a violation of the law. . . .
There must be a decree undoing . . . that which has been achieved in
open, notorious, and continued violation of its provisions." Day also
acknowledged that the corporation's ability to control the market at
whim was self-evident. But he could not agree that mere size was an
issue. Neither could he agree that the Sherman Act applied to a company if its size and power had been obtained by lawful means and natural growth.[25]

In England, where he read McKenna's and Day's opinions six weeks later, Davis had a momentary flash of resentment. "At the risk of appearing contemptuous," he said, "I must say that I do not think they will shed enduring lustre on that great tribunal." [26]

« III »

Meanwhile, Davis defended the most humanitarian of all the Progressive era's legislative enactments—the Keating-Owen Child Labor Act of 1916. The evolution of his views toward a federal child labor law paralleled the President's. In 1908, Wilson had termed federal action "obviously absurd," in the campaign of 1912, he had relegated the issue to the states, and as late as 1914 he had refused to urge Congress to act. Davis had opposed federal action in his presidential address to the West Virginia Bar Association in 1906, and in running for re-election to Congress five years later, he had neither condemned Roosevelt's call for a national child labor law nor defended Wilson's insistence that it was a state matter. He left no record of his reaction when Wilson reversed himself and drove the Keating-Owen bill through Congress shortly before the presidential campaign of 1916.[27]

The new law was soon tested, at the instance of the North Carolina Cotton Manufacturers' Association. The Association found an underpaid mill worker who needed the wages of his two young sons to sustain his family, and it arranged for the general counsel of the American Tobacco Company to file suit in his name. When the suit reached the Supreme Court in the fall of 1917, Davis assigned it to himself. Julia Lathrop, former Chief of the Children's Bureau and one of the unsung heroines of the era, complained that Davis was so conservative that he might not do justice to the case. But Secretary of Labor William B. Wilson and Assistant Secretary Louis F. Post expressed "intense" satisfaction with the Solicitor General's decision to participate. The case was docketed as *Hammer v. Dagenhart*.[28]

After rereading his address to the West Virginia Bar Association, Davis said privately that much that he had then said had been made obsolete by recent decisions. He also remarked that the new law "is perhaps the furtherest reach that has yet been attempted under the Commerce Clause." But not even to Szold, who wrote most of the brief, did he disclose what he thought of the child labor law as a matter of public policy.[29]

On March 21, 1918, Davis sent galleys of Szold's seventy-page brief to Roscoe Pound, who had been one of the government's special counsel in the lower court. The Harvard Dean termed it "full, complete and convincing." His enthusiasm was understandable, for Szold had included the pertinent sociological underpinning and yet had focused sharply on the issues at law. Standing on Marshall's opinion in *Gibbons v. Ogden,* the brief asserted that the Constitution's grant of commerce power to Congress was "plenary and embraced all the power which the States had previously enjoyed." It further contended that the Act was a regulation of interstate commerce both in terms and in fact, that it aimed to eliminate unfair trade practices caused by disparities between state laws, and that it did not violate the Fifth Amendment. It also denied that the measure's real purpose was to regulate child labor within the states. "Congress did not seek to do indirectly what it could not do directly. It sought only to prevent the evil resulting from the interstate transportation of child-made goods." Finally, the brief dismissed as irrelevant charges that the child labor bill had been passed for reasons of political expediency.[30]

Significantly, Davis and Szold also insisted that Congress could regulate the products of child labor because such labor was morally wrong. A five-page section emphasized that work which was once regarded as "harmless or beneficial" was now thought to be "immoral and injurious." A thirteen-page section contended that the health of children in competing states was "injuriously affected" by the interstate transportation of child-made goods. And numerous short, sharp assertions played on the proposition that citizens who bought the products of child labor were made "unwilling parties to practices deemed immoral." [31]

Davis' oral argument on April 17 dispelled any lingering doubts that his states' rights sympathies might compromise his presentation. In what Szold remembered as a "brilliant performance," the Solicitor General pointed up the brief's main contentions with eloquence. He forcefully reminded that Court that it had no power to inquire into Congress' motives. Yet several Justices were intent on doing precisely that; when Davis declared that "underlying this statute is the conviction that child labor is always and everywhere inherently an evil thing, and all statutes are a reflection of the prevailing opinion in the public mind," his friends White, Day, and McReynolds questioned him sharply.[32]

On June 3, 1918, Justice Day found the Child Labor Act unconstitutional for a five-to-four majority which included White, Pitney, Van Devanter, and McReynolds. In an indignant opinion which even misquoted the Tenth Amendment, he ruled that the Act not only exceeded Congress' authority over interstate commerce, but threatened to destroy "our system of government." [33]

Davis took comfort in Holmes' slashing dissent, the reasoning of which both paralleled and augmented his own. He also considered Szold's suggestion that they move for reargument, but concluded that the majority's views were so fixed that a new hearing would be fruitless.[34]

« IV »

Despite his powerful arguments in the eight-hour and child labor cases, Davis' political philosophy underwent no permanent change during his five years as Solicitor General. At heart, the private man remained a Spencerian or Social Darwinist; only his innate kindliness and respect for the persons of all men tempered his harsh conviction that the fittest would surge to the top, barring the caprice of fate or governmental interference with the natural order. The state, in his view, had no more than three or four functions: the prevention of monopoly, the maintenance of order and national security, and the preservation of property and liberty (which he deemed inseparable). It was not for government to intrude, uplift, or reform. It was not for government to confer special privileges on any individual or organization. It was not for government to compensate for the accident of birth, no matter how impoverished the cultural or economic inheritance.[35]

Only twice during his solicitor generalship did Davis strike an even vaguely progressive note in a personal letter. In 1914, after reading Mary Antin's *Promised Land,* he remarked that "to those of us who resent all immigration in general and that of the Russian Jew in particular, the book is a sermon." A year later he came close to resigning himself to the inevitability of change. "I wonder if anything is ever settled. This much seems certain: every generation . . . must thrash out the list for itself; and the individual who can escape the . . . process is fortunate." Otherwise the thrust of his comments was unqualifiedly conservative.[36]

Davis deplored the President's "retrogressive" decision to support direct presidential primaries. He complained that Congress had "piled one experiment upon another" by providing that the income tax of 1913 be collected at the source. He lamented Wilson's shift from the restorative principles of the New Freedom to the advanced progressivism of Roosevelt's New Nationalism. "I shall keep my mouth shut until called upon to speak," he grumbled when the President came out for a strong federal trade commission in January 1914, "but I have no great want for the . . . ideas—both because I do not like government by commission . . . and because I regard it as centralization final and complete." Monopolies could be dissolved by suits brought under the Sherman Antitrust Act or by consent agreements; Wilson's proposal was so much like Roosevelt's that it would result in federal control of all business.[37]

Although states' rights were and remained a motivating factor in Davis' political thought, his root concerns were taxation, regulation, and paternalism on all levels of government. His support of an attack by his father on Governor Henry Hatfield of West Virginia in 1915 is illustrative. Outraged by Hatfield's call for woman suffrage, abolition of child labor, stringent mine safety laws, state departments of health and labor, and new taxes, old John J. questioned the Governor's "sanity" in a vitriolic, unsigned letter: "There is not a fad, or ism or fancy or whim . . . that he does not recommend. . . . Offices, offices, more offices—taxes, taxes, more taxes. Pile up the burdens . . . and to hell with the prosperity of the Commonwealth." Should he publish the letter? he asked his son. John W. replied that the assertions were "all true as gospel" and that he would not even "tone them down." [38]

Davis' reflections on Woodrow Wilson suggest that his perception of men and events was considerably sharper than his insight into ideas and issues. He admired the President's strength. "He was a full-grown man. No doubt about it. He was a powerful, driving person." He was also bolder than Theodore Roosevelt. "Wilson . . . had confidence in his own reasoning about something. If it satisfied him, he'd go through with it no matter what it cost. I don't think Teddy would have done that." Moreover, his concern for the welfare of men in the mass "was thoroughly genuine, almost apostolic." Still, he was a hard man to work for. "It was a feeling of, 'Well, the boys in the schoolroom had better look out.' " He was simply incapable of inspiring the kind of affection felt for T.R. by the man in the street and Roosevelt's intimates. "Wilson . . . was not a man that you would instinctively love. You might follow him. You might approve him. You might admire him. It was difficult to feel personal love for him, however. . . . I don't think the individual man meant much to him. . . . I don't think it pained him to give pain to other men." [39]

Nevertheless, Davis supported the President loyally. He campaigned for the election of a Democratic Congress in 1914, and he stumped for Wilson's re-election two years later. In between, he dismissed Elihu Root's memorable assault on the Administration in February 1916 as an act of special pleading. "It is Root the lawyer, making the best case he can for his client, the Republican Party. The Old Guard would nominate him for the Presidency if they dared—which they do not." But it was against Wilson's opponent, Charles Evans Hughes, that Davis leveled his most damning indictment:

> Poor Hughes, to be taken to the high mountain and shown all the kingdoms of earth, and then to be dashed from such an eminence overnight. . . . And yet I cannot help feeling that in a measure it serves him right, (a) for permitting himself to be tempted while on the bench, (b) for cowardice in facing the hyphenates, (c) for hypocrisy in some criticisms of the administration, (d) for trying to fish for votes in every pool.[40]

Actually, Davis' forays into politics were infrequent. His work as Solicitor General consumed most of his energy and engaged most of his interest. He continued to impress upon his staff the view that clarification of the law, not victory, was the ultimate goal. "More than once we confessed judgment against the Government," Szold recalled, "more than once Mr. Davis observed to me that we could not lose, that all we wanted was a just and right decision." Davis also continued to be shocked by Holmes' strain of cynicism. "Mr. Solicitor," Holmes once asked, "how many more of these antitrust cases have you?" "Quite a number, Mr. Justice." "Well, bring 'em on and we'll decide 'em. Of course I know and so does every other sensible man that the Sherman Law is damned nonsense, but if my country wants to go to hell I am here to help do it." [41]

Davis was delighted in 1916 when Brandeis joined the ranks of those who found it "a pleasure" to hear him. But he was even more gratified by a remark of John G. Johnson, to whom he was already being compared favorably. Told that the Solicitor General had only a few minutes in which to complete an argument against him in an antitrust case, Johnson said, "Yes, but he is one of the most concise talkers at this bar—and one of the most dangerous." He added that Davis was the best Solicitor General he had faced in his long practice before the High Tribunal.[42]

Nevertheless, commendations were not enough. By the spring of 1917 the job had begun to pall and Davis' horizons to widen. He felt, he confided to his mother, that he would never have more important cases or greater successes; the solicitor generalship had become a "blind alley" and he was "firmly resolved to go *up,* or *out* but not *on.*" He did not add, for she already knew it, that rumor, three times in three years, had put him on the Supreme Court.[43]

Speculation of an appointment for Davis had first occurred in May 1914, when each member of the Court said that he would be gratified to have him succeed Justice Horace R. Lurton. "I do not want that bee to buzz in my bonnet no matter how softly," Davis wrote his father. On McReynolds' elevation, three months later, he said only that he spurned the thought of a "life sentence to monastic seclusion." [44]

The following year, Davis almost became counselor to the State Department on the recommendation of Secretary of State Robert Lansing, to whom he had become close through the friendship of their wives. Davis' father warned that if he made a mistake as counselor it would become known all over the nation, and Chief Justice White disapproved on other grounds. "The auger," he said, "is too big for the hole." President Wilson agreed. It would be unwise, he assured Attorney General Gregory, who wanted to hold Davis, "to disturb one who is so clearly the right man in the right place." [45]

Gregory also figured in the Solicitor General's failure to be nominated for Justice Lamar's seat in 1916. Davis conceded that an appointment to the Supreme Court would fulfill any lawyer's ambition and that it could not be declined. But he refused to encourage his numerous supporters. "If there is one office . . . which ought to come to a man unbidden it is certainly this one; and I would not for the price of the place itself, be in the attitude of campaigning for it, or permitting my friends to do so." He also agreed with Gregory that his own appointment would be inexpedient because two Justices—he and McReynolds—would then have to disqualify themselves from the *U.S. Steel* case and the rehearing of the *Harvester* case.[46]

Gregory meanwhile commended Louis D. Brandeis to the President, and on January 28 Wilson sent Brandeis' name to the Senate. Davis showed no envy, nor did he express resentment when the President nominated John H. Clarke of Ohio for Hughes' seat that summer. "I have reached a stage of extraordinary indifference. Familiarity has done . . . its deadly work, and if I do not despise it, at least I do not yearn for it." [47]

Still, Davis was restless. He knew that he could command his government salary several times over in private practice, and in late

March of 1917 he began to negotiate with the eminent New York firm of Cravath & Henderson. ("They are distinctly counsel for the predatory rich," he told his mother, "railroads, Trust Co.'s, combines and such.") But it was the national emergency, not Cravath & Henderson's clientele, that bothered him. He had "a gnawing of conscience," he confessed, at the thought of leaving government service during the war.[48]

« V »

Under his wife's tutelage, Davis began to feel more at ease socially during this period. He had stood speechless as the guests arrived for their first formal dinner for the Supreme Court, and Nell had been compelled to carry the conversation. "Goodness," she confided to her sister, "if he had married a woman as timid as he is he would never have had his head above water outside the law." (Adding that she had spent $75.00 on flowers, she warned her against telling anyone in Clarksburg.) Yet, even as he overcame his shyness, he continued to resent forced conversations and effusive women.[49]

Then and later, Davis found politically minded women insufferable. He once remarked, after drawing as a dinner partner the "deadliest" peace advocate he had ever encountered, that if she were necessary for peace, he was for war. The suffragettes were the most intolerable of all: "As long as I believe that suffrage will add nothing to the happiness of women, and contribute no resultant benefit to the state, I am and shall continue to be against it." He could not conceal his delight when President Wilson invited a group of picketing suffragettes into the White House one bitter cold day. "Not they," Davis remarked, "the crown of martyrdom shall not be so snatched from their brows. How grand it would be for 'the cause' if they could only get their toes frozen or develop a case or two of pneumonia. Rien va plus." [50]

Meanwhile, Nell's possessiveness prevented Davis from seeing much of Julia, who was then in her teens. Nell rarely asked her stepdaughter to Washington; when Julia did come, Nell made her uncomfortable. Julia never complained to her father. But, as one of her cousins said after a visit, "we never dare to speak to Mrs. Davis unless she asks us a question. . . . Everything is so formal we are so afraid we will do something wrong. I don't think Mrs. Davis cares very much about having us." The father did what he could. He saw Julia on holidays, wrote to her regularly, and mentioned her often to Szold and others.

"Our personal life was warm and passionately fond," Julia remembered, "and all the more because it was not unrestrained." [51]

Both of Davis' parents died during his solicitor generalship, his father in 1916, his mother a year later. Over the years he returned to Clarksburg periodically to visit his sister Emma, who lived on alone in the big house on the side of the hill. He also renewed some of the friendships of his youth and early manhood. Yet the intervals between visits stretched out longer and longer, and by his late middle age the missing faces and changing scenes had drained the trips home of most of their pleasure.[52]

« VI »

Davis' decision to forego a remunerative private position as war impended in 1917 reflected more than ordinary patriotism. He believed, as he had not believed in 1898, that America's cause was just, and he declared early in the war and repeatedly thereafter that he never had less neutrality in his soul. History he said, showed "no blacker crime" than the German attack on Belgium; he hoped that the tribal god of the Germans would slumber "until a hundred drops of German blood shall have atoned for every drop drawn from the Belgians." Subscribing unreservedly to President Wilson's construction of neutral rights, he chafed under Wilson's reluctance to take the ultimate step. "The school of Moltke, Bernhardi, Nietzsche, and the rest who taught that war is a thing desirable for its own sake," he wrote, was at last discredited. "Belgium replied to Germany: We are a country, not a road." The right of Americans to travel through the war zones on the ships of belligerents was inviolable, and it devolved upon the United States in general—and lawyers in particular—to stand as the "defender and champion of the sacred right of law." As he confided to Assistant Attorney General Charles Warren when the President finally severed relations with Germany in early February, for the first time in three years his head and his heart were as one. (So strongly did Davis feel that *Current Opinion* later termed him an extremist, and Warren, an anglophile himself, labeled him "The Germaniac.") [53]

Consequently, Davis heard Woodrow Wilson deliver his war message to Congress, on April 2, 1917, with relief bordering on elation. "I may live to be a hundred, but it is not likely that I shall ever witness a more thrilling scene or be more stirred myself." The President made it clear that "we fight for no selfish purpose, but only for our rights and the rights of all the world." Immediately afterward Davis brushed against the French Ambassador, Jean Jules Jusserand. "Mr. Ambassador," he exclaimed, "I want to take your hand." Jusserand, his eyes glistening with tears, replied, "Ah, we are allies now—no, allies *again*." [54]

Nine months after the United States entered the war, Davis defended the Selective Draft Act of 1917 in an omnibus suit brought by several radicals and non-religious conscientious objectors who had been charged with failing to register, aiding someone in not registering, or conspiring to dissuade persons from registering. He also represented the government in a separate suit involving Emma Goldman, the fervent anarchist and pacifist. All told, these suits challenged the constitutionality of the draft law on eighteen separate counts. The most novel, put forth by Harry Weinberger, counsel for Miss Goldman, contended that the exemption of members of "well-recognized" pacifist sects created a religious privilege. "Whatever establishes a distinction against one class or sect," read one of Weinberger's excerpts from Cooley's *Constitutional Limitations*, "is . . . if based on religious grounds a religious persecution." Nothing was more plainly expressed than the Founding Father's determination "to guard against the slightest approach towards the establishment of an inequality in the civil and political rights of citizens, which shall have for its basis only their differences of religious belief." [55]

Virtually the entire proceeding, from the original arrests through the arguments and opinion of the Court, testified graphically to Norman Thomas' observation that "when a nation is at war, Mars becomes a mighty evangelist in his own behalf." Davis' brief, which was prepared by the overburdened Szold, who utilized, in part, research done by his wife, was highly persuasive on the main point. It emphasized that compulsory service had often been required in emergencies, that colonial statutes had provided for the same, and that English and American courts had uniformly upheld acts of conscription. Society, it argued, had no recourse but to resort to compulsory service in time of crisis:

> It would be strange indeed if, alone among the nations, the Government of the United States, ordained and established to "provide for the common defense" . . . were prohibited by its organic law from using those means approved by the common experience of mankind as essential to such protection and security.

The brief failed, however, to grapple with most of the plaintiffs' flank attacks, including the one on religious privilege. Three declarative sentences dismissed Weinberger's contentions.[56]

The case was heard in December 1917 in a chamber bursting with patriotic fervor. Chief Justice White was hard pressed to control himself, and when a country lawyer said that the people had never approved the declaration of war, he admonished him for making an "unpatriotic statement." The old Chief Justice also listened to Weinberger's wide-ranging assault in seeming disbelief. Even Davis was infected by the emotionalism of the moment. He asserted that the efforts of Emma Goldman and her "cohorts" to prey upon the minds of the ignorant approached treason, and he dismissed as "frivolous" their contention that the Selective Service Act was unconstitutional. Only because they had broadcast their views to the nation did the government bother to appear in Court to refute them; they had sought to impair the country's defense, and they deserved maximum punishment.[57]

One month later, the Chief Justice upheld the Selective Service Act for a unanimous Court. White cogently defended Congress' right to conscript, but refused to dignify the religious privilege argument with a detailed rebuttal:

> And we pass without anything but statement the proposition that an establishment of a religion . . . resulted from the exemption clauses . . . because we think its unsoundness is too apparent to require us to do more.[58]

Davis was later to broaden his conception of the scope of conscientious objection. But on the main issues raised by Goldman's counsel—the establishment of a religious privilege and the right of Congress to compel military service—he never changed. "Opposed as I am to the expansion of the powers of the Federal Government," he said in 1936, after reading an undelivered opinion by Chief Justice Taney which had attacked the Civil War Conscription Act, "I nevertheless think that . . . Taney was wrong and the Supreme Court in the Draft Cases of 1918 reached the proper conclusion." [59]

By then Davis had already helped Charles Warren draw up a presidential proclamation, based on an Act of 1798, authorizing internment of enemy aliens under certain conditions. He also seems to have given qualified approval to Warren's draft of the Espionage bill of 1917. As sent in to Congress on the President's insistence, this measure prohib-

ited publication of any information "declared by a Presidential proclamation to be useful or possibly useful to the enemy." Although
Congress rejected that sweeping language, it did accept passages
which inadvertently allowed Postmaster General Albert S. Burleson
to become a virtual press czar.[60]

Davis' support of the "Spy Bill," as the Espionage Act was called
by civil libertarians, was characteristic of the broad construction he
gave the government's war powers in this and later wars. He declared
that "only those things which the Constitution [forbids] in express
and literal terms" were prohibited. And he denied that the Sedition
Act of 1918, which went far beyond the Espionage Act in its repressive features, violated the First Amendment.* "Those who so contend,"
he warned the Kentucky Bar Association, "mistake the meaning of
the liberty which it was the purpose of that amendment to preserve.
As remarked by Lord Mansfield . . . , 'The liberty of the press consists in printing without previous license, subject to the consequences
of the law.'" In time of war, he added, in a reference to *Patterson v.
Colorado,* "punishment may extend as well to the true as the false."
Fortunately, Davis was no longer Solicitor General when the Sedition
Act came before the Court in *Abrams v. United States,* so he was
spared the agony of a dissent by Holmes which has been termed "the
most eloquent and moving defense of free speech since Milton's
Areopagitica."[61]

For many months Davis served as a buffer between Warren and
John Lord O'Brian, the upstate New York Republican and civil libertarian who headed the War Emergency Division of the Justice
Department. O'Brian conceded that Warren's bold order to intern
German and Austrian master agents on the night war was declared
paralyzed the enemy's espionage system. But he protested that loose
interpretation of the Espionage and Sedition Acts by Justice Department officials in the field "gave the dignity of treason to what were
often neighborhood quarrels or barroom brawls." He also condemned
the activities of the American Protective League, a volunteer organization of some 250,000 professional patriots who served as amateur
secret service agents.† Davis left no record of his own views on these

---

* Neither Davis nor Warren participated in the framing of the Sedition Act,
which was a congressional measure from its inception.
† Zechariah Chaffee, Jr., the great historian of civil liberty in the United
States, later summed up the darker side: "It became criminal to advocate
heavier taxation instead of bond issues, to state that conscription was un-

excesses. Unquestionably, however, he agreed with Attorney General Gregory's assertion that the Justice Department was "responsible for the protection of civil liberty" no less than for enforcement of counter-espionage measures.[62]

Davis' conciliatory spirit enabled him to remain on cordial terms with Warren despite the latter's desire to institute near police state procedures. Davis warned the future historian of the Supreme Court that his views on treason went to the extreme verge of legality. (Warren insisted that the constitutional provision that treason must constitute an "overt act" could be interpreted to include "words as well as deeds if they can be proved by direct evidence.") Upon receipt of a letter from former Assistant Attorney General William Wallace proposing that sundry Germans be summarily shot or hung, Davis also sent Warren a chiding note. Said the Solicitor General in forwarding Wallace's letter: "Referred to the great destroyer of the constitution, as the reward of a kindred spirit." There can be little doubt, moreover, that Davis sided with the President, Gregory, and O'Brian against Warren's unauthorized effort, in the spring of 1918, to persuade the Senate to subject civilians to trial by military tribunals. But with customary grace, he sent Warren two highly appreciative notes when Gregory forced the Assistant Attorney General to resign in April of 1918.[63]

« VII »

By the time of Davis' own resignation in the fall of 1918, he had argued sixty-seven cases orally and had won forty-eight. He had also appeared on the brief in twenty-one other cases, and had signed four *amicus curiae* briefs. He had earned the respect and affection of all his associates. And he had drawn warm tributes from every man who served on the Court between 1913 and 1918. Chief Justice White, who ranked him second only to Taft as a lawyer, once remarked half seriously, "Of course, no one has due process of law when Mr. Davis is on the other side." Hughes called him the "clearest thinker and the best informed and prepared man" to argue before him during his

constitutional . . . , to say that the sinking of merchant vessels was legal, to urge that a referendum should have preceded our declaration of war, to say that war was contrary to the teachings of Christ. Men were punished for criticizing the Red Cross and the Y.M.C.A." Chaffee, *Thirty-Five Years with Freedom of Speech,* 1 U. OF KAN. L. REV. 6 (1952).

six years as Associate Justice. And Holmes regarded him as the most complete advocate he had ever heard. "Of all the persons who appeared before the Court in my time," he said near the end of his life, "there was never anybody more elegant, more clear, more concise or more logical than John W. Davis." [64]

CHAPTER 9

Prisoners of War Conference in Switzerland

Mr. Davis is a lawyer of distinguished ability. . . . He will be in every way a worthy representative of the country. Aside from his ability as a lawyer, he is a most effective speaker and a man of rare personal charm.

CHARLES EVANS HUGHES

« I »

"For God's sake, read this," Davis exclaimed to young Christian Herter, as they walked up the great stairway in Claridge's Hotel in London on September 6, 1918. He handed Herter a decoded cablegram from Secretary of State Robert Lansing, asking the Solicitor General to accept appointment as Ambassador to the Court of St. James's. A companion message from Davis' wife was more peremptory: "I insist you accept the President's offer regardless of personal interests or sacrifice. You must not decline." He felt, Davis said, as though the dome of St. Paul's had fallen on his head.[1]

Davis cabled Lansing that he lacked the financial resources to accept, then sent a long, reflective letter to Nell. He told her that he was utterly dependent on her, and that the offer was more frightening than alluring. "I am . . . an indifferent as well as an uncommunicative beast, who likes to go his own way for his own special affairs & let others do the same & d——d to them. To cruise around & accumulate impressions of men, things & coming events is distinctly not my *métier*." He doubted, furthermore, that he could afford to accept. He did not care to be wealthy, but no amount of "tinseled honor" could compensate for a penniless old age. Adding that Nell and Julia entered the equation, he said that he could not *"bear"* to put the ocean between them and Julia, who was then at Wellesley. He closed on a plaintive note: "What a life I have had in my small way; hankering always for the Bar & dragged from it again & again." [2]

Nell replied that she had carefully considered Julia's interest and that she was sure that the appointment would be to her advantage. Davis answered that if he did accept, it would only be by bidding the last trick in his hand in the way of self-confidence. "A mad adventure —I call it." Meanwhile, Lansing wired that Davis could draw on his capital or Lansing could arrange a loan for him through friends.[3]

Davis also discussed the offer with Rufus Isaacs, Lord Reading, the British Ambassador to the United States, who was then in London on leave. The former Lord Chief Justice and the Solicitor General had become close friends in Washington. Both men had achieved eminence through hard work and dedication; both had a consuming respect for law and the legal profession. They also shared a sharp but quiet sense of humor. Diplomacy, Reading assured his friend, was not an occult science. No doubt he was right, Davis replied, but "a Solicitor General is no fair exchange for a Lord Chief Justice." [4]

To the relief of Nell and Lansing, Davis finally accepted. "You can hardly realize the contentment which I feel in having an intimate friend . . . at our most important diplomatic post," the Secretary wrote; after all, diplomacy "is nothing more nor less than tactfully applied common sense." [5]

Davis was better cast for the post than he realized. Fresh from matching wits with the finest legal talent in the corporate world, he was at the zenith of his intellectual power; never would he be more flexible, less disposed to stand uncritically on the "first principles" of his formative years. For almost a decade he had forced himself to adapt to the changing dictates of law and politics, and for more than twenty years he had displayed an extraordinary facility for discerning the essential point in an argument or discussion. Surely, as Lord Reading urged, these talents were transferable: "You deal with people who have ideas, and you try to see that their ideas are the ideas you'd like them to have. I'd never been in diplomacy till they sent me over there, but I found it was just a lawyer's job." [6]

The Ambassador-designate even looked the part. His erect carriage, silver hair, and long, Anglo-American face gave him a passing resemblance to Woodrow Wilson, though his expression was less austere and his manner more receptive; at forty-five he was the epitome of dignity, maturity, and quiet force. He dressed fashionably, yet conservatively, and although too much the private man to be the "ordinary good fellow" some reporters described him as being, his charm was remarkable for one of his caution and prudence. Men of all stations were drawn to him by his ready, soft smile, twinkling blue eyes, and underlying warmth; it was a rare acquaintance who failed to solicit his approval or offer a confidence. He was the master of his emotions, except for a tendency to blush when praised, and most of his friends never saw him ruffled or irritated; even when wracked by self-doubt, he maintained an air of self-possession. As the London *Times* observed, "he has the ease and quiet finish of the South and its mellow humour mingling with the sterner qualities, the competence, the decisiveness one associates with the North." [7]

Nevertheless, Davis' appointment as Ambassador met with a flurry of criticism. Many commentators thought that the President should have selected Taft, Root, or Roosevelt, and a few even questioned Davis' capacity. But the main objection was his lack of reputation outside the legal profession. "His name means absolutely nothing to the mass of people," commented the New York *Evening Post*. "In England, it is safe to say, he has never been heard of by the public." Among those who knew Davis well, however, there were no reservations. Justice Holmes commended him to his English friends. Every West Virginia paper save one endorsed him. And scores of Republicans in Congress applauded the selection. "My pride," wired his classmate and best man, Sam Halley of Louisville, "has gone on an awful spree." [8]

« II »

At the time of the appointment, Davis had been en route to Berne, Switzerland, as one of four high commissioners to a conference with the Germans on prisoners of war. He was instructed to fulfill the mission before assuming his duties as Ambassador.

For more than a year, reports of harsh treatment of prisoners had been filtering into Washington. Yet not until the great German offensive of 1918 was turned back did the Imperial Government agree to meet with an American delegation. The conference was to be held in late September. The Department of State, which was receiving frequent pleas from the relatives of the one hundred American civilians interned in Germany, named John W. Garrett, Minister to the Netherlands, as head of the American delegation. Major General Francis J. Kernan represented the Army, Captain Henry H. Hough the Navy. The Justice Department was reluctant to appoint a man of rank to the commission, for Attorney General Gregory wanted to avoid formal discussion of the 2000 Germans interned in the United States. Under pressure from the Department of State, however, Gregory agreed to recommend Davis. "We are going to try to confine the conference to a discussion of prisoners of war and to internment camps," Frank L. Polk, the department counselor, explained, "but there are certain civilian matters which will almost certainly be brought up." [9]

By then, Davis was so anxious to participate directly in the war effort that he accepted the assignment with rare enthusiasm. It was "quite wonderful and important," he wrote Julia. Late in August he sailed for Liverpool on a drab, dirty transport that was jammed with 4000 troops who slept in three shifts while the ship zig-zagged across the Atlantic for thirteen days. After spending a week in London, Davis joined the other commissioners in Paris. There he watched his first air raid from the *porte cochère* of the Ritz instead of taking refuge in the great vaulted wine cellar of the hotel. A day or two later he inspected the A.E.F. prison camp outside Tours, finding it up to the standards his group was prepared to demand at Berne. (The German soldiers complained only that their 3500-calorie diet included too much meat and white bread.)[10]

On September 24, 1918, the President of the Swiss Federation formally opened the German-American Conference on Prisoners of War in the directors' room of the Swiss National Bank in Berne. Neither the Germans, whose delegation was headed by Prince zu Hohenlohe Langenburg, nor the Americans shook hands or spoke directly to each other, nor did any sign of recognition pass on their chance encounters around town. For several weeks, in fact, all remarks were addressed to the Conference's neutral president, Paul Dinichert, Minister of the Swiss Department of Foreign Affairs. Dinichert, a gracious, cheerful gentleman, spoke French, German, and English with equal fluency; his consummate tact and fair-mindedness reduced the tension and may well have saved the Conference.[11]

A five-man subcommittee—Christian Herter, Moorfield Storey, Jr., Commander Raymond Stone, Colonel Ulysses S. Grant III, and Charles H. Russell, Jr., Secretary of the American Legation in Paris— did the hard, detailed work for the Americans, although Davis spent many hours mulling over their proposals and offering counsel. He also spent a great deal of time sightseeing and talking informally to Swiss leaders and visiting Americans, including the Morgan partner Henry P. Davison, who was chairman of the American Red Cross. Time dragged, nonetheless, and he wrote often and longingly of the "dear, sweet women" he had left behind.[12]

Both delegations strove to protect their countries' larger interests. The Americans refused to agree to repatriate captured submarine personnel because they had received reports that the Imperial Navy had more submarines than crews. Conversely, the Germans insisted that any agreement on the use of prisoners as laborers apply only to Americans, presumably because they wanted to avoid modification of the severe conditions under which they were working tens of thousands of Frenchmen, Belgians, and Russians.[13]

The Germans were soon complaining that most of the discussion was directed against them, as in truth it was. The Americans possessed what they deemed to be well-authenticated reports of German mistreatment of both Allied and American prisoners. The reports indicated that captives were issued inferior clothing, employed dangerously close to the lines, and forced to clear mine fields. They were also deprived of their personal possessions, given inadequate medical treatment, forbidden to converse with each other, and cruelly punished for minor infractions of rules. In addition, women prisoners were said to be sexually abused.[14]

A firm agreement was more in Germany's interest than in the United States'. The Imperial Government held less than 5000 American military prisoners and was not likely to capture many more. United States forces had more than that number of German captives when the Conference began, and they were daily adding to the total. Furthermore, there were only 2000 American citizens in all Germany (the Germans said 7500) as against 1,800,000 Germans in the United States. Nevertheless, the German delegation negotiated for some weeks as though it were in a position of strength.[15]

The most vexatious problem was the specific wording of the articles of agreement, 180 of which were eventually adopted. The Germans wanted to confine the articles to statements of principle; the Americans wanted to set forth both the principle and its application. The Americans prevailed, although not without compromise. They originally proposed that officers (but not enlisted men) be transferred to a neutral country for internment. Urbanely, the Germans responded that this would be "undemocratic," that German military authorities had always entertained "conspicuous consideration" for the men in the ranks, and that they could not countenance "so gross a distinction." In obvious embarrassment, the Americans withdrew the proposal.[16]

On the other hand, the United States delegation won acceptance of the American definition of citizenship. Many naturalized Americans were still regarded in German law as German citizens, and it was rumored that the Imperial Government intended to treat such men as traitors if they were captured. An article guaranteeing normal treatment of captives of German origin was drawn up, apparently by Davis; but not until the Americans threatened retaliation did the German delegation accept it.[17]

Meanwhile, American intransigence over repatriation of captured submarine crews precipitated an angry adjournment. The Germans feared that a repatriation agreement that excluded submarine personnel would destroy the submarine service's morale. The Americans, who were quite aware of this, refused to discuss the matter, and the Conference seemed to be on the verge of breaking up. After a day or two of patient negotiating by Monsieur Dinichert, however, the two delegations resumed informal discussions; then, late in the Conference, the United States agreed that submarine personnel could be interned in neutral countries, but that there would be no obligation to repatriate until after the war.[18]

By then the war had almost ended. Between the opening of the Conference and the first of November, Bulgarian and Turkish resistance collapsed and the Hapsburg realm virtually fell apart. The British and Americans pushed the Germans back in the west, Metz came within range of siege guns, and General Erich von Ludendorff persuaded his government to appeal to President Wilson for an armistice. Yet even as their world disintegrated, the German delegates took vigorous exception to American insistence on inspection of prison camps within the war zone. They mounted their most forceful opposition, however, against an American proposal that the prisoners should be fed and clothed as well as the captor's armed forces were. If the proposal were put into effect, American military prisoners would fare better than German civilians. The German delegation resisted, so Commander Stone reported, until they "divined that in the near future they would probably be without any American prisoners" and should therefore do all they could to safeguard their own men.[19]

Although Davis usually deferred to Minister Garrett and the other two high commissioners at the infrequent plenary sessions, he followed

all deliberations attentively. His special concern was civilian internment, on which subject he wrote the entire section of the final agreements. During debate on the matter, Prince Hohenlohe pleaded for inclusion of a clause forbidding internment of civilians in prison camps.
Davis wrote privately that the enormous alien population of the
United States made it the last nation which "could afford to surrender
this right in time of war." But in his response to Hohenlohe, he said
that total repatriation of civilians was outside the American delegation's authority, would require a change in international law, and
would violate an American statute of 1789. "That being true, it seems
to the American delegation hardly worthwhile . . . [to discuss the mat-
ter]. We have, however, thought it might be worthwhile to make some
remark . . . on the extent to which internment has been resorted to."
He then pointed out that less than 2000 of the 1,800,000 German,
2,700,000 Austrian, and 1,700,000 Hungarian subjects in the United
States had been interned.[20]

"That jarred the Germans," Davis recalled years later. "They
couldn't understand how that could possibly be true, how we could
leave that many unnaturalized aliens, citizens of enemy countries, at
large." Neither did they have an answer when he added that it was "a
great tribute to their law-abiding quality, that they are there, are be-
having themselves, and are not being interfered with. It is only the
men against whom there is some ground for reasonable charge that we
are interning."[21]

Final accord came on November 9. Then, ten hours after the Armistice of November 11 made the agreement academic, the commissioners met for the last time and signed copies in parallel English and German texts. "Vale, our agreement," Davis scrawled in his diary.
Monsieur Dinichert gave a brief farewell address, to which Hohenlohe
and Garrett responded with emotion. The delegations then exchanged
formal bows and departed. "We felt towards . . . [the Germans] no
spirit of fraternity," said one of the participants, in a sentiment Davis
shared, "not because of their individual personalities, but because of
the system and the government they are representing and the practices
for which they had stood and would, if victorious, [have] continue[d]
to stand."[22]

Davis rarely referred to the Conference in later years. But at least
once, with feeling rather unusual for him, he expressed to one of his
partners his sense of the importance of safeguarding prisoners of war.
He felt profoundly their helplessness, the dangers of abuse or neglect,

and the obligation of humane treatment as an essential of civilization.[23]

« III »

All through the Conference, Davis had suffered moments of "vast
terror" over his impending debut at the Court of St. James's. "I confess," he remarked after perusing a bundle of clippings on his appointment, "that I do not sense the universal approval of which Lansing
speaks." The prospect of drawing on his capital was especially depressing. What a turn of fortune, he wrote his wife, that their expenses
would be increased just when he had expected to build up their reserves by going into private practice! "Gosh! Where *are* we to get the
money? Yours must not be spent, that is certain." Nell saw no problem: the ambassadorship would enhance his stature so much that his
potential earning power would increase enormously. He had less confidence in himself than she did. What if he became ill? What if he
should fail? Concluding, finally, that he simply would not live on the
scale of such rich predecessors as Whitelaw Reid and Joseph Choate,
he resigned himself to his fate:

> I do not intend to pretend to be anything other than I am—an Ameri-
> can citizen of modest means—living like a gentleman, i.e., neither
> meanly nor extravagantly—doing his best to bear himself with the
> dignity befitting his office, but putting on no "side"—not taking him-
> self too seriously, but realizing that he has a tremendous job on his
> hands & giving it all the steam in the boiler.[24]

Davis returned to New York in late November to learn that he was
to sail back within the week with President Wilson and the American
delegation to the Peace Conference at Paris. (The Senate had earlier
confirmed him for the ambassadorship unanimously.) On Wednesday
morning, December 4, the Davises strode briskly under arches of flags
along a pier at Hoboken lined with troops and boarded the *George
Washington* with the President's party. "Here we go, Julia! Soldiers,
sailors, bands, flags, et cetera. . . . Thank you for your sweet steamer
letter." [25]

Only once during the passage did Wilson confer with Davis. The
President related his well-known views on freedom of the seas, the disposition of Germany's colonies, and the League of Nations, then re-

marked that they should wait for the Russians to resolve their internal problems themselves.[26]

At Brest, the Ambassador and his wife were transferred to Admiral William S. Sims' flagship and taken directly to England. Following a rush fitting of a frock coat, Davis presented his credentials to King George V in a brief and pleasant ceremony. His Majesty talked informally about a wide range of matters—the communist excesses in Russia; the devastation in France; the magnitude of the French demands for reparations; their refusal to make English the official language of the Peace Conference in return for holding the Conference in Paris. He spoke most feelingly, however, of his desire for intimate relations with the United States. In particular, he praised Admiral Sims and commented approvingly on the fraternization of British and American naval officers. He also alluded, with an understanding smile, to disorders in Cork provoked by the Irish girls' preference for Americans.[27]

The new Ambassador soon had the first of many fascinating conversations with David Lloyd George at a dinner given by the Readings. The stocky little Prime Minister, son of a Welsh teacher, radiated vitality. "When he came into a room," Davis recalled, "it was as if the room lit up. He was one of the nimblest men I ever knew. He could start one way and change his gait to another so fast you wouldn't even see the change." Unquestionably, said Lord Reading, Lloyd George was the most unfairly gifted man he ever knew; he combined all the virility of a man with the subtlety and attractiveness of a woman.[28]

Over port and cigars that night, the Prime Minister discussed the dramatic possibilities of trying the Kaiser as a war criminal. Such a trial, he insisted with passion, could establish for all time that men could not break treaties and wage unjust wars with impunity. He added that, although many bad English kings had lost their lives for one reason or another, the trial and beheading of Charles I had had the most lasting effect on the monarchy. Lord Reading urged that nothing be attempted without support of competent evidence, and Davis warned of the danger of turning the Kaiser into a martyr. "The more I deliberate . . . the less I lean toward a trial," he wrote in his diary afterwards.[29]

By then the Ambassador and his wife were settling into a house on Berkeley Square which had been lent to them by Arthur Glasgow of Richmond, brother of the novelist Ellen Glasgow. The leafy garden of the Square, surrounded by stately brown porticoes, was then the heart

of Mayfair, a more fashionable address than the Davises would be able
to afford on their own. Nell staffed the house with some servants left
by the Glasgows and some inherited from the Walter Hines Pages (including a positive little lady's maid who was well versed in court eti-
quette). She had hardly organized the household of fifteen or more
than she gave a formal lunch for Mrs. Woodrow Wilson, who came
over from Paris with the President just after Christmas. Meanwhile,
amidst the pomp and ceremony which had returned to London for the
first time in five long years, the Ambassador was standing out among
the English and his fellow diplomats as the only man in plain black
evening clothes, entirely unadorned. ("What swank!" said Sir Eric
Geddes.) [30]

The first of Davis' many observations of President Wilson's insensi-
tivity came at a glittering state dinner at Buckingham Palace, served
on gold plates brought up from the vaults of Windsor Castle for the
first time since 1914. His Majesty toasted the President and the American people warmly, generously, and felicitously. But as Lloyd George
complained, Wilson responded "with the perfect enunciation, measured emphasis and cold tones" which were to become all too familiar
in the months to come. "There was no glow of friendship or of glad-
ness at meeting men who had been partners in a common enterprise
and had so narrowly escaped a common danger." Neither was there
any recognition of Britain's enormous sacrifices. "Not a word of appreciation, let alone gratitude, came from his lips." [31]

The Archbishop of Canterbury protested to Davis afterwards, and,
whether by the Ambassador or others, word was passed to the President. Wilson redeemed himself partially in a speech at the Guildhall
the next day. Then, to the thunderous cheers of hundreds of thousands of common people who strewed his route with flowers, he made
a triumphal three-day tour through England. At its end, the President
pronounced his visit a "qualified" success and told Davis that the
British people would "stand no nonsense"; they deserved to know as
soon as possible the new rules by which the world was to be regulated.
He added that Lloyd George was a second-rate politician with no
more program than Georges Clemenceau, and that he would return to
England, if necessary, to muster popular support for the League of Nations.[32]

Davis made no comment on the President's remarks. But he did report that talks with Lord Bryce and others convinced him that Wilson's visit had "stiffened the already predominant sentiment in favor

of the League" and "increased the general good will toward the
United States." [33]

Less than two weeks later, Davis set the tone of his ambassadorship
before a British-American audience at the Pilgrim's Club:

> I would not wish to weaken by any exaggeration of phrase the tribute
> of America and her people to the manner in which Great Britain and
> the Britons have borne themselves . . . but it would not be easy to ex-
> aggerate, if one desired, their admiration for your courage, your stead-
> fastness, and your dogged endurance.

The new American Ambassador, the London *Times* announced the
next day, was a worthy successor to Lowell, Choate, and Page.[34]

CHAPTER 10

Ambassador to the Court of St. James's

I look back on it with great pleasure. Once you have the confidence of the English, they are amazingly frank and they have the valuable quality of not resenting frankness in others. I never found it necessary to be anything other than frank in defense of the American position.
DAVIS TO JOSEPH P. KENNEDY,
JANUARY 25, 1938

While Davis was captivating the British with his charm and sensitivity, relations between England and the United States were deteriorating—and so rapidly that he despaired of his usefulness before his tenure had fairly begun. Ignored by the President he represented, embarrassed by the crude pronouncements of his countrymen, and humiliated by the Senate's rejection of the Treaty of Versailles, he yearned to return to the practice of law.

Of the tensions between the two great wartime allies, America's failure to join the League, its undisguised sympathy for Ireland, and President Wilson's tendency to read "high moral lectures to the world" were merely the most obvious. Others, more deeply rooted, involved trade rivalries, Britain's drive to monopolize Middle Eastern oil, and her resolve to maintain control of the seas. Proud in her leadership of the Empire in the greatest of wars, Britain was more exhausted and more thinly spread than she realized. Idealistic, self-righteous, and far stronger than even her leaders knew, the United States wanted both to remake the world and to withdraw from it, to invoke the prerogatives

of power and to reject its responsibilities. "America was handed the
sceptre of the world," Lloyd George said to the unhappy Ambassador,
"and she has thrown it into the sea." [1]

« I »

Twice during the winter and spring of 1919 Davis visited the Peace
Conference in Paris, each time to return with relief at escaping an atmosphere he described as "mephitic." Americans of all persuasions, he
reported in late January, felt that Wilson was winning acceptance of
his ideas and had more than vindicated his decision to head the American delegation in person. Yet the President was wearing down physically: "the large supply of intelligent men at his disposal are not being
utilized; his habit of reticence is breeding discontent and discouragement among the leaders which . . . is communicated necessarily to the
rank and file. The commission forces lack organization. Things are
going so much his way . . . as to lead one to fear that there is a deliberate purpose to give him the line until they are ready to 'snub' him
or until his time is out." [2]

Four months later Davis found Wilson still playing "a lone hand."
The President opened a meeting of the American Peace Commissioners by declaring they had met "to lay their minds down alongside each
other," then did virtually all the "laying down" himself. He even discouraged Lansing's suggestion that some of the American experts be
asked to outline their views on reparations.[3]

A dispute over the Rhineland had drawn Davis to Paris the second
time. Fearful of an eventual resurgence of German power, Marshal
Ferdinand Foch was determined to keep the area under tight military
control during the projected fifteen-year occupation. At his instance,
the Supreme War Council drafted an occupation agreement patterned
on the one the Germans had imposed on France at the end of the
Franco-Prussian War. The American member of the Rhineland Commission, Pierrepont B. Noyes, was so appalled that he protested to the
President. Terming the agreement "more brutal . . . than even its authors desire," he warned that it would subject six million people to
"unendurable oppression"; instead of martial law, the Rhinelanders
should be given complete self-government, with a civilian commission
empowered to enforce the Treaty of Versailles.[4]

Wilson himself was at "wits' end" over the repressive features of the
War Council's plan. He persuaded Lloyd George and Clemenceau that

a new convention was imperative, then asked Davis to head the American delegation on the drafting committee. The Ambassador accepted with unwonted enthusiasm; nothing, he assured the President, could give him more pleasure than to soften the occupation.[5]

For ten days in early June 1919, Davis and his British and French colleagues struggled to convert Foch to their civilian point of view. The Marshal believed that force alone could contain the Germans; and although he professed to favor Davis' plan to give ultimate power to a multi-nation civilian commission, he remained intractable. Each day he would come to the meeting, pull on his great white moustache and say "bon, bon" as the others talked, then press anew for military control. Davis' patience grew precariously thin:

> Marshal Foch delivers himself at length on the necessity for leaving the matter to the military. . . . We reassembled and the draft was read . . . the Marshal again protesting, with a suggestion from [General Maxime] Weygand whenever he ran down. . . . Marshal Foch nothing daunted returns to the attack on the whole plan. . . . In order to hold the ground we had gained, I made bold, under the guise of inquiry, to make a resume of our conclusions to date.[6]

Meanwhile, the other delegates agreed to grant France the presidency of the Commission and a tie-breaking vote. Davis preferred a rotating presidency, but acquiesced because almost the entire army of occupation was to be French. He also accepted the proposal of the British representative, Lord Robert Cecil, who hoped for a short occupation, that they recommend revision of the agreement in two or three years. Otherwise, the final report embodied most of Davis' and Noyes' views. The Civil Commission was given supremacy; the army's powers were limited chiefly to those essential to its own maintenance and protection; and the jurisdiction of the Civil Commission was confined to enforcement of the terms of the Treaty of Versailles. The principal weakness was the exclusion of the suggestions of Noyes and the British that the Commission be empowered to intervene in German economic life if necessary.[7]

« II »

On June 11 Davis returned to England, where one abrasive incident followed another. Secretary of the Navy Josephus Daniels inflamed all England by calling for an "incomparably large" American Navy. Admiral Sims disclosed that just before he sailed for Britain in 1917 another ranking American naval officer had said to him that the United States "would as soon fight England as Germany." General John J. Pershing baldly declared that America had won the war.[8]

The Ambassador labored unceasingly to undo the damage. He told an audience studded with Royal Navy officers that the American Navy's services "were slight indeed" compared to Britain's "long and arduous. vigil." He remarked to the Pilgrims' Society that, with so many million English-speaking people "all *speaking*," it was not surprising that even a Brother Pilgrim (Admiral Sims) could be indiscreet. He referred often to the untold sacrifices of the British people. Yet he never apologized, never spoke abjectly, never conveyed the impression (except on the Irish question) that he was representing his country in any but the fullest sense.[9]

The press responded as warmly as his audiences did. A northern Irish paper compared him to that "greatest living master of the English language, President Wilson." The *Jewish Guardian* reported that he had captivated everyone. Dozens of others commented on his dignity, sincerity, and rare gift of concise and balanced eloquence. Enthusiasm for Anglo-American friendship inspires his every utterance, the London *Evening News* observed; he speaks "like a poet of the Stars and Stripes and Union Jack floating together over the Houses of Parliament and Westminister Abbey." [10]

Nevertheless, the mounting criticism of President Wilson and the peace settlement weighed heavily. Although Davis later conceded the brilliance of John Maynard Keynes' polemic, *The Economic Consequences of the Peace*, he did not see how the political arrangements could have been altered substantially. The President, he wrote, bestrode the Conference "like a colossus," forging as reasonable a peace as conflicting interests allowed; the Treaty's harsher features could be softened later by the League of Nations.[11]

The League itself was another matter. Davis shared many of Lloyd George's own reservations, and he was hard put not to assent openly to the Prime Minister's contention that the Convenant was too specific. "I held my tongue," he reported, "but the truth is that I entirely agree with him. Lansing had the right idea in his skeleton form of general principles which the President so curtly brushed aside." [12]

Davis insisted, however, that it would be "madness" to reject the League. Men who failed to see that the United States would be affected by the disintegration of Europe were beyond the pale: Henry

Cabot Lodge, the architect of the Treaty's defeat, was a "contemptible obstructionist"; James M. Beck, a pompous Philadelphia corporation lawyer who made an anti-Wilson speech in London, was full of "egotism and partisanship"; William C. Bullitt, the young pro-Soviet aristocrat who resigned from the peace delegation in May 1919 and revealed numerous confidences to the Senate foreign relations committee, was "a sneak" who could be "counted upon to lie in his betrayal." [13]

Yet neither was the President faultless. Davis deemed his Jackson Day demand of January 1920, that the United States "take" the League Covenant without substantial changes, a blunder of the first order. When William Jennings Bryan replied that the talk of a "solemn referendum" was foolish and that the Democrats should work out a compromise before the presidential election, Davis found himself on the Great Commoner's side for the first time in years. What would his duty be, the Ambassador asked himself, if Wilson held to his all-or-nothing policy? [14]

Davis concluded that his duty was to put his country in as dignified a light as possible. He encouraged Lord Charnwood, Lincoln's biographer, to publish an article explaining the Republican party's right to reject the Treaty. He himself, in countless private conversations, defended the United States against the charge of breaking faith. And at Oxford, he lucidly explained the Senate's prerogatives in a widely noticed address. (Davis privately regarded the two-thirds rule as obsolete.) [15]

Only one small diplomatic triumph brightened the gloomy fall and winter of 1919–20. On December 1, Edward, Prince of Wales, returned from an extraordinarily successful good-will visit to the United States. "Had I not urged the matter," Davis said in one of the few self-congratulatory passages in his diary, "I believe his invitation, if it came at all, would have been so delayed that it would have been refused; and if I had not pressed it after the President's illness I think the authorities here would have cancelled it." [16]

The King, who had deferred to Davis' judgment despite his own fear of Irish-American demonstrators, was delighted. At the Palace dinner given the night his son returned, he took Mrs. Davis in on his arm and seated the Ambassador on the Queen's left. Just before retiring, His Majesty summoned the Davises from among the sixty guests and bade them good night. "You are celebrating the anniversary of your arrival shortly," he said, "I hope you may have many more years with us." [17]

« III »

The King's gesture failed to weaken Davis' intention to resign as soon as he could gracefully do so. Assuredly, he delighted in London, the British people, and in the English countryside, where he and Nell spent many weekends as guests of important personages of the realm. He complained of "too many dinners, too much wine, too little vigorous work"; but he also conceded that life had never been "so full of novel incident and valuable experience." His early letters described the splendor of the dinner services, the glitter of his bemedaled diplomatic colleagues, the oddity of sprinkling his own conversation with "Your Highnesses." He told his West Virginia friends of learning to bow and walk backward out of the royal presence. He jested that he had a figure that could "shine" in silk stockings and knee breeches. He compared parceling out tickets to Ascot and presentations at Court to handing out fourth-class postmasterships in West Virginia.[18]

In the great country houses, surrounded by lush, green lawns and beautifully maintained gardens, Davis saw a way of life which struck him as the most agreeable in the world. He loved the casual grace, the instinct for form, the well-stocked minds, the feeling for language. And he was enchanted by the great houses' historical treasures: at Sutton Place, the Holbein portrait of Henry VIII; at Warwick Castle, the suits of armor that lined the Great Hall; at Holkham, the will of Sir Edward Coke, James I's Chief Justice, calling down maledictions on any descendants so feckless as to dissipate the property—all this and more was an unending stimulation to a man whose greatest fascination outside the law had always been the history of the British people.[19]

The great house parties also served a useful function for both Davis and his hosts. He became acquainted socially with government leaders, gained their confidence, and learned their manner of thinking. Affairs of state were often discussed on long walks in the countryside, or over whiskey and soda by the roaring fire in an ancient library stocked with first editions of the classics he loved. The English liked his lack of "side," his open but not invadingly friendly manner, his quiet humor, so much like their own. They appreciated his respect for their opinions, and they admired the integrity of his. They also sensed his at-

tachment to the Magna Carta and the English Bill of Rights, his faith
in the future of the English-speaking people, his belief in the civilizing
force of the British Empire. For these reasons and many more, the
King, Lloyd George, and countless other men gave him their friendship, their trust, and their private views on matters of moment. "John
W. Davis," said King George, "was the most perfect gentleman I have
ever met." [20]

There had been just one untoward incident. At his first large party
Davis walked over to a group of men conversing in a corner and introduced himself. They nodded coolly and resumed talking among themselves. Mortified, he swore never again to take the initiative. Three decades later the incident was still on his mind when Joseph P. Kennedy
was appointed Ambassador to the Court of St. James's. "The important thing . . . with the Englishman," Davis warned, "is to give
him plenty of time. He moves slowly and to rush only arouses his distrust. . . . [He] is like a horse in the pasture. If you rush up to him
with the bridle, he is off and away. If you give him time to look you
over, he will let you put your hand on his mane." [21]

Nell reveled in English life, and was never more fulfilled than during her two years at the Court of St. James's. By the spring of 1919 she
had found an adequate house in Belgravia. Six stories high, it rented
for $5500 (considerably less than the one in Mayfair). It seemed to
young Julia, on her arrival that summer, "very grand and elegant."
Actually, it was the smallest house that any American Ambassador had
lived in during this century. Only by opening up a reception room
could the dining room be made to seat thirty-six, at three round tables
for twelve. A first secretary of the Embassy, heir to a steel fortune, had
a much larger house around the corner on Belgrave Square. To econo-
mize further, Davis bought a second-hand Pierce Arrow from an American General and had its army khaki painted black. [22]

Because it was customary for each Ambassador to leave a portrait of
himself in the chancery, Mrs. Davis persuaded her husband to sit for
Lazlo, the most fashionable portrait painter of the day. Struck by
Nell's beauty, Lazlo insisted on painting her also. Then, not wholly
satisfied with the blandness of the official portrait of the Ambassador,
he did a second one of him. [23]

Nell had a genuine gift for entertaining, and even the King, notoriously early to bed, once remained until 12:15 after one of her dinners. Sooner or later, everyone in London came to her Thursday after-

noons at home. She could be gracious or aloof, charming or impersonal, as it suited her purposes. She also made some enduring friendships. "You will remember, perhaps," wrote Lady Charnwood, "that at first I was cowed by your perfection of dress and manner and how I got to the heart and ceased to be afraid! Oh, do let us see you again." [24]

Often, Nell's political instincts were helpful. Once, during a lull in the conversation at a dinner party, an English General asked her in a booming voice what she thought of President Wilson's interpretation of "freedom of the seas." (The British feared it as a threat to their naval supremacy.) Demurely, she replied that she knew little about it but thought it "had something to do with mixed bathing, hadn't it?" The next day the grateful embassy staff filled her drawing room with flowers.[25]

As the Ambassador came to feel at ease, he perceived the essential humanity in royalty and aristocrat, chambermaid and footman. He was amused at hearing some of the court members from the era of Victoria and Albert denounce the Germans in thick Teutonic accents, and he chuckled over the Prince of Wales' remark that "at least the war has kept me from having to marry one of those damn German princesses."[26]

Davis also enjoyed the King's confidences, small and large. "Nobody pays any attention to what I say around here," His Majesty complained to him one day. Or again, with the fate of the Czar and his family in mind, "It is very stupid to assassinate a president, for you can always elect another, but they could get rid of all of *us* without much trouble." Or still again, explaining why an independent Ireland was impossible, "I have *myself* seen a letter from De Valera inviting the Germans in. Did you know that?"[27]

Most of Davis' impressions of the middle and lower classes came from the press, conversations with Liberals in the coalition government, and, very rarely, officials of the Labour party. (Lady Astor liked to throw the incongruous together, and at Cliveden Davis became acquainted with the radical socialist J. H. Thomas, whose father had been a caretaker there.) Within months he developed an extremely warm feeling for the British people—for their fortitude, steadfastness, and stability, which, as he said, "one need not be an Anglo-maniac to admire." For a while, during the bitter strikes of 1919, he viewed the workers' cause with considerable sympathy:

The employer whose whole philosophy is based on the idea that he is
the owner of his factory and may do as he pleases with his own, is in
for a severe awakening. Labour is demanding an increasing share in industrial management and on the whole I think it is entitled to more of
it than it has had hitherto. I am inclined to think that it would be a
good thing to have Labour directly represented not only in the subordinate positions but on the Board of Directors itself.[28]

Yet it was hard not to see Britain through the eyes of her ruling
classes. Davis came to echo their charge that the strikes were political.
He was shocked by the old Duke of Richmond's complaint that he
had only a half crown left from each pound after taxes. ("How can
they stand it?" Davis asked himself.) On meeting a Franciscan friar at
Lord Sandwich's country house, he was surprised to learn that the
young man was an ex-officer of the Guards and had chosen to make
"his bed with the lowly out of sheer conviction." He listened sympathetically, though with some reservations, to the lament of Lord Midleton, former Secretary of State for India, that the peerage was being
diluted.[29]

Meanwhile Davis continued to win the English people's esteem and
affection with his speeches—over a hundred in a little more than two
years. He and Lord Reading, who was hardly less fluent, spoke back-
to-back so often that Lloyd George called them "that famous after-dinner team, Reading and Davis." Reading himself told Colonel Edward
M. House, the President's closest adviser, that Davis was an adornment
of English public life, "always making good speeches, never losing
sight of American interests and yet understanding us and our point of
view." Occasionally, of course, Davis disappointed himself. Once, after
a long, deadly evening at the Lyceum Club, he said to his wife that his
speech was "the worst" he had ever made. "It was more than that,"
Nell responded, "it was the worst speech *anybody* ever made." [30]

Of all his honors, Davis most treasured his membership in the Middle Temple. "If you don't know," he wrote Julia, "let me tell you that
the Middle Temple is one of the old Inns of Court or lawyers' societies. . . . [The] honor conferred is one which has been given to but
one other foreigner, my predecessor Mr. Choate, and is quite one of
the nicest things that the lawyers of England can do for me." He always remembered his sessions with his fellow lawyers as among his
most engaging and rewarding experiences in England.[31]

Neither the recognition nor the gracious social life sufficed to relieve
Davis' frustration over the growing tension between the American and

British peoples. In February 1920, fourteen months after his arrival, he unburdened himself in his diary: "Never since I have been here has sentiment been as unfavorable. . . . The press is daily more critical and caustic and the feeling of the general public is unmistakable." The reasons were clear and numerous. The fall of the pound sterling as against the dollar and the resultant increase in food prices was "being exploited as due to American greed and . . . her absorption of Europe's wealth during the war"; the Senate's failure to ratify the Treaty of Versailles converted "hope into bitterness"; the yellow press was refusing to put the Sims and Daniels incidents into perspective; Pershing's boast that the United States had won the war was still being condemned as "America's insult to our dead"; Secretary of the Treasury Carter Glass' opposition to loans to Europe was viewed as unnecessarily callous; American support of the Irish Independence movement was bitterly resented as interference; and, finally, Prohibition was depressing the British liquor industry. The Ambassador concluded that beneath it all lay "a latent trade jealousy, a fear for threatened marine supremacy, a dread of competition in naval armament, and a heavy realization of the legacy of financial and economic disadvantages which the war has bequeathed." [32]

The drain on Davis' financial resources intensified his depression. Although his expenses ran $20,000 or more above his salary and allowances, he might have put the short-term sacrifice in perspective had he deemed his services vital. But, as he complained to Lansing, his government had not even given him a real brief to argue; indeed, the Senate's rejection of the Treaty had virtually destroyed his usefulness. "I read countless reports from Paris and elsewhere on the state of the Universe; I send you or the Department a great deal of literature of questionable value; and I utter an unending stream of platitudes to yawning diners, but what am I really doing to help the wheels go round?" [33]

On February 13, 1920, just six weeks after he wrote that letter, Davis was startled to read at breakfast that Lansing himself had resigned at the request of the President. The Secretary of State, reported the London *Times,* had aroused Wilson's ire by holding Cabinet meetings during the President's illness. "I don't believe it," Davis exclaimed. "Bert would have told me." Young John Foster Dulles, Davis' house guest at the time, also disbelieved the news about his uncle; together they sent a coded cable to Washington. Informed that the report was true, the Ambassador wrote his dear friend that the President's atti-

tude was fantastic. "As Reading said to me this morning, 'What in the
world was Lansing to do? The world will not stand still because any
man is sick.'" Even King George was exercised. "I would not have dismissed my butler that way," he told Davis, adding that the President
seemed not to realize that the world had moved ahead during his long
seclusion.[34]

Within a week Davis drafted a letter of resignation of his own. He
had agreed to serve, he reminded the President, only because "all personal considerations were for the moment insignificant." Now, more
than a year later, actual peace seemed as remote as ever. His expenses
were out of all proportion to his private income, and his sense of duty
to himself and his dependents dictated an early return to private life.[35]

Davis never sent the letter. By then he himself was being frequently
mentioned for the presidency, and he was advised that his resignation
would be viewed as an open bid for the nomination. So with less heart
than ever, he turned again to the conflicts between the United States
and Great Britain.[36]

« IV »

The revolutionary heritage of the American people, the long repression of Irish-Catholics by the English and the Ulstermen, the movement for self-determination in Europe—all gave the Irish nationalist
movement an irresistible appeal in the United States. Even President
Wilson was moderately sympathetic. He had told his personal secretary before the war that there could never be "real comradeship" between England and the United States until the Irish question was settled, and he had been discreetly responsive to Irish-American
nationalists at Paris. Had the latter not been so impolitic, and had the
President not needed British support of the League, he might well
have pressed the Irish case.[37]

Davis' private views reflected both his instinctive distrust of most agitation and his tendency to accept the English view of Britain's national interest. He believed that some home rule was essential, if only
to avert a bloodbath, and he deplored the intransigence of the Protestants in northern Ireland. "How blind they are!" he wrote after reading a secret report of their tactics during the long Irish Convention of
1917–18. He also agreed with Sir Horace Plunkett, the southern Irish
Unionist and moderate Home Ruler, that England's conduct
throughout had been marked "by cowardice and stupidity." Yet he

never alluded to England's economic exploitation of Ireland, never commented on the incongruity of her support of self-determination on the Continent and her opposition to it in Ireland.[38]

Repelled by the ambushes and political assassinations of the Sinn Feiners, Davis asserted at one point that the Irishman's vice was "a lack of moral courage." He warned Lansing, Polk, and others, including the mayor of Boston, that military considerations alone made independence inconceivable: "The British will never consent to an independent nation on their western flank any more than the [American] Union would permit the voluntary secession of a single State." He doubted, moreover, that the Irish themselves had any real expectation of such an outcome—"perhaps not even a real desire for it." Indeed, he was so convinced that the Irish temperament would not permit a definitive solution that he relished the spirited response of the passionately Irish wife of Sir John Simon to his question, what do the Irish really want: "They don't want what they've got." [39] Privately, Davis bemoaned New York Governor Alfred E. Smith's heralding of Eamon de Valera "as the heroic head of the youngest republic." He fumed over the numerous expressions of support for Ireland in Congress. He labeled Republican National Chairman Will Hays' admission that the G.O.P.'s objective was the Irish-American vote a "callous avowal of political opportunism." The trouble with Americans, he confided to Charles Warren, is that they want to reserve to themselves "the sovereign privilege" of meddling in other people's business:

> I deplore the cheap demagoguery which is going on about Ireland, among other reasons because I think it the worst of services to Ireland herself. While a large majority of the Irish are dissatisfied with British administration (which really seems to have run the whole gamut of error—this in private), the best information I can obtain clearly shows that the majority do not desire an independent republic.[40]

Behind the scenes, Davis worked quietly to discourage American hopes for an independent Ireland. "I didn't, of course, undertake any active intervention. However, whenever I got a chance to put in a word, I put it in." He suggested to a prominent Englishman who was about to make a visit to the United States that he state frankly that there was no possibility of independence. He canceled an address to the Irish Society in London because "there is no sense in a useless trip into a powder magazine." He advised Sir Horace Plunkett not to testify before an ad hoc committee of investigation sponsored by Oswald

Garrison Villard of *The Nation*. He even gave an impression in some
of his speeches, so Irish newspapers charged, that he was "too much of
a pro-English partisan." [41]

Davis' abhorrence of violence made it increasingly difficult for him
to justify official British policy. He said nothing when Plunkett argued
that English repression of the Irish during the war had been defensible on military grounds, but that the postwar repression was indefensible on any ground. He was badly shaken when Sir Horace proved that
the government was deliberately misleading the English public by doc-
toring photographs of Sinn Fein atrocities; the pictures, wrote Davis in
disgust, are "a clear fake." Plunkett's insistence that the Irish had
hardly done "more than could be expected of any white people whose
liberties were so tramped upon" also forced Davis to reflect on, though
hardly to abandon, his notion that the Sinn Feiners should not be
compared to the American revolutionists of 1776. Neither did Lord
Bryce, then eighty-two years old and as intellectually vigorous and
prescient as ever, ease the Ambassador's mind. The author of *The
American Commonwealth* denounced British reprisals, condemned the
entire Irish policy, and asserted that a Labour government would be
quite capable of granting independence to Ireland, and to India as
well. [42]

Under these influences, Davis questioned Lloyd George's decision
to impose martial law on Munster, the largest province in Ireland. He
warned Sir Campbell Stuart, the newspaper executive, that rigorous
measures would leave a dreadful "legacy of hate." (Crown forces killed
203 unarmed Irish civilians in 1920 alone.) And he was outraged when
Major-General Sir Edward P. Strickland ordered seven houses in Cork
burned in retaliation for an ambush of English troops. The order,
Davis scornfully wrote in his diary, was an act "not to be distinguished
from the German methods in Belgium." [43]

Yet none of this convinced the Ambassador that Ireland was not
destined to remain part of the United Kingdom, that it should become
free, that revolutionaries should be recognized, and that Irish independence was more important than Anglo-American harmony. He recorded, with implied approval, Lloyd George's admonition to an Irish
priest that "we Welsh are content . . . as equal partners in the realm"
and that "Ireland [should] be likewise since—for good or ill—these
islands have been put here together . . . [by] Providence." He denounced as "madness" Massachusetts Senator David I. Walsh's resolution for Irish independence. He expressed agreement with the King's

private assertion that the government "would fight to the last Englishman or Irishman" and that it could not "raise the white flag while the
country is in the grip of a gang of outlaws and murderers." [44]

« V »

Meanwhile, events in revolution-wracked Russia put Davis' repugnance of the use of force in even sharper relief. He advised Lansing
that it would be unwise to recognize the Bolsheviks either "expressly
or by implication," but he had no sympathy for the Secretary of State's
desire to repress them with arms. He was especially discouraged by the
transformation of the Allied expedition to Archangel from an anti-
German to an anti-Soviet operation. "Call this morning from a ser-
geant U.S.A. wounded on the Archangel front," the Ambassador reported in February 1919. "Says the men there have no idea what they
are fighting for and demand to be told; a Captain reading the burial
service over a dead comrade said 'He died for a great cause, but we do
not know what it was.'" The whole expedition, Davis added, was a
miserable failure; he wished the United States were out of it.[45]

On September 27, 1919, Winston Churchill, then Secretary of War,
called on the Ambassador unannounced. He explained that he had
come to talk informally about the Russian situation. In Siberia, Admiral A. V. Kolchak, whom Lloyd George had written off, was leading a
White Russian force against the Bolsheviks. In Southwest Russia, General Anton Denikin, also a White Russian, had advanced to within
one hundred miles of Moscow and held five principal cities and a territory with thirty million inhabitants. Churchill was so confident that
Denikin would prevail that he planned to ask for another fourteen
million pounds' worth of army stores for him; however, he had just received a telegram from Kolchak, announcing a victory and reporting
that he needed further supplies in order to hold out. If Kolchak failed,
he went on, Siberia would probably fall into anarchy and come under
the control of the Japanese. Would America support Kolchak with
munitions and supplies, if not with men? "The Peace Conference has
lost its power," said Churchill grimly, "and is no longer able to control
the European situation." Davis promised to forward the request to
Washington along with a copy of Kolchak's telegram.[46]

Throughout the interview Churchill was intensely restless, pacing
the office, sitting down and jumping up, constantly in motion. "His
nature is distinctly that of the adventurer," the Ambassador noted,

"and given a free hand he would certainly be deeper in Russia than at present, and would be ready to take on new enterprises all over the world. He is an incurable optimist in regard to any enterprise of which he has once approved." [47]

Shortly after Churchill's visit, Lloyd George, with apparent casualness announced at a Guildhall luncheon that there would be no further aid to Russia beyond what had been promised. Davis saw Churchill, who had been discredited by the disasters in Gallipoli five years earlier, start and redden; Davis felt sure that he had not been consulted. Lloyd George admitted it afterwards; "I did it to stop his adventures." [48]

Two weeks later, Davis had a long, private conversation with Lloyd George and Sir Auckland Geddes, who was soon to become Ambassador to the United States. Davis was aghast to learn that neither man had a "fixed prejudice" against coming to terms with the Bolsheviks:

> Both of them brush aside the "shaking hands with murderers" argument, insisting that the Bolsheviks are no worse than the Germans; and to my insistence that it was impossible to make terms with a government which denied the sanctity of agreements, and sent its agents out to undermine the governments by whom it was recognized, they answered that the Bolsheviks, if they had not already come to their senses would do so when the pressure of foreign and domestic war was removed. They have lost faith in Kolchak and Denikin and made no secret of the difference of opinion between themselves and Churchill on the subject. . . . What the P.M. is really aiming at is the ultimate dismemberment of the Russian Empire and its separation into a number of independent states. He is still obsessed with the danger—especially as I think to Persia, India, etc.—of a restored nation of two hundred million souls. [49]

In mid-winter of 1920, the Ambassador and the Prime Minister had another lengthy meeting. "You in America are in about the frame of mind we were in a year ago," Lloyd George exclaimed, waving a bundle of dispatches bearing on trade between British and Russian businessmen. "You are filled with the idea of the Bolshevik horror, and do not want to shake hands with them, and you see a Bolshevik in every bush. We have recovered from that stage by way of a little blood letting of one hundred million pounds." [50]

"I want peace with Russia," the Prime Minister continued, "If you do not want to shake hands with the Bolsheviks you had better let us do it and then you can shake hands with us." He added that he did not plan to recognize the Soviet Government, that the terror had ended, that the Bolsheviks would change color once trade was opened, and that the Russians were a barbaric people accustomed to autocracy and had found the autocracy they wanted. "Barbaric enemies fight only for loot," he said. "There is no loot in Poland." He was willing to wager that Lenin and Trotsky were not military adventurers; if the Poles had any sense, they would make peace rather than let the French prod them into an attack on the Russians. (On April 25, 1920, Poland invaded the Ukraine in an ultimately abortive effort to wrest the territory from Russia.) [51]

Davis quite agreed that military intervention against the Soviets was out of the question. He had already said that he would make terms with the Russians were he in the Poles' place, and he was to tell the British Foreign Secretary a few months later that inclusion of Russian Poland in a united Russia was inevitable and that American aid to Poland would be pointless. As tactfully as he could, he took exception to a call from Lansing, by then in retirement, for an Allied offensive against Petrograd in July. No British government, he pointed out, would dare engage in further military adventure; besides, it was "practically certain that . . . the Soviet must fall from its own inherent weakness." [52]

Davis was gratified, accordingly, by the State Department's decision in June 1920 to permit individual American businessmen to trade with the Russians but to withhold diplomatic recognition of the Soviet government. This, he believed, would avoid the "ill-disguised recognition" implicit in Lord George's formal trade negotiations; more important, it would "take out of the mouths of the Soviet the excuse that the economic condition of Russia is due to the trade restrictions imposed by the Entente." [53]

« VI »

Neither the Irish nor the Russian question had compromised Davis' personal relations with his hosts; on the contrary, his transparent disapproval of his countrymen's sympathy for Ireland strengthened them. On the Near and Middle Eastern questions, however, he found himself caught between approval of the larger aspects of British policy and gradual realization that the government sought nothing less than a monopoly of oil.

Tension first developed over Lloyd George's decision in the summer of 1919 to withdraw the British army of occupation in Armenia. Late

in the Peace Conference he had persuaded Wilson to urge the Senate
to accept a mandate over that hapless land. This, Lloyd George said,
would protect the Armenians from annihilation by the neighboring
Kurds and Georgians. It would also lighten Britain's financial burden,
reduce tension between France and England, and engage America in
permanent peacekeeping. Above all, it would ease Britain's assumption of mandates in Persia and Mesopotamia, both of which were rich
in oil and integral to the lifeline to India.[54]

The British decision to abandon Armenia put Washington in a
cruel dilemma. Wilson dared not ask the Senate, which was then gird-
ing for the fight over the Treaty of Versailles, to ratify a mandate in the
Near East. Neither could he condone by inaction the massacre of the
Armenians, a tragedy sure to follow Britain's withdrawal. So he did
the only sensible thing: he had Lansing instruct Davis to urge postponement. There followed a protracted exchange between Davis and
Lord Curzon, the Foreign Secretary.[55]

George Nathaniel Curzon, first Earl Curzon of Kedleston, fifth
Baron Scarsdale, a brilliant but notoriously difficult man, had been
Viceroy of India and, since 1916, leader of the House of Lords. He
came from the impoverished aristocracy and was driven to rescue the
family name from mediocrity. Tall, imperious, with a broad bland
face and scanty hair, Curzon was cold or charming, reserved or exuberant, as mood or situation dictated. Most often, he wore his sense of superiority like an impermeable cloak. "I have married two women of
the middle classes," he said of his two rich American wives. He believed, profoundly, that the British Empire was "under Providence,
the greatest instrument for good that the world has ever seen," and
there ran through his speeches, as Harold Nicolson noted, "a recurrent
contrast between those who regarded the Empire 'as an irksome burden' and those for whom it was 'the most majestic of responsibilities.' "
Rigid and combative in most of his official dealings, he could be su-
percilious even with Davis. "You Americans," he loftily remarked during one of their discussions of mandates, "are inexperienced in such
matters." [56]

Davis sensed that Britain's dread of pan-Islamism would compel
Whitehall to hang on in Armenia, and he gave Curzon no encouragement that the United States would accept a mandate. Sentiment
against "trans-Atlantic adventure," he told him, was one of the two
cardinal tenets of American foreign policy. Why then, asked Curzon,
did not the United States openly request the British to stay on, given

America's professed concern for the Armenians? Davis made no reply. Neither did he respond when the Foreign Secretary said that Lloyd George felt that if the natives wanted to cut one another's throats it was deplorable but unpreventable.[57]

Curzon finally implied that Britain would accede to a direct request from President Wilson to remain in Armenia temporarily if the United States would underwrite part of the costs and accept a mandate eventually. Davis forwarded this proposition to Washington with a warning: anything less than complete refusal should be worded so as to avoid charges of bad faith were the mandate later declined. Lansing's reply closed the matter. For the President to ask Congress to support the British in Armenia would be to add fuel to the flames already raging over the Treaty; the Ambassador should so inform the British. He should also remind them that world opinion would be outraged if massacres followed withdrawal of their 22,000 troops. Reluctantly, the Foreign office postponed withdrawal.[58]

By then Davis was immersed in the politics of oil. Three times at Paris the Americans had urged the British to admit a Persian delegation to the Peace Conference, and three times the British had refused. Forced thus to deal directly with the Foreign Office, the Persians granted Britain virtual hegemony over their country in the Anglo-Persian Agreement of 1919. When the agreement was published in August 1919, Curzon apologized to Davis for failing to notify him in advance, but he assured him that he had earlier told Colonel House of the negotiations. Davis promised to transmit to Washington Curzon's request that the American Minister at Teheran, who was openly endorsing French criticisms of the agreement, be instructed to maintain a friendly and benevolent attitude toward the British.[59]

Lansing replied that the British had not been frank, that he and the President regarded the agreement unfavorably, and that they were not disposed to have the American Minister assist the British. A few days later Colonel House told Davis that Lord Curzon never had confided in him. When Lord Reading subsequently remarked that Curzon had "a streak of the cad in him," Davis silently acquiesced.[60]

Neither Curzon's lack of candor nor the revelation of the influence of the oil question on government policy destroyed the Ambassador's conviction that the Anglo-Persian Agreement was a strategic imperative for the British. By the summer of 1919, if not before, Davis had become a staunch defender of the British Empire's stabilizing role in world politics—one who shared Lloyd George's hope that the American people would "come to feel that . . . [Britain] was not a land-grabbing institution but was engaged in the discharge of duties forced upon it." (The Prime Minister did not, of course, tell Davis of Curzon's memorandum of August 9 to the Cabinet, a key passage of which read: "Lastly, we possess in the south-western corner of Persia great assets in the shape of the oil fields, which are worked for the British Navy, and which give us a commanding interest in that part of the world.") [61]

Davis assured Lansing that he too disapproved of the way the agreement had been negotiated. "But that aside, am I right or wrong in thinking that Persia needs outside help . . . pretty badly; that we are not ready to . . . [give it] and that Great Britain is the only nation that is able and willing to do so." He conceded that he would be more free from doubt if the Anglo-Persian Oil Company had not been granted exclusive right to lay pipelines within the kingdom; nevertheless, the United States had no basis for action "if we profess faith in the power of the League of Nations to redress any future abuses." [62]

Thereafter Davis repeatedly asked Lansing to spell out the American position on the agreement. "I am rapidly coming to the conclusion," he grumbled, "that a diplomat's duties are confined to wondering about matters as to which he is ignorant and worrying about questions as to which he is powerless." Meanwhile, without informing Davis, Lansing directed the American Minister in Teheran to disassociate the United States from the agreement. He then cabled London that American approval was conditional "until and unless it is clear that the Government and the people of Persia are united in . . . support of this undertaking." Still unwilling to believe the worst of the British, Davis blamed the State Department's attitude on unreliable information out of Teheran. "How," he testily wrote in his diary, ". . . has that approval been evidenced . . . by the people of Persia except by the action of their lawfully constituted authorities?" When Curzon called the American note grudging and ungenerous, Davis was so much in agreement that he did not argue the point at length.[63]

On April 20, 1920, Davis went to Parliament to hear Lloyd George defend the Treaty of San Remo: Syria to France, Mesopotamia and Palestine to Great Britain, the oil divided between them. Concluding that Britain intended to acquire all the oil fields possible, the Ambassador for the first time urged the State Department to pursue a hard line. His diary reveals his disgust:

No part of the peace making has worn an air of more undisguised self-
seeking than this Turkish treaty and after possessing themselves of all
the assets of the deceased which they think have any realizable value,
[the powers] . . . turn to America and ask her to accept the most difficult, thankless and impossible task of all [the Armenian mandate]. It
is bald to the point of indecency.[64]

Yet even as Davis scorned Britain's ulterior purposes, he continued
to defend her stabilizing role. He privately maintained that the
United States should give Britain moral support in the Middle East
lest chaos ensue, though he hoped that the British would open the Mesopotamian oil fields to American companies. In mid-May he and L. I.
Thomas, the Standard Oil Company official, forcefully presented the
American case to Sir John Cadman, the head of the British petroleum
office. "I told him," Davis reported, "that American opinion would be
offended by . . . monopolistic concessions; that all that America
wanted was the open door and fair treatment; that competition between American and British commercial interests was inevitable and
helpful but if it went to the point of a trade war . . . it would be an
unmitigated calamity." Sir John professed to agree, though he refrained from endorsing the open door categorically.[65]

Lloyd George and Curzon remained adamant. The Prime Minister
remarked at a private dinner for Davis in the House of Commons that
the United States was producing 70 per cent of the world's oil, Britain
only 4 per cent; charges of conspiracy to monopolize were therefore absurd. In reply, Davis challenged the figures. Then, just before he returned home on leave in August, he received from Curzon a long, tart
note which he deemed too important to acknowledge himself. The
Foreign Secretary pointed out that the United States reserved control
of American resources for American interests, and also excluded British interests from countries "amenable" to American control; the Mesopotamian mandate would increase the British total to 4.5 per cent—
hardly "justification for supposing that Great Britain . . . can
seriously threaten American supremacy." He added icily that the
terms of mandates could be discussed properly only by members of the
League of Nations.[66]

In Washington, Secretary of State Bainbridge Colby, Lansing's successor, and Davis worked on a draft of a reply to Curzon's note. Back
in London that November, Davis was eating dinner when a messenger
handed him the final version of the note. It was signed by Colby and

was addressed directly to the Foreign Secretary, instead of to the Ambassador, as diplomatic form required. An accompanying dispatch said that the text would be released to the press two days later. A forceful restatement of the American position, the note charged that the British-controlled Turkish Petroleum Company had not been granted prewar concessions by the Mesopotamians as Curzon contended; it took particular exception to a stipulation in the San Remo Agreement that any private company in the Mesopotamian fields should be under permanent British control.[67]

Davis approved the note's tenor and content, but lamented the plan to publish without Britain's consent; he was also furious over being bypassed. He cabled a vigorous recommendation against publication (his advice was followed), then warned Colby by letter that direct communications to the Foreign Secretary would eliminate the Embassy as a channel of communication with Whitehall.[68]

Colby's reply confirmed Davis' suspicion that President Wilson had been behind the snub. He said that he felt "no grief," but he was in fact deeply embittered. "As for Wilson," he wrote in his diary, ". . . I am quite sure that I do not [enjoy] and never have enjoyed his confidence, notwithstanding the fact that I am not ashamed of the service which I have rendered to his administration." He added:

> Such admiration as I have for him as a leader is due solely to his boldness, his devotion—which I take to be real—to democracy, and his genuine hatred of Privilege. For the man himself I confess that his patent pettiness of soul fills me with the same disgust which has infected all those who have been near him, save the sycophants and time servers, and is responsible for the cold hatred which denies him sympathy even in his illness.

Yet Davis retained his sense of proportion. With characteristic fairmindedness, he privately termed the award of the Nobel Peace Prize to Wilson two weeks later "a deserved tribute." [69]

« VII »

The Mesopotamian incident strengthened Davis' resolve to resign. While on leave, he had completed arrangements to join a prominent New York law firm; after ten years of public service, he was anxious to build up his shrinking capital. On December 23, 1920, he sent in his resignation. Wilson reacted curtly: It would be injurious to the public interest for such an able representative to leave such an important post; Davis should remain until the change of administration on March 4. The Ambassador's new partners also urged him to stay on, and he reluctantly agreed not to sail until after Warren G. Harding took office. "Nothing but a squad of policemen at the gangplank will prevent my embarkation," he wrote Lansing on booking passage for March 9, 1921.[70]

For all his pique, the Ambassador never lost sight of what he conceived to be his larger mission—the advancement of Anglo-American harmony. At dinner after dinner, and in speech after speech, during these final months he strove to prevent further deterioration of relations. On Armistice Day he touched that deep sentimental strain which is such an unmarked feature of the English character by laying on the cenotaph of the "Unknown Warrior" in Westminster Abbey a wreath bearing the legend: "America will not forget." He drew enormous applause with a moving peroration in a speech on the unguarded boundary between Canada and the United States. He suggested (to no avail) that the President reply to a personal letter from Lloyd George that had lain unacknowledged for more than five months. He persuaded two American Mormons not to sue several British newspapers for libel. (The Apostle Paul did not exactly have an easy time, he explained.) He advised Winston Churchill, who bustled into the chancery one day with a book on the war "in his head," that serial publication by William Randolph Hearst would enable him to present the British point of view to a "presumably hostile clientele." (He also urged him to demand guarantees against garbling.) In a panegyric on the English origins of the American Constitution, he even quoted Alexander Hamilton's assertion that "the British Government is the best in the world," adding his own testament that Congress was as much the "spiritual off-spring" of the ancient Saxon moots as was Simon de Montfort's Parliament of 1265.[71]

Meanwhile, Davis had yet another series of memorable conversations with Lloyd George, this time at Trent Park, the country house of Sir Philip Sassoon. For two days, relieved only by the Prime Minister's naps and the evening recitals of a Welsh soprano, Lloyd George talked —at table, in the library, on the fairways. "I like Wilson," he said at the outset. Ignoring Mrs. Davis' retort that he need not apologize, he then spoke with feeling of the President's hatred of the privileged classes; no matter what Wilson did, he insisted, they would never forgive him.[72]

The Prime Minister hoped that the incoming Secretary of State

would visit England before the inauguration, and he lamented that
there was no one to do business with during the interregnum. ("A
clear intimation of my status," Davis ruefully noted.) Lloyd George
seemed to understand, however, that Harding's campaign statements
were not to be taken literally; even a man so devoted to principle as
Gladstone, he reflected, had been compelled to compromise. All he
really resented, he explained, was the call for an independent Ireland
by the Democratic candidate, James M. Cox. As for the League of Nations, Britain was amenable to modifications in the Covenant, but
doubted that the French would consent. (Davis surmised that Lloyd
George was willing to make almost any sacrifice to bring the United
States into the European orbit.) [73]

The Prime Minister further asserted that the French had had "one
continuous ambition from the day of Charlemagne, namely, to be the
military masters of Continental Europe, and . . . they were still—
under the leadership of Foch—nursing this ambition." When Davis
interjected that the French were "crazy" to hold to that aim, Lloyd
George implied that the British would continue their historic opposition to domination of the Continent by a single power. He also clung
stubbornly to the notion that trade would restore order in Russia; indeed, Davis deduced that he rather welcomed the collapse of General
Wrangel's campaign in south Russia as "a severe loss of face for the
French." [74]

Davis tried unsuccessfully to draw the Prime Minister into a discussion of the Mesopotamian oil question, then remarked that the system
of Imperial Preference "would put a ringed fence" around much of the
earth's surface and that the world "would resent any effort to monopolize all the resources of the Empire." Lloyd George replied that he too
regarded the policy as unwise, but that it flowed logically from the
protectionist policy which so many foolish people were advocating.[75]

On the last day of the meeting, after breakfast, the two men tarried
to discuss the United States' competitive naval program. Lloyd George
emphasized that the Royal Navy must be predominant in European
waters and that the British people would "spend their last shirt" to
keep it so. Davis suggested that an understanding might be reached
through informal conversations, but cautioned that Harding's campaign had been conducted on strongly nationalistic lines and that it
was easy to excite the American people's "vanity." [76]

As always, Davis had been exhilarated by the Prime Minister's life
force. All who had known him, Davis reflected in 1947, could testify

amply to his faults. Nevertheless, he had been a "great" man, possibly even surpassing Churchill as a wartime leader. He had also been a magnificent orator:

> His speeches rarely moved on the same tenor throughout. They weren't as finished, for instance, as Churchill's speeches, but there were in them passages of great eloquence.[77]

Two months before the Davises sailed, they participated in a ceremony of minor moment and unique poignance—the presentation to the government of Chequers Court, the historic country house of the Lees of Fareham. An Elizabethan building with six peaked gables and eight mullioned windows along each front, it stands on terraced gardens leading down to a wide and stately lawn. It hugs the earth, and neither porches nor porticos break the transition from indoors to out-of-doors; ivy climbs its mellow stones to the second story. Behind the house, on Beacon Hill, the first bonfire was lit to announce the approach of the Spanish Armada. The Celtic King Caractacus is said to have been born on the site, and gold Roman coins have been plowed up in the surrounding fields. The house once belonged to the daughter of Oliver Cromwell, and Cromwell's death mask hangs in the hall beside the letter he wrote announcing the defeat of King Charles' troops at Marston Moor: "The Lord made them stubble as to our swords." Everything in this veritable museum, from Elizabeth's ring and a mother-of-pearl locket with ER in diamonds on the cover and miniatures of Elizabeth and Anne Boleyn inside, to "The Arithmetician" by Rembrandt and a self-portrait of Sir Joshua Reynolds, was part of the transfer.[78]

The ceremony began with a long, funereal dinner, attended by Lloyd George, the Readings, and several other notable personages. Afterwards Lord Lee, who was childless, rose to explain that he and Lady Lee (an American) were giving the property to the government because they believed Britain would be better served if its leaders had a place for periodic rest and recreation; they especially felt that Chequers would "steady" any future Labour or radical ministry by reminding it of all that gone into England's memorable past.[79]

Lloyd George, who was never comfortable among aristocrats and was rarely to use Chequers himself, responded with a uniquely personal statement. He had come into politics, he said, as an iconoclast, determined to tear down; such men, he insisted, were necessary, but it was also necessary to preserve and build up. He added that party life imposed a much greater strain than outsiders realized. The constant criticism made one feel like a hunted animal, peering first here and then there in anticipation of the next attack and feeling always that one's claws must be sharp and ready for use. This, he noted, was not unique to England. Just the other day he had read in an American newspaper on attack upon President Wilson so scurrilous that he almost threw the paper into the fire.[80]

On that somber note the party adjourned to the Hawtry room to witness the signing of the deed, after which Lord and Lady Lee drove away, leaving all their personal belongings in the house—and leaving the butler, who was to stay behind, in tears. The guests felt, so Davis remarked, as though they had returned to the house of the deceased after the drive to the cemetery—an analogy made more exact by the fact that the Lees' tomb was then being prepared on Beacon Hill.[81]

"Altogether," Davis mused, "it was a depressing ceremony. No one present, I think, could appreciate the spirit which moved them to give up so handsome a home on which so much care as well as money had been spent and which represented such a large part of their individual fortune, and the form in which it was done . . . [made] the hair-shirt as rough as possible. . . . Nonetheless the gift is a very splendid and generous one and the idea behind it entirely noble." [82]

« VIII »

One last diplomatic crisis intruded. President Wilson had proposed to the Council of Four at Paris in April 1919 that the island of Yap, a former German possession and the point of convergence of all major cables in the Pacific, be internationalized. Lloyd George objected, the British having already promised the Japanese a mandate over Yap. For various reasons neither Wilson's opposition to the Japanese mandate nor his proposal to internationalize the cables appeared in the official record. Eighteen months later the British brusquely rejected an American request to reopen the matter. Then, on February 11, 1921, Secretary of State Colby sent Davis a crudely phrased protest for transmission to Curzon.[83]

The Foreign Office's November note, said Colby, showed that the British were willing to destroy all possibility of future cooperation by "substituting sinister diplomacy for square dealing or even enlightened selfishness"; serious protest would follow unless the British agreed to negotiate within a few days. Fearful that the President would fuel the crisis with a special message to Congress, Davis quickly arranged to see Curzon and Auckland Geddes, who was home from Washington on leave.[84]

Geddes conceded that the Foreign Office's own note had been wretchedly drawn, and Curzon advised Davis to inform Washington that Britain would not feel bound to support either the Japanese or American claim at a future conference. Then, unbending more than he had ever done before, the Foreign Secretary admitted that the United States had been badly used. Davis replied that, although the Americans were not blameless, the President attached such importance to the Yap matter that he might act precipitately. He closed on an ominous note: the Harding administration "would come fresh on the bit." [85]

The Ambassador's success in drawing a conciliatory statement from the British seems to have eased the tension in Washington. Nevertheless, Colby again bypassed him. On February 26, without prior warning, Davis read in the London papers the text of an American protest to the League of Nations. Relieved by its restrained and dignified tenor, he said simply, "I entirely approve." Two days later he used his valedictory to the Pilgrims' Society to make a felicitous allusion to the dispute. The United States and the British Empire, he said, were like two great ships in the same waters. "Neither can hope to maneuver without taking account of the other's whereabouts. . . . But God pity the steersman of either who brings them into collision." [86]

By then Davis was receiving too many tributes to brood over the State Department's discourtesies. Before he left for home, virtually every newspaper in England praised him for his dignity and sincerity, for the eloquence of his formal addresses and the charm of his after-dinner talks, for the sensitivity that had softened conflict and kept the "mutual interests of the two great democracies in the foreground"—for all the qualities that made almost everyone who knew him and his work agree that the United States had never had a more beloved representative at the Court of St. James's.[87]

Four days before they sailed on the *Olympic,* the Ambassador and his wife took lunch with the King and Queen at Buckingham Palace. They talked discursively at table, King George sipping a whiskey and soda and commenting fondly on the wooden desk chair he had used for twenty-two years and the broken settee Queen Mary was threatening to remove for repairs. He also remarked, with some asperity, that

early in the war Lloyd George had forced him to pledge publicly to
discontinue serving alcohol until victory, and that he had kept the
pledge religiously until his physician ordered him to resume a stimu-
lant. Prohibition, he said with emphasis, would never come to Britain.[88]

After the meal, the Ambassador and the King remained at the table.
His Majesty lit a fresh cigarette and reviewed Anglo-American relations. It had always been his own and his father's dearest wish, he
said, that the two countries should work closely together. He opposed
a formal alliance because the rest of the world might combine against
them, but saw no reason why the United States and Great Britain
should come into conflict. He added that his country had taken on too
great a burden in accepting mandates in Palestine, Mesopotamia, and
Egypt.[89]

King George then asked Davis' pardon for speaking to a point on
which British opinion was keenly sensitive—supremacy at sea. The
ill-feeling with Germany had begun, he noted, when the Kaiser started
to build a large navy and displayed even greater vanity over it than
over his army; similar competition between the United States and
Great Britain would induce similar feelings. Davis replied that, although a naval race would ruin both countries, the United States felt
that its need to defend the Panama Canal and outlying possessions
mandated supremacy in her own waters.

The discussion turned to the Far East, Davis suggesting that Japan
was arming not for aggression against either the United States or
Great Britain, but because of her determination to be supreme in
Asia. Clearly, she would "resent any challenge or interference with her
ambitious plans"; hence the desirability of the proposed naval conference among the three nations. The King volunteered that the Anglo-
Japanese Treaty of 1902 had never been intended to operate against
the United States. The Ambassador acknowledged that informed
Americans understood this, and that the Foreign Office had assured
him that it would be made clear if the Treaty were renewed. Nevertheless, the Treaty's existence was an irritant to anti-British elements
in the United States, especially, he added with a smile, to the Irish
"you send over to us." [90]

Early Wednesday morning, March 9, 1921, Davis and his wife left
the Embassy for the last time. A few nights earlier, Sir James Barrie,
author of *Peter Pan,* had told him, in an odd, diffident way, that he
had "done magnificently." Now Lady Charnwood, who had come to

see them off, whispered that he would have made a better inaugural address than Harding. The Davises then drove to Victoria Station, where Curzon, the diplomatic corps, Lord and Lady Bryce, Lords Midleton, Sandhurst, and Reading, and many other friends gave three hearty cheers as their train pulled away.[91]

As the *Olympic* slipped out of her berth at Southampton, a British destroyer with the Stars and Stripes at its peak and an Admiral in command eased ahead of her bow. Two squadrons of destroyers, all flying the United States flag, fell in, port and starboard. They escorted the ship to mid-channel, then turned about and passed in review, their decks lined with cheering sailors. No American Ambassador had ever before been thus honored. From the bridge of the *Olympic* the Ambassador radioed a final message: "Mr. Davis . . . is glad to have as his last sight of England the representatives of the valiant British Navy which has done so much to make the seas secure for the commerce of the world." [92]

CHAPTER 11

Reluctant Dark Horse: A Note on the Campaign of 1920

I was not willing to forfeit my own self-respect by running away from what looked like a difficult adventure, but on the other hand did not feel under any obligation to put myself forward.

JOHN W. DAVIS

« I »

Months before Woodrow Wilson's stroke in the fall of 1919 foreclosed his nomination for a third term, influential West Virginians were boosting Davis for the office many had long believed he would some day hold. They were led by former Senator Clarence A. Watson, mine owner, entrepreneur, and ultra-conservative, but their ranks included most of the state's secondary Democratic leadership and much of the press. Doc Johnston, the genial plotter of Davis' nominations to the legislature in 1898 and to Congress in 1910, was threatening again "to take the bull by the horns." And many others were doing the same. Even in Maryland, Pennsylvania, Virginia, and Kentucky, prominent Democrats were reported to be partial to Davis. The time had come, Governor John J. Cornwell of West Virginia wrote the Ambassador in July, to give them a sign of encouragement.[1]

Davis framed a reply to Cornwell, then let it lie on his desk while he poured out his feelings in his diary:

> I dread the burdens of the office; have never nursed any ambition for it; would certainly not refuse a nomination . . . if it came my way; cannot become an active candidate at this time . . . ; to resign now in order to run for the nomination would defeat its own ends; . . . any boom started now would not outlive the winter frost . . . but if the fates so will it, let it be.

He added that his chances were bound up in the Irish question. A satisfactory Home Rule bill that autumn might bring his name to the fore; an unsatisfactory measure, or none at all, would damn him along with the British.[2]

Late in July Davis recast his letter to Cornwell. "Only a self-intoxicated egoist," he wrote, "can think of . . . the Presidency . . . without shivering at the burdens and responsibilities it entails. I claim not to be in that class." He added that he did not want the British to think that he was serving his personal interests when pressing a diplomatic point. He subsequently shocked Lord Reading, who had remarked that the presidency was the greatest office in the world, by saying that he had "no stomach" for it. He also told Colonel House that there were no "presidential bees" in his bonnet. Finally, he warned his West Virginia friends that he was not going to be used "as a stalking horse or a club to beat out other men's brains." [3]

Davis' supporters were emboldened, nevertheless, by predictions that William Gibbs McAdoo, the President's progressive, pro-labor son-in-law, and Attorney General A. Mitchell Palmer, a Pennsylvania Quaker turned witch-hunter and strikebreaker, would deadlock the Democratic convention. "You can have your native state for anything," one of the West Virginians wrote, "for we know you and you know us." They made short shrift of Governor Cornwell's effort to become West Virginia's favorite son himself. Davis viewed the Governor's ambition with indulgent acquiescence, saying that it would be wrong for Cornwell to step aside. As for his own nomination, it would have to come, if at all, "under the Selective Service Act." [4]

Cornwell bowed out for lack of support on March 9, 1920, and the State Democratic Committee endorsed Davis the following day. "Give us a warm shower," Watson cabled the Ambassador. Davis' response was tepid at best:

> A nomination for that office when it represents the deliberate wish of one's party is a call to duty which no man can or should refuse. Let me say, however, in all sincerity, that I do not seek the nomination and cherish no higher ambition than to perform the duties of my present position.[5]

By then Lansing, though still Secretary of State, had already urged
Davis to return home and become an active candidate. The Ambassador, he pointed out, was identified with the Wilson administration to
just the right degree; to be its actual heir would be to suffer a heavy
handicap. Davis replied that, McAdoo aside, Palmer had too much
going for him. "No little grist has been brought to his mill . . . by his
victory over the beef trust, which stamps him as an enemy of predatory
wealth; his fight with the Miners, which squares the other side of the
circle—although I thought the injunction a mistake; and lastly the
hordes of Bolshevik fleeing before his conquering sword. . . . Woman-
suffrage, prohibition, tariff-reform, child-labor—on my word he has
been up with the field on all of them. His quiver is pretty well filled.
Palmer—well, why not?" Davis added that the Irish question destroyed his own chances. The Democratic party could not take a candidate "fresh from the court of the hated Sassenach . . . [and he] could
not and would not buy the Presidency at the price of giving encouragement to the baseless and impossible dream of an independent Irish
Republic." [6]

Davis' irony pricked Lansing's sensibilities. The Secretary of State
had himself contributed to the pressures on Palmer that had led, in
January 1920, to the most wanton violation of the Bill of Rights to
that time—the dragnet arrest of thousands of aliens, Communists, Socialists, radicals, liberals, conservatives, naturalized citizens, and native-born Americans by Justice Department agents led by J. Edgar
Hoover, then head of the department's alien radical division. Cour-
teously but firmly, Lansing replied at the end of March that Palmer
was a strong, capable Attorney General and might make a good conservative President. He conceded, however, that his labor policies, "the
best evidence of his fearlessness," would give the politicians pause.[7]

Lansing then assessed the entire field. McAdoo was in trouble because many people suspected that he harbored "a Machiavellian love
of power." Neither Governor James M. Cox of Ohio, a hazy figure, nor
Governor Edward I. Edwards of New Jersey, an unreconstructed wet,
had much chance, and those of the others were even slimmer. "Nobody knows whether [Herbert Hoover] . . . is a Democrat or Republican, and he himself seems in doubt." Influential men in both parties
were speaking sarcastically of his independence of party and his declaration that he was not a candidate. The President? His nomination
was impossible, the notion of his candidacy absurd. There was only
one other possibility—Vice President Thomas R. Marshall. Marshall
wanted the nomination and had issued a conservative statement of

"sound" but politically impractical principles. Consequently, the State Committee's action might be far more important than Davis realized.[8]

Lansing's observations increased the Ambassador's inner stress. His feeling that no Democrat could win in 1920 deprived him of what "little exhilaration" the prospect of running might have given him; and his realization that he could not support Wilson's uncompromising plank on the League of Nations depressed him further. In no event would he resign before the Convention in July. "I become a mere ex-Ambassador," he explained to his sister Emma, "and a live dog is better than a dead lion; if I am not nominated I shall be charged forever with . . . having dropped the bone I am carrying to snatch at the shadow in the stream." [9]

Yet circumstances had made Davis a candidate, and he knew it. He could refuse to file a formal announcement in West Virginia, but he could hardly stop State Chairman Clem L. Shaver of Fairmont from organizing a Davis-for-President Club underwritten by a $25,000 contribution from Watson. Resigning himself to his fate, he authorized Shaver to decide whether to put his name forward at the convention in San Francisco. "I promise to be entirely content with your decision as long as you don't run me on a wet platform or in favor of government ownership." [10]

Through most of the spring the Ambassador pursued his duties in England, serene in the conviction that he was in no actual danger of winning the nomination. But suddenly, on May 23, an unprecedented three-column editorial in *The New York Times* transformed him into a serious contender. "Mr. Davis," declared the *Times,* after reviewing the highlights of his congressional career, "contended for justice to all parties, for right and reason. He is not a man of nostrums. His personal qualities have won the friendship, confidence, and admiration of everyone he touched. . . . JOHN W. DAVIS is a great man, a great American, a great Democrat." [11]

The editorial gave the Ambassador a cold chill. What sort of a candidate would he make, he asked Lansing, when he disapproved—

(1) Irish Independence . . . , (2) An Armenian Mandate, (3) A death struggle for the unconditional ratification of the treaty, (4) the emasculation of the prohibition amendment, (5) Government ownership, (6) Federal interference with the right of suffrage—a fait accompli, it is true, (7) et id omne genus.[12]

Governor Cornwell, who was to prove a loyal supporter, meanwhile urged Davis on. He reported that he was objectionable to neither the

Administration nor the anti-Administration forces, and he predicted that the McAdoo people would be "very glad" to fall in behind Davis if they failed to nominate their own man. By late May, the Ambassador realized that all he could really do was shape the character of his candidacy. Reluctantly, he asked Cornwell to place his name in nomination, adding that it might be necessary to frame his own platform following the nomination—but not in a way that would imply that official party platforms "are mere scraps of paper." He feared most, however, that his stature would be enhanced just enough to make him the vice presidential nominee. "No man ought to run for an office which he could not afford to hold if elected." [13]

The New York Times' endorsement had set off a wave of favorable comment all over the United States. Even the Letters-to-the-Editor columns burgeoned with tributes. As one of Davis' former colleagues in Congress typically wrote, the Ambassador was "intensely human, with a superb intellect to give that humanity discipline and direction." But the most heart-warming statements came out of Clarksburg. "Not one Republican had anything else to say of Mr. Davis except praise for his manliness, personality and mental strength," reported a metropolitan newspaperman after spending a day in the town. Even the editor of the West Virginia Labor News spoke highly of him.[14]

Was it all too late? Mark Sullivan, the New York Evening Post's seasoned correspondent, thought not. Although the strongest partisans of McAdoo, Palmer, and Cox had adopted the defeatist slogan, "Let us nominate a clean candidate on a clean platform and take a clean licking," this did not have to be. Davis, said Sullivan, had all the President's good qualities and none of his bad ones; his nomination would restore the party's morale and give it an even chance in November. The New York World, the Administration's unofficial organ, was less enthusiastic: "In spite of a certain niceness in dress, [Davis] . . . has had enough of the rough-and-tumble of politics to keep him out of the exquisite class." [15]

Yet there were also some ominous rumblings. Bernard Baruch privately deplored Davis' lack of commitment to men or issues. The Times itself conceded that most of his actual endorsements came from conservatives. And Villard of The Nation questioned his broader qualifications: "John W. Davis would bring a new and interesting personality into public life, marked ability, and a well-trained legal mind— just when we need least of all the legalistic mind so cold and clear-cut." More important, the big-city delegations were already insisting that the party platform express "sympathy" for Irish aspirations for self-determination. Still, McAdoo had failed to win the President's endorsement and was soon to announce his formal withdrawal; the party's powerful Prohibition wing regarded Cox as "too wet"; and labor, which had already buried Palmer in the Michigan primary, was determined to blackball the Attorney General at the convention. Furthermore, three-fourths of the delegates were unpledged.[16]

In London, 3000 miles away, it all seemed unreal. The British press (excepting the Irish papers) had reported the endorsement of *The New York Times* with such enthusiasm that Davis professed not to recognize himself as the subject; the editorials read "like the obituaries of some deceased friends," he said. At times he was almost morose. "I dread the labors and exhaustion of the campaign. I dread still more the cares and burdens if one be elected." His wife's ambitions, he confessed, far outran his own.[17]

« II »

On Monday, June 21, 1920, Stephen Jackson of Clarksburg led an advance party of West Virginians into San Francisco, where they opened modest headquarters on the fourth floor of the Palace Hotel. They hoped, they said, to leave the convention with everyone's goodwill after winning the nomination through a "family council" rather than a "family quarrel." They added that they had been impressed on the trip out by the number of Republicans who said they preferred Davis to Harding, and that they were confident President Wilson was cordial toward the Ambassador's candidacy.[18]

The West Virginians were unaware that the President had already expressed himself on Davis. On May 30, seated in a wheelchair on the portico of the White House, with his left hand paralyzed and his eyes so prominent that his face had an owl-like cast, Wilson had talked at length with National Chairman Homer Cummings. Early in the conversation the President indicated that he had no preference among McAdoo, Palmer, and Cox, but that there might be serious objections to certain other men. The thought seemed to linger on his mind, and some minutes later he came back to it: "Now there is Davis. He is a fine man but he is a formalist. If you want to stand still, he is just the man to nominate." Revolution was everywhere, the President added; governments must respond to the needs and wishes of the people, and those who would drive down stakes were the nation's "most dangerous enemies." [19]

The first real surge of hope for Jackson's little band came on June

23, when the Wall Street betting odds put Davis, at three to one, ahead of all candidates except Cox. That same day, charges by women delegates that the Ambassador opposed woman suffrage induced a mild crisis aboard the train carrying the main body of the delegation. "Cable me your record," Watson wired the Ambassador in London. Davis now faced his first intellectual crisis. He conceded privately that to extend the franchise by federal action would "almost pull my heart out by the roots"; yet he regarded ratification of the Nineteenth Amendment as inevitable. He replied as smoothly as possible:

> No record other than refusal to support Federal Amendment when member Judiciary Committee Congress.
> While I have never advocated Federal control of suffrage, I recognize that question as passed. Believe Woman Suffrage inevitable and favor speedy disposition.[20]

At the chancery the next morning, Davis gave a long interview to a reporter from the *World,* then refused to authorize publication for fear he would seem to be promoting his candidacy. In San Francisco, at the same time, his supporters were lamenting the vagueness of his image. As one friendly Senator remarked, "Mr. Davis would make a great President, but people from Kull Knob and Coon Hollow don't understand the importance of the ambassadorship or the ability required to fill it." [21]

Friday, June 25, brought the main body of the West Virginia delegation into San Francisco with a new problem—Prohibition. Earlier, Watson had urged Davis to avoid the liquor question "like a rattlesnake"; now, shaken by soundings he had taken en route, he urged him to come out for the sale of wine and beer. The Ambassador's forthright reply destroyed his slim chances of becoming the second choice of Cox's urban delegations:

> Believe amendment adopted after due deliberation and should be honestly enforced. Duty of Congress to draw line in good faith and without evasion between intoxicating and non-intoxicating regardless of name.[22]

Nevertheless, the closely reasoned nominating speech of Governor Cornwell and the flowery seconding speeches of Izetta Jewel Brown of West Virginia and Lucy Dudley of Tennessee sparked considerable interest and enthusiasm. Numerous favorite-son delegates promised to switch to Davis at the opportune moment, and all through the week of June 28 Watson fired short, buoyant cablegrams to London: "You are gaining strength." "If McAdoo . . . collapses your chance best." "Situation improving." "This minute it is McAdoo or Davis." [23]

By Saturday night, Davis' supporters were brimming with confidence. Tennessee had transferred twenty-four votes from Cox to the Ambassador on the sixteenth ballot, and Palmer had stormed out of a conference when McAdoo's lieutenants suggested that he concede defeat. "If I am not nominated," the Attorney General exclaimed, "you can be assured that the nominee for President will be someone other than McAdoo or Cox." That meant Davis, or so it seemed.[24]

From six o'clock Saturday evening until eleven o'clock Monday morning much of the press and many delegates regarded Davis as the nominee; even Franklin D. Roosevelt, who cast a number of votes for him, thought that he would win. But in the end, the concerted hostility of the McAdoo supporters and the big-city bosses proved impossible to overcome. Davis reached a high of seventy-six votes on the fortieth ballot, and Cox was nominated on the forty-fourth. The Ohio Governor was selected, concludes the historian Bagby, because he was "non-administration, a politician's candidate who would listen, and a wet." [25]

Five themes dominated the letters that poured into the chancery afterwards: Davis would have been nominated if the delegates could have met him; he would have won if the deadlock had lasted one more hour; many Cox, Palmer, and McAdoo delegates, especially the lawyers, personally preferred him; the Irish and liquor questions had hurt him badly among big-city bosses, such as Charles Murphy of Tammany; and Davis had emerged as a serious contender for 1924. "Rest assured," wrote Clem Shaver, "you will have a h—l of a time living up to the standard we fixed out there." [26]

Arthur Koontz, the West Virginia gubernatorial candidate, was more urbane:

When you were accused of not being fair to labor we could combat it; when you were accused of not being regular in politics we could correct it; when you were accused of being against woman suffrage we could explain it . . . but when you were accused of attending the King's reception in knee breeches, and red at that, it was wholly impossible for novices, as we were, to convince the Maloneys, the Murphys, the Mooneys, the O'Briens, etc., that there was not an inkling of truth in it, or if it were true, that it did not necessarily mean you were an enemy of old Ireland.[27]

« III »

While the bulletins were coming in from San Francisco, the Ambassador was spending a leisurely afternoon with Lord Astor, saluting Canada as the keystone of the English-speaking arch in a Dominion Day speech, and casually discussing his chances with Herbert Asquith. "My dear Ambassador," said the former Prime Minister, "my best wish for you is that you do not get it." [28]

Not until Saturday, July 3, did Davis begin to feel the strain. On Monday, the decisive day at San Francisco, he received hundreds of guests at the Embassy's annual Fourth of July reception, then bet two boxes of cigars against himself with the toastmaster of a dinner at the Savoy. On learning the outcome, he immediately cabled Watson to stop any movement to nominate him for Vice President. Afterwards, he wrote the first of many letters to his supporters. He was "relieved but not surprised"; Cox was a man of "imagination and aggressiveness"; he thought "well" of Franklin D. Roosevelt, the vice presidential nominee. [29]

Seven weeks later Davis came home on leave. He explored overtures from several law firms in New York, checked in at the State Department in Washington, and then visited the Lansings in Maine. There he persuaded the former Secretary of State not to publish his acid sketches of the Big Four at Paris until Wilson left office, so as not to "furnish ammunition to the enemies of the Treaty." Early in September the Davises went down to Clarksburg for a reception in the county courthouse. A day or two later, the Ambassador made a painful pilgrimage to Media, walking alone through the fields with his memories of his first wife. Back in New York, he met with officers of the American Petroleum Institute and responded sympathetically to their plea for diplomatic support of their interests in the Middle East. Not until six weeks after his return was he received at the White House by Mrs. Wilson; the President, she explained, suffered a "nervous dread" of seeing people. "A curious inaccessibility for the leader of a great party and Chief Magistrate of a Nation," the Ambassador commented in his diary. [30]

Late in September, Davis sent James M. Cox a tightly packed statement of counter arguments to Republican charges that Article X of the League Covenant would commit the United States to war. He then made four campaign speeches on the League of Nations. In Clarksburg, 5000 people turned out to give him a prolonged ovation. But in

Lakewood, Ohio, a miniscule group received him. Irritated by the arrangements—no one met his train and the speech was scheduled for a tent on a corner lot—he attacked Harding with rare fervor. He also assailed Elihu Root for saying what he knew to be untrue—that the United States, under Article X of the League Covenant, could be required to go to war against its will. His anger vented, Davis' sense of humor broke through. Just before boarding the train he fired off a telegram to his old friend B. P. "Pat" Harrison of Mississippi, head of the National Speakers Committee:

> Meeting on outskirts of city near Indiana line. Adjourned from tent to village lodge-room because of inclement weather. Great enthusiasm enjoyed by all. Attendance two hundred.[31]

BOOK III

The Law and Politics 1921-1937

Return to the Law

I never looked forward to anything with so much eagerness as I do to my approaching return to the Bar. Bismarck, I think it was, who said that ten years are all any man should devote to public service. He was entirely right about it.

JOHN W. DAVIS, 1921

Within a month of his resignation as Ambassador in March 1921, Davis had moved into the offices of his new law firm in downtown Manhattan. Although he had to wait six months for admission to the New York Bar, he was free to practice in Virginia, West Virginia, and the federal courts. In mid-May he prepared to go to Richmond for his first case in almost three years. "How far, I wonder, has my hand lost its cunning?" he wrote Julia, with just a tinge of the old anxiety. "That is the great question which this journey is to solve. There was a day when your Dad was considered a fair, run-of-mine lawyer." [1]

« I »

Davis' choice of a firm had reflected his desire for congenial partners and a remunerative situation. Recognition at the bar, self-satisfaction in work well done, physical and financial comfort, leisure for travel abroad—that is what he wanted, and that is what his new connection gave him.

During Davis' twenty-eight months at the Court of St. James's, law firms seeking his services had increased their offers to the point that he was assured of making up in one year in private practice all that the ambassadorship had cost him. It was borne upon him, moreover, that guarantees were a mere form and that he could earn "a very large income immediately and a comfortable fortune in a few years." John Foster Dulles proffered a 10 per cent interest in Sullivan & Cromwell. Former Assistant Attorney General William Wallace, Jr., offered a one-third interest in Chadbourne, Babbitt & Wallace. And Paul D. Cravath sought out the Ambassador in London to renew and raise the offer he had first made in 1917. As Davis sifted these and a dozen other overtures while home on leave in the summer of 1920, he had only to decide whether he preferred New York to Washington, a large firm to a small one, corporate to general practice, and leadership of a firm to a subordinate, but senior, partnership.[2]

Davis made two crucial decisions at the outset: he would neither form a new firm nor go into practice in Washington. The labor and uncertainties of starting all over again were too great, the chances of success in Washington too slight:

> Many [Washington lawyers] were ex-occupants of political office, of whom a residuum is left at the end of each administration like sea-weed cast up on the beach by the receding tide. I firmly made up my mind that I would not be in that class. The great trouble about a Washington practice is that it rarely builds up a clientele that can be relied on to return from year to year. One job done and out they go.[3]

In the end, the Ambassador considered only two firms, both in New York: Stetson, Jennings & Russell, and Cravath & Leffingwell. The former's interest in him went back to a shipboard incident in November 1918. Asked to give a five-minute talk on the Conference on Prisoners of War at Berne, he had spoken with grace, modesty, and clarity. Afterwards Allen Wardwell of Stetson, Jennings & Russell, who was returning from a Red Cross mission to Russia, introduced himself, and the two men enjoyed a cordial relationship the rest of the voyage.[4]

In March 1920, Wardwell wrote the Ambassador that all his partners were anxious for Davis to join them in a leading capacity. Their firm, he explained, served as counsel to J P Morgan and Co. in financial transactions and was general counsel to the Guaranty Trust Company of New York. Among its most active clients were the Associated Press, the Erie Railroad, and the International Paper Company. The firm also handled many large estates, did considerable trial work, and touched almost everything except admiralty and patent law.[5]

Davis' interest in Stetson, Jennings & Russell was heightened by the enthusiasm of his close friend Frank Polk, a man of surpassing charm and an unfailing instinct for the wise and humane. Polk was already entertaining an offer, and he hoped that Davis would also be receptive. "It is a firm with a splendid name and a great reputation for conservatism," Polk wrote the Ambassador, "has a wonderful business, and not only has your friends the Morgan people but . . . many other big concerns. Stetson is a hopeless invalid . . . and Jennings and Russell are not up to much work. If they made you the head . . . that would be the most attractive position in New York." Polk's only concern was that he himself, who was being brought in to attract new clients, might prove "a gold brick." Accordingly, Davis arranged to see Wardwell in New York when he returned on leave in August 1920.[6]

Allen Wardwell was a broad-gauged man of deep human concerns. He had entered the office as a clerk upon graduation from the Harvard Law School in 1898, and had become a partner in 1909. He realized that the infirmities of the three senior partners made it imperative that a man of eminence be brought in to hold the firm's important clients as well as to draw new business; and, though slated for leadership of the firm himself, he had decided even before Frederic B. Jennings' sudden death in late May to offer Davis the top position.[7]

Two days after Davis' arrival in New York, Wardwell spelled out his terms: leadership of the firm, a $50,000-a-year guarantee, and 15 per cent of the net ($469,000 in the first seven months of 1920). With any new business at all, this meant that Davis could expect upwards of $150,000 a year. The pressures soon mounted. The general manager of the Associated Press told Davis that he could have the general counselship of the AP *if* he joined Stetson, Jennings & Russell. In mid-September Henry P. Davison, the driving, dynamic Morgan partner, had his yacht take the Davises to his Long Island house for a weekend of golf at the Piping Rock Country Club and talks with Thomas W. Lamont and other Morgan partners. On a three-hour drive through the rolling estate country, Davison urged Davis not to join Chadbourne, Babbitt & Wallace. Davison complimented Cravath & Leffingwell, but made it clear that he preferred Stetson, Jennings & Russell. Back in the city on Monday, Davis was offered the general counselship of the Standard Oil of New Jersey by the president and the chairman of the board. Unperturbed when he replied that he had resolved never to serve a single client, they intimated that they would retain him anyway if he went with Stetson, Jennings & Russell.[8]

Meanwhile, Davis saw Paul Cravath a second time. Cravath was the prototype of the new breed then transforming Wall Street law offices into so-called "law factories"; he eschewed litigation, hardly ever appeared in court, and was more a master of men than of law. A huge, dominant figure who stood six feet four and weighed 250 pounds, he was known about town for his "massive elegance," "glittering presence," and overbearing pomposity. He was ill-tempered and irascible, contemptuous of his inferiors, rude to his associates, and inconsiderate of his partners; to work for him was to be consumed by him. Yet he could be patient in the pursuit of his immediate ends; rarely did he fail to bend a conference to his imperious will. Above all else, he prized intelligence, knowledge, and industriousness. Every year he brought in a number of bright young men from Harvard, Yale, and Columbia, and from the best of them he selected partners after six or seven years; only once since 1906 had he gone outside the firm for a senior man. So greatly did he covet Davis' services, however, that he offered him 15 per cent and a minimum guarantee of $50,000 a year. He proposed to retain leadership of the firm and a 25 per cent interest for himself.[9]

Wardwell countered by increasing Davis' guarantee to $60,000 and agreeing to raise his share to 18 per cent and possibly more as soon as Russell retired. Davis probably would have accepted without the added inducement, for he liked Wardwell, wanted to be with Polk, and was attracted by the prospect of heading the firm. He was also drawn to the two other leading partners, George Gardiner and Lansing Reed, both of whom were warm and engaging men; from the beginning, indeed, Davis was captivated by the sparkling humor of Gardiner, a hunchback who had been Stetson's secretary before earning an LL.B. in night courses at New York University in 1900. On September 28, 1920, from the Homestead at Hot Springs, Virginia, where he had gone to mull over matters, Davis wrote Wardwell, accepting his offer.[10]

The House of Morgan was as delighted as the Ambassador's new partners were. Davison wrote that Davis should wait to commit himself on a house. "We must find the right place in our own island neighborhood." Thomas W. Lamont sent an effusive letter. And Morgan, whom the Ambassador had met and liked in London, made an Olympian gesture. "Please communicate to Davis my great satisfaction," he cabled Lamont; "I also consider the firm very much to be congratulated." [11]

Others were not so pleased. Davis' political friends feared that Stetson, Jennings & Russell's connection with Morgan would destroy his

chances of winning the presidential nomination in 1924. As one of
them observed, "the very nature of [the firm's] business and clientele,
must have forced a final choice as to a political career." Lansing was of
the same mind, although he passed over politics in his congratulatory
letter. The firm's high standing in the profession, he wrote, was the
best possible reason for joining it.[12]

« II »

The seventh-floor corner office in the old Mills Building at 15 Broad
Street, which Davis moved into on April 1, 1921, was the same one
Grover Cleveland had occupied between presidential terms in the late
1880's. A plain, square room from which the eaves of the Stock Exchange and several stories of the towering Postal Life Building were
visible, it was lined with bookcases and furnished with the large double desk used by Cleveland, a swivel chair, and two or three uphol-
stered chairs for clients. On the walls Davis hung some family pictures
and a few prints he had brought from England, and on the desk he
placed a small, framed engraving of Thomas Jefferson. The building
itself rose nine floors above Exchange Place and Broad Street. Faced
with sculptured red stone and finished inside with California redwood,
it had been the plushest large office structure in New York when
erected in 1881–82. A bank of modern, cable-type elevators added to
its distinction. Age and pollution had dimmed its luster, however, and
by Davis' time it was becoming dark, grimy, and close.[13]

Stetson, Jennings & Russell's predecessor firms dated to the 1850's.
The founder, Francis N. Bangs, was one of the more colorful and
gifted lawyers of his era. But it was the man Davis replaced, Francis L.
Stetson, who imbued the firm with most of its traditions and brought
in its most important clients. A graduate of Columbia, Stetson served
as an aide to Samuel J. Tilden in his fight against the Tweed Ring
and then spent three years as Assistant Corporation Counsel of the
City of New York before entering partnership with Bangs in 1880. In
1895 he accompanied J. P. Morgan to the White House during the financial crisis in which Morgan and his associates shored up the government's gold reserves by buying $65 million worth of bonds. Deeming
his services a patriotic duty, he declined to charge Morgan a fee despite the $6 million profit reaped by the financier and his syndicate.[14]

For many of the same reasons that later brought Davis to eminence,
Stetson became one of the most prominent corporation lawyers in the

nation in the 1890's. Like Davis, he was courteous, cordial and dispassionate; and, like Davis, he was transparently fair-minded. He had the same knack for weighing disputed views impersonally, the same facility for avoiding acrimony, the same aversion to imposing his will on others. He also had little more than a surface interest in the careers of his associates, and not much more in the destiny of his own firm. If he led, and in an inconclusive way he did, it was by example rather than by command. A superb legal craftsman, he built his early reputation on trial work and his later one on his services to the financial and corporate community. He pioneered in transforming the corporate mortgage from a simple real estate lien into a complex agreement running to as many as two hundred pages, and he eventually became the country's foremost specialist in corporate reorganizations.[15]

In 1898 Stetson formed the Federal Steel Company by merging the Illinois Steel and Minnesota Iron companies. (This company, said Davis in 1900, had been formed as a trust by lawyers "hiding . . . behind a legal quibble," and it had thrown thousands of men out of work in order to limit production.) In 1901, in the same room Davis occupied twenty years later, Stetson helped draw up the mortgage for the Carnegie Company, the main legal feature in the formation of the mammoth, overcapitalized United States Steel Corporation. (Its creation, Davis contended in 1917, was "abnormal, immoral, [and] the very negation of normal business growth.") [16]

Stetson also represented Morgan in the formation of the Northern Securities Company in 1901. He subsequently reorganized the United States Rubber Company, formed the International Harvester Company, and advised J P Morgan and Co. on mergers involving the Guaranty Trust Company of New York. In 1912 he served as Morgan's emissary to President-elect Woodrow Wilson in a fruitless effort to persuade Wilson to adopt Wall Street's proposal for a banking system fully controlled by bankers.[17]

Stetson became counsel to many of the corporations he had helped create, and several of his partners became counsel to others. Yet he never conceived of the firm as a true partnership. Like Davis, he was more law-minded than commercial- or organization-minded, and, like Davis, he preferred the informality of a small office. He was reluctant to assign his clients to other partners or associates, though he sometimes did so, and he shrank from the responsibility of heading a large firm.[18]

From 1896 until the outbreak of World War I, the number of part-

ners in Stetson, Jennings & Russell never rose above seven, and between 1911 and 1914 the firm's average annual income was only
$287,197. As Lansing P. Reed, who had been advised not to enter the
firm in 1908, reflected years later, "the firm was a firm only in name
. . . [and the] only reason that we remained counsel for J P Morgan
and Co. after Mr. Stetson's decline in health was that their admiration
for the character and ability of Mr. Gardiner was such that they could
not go to anyone else." Inevitably, the younger men, including Wardwell, who was related to Stetson by marriage, grew restive. They did
much of the real work without full remuneration; they saw prospective
business go to other offices; and they feared that important personal
clients would also go elsewhere after the senior partners retired or
died. Not until after Stetson had become senile and Jennings and Russell had gone into partial retirement was a true partnership formed.
This was in 1919, the year before Wardwell, acting as de facto head,
arranged to bring in Polk and Davis.[19]

« III »

Davis' concern that his hand might have "lost its cunning" vanished
the moment he began to speak in the United States Circuit Court of
Appeals in Richmond on May 13, 1921. As counsel for the Federal
Trade Commission in an appeal brought by a group of Norfolk ship
suppliers, he defended the Commission's ruling that the suppliers desist from giving gratuities to ships' officers. The custom, he declared in
an argument which the local press called "one of the most powerful
. . . yet presented to the tribunal," had both a bad moral effect on the
officers and a detrimental impact upon business competition; the Commission's ruling should be upheld.[20]
Meanwhile, Davis' work habits were surprising Wardwell, who had
assumed he would maintain short hours, delegate most of his duties,
and spend little time in court. Not only did the former Ambassador
hold old clients and attract new ones, he proved to be a hard-driving,
industrious advocate who ground out as much or more work as anyone else. Soon after entering the firm he had been driven into almost
frenzied examination of the New York statutes by his inability to answer a client's question. Yet he loved the forced study, and his correspondence during these first months was almost euphoric: "You have
no idea with what pleasure and enthusiasm I return to [the law]. . . .
I was never happier, either in my work or in my surroundings. . . .

The only thing which makes me distrust the permanence of my professional vigor is that the loss of a case no longer depresses me as hopelessly as in days gone by." [21]

Neither did Davis regret giving up, as he thought, his chances for the presidential nomination in 1924. He had no intention, he wrote an old West Virginia friend, of being weaned from his new practice by vague suggestions of future political honors:

> The only thing which will keep me from becoming a corporation lawyer will be the unwillingness of said corporations to contribute to the support of a member of the most deserving class of the community. I have already become a member of the board of directors of the United States Rubber Company and of the Atchison, Topeka & Santa Fe Railroad, and will shortly go on the board of the National Bank of Commerce, so you can see where I am headed. Do not, I beg you, disturb my repose. [22]

Despite the pressure, Davis insisted that "hour by hour and minute by minute," Wall Street lawyers worked no harder than other busy men. The difference was that commuting made the day artificially brief and forced them to pack into seven or eight hours the work of ten or twelve. Yet the compensations were considerable. Davis rented a pleasant, spacious house in Locust Valley, Long Island, from George Baker, Jr., the banker. On Sundays, following services in the local Episcopal church, where he became a vestryman, he played a round of bad, though companionable, golf at the Piping Rock Club. And on weekdays, relaxing over pinochle or backgammon, he went to and from Manhattan on J. P. Morgan's launch or in a special car rented from the Long Island Rail Road by a group of Wall Street lawyers and executives. In the city, when not tied up in court, he usually took lunch at the round table of the Broad Street Club. Almost every summer he and his wife visited England and the Continent for six weeks or more. [23]

Davis' devotion to the law, his love of comfort and elegance, and Nell's delight in their new social circle would have made life idyllic had it not been for the incessant civic demands. "I am trying to give 100% of my time to the earning of a livelihood and still retain 25% for outside activities," he grumbled to former Secretary of War Newton D. Baker. "The mathematics of the thing is all wrong." Even informal talks taxed his energy, and he envied men like Baker who had the "versatility of intellect" to deliver them at will. Reluctant to offend and burdened always by conscience, Davis accepted far more engagements than he could carry with justice to himself. As a result, most of his talks and speeches were inconsequential or topical, though they were invariably phrased with grace and delivered with a fine sense of the occasion. Within a few years he was perhaps the most sought-after ceremonial speaker in New York.[24]

Of the dozen or so speeches Davis made the spring of his return to the law, two remain interesting. The first was a call for increases in the salaries of diplomats and members of the Foreign Service: "Nothing is less democratic in our democratic country than our refusal to compensate those who serve us. The nation has the right to the services of all her sons, rich and poor alike, but she should not ask for it upon terms such that none but those with private means can afford to serve." The second was a thoughtfully conceived and charmingly written paper on the English legal profession. He conceded that the separation of the roles of the solicitor and barrister had many attractive features, but concluded that the American system served the client better because it concentrated responsibility; it also enabled the lawyer to perform either role "as his opportunity or his taste may dictate." (A decade and a half later, drawing on his rich experience at the appellate bar, he decided that the English system probably served justice better.) [25]

Although Davis immediately went on the boards of the Rockefeller Foundation and the Carnegie Endowment, he did escape one onerous duty that first year. Shortly after the Washington Naval Conference was announced in August 1921, former Republican National Chairman Charles D. Hilles urged President Harding to add Davis to the American delegation:

> he is a man of broad learning, fine character, and has a wide acquaintance among public men. . . . He was the ablest and most effective of all the diplomats who were located in the war area during the Wilson regime. He is big enough to follow and support Secretary Hughes in his nation's programme, and he would bring some of the influential statesmen to your standard.

Harding decided, however, to limit the delegation to Secretary of State Charles Evans Hughes, Elihu Root, Henry Cabot Lodge, and Oscar Underwood.[26]

Davis would have suffered considerable intellectual anguish had he served, for though he regarded Hughes' dramatic call for a ten-year naval construction holiday as "bold and courageous," he felt that the

Four Power Treaty was marred by "the vice of exclusiveness." He believed that the Senate should ratify it in order to avoid the stigma of again rejecting the work of a conference in which the United States had participated. But he fervently hoped that the Senate would also insist that other nations with interests in the Pacific be invited to adhere to the Treaty on equal terms.[27]

« IV »

Eighteen months after Davis joined Stetson, Jennings & Russell, he made the most fateful decision of his post-ambassadorial career. Many members of the Supreme Court had long hoped that he would join them on the bench. In the fall of 1918 Chief Justice White implied that he would resign if the President would make Davis his successor. Fifteen months later, in London, Brandeis remarked that he would like to see him on the Court. And in October 1920 McReynolds also offered to resign if the President would replace him with Davis. (To his own account of the offer in his diary, Davis added one word: "nonsense.") McReynolds, of course, had made an idle gesture, and White later told William Howard Taft that he intended to hold the post until a new Administration could give it to the ex-President.[28]

Harding's appointment of Taft as Chief Justice in June 1921 finally opened the way for an overture to Davis. The former President was determined to mould the Court in his own image, and he conceived Davis, more than most others, to be in that image. As an eminent student of the Taft Court has observed, Taft never fully accepted the myth "that it was the Constitution, not the judge, which spoke through judicial decisions." He understood, as many abstractionists did not, that the Court reads policy into the Constitution even when affirming the status quo. "Courts are composed of judges," Taft wrote in 1914, "and one would be foolish who would deny that courts and judges are affected by the times in which they live." He had also made it clear on occasions too numerous to list that he regarded the Constitution conservatively interpreted as the last remaining bulwark against "socialists," "anarchists," "radicals," and even Roosevelt and Wilson "progressives." In 1920 he wrote in the *Yale Review* that the probable retirement of four Supreme Court Justices within the next few years made the choice of their successors the most critical domestic issue of the presidential campaign. And in 1922 he vented his spleen on the legal realists:

The influence of the Harvard Law School through Frankfurter and Pound is to break down that fundamental instrument the Constitution and make it go for nothing. That I think was Wilson's purpose in appointing Brandeis and Clarke.[29]

Yet Taft did not want a reactionary. In spite of an anti-labor bias so strong that he had scored the very provisions of the Clayton Act that Davis had originally framed, he wanted a man with proper regard for due process. "I feel," he told Elihu Root in December 1922, "as if we ought not to have too many men on the Court who are as reactionary . . . as McReynolds, and that we need men who are liberal but who still believe that the cornerstone of our civilization is in the proper maintenance of the guarantees of the Fourteenth Amendment and the Fifth Amendment." [30]

As Chief Justice, Taft had no influence on the appointment of Harding's intimate friend, Senator George Sutherland of Utah, to Justice Clarke's seat. Nor did he influence the selection of Edward T. Sanford of Kentucky for Pitney's place. But he did play an important role in filling Justice Day's slot, the opening for which Davis was considered. No sooner had Harding nominated Sutherland than Taft and Justice Van Devanter, his confidant, concluded that it would be wise to add a Democrat. The Chief Justice's thoughts at once turned to Davis. (Taft regarded Pierce Butler of Minnesota, who was more conservative on civil liberties and had the advantage of being a Catholic, as the next best qualified man.) Meanwhile he had his former Attorney General, George Wickersham, sound out Davis.[31]

Davis was more disturbed than pleased by the prospect Wickersham opened. Long before he had left Washington in 1918 the Court had lost most of its aura, and by 1922 he had tried enough cases in the state and federal courts in New York to know that the quality of argument there was generally superior to that in the Supreme Court. On the day of Clarke's resignation, in fact, he had remarked that anyone familiar with "the severity of the daily grind of the Supreme Court can hardly blame another for seeking to escape." There was far more "fun" on the bar's side, he said again and again. Yet, as he also acknowledged, a seat on the Supreme Court was the highest honor a lawyer could hope to receive.[32]

Davis might have accepted had his wife not been depressed by the difference between official entertainment in Washington and the splendor she had been part of in England. And he would doubtless have accepted had he himself been more interested in the abstract or philosophical aspects of law. Certainly, he would have been responsive had he been willing to forego the large income that he was now, for the first time, beginning to earn. But, as he lightly phrased it to the Wall Street lawyer, Charles C. Burlingham, "I have taken the vows of chastity and obedience but not of poverty." [33]

While Davis was turning over the matter in his mind, Taft commissioned Thomas W. Shelton of Virginia to marshal political support for him. Shelton soon reported that many prominent Democrats, including Carter Glass, strongly endorsed the former Ambassador. Then, on October 26, Taft had Van Devanter write to Davis. "The Chief Justice and I," said Van Devanter, ". . . conceive you would deem it a patriotic duty to accept." [34]

Two days later, Shelton sent Davis an impassioned appeal:

> Destiny has cast some few men for public service and for the great honors incident to that trust. When the names of J. P. Morgan or Carnegie have been forgotten; when Choate and [James C.] Carter will be meaningless, the words of Mr. Justice Davis will be fresh in mind; will be educating generations in fundamental principles and will be measuring civil liberty and property rights amongst millions. . . .

"You are a young man," Shelton continued, "and are . . . sure to become Chief Justice. . . . What great lawyer is it that would not prefer that post even to the Presidency? . . . There are times in the life of a nation when a call to civil service is as impelling as one to the sacred Altar." [35]

By then Davis had already declined. He conceded that Van Devanter's remarks on patriotic duty had touched his conscience, but he protested that he had already given the ten most fruitful years of his life to public service. He added that he still hoped to do his share, though out of office rather than in it; "all that I ask is a breathing spell." He had entered practice in New York with the fixed intention of remaining in private life until he had accumulated "not a fortune, for that is beyond the reach both of my desire and my opportunities in these income tax days—but some economic independence." That now seemed measurably within his grasp. After extolling his clients and partners, he observed that "no sober man reaches middle life without feeling the increasing necessity for making some provision for the future." [36]

Davis' letter shook Van Devanter and Taft profoundly. Van Devanter acknowledged that Davis had done much for the public, and had done it "exceedingly well." Yet he could not resist a thrust. "Could you know the estimates of you which have been called forth in this matter, I am sure you would feel a deep sense of gratification and would realize that high duty well performed has its real reward." The Chief Justice agreed that Davis' earlier service entitled him to look after his own affairs, but he also thought that he would live to regret the decision. "While he is young enough to wait some years, by that time he will have become so identified with the Morgan interests that no President would feel like taking him from the center of Wall Street and putting him on the Bench." [37]

The Chief Justice could not understand why Davis was unwilling to live on $15,000 a year. It was more difficult to select a judge than reformers realized, Taft wrote Burlingham in irritation two months later. "If you people in New York were not so eager for money and would be content to live on a reasonable salary . . . you might have some representatives on our bench, but you are all after the almighty dollar." [38]

Davis never had more than passing regrets. He admitted feeling at times that perhaps it had been "call to duty." He always said that he would have accepted had the overture come while he was still Solicitor General or after he became financially secure. Yet he evinced no interest when his name was raised on subsequent occasions, and for thirty-three years thereafter his letters were those of a man supremely happy in his work. His riposte to President Harding, who told him the last time he saw him that he had come close to making him a judge, was characteristic: "You could have gone further and done better." [39]

CHAPTER 13

The Presidency and the House of Morgan

The only limitation upon a right-thinking lawyer's independence is the duty which he owes to his clients, once selected, to serve them without the slightest thought of the effect such a service may have upon his own personal political fortunes.

JOHN W. DAVIS, MARCH 1924

« I »

By June 24, 1924, when the Democratic Convention opened in Madison Square Garden, Davis was a leading compromise candidate for the presidential nomination. His West Virginia friends had formed an informal Davis organization in October 1921, and from then until the convention ground to a halt, nearly three weeks after it had begun, they worked single-mindedly to convince the great power blocs that he was the only man who could unify the party. Their strategy, as in 1920, was to make Davis the second choice of delegates pledged to other candidates, and they were again to draw moral support from *The New York Times*. This time, however, they faced a more formidable obstacle than the Irish question and popular prejudice against the Court of St. James's: their candidate's connection with the House of Morgan.[1]

Although Davis still deemed the presidency more a burden than a blessing, the prospect of occupying the White House no longer terrified him; consciously or unconsciously, he had taken the measure of Harding and Coolidge and found himself not wanting. For reasons both idealistic and practical, however, he had refused for two and a half years to encourage his supporters.[2]

The former Ambassador was determined that the nomination would come on his own terms, if it came at all; at no time did he turn down a client to curry favor with the party's progressive wing. He argued in one Supreme Court case that a Pennsylvania law to protect small property owners from cave-ins beneath their dwellings deprived mine owners, who held title to the sub-surface land, of due process. He contended in another that West Virginia's effort to assure a flow of natural gas to its own residents by limiting transmission outside the state was unconstitutional. He represented the Coronado Coal Company against the United Mine Workers. He accepted a retainer from the Bituminous Coal Operators Committee, the member companies of which were engaged in anti-union practices comparable to the ones he had declaimed so eloquently against while in Congress. At the instance of J P Morgan & Co., he urged Governor Alfred E. Smith to veto a bill to tax private bankers. He even won an unpopular 10 per cent rate increase for the New York Telephone Company on the eve of the convention.[3]

Neither did Davis court the progressives in his political and legal addresses; on the contrary, he emphasized the party's pre-Progressive era values. "Belief in the liberty and freedom of the individual man . . . equality of human rights, equal rights to all and special privileges to none—that is the cardinal essence of the Democratic creed," he declared in 1922. The party stands for economy, believes in local self-government, and opposes a single, centralized government. It further holds that "the man or the political party or the nation that takes as the motive of its existence and creed 'Am I my brother's keeper?' will suffer just as surely the malediction of the Divinity as he by whom those words were first uttered." * [4]

As president of the American Bar Association in 1923, Davis expressed his philosophic opposition to the incipient welfare and regulatory states even more emphatically: "Increased solicitude for the health and physical comfort of the individual has led men to speak and to think quite mistakenly of so-called 'human rights' as of something which can be divorced, either in practice or in legislation, from so-called 'rights of property.'" The view that government's greatest duty was the encouragement of individual effort was giving ground to the

* This was a misconstruction of the implications of the Biblical text. Cain, of course, used the phrase to deny responsibility.

theory that government should supplement, if not supplant, such effort. Regulation of coal, iron, and gas by commissions created a body of administrative law which was nothing less than a "naked . . . attack upon our theory of government under a written constitution." Following a cavalier reference to the proposed equal rights amendment for women, Davis added that the easy adoption of the income tax, Prohibition, and woman suffrage amendments cast doubt on whether Americans were quite as immune as they thought from "that appetite for organic change which Lecky declares to be one of the worst diseases that can afflict a people." [5]

In other addresses, Davis extolled Anglo-American friendship, called on the United States to join the World Court, and opposed passage of the veterans' bonus. Only on taxation did he hedge. Privately, he favored the Mellon Plan to reduce taxes sharply in the upper brackets. "Our true policy," he wrote in December 1923, "is to out-Mellon Mellon." But in a speech on taxation in January 1924 he failed to comment on either the Mellon Plan or a Democratic proposal to make greater reductions in the lower brackets. Instead, he scored government spending and urged his party to eschew new programs "no matter what pleasing name or persuasive reason may attend them." He also urged the Democrats to avoid the Republicans' policy of making tariff-protected manufacturers the "petted beneficiaries of governmental privilege." [6]

The anti-progressive thrust of Davis' speeches escaped wide notice, and by the fall of 1923 he had moved into the ranks of the serious contenders for the nomination. Reports that he was the second choice of many Smith and McAdoo delegates were multiplying. Former Governor John J. Cornwell was preparing to lead a group of West Virginians to New York to raise funds, though he himself was "lying low" because of his position as general counsel of the Baltimore & Ohio Railroad. And dozens of Davis-for-President clubs were forming spontaneously. ("Folks just go ahead and form them and tell Mr. Davis about it later," explained one of his self-appointed managers.) Then, early in the new year, a *New York Times* editorial reminiscent of the one that had made Davis a national figure in 1920 pushed him into the forefront of the second-line candidates. [7]

Davis sometimes intimated in the next few months that he lacked the political and financial support to become a candidate on an impressive scale. But as his rejection of requests to speak (as many as eight in one day) indicates, he could have had maximum exposure at minimum cost had he wanted it. He declined invitations to address the state legislatures of Missouri and Mississippi. He told the Hartford *Times* that he could forward no biographical data beyond that in *Who's Who*. He persuaded a newspaperman not to publish a sketch about him in the Washington papers. He even appealed to *The New York Times* to hold back: "I have taken in good faith the position that I am not a candidate. If I should give an interview . . . on political subjects, would it not be said at once that my position was a mere cloak for an ill-concealed ambition?" [8]

« II »

Hardly a week passed in 1923 that Davis was not reminded that his connection with J P Morgan & Co. was his main liability. Most commentators conceded that his choice of clients was his own business. But as someone said of reports that he was to represent the Coffee and Sugar Exchange in an antitrust suit, a victory would make him "The Enemy of the American Breakfast Table." In January 1924, the Democratic National Committee wrote Davis off informally because of his connection with Morgan. The next month Theodore Huntley of the Pittsburgh *Post,* Davis' most insistent supporter in the Washington press corps, implored him to give up his New York practice: "The . . . public, my dear Mr. Ambassador, is hardly in a mood to philosophize over Wall Street. . . . You can damn Wall Street or you can deplore Wall Street, but you can't do business with Wall Street & be elected President of the United States." [9]

Davis inclined at first to shrug it all off. "While I . . . have always kept my clients' business and my political views in two separate compartments, I know that a man on the street does not always look at things that way." Yet the inference that he was a kept man rankled, and his responses grew more acidulous. He wrote that one who sacrificed his independence in order to gain the presidency could not hope to regain it after he became President; he complained that some of his political friends were deploring what otherwise might be considered his good fortune.[10]

Suddenly, in mid-winter, the political situation changed dramatically. William G. McAdoo, the odds-on favorite for the nomination, was disclosed to have received $150,000 to represent Edward Doheny, one of the architects of the Teapot Dome scandal, in negotiations with the Mexican government over Doheny's oil lands. The former Secretary of the Treasury was to receive an additional $900,000 if Mexico agreed not to expropriate Doheny's property, as provided by the Mexican Constitution.[11]

In an appearance before a Senate committee in February, McAdoo defended himself vigorously. He asserted that his employment had been open, that the United States government itself opposed expropriation, and that he had acted as an attorney rather than as a lobbyist. The explanation satisfied Davis, though he realized that it would not stand up politically. He also predicted that the incident would reduce his own chances. As he wrote his sister Emma, the party would probably become "even more gun shy . . . of selecting a lawyer whose capacity entitles him to be employed in matters of importance—for that is what it all comes to." Davis also deplored the Teapot Dome investigating committee's insistence on employing as counsel only lawyers "untainted" by corporate affiliations. "What distresses me is that in a Congress made up of a majority of lawyers . . . , no one seems to have the courage to come forward and defend the professional integrity of the bar." [12]

The popular reaction against McAdoo's involvement with Doheny prompted Theodore Huntley to renew pressure on Davis to sever his connection with Morgan. "I still think you can with dignity and decency and entire honesty trim your sails to what I believe to be a genuine demand for your candidacy," the reporter wrote. On March 4, just as Huntley was giving up hope, Davis sent him a long, impassioned letter:

> If I were in the market for the goods you offer, I would not complain of the character of this consignment, although I notice you do not guarantee delivery. The price you put on them, however, is entirely too high. You offer me a chance to be the Democratic nominee for the Presidency which carries with it in this year of grace more than a fair prospect of becoming President of the United States. In exchange, I am to abandon forthwith and immediately a law practice which is both pleasant and, within modest bounds, profitable; to throw over honorable clients who offer me honest employment; and desert a group of professional colleagues who are able, upright and loyal. If this were all, I would think your figures pretty stiff, but you are really asking something still more.
>
> I have been at the bar nearly thirty years, and with the exception of ten years spent in public life I have enjoyed during the whole of that time a practice of an extremely varied character.
>
> At no time have I confined my services to a single client, and in consequence I have been called upon to serve a great many different kinds of men; some of them good, some of them indifferently good, and oth-

ers over whose character we will drop the veil of charity. Indeed, some of my clients—thanks perhaps to their failure to secure a better lawyer —have become the involuntary guests for fixed terms of the nation and the state. Since the law, however, is a profession and not a trade, I conceive it to be the duty of the lawyer, just as it is the duty of the priest or the surgeon, to serve those who call on him unless, indeed, there is some insuperable obstacle in the way.

No one in all this list of clients has ever controlled or even fancied that he could control my personal or my political conscience. I am vain enough to imagine that no one ever will. The only limitation upon a right-thinking lawyer's independence is the duty which he owes to his clients, once selected, to serve them without the slightest thought of the effect such a service may have upon his personal popularity or his political fortunes. Any lawyer who surrenders this independence or shades this duty by trimming his professional course to fit the gusts of popular opinion in my judgment not only dishonors himself but disparages and degrades the great profession to which he should be proud to belong. You must not think me either indifferent or unappreciative if I tell you in candor that I would not pay this price for any honor in the gift of man. . . .

What is life worth, after all, if one has no philosophy of his own to live it by? If one surrenders this to win an office, what will he live by after the office is won? Tell me that! [13]

Huntley was stunned. Davis had destroyed all chance for the nomination, or so it seemed. Shortly, however, it occurred to him that the former Ambassador had "simply and spontaneously" done what he could not have done by premeditation. "Urged to dramatize his democracy, he had . . . dramatized his honesty." How, Huntley wondered, could he capitalize on Davis' eloquent candor? He decided to risk one more rebuff by requesting permission to publish the letter.[14]

By then Davis was at the end of his tether. "There is nothing I resent more than the idea that a lawyer sells himself body & soul to his clients. I have always loved the practice of the law better than anything in the world, unless it would be my wife & child, & a blow at the honor of the profession . . . hits me near the heart." It was time that society understood the lawyer's role. He authorized publication.[15]

On March 30 the Pittsburgh *Post* printed Davis' statement in its entirety. "The letter has gone like wildfire," Huntley scrawled from the Senate Press Gallery the following afternoon. "It *is*—in spite of you! —the dramatization I sought." Washington correspondents of all political stripes were overwhelmed by sentiments of "friendship, respect and belief." Within twenty-four hours virtually every daily in the country had published portions of the letter, and by the end of the week scores of editorial writers had rhapsodized on Davis' candor, courage, and devotion to principle. Although they differed on the letter's political import, they were as one in terming it a noble service. The Springfield *Union* summed it up, "Mr. Davis deserves the warmest thanks . . . for his forceful rebuke of the suggestion that a lawyer cannot service a rich client without injury to his character or without sacrificing his claim to public confidence and trust.* [16]

Thereafter, the Morgan connection did not appear so formidable. Congressmen James F. Brynes, Pat Harrison, and Cordell Hull, among many others, spoke of the former Ambassador with new enthusiasm. In Texas the legal community swung behind him almost as a body. Elsewhere signs of new second-line support sprang up as admiration for Davis' forthrightness began to overcome reservations about his conservatism.[17]

« III »

Actually, the question was more subtle than either Davis or his admirers perceived. The former Ambassador had been honest in asserting that none of his clients had "ever controlled or even fancied that they could control" his personal or political conscience; his indifference to the demands of mining, manufacturing, and railroad constituents while he was in Congress testified graphically to that. Nevertheless, as his father had angrily implied when the young Davis became a part-time railroad counsel early in the century, to accept a regular retainer was to change the character of one's practice and to restrict one's political and professional independence. It was also to subject oneself to the unconscious influences that bear on all men. William Ernest Hocking, the noted philosopher, spoke directly to this point in the *Yale Review* that summer: "When Mr. Davis scorned the suggestion that he should change his occupation to make himself a fitter possibility for the presidential nomination, he was right; when he asserted that occupation

---

* Almost forty years later members of the bar were still hailing Davis' words. "His letter is an eloquent statement of the dignity inherent in the profession of law and the self-respecting satisfaction that no alternative way of life is superior to the practice of one's profession in accordance with the highest standards. Davis held to the image of himself as a lawyer and to his profession's image of itself as a *true* profession. . . . He was really and truly not interested in political office as something more to be desired than a lawyer's practice." B. H. Levy, *Corporation Lawyer . . . Saint or Sinner?* (New York, 1961), 84.

and activities have no psychological influence upon perceptions of public policy, he was wrong. Associations alter interpretations." [18]

Felix Frankfurter, then a Harvard Law School professor and contributing editor to the *New Republic*, was one of the few others to probe beneath the surface. Frankfurter had known Davis casually in Washington and was later to write that he was "the most charming of men . . . an admirable type—in the sense that he was one of the few successful lawyers who cared strongly about the standards of the profession." But Frankfurter seems also to have felt for Davis the contempt of the academician who knew that he too could have had a remunerative corporate practice had he been willing to accept the restraints on his freedom of action. He was especially disillusioned by Davis' failure in 1922, and again in early 1924, to join Senator George Wharton Pepper, Moorfield Storey, Sr., and other leaders of the bar in appealing to Presidents Harding and Coolidge to pardon the victims of the wartime Sedition Act. Surely, wrote Frankfurter in the *New Republic*, after exhuming Davis' address to the American Bar Association, the president of the organization that professed to represent the guardians of the law was under obligation to address the subversion of the law by both the bench and the bar. But in the face of the Association's disregard of the Bill of Rights and its continuing drive against political "radicals"; of the judiciary's near emasculation of the anti-injunction clause of the Clayton Act; of the legal profession's acquiescence in a dual standard of justice for rich and poor, black and white—in the face of all this, Davis had been "wholly silent . . . truly eloquently silent." [19]

Frankfurter elaborated on these and kindred themes in several unsigned articles that spring. Since the former Ambassador's return to the United States in 1921, Frankfurter asserted, he had either failed to speak on the testing issues of domestic politics, or had taken an antiliberal position, "or [had] contented himself with fluent repetition of hollow party shibboleths," while denying that his connection with the most powerful banking firm in the world had any relationship to his fitness for the presidency. "One does not know which interpretation of this attitude disqualifies Mr. Davis more—that he believes it, or knowing better, seeks shelter behind it." Frankfurter also dilated on Hocking's theme. "Like the rest of us, [Davis] . . . is mastered by the material with which he works. . . . Of course Mr. Davis resents the suggestion that any client of his 'could control' his 'political conscience' . . . No man could possibly 'control' Mr. Davis." But conscience was not a thing apart from the totality of daily life. Davis was no longer a small-town West Virginia lawyer with a highly diversified practice; nor was he merely a distinguished advocate. Rather, he was a director of economic enterprises of vast power. The subtle alchemy of those associations was strikingly evident in his reference to his law practice as "within modest bounds, profitable." [20]

"Mr. Davis," Frankfurter continued, "is not content to rest his Morgan retainer on those ultimate grounds of preference which are open to every free man. He must account for himself on the score of duty." Yet the leaders of the bar had never fulfilled their duty. Joseph H. Choate had refused a call to argue the constitutionality of legislation limiting the hours of labor for women. Attorney General Palmer had openly criticized certain lawyers for defending radicals. The bar as a whole had not even attempted to extend equal protection of the law to everyone. The simple truth, Frankfurter sorrowfully concluded, was that the leading lawyers of the United States had been engaged mainly in supporting the claims of corporations, while the people and their interests had been represented generally by men of very meager legal ability. Had John W. Davis chosen differently, he could have set a monumental example for lesser men:

> Few lawyers ever were confronted with a clearer choice than that which faced Mr. Davis on his return from London. Experience, circumstances, and endowment combined to offer him the great rewards and the ancient freedom of the unattached advocate. It was his to choose, and he chose a different path. . . . Now, with all his gifts, he befogs the public mind with false conceptions as to the social implications of the legal profession.[21]

As Davis himself had proudly observed, not only did his firm number a dozen or more of the greatest corporations in the country among its regular clients, he himself was a director of several of them. This closed him off from public debate on such cardinal issues as the concentration of economic and financial power and the relations between capital and labor. The United States Steel Corporation, one of the firm's regular clients, forcibly resisted labor's efforts to organize until well into the New Deal. The Erie Railroad, another client, owned or controlled coal mines that still employed children and still had part of the work force on a twelve-hour day. The Atchison, Topeka & Santa Fe, on whose board Davis had sat, had played an aggressive role in the issuance of the most sweeping injunction in history (the "Wilkerson Injunction") during the Railway Shopmen's Strike of 1922. Many other clients had a vested interest in low taxes, the anti-union shop, loopholes in the antitrust laws, and minimal regulation of public utilities.

Assuredly, neither Davis nor his firm was directly responsible for any of this. The Atchison, Topeka & Santa Fe's action in the Shopmen's Strike was ordered by its operational managers; the anti-union activities of United States Steel were part of a broad offensive which no legal counselor could have blunted, much less reversed. Furthermore, Davis privately opposed some of these policies in principle. He deplored child labor. He disapproved the abuse of the injunction. He discountenanced monopoly in the abstract. Indeed, the realization that he did hold such views was probably central to his carefully chosen words about "conscience" in the Huntley letter. He also knew—and so did every one who had ever served with him in government—that as President of the United States he would be absolutely incorruptible, absolutely dedicated to the national interest as he understood it.

Nevertheless, Davis could not perceive, or would not admit, that his permanent retainers and membership on corporate boards proscribed his freedom. He could not, during his three decades on Wall Street, have served as counsel to any of the congressional committees that investigated banking, monopoly, the securities industry, and the repression of labor. Neither could he have criticized the Wilkerson Injunction directly. (In his one full-dress political speech, made in the fall of 1922 when debate over that injunction was at its height, he ignored it.) It is also inconceivable that he could have attacked the labor policies of the U.S. Steel Corporation as he had attacked those of its predecessor companies in 1900. The implication was clear: The delegates to the Democratic Convention would have to accept Davis in the faith that his philosophy was the one he had seemed to hold when arguing the great progressive cases of the Wilson era.[22]

CHAPTER 14

Madison Square Garden

I have seen a good many men under the awful temptation of the Presidency. I have never seen another who had such absolute respect.

WALTER LIPPMANN

« I »

Davis' silence on the divisive issues probably strengthened his candidacy. Conservatives and moderates felt that he was one of them at heart. Progressives believed, or wanted to believe, that his record in Congress and as Solicitor General was a more accurate index of his real commitments than his Wall Street practice was. Proponents of the League of Nations were confident that he still stood with them. And, though some residual resentment remained in the big-city delegations, the creation of the Irish Free State in 1922 had made the Irish question academic. Manifestly, only a Sherman-like declaration could have removed Davis from contention by the spring of 1924.

Of the front-runners, McAdoo would go into the convention with firm pledges from about one-half of the delegates. These included almost all the Prohibitionists, the majority of rural progressives and labor people from the South and West, and at least two-thirds of the Ku Klux Klan sympathizers. They also included scores of old friends from the Wilson era who regarded him as the most capable man in the party. Still, his involvement with Doheny made it extremely doubtful that he could pick up the extra two hundred votes necessary for nomination under the two-thirds rule. As Senator Thomas J. Walsh of Montana, who had pronounced the Doheny retainer a red

herring in the winter, bluntly asserted early in the spring, McAdoo
was politically dead.[1]

The prospects of the second front-liner, New York's brilliant, three-
time Governor, Alfred E. Smith, were even poorer. Until early spring
Smith had been merely a stalking horse for the urban Catholic bosses
who aimed to force the nomination not of a Catholic (they could have
had Walsh, a progressive and a dry), but of a conservative and a wet.
Although Smith was more liberal than McAdoo on civil liberties, he
shared Davis' concern for states' rights. "[In] recent years," he said in
a rare statement on national policy in 1923, "there has been too much
interference by the Federal Government with the affairs of the different states, and we have abundant evidence that violence has been done
to the old-time Democratic theory of the rights of the states . . . guaranteed by the Constitution." Many old-line Wilsonians also questioned
Smith's knowledge of foreign affairs. More serious still, the Governor's
unabashed wetness and rasping Lower East Side accent, his associations with Tammany and his open devotion to the Roman Catholic
Church, symbolized all that rural, old-stock America feared and
loathed.[2]

Nevertheless, Smith's unexpected victory in the Wisconsin primary,
where Catholicism was strong and resentment of Prohibition pronounced, convinced many of the Governor's near-fanatical followers
that he should make a serious bid. By the first of April they had for-
mulated their strategy: they would deadlock the convention, pack the
galleries, and stand firm until McAdoo's lines broke. Smith, meanwhile, decided to discourage a "sidewalks" movement to condemn the
Ku Klux Klan explicitly in the platform. "I did not feel," he later explained, "that anything would be gained by the passage of a resolution
denouncing any large group of delegates or finding fault with their
theories." Only when he realized that it was "hopeless" to try to stay
neutral did he agree to join the issue.[3]

The third avowed candidate, Senator Oscar Underwood of Alabama, was out of the running before he fairly started. Like Davis, Underwood was personable, courageous, and conservative, but he was also
more outspokenly negative. "He had no constructive suggestions or
principles with which to replace that which he criticized," observed a
Texan who had observed him on the stump that winter. Months before Underwood alienated much of the South in the fall of 1923 by
boldly denouncing the Klan, he had been written off by all but the
militantly anti-KKK and anti-Prohibition East. Defeated in every pri-

mary he entered save that of his home state, he would arrive in New
York with Alabama's twenty-four votes, the second-line support of
many Easterners and some Southern conservatives, and a fierce resolve
to storm the convention on the Klan issue.[4]

Of the dark horses, Senator Carter Glass was one of the most potent
threats to Davis. The peppery Virginian possessed few of the former
Ambassador's ingratiating qualities, though he shared his philosophy
and held many of the same tactical advantages. He had managed to
oppose woman suffrage without offending its proponents irreparably.
And he disapproved of, but had never publicly denounced, the Ku
Klux Klan.[5] Glass professed to be without presidential ambitions. Yet
even as he arranged to become Virginia's favorite son (ostensibly to
hold the delegation for his close friend McAdoo), he envisioned himself as the legatee of a deadlock. He felt that Easterners committed to
Smith would never accept McAdoo, and he urged his supporters not
to embitter them. There was a real possibility, he explained, that the
convention would turn to a "sane" Southerner; in that event, he would
need the cooperation of both the Smith and the McAdoo people.[6]

The most likely dark horse was 300-pound, sixty-six-year-old Samuel
M. Ralston of Indiana. He had been a mildly progressive Governor
from 1913 to 1917, and had been elected United States Senator in
1922. As one of the few students of his career writes, he was "a Protestant, perhaps a little tinged by the Klan, yet beloved by the Catholic
Democracy of the state he had long served." He had considerable executive ability, but "said little, made very few opponents, and no enemies." Although Ralston had earlier denied any connection with the
Klan, he had pointedly added that he would appreciate the aid of all
voters. Behind him stood the wiliest boss of them all, Thomas "Uncle
Tom" Taggart. More even than Davis, Ralston lacked the will for
power: "There is something about the greatness of the exalted position
. . . that admonishes me against wanting to undertake the execution
of its grave and solemn duties."[7]

« II »

Despite the favorable reaction to the Huntley letter, Davis continued to insist that he was not a candidate and would do nothing to become one: the presidency should not be an object of personal ambition, and no one should impose himself on the party in such a
favorable year. Even so, he could not ignore the signs. Delegates from

Delaware, Kentucky, Mississippi, Tennessee, Missouri, Louisiana, North Carolina, Texas, and even Rhode Island reported that he was the second choice of their delegations. Davis-For-President clubs continued to proliferate. A poll of 1900 lawyers, politicians, businessmen, and labor leaders gave him 44 per cent, McAdoo 29, Ralston 13, Underwood 8, and Smith 4. (Only the labor leaders gave McAdoo a majority.) [8]

By early April Colonel House, an original McAdoo man, was thinking of pushing Davis quietly. (House believed that he could persuade business and financial leaders to support Davis over Coolidge by telling them that repudiation of their lawyer would reflect on themselves.) He was disappointed, especially, by McAdoo's refusal to support even associate membership in the League of Nations. But in the end, House was swept along by McAdoo's buoyancy. "McAdoo was militant and confident," he reported after talking to him in late May. "The man has great charm, unlimited courage and fine imagination." [9]

By then Davis had already resigned himself to a minimal effort. In mid-March he authorized Louis Johnson of Clarksburg to send campaign literature to Washington and Lee alumni. He also returned a pamphlet drawn up by Clem Shaver for a nationwide mailing to county chairmen with a stern admonition to make it less apologetic: "I think we will make a mistake if we assume a purely defensive attitude on the Wall Street bug-a-boo. Should not our note be that it qualifies rather than disqualifies men for public service to have been called in to advise about large affairs in private life? Let us show a bold front and wind up on the 'take me as I am' note." [10]

That "note" included a brief account of Davis' Wall Street practice, a longer account of his liberal record in Congress, and a progressive-slanted review of his service as Solicitor General in the *Midwest Oil,* child labor, and eight-hour-day cases.[11]

As the convention drew nearer, it became more and more apparent that the rank and file wanted at least a mild progressive. Even the delegations from the great urban states were sprinkled with men and women unsympathetic to the bosses' determination to nominate a wet regardless of his economic philosophy. Thus Sing Sing's great penologist Thomas Mott Osborne confided to Franklin Roosevelt: "Of course I shall have to vote for . . . [Smith] as long as there is a chance; but I don't think there is much chance, and I hope to Heaven there won't be. He is not a really good Governor and would make a damned poor President. . . . As for Ralston, I'd as soon vote for Coolidge. Ditto,

Underwood." They should plan, Osborne urged, to fasten onto a progressive, any progressive—Brand Whitlock of Ohio, Josephus Daniels of North Carolina, Governor William E. Sweet of Colorado. Even Bryan would be acceptable "if it were not for his ridiculous and pre-Adamite fundamentalism." [12]

To forge ahead of Ralston and Glass, Davis had only to declare himself a moderate progressive. But in the face of his friends' importunings, he continued to hold that he had already expressed himself on everything that promised to be an issue. Actually, he had spoken on the League of Nations, the World Court, and the tariff; he had also outlined his laissez-faire, anti-social-welfare philosophy in his address to the American Bar Association. But he had said little or nothing about the searing domestic issues that threatened to produce a massive third-party movement if the Democrats nominated a conservative. Farm relief, railroad regulation, development of Muscle Shoals, control of natural resources, the Mellon Plan, federal aid to education, the still unratified child labor amendment, the resurgent abuse of the labor injunction, the denial of civil liberties to radicals, the persistence of lynching, even the Ku Klux Klan itself—on not one of these matters had Davis spoken publicly, and on only two or three had he commented privately.[13]

The problem, in part, was Davis' integrity. To make a statement, he explained to Huntley, would be to issue "a campaign manifesto . . . the very thing I have endeavored to avoid." Not even Lansing, who begged him to say a few chosen words when he went to Princeton to receive an honorary degree in June, could budge him. If forced to speak, Davis told the former Secretary of State, he would dilate on that "illustrious company of warriors, scholars, scientists and statesmen who . . . have turned and turned again for light and leading to those whose torches have been lit at the never dying flame that burns, never more brightly than today, on the vestal altars of old Nassau, consecrated in song and story." [14]

Thus it was that Walter Lippmann would write that Davis' nomination "was the result of confidence in his character rather than of studied agreement with his views."

> He made no active campaign for the nomination, and had nearly broken the hearts of his friends by a cavalier refusal to make even one gesture which would seem to reflect on his clients, or to betray the slightest distrust of the soundness of the legal services he was engaged in. . . . He has ambition, of course, for worldly things. But it does not

torture him. He has little lust for power . . . it seems to fascinate him
far less than it does most men.[15]

« III »

The divisions that would make the Democratic nomination an
empty honor were almost beyond repair when the convention opened
in the old Madison Square Garden on June 24, as the most oppressive
heat wave in years settled in. There was a burst of enthusiasm when
keynoter Pat Harrison, his words rolling around his mouth like a quid
of tobacco before passing into the battery of microphones which carried the proceedings over the air for the first time in history, labeled
the Republicans the "Grand Oil Party." And there was a spontaneous
demonstration when he eulogized Woodrow Wilson, who had died in
February, bitter yet unbroken. But those were the last displays of
unity until Davis addressed the remnants of the convention more than
two weeks later. The assemblage's real tone had been set when the galleries, packed with Tammany hacks and sprinkled with priests, un-
loosed a cheer when they thought Harrison said, "What this country
needs is a real beer." (He had said, "What this country needs is another Paul Revere.") [16]

Smith and McAdoo had come into New York a few days earlier,
both brimming with surface confidence and determined underneath to
rule or ruin. "I believe that when they get around to naming the real
man, after distributing the complimentary votes, I'll be nominated,"
Smith boasted. "The rank and file of the people of this country want
me. . . . This may sound a bit chesty, but it isn't at all. . . . It's a
mere statement of fact." McAdoo, who had considerable cause for opti-
mism, was more ideological. Only a progressive can win the election,
he told 3000 roaring supporters who met him with a brass band at
Pennsylvania Station. He then damned "this imperial city . . . , [this]
seat of that invisible power represented by the allied forces of finance
and industry . . . , reactionary, sinister, unscrupulous, mercenary, and
sordid." Even Underwood breathed resolution. Emboldened by the
Smith forces' decision to fight it out on the Klan, he seemed confident
that they would eventually shift to himself. The night before the first
session he issued an ultimatum: the platform would condemn the Klan
by name or he would withdraw his candidacy and, by implication, disrupt the convention.[17]

William Jennings Bryan, beads of sweat pouring off his still unfurrowed brow, meanwhile cornered delegates in the hotel lobbies. As for twenty-eight years past, the Great Commoner sought to make the party progressive; he also retained a glimmer of hope that it would turn to him for the fourth time. In the pockets of his rumpled palm beach suit he carried a bundle of planks on federal aid to education and strict control of natural resources, and a referendum on entering wars not begun by enemy attack. "Really, he was most reasonable," reported Robert Woolley, one of the handful of McAdoo men also sympathetic to Davis; he did not intend to make Prohibition an issue, and he was supporting an "Anti-Ku Klux plank which does not mention the Klan by name, but handles it without gloves." Woolley added that Bryan had attacked Davis unmercifully in his column in Hearst's *New York American*.[18]

As the tension mounted, the former Ambassador remained in the background, almost unattended. *The New York Times* announced on June 20 that he would respond to his party's call, though he did not consider himself a candidate. Then, on the eve of the convention, he gave the West Virginia delegation a buffet lunch at his house in Locust Valley, Long Island, before moving into Frank Polk's midtown residence. Clem Shaver issued a statement praising Davis' liberalism that same day, and from then until the balloting ended most of the West Virginia delegates worked feverishly to portray their man as a genuine progressive. They also tried to offset the lingering Irish resentment by emphasizing that his law firm was then representing the Free State in litigation. But Davis himself remained silent. He ignored Bryan's piercing strictures. He made no effort to restrain Senator Matthew Neely of West Virginia, who was denouncing him and his conservative backers to anyone who would listen. And he refused to see newspapermen, much less issue a statement.[19]

Although Davis' iron discipline worked against him with the progressives, it did remove him from the bitter struggles over the platform. By early June he had fallen in behind the party in opposition to the Mellon Plan. One of the differences between the Republicans and Democrats, he explained, was that the former had more "favor seeking, privilege hunting corporations" within their ranks; hence their desire to give special relief to the very rich. But that was his only pre-convention comment on a domestic issue, and it was made privately. His conciliatory spirit probably made him sympathetic toward Bryan's plan to avoid indicting the Ku Klux Klan by name, a plan which many prominent Catholics also endorsed. Davis' sympathies must also have been

engaged by Newton D. Baker's brilliant, heart-rending plea for unqualified entry into the League of Nations. (The convention adopted
Bryan's plank for a national referendum.) Yet, just six weeks earlier,
Davis had written that although he opposed retreat, he was not greatly
concerned about the terms of American adherence. At any rate, he
made no overt effort to bend the West Virginia delegates to his views
on either the Klan or the League. They split seven to nine on indicting the Klan by name, and they voted unanimously for Baker's plank
on the League.[20]

« IV »

Davis' nomination, the last of nineteen, evoked one of the more mechanical demonstrations of the convention. Despite Elmer Davis' pre-
diction in *The New York Times* that the seconding speech by that
"most suave and gracious of lady delegates," Izetta Jewel Brown,
would be worth a hundred votes, they failed to materialize. West Virginia gave Davis its sixteen votes on all 103 ballots, and Louisiana
switched to him on the seventh ballot in anger over Underwood's intransigence on the Klan. But not until the nineteenth ballot, when
Mississippi abandoned Senator Joseph T. Robinson of Arkansas, did a
swing to Davis become a real possibility. By then Al Smith was hanging on only to drive McAdoo into oblivion, and many of the Californian's supporters were talking of compromise. If Davis could pick up
the favorite-son delegations, especially James M. Cox's large Ohio bloc,
the stampede might begin. Perceiving this, Bryan rushed over to the
Mississippi delegation to remonstrate.[21]

Earlier, in a speech interrupted thirty times by cheers or hisses, the
Great Commoner had implored the convention "in the name of the
Son of God and Savior of the world" not to condemn the Klan by
name. The Democratic party, he warned, must not be diverted from
its common cause—the wresting of American society from control by
the giant corporations and capitalists. Victorious on that issue by the
narrowest of margins, he now strove to prevent the nomination of the
man he regarded as the servant of those same interests.[22]

"This convention must not nominate a Wall Street man," Bryan
shouted. "Mr. Davis is the lawyer of J. P. Morgan." Unruffled by someone's rejoinder, "And who is Mr. McAdoo the lawyer for?" he pointed
out what conservative leaders never did grasp: only the nomination of
a progressive could prevent Senator Robert M. La Follette's third-

party candidacy from drawing more votes from the Democrats than from the Republicans.[23]

In the press gallery that night, Bryan amplified his views. "I have no personal objection of any kind to Mr. Davis. He is a man of high character. So is Mr. Coolidge. There is no difference between them." After conceding that Davis had a perfect right to choose his own clients, he added that "when a man makes a decision, he takes all the accessories that go with it"; the presidency ought to go only to those who champion causes.[24]

Had Davis been an opportunist, or even truly ambitious, he would have seized the occasion to declare himself a progressive. But to his friends' distress, he said nothing, absolutely nothing. Modest, detached, tolerant of difference of view, he remained tacitly scornful of the bombast and deceit of the political arena, neither blind to nor greedy for the honor at stake.

McAdoo's lieutenants now took up Bryan's theme, while labor delegates warned that the nomination of Davis would cost the party a million votes between New England and the Alleghenies alone. On the thirty-fourth ballot, Mississippi went over to McAdoo. Five ballots later, Missouri, the only other full delegation to join Mississippi's original swing to Davis, also fell in behind Wilson's son-in-law. This dropped Davis from a high of 122 votes to 71, where he hovered until near the end. McAdoo rose to 499, 230 less than the two-thirds needed for nomination, and Smith held fairly steady at 320.[25]

And so the convention dragged on, day after day and night after night, the temperature in the mid-eighties, the humidity and cigar smoke almost stifling. Even the bunting and the 3500 flags seemed to be wilting. Tempers became frayed, charges and counter-charges more bitter, the confrontations between wets and drys, Catholics and Protestants, conservatives and progressives, more frequent and harsh. The Imperial Wizard of the Klan fell ill of ptomaine poisoning, and only the 1200 policemen assigned to the convention prevented the Texas delegation from burning a cross outside the building. A man was arrested for vending an anti-Catholic sheet outside the Garden's doors. The Smith forces admitted that they aimed to prolong the meeting until the McAdoo delegates' money ran out. ("Gentlemen," said the chairman of the pro-Smith Massachusetts delegation, "we've got to . . . pick a cheaper hotel or a more liberal candidate.") Tammany plied the driest of McAdoo's leaders with liquor. "Some of my best men have been hopelessly drunk ever since they landed in New York," the Californian complained.[26]

Nevertheless, McAdoo refused to release his delegates until the ninety-ninth ballot. He had known since spring that he could not hope to win two-thirds of the delegates, though he believed that he could carry a simple majority. Rather than harden lines before the balloting began, he had fastened on a bold, yet uniquely devious, plan to scuttle the two-thirds rule during the balloting. At the "psychological moment," after a deadlock had developed and after he had mounted a majority, his supporters would denounce "the obstructive minority" and move to drop the two-thirds rule. They would then overrule an unfavorable decision by the chair and drive through his nomination. This was the reason McAdoo could predict, as his total came within twenty votes of a majority on the sixty-ninth ballot, that "courage and consistency" would result in "inevitable victory." [27]

« V »

At Frank Polk's house on Sixty-sixth Street Davis passed the time playing Mah Jongg, writing personal notes, and chatting with delegates who dropped in to take his measure. Sometimes he went into the radio room to hear the roll call, but usually he waited for an assistant to bring him a tally. He showed little strain, and complained only once—he must go somewhere, do something, he burst out. A few nights later he fell asleep in a chair; awakening in obvious embarrassment, he remarked to one of the ladies that dozing in chairs "is never allowed in our house." Meanwhile he brooded over the convention's "suicidal" course. He suggested to one friend that he divert his prayers from him to the party. He confided to another that if he sent him his real thoughts he would be arrested for violating the postal laws. He told a third that if the Democratic party threw away its greatest opportunity since 1912, it would be "due primarily to the ambition of certain men [McAdoo and Smith] who are putting their own advancement before the party welfare." [28]

By the sixtieth ballot, on the Fourth of July, Davis had had enough. With characteristic highmindedness, he drafted a letter of withdrawal addressed to the head of the West Virginia delegation: "Manifestly, the situation is fraught with the gravest possibilities not only to the party, but to the country which it seeks to serve." He was anxious to avoid responsibility for continuing the deadlock, and he wanted to do all in his power to bring the convention "to a prompt, a fruitful and satisfactory end. . . . This is no time for the pursuit of personal ambition." [29]

The letter was never used. Polk may have persuaded Davis not to send it, or the West Virginia leaders may have decided to suppress it. At any rate, the West Virginians held firm when McAdoo made his last desperate bid on the sixty-ninth ballot. They also voted solidly for Davis following the failure of McAdoo and Smith to agree on a compromise choice. Yet their efforts to mobilize Davis' second-line support met only frustration. As Davis recalled, "every time I'd reach out into the eastern group personalized by Al Smith, the McAdoo group would run away from me. Then when I'd reach out and try to get the McAdoo group somewhere back into the corral, the Smith group would run away from me." [30]

For a half-dozen ballots near the end it seemed that Davis had no chance at all. Mississippi had broken for Ralston on the eighty-second ballot, and by the ninety-third the Indianan was leading Davis, 196¼ to 65. Confident that he had become a President-maker at last, Tom Taggart began to receive a stream of Smith and McAdoo men in his room high up in the Waldorf-Astoria. Suddenly, through the hum of low-pitched conversations, the telephone sounded. Ralston, back home, was on the line. "My family does not wish me to take it, and my own views coincide with theirs." [31]

Uncle Tom protested long and volubly, but to no avail. Pat Harrison then exclaimed that Davis would be the nominee. Others agreed. James Cox and Mayor Frank Hague of Jersey City had been "talking" Davis for some time, and Franklin D. Roosevelt, Al Smith, and George Brennan, the Illinois boss, were discussing him in Smith's quarters in the Biltmore at that very moment. Yet nothing was really settled. [32]

Sometime that same day, Tuesday, July 8, Carter Glass and Davis conferred privately for an hour and a half. Each said that he wanted the other to have the nomination, and each said that he would accept it himself only as a matter of duty. They agreed, so Glass reported, "that the platform was the most atrociously undemocratic document ever issued from a National Convention and that neither would accept the nomination on it without having it distinctly understood that we [sic] should be at liberty to discard anything . . . that was unsound." They also agreed that Davis should make his second try for the nomination at once, then throw his support to the Virginian. Glass then arranged what he thought would be a temporary shift of twelve of Virginia's twenty-four votes to Davis. ("In all of my career," McAdoo later wrote, "I have had nothing to grieve and shock me as much.") [33]

Yet even while he was conferring with Glass, Davis was gaining momentum on the floor. After McAdoo released his delegates, Davis moved ahead of him on the hundredth ballot, the last that night. Nevertheless, victory was far from certain. Most of the McAdoo people remained wary of Davis because of his Morgan connection and because McAdoo regarded him as the "tool" of his own Wall Street enemies; moreover, the Smith forces were planning to vote for Underwood, their sentimental second choice, before turning to Glass. This enabled the popular convention chairman, Senator Walsh of Montana, a dry, a Catholic, and a progressive, to develop significant strength. [34]

Red-eyed and spiritless, their shirts unlaundered and their suits unpressed, the delegates trooped into Madison Square Garden for the one hundred and first ballot on Wednesday morning, July 9. The cavernous hall was half empty—maids, chauffeurs, even boot-blacks were turning down tickets—and there were not enough alternates on hand to fill out the delegations. Listlessly, the balloting proceeded. Davis picked up a hundred or so votes, but Underwood added more than 180 and Walsh moved up to 98. Davis climbed another hundred on the next ballot, but so did Underwood. Even Tom Taggart, groping frantically for the right bandwagon, was beset by doubt; he gave ten of Indiana's thirty votes to Davis, ten more to Underwood, and ten to Glass. [35]

Now, for the first time, Carter Glass savored victory. The leaders of the New York, New Jersey, Ohio, Illinois, and several other wet, urban, conservative delegations had given him "direct authoritative word" that they would put their full strength behind him on the one hundred and fourth ballot. And Pennsylvania's industrialist-political boss, Joe Guffey, was in his room pledging the Keystone State's seventy-six votes to Glass when the one hundred and third ballot began. They were confident that Davis had already reached his peak. [36]

Down on the floor, however, the drys, KKK sympathizers, and pure McAdoo progressives feared that Underwood might slip in; they began in driblets, two delegates here, three or four there, to shift to Davis. Late on the one hundred and second ballot, Governor Pat N. Neff of Texas was recognized. Neff had been saying all along that McAdoo was "too oily" and Smith "too wet." Now he announced that Texas was switching from former Secretary of Agriculture Edward T. Mere-

dith of Iowa to "that great outstanding liberal, John W. Davis."
(Neff's statement, wrote Elmer Davis, "was news to a good many people who have supported John W. Davis because he seemed to them
representative of the finest type of conservative Democrat. But who can
refuse forty votes?") [37]

Taggart was now ready to make a running jump—almost. He gave
Davis twenty-five votes on the one hundred and third ballot, but doled
out five to Underwood, just in case. (Among the pro-Davis delegates in
the Indiana delegation was a young internationalist named Wendell
Willkie.) All at once, Davis was everybody's man. New York held off
temporarily to spare him the odium of receiving the decisive shove
from the most despised state in the convention. But Ohio, where Cox
had been slowly building up strength for Davis, gave him forty-one of
its forty-eight votes. Other delegations began to do likewise, and as
soon as the roll call was completed, half a dozen chairmen were
clamoring for recognition. Soon the leader of almost every delegation
that had not voted solidly for Davis was standing on his chair shout-
ing and waving at Walsh—all except Franklin D. Roosevelt, whose
"Happy Warrior" nominating speech for Al Smith two weeks earlier
had sparked a ninety-minute demonstration. As the crowd fell silent,
Walsh recognized Roosevelt, who raised his great body painfully,
leaned heavily on his crutches, his legs dangling almost uselessly, and
announced that New York cast sixty of its ninety votes for John W.
Davis. A few moments later Senator Claude E. Swanson of Virginia, a
handsome, heavily moustached man who could have passed for a mati-
nee idol, took the floor. "The wound of 1863 is closed," Swanson in-
toned. "Virginia falls in behind West Virginia. Righteousness and
peace have kissed each other; Virginia casts twenty-four votes for
John W. Davis." [38]

One last little drama remained. While Senator Walsh stiffly ignored
the frantic cries for recognition of the head of the Klan-ridden Georgia
delegation, Tom Taggart moved that Davis be nominated by acclamation. The motion carried with a roar, and at 3:25 Wednesday afternoon, July 9, the ninth day of the balloting and the fifteenth day of
the longest convention in history and the most discordant Democratic
assemblage since before the Civil War, John W. Davis was declared
the nominee for President of the United States. There followed a per-
functory demonstration which Walsh stopped with a wave of his gavel
fifteen minutes after it began.[39]

« VI »

The candidate did not even hear the final balloting. He was musing alone in the Polk library when his wife called from the stairwell: "You've won, you've been nominated." He put down his cigar, dashed up the stairs and embraced her, his face beaming. Late that night he almost broke down in the privacy of his bedroom. Taking Nell's hands in his own, he swore that the job was too big for him, that he could not go on with it. Then, recovering a little, he begged her to stand by him.[40]

Outside the house the street quickly filled with policemen, reporters, and newsreel cameramen. A few minutes later Davis received the newspapermen in the hall, chatting cordially with those he knew and answering questions with disarming candor until someone asked him how he could square his position on the League of Nations with the party platform. Before he could reply, Polk interjected that the question was "unfair at this time." Davis added that he would set forth his views in his acceptance speech. Then, wearing a fresh white shirt, a black tie with white figures, and a dark, pin-striped suit with a pair of tortoiseshell reading glasses protruding from the upper coat pocket, he stepped outside to face the camera. His expression was solemn until he responded graciously to a command to "smile like a President"; he at once looked younger than his fifty-one years. His wife appeared drained as she stood beside him, her pale skin contrasting starkly with her black satin dress and hat. She smiled weakly and said simply that she was "very proud and happy." Davis then went back in and told Carter Glass over the phone that he "fully understood" what the Virginian had done for him.[41]

Out in Locust Valley Davis' servants danced a jig; down in Clarksburg an impromptu crowd paraded joyously through the streets while giant firecrackers boomed in the surrounding hills; and in Charleston, West Virginia's Republican Governor issued a statement praising Davis' character. Elsewhere the reaction was more measured. Deep in the financial district of Manhattan, J. S. Fried and Company announced that the odds on Coolidge, eight to five the preceding week, had shot up to five to two, with few takers for Davis.[42]

Back at the Polk house that afternoon, Davis prepared his first campaign statement. "I shall hope," he said, "to rally . . . that great body of liberal, progressive and independent thought which believes that 'progress is motion, Government is action,' which detests privilege in whatever form and which does not wish the American people or their Government to stand still or retreat in the midst of a changing world." He closed with a direct appeal to the progressives who had so bitterly opposed his nomination: "There can be no compromise with reaction. Liberal principles must and will prevail. This is the mandate of the hour and I shall obey it." [43]

The professionals had their cue. Bryan, who had announced immediately that he would support Davis, told reporters the next afternoon that he had had a delightfully frank discussion with him and that Davis' first statement—"that there can be no compromise with reaction"—was important. James M. Cox asserted that Davis "was a platform in himself." And McAdoo's campaign manager announced that "from what has been told me by men who are themselves thoroughly progressive, I have every reason to feel that Mr. Davis is progressive." But McAdoo knew differently. A long, probing talk with the nominee on July 10 confirmed his view that he was an economic conservative. McAdoo commended Davis' integrity and promised his cordial support as he boarded ship for Europe two days later, but his words were not of a kind to inspire. There was promise in the Democratic party, he said, "if [its] . . . progressive influence is wisely and vigorously used." [44]

Al Smith's behavior was hardly more calculated to rally his friends around Davis. After scotching reports that he intended to campaign intensively for the nominee, he was persuaded to address the delegates. Then, in one of the most tasteless performances of the entire convention, he fired the first round of the campaign of 1928. For ten long minutes he described the "enlightened" achievements of his three gubernatorial administrations before calling Davis a "wonderful" candidate at the very end. "I am the leader of the democracy of this State," he finally declared, as a thunderous wave of applause rolled down from the galleries, "and . . . I shall take off my coat and vest" and work for him. It was a speech, wrote Smith's friendly biographer, Henry Pringle, that could have been written for Mayor Hylan.[45]

All that night and the following day Davis worked feverishly to bind the party's gaping wounds. Subordinating his personal predilections, he decided to select a progressive for the vice presidential nomination. He first asked Walsh, who would have been nominated by acclamation that afternoon had he not declared a recess and walked resolutely off the platform to a deafening chant: "WALSH, WE WANT

WALSH." The Montanan, who was caught between party loyalty, his desire to be reelected to the Senate, and his belief that Davis' nomination had been a tragic mistake, rejected the offer. Davis then turned to Meredith, who earlier had been delighted at the prospect of running with McAdoo. He too refused.[46]

The situation became acute when Newton D. Baker also backed away. Governor William E. Sweet of Colorado and Huston Thompson, then a Federal Trade Commissioner, were considered, but they were dropped because of opposition within the Colorado delegation. Taggart, ever the optimist, suggested his fellow Indianan, former Vice President Thomas R. Marshall, a seventy-year-old arch conservative best remembered for the pronouncement, "What America needs is a good five-cent cigar." By midnight, when Davis went before the convention to make a brief speech, no decision had been made, though Bryan's younger brother, Charles, the popular and progressive Governor of Nebraska, was being discussed increasingly.[47]

As Davis and his entourage walked onto the speaker's platform, Robert Woolley slipped in beside Polk. Putting his arm around his shoulder, he whispered, "For the Love of God and the good of the Democratic Party, don't permit anyone from east of the Mississippi River to be selected. . . . the situation calls for Bryan." Polk agreed: "Boy, you are dead right. . . . Bryan is the man we will name." [48]

Early that morning Davis decided on the Great Commoner's brother. A reasonable choice on one level, it was self-destructive on others. It undermined Davis' greatest asset—his reputation for honest independence. It also terrified Eastern conservatives, mocked Western progressives, who felt that he was trying to buy them off, and antagonized unnumbered Catholics who identified the name Bryan with the Ku Klux Klan. Al Smith later recalled that during the campaign "not hundreds but probably thousands of people, particularly women, asked me if there was any way they could vote for Davis and not for Bryan." Carter Glass was more acerbic. "The one haunting thing," he wrote, ". . . is . . . that a man like John Davis would consent to have on the ticket with him a fellow like 'Brother Charlie,' a cheap edition of the party's most pestiferous harlequin . . . his support is not worth a bauble . . . it will weaken Davis in those debatable Eastern States which he must carry in order to be elected. The nomination of Bryan was a transparently foolish attempt to capture States in the West which are as certain to go to La Follette as election day is sure to come." [49]

The only good sign was the convention's enthusiastic response to Davis' brief speech at midnight. "He said little," Elmer Davis wrote. "He had no need to say more. In an eight-minute talk he . . . did all he could . . . to silence the sectional and racial and religious antagonism which had been stirred during the long fight in the convention." [50]

CHAPTER 15

The Presidential
Campaign of 1924

*Mr. Davis is an honorable and likable gentleman; he has made a skill-
ful, persuasive campaign which is perhaps the outstanding personal
achievement of the contest; but he has shown throughout that he is
. . . an instinctive conservative.*

"NEW REPUBLIC"

"Thanks," Davis said to a friend the night of his nomination, "but you
know what it's worth." He was doomed from the beginning, and at
that moment he knew it. Long before the disaster at the Garden an
aura of granite-like integrity had settled in on Calvin Coolidge; any effort to link the President with the Harding scandals was destined to
fail. Furthermore, the third-party candidacy of Senator Robert M. La
Follette threatened to draw off more Democratic than Republican
votes. Worse still, it was not in Davis' or anyone else's power to unify
the Democratic party. No endorsement of Davis by McAdoo, no tribute to his humanity by Al Smith, no characterization of him as a progressive by William Jennings Bryan could alter the central fact: the
party was irreparably split on every important issue of the day—the
Ku Klux Klan, Prohibition, the League of Nations, and most of the
economic questions that fell under the rubric of progressivism. Wise
and sensitive leadership might hold the Democratic organization together, but for more than that one could not hope.[1]

« I »

From the moment the weary delegates had turned to him on the one hundred and third ballot, Davis was torn by conflicting advice. He was urged to concentrate on the Republican East, on the theory that La Follette would cut deeply into Harding's 1920 ethnic support. He was told to write off the East and campaign vigorously in the old Bryan states in the Middle West. "We're going to win this campaign between the Alleghenies and the Sierras," Robert Woolley assured him. He was advised to stay out of Minnesota, the Dakotas, and other states La Follette might take from Coolidge. He was warned not to hammer the Wisconsin Senator too hard. And he was urged "to train . . . heavy guns" on him. Westerners, wrote A. Mitchell Palmer, feared that an attack on La Follette would drive progressives out of the Democratic party; that in itself, the former Attorney General added, "would justify doing it." [2]

The result was irresolution and confusion. "Davis . . . doesn't act with the decision and promptness he should," Woolley was soon complaining. Instead of making McAdoo's man, Daniel Roper, national chairman, Davis offered the position to Frank Polk. After Polk declined, he deliberated a full week before selecting Clem Shaver, the inarticulate and easygoing lawyer-promoter from Lost Creek, West Virginia, who had served him so devotedly at San Francisco in 1920. [3]

Meanwhile, Davis severed his partnership and resigned his directorships in the United States Rubber Company, American Telephone and Telegraph, the National Bank of Commerce, and one or two other corporations. Then, before leaving for Seven Hundred Acre Island in Penobscot Bay, he arranged for Gordon Auchincloss to establish campaign headquarters in the Murray Hill Hotel. Allen Wardwell handled finances temporarily, and Montgomery Angell, a young associate in the firm, coordinated the numerous campaign committees. Another young associate, Harold Hathaway, answered routine mail, imitating the candidate's signature almost perfectly.

In Maine, Davis worked on campaign plans between daily rounds of golf for almost two weeks. He conferred with a stream of politicians and men of affairs, mainly Easterners. He employed William Howard Taft's throat specialist to accompany him on his campaign train. He sent a thoughtful request for advice and information to all Democratic members of Congress, all delegates to the convention, and numerous private citizens, especially lawyers. And he asked several of his former Washington assistants to do research on legal questions. Norman Davis, former Acting Secretary of State, advised him on foreign policy, as did John Foster Dulles to a much lesser extent. Gray Silver, head of the conservative American Farm Bureau, served as the principal adviser on agriculture. Between conferences and exchanges of letters with these and many other men, Davis drafted his formal speech of acceptance for delivery in Clarksburg the second week of August.[4]

The first untoward incident of the campaign occurred in Maine. Asked by reporters to comment on the traumatic battle over the Klan at Madison Square Garden, Davis cavalierly replied: "It wasn't my party. The fight was over before the movement for my nomination began. The court is closed and I having nothing to say on the matter." His words spread consternation throughout the East. "I shivered myself when I saw it [the interview]," Polk wrote Walter Lippmann, who had fired off an anguished protest. "I have been warning him because I thought something might slip. He has been rather too good-natured and not firm enough in refusing to let them quote him in any way."[5]

Hard on the Klan incident came a contretemps with President Samuel Gompers of the American Federation of Labor. Despite the Democratic platform committee's rejection of the A. F. of L.'s planks, Gompers had been unsympathetic at first to La Follette's Progressive party movement. Only after McAdoo's drive had collapsed and La Follette had come out for the complete abolition of the labor injunction did he decide to endorse the Wisconsin Senator formally, and then he did so in the persuasion that a strong showing by La Follette would force the Democratic party to reorganize along "constructive, progressive" lines or suffer extinction.

The more progressive labor elements had been bitterly disappointed by Davis' nomination. Frank P. Walsh, the former co-chairman of the War Labor Board, felt that he had been the "most reactionary" man in the convention, and Daniel Tobin of the Teamsters professed to see no difference between Davis and Coolidge. Nevertheless, energetic action might have kept the A. F. of L. neutral. Many Federation leaders had intimate ties with Tammany, and some held office in the Smith administration. This group took vehement exception to Gompers' plan. Gompers himself seems to have had second thoughts as his executive council meeting drew near, and he indicated that he was anxious to talk to Davis.

The matter had special importance because of the huge swing of ethnic-labor voters to Harding in 1920. Much of this vote had shifted back to the Democrats in 1922, and it devolved on Davis to hold it. Gompers, who was seriously ill, wanted Davis to meet him in New York before the executive council met on July 31, but Davis declined to interrupt his "very-much needed rest" in Maine. (He believed that the A. F. of L. would endorse La Follette regardless of what he himself did or said.) He suggested instead that Gompers send him a list of subjects labor was interested in "at the moment." This Gompers peremptorily refused to do.

Meanwhile, Davis had former Secretary of Labor William B. Wilson send Gompers a long, favorable review of his labor record as a Congressman and as Solicitor General. Wilson's letter failed to move the A. F. of L. leader; over the protests of Vice President William Green and others, he drove through an endorsement of La Follette at the executive council meeting on July 31. He then wrote Davis that Wilson's letter had been too late to be effective. He also denied that Davis had originally drafted the liberal labor provisions of the Clayton Act. A more measured closing statement illumined his own and the labor movement's real grievance: "The executive council . . . has weighed in the balance . . . [Davis'] later utterances and courses, associations and training." [6]

The incident exposed the West Virginian on both flanks. Conservatives chided him for his "readiness" to make concessions to unions; progressives quipped that he was the type of candidate who had to "stop in mid-campaign and prove by the book that he [had] served in the cause of labor." Although Davis was nettled, he avoided a direct confrontation by having Wilson refute Gompers' misrepresentation of his record. At the same time, he ignored the demand of Norman Thomas, the Socialist candidate for Governor of New York, that he protest the "illegal evictions" of striking coal miners from their homes in West Virginia. [7]

One more sharp blow fell during these first few weeks. On July 19 Montana's junior Senator, Democrat Burton K. Wheeler, became La Follette's running mate. The maverick Montanan had won an early reputation for courage by defending miners against the mammoth Anaconda Copper Company. Later, as a United States Attorney, he had dismissed what he termed the company's effort to make law enforcement agencies "ready accessories in putting down strikes and other threats to their feudal sovereignty." He had also opposed the "persecution" of German-Americans during the war and had refused to indict members of the Industrial Workers of the World on flimsy pretexts. In 1920 he was defeated for Governor after being run out of one company town at rifle point, but two years later he won election to the United States Senate. There his brilliant prosecution of Attorney General Harry Daugherty brought him to prominence in the spring of 1924.

Wheeler had accepted La Follette's mandate with a flourish. "I do not abandon my faith in the democracy of Thomas Jefferson. I shall give my support . . . to those candidates . . . who have proved their fidelity to the interest of the people." These included neither the Republicans, "who frankly admit their reactionary standpat policies, [nor] the Democratic candidate who may claim in well-chosen phrases that he is a progressive but whose training and constant associations belie any such pretension." Wheeler's popularity among miners and German-Americans stood to offset that of Charles Bryan; furthermore, his reputation as a "people's lawyer" put Davis' image as Morgan's counsel in sharper relief than ever.[8]

To compound Davis' difficulties, Shaver was proving a singularly ineffective chairman. He deferred reorganization of the National Committee for three critical weeks, was slow to set up division headquarters in New York, Washington, and Chicago, and never did establish any headquarters on the West Coast. He insisted on serving as campaign manager himself, refused to appoint a publicity chairman until very late, and neglected to coordinate the state speakers' bureaus in the interim. He also exposed Davis' predictions of victory to ridicule by announcing that the election would be decided in the House of Representatives. In addition, Shaver allowed Al Smith's friends to dominate the selection of vice chairmen and to supplant McAdoo's man, David L. Rockwell, with Mayor Frank Hague of Jersey City. As Robert Lansing remarked, "no party ever had a more flabby and useless [national committee]. . . . I cannot think of what was done, or rather what was not done, without indignation and contempt."[9]

A month after the nomination, headquarters in New York were still in near chaos. Records were lost or misplaced in a move from the Murray Hill Hotel to the Belmont, and letters, telegrams, and even long distance telephone messages were failing to reach the candidate. "Nothing has yet been done there, everything is upside down," complained Claude Bowers, on leave from the *World*. "I have no hopes of anything from Shaver. Frank Polk and Norman Davis are not practical politicians nor organizers, and unless some of the old war horses get into harness I am afraid we shall enter the campaign in worse shape than ever before." Six weeks later Woolley found conditions in Washington just as bad. "Davis is terribly worried," he told Colonel House. "He is a wonderful candidate, but his Chairman should have been the recipient of the sap bucket of Coolidge." Chief Justice Taft, who, privately, remained true to his Republican faith, was relieved. "The truth is," he confided to his brother Henry, "that John Davis is too good a candidate for the Democracy to succeed with." [10]

Only one small advance punctuated this dreary string of setbacks. Late in the summer Al Smith reluctantly agreed to stand for reelection as Governor. Like Davis in 1920, Smith yearned for financial security. More important, he was still smarting from charges that Tammany had knifed Cox and Roosevelt in 1920 when he led the national ticket in New York by nearly a million votes; his advisers feared that another "runaway" would reopen the wounds of Madison Square Garden and assure Smith's "crucifixion" in 1928. Davis understood Smith's plight, but he also knew that his only chance of carrying New York was on the Governor's coattails. Brushing aside warnings that Smith's involvement would dramatize the Klan issue and weaken his own candidacy in the Midwest, he persuaded the Governor to run. "I told him that there would be no room for misunderstanding, least of all on my part." [11]

Smith's support proved nominal. He and his wife received the Davises at Albany, and Tammany staged the most gigantic rally in its history at the end of the campaign. But after making two or three speeches for Davis in New England, the Governor canceled the remainder of his schedule because of "rheumatism." [12]

« II »

While Davis worked feverishly on his acceptance speech ("it is giving me no small concern because of the conflicting advice I receive"), his friends fretted over his lack of forcefulness. Everyone was captivated by his graciousness, sincerity, and modesty. "In all the bitterness of the campaign," letter after letter said later, "I never heard one word against you as a man." Yet, as Franklin D. Roosevelt suggested, following a "charming and beautifully expressed" talk by Davis at a Duchess County picnic, he would have to be more dramatic on the stump. Reports that Eastern workingmen were defecting to La Follette were pouring in daily; and in the movie houses on the lower East Side talking newsreels of La Follette gesticulating forcefully were drawing cheers, while those of Davis, dignified and stiff, were evoking boos and hisses. Even within Democratic headquarters Davis seemed shy and embarrassed, unable to establish rapport with the Irish workingmen who were mustered in to shake his hand. (He did handle one situation with aplomb. One day at headquarters, Davis, Bowers, and Arthur Krock walked into the office of a party leader. As they opened the door, the leader's secretary slipped off his lap. Seemingly unperturbed, he said, "How are you, Mr. President?" "Fine," Davis replied, "but I think you had better go on with your dictation.") [13]

The acceptance ceremony at Clarksburg on August 11 confirmed the inner circles' fears. A huge and responsive crowd welcomed Davis at the station on Saturday afternoon, August 9. Standing bareheaded in an open car, his face beaming and his arms rising and falling in greeting, he was driven between throngs of people who lined the sidewalks four and five deep and called out to him by his first name. The motorcade wended its way to the large house on Lee Street where his sister Emma lived alone. Five thousand people swarmed over the grounds as Davis walked slowly up the steep row of steps to the veranda, looked down with glistening eyes, and faltered momentarily. He then made a few gracious remarks and went inside. The next morning he attended services in the little Presbyterian church his father had served so faithfully and on whose board of trustees he himself had sat since his father's death.

On Monday night Senator Thomas J. Walsh formally notified Davis of his nomination before a throng of 50,000 which was driven to cover by a drenching rain before the candidate could complete his response. "Your practice," the Montana Senator said, in words written by Davis, "has been general, one day speaking for some great and possibly ruthless corporation, the next for an impoverished contender against the massed wealth of such." Davis then began a long address:

> You will understand . . . the feelings which have prompted me to fix our meeting at this spot in the hills of West Virginia. These are the hills that cradled me and to which as boy and man I lifted up my eyes for help. In this soil rest four generations of my people—artisans, tradesmen, farmers and a sprinkling of the professions, laborers all, who played in simple fashion their appointed parts in the life of this community. Among them now lie those who gave me life, and to whose high precept and example I owe all that I have ever been and all that I can hope to be.

He went on to affirm his support of the party platform, to report that he had severed his connection "with the honorable gentlemen" who were his law partners, and to declare that he had "no clients today but the Democratic Party and, if they will it so, the people of the United States."

The entire speech was felicitously phrased and smoothly delivered; even *The Nation* conceded that Woodrow Wilson "at his best seldom surpassed [Davis'] . . . beauty and occasional eloquence." Yet his words had none of the moral fervor that had distinguished the late President's addresses. Only on corruption did Davis speak with the indignation that sears; only on the tariff and the League of Nations did he display real perception. Commentator after commentator remarked on his lack of force, his vagueness, his failure to convey a sense of mission. The Democratic candidate, independent observers tended to agree, had been charming rather than convincing. As *The Nation* concluded, there was not "one syllable . . . to recall Woodrow Wilson's 'New Freedom' with its passionate and moving appeal to rise against the big-business mastery of the Government of the United States." Even Davis' old Clarksburg friends were disappointed. "He made a Republican kind of speech," Charles Johnson sadly reflected years later.[14]

Davis returned to New York in deep trouble. His silence on the Klan was being contrasted with La Follette's condemnation of the organization five days earlier. The Smith people, growled Claude Bowers, "are putting us all down as Klansmen and practically all the Irish and Catholic papers are denouncing Davis as one." Letters-to-the-editor in the New York *World* were running fifty to one against Davis. And reports of a massive swing of Catholic workingmen to La Follette were pouring in from all over New England.[15]

La Follette's own denunciation of the Klan had been made under duress. The Wisconsin Senator agreed with Bryan that "the combined power of the private monopoly system over the political and economic life of the American people" was the central issue of the campaign. He was also aware that the Klan-ridden supporters of McAdoo comprised one of his greatest potential sources of Democratic votes in the West. His personally dictated platform, adopted a full week after the epochal struggle over the KKK at the Garden, had ignored the Klan. Nor had he mentioned it in the ensuing month despite a deluge of appeals by liberals and their allies of the moment, the Roman Catholics. But on August 5, prodded by the *Irish World* and Robert P. Scripps of the newspaper chain, La Follette resentfully announced that he would say again what anyone familiar with his record already knew: "I am unalterably opposed to the evident purposes of the secret organization known as the Ku Klux Klan, as disclosed by its public acts." [16]

La Follette's action put Davis in a bind. Samuel Untermyer was reporting rampant restiveness among Catholics, Jews, and "the best citizenship of the Protestant faith"; Jim Farley was saying that, if Davis did not denounce the Klan, many Democrats would turn to La Follette; scores of other prominent Easterners were imploring Davis to speak out. Numerous Southerners and Midwesterners were warning that "an unjust attack on the Knights of the Ku Klux Klan" would drive to Coolidge the only states the Democrats could possibly carry.[17]

Davis had not yet made up his mind when he learned that the Republican vice presidential candidate, Charles G. Dawes, planned to denounce the Klan on August 23.* This meant that Davis would have to face the question constantly on the stump. "Even 'Cautious Cal,' " he explained, "would have been compelled to do so if he had so much as shown his nose outside the White House." He decided to speak out in New Jersey on August 21. The night before the speech a representative of the Grand Kleagle handed him a letter offering to deliver the solid South in return for silence. "Is that all?" Davis asked after reading the letter. "Yes," the emissary replied. Davis then tore up the letter. "You may say there is no answer," he said. Before a huge crowd of roaring Democrats at Sea Girt the next day, Davis condemned the Klan:

> If any organization, no matter what it chooses to be called, whether it be KKK or any other name, raises the standard of racial and religious prejudices, or attempts to make racial origins or religious beliefs the test of fitness of public office, it does violence to the spirit of American institutions and must be condemned by all those who believe as I do in American ideals.

He then appealed (in vain) to Coolidge to join him in removing prejudice from the debate.[18]

Davis was in a rare state of exuberance afterwards. He could hardly wait to hear from Polk, who had urged him to face the issue squarely. "I wonder what Frank will say," he said to his bodyguard. "When will Frank get the New York papers?" [19]

Thereafter Davis, alone among the candidates, attacked the Klan

---

* Dawes' denunciation was so equivocal that it almost constituted an endorsement.

regularly, sometimes in his prepared remarks, more often in replies to carefully planted hecklers. His forthright stand kept many Catholics and Jews loyal to the party. It also won over a sizable minority of Negroes in New York and Indiana. In both states Davis came out for equal rights, and in Harlem he capitalized heavily on his arguments in the Alabama peonage and Oklahoma grandfather clause cases. Negroes received him with special warmth in Missouri, where the Klan was strong and pressure to remain silent heavy. They gave him a three-foot-high silver loving cup:

> A TOKEN OF APPRECIATION
> PRESENTED TO THE HON. JOHN W. DAVIS
> BY A GRATEFUL PEOPLE . . .
> FOR HIS MATCHLESS EFFORTS IN FIGHTING
> THE CAUSE OF HUMAN RIGHTS of the NEGROES
> OF WEST VIRGINIA and the NATION.[20]

Just as Davis had feared, his attacks on the Klan infuriated many of the McAdoo people. "His untimely and unnecessary denunciation has lost him strength," grumbled former Assistant Secretary of State Breckinridge Long. Davis' entire campaign has been "Tammanyized," snarled another McAdoo man. Many West Virginians believed that his anti-Klan statements cost him his native state. "The KKK played hell with us here," Doc Johnston reported. For reasons unexplained, however, the Imperial Wizard vented his spleen on La Follette alone. He labeled the Wisconsin Senator "the arch enemy of the nation" and announced in mid-campaign that Klansmen were free to vote for either Coolidge or Davis.[21]

Courageous as Davis' speech was in the context of the campaign, it failed to satisfy those reformers who regarded the Klan as merely one of the uglier manifestations of the race problem. The Democratic candidate, conceded *The Nation*, had spoken "brave and welcome words about race prejudice." It wondered, however, how far he was prepared to go:

> Mr. Davis waxes eloquent as to the Constitution. . . . But, like everybody else, Mr. Davis knows that sacred document to be violated constantly in the disfranchisement of millions of Americans because of the color of their skins. Will he have us understand that if elected he will right that wrong, that he will help cut down the Southern representation in Congress as the Constitution specifies shall be done? [22]

Davis never addressed that larger question. (Neither did La Follette, Coolidge, nor any subsequent presidential candidate until Truman.) Although he was certain that his speeches had hurt his cause by driving tens of thousands of Klansmen into the party of Lincoln, he believed, understandably, that he had fulfilled his moral responsibilities. "I shall always be proud that I lined up where I did." [23]

Davis' general declarations on civil liberties also evoked a cynical response. Both *The Nation* and the *New Republic* contrasted his "vindication of the . . . Constitution as the . . . invincible guardian of the rights of the individual" with the open assault on radicalism made by elements of the American Bar Association during his presidency of that organization. They also assailed him for voicing conventional objections to criticism of the courts, while failing to remind the bar of its obligation to defend peaceable assemblage and free speech. Sardonically, *The Nation* congratulated him on his sudden "discovery" of the tradition of free speech after being "tongue-tied" throughout the "gallant struggle" of the American Civil Liberties Union to defend individual rights in postwar America:

> Let him denounce by name the public officials and the mining companies in his own West Virginia who have made of democracy in that state a mockery and a sham. Let him denounce the mayors in those Gary-owned Pennsylvania towns who today refuse to permit meetings to be held if they do not like their purpose.[24]

« III »

Davis' effort to conciliate labor continued to meet sullen indifference or active resentment. Robert Szold and others prepared a list of his pro-labor arguments as Solicitor General, and he himself often mentioned the Adamson eight-hour and the child labor cases in his speeches. Yet no review of his prewar record could offset the fact that he had become "Morgan's lawyer"; no affirmation of the rights of "free contract" or "voluntary agreement" could convince labor that he would thwart management's (and, to some extent, the judiciary's) grand offensive against unions. Repeatedly, however, he invoked such phrases. In his Labor Day address at Wheeling he also rebuked La Follette by implication for proposing federal support of the organizing process. "We cannot and should not take a paternalistic attitude [toward] grown men and women," he declared.[25]

The progressive Wall Street lawyer and McAdoo intimate Thomas L. Chadbourne read Davis' remarks in disbelief. He wired:

TAKE IT FROM ME, JUDGE GARY HIMSELF NEVER EXPRESSED HIS ANTAGONISM TO UNIONISM MORE. . . . AS A MATTER OF FACT HE HAS EXPRESSED IT TIME AND AGAIN IN ALMOST IDENTICAL LANGUAGE. . . . IF YOU ARE EXPRESSING YOUR WELL CONSIDERED CONVICTIONS THERE IS NOTHING MORE FOR ME TO SAY. . . . WE ARE TWENTY-FIVE YEARS BEYOND THE TIME WHEN LIBERTY OF CONTRACT BETWEEN THE INDIVIDUAL EMPLOYEE AND INDIVIDUAL EMPLOYER CAN BE ADVOCATED BY ANY PARTY WITH A LIBERAL INSTINCT.[26]

The trouble was that Davis *was* expressing his "well considered convictions." As Chadbourne perceived, these were ill-adapted to the harsh realities of the labor movement's struggle for survival, much less its growth. Davis had failed to mention the bloody repression of the attempt to organize steel in 1919. He had said nothing of the more than one hundred lives lost in the United Mine Workers' abortive effort to organize southern West Virginia during the so-called Mingo War of 1919–23. He had passed over a half-dozen Supreme Court decisions that stripped the anti-injunction clause of the Clayton Act of its effectiveness and virtually legalized management's campaign to destroy the labor movement. He had made no reference to the collapse of the bituminous unions. And he had seemed unaware of the fact that, at the moment he spoke, 10 per cent or more of the industrial labor force was unemployed. Except for pro forma endorsements of the child labor amendment and the Democratic plan to reconstitute the pro-management Railway Labor Board, he had said little that Coolidge did not also say in *his* Labor Day address. Only in a tepid criticism of the abuse of the injunction—one that lacked the moral and intellectual force of his memorable indictment of 1912—did he go beyond the President. "If the legislation already passed is not sufficient guidance in this matter," he said, "we must write it in plain terms." As sophisticated businessmen realized, this meant that the Democratic candidate posed no threat to the established order; soon afterwards the superintendent of a Western railroad urged all his agents and foremen to form *either* Coolidge or Davis clubs among their workmen. Yet as Harold Ickes perceived, there was a subtle difference. "I will not vote for the political bell-hop who is . . . masquerading as President," Ickes wrote Hiram Johnson. "Davis is at least an upstanding man and when he serves the House of Morgan he charges for his services. Coolidge is an even more facile servant of the same master, but he does it for nothing." [27]

If the Labor Day address was the measure of Davis' bedrock conservatism (or nineteenth-century liberalism), it was also the gauge of his personal integrity. By then he well knew that La Follette's full-throated call for the outright abolition of the labor injunction was exerting a powerful pull on workingmen. But for Davis the formalist, such a solution was worse than none at all; just as he had refused in 1912 to "tear down the pillars of the temple" on labor's demand, so did he refuse at this critical juncture to trade on his conscience.[28]

As it turned out, Davis' broad generalizations gave the old-line Democrats in the A. F. of L. hierarchy the rationale they needed to defy Gompers, who was then near death. Fearful that the spill-over to the gubernatorial line from a heavy vote for La Follette would hurt Al Smith, the Central Trades and Labor Council of Greater New York rescinded the endorsement of the Wisconsin Senator five days before the election. For the Railroad Brotherhoods and some of the more militant union leaders, however, there was no backtracking. They derided Davis' contention that "the upright lawyer sells his services but never his soul." They ridiculed the notion that his corporate directorships and retainers neither delimited his freedom nor shaped his practice. And they hit him again and again for his appeal in the *Coronado* case, his defense of the Pennsylvania Coal Company's "right" to mine beneath workers' houses, and his briefs for higher rates for the New York Telephone Company. They also attacked him for his indirect involvement in the Wilkerson Injunction: "He comes out to [the Midwest] . . . to make a Progressive talk to the common people of this country and denounces injunctions when he himself was a director of the Santa Fe Railroad at the time it appealed for an injunction against the working men during their strike."[29]

McAdoo, sulking first in Europe and then in The Johns Hopkins Hospital, where he underwent a minor operation, might have helped. But he was under open pressure from the railroad unions to avoid damaging La Follette, and in any event he was too bitter to view Davis' predicament with less than ill-concealed pleasure. "I am not responsible for the present situation," he wrote, "and there is really no reason why I should respond to the Macedonian cries for help from those who created this situation. . . . They have finally discovered that the strength that my nomination would have brought them is the very strength that is necessary to victory."[30]

More often McAdoo attributed his silence to policy differences. Davis was a fine fellow, he wrote Mrs. Woodrow Wilson, but he disagreed with him on almost every issue. "What is there I can say for him?" he asked his shipboard companions en route home in September. Davis' views were so opposed to his own, he told the Democratic National Committee, after reading a sheaf of his speeches, that he could not campaign for him with conviction.[31]

Still, McAdoo had to make a gesture. Following a personal request by Davis, he released a long, tortuous letter which proved more redolent of respect for La Follette than of support for the Democratic candidate. The Wisconsin Senator, said McAdoo, "represents a vibrant and wholesome movement in our public life . . . and deserves admiration and respect for the courageous fight he has made against entrenched privilege and the invisible forces of government and for the fight he is now making to drive the corrupt and incompetent Republican administration out of power." Nevertheless, La Follette had no chance to win, and Davis did. The Democratic platform was a distinctly progressive document, and, as championed by Davis and Bryan, it was "worthy of the confidence and support of the American electorate." The letter fooled no one, including Davis. McAdoo, he remarked in uncommonly acid tones, had been disloyal and treacherous.[32]

With William Jennings Bryan it was different. The Great Commoner scrawled friendly letters of advice, tried to create an impression of unity, and campaigned for six weeks on the West Coast at his own expense. He wrote Davis that his denunciation of the Klan was "admirable," and he said as much to newspapermen. He suppressed his disappointment when Davis gave in to the urban bosses and jettisoned a plan to bring Charles Bryan East for a few speeches. He even overlooked Davis' tacit rejection of his plea to make monopoly the key issue. ("We must protect competition *wherever competition is possible*," Bryan urged. "& favor govt. ownership *wherever competition is not possible*.") He was also gracious after the election. The Democrats, he wrote Shaver, did as well as could be expected, given their lack of editorial support in the North and West. "We had no way of getting before the public the splendid speeches made by Mr. Davis." [33]

Everywhere Bryan went he evoked the old enthusiasm and affection among the truly faithful. As Davis' representative to Charles Bryan's notification ceremony reported, "Both men and women were saying: 'From where I sat, the light shining on his face as he pronounced his blessing, W. J. looked saintly.'" Even columnist David Lawrence was impressed. "Mr. Bryan is speaking to enormous crowds. His powerful voice, his eloquence, his dynamic personality are still as fascinating as they were years ago. . . . He has kept many wavering [Democrats] from going to La Follette." [34]

« IV »

By campaign's end, Davis had delivered some seventy formal speeches, had made countless whistle-stop appearances, and had covered 12,000 miles. He made two trips into the Middle West, one of which was extended to Denver and Cheyenne. He wrote off most of New England, though he spoke once in Rhode Island. Otherwise he concentrated on the Middle Atlantic region, Maryland, Tennessee, Kentucky, and especially West Virginia, where he spoke four times. He felt that the regimen was too arduous for women and believed, in any case, that they should not participate in politics; neither his wife nor his daughter accompanied him. He lived in a Pullman car with his throat specialist, Dr. J. J. Richardson; his secretary, Harold Hathaway; and William F. Nye, his colorful bodyguard and factotum. Senator Key Pittman and John E. Nevin, a publicity man, traveled with him, as did his partner Edwin S. S. Sunderland. Norman Davis was on and off the train, Cordell Hull made the first trip into the Midwest, and numerous state and local leaders came aboard at various points. A number of reporters, several typists, and two telegraph operators rounded out the entourage.[35]

Davis drafted most of his speeches and edited all of them; ghostwritten speeches, he said, "were a fraud on the public." He usually limited them to between fifteen and twenty double-spaced pages, which took about half an hour to deliver. His impromptu rear-platform talks were rife with homely illustrations, and his ability to catnap between stops kept them fresh. Both his diction and his literary allusions in the formal speeches often went over the heads of his audiences (Adlai Stevenson was later compared to Davis), but his sincerity and idealism were transparent:

> We believe that at bottom the vital issue in this campaign is whether America is to continue to blunder in a morass of material aims and purposes, or whether, guided by the torch of high ideals, she is to enter into the fulness of that peace and prosperity, and reap the benefits of that enduring brotherhood which are the just inheritance of a nation exalted by righteousness. Such is our faith and such our purpose. We join issue for them under the old battle-cry that comes ringing through

the centuries: "God defend the right!" I cannot be otherwise than confident of the outcome.[36]

Yet almost everything Davis said or did not say offended one or the other of the party's dissident elements. Many observers felt that his internationalism was his chief qualification for the presidency, and he yearned to call unequivocally for American entry into the League of Nations. But the rejection of Baker's plank at the convention, the seething resentment of German-Americans, and his own feeling that he must form a consensus all militated against it. He also believed strongly that, by making the League a partisan issue in 1920, Wilson had given a veneer of plausibility to the notion that that election had been a referendum on American membership. He therefore confined himself to an educational campaign—an informed, prescient, and high-minded one, but an educational campaign nonetheless.[37]

Even this reasoned approach antagonized many isolationists and some internationalists. Irish-Americans smiled wryly over the former Ambassador's enthusiasm for the new Irish Free State. ("Ireland, I rejoice to say, has shaken off her long subjection, and once more a nation has made her entry into the League the sign of her glorious rebirth.") German-Americans were unmoved by Davis' assurance that Germany would soon take the seat in the League of Nations to which "she is rightly entitled." And Mrs. Woodrow Wilson was so disappointed by his failure to repudiate the platform's call for a referendum on the League that she refused to write a public letter of support. As Hamilton Fish Armstrong, editor of *Foreign Affairs*, sadly and perhaps too harshly concluded, Davis' effort to conciliate the isolationists was "more opportunistic than inspiring." [38]

This left little to differentiate Democratic from Republican policy. Foreign trade, of course, remained, and on it Davis spoke with insight and imagination; his forthright calls for tariff reduction were the most compelling statements of his entire campaign. Nevertheless, the Washington Naval Conference, the Dawes Plan for scaling down German reparations, and Coolidge's call for membership in the World Court all blurred the G.O.P.'s isolationist image. Forced thus to grasp for minor issues, Davis charged that foreign policy was in the hands of a Senate minority "to whose slightest nod both President and Secretary have bowed without complaint." He also criticized the Administration for failing to maintain naval parity with Great Britain.[39]

As for the rest, Davis ignored La Follette's (and Bryan's) demand for

a referendum before the nation could enter a war "not begun by
enemy attack." He failed, as did Coolidge, to link German reparations
with the Allies' war debts to the United States. And although he endorsed the Democratic plank on Philippine independence, he paid no
attention to the La Follette group's bitter, specific, and somewhat over-
drawn indictment of the Morgan firm's support of "oil diplomacy" in
Mexico and "financial imperialism" elsewhere in Latin America.[40]

Davis also passed over direct comment on the restrictionist immigration law that had been enacted earlier in the year by an overwhelming
bipartisan majority. Pressed by Poles, Czechs, and others to condemn
it *in toto,* he responded with ringing affirmations of the rights of those
already admitted. "I don't think that Americanism is a question of the
length of our stay in this country," he said to an Italian-American audience in Providence. "What are all of us but immigrants!" [41]

A single sentence in one of Davis' speeches summed up that uncritical acceptance of the existing social and economic order which made
him the despair of the progressives: "There is nothing in the purpose
of the party I represent that holds for any legitimate business in this
country any threat or menace whatever." Repeatedly, to be sure, he
condemned Republican subsidies to business with the traditional
Democratic rhetoric against "special privilege." Late in the campaign,
furthermore, he censured the G.O.P. for indifference to heavy unemployment in the Northern textile industry. But he blamed the unemployment on high prices induced by the tariff rather than on low
wages and child labor in the South, and he said nothing of relief for
the unemployed. (Neither, of course, did Coolidge.) [42]

Even as he dutifully denounced the Mellon Plan, Davis made it
clear that reduction of the federal budget was his deeper concern. "It
is healthy for every government . . . to be kept on a restricted if not a
starvation diet." He weakened his calls for construction of federal
dams by failing to relate them to multi-purpose river valley development, as George W. Norris was then doing. And he ignored the
suggestions of Bryan, Huston Thompson, and other progressive Democrats that he attack the enormous concentration of financial and industrial power. As a result, some businessmen regarded him as a mild
liberal of indefinite commitments, others as a fish out of water. "They
saw in him a conservative of the most respectable and distinguished
type, but . . . a conservative at the head of the wrong party; they
found conservatism well presented by Coolidge." [43]

Davis' statements on farm policy were considerably more realistic than either Coolidge's or La Follette's. He believed that the McNary-Haugen bill to raise prices by dumping the surplus abroad would stimulate production; and like Coolidge—but unlike La Follette, who endorsed the bill despite personal reservations—he opposed it. His main emphasis, however, was on international trade. Republican tariffs, he said, forced farmers to pay more for manufactured goods and made it difficult for foreign nations to purchase American farm products. Reduction of freight rates, improvement of internal waterways, expansion of cooperatives—all this, Davis acknowledged, was desirable. But trade alone offered a long-term solution.[44]

Meanwhile, the Harding scandals brought no return. Few people believed that Coolidge shared responsibility, and fewer still seemed to care. Davis' early comments were mild and impersonal. "I make no charges against the honesty and integrity of the present occupant of the White House. I think no man truthfully can." Urged to strike harder as the campaign lengthened, he criticized Coolidge for failing to move promptly against those implicated:

> Would Andrew Jackson have so dealt with that situation? Would Grover Cleveland have so dealt with that situation? Would Theodore Roosevelt have so dealt with that situation?

Patently, Coolidge lacked "the eager, burning zeal to drive its end, or the creative indignation that cannot rest until justice has been brought." [45]

Yet even those self-evident truths were stillborn. The Republican press pounced upon Davis for attacking the President. Senator George Wharton Pepper blandly noted that "seventy per cent of honesty in public affairs is a fair average." A New York stock broker remarked that "Davis may promise honesty, but Coolidge is for prosperity, and so am I." The cowboy humorist Will Rogers reached the core: "Davis announces that his Policy will be Honesty. . . . That [is not] an issue in Politics. . . . It's a miracle. . . . Can he get enough people that believe in Miracles to elect him?" [46]

Davis' persistent efforts to draw out the President were no more productive. "I did my best . . . to make Coolidge say something," he recalled with a twinkle thirty years later. "I was running out of anything to talk about. What I wanted was for Coolidge to say something. I didn't care what it was, just so I had somebody to debate with. He never opened his mouth." At the time, however, Davis was indignant.

He charged the President with trying to "tip-toe in international affairs for fear the Senate might overhear him." He termed the Republican campaign "a vast, mysterious, and pervading silence." Finally, in total exasperation, he burst out:

> If scandals break out in the Government, the way to treat them is—silence.
> If petted industries make exorbitant profits under an extortionate tariff, the answer is—silence.
> If the League of Nations . . . invites us into conference on questions of world wide importance, the answer is—silence.
> If race and religious prejudices threaten our domestic harmony, the answer is—silence.[47]

It was no use. For, as Coolidge disarmingly confessed, "I don't recall any candidate for President that ever injured himself very much by not talking." [48]

While Coolidge's aloofness was driving Davis to cold fury, he himself was frustrating his friends and advisers. "I am afraid," Colonel House lamented, "that the same qualities he lacks in directing a political campaign would cause him to fall short of being a great President. He has shown no aptitude for organization or judgment of men." His speeches were failing to transport the crowds. "He had them leaning half out of their seats at times," Nye wrote Polk after a major address in Ohio, "and if he just followed it up they would have fallen over on their faces." In vain, House, Woolley, Huntley, and others urged him to change his style. "I tried to get him to rise to . . . the necessary heights . . . ," House said after a three-hour conference with the candidate in October. "If I had given the same talk to Woodrow Wilson . . . a speech electrifying the country would have been the outcome. . . . Davis . . . has failed to . . . carry conviction. He comes up to the edge and when you think he is about to put it over, he falls just short of the right words and right effect." Even a pro-League speech in Newark that almost broke with the platform failed to move his audience. At least a dozen people, Woolley reported, said that "you have to be more fiery . . . and give more evidence of a soul stirred within, if you are to lift your fight eventually to a spiritual plane." [49]

Davis blamed his legal background. All his life, he explained to House, he had been trying to eliminate emotion from his briefs and oral arguments. Yet no counsel who had shrunk before his dissection of a faulty argument, no judge who had observed him march to an irrefutable conclusion, could believe that he lacked verbal or intellectual power. John W. Davis did not need to pound the lecturn, wave his arms, and sound the shrill, frenetic note. Everything about him— his heavy jowls, stately bearing, pure white hair, rich deep voice, even the rectitude that made him disdain the little acts of the crowd pleaser —would have inspired confidence had his words been compelling. But partly because he deemed it his duty to be a consensus candidate, and largely because he had no real grievance against the existing order, he proved incapable of writing a convincing brief for his own and his party's election. As a memorandum circulated in mid-October among White House staff members said with only a modicum of exaggeration, Davis had endorsed everything of importance that President Coolidge himself had advocated.[50]

« V »

More illuminating of the nation's problems than the speeches or silences of the candidates was the ferment the campaign generated in intellectual circles. Long before the debacle at the Garden a great host of reformers had been champing to form a third party. By summer's end not only the Socialists, Single Taxers, vegetarians, and theosophists; not only the legendary General Jacob Coxey, the gentle poet Edwin Markham, the idealistic muckracker Upton Sinclair; not only the Grand Chief of the Brotherhood of Locomotive Engineers and the NAACP's W. E. B. Du Bois; but virtually the entire leadership of the American reform movement had come out for La Follette—Jane Addams, John Dewey, Frederick C. Howe, Amos Pinchot, Oswald Garrison Villard, Frieda Kirchway, Donald Richberg, John Haynes Holmes, Ernest Gruening, Helen Keller, Fiorello La Guardia, Harold Ickes, Peter Witt, John R. Commons, Herbert Croly, and Felix Frankfurter. Walter Lippmann, then editor of the *World,* was almost alone in endorsing Davis.[51]

Few of these men and women thought that La Follette could win, and many took exception to one aspect or another of his platform. The Socialists deplored his failure to espouse government ownership on a wide scale, and Felix Frankfurter felt that nineteen of his twenty planks were impracticable. The intellectuals were also disappointed by his refusal to form a true third party. (La Follette's electors were listed under a variety of labels, and there were no Progressive candidates for Congress or state and local offices.) They believed, however, that Davis' nomination proved that the Democrats were no more willing to tamper with the foundations of economic power than were the Republicans, and in article after article in *The Nation* and the *New Republic* they dissected the Democratic candidate and the existing party system. The real trouble, said the *New Republic,* was that Davis was "wholly unaware of the class-creative activities of Big Business and . . . conceives the American Republic of today as an actual embodiment of Jeffersonian Democracy and consequently an essentially fulfilled ideal." If Davis' candidacy did nothing else, the *New Republic* continued, it dramatized the similarity of the Democratic and Republican parties; to accept the *World's* contention that America would not support a party system based on divergent economic interests was to submit to a permanent veto on progressivism by the solid Democratic South. Just as a large vote for John C. Frémont in 1856 had paved the way for Lincoln in 1860, so would a heavy turnout for La Follette in 1924 enable him or some other progressive to win in 1928.[52]

Behind the scenes, Frankfurter tried to persuade Newton D. Baker, Charles Burlingham, Rabbi Stephen S. Wise, and Walter Lippmann to support La Follette. Baker agreed that the Democratic party's stand on the League of Nations was far from satisfactory. But, as he also emphasized, Davis was for the League and was "saying so frankly." On less firm ground, Baker also cast the former Ambassador as a fighter against plutocracy. Frankfurter, he said, was "not moved by animus," but he was wrong in characterizing Davis as a creature of Wall Street; his father had "fought the powers of organized wealth to the end of his life, and [had] left the fight to his son to finish." [53]

Wise was torn by Baker's argument. "I don't like the airy, fairy socialists . . . [supporting La Follette]. I like still less the anti-Wilsonians." It was also true that the La Follette movement lacked coherence and that Davis commanded respect as an individual. Yet beneath all the differences, La Follette and his supporters were moved by "common devotion to the end of wresting the control of our country's affairs from the two groups that have ineptly at best, and criminally at worst, mismanaged for many years." What should he do? Vote for Davis and the League, or for La Follette and his "discordant yet plastic" progressivism? [54]

For Frankfurter the question was idle. In a reply to Wise, who sent him Baker's letters, he clarified and amplified the charges he had been making in the *New Republic.* He had never said, he pointed out, that Davis would be anybody's "creature"; he had simply argued that the former Ambassador's decision to serve corporate interests should be viewed as a function of his temperament, predilections, and experience. "Davis' father may have 'left the fight' to his son to finish, but never once after Davis . . . had a commanding position at the bar did he lift his finger or his voice for those causes which, Baker says, the father handed on to the son. On the contrary, the whole power and prestige of the man was on the other side." Davis' record as Solicitor General no more made him a liberal than the arguments of James Beck made him one; he had simply taken whatever government cases came up.[55]

The Harvard professor then bared his soul in a long letter to Burlingham. "You know the quality of the lads that come to this school—the best there are in the country. And yet, on the whole, a pretty crass materialism is their dominating ambition. . . . Davis' career is as subtly mischievous in its influence on the standards of the next generation of lawyers as it would have been to nominate McAdoo." It would be utterly wrong at a time "when we need the discouragement of material ambitions, and the instilling of spiritual concerns" that the presidency should go to a man of Davis' values:

> Coolidge was endowed with a mediocre mind and spirit; not much is to be expected from him. But Davis is a man of great ability. *Noblesse oblige!* What's he done with it? . . . What meaning has he? . . . [His] career is one that reinforces . . . the tendencies that seem to me most baneful to our profession and, therefore, for the unfolding of a reign of law. . . .[56]

Burlingham was too conscious of Davis' capacity to act with disinterest in a structured situation to be persuaded. Davis, he insisted, would surmount his philosophical predispositions when forced to face reality, just as he had done as Solicitor General. He conceded that the former Ambassador liked money and was not "a very enlightened person, socially or industrially," but he insisted that he was so intelligent that he would learn if elected. His chief defect "is a lack of enthusiasm—a fatal defect as a campaigner. He has nothing of the crusader in him. He is too calm, too humorous, possibly too cynical." He was certain, however, that Davis would be a courageous President: "he would lead his party, he would not truckle to the 'interests' and he would get on with Congress if any president can." La Follette? His movement was purely personal and egotistical. Unintelligent in conception and misleading in program, it lacked the definite purpose and direction of the British labor movement.[57]

Walter Lippmann saw no need for a programmatic new party. He asked Frankfurter to explain further the *New Republic* group's objective. "[The] immediate results of the 1924 election do not appear very important," Frankfurter replied; "the directions which further or retard . . . are tremendously important. Coolidge and Davis have nothing to offer for 1944; they have no dreams . . . except things substantially as is [sic]. The forces . . . behind La Follette are, at least, struggling and groping for a dream." Irritated by Frankfurter's suggestion that the *World* should explain why it had called Davis a conservative in April and a liberal in August, Lippmann broke off the correspondence.[58]

Late in October Lippmann reworked his *World* editorials into a long article for the *New Republic*. He wrote that he supported Davis not only because the need to cooperate with Europe made it critically important that the next President "be neither bewildered, apathetic nor obtuse," but also because Davis' "strong Jeffersonian bias against the concentration and exaggeration of government is more genuinely liberal than much that goes by the name of liberalism." La Follette merited warm respect as a man. But his party was "a gathering of the disfranchised and dissatisfied," and its leader was "shrewd enough to know" that to unite his followers he had to avoid the issues that divided them:

> On foreign policy, on the question of whether to break up monopoly or socialize it, on immigration, on prohibition, even on the Supreme Court, the La Follette movement speaks with an uncertain voice or none at all. . . .
> . . . His political program is almost violently nationalistic and centralizing. . . . His policy in respect to large corporations seems to me an illogical mixture of the individualism of 1890 . . . and pre-war Socialism. His foreign policy seems to date about 1919.[59]

« VI »

Despite his realization that he could not win, Davis maintained his morale by reading the signs optimistically. Although he later said that the best he could ever see was a contest in the House, all of his campaign letters were infused with hope. He wrote that his first trip through the Middle West was successful beyond expectation. He predicted that La Follette would draw more Republican than Democratic votes in Rhode Island and Connecticut. He contended that he had a fighting chance in New York. He denied knowledge of a *Literary Di-*

gest straw vote that forecast Coolidge's victory with fateful accuracy. "As things stand today," he declared in mid-October, "we should carry it in the electoral college." [60]

It seemed for a while in October that Davis and La Follette might actually win enough states to throw the election into the House. La Follette seemed to be sweeping the West. Republican editors were treating Davis, if not his party, with respect. And there was a vague feeling in the Democratic party's inner circle, best expressed by John Foster Dulles, then a Democrat, that sophisticated conservatives would abandon Coolidge in the realization that "extreme conservatism quickly bears fruit in a radical party of increasing menace and power." [61]

To avoid cutting into La Follette's strength, Davis canceled plans to go out to the West Coast. Some McAdoo men labeled the cancelation a sell-out and blamed it on Al Smith. "Davis was urged at the very beginning . . . to come out here, hammer Wall Street and adopt a liberal attitude on the railroad and similar questions," a Californian complained. "The Tammany crowd advised him to the contrary [and now] accuse McAdoo of deserting Davis in the west!" Yet McAdoo himself thought that the Democrats should lie low wherever La Follette had a chance and Davis had none. The state chairmen of Minnesota and Wyoming also agreed with this strategy, and throughout the West many Democratic leaders worked quietly for La Follette. [62]

The Republicans countered by predicting that Charles Bryan or La Follette would become President if the election went to the House. "Coolidge or Chaos"; "A Vote for Davis is a Vote for Bryan"—such was the thrust of the pamphlets they printed by the ton and the speeches they made by the thousand. "Look out! Look out!" cried Charles Dawes as he stormed across the country firing alternately at Bryan and the Wisconsin Senator:

> You face now the master demagogue. Don't be deceived on this issue. Where do you stand? On the rock of the Constitution of the United States under the American flag and behind President Coolidge—or on the sinking sands of Socialism, with the red flag? [63]

Dawes' heady emphasis on La Follette's radicalism forced Davis to alter his tactics further. Much as he loathed the G.O.P.'s stand on the tariff and the League, he disdained La Follette's program more. No proposal distressed him more than the Progressive demand for the recall of judicial decisions; no passage in his address to the American

Bar Association in 1923 had carried more feeling than his condemnation of it. Yet to attack the Wisconsin Senator's radicalism now was to reinforce the Republican argument that conservative Democrats should ensure La Follette's defeat by voting for Coolidge. Accordingly, he admonished La Follette in one sentence and explained him in the next: The doughty Wisconsin Progressive was unwise and impractical, but the Republicans' characterization of him as "rawhide and bloody bones" was unreal and unjust; his scheme for circumventing the Supreme Court was not "bolshevistic," it was merely "the old British theory of supremacy of Parliament." The real threat to American institutions was the Grand Old Party's tolerance of corruption and subservience to special interests.[64]

Davis proved powerless to allay conservatives' fears of Bryan and La Follette. Sustained by a $4 million war chest, the G.O.P. attacked La Follette with increasing ferocity all through October. "We are confronted by the possibilities of a violent social and industrial revolution," declared the president of the Pennsylvania Manufacturers Association. "We have in La Follette and Wheeler, a Lenine [sic] and Trotsky with a formidable band of followers made up of the vicious, ignorant and discontented element, openly organized for battle." Mobs pulled La Follette speakers from platforms, stoned their cars, and intimidated them in a score of reported incidents, often with the acquiescence of public officials and sometimes with their active cooperation.[65]

La Follette received only token contributions from labor, little editorial support beyond the Scripps papers, and unfair coverage from the rest of the press except for *The New York Times.* Forced to charge admission to his rallies, he became so shrill and strident as his fortunes ebbed that his managers implored him to stop playing on the passions of the German-Americans. Even the *New Republic* admitted that his speeches had weakened rather than strengthened his campaign.[66]

Davis' campaign faltered with La Follette's. In states where he had a chance to win, Davis argued that it was pointless to waste a vote on the Wisconsin Senator. He also tried to supplant the Republican slogan, "Coolidge or Chaos," with a variation of his own: "Coolidge and then Chaos." But it was no use. From all over the nation reports of apathy poured in. "There is no evidence of any desire or will to win," a Nevadan lamented. "Davis is being unfairly treated, and universally neglected." Party workers in Connecticut, said another report, were "doing nothing but going through the motions." As the Tennessee editor George Fort Milton remarked, "the jig is up . . . , and I frankly confess that I am not putting on crepe." Contributions lagged to such an extent that the National Committee was forced to borrow to meet its scaled-down budget of less than a million dollars. The St. Louis *Post-Dispatch* reached to the essence:

> On the Democratic side there was only John W. Davis, making an able, eloquent but lonely campaign, with little money, a poor organization and not much support from the leaders of the party.[67]

For all the discord and disloyalty, Davis was never gloomy or depressed, never discourteous or unkind. Occasionally he entered a mild complaint: "Hard at it all day—Shaver-White-Roper-Noonan, etc." "This is a —— of a job you handed me." "The task of preparing speeches I find a heavy burden." "I am living now in terms of minutes & not hours." He made time, nevertheless, to write gracious personal notes between speeches. (Just a week before the election he recommended the board chairman of Standard Oil for membership in the University Club.) He overlooked the failure of most Democratic candidates to identify themselves with his candidacy. "Curley is stressing Curley, Walsh is stressing Walsh," read a typical report from Massachusetts. Davis even smiled at their tendency to upstage him. In Maryland, where Governor Albert C. Ritchie introduced Davis with a prolonged build-up of himself, an old friend remarked afterwards that Ritchie had not been very hospitable. Davis mused a moment, then, his eyes brightening, replied, "Well, Morgan, it's all right by me. He's probably got more to gain than I have." [68]

Sometimes Davis relaxed at whistle-stops by reading humorous extracts from his mail. The story he liked best, however, he told only in private: "Marty," a young Irish woman from Brooklyn's Gashouse District, had confided to her ward leader after meeting Davis, "you kin tell your mon he kin park his shoes under my bed anytime he wants." [69]

Not until a few days before the election did Davis' spirits begin to sag. He confessed that he was mentally tired and that he could never be as happy in office as in private life. He added that whatever the verdict, he was prepared to accept it philosophically; all he hoped was that the party would "feel that it has had a run for its money." By election morning he was resigned to defeat. Asked how he felt, he responded, "Fine, but not bouyed up by hope." But even then he had no foreboding of disaster. "Nowhere that I went," he later said, "was there any evidence that a landslide was impending, although there was general agreement that the 'silent' vote was larger than had ever been known." [70]

« VII »

The returns gave Davis 8,385,283 votes to Coolidge's 15,718,211 and La Follette's 4,831,289. In the electoral college he carried only the Old South and Arkansas, Oklahoma, Tennessee, and Texas. He lost four of the border states—Maryland, West Virginia, Kentucky, and Missouri —and came close to victory nowhere in the North. In twelve states from Michigan to the Pacific Coast he trailed La Follette, and in Minnesota, North Dakota, and California he won less than 9 per cent of the vote. He failed to reach 20 per cent in Pennsylvania; and in New York, where he ran almost a million votes behind Al Smith, his 29 per cent was less than one point above his national average.[71]

As Davis listened to the early returns with his wife and daughter, the Lansings, and a few other friends at the Polks' house, he was the most cheerful person in the room. Only when the announcer reported that he had lost his own precinct in Clarksburg did his eyes show disappointment. At Democratic headquarters a few hours later he was again the most cheerful person present. He said a few pleasant words to party workers, urged them to work for unity, and went home to bed, grateful, so he told a few intimates, that he had "not been sent up for four years." [72]

All post-election analyses indicate that La Follette cut much more deeply into Davis' nominal strength than into Coolidge's. Davis ran 13 per cent behind the Democratic congressional vote, the President only 4 per cent behind the Republican congressional vote. This reflected La Follette's heavy inroad into the Democratic ethnic vote in Eastern cities as well as his strong showing in rural areas from the Midwest to the Pacific Coast. The Wisconsin Senator did especially well among Germans and Scandinavians. Besides winning three million or more Democratic votes, he apparently drove tens of thousands of conservative Democrats to vote Republican. His candidacy also contributed to Democratic apathy by dramatizing Davis' conservatism; a great number of Eastern Democrats stayed home in the persuasion that there was no real difference between Davis and Coolidge and that La Follette had no chance of winning. As Franklin D. Roosevelt concluded after surveying the wreckage, "it is hopeless for the Democrats to try and wear the livery of the conservative." [73]

The Ku Klux Klan issue apparently cut both ways. Charles Bryan's presence on the ticket seems to have encouraged many Eastern Catholics to sit out the election. On the other hand, Davis ran better among rural Protestants in Maryland and Missouri and better in the Klan-ridden South as a whole than Cox had done in 1920, when there was no Klan. He carried Oklahoma despite the election of a Klan-supported Republican senatorial candidate, and in West Virginia, where the head of the Klan called him "the best man" even after he had denounced the organization, resentment of his anglophilia and postwar labor record was reportedly decisive.[74]

Prohibition seems to have worked against Davis to La Follette's advantage. The urban Democratic machines billed Davis as a wet, and the dry leader, Wayne Wheeler, attacked him for his repeated use of phrases such as "personal liberty," "illegal search and seizure," and "home rule." Nevertheless, his scrupulous observance of the platform's call for enforcement probably disaffected hundreds of thousands of workingmen who might have supported an outright wet.[75]

Davis himself believed that the election turned on a sharp rise in farm prices and on the Republican's broad appeal to the "belly." He also felt that he had been crushed between conservatism and radicalism. No Democrat, he maintained, could have won in 1924. Yet, with characteristic modesty, he also insisted that someone else might have done better. Saddened and embarrassed by the number of congressional candidates he had dragged down to defeat, he sent out numerous letters of commiseration immediately after the election.[76]

Not once in the aftermath did Davis display real bitterness. He expressed pleasure in Smith's resounding victory over Theodore Roosevelt, Jr., in the New York gubernatorial race. "Al is a political wonder," he said to the leader of Tammany. In time he even forgave Samuel Gompers. "I had respect for . . . [him]. Some of Gompers' speeches were pretty inflammatory but I always thought that he felt that necessary to keep the Radicals from scorching his coattails." McAdoo alone remained outside the pale. The Californian, he said, had been "distinctly unfriendly." [77]

Only to a few friends did Davis reveal his inner anguish. "I believe I have been a fair success in life except as a candidate for President," he said to Jouett Shouse. To Norman Davis he confided that there seemed to be less rather than more glory as the days went by and that he now saw many things which might have been done differently. The one great comfort was that he had not sold "the truth to serve the hour." His greatest satisfaction, he wrote Lord Charnwood, was that he had said nothing he did not believe and had spoken his mind on every question he thought material.[78]

Solace came in the post-election mail. Newton D. Baker wrote that the campaign had been errorless. Jesse Jones said that Davis more nearly approached the ideal citizen than any man he had ever met. Robert Woolley asked for an inscribed photograph to hang in his study beside that of Woodrow Wilson. Dozens of others praised him for the moral tone and high intellectual content of his speeches. Even McAdoo's daughter-in-law wrote warmly: "when I reflect upon the gross materialism of some of our friends in Wall Street, it is inspiring to know that there is one man who, though intimately associated with that 'menage', has kept his idealism intact." The most moving statement came from Davis' young secretary, Harold Hathaway.

I've seen you under the greatest strain anyone could undergo . . . and the admiration I had for you at the beginning has grown far beyond my power of description. I can't answer your letter, sir, or tell you what it means to me, but you know I am entirely sincere in saying that I would rather be near you in any capacity than to be myself president of the United States.[79]

Rarely in later years did Davis speculate on what he would have done had he become President. James M. Cox believed that he would have given the country an able, liberal administration. "His keen sense of justice would have balanced well the equities as between classes and no man would have met his responsibilities with better understanding." But others doubted that he would have done much more than Coolidge to change the fateful course of the economy. Certainly he himself never claimed that he could have averted the Great Depression. The most he ever said was that he would have held "a tight rein" or that he would have made more legislative proposals than did Coolidge, though "with what result it is impossible to say." Neither did he believe that he could have taken the United States into the League of

Nations. But surely he would have been more internationalist in tone, more disposed to cooperate with the League, than Coolidge or Hoover. Usually he parried questions on what he might have done with a story:

> After the campaign was over one of my rather rigidly pietistic friends said, "Did you say anything . . . you didn't believe?" "Oh yes," I said, "I went around the country telling people I was going to be elected, and I knew I hadn't any more chance than a snowball in Hell." [80]

CHAPTER 16

Wall Street Lawyer

I should say . . . that success lies in contentment. To be content requires three things: The approval of one's God; the approval of one's self; and last and least important, the approval of one's fellow men.
JOHN W. DAVIS, 1932

John W. Davis was no more capable of prolonged inactivity than of sustained bitterness. Two weeks after the election, feeling "like a sucked orange," he sailed for a four-month vacation in the Mediterranean. Less than three months later he was back at his desk, to the delight of his partners, who had renamed the firm Davis Polk Wardwell Gardiner & Reed in his absence.

« I »

By 1925 the tendency of the large Wall Street firms to concentrate on corporate reorganizations and other forms of office law was even more pronounced than it had been in 1921. As Allen Wardwell said, in words that applied to almost every large firm in Manhattan, "some of my partners can't find their way to the courthouse." One result was the deterioration of the appellate bar. "Hardly any of the leading partners of the big New York firms come down . . . [to the Supreme Court] any more," Chief Justice Taft grumbled in 1927. "They send their juniors, and we rarely hear a good argument." Learned Hand's concern ran deeper. "In my own city," the great Second Circuit Judge observed, "the best minds of the profession are scarcely lawyers at all."

They may be something much better, or much worse; but they are not that. With courts they have no dealings whatever, and would hardly know what to do if they came there. . . . I cannot quite see how a system of jurisprudence dependent upon precedent is permanently to get on at all with its best talent steadily drawn away from the precedent makers.[1]

Davis' greatness as an advocate in the grand tradition gave Davis Polk, as the firm was commonly called, unusual balance and distinction. "Under him," Wardwell recalled, "we got . . . men . . . who came to make the trial of cases their chief object in life. They attracted cases to this firm because they were trial lawyers, not because it came out of business we had elsewhere. . . . People come in here and want to get John to try or argue a case for them. . . . That, I think, is something that was not true of most of the other large firms that were about our size or even a little bigger." [2]

Davis, like Stetson before him, led mainly by example. A "lawyer's lawyer" and a "partner's partner," in the apt characterization of the firm's historians, he had not the time to handle administration or to conceive and initiate policy, nor had he any interest in doing so. He presided over partners' meetings with grace, wit, and quiet persuasiveness, and he displayed an extraordinary facility for summarizing complex and strongly held views in a way that drained them of emotion. But he rarely went beyond forming a consensus, and he almost never imposed the majority's view upon a deeply feeling minority. The administrative matters that accompanied the firm's growth—from thirty to more than ninety lawyers during his thirty-four-year tenure—were guided first by Lansing Reed, then by Frank Polk, and after World War II, by George A. Brownell.[3]

Only in the tax field did Davis supply the initial thrust for expansion. Early in the 1920's he asked his young assistant, Montgomery Angell, to devote himself to tax law. No tax specialist had become a partner in a large firm to that time, and Angell aspired to be a generalist like Davis. "Don't fool yourself," Davis said to him. "Taxes have now reached into every branch of law. If you take on this tax business you'll find you'll need all the law you've ever learned and a good deal more, which may have nothing in the world to do with taxes, but which affects tax. If you don't like it, you can give it up after a year. We'll raise your pay, of course." [4]

The assignment proved congenial. Angell was made a partner a few years later, and he eventually became one of the nation's foremost tax lawyers. Meanwhile, new specialists were developed within the firm, and by the late 1940's Davis Polk had three partners and six or seven associates working exclusively on tax matters. Davis always held that the expansion had been necessary for survival:

> [One] man says, "I can't handle this. We'll have to get another man." Then, if two can't handle it, "Let's get another man." . . . We don't try to departmentalize consciously but it works out that way. . . . For instance, in corporate questions, the issuance of corporate securities and all of that, the tax angle has to be considered constantly. . . . So it is with estates and corporate finance. . . . They must settle down to doing that kind of work, and little by little you find your firm growing. The main aim . . . is simply to answer the problems brought to you. That's all. If you don't answer them, they go elsewhere. Or, if you answer them in a slipshod manner, you'll lose them. . . . Unless you can give them the best there is, you have no business trying to hold a client.[5]

Davis' strong feeling for the individuality or personal quality of practice made him regret the growth. "I wouldn't have wanted to head a firm like this," he once said, "if I couldn't feel that at least the partners' names appeared separately on the letterhead." He disliked going into court without having met his client. He was embarrassed by the failure to remember the names of the young associates he passed in the corridors. (His partner Theodore Kiendl once mistook one of the associates for opposing counsel and introduced himself in court.) He shook his head over the division of labor, saying that "no six lawyers can draft anything." And he himself refused to specialize. "I still think of the lawyer as an advocate and an adviser," he said in 1954. "That has helped to keep me from going into something like tax-work. I'd have been a flat failure if I had." Small-town practice was the best training for a young man. "There is one thing you've got to learn as a country lawyer, and that is, to take care of yourself, to be confident in your own decisions and efforts." [6]

Davis never really faced the contradiction between his views on small-town training and his firm's practice of hiring associates directly out of law school. The character of the practice demanded early specialization. As one of the partners once remarked, "We corporate lawyers can't take chances. . . . If we make a mistake and give an opinion based on something wrong, we may ruin the [company]." Each year a number of bright young men, usually from Harvard, Yale, and Columbia, but occasionally from Michigan or Virginia, were brought in as associates. Many would move on before they came up for partnership, some because they lacked the qualifications or disliked the work, others because they were offered greater opportunity elsewhere. The best of those who remained were taken into the firm eight to twelve years later. Most of the others would then leave, although a few stayed on to become partners in late middle age.[7]

There was a sense, surely, in which the firm observed Paul Cravath's maxim: "Brilliant intellectual powers are not essential." But what that really meant was that judgment was more critical to the successful practice of law than pure intellect was. In fields such as trusts and estates, where many of the clients were wealthy widows, social contacts were also important. As a senior partner once explained to a group of law students, "Even the big firms notice if you bring in business." Yet, as another senior partner insisted and as the firm's reputation attested, "the office always tried to get the best brains it could." Of the forty or so men who became partners during the Davis era, half had been graduated from college with honors, had been elected to Phi Beta Kappa, or had made their schools' law reviews. Among them was a Rhodes Scholar. Most of the others had first-rate minds.[8]

By the late 1930's Davis Polk was known as the most socially exclusive office on Wall Street. With some exceptions, the partners comprised more an aristocracy of talent than of birth. Many came from small towns across the nation, and most of them were more representative of the professional and small business classes than of inherited wealth. Although predominantly Anglo-Saxon Protestant, there were a few Roman Catholics among them. One Italian-American and several Jews also served as associates during Davis' time, but the former went into politics before his promotion came up and no Jew was admitted to partnership until 1961.[9]

The associates' salaries ran considerably above those of young government lawyers or law school instructors. As they became established in uptown apartments or the more fashionable suburbs, they moved almost automatically into New York society. A higher proportion— twenty-six of thirty-eight—of Davis Polk partners than of any other Wall Street firm were listed in the *Social Register,* and most of the unlisted ones could have been included had they bothered to fill out the form and pay the fee.[10]

Davis seems simply to have acquiesced in this pattern. Certainly he numbered many Jews, including Lord Reading and Judge Joseph M. Proskauer, among his intimates. He said that he had "no better friend in the world" than Reading, and three years after Davis' death Proskauer was still writing emotionally of the "deep love and respect" he felt for him. He took a kind of perverse pride in what he euphemistically called his "humble origins." And he was mildly contemptuous of the vulgar rich. "Whenever I can detect what high society wants," he said, "I gravitate inevitably to the opposite side." [11]

Yet his grace and sensitivity, his charm and civility, drew men and women of refinement to him and he to them. Under the influence of his upper-class English friends, he gradually lost his mild reservations about the British social structure. He compartmentalized his own social life rigidly, and he seems to have shared the general feeling, as expressed by one of his partners, that "this business of taking a partner into one's house is almost more important than choosing a wife." [12]

Davis Polk also had a reputation for continuing family connections. Allen Wardwell and J. Howland Auchincloss, both of whom preceded Davis, were related to Stetson and Russell. During Davis' long tenure, however, only three sons of partners or deceased partners were taken into the firm: Edward R. Wardwell, Frank L. Polk, Jr., and Ewen MacVeagh. Another of Polk's sons left before it was time to decide on his partnership, and two other close relatives of partners failed to become members. Davis, of course, appreciated the intimacy and sense of tradition that blood relationships brought. But he also perceived the potential problems. He insisted that relatives of partners make their own way, and he often said that they carried an additional burden.[13]

« II »

Davis' presence was felt everywhere within the firm. His genius as an advocate was an inspiration to all, and it was universally agreed that no one matched him in the ability to extract the pith of a complex legal matter; even the specialists in corporation law had him review their more important opinions. Everyone regarded him as a great teacher in conference because of his unwearied patience in opening the many folds of a problem and marshaling the elements of judgment around its central point. No matter what the underlying tensions, he never seemed perturbed.[14]

Davis' work habits continued to astound his partners. "How he did it I don't know. I simply don't know. He never wasted a moment." He sometimes prepared his arguments aboard his train or in his hotel room. And though he joked that it was amazing how much it helped in argument to know what the case was about, the pressure was acute. As he wrote Charles Warren after a brief trip to Washington in 1925: "I had two cases on the docket in quick succession. I went at once to a room in the Metropolitan Club, sequestered myself for their study, went to the court room and argued one, came back and dug on the other." [15]

Six years later there was still no letup. For ten months, Davis wrote a Scottish friend in 1931, the pressure had been absolutely unintermittent.

> There was not a day . . . when I was not either in court or engaged in breathless preparation for the next assault on my clients' enemies. In February I had what was denominated a two weeks' holiday, in the course of which time I argued one case on appeal in New Orleans, two in Philadelphia and prepared for another in Washington. Now I am prepared to kick up my heels for a month or six weeks and tell the embattled legal world that they can go hang. . . . My practice has ranged this winter from Boston to Denver, Denver to New Orleans, New Orleans to Charleston, South Carolina, and back along the seaboard. If it could all be done in one swing around the circle, it would not be so bad, but each case is a separate foray. *Quis fit Maecenas?*—how I would like to be a Scottish laird, buried in the seclusion of my Caledonian hills.

Only his self-confidence and ability to relax enabled him to maintain the pace. His preparation completed, he would fold up his papers, say that "the case is sound as a nut" or something of the sort, and turn to a game of cards or to storytelling.[16]

Davis' integrity and industriousness set the firm's tone. In his office, he was pleasant but slightly withdrawn. He guarded his privacy closely, talking only about the externals of his personal life, and then only seldom. "I think he wanted more children, but he wouldn't discuss it," his most intimate friend mused. One sensed, another partner said, that the coldness and precision of his mind were in constant tension with the humor and sympathy of his heart. He welcomed anyone who entered his open door, but he also drew a line which only a few senior men ever crossed. Rarely did he initiate small talk when at his desk, and often he ended an intrusion as briefly as courtesy permitted.

Davis rarely lost his temper. One of the few times that he did, he was in his office, late one afternoon. He was reading proofs on a brief to be filed the next morning, when Frank Polk walked in and asked a question. Davis looked up, slammed his hand on the copy, and almost shouted: "I am only capable of doing one thing at a time. For the moment I am doing this!" Polk apologized and withdrew. A similar incident occurred during a jury trial in the early 1930's. While Davis was interrogating a witness, his partner Kiendl tried to get his attention by pulling on his coat. In exasperation, Davis turned around and said: "How in the world can I cross-examine with you tagging on my tail?" Usually, he displayed annoyance more subtly. Some years later, an important but unsophisticated government official, who had recently taken up golf, joined him in a foursome. For several holes the official bubbled over with talk of books he had been reading. Then, just as Davis stepped up to the tee and went into his backswing, the official asked him if he knew of Dante. Davis, his club poised high in the air, drily responded, "Yes, he's been well spoken of." He then teed off.[17]

As one of Davis' right-hand men reflected, "Mr. Davis was a peculiar combination—an aristocrat with great humility. He was choosy about his associates. Yet he was different. He was a hail-fellow-well-met up to a point. Wardwell had no barrier, but Mr. Davis had reserve. Not that he was a stuffed shirt. He was socially light, never heavy or ponderous, never vulgar. He did everything with elegance and grace."

Davis loved fine clothes, and he was invariably correctly appointed, down to a cane. Long after counsel had begun to plead before the Supreme Court in business suits, he continued to wear a cutaway. Even on the golf course, he wore knee breeches, a cravat, and a sports jacket for some years after informal attire had become common. *Vanity Fair* once ran a picture of Davis and Frank Polk, who dressed just as elegantly but liked to tease Davis about his "high button shoes," facing each other in a general atmosphere of sartorial splendor. Davis expected the firm's young men to uphold the forms, and once, in a gesture softened by a smile, he handed a very junior associate a ten-dollar bill and told him to buy a hat. Yet he never let appearance become an end in itself. He sometimes worked in his shirtsleeves. (He refused to allow air conditioning in any of the offices because he believed it to be unhealthy.) And he once appeared in the Supreme Court with a pencil over his ear.

A few of Davis' partners perceived his limitations. Several recognized that he had run a poor campaign for the presidency, and a few were unsympathetic to his strict constructionism and resistance to social and economic change. "I have no doubt of his brilliance," one said, "yet I'm not sure that he was brilliant outside the law. He had great forensic ability and a marvelous memory. He was also capable of adapting himself to changes once they were made. But he was not really flexible intellectually. He was too rigid in his belief in the soundness of fundamental principles. He would not have made a brilliant scientist." Even so, they revered him: "He had the highest principles." "He was a very lovable man." "He had intellectual courage of a high order." "He had an utter disregard for what people thought of him." "He was the only man I ever considered a hero." An outsider summed it all up: "He was such a warm and deep respecter of personality. I've never known anyone in the firm who didn't glow when his name was mentioned."

Almost all the younger men felt that Davis' modesty and honesty made him the easiest partner in the firm to work for. Until late in life he had each junior associate go on at least one case with him shortly after being hired, and he invariably made it an educational experience. Despite his feeling for form, he criticized only on substance, and always he leavened his remarks with humor. Once, for example, he chose to impress the need for thorough preparation upon a young associate by twitting him for not knowing the *species* of bedbugs involved in a case. Yet never did he censure in the presence of others or talk down to the rawest recruit.

Neither was Davis effusive in his praise. He expected good work, and he usually commended only in passing. He also refused to take credit he did not earn; whenever he won a case on the brief, he made sure that the junior who wrote it knew that he appreciated his work. He never bragged about his victories, although a note of self-satisfaction sometimes crept into his letters. He insisted on accepting responsibility for defeat unless he thought the decision was bad, and then he would grumble about the court. More commonly, he was tight-lipped. He told his daughter in confidence that a certain partner had "failed for years to pull his oar." He also disclosed to her his deep affection for Frank Polk and Edwin S. S. Sunderland and his respect for the intellects of several of the younger men. Otherwise his letters, his conversations, and his two-hundred-page Oral Memoir are virtually barren of judgments or comments on his partners and associates.

When a client was ushered into Davis' office, Davis usually called in an associate and introduced him. The associate would prepare a memorandum or opinion, but if a serious complication developed, Davis would go over the papers and the record himself. He was always warm and informal in the ensuing conferences, and once, in an especially bad case, he exclaimed: "Tell me how to argue it and I'll argue it." Normally he used only one assistant at a time, but during the New Deal he argued so many important cases that he assembled a special staff of able associates: Edwin F. Blair, Luke W. Finlay, Jr., Paschall Davis, and John M. Polk. He would call them in singly or in a group, comment on the points to be researched, cite the volumes of the reports in which the pertinent cases could be found, and then dismiss everyone with a witty remark. On their return he would absorb their findings and formulate final strategy on the spot.[18]

Davis' strength as a teacher was also a function of his gift for language, which was pungent and descriptive in court and conference alike. He invented his own colloquialisms and inclined toward simple Anglo-Saxon verbs: "He was like a man speaking in blank verse," a partner recalled in awe. He conveyed his passion for clarity through a style sheet he drew up for new men (no one who read it dared lean again on "and/or"). His revision in 1953, his eightieth year, of a bar committee's recommendation to the Attorney General, is notably illustrative:

As drafted by the committee:
To you, Sir, has been entrusted the enormous responsibility of recommending to the President the best qualified available persons to fill the vacancies on the United States Court of Appeals for the Second Circuit. Upon the wisdom of your recommendation depends the preservation of the prestige of this great Court and other courts to which you will recommend appointments in the future. We pray that in making your recommendation you will adhere to the fundamental principles outlined above, to the end that the Court in which we either for long have been privileged to sit or before which we have appeared as advocates these many years shall be the beneficiary of your best endeavors. May the banner of greatness of this Court never be hauled down!

As revised by Davis:
We recognize the great responsibility you bear in making recommendations to the President for appointments to vacancies on the federal bench. Perhaps no function of your office has more lasting character. We do not doubt either your desire or your ability to perform this important duty to the best interests of the Country that you serve. We offer these suggestions therefore with a sincere purpose to aid and support you in the carrying out of this great task.[19]

« III »

Within a few years of going to Wall Street Davis had more or less fulfilled his lifelong dream of financial security. His pre-tax income from practice soared far above expectations, reaching a high of $400,-000 in the late 1920's and averaging $275,000 during the five worst years of the Depression. His connections with the leaders of finance and industry enabled him to invest wisely, and he also built up a comfortable portfolio for his daughter. He survived the Great Crash of 1929 reasonably well by disposing of his most speculative stocks between the first break in the Market on October 15 and the calamitous decline on Black Thursday, October 24. "While I shipped some water, I lost no cargo."

All through the 1920's Davis' complaints about taxes increased in frequency and acerbity. He resented the fact that professional men did not receive the same tax breaks as businessmen did, but he invariably called for general reductions rather than for the elimination of inequities. Not once in a dozen or more comments did he propose that the loopholes be closed; and despite his attacks on the Mellon Plan in 1924, as early as December 1925 he reverted to his pre-campaign position that the surtaxes were too high.[20]

Although some acquaintances thought that Davis was far more concerned about income than a professional man should be, no one who knew him considered him small or avaricious. "[He] has not been a 'green goods man'" Charles Burlingham, that shrewd observer, admonished Felix Frankfurter in 1924. "He likes . . . to earn money but his money-earning is only incidental." One of Davis' own reflective remarks made the same point: "I think my chief ambition is not for money as money, but for the 'glorious privilege of being independent.'" He often joked about creeping in and out of the office on days when a director's fee was in the offing. And he once said to the Clerk of the Supreme Court in a stage whisper: "Tomorrow I have a date with J. P. Morgan, the day after that with Rockefeller. God, how I hate to take their money!" Yet most of his younger partners and assistants never heard him discuss the stock market or saw him study the financial pages. "Those people down town . . . worry all the time," he would say to Julia. "When I buy a stock I ride it down, and never look at it again . . . Anybody can get rich if he cares more for money than he does for anything else." This, of course, was romanticizing. Still, a stratum of truth underlay it. As the executor of his estate exclaimed on examining his portfolio, "Mr. Davis violated almost every principle we followed in the trusts and estates department!"[21]

Davis was exceedingly generous in his private relationships. "I've never kept track of what I've given away," he said in his old age, "but I expect it is as much as I've kept." He treated his daughter, sisters, nephews, and nieces with great liberality and was "a soft touch" for old friends and even casual acquaintances; over the years he made uncounted permanent "loans" in amounts between $25 and $500. On the other hand, his contributions to institutions and organized charities were modest, partly because he lived surprisingly close to his income, especially after 1946. His taxes were high, and, depending on his mood of the moment, he estimated them at one-third, one-half, or two-thirds of his gross. His fixed expenses were comparably high. Besides his estate in Locust Valley, he maintained a Fifth Avenue apartment and a cottage at Yeamans Hall, a wintering place in South Carolina. Both the Long Island and the Fifth Avenue establishments were modest by the standards of his financier friends, but they required a staff of six or seven and were furnished in costly antiques, one of Nell's passions. To all this was added the expense of nine club memberships, from the Links to the Century; a chauffeur-driven Pierce-Arrow or Cadillac; and annual trips to the British Isles and the Continent. "I am lucky," he wrote in rejecting a request for a contribution in 1939, "to get out with my living expenses." [22]

In Davis' persistent complaints about taxes he did himself an injustice. His private correspondence indicates that he often set fees well below what some of his partners thought was appropriate, and, unlike some of the other heads of Wall Street firms, he periodically reduced his percentage of the firm's profits—so much so that Kiendl remarked in the 1950's that "we have never been able to prevail upon him to take . . . the full measure of his contribution." He first cut his percentage by one-eighteenth in 1934. Three years later, at the same time that he was protesting President Roosevelt's "soak-the-rich" tax program, he reduced it an additional one-sixth. Five years later he lowered it by another fraction, bringing the cumulative reduction to a full third. Then, in 1946, partly to accommodate the young men returning from the war and partly because of the diminution of his own activity (though not his faculties), he contracted it by a second full third. "Gentlemen," he said when his partners protested, "if there's one thing I can do in this firm, it is to reduce my own percentage." [23]

Nor was that the sum of Davis' generosity. Between 1929 and 1954, he gave perhaps a full year of his own time and, in addition, the time of several partners' and associates' to cases for which he charged no fee.* He also made numerous endearing small gestures. Early in Montgomery Angell's service he had Angell's salary increased by the exact amount of the initiation fee and dues of a country club the young as-

* See Chapters 18, 19, and 28.

sociate aspired to join. For many years he took a group of fledgling lawyers to Washington at his own expense to move their admission to practice before the Supreme Court. He also insisted that the firm carry partners or associates at full percentage or salary in the event of prolonged illness.[24]

One of Davis' greatest charms was his playful strain. Once, in the late 1920's, he strode into court in West Virginia, stared stonily at an old friend in the opposing counsel's chair, and thumbed his nose at him. A decade later, at the unveiling of a portrait of his old friend Reynolds Vance at the Yale Law School, he said, in the presence of Vance and his wife, "I think I've known the subject longer than anyone in this room, including the charming lady who shares his name. In fact, I slept with him before she did." On another occasion, when he was in his mid-seventies, he walked up steathily behind a partner's wife on Fifth Avenue, snatched her purse, and disappeared momentarily into the crowd.[25]

The young associates who worked for Davis loved him. "He was really a warm, simple man, the kind we could take our problems to," said one. "He treated me like a son," said another. On only one count did they have a grievance: he failed to press hard for their advancement. It was customary for an ambitious associate to make himself indispensable to a partner, in the expectation, as one of the senior partners candidly put it, that "he will . . . push you along so that you won't want to leave." But Davis was so determined to be fair, so sensitive to the use of power, that he would not force his will on the more aggressive partners. As a result, some of his finest assistants were never taken into the firm. Such was their respect and affection for him, however, that they never let their disappointment turn into bitterness toward him. Similarly, he never made anyone his protégé and never took any interest in grooming a successor. He also said that his name should be removed from the firm name upon his death, presumably because the institutionalized practice of law was not the kind he loved and most respected.[26]

One of Davis' more frustrating pleasures was his relationship with West Virginians who had run afoul of the law in New York. Rich and poor, friend and stranger, resident and transient, they made their way to the firm's offices. The receptionists had standing instructions to admit anyone who claimed Davis' acquaintance, and during the 1930's the firm put some twenty matters on the "West Virginia Calendar." These ranged from traffic violations to assault and battery charges, and, although they were normally handled by an associate, Davis rarely escaped involvement. Nor did he want to escape it, for the cases kept him in touch with his origins.[27]

Even West Virginians practicing law in New York came in for advice. Davis once read a memorandum on an important business transaction for a young graduate of Washington and Lee. "I think you've told him properly," Davis said. Relieved and gratified, the young man offered to have his client send Davis $500. "No, George," Davis replied. "I put no charge on the books for less than $2,500. You just tell your client I said he's right and forget about it." [28]

Every year Davis also wrote a half-dozen or more letters full of free legal advice for West Virginians. He advised on divorce proceedings and investments. He explained to a Clarksburg widow how she could claim patent rights on a wire knife her husband had perfected. He counseled a Clarksburg legislator on proposed changes in the West Virginia laws on corporations. And he wrote lengthy opinions on various matters for small businessmen.[29]

One of the few West Virginia cases Davis did argue—a suit by Clem Shaver for a commission in a big coal deal—angered him as much as any case he ever had. He won a verdict for Shaver in a jury trial in the Marion County Circuit Court, but the Republican majority on the West Virginia Court of Appeals reversed judgment by a strict party vote. Convinced that the decision was a personal insult, Davis called it "one of the most infernal outrages" he had ever encountered. Never, he swore, would he argue before that tribunal again; the only consolation was that he had paid his "last political debt." [30]

« IV »

While the "West Virginia Calendar" was reaffirming Davis' humanity, his corporate practice was making him more and more tolerant of the concentration of wealth and power in America. Fundamentally, his concerns remained strictly legal. "He knows little or nothing about reorganizations, etc.," Burlingham observed. "He is just a law lawyer." Davis usually avoided comment on the strictly economic elements of a problem, and even at directors' meetings he remained silent until a legal issue was raised and his opinion was solicited. He would tell his corporate clients what they could or could not do within existing interpretations of the law, but he never devised novel or ingenious ways to circumvent the law. Preventive advice, in his view, was one of the lawyer's primary obligations; more than once when he told a client what he did not want to hear, the client went to another lawyer in search of a looser construction.[31]

This indifference to management and corporate policy strengthened Davis' conviction that he was a free moral agent, that his legal counsel had no relation to his social and political conscience. On Wall Street, no less than in Washington a decade earlier, he adhered absolutely to the principle that the lawyer's duty was to represent his client's interest to the limit of the law, not to moralize on the social and economic implications of the client's lawful actions. From the perspective of the bench, Holmes and Learned Hand agreed. Once, in the 1920's, Hand closed a talk with Holmes by saying, with mischievous intent, "Goodbye Mr. Justice, now go and do justice!" Holmes, who was leaving, turned around and said, "What's that you said?" Hand repeated the remark. Holmes retorted: "You know better than to say a thing like that. All we do is apply the rules of the game." [32]

Yet, as Frankfurter had contended in 1924, Davis' political eminence gave the entire quesion an added dimension. As a former presidential candidate and as one of the most respected leaders of the bar, Davis' legal involvements and pronouncements in his political and bar association addresses were of considerable influence. The nature of his practice and the degree to which it and his board memberships influenced his public philosophy is, therefore, a matter of historical moment as well as of biographical interest.

Actually, Davis represented one corporation against another corporation in most of his cases in the state and lower federal courts. Even some of his Supreme Court arguments had little political significance. Many hinged on technicalities, and several involved the assessment of damages against one corporation in favor of another. To take an example unique only for its color, in 1927, he successfully defended the P. Lorillard Company's use of the trade name "Beech-Nut" on chewing tobacco against the Beech-Nut (chewing gum) Packing Company's contention, as Holmes phrased it in his opinion, that the association of the Beech-Nut name with chewing tobacco would be distasteful to the gum company's more "refined female customers." [33]

Nevertheless, from 1925 to the New Deal, when he emerged as a national spokesman for conservatism, most of Davis' Supreme Court cases pitted him against the government. Six times he represented corporate or individual wealth in tax cases, and twice he signed *amicus curiae* briefs in kindred cases. Seven times he contended, for railroad, natural gas, or oil companies, that various state and Federal Trade Commission regulations were unconstitutional. And three times he defended corporations in antitrust proceedings. He even argued (unsuccessfully) that a West Virginia tax on natural gas at the well was unconstitutional. He also defended a stock option plan for the American Tobacco Company's directors and managers which, although found to be within the law, has been trenchantly described by one legal commentator as little less than "a fraudulent device to obtain huge bonuses of cheap stock for the managerial officers at the expense of the stockholders." * [34]

Inevitably, these cases exercised a subtle influence on Davis' thought, reinforcing his conservative strain in some instances and modifying his liberal strain in others. This was implicit in the contrast between his full-throated attacks on monopoly between 1900 and 1912 and his muted response to La Follette's assault on private economic power in 1924. It was explicit in his changing views on monopoly. He remained a proponent of the antitrust laws in the abstract. The alternative, he wrote as late as 1944, "is government regulated monopoly." He also contended that the Sherman and Clayton acts were more effective than commonly realized. "I feel sure they have prevented far more violations than they have ever punished. Any lawyer familiar with the subject can verify this. Transactions innumerable are vetoed by counsel every day in the year on antitrust grounds." Yet his defense of the antitrust laws was heavily qualified. He favored partial suspension during the early New Deal, he disapproved proposals to increase the criminal penalties, and he advocated an amendment that would have sapped them of their strength by permitting companies to form voluntary agreements. As early as 1925, in fact, he confided to Robert Lansing that he had virtually lost all faith in the Sherman Act:

> . . . after no small experience on both sides of cases brought to enforce it, I confess to you that I am skeptical as to the practical value to the public of any judgments which the government has secured under & by reason of it. Certainly anthracite costs us much more than it did in the old days of unregenerate combination & I am inclined to think the same thing can be said of petroleum & its products. "Striving to better, oft we mar what's well," & if the operation of natural economic laws does not save us I fear, Mr. Lansing, that we are doomed men. All of

* In addition to salary and bonuses of $2,077,000 for the year 1930, George W. Hill, president of the company and originator of the plan, received an allotment of stock worth $1,169,280. One retired officer of the company was also assigned an allotment.

which you may take for Laissez Faire or any other condigned thing you please.[35]

Davis' employment by utilities companies seems also to have intensified his long-standing opposition to government regulation. His call for increased regulation of railroads during the campaign had been more a function of his desire to hold the party together than of his personal philosophy, and the election was no sooner over than he returned to his anti-regulatory posture of earlier years. Convinced that state utilities commissions unfairly favored the consumer by issuing decrees more "political" than economic, by the fall of 1925 he was writing that the "constant fight to get a fair rate is disheartening." Neither then nor later did he face the question of how telephone, transportation, gas, electric, and other necessary monopolies could be made to levy reasonable charges in the absence of rate-fixing by government bodies.[36]

Davis' close ties to what he had once called the "predatory interests" saddened many of his friends from the Wilson era. John Lord O'Brian believed that he never gave as much to public service after he left London as he should have done, that he lacked the dedication of Taft, Hughes, and Stimson. Robert Szold, who had called him a "great man" as late as 1924, was ambivalent. "I don't think Mr. Davis' career in New York is the one that should be perpetuated," he said a few years after Davis' death. "The story of the man who represented the telephone company and Morgan is an epilogue." Yet Szold also said that his biography should be an inspiration if it were honestly written. Huston Thompson, who had remained in the public service, was most grieved of all. "I wonder what's got into John, I wonder what's got into him," he often said to his wife during the 1920's and 1930's. Finally, he asked Davis why he always seemed to be representing corporations or other conservative interests. Coolly, Davis replied, "I'll take any case that comes into my office." Thompson retorted: "John, you kind of shock me. That's just what Newton Baker [then the nation's foremost defender of utility corporations] has done!" [37]

Davis' formalism made it impossible for him to perceive, as his partner Wardwell did, that the views of most Wall Street lawyers reflected their corporate association in some degree. He liked to maintain the illusion of disengagement by jesting about his clients' crimes. "Just how guilty are you?" he sometimes said in opening a conference. He also enjoyed quoting John G. Milburn: "Who is going to tell the lies when they start asking the questions?" But he firmly insisted that "an advocate isn't worth his salt unless he winds up seeing only his own side of the case," and he invariably leaned far to see his client's point of view.[38]

A few acquaintances felt that Davis' life-style, rather than his corporate clientele, was responsible for the reinvigoration of his conservative strain. "He greatly enjoyed his associations with the rich," Arthur Krock mused a few years after his death. "This made him more conservative." But others, men who knew the real cast of his mind, believed that his style of life was simply a function of his root convictions. Thurlow Gordon, who had worked closely with Davis during his solicitor generalship, felt that he had changed hardly at all. Justice Brandeis was of the same mind. In agreeing with Huston Thompson in 1941 that Davis was a brilliant, charming conservative, Brandeis asked Thompson how Davis had acted when he saw him. "He acted as if he were a happy man," Thompson replied. "Well," said Brandeis, "that was what I would expect because he loved good living and he was a natural conservative and he was doing what he liked." [39]

Davis' resurgent conservatism did not isolate either him or the firm from public service. On the contrary, he gave his name and a very substantial amount of his time to civic pursuits. Besides taking several public interest cases, he served faithfully on the boards of a dozen or more foundations and associations and on scores of committees. Moreover, he encouraged his partners to do the same. A tradition of service had been established by Francis Stetson, Lansing Reed, and Allen Wardwell, but under Davis' leadership the partners' participation in governmental, educational, charitable, religious, hospital, and bar-association affairs increased greatly. Davis liked to quote Bismarck's maxim that every man owes ten years of his life to his government, and he urged his partners and associates to follow it in one way or another. "The time you spend," George Brownell reports him as saying in substance, "can be for the country or the state or the city, or for colleges, schools or churches, or professional organizations or what have you. And it can be by the day, by the month, or by the year—that's all up to you." Leaves of absences for government work were granted automatically, and the younger men became so infected with enthusiasm that they drafted a public-service stipulation for inclusion in the partnership articles. Davis approved the proposal at first, but he finally decided that a uniform requirement would be unworkable and that he should simply continue to encourage the principle.[40]

The firm prided itself on its support of the Legal Aid Society. With Davis' encouragement, Allen Wardwell was the Society's president for ten years and its "guiding light" for as many more. Since then the firm has been among the Society's liberal benefactors and one of the partners has always been an active member of its board. As chairman of the New York City Bar Association's committee on professional responsibility for several years, Brownell participated in setting up the city's program of legal assistance to the poor, which was supported primarily by federal funds under the Economic Opportunity Act.*[41]

By precept and example, Davis also imbued the associates and younger partners with an urgent sense of the majesty of the law and the courts. He was especially fond of a paper by Lord Moulton on law and manners, a key passage of which reads: ". . . to my mind the real greatness of a nation, its true civilization, is measured by the extent of this land of Obedience to the Unenforceable." So strongly did Davis subscribe to that view that he tended to invest the advocate's supporting role in rendition of that almost mystical concept, "justice," with a kind of priestly sanction. In the 1940's, for example, as Davis and a young associate left the courtroom, the associate expressed wonder that Davis had bothered to make a polished argument and smooth and subtle presentation of an extremely complex point before an ex-Tammany judge of limited legal background. To his great surprise, Davis stopped and said: "Young man, never let me hear you say that again. I couldn't be a lawyer and argue cases as I do unless I believed that the man on the bench, no matter what his origins, was doing his level best to do the right thing."[42]

Davis' attitudes and values had an elevating impact on everyone he touched; the firm's reputation for integrity, always high, became so fixed during his tenure that even the courts were prone to defend it. Once, about 1940, an opposing counsel charged one of Davis' partners with making a fraudulent contention in argument. Immediately, the judge interrupted him. "Wait a minute, counsel," he said. "The firm you're talking about is Davis Polk Wardwell Gardiner & Reed. You can't charge them with fraud!"[43]

---

* For a highly sophisticated analysis of the long-term failure of *pro bono* impulses, especially in the profession as a whole, see the American Bar Association's recent publication, F. Raymond Marks (with Kirk Leswing and Barbara A. Fortinsky), *The Lawyer, The Public and Professional Responsibility* (Chicago, 1972). Note, in particular, the final chapter, "The Practice of Law Is a Public Utility."

CHAPTER 17

Al Smith and Religious Toleration

But stay a moment and contemplate that Statute of Religious Freedom as Jefferson wrote it; how trumpet-like its words ring out across the years.

JOHN W. DAVIS

« I »

"I don't mind telling you," Davis said in 1926 to an old friend who suggested that he run for the presidency again, "that there are few things I want so little"; furthermore, there was not "the slightest possibility" the party would have him. Even dead politicians fall into two classes: those who do not know they are dead, and those who know it and are glad of it. He put himself in the latter class:

> I have had my fling and a good one, done my share of the work according to my lights and am now a candidate for a comfortable arm-chair in the ranks of retired statesmen. There is a feeling of satisfaction of getting such things out of one's system. From this time on, I am for the mammon of unrighteousness. I don't wish to be uplifted, reformed or exhorted. All I ask is a comfortable enjoyment of my own sins.[1]

Davis had rejected even nominal leadership of the Democratic party following the debacle of 1924; control of the national organization, he insisted, reposed in Congress. Privately, he wrote that the Democrats should find the lowest common denominator for East, South, and West, "bowing neither to conservatism . . . [n]or radicalism." In particular, they should disabuse high-minded businessmen of the notion that they were solely the party of the unsuccessful, by distinguishing between "financial comfort" and "special privilege." They should also allow Prohibition to "slumber" until a unifying issue emerged. But what that unifying issue would be, Davis did not profess to know. He evinced no interest in farm relief, tax reform, regulation of securities, abuse of the injunction, multipurpose river-valley development, or control or dissolution of monopolies. He protested that Franklin D. Roosevelt's proposal for a policy conference in 1925 would produce "an incipient riot." And he warned against "clarion calling"; the people, he said, "would not believe Moses though he rose from the dead." [2]

From time to time, again, mainly in private, Davis asserted that the United States had a duty to join the League of Nations and that it should remove debilitating "vital interests" and "national honor" clauses from treaties. He also chided Coolidge for his evasiveness on the World Court. "Without meaning to be flippant," he remarked to newspapermen the day before the inauguration, "I do not know what President Coolidge's idea about [it] is." Yet he supported the Administration's non-recognition policy toward the Soviet Union. He also approved its effort to maintain order in the Caribbean: "If a handful of American Marines will give the people of . . . [Nicaragua] a temporary respite from the armed bands of marauders who take the name of 'armies,' I should consider it a charitable act to loan them for that purpose." He was doubtful, however, that the controversy over Mexico's expropriation of American-owned oil lands could be resolved; and in January 1927, nine months before the Morgan partner Dwight W. Morrow began his successful mission, he wrote that it would be bootless even to suggest arbitration. [3]

Neither was he receptive to Newton D. Baker's report that Democrats from all regions were asking him to urge Davis to formulate and announce party policy on Mexico and Nicaragua. This could be done, Baker suggested, through a conference, headed by Davis, which would include Bernard Baruch, Franklin D. Roosevelt, Norman Davis, and, presumably, himself. Davis graciously dismissed the proposal, explaining that such a conference would alienate Congress. He also questioned the propriety of private citizens making public declarations on foreign policy. "I have great aversion to going off half-cocked and perhaps embarrassing those . . . [in] responsibility." [4]

« II »

Meanwhile, Davis became increasingly sympathetic to Al Smith's presidential aspirations. He felt indebted to the Governor for running for reelection in 1924, and he feared that the party would rend itself in two if its urban Catholic constituents were denied their choice a second time. He was convinced, furthermore, that Smith was of presidential stature. "He still carries in his conversation and public speeches many of the colloquialisms of his early surroundings," he explained to his friend Lord Shaw:

> High society is pained at the thought of his entering the White House, but . . . Smith has a great gift of popular leadership, wit, humor, courage, and one of the most direct and honest intellects I have ever encountered. I have sometimes wondered whether, if he had had a collegiate education, the blade might not have lost some of its temper in the effort to sharpen it. He is a thoroughgoing liberal and democrat; he is a man of great personal independence, and as such I support him with zest, although on questions like the tariff he leans nearer to the protective point of view than I do.[5]

Davis made no announcement of his decision to support Smith; nor did he otherwise try to impose his views on the party. Even his private policy statements were little more than polite responses to direct inquiries. He said that he hoped the Democratic platform would call for American membership in the World Court, warned against taking "any backward" steps on the League, and agreed with Roosevelt that the two-thirds rule on nominations should be abolished. Significantly, however, he did speak out on the most divisive issue of all: religious freedom.[6]

Smith's Catholicism had become a matter of national debate in the spring of 1927, when Charles C. Marshall, a New York attorney and an Episcopalian, questioned the fitness of any Catholic to be President in an article in the *Atlantic Monthly*. Citing numerous papal bulls and encyclicals, Marshall contended that the Roman Church still adhered to the Two Powers, or dual allegiance, theory, and that Catholic policy differed from American policy on marriage, education, and the Mexican situation. Was Governor Smith prepared to put American interests above those of the Roman Catholic Church? he asked rhetorically. Patently, he thought a satisfactory reply impossible.[7]

Smith read an advance copy of Marshall's article in disbelief. "I've been a devout Catholic all my life and I never heard of these bulls

and encyclicals and books," he said. Warned by Roosevelt and others
that he had to respond, he resentfully agreed to reply in the next
issue. With the help of Father Francis P. Duffy of World War I fame
and State Supreme Court Justice Joseph M. Proskauer, a Jew, he hammered out a defense of his career and faith—one that emphasized his
vigorous support of public schools as Governor and the diverse religious affiliations of his appointees. He concluded with a moving personal testament:

> I believe in the worship of God according to the faith and practice of
> the Roman Catholic Church. I recognize no power in the institutions
> of my Church to interfere with the operations of the Constitution of
> the United States. . . . I believe in absolute freedom of conscience for
> all men and in equality of all churches, all sects, and all beliefs before
> law as a matter of right and not as a matter of favor. I believe in the
> absolute separation of Church and State. . . . And I believe in the
> common brotherhood of man under the common fatherhood of God.

Moved by Smith's simple eloquence, Davis sent him a wire:

> YOUR REPLY IS WHOLLY ADMIRABLE. IT HITS THE BULL'S EYE. YOU HAVE
> DONE A SERVICE TO THE PEOPLE OF THE COUNTRY.[8]

Davis himself had first spoken to the issue in August 1926, in a
speech to the Virginia Bar Association on Thomas Jefferson's career as
a lawyer. After praising the Virginia Statute of Religious Freedom in a
long, calculated digression, he had cautioned that "some recent manifestations in the United States warn us not to be too vain over our
spirit of tolerance." Within a generation, he noted, a Jew had been
Prime Minister of Great Britain; a Catholic, Premier of Canada; and a
Protestant, President of France. He would be ashamed of his country
if it proved to be less liberal than those "great sister democracies."[9]

Davis' faith was at once idealistic and pragmatic. As a believer in
natural law, he deemed freedom of expression a near absolute; as a
man of affairs, he understood that few men are ruled by abstractions.
Jefferson's definition of religious freedom, he said on the one hand,
was philosophically complete. Individual Catholics, he said on the
other, had repeatedly proved their capacity for disinterested action; to
require them to renounce an outdated and theoretical substructure
that few laymen understood, much less acted upon, would be as unwise as it was unjust. There was no possibility that Smith would honor
the more distasteful "politico-religious teachings" of the Church, and it

Anna Kennedy Davis (1841–1917)　　　　John J. Davis (1835–1916)

The Davis house in Clarksburg　　　　John W. Davis at fourteen

Judge John W. Brockenbrough

The Rev. Dr. James A. Quarles

The Colonnade of Washington and Lee

Professor Charles A. Graves

Dean John Randolph Tucker

ABOVE: Media, the Mc-
Donald farmhouse

John W. Davis and Julia
McDonald at the time of
their engagement in
1893

amily group about 1907. SEATED: Hilary Richardson, Walter C. Preston, Anna K. Davis, John
Davis, Julia Davis. STANDING: Lillie Davis Preston, Emma Davis, Nan Davis Richardson, John
W. Davis, John J. D. Preston.

JUDGE JOHN J. JACKSON.

The judges in the miners' case of 1897

Nathan Goff, Jr.   John J. Jackson

John G. Johnson, the most feared appellate   Assemblyman John W. Davis, 1899
lawyer until 1917

bert Szold, Davis' assistant, and his principal brief writer

Solicitor General Davis, 1918

e United States Supreme Court in 1916. SEATED: William R. Day, Joseph McKenna, Chief
tice Edward D. White, Oliver Wendell Holmes, Jr., Willis Van Devanter. STANDING: Louis D.
Brandeis, Mahlon Pitney, James C. McReynolds, John H. Clarke.

Davis' daughter, Julia

The Lazslo portraits of the Ambassador and
his wife, Ellen Bassell Davis

A weekend at Chequers

vid Lloyd George, Lord Curzon, and the Ambassador

Lord Reading, Davis, and Lloyd George

ward, Prince of Wales, General John J. Pershing, unidentified officer, Minister of Munitions Winston Churchill, and Davis reviewing American troops at Hyde Park

Davis and the men who attracted him to Stetson Jennings & Russell in 1921. SEATED: Davis a
George H. Gardiner. STANDING: Frank L. Polk, Lansing P. Reed, Allen Wardwell.

was preeminently in the national interest that the presidency be opened to non-Protestants:

> This country cannot endure if its citizenship is divided into mutually suspicious groups along religious lines. There are said to be eighteen million Catholics; there are certainly several million Jews, and certainly millions without any church affiliation whatever. If you serve notice on these groups that the avenues of honor and public service are closed to any one of them, what effect do you think that would have on their feelings toward America, American institutions and their fellow-citizens?

Many powerful party leaders had already come to the same conclusions, though none expressed them so well.[10]

As the movement to nominate Smith gathered momentum, the opposition began to attack the Governor's flanks. Catholicism, the Shepherdstown [West Virginia] *Register* artfully asserted, was not the issue. Neither was Prohibition central, although it was foolish to believe that "these ardent temperance folks would stultify themselves by voting for a man who would be pledged to undo the work that they have done." Manifestly, the real objection to Smith was Tammany's treatment of John W. Davis; the Wigwam had "slaughtered," "knifed," "treacherously betrayed," and "deliberately destroyed" him in 1924.[11]

On January 18, 1928, the same day Davis wrote privately that "as a non-Catholic—who dissents on pretty much every point of Catholic doctrine—I am willing to go to the mat at any time on the right of a Catholic to hold any office for which he is qualified," two Southern demagogues attacked Davis himself. In 1924, charged Senators J. Thomas Heflin of Alabama and Cole Blease of South Carolina on the floor of the Senate, the West Virginian had sold out to the Catholics:

> *Mr. Heflin* . . . John W. Davis—a very able, clever gentleman but the poorest politician that ever stood in front of a political army—permitted these gentlemen, not as Americans, not as Democrats, but as Roman Catholics, to insist that he denounce the Ku Klux Klan and finish our chances of success at the polls after the convention had rejected that notion.
> Then they sent word to Mr. Coolidge, so it is said, to join Mr. Davis in denouncing the Klan. A bunch of priests called on him and told him Davis was going to denounce it. . . .
> Coolidge said he did not make a chatterbox out of his mouth about things that were not in the platform. [Laughter] And he got elected. . . . But what did John Davis do?
> *Mr. Blease.* He got what he ought to have gotten; he got beaten.[12]

274 The Law and Politics 1921–1937

Even Davis' sister Emma was troubled. What did her brother think of the oath of the Knights of Columbus, copies of which were flooding rural and small town post offices? (According to this spurious document, Knights swore in their "own blood" to "wage war" on Protestants and Masons by any means, including poison.) Davis replied that the oath was credited only "by bad men," and that the people circulating it were hurting the country more than the Church itself could possibly do. "Burn it and forget it." [13]

« III »

While Davis was privately defending Smith, Tammany was treating the Wall Street lawyer with contempt or indifference. It coldly rejected suggestions that he nominate Smith at Houston that summer; and neither before, nor during, nor after the convention did it take him into its confidence, much less its councils. Yet Smith himself remained cordial, and with good reason.[14]

Shortly after the convention, Davis accepted the chairmanship of a national committee of lawyers for Smith. To his partner Frank Polk, president of the College League for Alfred E. Smith, he sent an endorsement for publication: "No man now in public life has more consistently proclaimed the doctrines of equal rights to all and special privilege to none, of local self-government, of obedience to law, of governmental honesty and national fair dealing, and of political courage than he has done." [15]

Despite pledging $10,000 to Smith's campaign, Davis refrained from giving unsolicited advice. Even complaints about the Smith group's clannishness failed to budge him. "Life-long Democrats are feeling pretty sore because they are given no consideration," Lansing reported, "while the heads of the committees are a lot of second raters whom no one knows and in whom they have absolutely no confidence." Would not Davis urge Smith to arrange the nomination of Peter Ten Eyck, a Protestant, for the New York Senate seat? "Franklin D. Roosevelt might do, but his affiliations with Al Smith and his crowd would counteract the full value of his nomination, fine fellow though he is." Gently, Davis refused to act. He also ignored mounting requests that he urge Smith to soft-pedal his attacks on Prohibition. Indeed, when the Governor broke with the platform and called for repeal in his address of acceptance, Davis fired off a generous telegram:

CONGRATULATIONS ON YOUR SPEECH. FOR CLEARNESS, DEFINITENESS AND COUR-
AGE IT CANNOT FAIL TO IMPRESS THE COUNTRY.[16]

One of Davis' first actions as head of the lawyer's committee was to
delete a number of passages offensive to blacks from a pamphlet prepared by his old chief, former Attorney General Thomas W. Gregory.
"There is a very strong feeling that we are going to get a number of
negro votes in the Northern States," he explained, "[and] . . . I think
it would be wrong to send out any literature that the Republicans
could quote in an effort to drive them back." Later that fall, Davis
tried unsuccessfully to persuade the Postmaster General to remove the
mailing privileges of a self-styled "Rail Splitter" from Illinois named
W. Lloyd Clark. On a widely distributed postcard, Clark had charged
that Smith's running mate, Senator Joseph T. Robinson of Arkansas,
was "putting his O.K. on the program to catholicize, mongrelize and
debauch America"; that the Catholic Church wanted the "return of
the saloon and the brothel to people hell with lost and damned souls";
and that "every K. of C., whiskey vandal, gambler, white slaver and
derelict of the underworld is for Smith." [17]

The libel question again came up in mid-October, when the Reverend J. Frank Norris of the First Baptist Church of Fort Worth,
Texas, said in a radio sermon that "Smith came home drunk every
night at twelve," "has always been on the side of liquor drinking and
prostitution," and "is a crooked tool of Tammany." Boldly, Norris
challenged Davis to file suit against him in any court in the United
States. Although Davis was tempted, he realized that a trial would
dramatize the charges. "The great trouble with the truth," he sadly
observed, "is that it travels more slowly than the lie." [18]

In the meantime, Davis sent a long open letter extolling Smith's
character and rare gift of leadership to the editor of a friendly West
Virginia newspaper. He repeated his judgment that the New Yorker
had "one of the most direct and honest intellects" he had ever known,
and he praised his refusal to equivocate on Prohibition. "Governor
Smith believes that the wrong road has been taken. He has the courage to say so." His "justly famous" reply to Marshall's *Atlantic* article
was similarly courageous. Adding that no one who had marked
Smith's conduct as Governor could take seriously the "grotesque" assertions that he was a tool of Tammany, he averred that Smith had given
him, Davis, such "cordial support and assistance" in 1924 that he had
polled 144,000 more votes in New York City that Cox had in 1920.

The Democratic Publicity Committee termed the letter one of the most compelling documents of the campaign and had it distributed through the entire South in pamphlet form.[19]

« IV »

By mid-autumn Davis was ready to make a full-dress speech on religious toleration. Reports that evangelical clergymen were urging their congregations to vote against Smith had been pouring in all summer long. "Most of them think and talk in terms of Tammany," an Indianan wrote, but behind their fulminations "was a religious complex, frequently sub-conscious." Unquestionably, a West Virginian concluded, the religious issue was basic: "People . . . say it is because he [Smith] is a wet man, but when we get to the bottom . . . we find that it is the influence of the cross-roads ministers." Not only were the preachers predicting that Smith's election would bring the return of demon rum and the mongrelization of the American people, they were assuring their trusting listeners that papal power, even the Vatican itself, would be transferred from Rome to the United States. "It's terrible, the impression these people have gotten," said a loyal North Carolinian.[20]

It was against this background that Davis addressed the nation over a National Broadcasting Company hookup on the night of October 11. For twenty-three minutes, his words rolling out with all the authority of one of his great oral arguments, he pleaded for restraint, wisdom, and perspective. Using Jefferson's statute on religious freedom as his text and history as his witness, he recalled how Quakers had been "whipped, mutilated, hanged and exiled in New England and New York"; how Catholics had been discriminated against in Colonial Virginia; how Baptists had been "cruelly scourged in Massachusetts." He charged that denominational papers had allied themselves with "certain publications that make an unwholesome living as peddlers of religious hatred." He denounced the National Lutheran Editorial Association for supporting broadcasts of the bogus oath of the Knights of Columbus. He cited explicit denials of the Pope's temporal authority by James Cardinal Gibbons and Archibishop John Ireland. He even included a statement by William Jennings Bryan:

Those who have come into intimate acquaintance with representative Catholics did not need to be informed that they do not concede to the

Church authorities the right to direct their course in political matters, but many Protestants, lacking this knowledge which comes from personal acquaintance, have been misled.[21]

Davis' thrust was again both philosophical and practical. "The Constitution has spoken on religious liberty and proclaimed it throughout the land," he declared. "There should be no debate." Yet there was debate, most of it between Protestant and Catholic. This was regrettable, for "this is not a Roman Catholic question"; it was, rather, a question of vital import to members of all faiths as well as to those who, like Jefferson and Lincoln, belonged to no church:

If a member of one faith is to be excluded today from a civil right or opportunity or privilege, is to be declared by reason of his creed unfit or unsafe for public place or honor, what faith may not be trodden down tomorrow? "He only is free," says the maxim, "who lives among free men."

The abstract issue raised in the *Atlantic* by that "able gentleman," Charles C. Marshall, was simply not germane. Indeed, the discussion it engendered was both futile and harmful—futile because there was "no possibility of such a misfortune," harmful "because merely to discuss such a contingency gives it a color of possibility to which it is not entitled." If there was one "infallible recipe" for producing a Catholic political party, it was anti-Catholicism:

Men do not cohere for long periods simply from sentiment or in the hope of common advantage. Ambitions and desires and hopes change too rapidly for that. But there is a force that will tie them together with hoops of steel—a force whose binding power is beyond all human strength to loosen. It is the stern and bitter force of a common grievance based on the denial of a common right.

Never, said Finley Peter Dunne, the creator of "Mr. Dooley," had a speech appealed more convincingly to his mind or more profoundly to his emotions.[22]

Late in October, Davis campaigned through the South. In Wheeling, 40,000 people cheered him in the streets and a record crowd heard him warn that the country could not "survive if any of the core principalities of human liberty are touched with the hands of any individual for political, personal or sectarian purposes." In Memphis, where the Reverend Billy Sunday had charged two days earlier that Smith's ranks were filled with "boot-legger politicians, pimps, crooks, and streetwalkers," Davis announced that it was beneath his dignity "to debate with a man with a mind so putrid and with tongue so foul." [23]

Davis also scoffed at rumors that Smith intended to repeal the immigration laws. The Governor's concern, he pointed out, "was to prevent the separation of families in cases where good people have come to this country and are making good citizens. . . . He does not want to increase the grand total of those admitted, but to prevent unfair discrimination." As for the Republican candidate, Herbert Hoover, he was straddling on Prohibition, water power, and the tariff in order to please voters in all sections of the country: "I have great respect for Mr. Hoover. If I wanted to say anything to his detriment I would have to resort to quotations."

Yet even as he censured Hoover, Davis commended him for divorcing himself from bigotry. He seems not to have realized that the future President's denunciations of what Edmund A. Moore has aptly termed the campaign within a campaign were so mild that they served only to create an illusion of straightforwardness. As the Catholic weekly *America* pointed out in a series of stinging editorials, a general condemnation of a specific evil carries no conviction:

> If it was not within the power of Mr. Hoover and the Republican party to kill this campaign of bigotry, it was within their power to disavow it, and repudiate in unmistakable language the political aid offered by its authors. But that they never did. . . .
> From first to last, every agency of bigotry in this country worked for the success of the Republican party. From first to last, not one decisive word against any of these agencies was spoken either by Mr. Hoover, or by anyone entitled to speak for the party. [24]

« V »

For all their force and eloquence, Davis' speeches had a minimal effect on the voting: Republican candidates had persisted in repudiating the vilifiers perfunctorily or not at all; and the resistance of hard-core anti-Catholics seems to have been stiffened, rather than weakened, by Davis' appeals to reason and principle. As one of his typical incoming letters said, "I read with interest—and a great deal more disgust—the Press account of your speech last Thursday. In my opinion, you are a plain unvarnished liar." Other correspondents dismissed the religious issue entirely. Former Governor William E. Sweet of Colorado, an anti-Klan Democrat, wrote that as a prohibitionist he would not have voted for Smith had he been a Baptist. Another liberal Democrat complained that Smith had echoed the Republicans on the tariff. "Is the Governor honestly confessing . . . that the Democrats have been wrong all these years . . . ?" [25]

Yet, as with most invocations of high ideals, Davis' ringing words had enriched the national heritage just a little. They had also shored up many Catholics' wavering faith in America. From all over the country and from all strata of society came letters applauding his "noble sentiments" and "inspiring" phrases. "I believe," wrote Wall Street lawyer and Catholic layman William D. Guthrie, "that [the NBC speech] will become a classic, and learned by our children for generations to come. . . . God bless you." No one, said another attorney, could "fully comprehend how deeply my Roman Catholic fellow-countrymen have been wounded by the shafts of malice and ignorance"; he had literally wept as he listened to Davis' words. "I thought," wrote a woman from Long Island, "how wonderful is a fine mind, but still more so . . . the will to use it for justice and for good will among men." [26]

Despite Smith's defeat by more than six million popular votes, many Catholic publicists saw reason for hope. It would be wrong, warned a Providence diocesan editor, for Catholics to condemn Protestantism indiscriminately:

> For to say Protestantism would be to include in the indictment of big-otry all of those valiant Protestant champions of religious liberty in the South and the North—such as John W. Davis, Senator Carter Glass, Senator Pat Harrison, Senators Blaine, Norris and Bruce, ex-Senator John Sharp Williams, Professor Henry Van Dyke, Professor Nicholas Murray Butler, Professor John Dewey, Ellery Sedgwick and scores of others equally admirable for their patriotic attitude and their courage —and also the 9,000,000 strong non-Catholics who stood their ground against every assault of the hosts of religious fanaticism. [27]

Davis himself was shaken by the magnitude of Hoover's victory. "I don't envy the Republican Party its illegitimate daughters the Ku Klux Klan and the Anti-Saloon League," he said. As for the Democratic party, it was stronger than it would have been had it denied Smith the nomination which was his "by right." Furthermore, the Governor had made "a square, honest fight." [28]

Davis' assessment of his own role was characteristically restrained: "I am glad to have had a chance to express myself on the religious question, about which I feel very deeply. It is humiliating to me to find the country following the lead of such men as . . . Billy Sunday." [29]

CHAPTER 18

Selective Conscientious Objection

I assure you very expressively that in my opinion the conscientious scruples of all men should be treated with great delicacy and tenderness. It is my wish and desire that the laws may be as extensively accommodated to them as the protection and the essential interests of the nation may justify and permit.

GEORGE WASHINGTON

Eighteen months after the campaign of 1928, Davis again put his views on freedom of religion on record, in the celebrated case of Douglas C. Macintosh, a Canadian-born theologian who reserved the right of selective conscientious objection in his application for American citizenship.

At issue were far-reaching questions of law, history, and national policy. Was conscientious objection a constitutional right or a legislative privilege? How was religion to be defined, and who was to define it? Could a government bureau arbitrarily reverse a practice hallowed by long observance? Did a person agree to bear arms when he swore to "support and defend" the Constitution? Could Congress require of a naturalized citizen what it did not demand of a natural-born citizen? But it was Macintosh's adherence to the Augustinian concept of the Just War, adumbrating as it did one of the issues to be raised by the trial of the Nazis at Nuremberg, that engaged the sensibilities of idealists, drew Davis' firm into the clergyman's defense, and evoked a memorable dissent by Chief Justice Charles Evans Hughes.

« I »

Douglas Clyde Macintosh was an old-school Baptist by inheritance, training, and conviction. Born in Ontario in 1877, he was ordained a Baptist minister at the age of thirty. In 1909, the same year he received a Ph.D. from the University of Chicago, he was appointed to the faculty of the Yale Divinity School. Macintosh was not, and never had been, a pacifist. During World War I he volunteered for the Canadian Expeditionary Force as a chaplain, serving at Vimy Ridge and in the Battle of the Somme before returning to the United States on a speaking tour for the Allies. He then went back to France to run an American Y.M.C.A. hut behind the lines at St. Mihiel. After the war he resumed teaching at Yale as Timothy Dwight Professor of Theology.[1]

Dr. Macintosh wore pince-nez and high starched collars, spoke in clipped accents, and was reserved among strangers and casual acquaintances. Although proud, stubborn, and independent-minded, he was neither vainglorious nor conceited. Intimates valued him for his warmth, unswerving devotion to principle, and inspiring qualities as a teacher. "The more passionately Mac felt about a position, the softer his voice became. When he started to whisper it was time to head for the hills." His doctrinal outlook was conservative, but his methodology was liberal. He established himself as a philosopher of note with *The Problem of Knowledge* in 1915 and as a theologian of distinction with *Theology as an Empirical Science* four years later. In 1928 Macintosh offended many of his co-religionists by contending, in a series of lectures in Calcutta, that non-Christian philosophies were often infused with religious values. Yet he considered himself a staunch defender of evangelical Christianity, and he maintained his Baptist connections throughout his life.[2]

Dr. Macintosh took out first citizenship papers in 1925. Four years later he joined 185 other applicants for naturalization in a crowded federal courtroom in New Haven. One of the other petitioners had been arrested three times in the preceding eighteen months; two would acquire criminal records during the following three years; one would be brought before the Humane Society for gross abuse of her children; and several were, or would become, prostitutes. All except Macintosh would be granted United States citizenship.[3]

Dr. Macintosh was determined not to fight in an immoral war. As he said on his written application, he wanted "to be free to judge the necessity" of bearing arms, he did not believe in having his moral

opinions settled by the majority, and he could not promise to act
against what might be the best interests of humanity:

> I do not undertake to support "my country, right or wrong." . . . I am
> not willing to promise beforehand, and without knowing the cause for
> which my country may go to war, either that I will or that I will not
> "take up arms in the defense of this country," however "necessary the
> war may seem to the Government of the day." [4]

Under interrogation by the court on June 24, 1929, Macintosh amplified those views. His counsel, Dean Charles E. Clark of the Yale
Law School, then argued for his admission on the ground that Dr. Macintosh's age made the question of military service moot. But District
Judge Warren B. Burrows, a simple, patriotic Baptist who was to resign to run for the state attorney generalship the next year, denied the
petition. No matter how estimable Macintosh's character, said the
Judge, if men of his beliefs were naturalized there would be no one to
fight "when the powder begins to burn and the bullets to fly"; patently, the Reverend Doctor was "not attached" to the Constitution of
the United States.[5]

Had Macintosh applied for citizenship before World War I, he
probably would have been naturalized as a matter of course, for the
right of conscientious objection was long established. The original colonies had all exempted members of recognized pacifist bodies from
bearing arms, and the Fundamental Constitution for the Province of
East New Jersey (1683) had not even required formal religious attach-
ments. In ratifying the United States Constitution, North Carolina
and Virginia had suggested that "any person religiously scrupulous of
bearing arms, ought to be exempt, upon payment of an equivalent to
employ another to bear arms in his stead"; and Madison had included
a similar statement in his original draft of the First Amendment. Although both that draft and a revision incorporating the phrase, "or to
infringe the rights of conscience," were struck out, apparently in the
interests of brevity, the rights of conscientious objectors were understood by many to be implicit in the final version.[6]

During the nineteenth century, several powerful pronouncements
defined religion in far less restrictive terms than those that twentieth-
century judges and legislatures came to use. In 1833, to cite one of
many examples, Joseph Story declared, in his *Commentaries on the
Constitution*, that the rights of conscience were beyond the "just
reach" of any human power. "They are given by God, and cannot be

encroached upon by human authority, without a criminal disobedience of the precepts of natural, as well as revealed religion." Almost sixty years later, Justice Stephen J. Field denied that religion had any necessary relation to membership in an organized church:* "The term . . . has reference to one's views of his relations to his Creator, and to the obligations they impose of reverence for His being and character, and of obedience to His will." It was not to be confused "with the cultus or form of worship of a particular sect," which was a definition Davis had rejected by implication in the *Selective Draft Law* cases of 1917.[7]

For many years the Naturalization Service had required an applicant for citizenship to prove only that he was a man of good character and to swear simply that he would "defend the Constitution." But in the Naturalization Act of 1906, Congress expanded the oath to read: "support and defend the Constitution and laws of the United States against all enemies, foreign and domestic; and to bear true faith and allegiance to the same." Polygamists and anarchists were barred from naturalization for the first time, though no mention was made of pacifists or of any obligation to bear arms. Not until 1916, a year of rising war fever, did a federal judge refuse to naturalize a Quaker. Then, in 1917, the Selective Draft Act limited exemptions from combatant service to members of "any well-recognized religious sect or organization" whose creed prohibited the use of arms. Liberal as that provision was (some 57,000 religious pacifists were excused from combatant service during World War I), it drastically narrowed the definition of religion.[8]

The Naturalization Service began, on its own, to ask all applicants if they were "willing if necessary to take up arms in defense of this country," and in 1923 it incorporated the query into the naturalization form as Question 22. Three years later, in response to an inquiry from Roger Baldwin, director of the American Civil Liberties Union and an applicant for a passport, the State Department ruled that it did not construe the oath "as necessarily involving physical defense of the Constitution" and did not perceive "any good reason" why pacifists should not take it; but if Baldwin continued to have conscientious scruples, the Department would consider his application if he simply swore to defend the Constitution "so far as his conscience would allow." [9]

---

* In that same opinion, *Davis v. Beason,* Field nevertheless proscribed polygamy.

« II »

Judge Burrows' refusal to naturalize Dr. Macintosh in July 1929 evoked an impassioned editorial endorsement in conservative nationalist circles. The New York *Herald Tribune* predicted that "national suicide" would result if citizens refused to surrender their will in crises of life and death. The Memphis *Commercial Appeal* announced that good citizenship could "permit of no reservations." Other newspapers thanked Burrows for saving the country from "anarchism." Almost alone among major dailies, Walter Lippmann's New York *World* attacked the ruling. "The absoluteness of this doctrine," it declared, "is as naïve as it is intolerable. The majority of wars in which any great Power engages are not life-and-death struggles in which its existence is at stake, but little wars of policy, interest, or accident. It is absurd to lay down a rule which makes it the absolute obligation of the citizen to give unquestioning support to every war. . . . The *Herald Tribune's* position is nothing more or less than a challenge to the principle of a moral responsibility." [10]

Even before Judge Burrows ruled against Macintosh, American Civil Liberties Union officials had assured the theologian that their "resources" would be at his disposal. Immediately after the decision, Roger Baldwin wrote Macintosh that the Civil Liberties Union would be gratified to help in the appeal. Baldwin also asked the Reverend Dr. Harry Ward of the Union Theological Seminary to "urge" Macintosh to let the ACLU enter the case. [11]

The American Civil Liberties Union's interest transcended Macintosh's appeal for citizenship. The ACLU's broad purpose was to strengthen civil liberties by winning landmark suits, and it hoped in this instance to secure modification of a ruling laid down two months earlier against Rosika Schwimmer, a Hungarian-born feminist, pacifist, and atheist. On May 27, 1929, with Holmes delivering his last searing dissent in a free speech case, the Supreme Court had declared Madame Schwimmer ineligible for citizenship for refusing to agree to bear arms or to desist from propagating her pacifist views. (Ordinarily, women were not asked Question 22; it had been propounded to Madame Schwimmer at the instance of the Women's Auxiliary of the American Legion.) [12]

The impact of *Schwimmer* had been felt almost at once, two Quaker women and one Mennonite being denied citizenship shortly after the decision was rendered. Meanwhile, Marie Averill Bland, a Canadian-

born nurse and Episcopal clergyman's daughter who had turned pacifist after rehabilitating shell-shocked soldiers, came up for naturalization in New York. Judge William Bondy did not ask her to respond to
Question 22. Nonetheless, she insisted on qualifying her oath with the
phrase, "so far as my conscience as a Christian would permit"; she also
announced that she would not serve in any war. This bound Judge
Bondy to *Schwimmer,* and he rejected her application.[13]

The ACLU thought that the conventional backgrounds and exemplary reputations of Dr. Macintosh and Miss Bland might induce the
Supreme Court to view the issues raised by *Schwimmer* in a new
perspective. So Baldwin asked Dr. Ward to suggest to Macintosh that
his case be coordinated with Miss Bland's. Ward had difficulty establishing rapport with the theologian. "Macintosh is a reserved person
and I have to get on with him gradually," he reported. At length,
however, Dr. Macintosh agreed to cooperate, for the larger principle
was preeminent to him as well. He also told Ward that the ACLU
could argue his appeal if pending arrangements with a prominent
New York firm failed to materialize.[14]

Within hours of Judge Burrows' ruling against Macintosh, Professor
Jerome Davis of the Yale Divinity School had asked his old friend
Allen Wardwell to take the case, on the theory that it would be better
if a leading Wall Street office handled the matter. He added that, although Macintosh was limited in means, he was one of the most distinguished theologians in the world. Four days later Professor Davis
reminded Wardwell that "faith in God and Freedom of Conscience"
were fundamental American traditions and that Macintosh was
"merely upholding the principle for which our forefathers came to this
country." Wardwell, a prominent Episcopal layman of strong liberal
convictions, did not need to be reminded. After conferring with Dr.
Macintosh, he recommended to John W. Davis that they take the case
without fee.[15]

Not only did Davis approve, he said with rare fervor that he wanted
to argue the appeal himself. At various times, he called Judge Burrows' ruling a "damn absurdity," commented on Macintosh's "Nordic"
background, and deplored the "fantastic and irrelevant" nature of the
Naturalization Service's questions. He also commented bitingly on the
"violence" the decision did to common sense. If any man ever fulfilled
the requirements of citizenship, he asserted, that man was Dr. Macintosh.[16]

Davis' partners believed that he took the appeal because it was brought to him, because it presented a debatable issue under law, and because it afforded him an opportunity to express his deep feeling for personal rights against governmental power. As he caustically remarked at the time, the framing of Question 22 by the Naturalization Service rather than by Congress made the question "a pure bureaucratic innovation . . . , an adornment and embroidery of the act which Congress itself had passed." He may also have been influenced, if only subconsciously, by a desire to purge himself of the illiberal statements he had made in his World War I cases, the tone of which had been wholly out of keeping with his abiding concern for the right of conscience. But however that may be, he felt more keenly about this case than almost any he ever argued.[17]

Dr. Macintosh's decision to turn the appeal over to Davis Polk rather than the American Civil Liberties Union probably brought the theologian closer to victory, although at some intellectual cost. In accordance with standard practice, the firm established the lines of authority at once. Macintosh was asked to agree that there be no direct connection with any other case, including that of Miss Bland. He was also requested to make no public statements. Davis then planned his strategy with Wardwell and Charles Poletti, a young associate who later served briefly as Governor of New York. Many laymen and some lawyers expected a frontal assault on *Schwimmer*, but Davis knew all too well that to ask a lower court to overrule the Supreme Court on a very recent decision was to lose before the judges left the bench. Dismissing suggestions that they attack *Schwimmer* directly, he instructed Poletti to distinguish *Macintosh* by underscoring Madame Schwimmer's non-religious outlook and her refusal to promise that she would not propagate her views.[18]

The brief Poletti drew up that spring in the names of Davis, Wardwell, Dean Clark, and himself denied that the two cases were related: The government had emphasized in *Schwimmer* that religion was not at issue, Madame Schwimmer having declared herself an absolute atheist. She had also avowed that she had "no sense of nationalism, only a cosmic consciousness of belonging to the human family." Furthermore, she had refused to promise that she would not propagate her pacifist views in wartime. Indeed, Justice Holmes had intimated in his dissent that the majority had acted in fear that Madame Schwimmer might engage in activities such as had been declared unconstitutional in

*Schenck v. United States.** Dr. Macintosh, the brief pointedly asserted, "does not anticipate" so doing.

The brief further contended that the rights of conscience were implied in the Bill of Rights. Brevity, it said, in explanation of the failure of the Constitution to include an explicit guarantee, usually implied a broad or general construction; but, in any event, "it should not be forgotten that Article IX . . . provides that the enumeration in the Constitution of certain rights shall not be construed to deny or disparage others retained by the people."

"Not all wars are just," the brief continued. "Unfortunately a few are unjust." International jurists had long recognized this, and the United States had made the premise part of the supreme law of the land by renouncing war as an instrument of national policy in the Kellogg-Briand Peace Pact of 1928. Had not the Supreme Court itself declared in *Schwimmer* that the Pact was "in harmony with the Constitution and policy of our Government?" Manifestly, Dr. Macintosh aspired to adhere to the same high purpose:

> Since it is to be assumed that the Government will carry out in full the obligation solemnly undertaken in the adoption of the Kellogg Pact, a Christian citizen will have slight occasion, indeed, to confront a clash between the military demands of his government and the dictates of his conscience.[19]

Davis had no illusions that the decision would hinge on the Kellogg-Briand Pact; nor is it likely that he believed it should, despite the emphasis he later gave it in oral argument. As he was to say in testimony before the House Committee on Immigration and Naturalization in 1932, "some of us have an opinion as to the efficacy of the Kellogg Pact." Accordingly, two long sections of the brief dilated on matters more likely to impress the legal mind. The first cited Chief Justice Marshall's opinion in *Osborn v. Bank of the United States:* "[A naturalized citizen] is distinguishable in nothing from a native citizen except so far as the Constitution makes the distinction; the law makes none." The second emphasized Congress' failure to enact a law requiring an applicant to bear arms. Question 22, it asserted, was merely informative to a court; an applicant was under no congres-

---

* Schenck had circulated anti-draft leaflets among soldiers during World War I; Holmes, for an unanimous court, had upheld his conviction under the Espionage Act in an opinion that denied that free speech had ever been absolute, either in peace or in war.

sional or constitutional obligation to give it "an unqualified affirmative answer." [20]

For all its force, the brief disappointed secular liberals. Although Roger Baldwin, on first reading, found it "clear, forceful [and] convincing," on reflection, he lamented its religious thrust. Some of Macintosh's colleagues at Yale also regretted the imputation that the philosopher-theologian had been governed by religious principles alone. "I did not so understand his position," one of them said. "It seemed to me that his intelligence, not religious scruples, was to be his guide." Should not the religious emphasis be reduced? Dean Clark agreed. "I wonder," he wrote Wardwell, "if the dilemma with which Dr. Macintosh was faced is not one with which any conscientious man could be faced as to certain things near and dear to his heart." Felix Frankfurter, who read Clark's copy of the brief, was of like mind. He commended the industry and research that had gone into the brief, but concluded that "it did sound pretty religious." The Harvard professor also noted that General Ulysses S. Grant had indicted the Mexican War in more sweeping language than had Lincoln, who was cited in the brief.[21]

"Of course . . . [the brief] is religious," Poletti replied to Frankfurter with a touch of asperity. "I regret . . . [this] as much as you do." Nevertheless, religious scruples formed the cornerstone of Dr. Macintosh's position, and both Davis and Wardwell believed that the only way "to slide by" the *Selective Draft Law* and *Schwimmer* cases was to emphasize the religious factor.[22]

« III »

Tension continued to rise during the two weeks between the completion of the brief and the opening arguments in the Second Circuit Court of Appeals on May 19, 1930, before Judges Martin T. Manton, Learned Hand, and Thomas W. Swan. At Wardwell's suggestion, Poletti advised Macintosh to demonstrate his concern by appearing in court. He added that Davis was very excited and wanted to meet him. Dean Clark told a reporter that if Judge Burrows' decision were allowed to stand, not only would Harry Emerson Fosdick and President Henry Sloane Coffin of Union Theological Seminary be ineligible for citizenship, Jesus of Nazareth would also be barred. Then, just before the hearing, the rector of Grace Episcopal Church declared in a sermon that true patriotism in the United States "means loyalty to a country which has signed the Kellogg treaties renouncing war." [23]

Davis thrust hard on the practical aspects of the case in his opening argument in the ornate federal courtroom in the old Post Office Building at Broadway and Park Row. He extolled Macintosh's character, emphasized that he was not a dangerous propagandist, and challenged the essence of an oath. It was doubtful, he observed, that any man had ever sworn allegiance "without making some reservation which would leave him some freedom of action." Near the end he moved the bench to laughter:

> If war ever came again to this country, I for one would not sleep any sounder if I knew that I was being defended by an army of middle-aged Baptist ministers with conscientious scruples against fighting.

Davis also seized the advantage when Judge Hand asked the befuddled government counsel if he believed that an act of Congress necessarily expressed the will of God. Would counsel, demanded Davis, bar naturalization to an alien who opposed the Prohibition Amendment? Davis also hammered on the distinctions between *Schwimmer* and *Macintosh* for the benefit of Judge Manton, who seemed to have difficulty grasping them. Finally, he declared that the Constitution "plainly does not require anyone to set aside his conscientious religious beliefs" and that it was "unconscionable to require an alien . . . to bind himself to conditions not imposed upon American-born citizens." Even the harassed government attorney was impressed. "Mr. Davis was, as usual, masterful," he said to Poletti.[24]

More important, Davis was persuasive. On June 30, in an opinion which paraphrased or incorporated large sections of both the brief and the oral argument, Judge Manton, for a unanimous court, reversed Judge Burrows' decision. He contrasted Madame Schwimmer's "absolute atheism" with Dr. Macintosh's "upright sense of obligation to his God." He affirmed Davis' contention that naturalized citizens should receive the same privileges as native-born citizens. He even upheld Davis' construction of the Kellogg-Briand Pact. "There is," said Manton, "a distinction between a morally justified and an unjustified war, as recognized in international law. Such recognition was given in the recent Kellogg Pact." [25]

Davis was so elated that he replied with lighthearted immodesty to a friend who wrote that he had "A SNEAKING SUSPICION" that Manton's opinion contained a good portion of the brief. "Many thanks," said Davis. "What the blank do you think briefs are for anyhow?" [26]

Others were not so pleased. Roger Baldwin could not understand the reasoning behind the court's distinction between *Macintosh* and *Schwimmer*. "I hope for the sake of light on the whole matter an appeal may be taken to the Supreme Court." Charles Howland of the Society of Friends felt that it was "a pity that the Court lost an opportunity to make a substantial contribution to American constitutional doctrine." A few newspaper editorials were especially perceptive. Why, asked the New York *Telegram*, should the courts "discriminate between hatred of war based on Christian conscience and hatred of war based on a more universal and more purely human form of conscience"? To base a grant of citizenship on particular religious beliefs, added the *World*, was to come "dangerously near to prescribing a religious test for citizenship." [27]

The elevation of Christian conscience above other forms of conscience had in fact implied a narrow, formalistic definition of religion, one at variance with Dr. Macintosh's broadly philosophical conception. It had also breached further the wall of separation of Church and State by giving special dispensation to those who fit that definition. Yet even if Davis had wished to support philosophical, as distinct from religious, conscientious objection—and there is no evidence that he did—he could not have done so in good faith. For as working counsel, he was morally bound to make the most effective argument possible for his client, not to propound theories that might prepare the ground for new law in a future case while assuring defeat in the case at hand.

« IV »

Davis altered his strategy in no essential in arguing against the appeal before the Supreme Court in April 1931. He told the bench with all his usual pungency that "the idea that a priest in his cassock, a nurse in her gown, a woman with her children hanging to her skirts, and a paralytic in his chair must all swear to bear arms before they become citizens reduces the process of naturalization to an absurdity." He declared that "what we want now is not more men who agree with the majority but [more] who are willing to go against the majority on occasion." And he pounded hard on the inconsistency of the government's adherence to the Kellogg Pact and its warlike demands upon

Dr. Macintosh. The government counsel, Solicitor General Thomas D. Thacher, gave almost as much as he took. How, he asked at one point, did Davis square his assertion in the *Selective Draft Law* cases, that it was the citizen's highest duty to defend his country by force of arms, with his present contention, that "the rights of conscience are inalienable rights which a citizen need not surrender and which no government or society" can remove? [28]

Davis' himself felt that he had fallen below his usual level. He left the chamber grumbling to the marshal that he could "think of nothing more foolish than a bunch of old men with broom sticks going off to war." And he confided to Charles Warren that he was dissatisfied with his argument. "The truth is I feel this case so deeply that it is hard for me to do it justice. I am sufficiently irreligious myself to have a profound respect for the religion of others, and the result reached in this case seemed to me so absurd from any standpoint of practicality —having so little relation, indeed, to the personality and fitness of the applicant—that I get hot all over whenever I think about it." [29]

Four weeks later, in an opinion almost unique for its indifference to the First Amendment, Justice Sutherland overruled the Court of Appeals for a five-to-four majority. He declared that Davis' contentions that exemption of conscientious objectors was "a fixed principle of our Constitution" and that applicants for naturalization were being discriminated against were "astonishing." Congress, not the Constitution, gave them such rights as they possessed, and Congress could remove them at will. Unlike the native-born citizen, Macintosh was "unwilling to rely . . . upon the probable continuance by Congress of the long-established and approved practice of exempting the honest conscientious objector." Passing over the Kellogg-Briand Pact altogether, Sutherland then rendered one of the most uncompromising endorsements of the war power ever made by a member of the Supreme Court. "Unqualified allegiance to the Nation and submission and obedience to the laws of the land . . . are not inconsistent with the will of God"; the only limitations on the war power were those in the Constitution or in international law:

> To the end that war may not result in defeat, freedom of speech may, by act of Congress, be curtailed or denied so that the morale of the people and the spirit of the army may not be broken by seditious utterances; freedom of the press curtailed to preserve our military plans and movements from the knowledge of the enemy; deserters and spies put to death without indictment or trial by jury; ships and supplies requi-

sitioned; property of alien enemies, theretofore under the protection of
the Constitution, seized without process and converted to the public
use without compensation and without due process of law in the ordinary sense of that term; prices of food and other necessities of life fixed
or regulated; railways taken over and operated by the government; and
other drastic powers, wholly inadmissible in time of peace, exercised to
meet the emergencies of war.[30]

Not until 1954 would Davis again be so outraged by an opinion of
the Supreme Court. "Dear Dr. Macintosh," he said in a one-sentence
letter to the theologian, "I blush for my country." The finding of the
majority, he acidly remarked in other letters, was as wrong in law as it
was in policy. It would doubtless meet the approval of 100 per cent
Americans, most of whom would not fight if "there were any way in
the world to wiggle out of it"; but by any thoughtful measure it was
"a sad reflection on the intelligence of Congress and the country." [31]

In his book-lined study in Timothy Dwight College at Yale, where a
reporter sought him out on the afternoon of the decision, Dr. Macintosh said that he had rather expected the result. He brightened momentarily on learning that Chief Justice Hughes had written a forceful
dissent in which Holmes, Brandeis, and Stone had concurred. But he
responded grimly when asked if he would modify his position in order
to gain citizenship: "I'm not budging from my stand one bit. I will
make no further attempt to obtain citizenship if my point of view is
unacceptable." [32]

Davis believed it hopeless to ask for a reargument. "What is written
is written so far as those gentlemen are concerned, and a petition for
rehearing is usually a 'self-denying' document." His associates were so
wrought up, however, that they persuaded him to file. They felt that
Justice Sutherland's failure to face the fact that the naturalization
oath, unencumbered by leading questions, was virtually the same oath
required of all civil officials gave them a substantive issue. (Davis had
emphasized this point in argument, and Hughes had taken it up in his
dissent.) They also hoped that Justice Owen J. Roberts, a moderate,
might reconsider in the light of Hughes' moving evocation of the central moral question. " [In] the forum of conscience," the Chief Justice
had said, "duty to a moral power higher than the State has always
been maintained." Many conscientious, law-abiding citizens had
unquestionably made such a reservation:

There is abundant room for enforcing the requisite authority of law as
it is enacted and requires obedience, and for maintaining the concep-

tion of the supremacy of law as essential to orderly government, without demanding that either citizens or applicants for citizenship shall assume by oath an allegiance to God as subordinate to allegiance to Civil power. . . . The attempt to exact such a promise, and thus to bind one's conscience by the taking of oaths or the submission to tests, has been the cause of many deplorable conflicts. The Congress has sought to avoid such conflicts in this country by respecting our happy tradition. It would require strong evidence that the Congress intended a reversal of its policy in prescribing the general terms of the Naturalization Oath. I find no such evidence.[33]

The feeling that Roberts might switch on reargument rested on more than intuition. Chided by Holmes for being "with the wrong crowd," Roberts had reportedly confessed unease over the authoritarian tone of some of Sutherland's booming periods. It was possible, Dean Clark suggested to Wardwell, that Roberts might welcome an opportunity to avoid being "permanently set down" as in agreement with the entire opinion.[34]

The petition for reargument drew fire, ironically, from one of Dr. Macintosh's staunchest supporters—the *Christian Century*. As a practical matter, declared a long editorial, the petition was so persuasive that it might lead to a reversal. But as a comprehensive critique of the un-American implications of the majority opinion, it was gravely deficient. "The consequences of the court's decision are far more penetrating than Dr. Macintosh's attorneys seem to discern." If the decision were enforced, not only would Quakers and Mennonites be denied citizenship, as Davis contended, but every citizen, naturalized or native-born, would be affected by the court's virtual mandate that all Americans subordinate their consciences to the will of Congress. This, manifestly, was "tyranny." [35]

Three months later, Justice Roberts having held firm, the Supreme Court denied the petition for a rehearing. The *Christian Century* and many churchmen continued to seethe, but some secular-minded liberals professed satisfaction. A reversal, wrote the historian-columnist Harry Elmer Barnes, would probably have made religious conviction the only legal basis for pacifism. This would have put those who refused to fight from philosophical or sociological convictions, unrelated to the supernatural world, at a distinct disadvantage. "The free thinking internationalist is now on the same plane with the religious objector." [36]

Davis never ceased to believe that the decision was a "farce." Nor did he ever lose his interest in the issues raised by the case. Even before the petition for reargument was denied, he had Poletti draft for the American Civil Liberties Union and the Society of Friends an amendment to a bill to revise the Naturalization Act:

> An alien otherwise so qualified shall not be denied citizenship under any provision of this Act solely by reason of his refusal on conscientious grounds to promise to bear arms, but every alien admitted to citizenship shall be subject to the same obligations in all respects as a native-born citizen.[37]

Davis also had Poletti draft a statement for submission to the Committee on Immigration and Naturalization in the winter of 1932 over his (Davis') signature. Then, late in March, he made a special trip to Washington to testify for a liberal, pragmatic approach to naturalization. "No more effective showing could have been made," a special ACLU newsletter said of his presentation. "The professional patriots who crowded the committee room were stunned and sobered." [38]

Nevertheless, Davis' eloquence failed to move a majority of the committee. The bill was never reported out, numerous other measures suffered the same fate, and a personal appeal by Davis to Secretary of Labor Frances Perkins that Question 22 be eliminated by administrative ruling brought no result. Not until 1942, when Congress amended an act of 1940 by authorizing the naturalization of conscientious objectors then serving in the armed forces in a non-combatant capacity, was the way opened for a possible reversal of the *Schwimmer, Macintosh,* and *Bland* decisions. (The Court had ruled against Miss Bland on the same day it had ruled against Dr. Macintosh.) [39]

Within a year, James Louis Girouard, a French-Canadian Seventh-Day Adventist, filed final naturalization papers in Massachusetts. Asked the usual questions, Girouard replied that he would serve as a non-combatant but would not bear arms. Over the vigorous protest of the naturalization examiner, the District Judge admitted him to citizenship. The government secured a reversal on appeal, after which the Supreme Court granted certiorari.[40]

To the dismay of the American Civil Liberties Union, Girouard's counsel, former Attorney General Homer C. Cummings, tried to distinguish the *Schwimmer* and *Macintosh* cases. Julian Cornwell, a Wall Street practitioner, then drew up an *amicus curiae* brief for the ACLU in consultation with Davis. A short document which bore Davis' stylistic imprint, it shot directly across Cummings' bow. After establishing that Girouard's case was distinguishable from the others on the facts, it held that the distinctions were irrelevant for two reasons: First, the Court had read into the oath in those cases "a Congressional intent which does not appear on its face, which had not previously been supposed to be there, and which agencies of government other than the Naturalization Service have generally assumed not to exist"; second, the 1942 amendment plainly showed that Congress did not intend that applicants promise to bear arms.[41]

Davis had argued the first proposition too often to believe that it would have any effect; after citing his standing aversion to *amicus curiae* briefs, he signed the ACLU brief only as a courtesy to Cornwell. But on April 22, 1946, to Davis' surprise and gratification, the Court ruled in their favor by a five-to-four majority. In an opinion which drew heavily on Hughes' dissent in *Macintosh*, Justice William O. Douglas reversed the lower court's ruling against young Girouard and overturned *Schwimmer, Macintosh,* and *Bland* in the process. Dismissing the notion that Congress' failure to change the oath implied that it supported the government's construction of it, Douglas said that it was "treacherous to find in congressional silence alone the adoption of a controlling rule of law." Furthermore, the "affirmative recognition" in the 1942 amendment, that one could be attached to the principles of the government without bearing arms, negated any inference that might be drawn from Congress' earlier silence. He added a moving coda to Hughes' dissent in *Macintosh:* "Throughout the ages, men have suffered death rather than subordinate their allegiance to God to the authority of the State. Freedom of religion guaranteed by the First Amendment is the product of that struggle." [42]

The decision prompted more than the usual flurry of interest in the Davis Polk offices. Poletti was no longer with the firm, but Davis, Wardwell, and Porter Chandler, who had helped on the second *Macintosh* brief, were all there to share in the vindication. Their thoughts turned to Dr. Macintosh. Fifteen years earlier Wardwell had written the theologian that he was confident that we would "return to the more liberal point of view of our forefathers" before long; now Wardwell suggested that Chandler inform the theologian that he was at last eligible for citizenship.[43]

It was too late. In 1942 Dr. Macintosh had suffered an incapacitating stroke. Sometime between 1931 and 1946, moreover, he had quietly reaffirmed to his wife his attachment to his Canadian heritage. It seemed best, Mrs. Macintosh replied, to let the matter drop. Lapsing into the past tense, she added:

Mr. Macintosh had stood for freedom of conscience no doubt since his boyhood—he was a Protestant evangelical Baptist or Non-conformist by inheritance for generations, and intellectually a Liberal, but with all he was a Canadian and a Britisher. I could do a Proustian piece on this case—on its history. He was deeply disappointed with the Supreme Court decision, but in the depths there was profound compensation. The ancient loyalties could prevail.[44]

CHAPTER 19

Brother at the Bar

John Davis was the kindest person to other lawyers. A brother at the bar was a brother. FELIX FRANKFURTER

There was no difficulty in getting John W. Davis to take unpopular cases. This was his greatest contribution. He gave courage to hundreds of lawyers. MORRIS ERNST

[The advocate] lends his exertions to all, himself to none. The result is . . . for the Court to decide. It is for him to argue. He is . . . an officer assisting in the administration of justice, and acting under the impression that truth is best discovered by powerful statements on both sides of the question. LORD ELDON

Three times in the 1930's Davis won the gratitude of his profession by defending members of the bench or bar charged with misconduct of one sort or another. In one case he conceived the issue to be the independence of the judiciary, in another the privileged position of a counsel whose clients had acted criminally. In the third he simply accepted his responsibility as a leader of the bar to represent an unethical attorney in disbarment proceedings. In no instance did he charge a fee, although one case involved two grueling jury trials, an inordinate amount of time, and the services of one of his partners and four associates.

« I »

Late in February 1929, an obscure Brooklyn Congressman named Andrew L. Somers sent to the Speaker of the House of Representatives several communications from three of his constituents. Their gist was that Grover M. Moscowitz, United States District Judge for the Eastern District of New York, should be impeached. The details of the allegations are still partly shrouded, for the subsequent hearing was closed and the body of the report sealed. But enough was said on the floor of the House and in leaks to the press to reveal their gravamen: Moscowitz had systematically favored members of his former law firm in the assignment of lucrative bankruptcy receiverships and had conspired with a group of lawyers to mulct the estate of a Brooklyn businessman.[1]

Judge Moscowitz brushed off the charges until it became apparent that Somers intended to press them in Congress. The Judge then asked for an investigation, and sought to enlist Davis as counsel. Davis was in Bermuda at the time, so Moscowitz talked to Theodore Kiendl. Kiendl immediately sent Davis a cable:

TED CONFIDENT HE CAN DO BULK OF WORK AND LIGHTEN YOUR BUR-
DEN VERY CONSIDERABLY. CONSIDER MATTER IMPORTANT AS UNWAR-
RANTED ATTACK ON JUDICIARY. HOPE YOU CAN FIND IT POSSIBLE TO
ACCEPT.[2]

Davis accepted by return wire. On Kiendl's advice, Judge Moscowitz then announced that he welcomed the investigation "in the abiding conviction that it will disclose that my career . . . has been irreproachable." He added that he would discontinue holding court until the investigation was completed.[3]

In Washington, meanwhile, Representative Emanuel Celler reluctantly revealed the charges during debate over a resolution to investigate. He did so, he explained, because, even after a trial, newspapers usually "only carry a very small notice with reference to the established innocence of the man previously condemned." According to Celler, Judge Moscowitz' difficulties originated in the bankruptcy of one Samuel Levine, a Brooklyn businessman. Just before declaring bankruptcy, Levine had converted mortgages into cash and had then withdrawn more than $100,000 from his bank account. Summoned to testify on those actions, he had committed suicide. Afterwards, in testimony before a special commissioner, one of Levine's two sons was so evasive that Judge Moscowitz cited him for contempt. In due course,

Moscowitz appointed Abraham J. Halprin, a member of his old firm, Strongin & Hertz, to handle the receivership. Halprin was awarded $27,420 in fees, a sum approved but not necessarily fixed by Judge Moscowitz.[4]

Embittered by the entire proceeding, the Levine brothers accused Moscowitz, before Representative Somers, of conspiring with Halprin and other lawyers. Some time later a Brooklyn manufacturing firm sent Somers correspondence purporting to show that the Judge had handled other receiverships in the same fashion. Although Celler conceded that the fees were larger than should have been allowed, he emphasized that nothing in the materials Somers had sent to the Speaker indicated whether Moscowitz or the bankruptcy referee had actually set the amounts. (He glided over Moscowitz' failure to reduce them.) "I have known this judge for many years," he added, "and I believe him to be . . . honest and upright." He and all other district judges were victims of a "vicious system" which required them to parcel out receiverships along political lines. "Do not fire your ammunition upon one judge in Brooklyn. . . . Investigate them all." In spite of Celler's plea, the House approved a joint resolution to investigate Judge Moscowitz three days later. Earl C. Michener, a Michigan Republican, was named chairman of the five-man investigatory committee.[5]

Soon after Davis' return from Nassau, Michener confided to him that he disapproved of instituting impeachment proceedings in this manner. He readily consented to Davis' request that the hearings be private so as not to impair Judge Moscowitz's usefulness should he be cleared. He also honored Davis' request that they begin as soon as possible. For, as Davis explained, "it would be a grave injustice to Judge Moscowitz to deprive him of an early opportunity to confront his accusers and make a prompt reply, a thing which clearly he cannot and should not attempt to do through the press." [6]

Protracted hearings followed behind closed doors at the Association of the Bar building at 42 West 44th Street in New York. Two weeks after the first phase ended in mid-April 1929, Representative Somers talked freely to a newspaperman:

> I expect impeachment of Judge Moscowitz. A judge can make one or even two or three mistakes in the assignment of bankruptcy cases to lawyers who loot the bankrupt firms or persons of almost all their available assets, without implicating himself in any way with a bankruptcy ring. But when he continues to make assignments to such bankruptcy looters there are only two conclusions to draw.

The judge is either assigning the cases to crooked lawyers with a knowledge of what they are doing or he has not enough intelligence to perform his official duties in a competent manner in order to maintain the dignity of the bench.

Pressed by Davis for an explanation, Somers replied that the quoted remarks were "decidedly" inaccurate. But he did not make a public retraction.[7]

Six weeks later, the New York *World,* whose reporters were picking up scraps of information from participants in the hearings, announced that Moscowitz had been receiving income from mortgages and rents through his old law firm. Bold and misleading headlines set off the story:

MOSCOWITZ GOT $53,000 FROM STRONGIN,
NAMED TO BANKRUPTCY
LINK MOSCOWITZ AS PROFIT TAKER WHILE ON BENCH

The New York *Evening Post* then commended the *World* for publishing evidence that would not otherwise have come out. This prompted a protest by one of Davis' partners to the editor of the *Post:* "I have the utmost contempt for the conduct of a paper like the *World.* [It] . . . starts accusations through its own reporters . . . based on charges of utterly unscrupulous characters, and then, to justify its position, presents every news item which it can get in an absolutely false and biased way." A week later Representative Michener tried to undo the damage with a clarifying statement:

> In so far as the articles suggest or intimate that Judge Moscowitz received any payments from Strongin & Hertz for anything that transpired after he ascended the Federal bench, the articles are contrary to the specific findings of the accountants.
>
> The accountants' report nowhere indicates that Judge Moscowitz received so much as one penny from the firm of Strongin & Hertz or from any other source, that he was not entitled to receive from investments made and services rendered prior to the time that he was sworn in as a Federal Judge.[8]

Nevertheless, other evidence confirmed that Judge Moscowitz had systematically assigned receiverships to members of his former firm and had consistently approved excessive fees. These were not indictable crimes, but they were palpable violations of Canon 12 of the Judicial Ethics code, which had been drawn up by an American Bar Association committee appointed in 1922 (the year Davis became president of

the Association) and headed by William Howard Taft. Canon 12 enjoined "undue favoritism" in assigning receiverships, directed judges to
"avoid excessive allowances," and declared that consent of counsel did
not relieve them of the obligation to be "scrupulous" in granting or
approving compensation.[9]

Infuriated by Davis' denial that Moscowitz had violated Canon 12,
Somers sent Davis and each member of the subcommittee a copy of
Davis' memorable summation in the Archbald impeachment trial of
1913. Among the many passages Somers underlined were these:

> We insist that the prohibitions contained in the criminal law by no
> means exhaust the judicial decalogue. Usurpation of power—
> unblushing and notorious partiality and favoritism, indolence and ne-
> glect, [are] all violations of his official oath, yet none may be
> indictable. . . .
> [W]hat he can do, ought to do, and must do, is to avoid putting
> himself in any position to which suspicion can rightfully or reasonably
> or naturally attach. More can not be expected of him, but nothing less
> should be permitted.

Davis never acknowledged receipt.[10]

Almost a year passed before the full Committee on the Judiciary issued a report. The majority concluded that, although impeachment
proceedings were unwarranted, Judge Moscowitz's appointment of
members of his former law firm to receiverships was indefensible:

> [T]he action of Judge Moscowitz . . . is not only not to be indorsed
> but is deserving of condemnation as unethical and dangerous and
> threatening the destruction of the confidence of the bar and the com-
> munity in the court and calculated to bring it into discredit.

A statement of "additional views" signed by Representatives Fiorello
La Guardia of New York and Hatton W. Sumners of Texas contended
that the evidence did justify impeachment.[11]

Relieved yet disappointed, Davis and Kiendl declared in a press release that the committee's criticism of Judge Moscowitz was without
any fair basis in the record. They also denied that he had indulged in
favoritism: "Much has been said about the repeated appointments of
his former partner and associates to bankruptcy and equity receiverships. Any informed person must appreciate that it has been the custom in both federal and state courts to appoint those in whom the
court has the utmost confidence."[12]

Four months went by before Judge Moscowitz could bring himself to write Davis. Ever since his ordeal, he explained, he had been trying to find words to thank him and Kiendl. Thereafter, until his death, he sent Davis a hand-written note every New Year. The message varied little: "You have always been so kind and gracious." "You have always been my great tower. of strength." [13]

« II »

Ten months after Judge Moscowitz's uneasy restoration to grace, Davis began a four-year struggle to save one of New York's leading trial lawyers, Isador J. Kresel, from Sing Sing. The case involved a mistrial, two separate jury trials, and an appeal, as well as a vendetta, a bribe-seeking juryman, and a "Gilbert and Sullivan" judge. It marked one of Davis' few arguments before a jury since leaving Clarksburg. ("I am interested in proving . . . that the old fiddle can still play a few tunes.") It saw him study Pitman shorthand to prove a crucial point, engage in fiery exchanges with the prosecuting attorney, and accuse a star witness of perjury. And it was climaxed by the most scathing appellate argument of his career. Never, in the view of his friends, did he perform more courageously or serve his profession more nobly. John Lord O'Brian summed up the sentiment of bench and bar alike: "the bravest thing Davis ever did was to take the Kresel case." [14]

The indictment of Kresel grew out of the failure of the Bank of the United States in December 1930. The president, Bernard K. Marcus, and the executive vice president, Saul Singer, were indicted for misapplying funds. Kresel, counsel to the bank and a member of its board of directors, was also indicted, but he was too ill to stand trial with Marcus and Singer. One-tenth of the families in New York were said to have had accounts in the Bank of the United States, and though the misapplication of funds had no bearing on the bank's failure, feeling ran so high that angry crowds picketed the courthouse and hurled epithets at the counsel for Marcus and Singer. A fifteen-year feud between Kresel and Special Assistant District Attorney Max D. Steuer, perhaps the most brilliant trial lawyer of the era, heightened the drama. [15]

A passionate little man of Galician birth, Kresel barely came up to Davis' shoulder and weighed hardly more than a hundred pounds. His stentorian voice, dark luminous eyes, drooping black moustache, and inquisitorial manner stamped him for what he was—a shrewd, probing investigator. He was known about the bar as "The Ferret." As warm, sensitive, and ingratiating outside court as he was cold and merciless inside it, Kresel aroused a vague protective feeling; among the many eminent men he numbered as friends were former Governors Alfred E. Smith and Nathan L. Miller, Judges Samuel Seabury and Joseph Proskauer, former Secretary of State Bainbridge Colby, and former Attorney General George W. Wickersham, All would testify to his reputation for integrity.

Kresel had been chief aide in Charles Evans Hughes' notable investigation of the insurance industry in 1905. Eight years later he had obtained the impeachment of Governor William Sulzer. Shortly after World War I he dug out the evidence upon which seventy-four cement manufacturers were indicted under the Sherman Act. Then, in 1928, his investigation of "ambulance-chasers" for the New York Bar Association resulted in that rare event, a mass disbarment of lawyers. At the time the Bank of the United States failed, he was Judge Samuel Seabury's chief counsel in the investigation that would induce the resignation of the playboy mayor, James J. "Jimmy" Walker. "Kresel," said Seabury, "served with an unflagging industry and devotion and . . . outstanding skill and ability. His contribution . . . cannot be overestimated." [16]

The Seabury investigation was the last in the sequence of events leading to Kresel's indictment. A decade and a half earlier Kresel had clashed with Max Steuer in a suit brought by a burlesque actress against a Broadway producer. Kresel charged Steuer with suborning perjury, and Steuer was subsequently brought up for disbarment. The charge proved to be false. Steuer then resumed practice, his income soaring to a million dollars a year in the late 1920's. In time he became the most influential adviser of Mayor Walker's hand-picked leader of Tammany, John F. Curry. As his own fortunes rose, Steuer's resentment of Kresel seemed to grow stronger, and about a year before the Bank of the United States proceeding, he charged Kresel with subornation of perjury in a hearing over a will. Nothing came of the charge.

Steuer seems to have been a curious blend of the realist and idealist. A small man physically, he had a reed-like voice, a bald, egg-shaped head, and a large, dominating nose. His slit-like lips often curled, and his characteristic expression was one of shrewdness and comprehension of the ways of men. By 1930, according to his friends, he was beginning to despise the political system he served and to think of going into public service, or at least public office. "To aspire to the [State] Supreme Court bench you must be subservient to your district leaders and at the same time sell your manhood," he resentfully told a group of Brooklyn law students. Steuer took the Bank of the United States case without fee, so he said, because "the depositors of this bank are people of my kind and I am interested in them." [17]

Whatever his motives, Steuer showed no disposition at first to implicate Kresel, the star defense witness, during his prosecution of Marcus and Singer; on the contrary, he tried to get him to pin full responsibility on the bankers. But Kresel, who seemed confident that he could save Marcus and Singer without injuring himself, insisted that they had simply acted on his considered advice as to what was within the law. On Kresel's third day on the stand, however, Steuer forced Kresel into an apparent contradiction of the testimony he had given before the grand jury, and Marcus and Singer were shortly found guilty. ("The only real crime committed here," their distinguished counsel Emory Buckner privately complained, "was the crime of the other New York banks which let this one go under.") Kresel was then indicted for perjury. Davis and Kiendl, who had earlier agreed to represent Kresel on the original indictment in the belief that he had really been charged with the crimes of his clients, readily assumed the additional responsibility of the perjury trial. It was, said Davis, "a most unjustifiable indictment against a fellow lawyer." [18]

Bitterness tainted with anti-Semitism was rampant when Kresel's trial for perjury began in May 1932. Marcus' and Singer's convictions were then on appeal, and many people were still demanding vengeance for the loss of their savings in the bank failure. As a Fifth Avenue resident wrote Davis, "How an American of breeding and background . . . can sully his reputation by defending the mean little band of cheap highbinders who wrecked the Bank of the United States is beyond my comprehension. Isn't it high time you Americans of good Anglo-Saxon antecedents reclaimed your country from the scum who have possessed it?" Harold Medina, who was not yet a federal judge, even concluded privately that Kresel "was faking, making himself sick by taking some kind of dope" in order to avoid being tried with Marcus and Singer. Yet much of the bar probably shared William D. Guthrie's view, that "poor Kresel [was] . . . being crucified and ruined for what was at worst an error of judgment without the slightest moral wrongdoing or unethical professional conduct." [19]

The charges against Kresel centered on his denial that he had told the grand jury he had warned Marcus and Singer there was "something suspiciously wrong" with an $8 million loan to some of the bank's affiliates, that he would have nothing to do with it, and that he deplored the fact that Singer's son, an associate in his own firm, had engineered it. Kresel disputed the wording of all these statements, insisting especially that the phrase "suspiciously wrong" had been part of a subjunctive rather than a declarative statement.

For Davis to create reasonable doubt that Kresel had made the statements in the form alleged, he had to show that the court stenographer had submitted an inaccurate transcript. This he did by mastering shorthand to the point that he was able to draw several damaging admissions from the stenographer, Louis Benson. But just as the cross-examination was building to a climax, Kresel reported that one of the jurors had secretly asked him to arrange a loan. The judge then declared a mistrial.[20]

Davis pursued the same line of interrogation in the new trial. He first forced Benson to admit that he had had difficulty deciphering some symbols quickly and that the perjury charge was based on a "corrected" copy of his shorthand transcript. He then induced the grand jury foreman, Lionel F. Straus, to retract his direct testimony and concede that Kresel had in fact used the subjunctive. Kresel's actual words, said Straus, had been "it would appear that this was a devious transaction" and "if it was I would have had nothing to do with it." Straus further admitted that Benson had consulted him about unclear symbols in the shorthand version of the transcript.[21]

These admissions made Steuer's testimony almost anticlimactic, though he came on strong at first. As he entered the witness box, he smiled broadly in the direction of Kresel, who turned his back on him; and throughout the direct examination his air was that of a man in complete control of himself and the situation. Under Davis' increasingly penetrating interrogation in cross-examination, however, he gradually lost his composure, and, finally, his self-control. "You interrupt me, Mr. Davis," he blurted out, "because you know that will prevent me from giving an accurate answer." He then conceded that he neither "could nor would" undertake to repeat verbatim a statement he had heard eighteen months earlier. Although he reverted to his original construction of Kresel's words before leaving the stand, the damage was done. "Yes," said Davis to an associate who complimented him on his skill in drawing out Steuer, "didn't I drive that nail through and bend it back on the other side." [22]

Confident that he had shown that the evidence was insufficient to permit a finding of guilt, Davis moved for a directed verdict. In a two-hour argument on June 21, he pointed out that the Appellate Division, in ruling on Marcus' and Singer's conviction, had said that the $8 million loan had not been material. He noted that one Justice had even dismissed Kresel's alleged statement as "an expression of opinion which could not have been competent for any purpose." He asserted that Benson stood exposed as an incompetent and unreliable stenographer. Then, as a tremor ran through the courtroom, he charged that Steuer had lied on the stand: "I assert that there is just as much ground for indicting Steuer for perjury . . . as there was for indicting Kresel." [23]

Justice Samuel J. Harris accepted only one of Davis' contentions, but that was enough. Kresel's words, he ruled, were not material. They were "purely and simply the viewpoint, characterization or opinion which he wished the grand jurors to believe was his as to the morality of the transaction. . . . This being so, as a matter of law I must direct a verdict of not guilty." [24]

Yet Kresel's ordeal was far from over. The appeal of Marcus and Singer had moved from the Appellate Division, which had upheld the conviction, to the Court of Appeals, where it was still to be heard. A reversal would relieve Kresel from standing trial on his original indictment; an affirmance would cause him to be tried for conspiring with the two bank officers. For ten long months he waited as his health deteriorated and he became so pressed for funds that he brought suit against a former client for a $25,000 fee. Finally, on March 14, 1933, the Court of Appeals upheld the conviction of Marcus and Singer in a divided decision. Justice Irving Lehman said, in a biting dissent, that not only was most of the testimony at the trial irrelevant, but "the admission . . . of the transcript of Mr. Kresel's testimony before the grand jury . . . was clearly erroneous and prejudicial." [25]

« III »

Late in September 1933, fifteen months after his acquittal on the perjury charge and a year and a half after his indictment for conspiring with Marcus and Singer, Kresel's second trial began. Justice George H. Taylor, Jr., emotional and undisciplined to an extreme, presided, and James G. Wallace, the prosecutor in the perjury trial, again represented the state. Gloom pervaded the almost empty court room through thirty-eight trial days and six thousand pages of testimony. Kresel passed the time rolling paper pellets. Only when he took the stand to claw like a caged tiger did the luster return to his eyes. "He's a lawyer; they all do that," the judge half-sneered when Wallace complained that Kresel was trying to get around direct questions with extended replies. "Give me a chance," Kresel cried, "I'm fighting for my life." Otherwise he sat listlessly, his strength gradually ebbing. Not even Davis and Kiendl, trying to force gaiety at lunch every day in a near-by Italian restaurant, could lift his spirits.[26]

Although most of the ground covered was familiar, the testimony did disclose that Kresel had tended to withhold rather than proffer advice on several questionable matters. It also revealed that, after warning Marcus and Singer against at least one probably criminal action, he had failed to report their conduct to the other directors.[27]

On November 9 and 10, in a passionate four-and-a-half hour summation, Davis contended that Kresel was a scapegoat accused of "a purely legal crime involving no moral turpitude." Kresel had been indicted, he said, in an allusion to the bank's embittered depositors, "in the days when the public was clamoring for a victim." Yet the transaction in which he was allegedly implicated "had no more to do with the collapse of the Bank of the United States than last week's weather report." Kresel's involvement was open and aboveboard; the prosecution had failed utterly to disprove his testimony that he had advised Marcus and Singer to take no action on the critical deal until the state superintendent of banking approved it. Patently, he was the innocent victim of an inaccurate stenographer. Then, as Kresel's eyes filled with tears, Davis made a stirring appeal for the sympathies of the jurors: Must this man lose "honor, liberty, and life itself" on this "flimsy" charge?[28]

An extraordinary spectacle followed. For ten hours, spread over two days, Wallace inveighed against Kresel. He charged that the defendant's personal relations with Marcus and Singer "prevented him from being the kind of a lawyer who would give candid advice." He riddled Davis' contention that Kresel had been indicted on a technical law. Of course it was a technical law, he thundered. "This law was not passed . . . with the approval of bankers or their counsel. It was passed to restrict them. . . . The legislators knew that bankers could not be caught in outright stealing because they are too clever for that. The law was framed to keep them from misapplying funds." As for Davis' intimation that Kresel had been indicted in order to discredit the Seabury investigation, it was utterly unfounded. He further assailed Kresel for failing to inform the other directors of the auditors' criticism of

Marcus' and Singer's policies: "He's no imbecile, no poltroon, but a great lawyer and a man of high repute. He lied, and you know in your hearts he lied." [29]

The worst was yet to come. Disregarding the lack of connection between the crimes charged to Kresel and the failure of the bank, Wallace implored the jury to "give a little attention to the poverty of depositors, who are mulcted by these people." Kresel, he said, was a "pilot fish" who guided "sharks that scour the financial seas." His character witnesses—Seabury, Wickersham, Proskauer, and the rest—were a troop of wooden soldiers who marched only because they had earlier "used him"; when the Bar Association "pundits" had cracked down on ambulance chasers, Kresel was "the bloodhound" they got to do the job. "He was cold, he was relentless, he was implacable in the pursuit of the little shysters, the little ambulance chaser, the pothouse politician." [30]

At 1:50 P.M. on the afternoon Wallace completed his diatribe, Justice Taylor began an even more remarkable charge to the jury. For hour on hour, standing most of the time and sometimes checking the accuracy of his dates with Kresel, he rambled on. At five o'clock he declared a ten-minute recess, and at 9:20 he recessed for another ten minutes. Finally, at 10:50, he stopped. He had filled 163 pages of the printed record.[31]

For an hour afterwards, too exhausted to move, Justice Taylor remained on the bench. Down below, Kiendl and another lawyer played checkers with an associate on an improvised board. For a while Davis strolled up and down the corridors, stopping occasionally to chat with Kresel and the other lawyers. About midnight a young man, two women in black, and an elderly man, apparently relatives of Kresel's, entered the courtroom. An hour or so later Davis stretched out on a bench, and Kiendl put an overcoat over him. At 6:50 A.M. the jury filed in to return its verdict: guilty. Kresel showed no emotion, but the elderly man who had come in at midnight gasped audibly and broke into a soft sob. As Taylor prepared to remand Kresel to the Tombs, Kiendl requested that he be released on the same bail he had put up before the trial. Wallace demurred briefly, then consented. Two weeks later Kresel's wife died.[32]

Immediately after Kresel's release, Davis and Kiendl went to Davis' apartment for breakfast. Deeply depressed, Davis said that they would have won if he had let Kiendl handle the trial. He added that criminal jury cases took too much out of him and that he would never try

another. Still, there were compensations, the most gratifying a letter
from Kresel:

> It isn't often that it is given to a man to see the soul of another. I have
> seen yours . . . it is divine. You have given to the bar an example of
> professional brotherhood and fine chivalry never before equalled in
> our jurisprudence, and you have done it at great personal sacrifice and
> in an atmosphere that I know was repugnant to you. Yet you stood by
> me these many weeks because of your fine sense of justice and because
> you believed that a brother lawyer was being persecuted.[33]

Many leaders of the bar felt almost as strongly. As William D. Guthrie wrote, in sending Davis a cherished bronze in recognition of his
"lofty and self-sacrificing devotion in the defense of the good repute of
our great profession," he hoped that the acclaim and gratitude of the
profession would be of some consolation for his bitter experience and
the cruel miscarriage of justice. If Davis had any reservations about in-
vesting himself in the appeal, these and other letters dispelled them;
his devotion to the case, in the words of one of his assistants, was
"fantastic." [34]

One year later, almost to the day, Davis stood at the bar of the Appellate Division in Albany, prepared to begin the greatest *tour de
force* of his career. For five hours on November 21 and 22, 1934, he defended Kresel and castigated Wallace in words such as he had rarely, if
ever, used in an appellate court. Gone was the gracious deference to
opposing counsel, the poetic allusions and swift flashes of humor, the
generous concessions on minor points—gone were most of the other
traits that had made him the most polished appellate lawyer in the nation. Kresel, he declared in opening, had been convicted for an "offense which involved no moral turpitude and which was based on a
transaction which caused no injury to any one and by which neither
the defendant nor any one else profited in the slightest, and which had
no effect on the closing of the Bank of the United States." Furthermore, the case had been seriously prejudiced by a summation "unparalleled in the history of jurisprudence" and "transcending all limits of
professional propriety."

Relentlessly, Davis continued. Wallace, he charged, had repeatedly
interjected certain elements into the case "in order to give a nauseat-
ing atmosphere of hypocrisy, bank-wrecking, personal gain and cun-
ningly conceived and clandestinely executed dishonest schemes to
profit at the expense of stockholders and depositors of the bank and

public." It was absolutely impossible from the dead page of the printed record even to approach an adequate portrayal of the effect the District Attorney's two-day diatribe had had upon his auditors. "Nor can we even begin to describe his unfettered ranting or his intemperate and inflammatory mode of address." Justice Taylor's charge to the jury fell into the same category. Not only was it "inflammatory, prejudiced and irrelevant," it was longer than "flesh and blood could stand"; no human being could be expected to deliberate fairly and intelligently after being subjected to such an ordeal.[35]

As Davis sat down, Kiendl whispered that the Court of Appeals had sent word that it was willing to wait until morning to hear his argument in an extremely complex insurance case involving Equitable Life. Davis replied that he was as ready as he ever would be and that he would appear in the court within fifteen minutes. He then walked across the street to the courtroom and completed his preliminary statement of the facts without referring to the eleven volumes on the table before him. So impressive was his performance that interested observers packed their bags and returned to New York, confident that the case was already won. The following morning, glancing infrequently at a few notes in his hand, Davis rounded out the most nearly perfect argument of his career—the only one in which he said everything he wanted to say in exactly the form he had wanted to say it. "In all my experience," said Kiendl, "I have never witnessed such a dual performance." [36]

On January 16, 1935, the same day on which a favorable judgment came down in the Equitable case, the Appellate Division reversed Kresel's conviction in an opinion which echoed Davis' oral argument. "There is no evidence," the court said, "that appellant urged or incited anyone to commit any offense. The extent of his offending is that he failed to forbid his clients to proceed. He swore that he believed the plan to be within the law." Besides, both the Appellate Division and the Court of Appeals were divided in their construction of the law. "A lawyer is not to be held criminally responsible because he honestly gives mistaken advice upon a doubtful question of law. . . . Infallibility is an attribute of neither lawyer nor judge."

Other passages sharply censured District Attorney Wallace and Justice Taylor: Wallace's denigration of Kresel's role in the investigation of ambulance chasers was in effect a denunciation of Kresel for his public services; Taylor should have rebuked Wallace for those and other slanders. Furthermore, Taylor himself had instructed the jury in language that confused rather than clarified. "It seems incredible to us that twelve laymen could intelligently comprehend and apply what the court said." [37]

For an hour or more that afternoon Kresel sat in his office sipping port, receiving callers, and talking over the telephone. "Isn't it grand, isn't it grand," he said again and again. At one point a faintly familiar figure was ushered in—William B. Scofield, one of the jurors who had found him guilty. He had come, he explained, to extend his congratulations. "What do you think of that!" Kresel exclaimed. Finally Davis entered with beaming countenance to chat and pose for photographs with Kresel. The decision, he told reporters, was just and warranted; "at no time has my confidence been shaken for a moment in Mr. Kresel's entire innocence and his personal and professional integrity." [38]

Even Wallace, basking in a nomination for a judgeship, seemed pleased. "I'm not entirely sorry to see Kresel get a little break the same as I got one." Only Max Steuer was bitter. "Mr. Steuer has nothing to say," his secretary told a reporter, "and doesn't want to hear about the case." [39]

Kresel was eternally grateful to Davis and Kiendl. For a decade or more he gave them an annual dinner, which was attended by some fifty judges and leaders of the bar, and every New Year until he died he sent Davis a gift of cigars or liquor and a warm, effusive message. "Mr. Kresel loved Mr. Davis," one of Kresel's associates recalled. "He couldn't find enough ways to express his gratitude." Yet the scars remained. Kresel remarried following the reversal, and he won some of his most important cases after resuming practice. But, as a former partner mused a quarter of a century later, "it was never quite the same." People always remembered that he had been implicated in some sort of scandal.[40]

For Davis there was only honor. Said *The New York Times:*

> He threw himself into the matter with as much devotion and tenacity as if Mr. KRESEL had been his brother. He was, in fact, a professional brother in need of help, and Mr. DAVIS gave of his best. In some of his pleas he displayed an emotion like that of ERSKINE, who once said to the jury, with tears in his eyes, "I shall go out from this court an unhappy man if you do not acquit my client."

Davis' own reaction was more low-keyed. "The Kresel case was a just outcome if ever there was one," he remarked to a partner. "If I had not won it this business of the law would have been too perilous for tender minded souls like you and myself to continue in. If we must all go to jail for the number of times we disagree with the appellate courts, I fear there would be few left outside." [41]

« IV »

Four years after Kresel's exoneration, Davis again represented a fellow attorney in a messy case, this time in a disbarment proceeding. But first he was drawn into an awkward situation in a concomitant matter.

Sometime in September 1938, Davis agreed to represent Louis Levy, of Chadbourne, Stanchfield & Levy, in the event that an investigation of Martin T. Manton, senior judge of the Second Circuit, also implicated Levy. Early in the new year, Thomas E. Dewey, the brilliant young District Attorney, informed the House Judiciary Committee that Judge Manton had apparently sold a number of decisions for sums ranging as high as $250,000. Among them was *Rogers v. Guaranty Trust,* the American Tobacco Company stockholders' suit which Davis had won on a technicality in the Supreme Court after winning on the merits before Manton. On May 22, 1939, Manton was brought to trial in New York. Never had a federal judge been charged with so many grave crimes. [42]

For two decades leaders of the bar had been uneasy about Manton, a mediocre judge with an erratic record. Unctuous, smooth-faced, and luxury-loving, he lived on the scale of a successful Wall Street lawyer. In 1922 Chief Justice Taft had rejected suggestions that he recommend him for a seat on the Supreme Court, one which Taft hoped at the time that Davis would accept. Manton, said the Chief Justice, had been "an ambulance chaser and had amassed a fortune through unwholesome associations with businessmen"; he was a "shrewd cunning, political judge . . . utterly unfit" for the high court. Early in the 1930's, Manton's colleagues, Judges Learned Hand and Thomas W. Swan, reportedly warned President Hoover against elevating Manton. A few years later, Charles C. Burlingham counseled President Roosevelt to the same effect. Davis knew Manton only casually. [43]

Late in the winter of 1939, Manton asked Davis to visit him in his chambers. Would he represent him in his impending trial? the Judge asked. "I don't want to," Davis replied. "I don't know what is involved." Davis was shaken and embarrassed at having to refuse to serve as counsel, and he lacked the heart to reject Manton's plea that he at least stand as a character witness. On May 30, Davis was one of a half-dozen witnesses, including Al Smith, a Catholic priest, the president of the Crucible Steel Company, and the head of the Moore-McCormick steamship line, who testified for Manton. Each was asked two questions: What was Manton's reputation for integrity and veracity among those who knew him? What was his general reputation as a citizen? All except Davis answered in superlatives—"the very best," "excellent," "unchallenged." To both questions Davis replied simply, "very good." A week later Manton was found guilty and sentenced to the penitentiary.[44]

Soon after the conviction, Charles Burlingham reported to Davis that several of their friends were puzzled by his testimony on Manton's behalf. "Since the Interboro receivership, *with the bar* Manton's reputation has not been good," Burlingham wrote, "but it may be you felt that his *general* reputation was something different, as it was." Burlingham added that he himself knew of several instances of unethical conduct by Manton, but that these were wholly different from "reputation." Davis replied that Burlingham was right. "Any man is entitled for what it is worth (which is ordinarily very little) to prove that he had prior to the events in suit enjoyed a good reputation." He closed with a gentle thrust: "Now I'll ask you one. If you knew of several 'occasions of unethical conduct' why didn't *you* do something about it?"[45]

Burlingham responded that Davis had given him exactly what he had wanted. "General reputation is not only different from specific charges; it is different from reputation *at the Bar*. I had thought Manton's reputation with lawyers has been pretty well shattered for some years." As for himself, Burlingham continued, he had done "nothing unless it is doing to have told Murray Butler and F.D.R. never to give him any honors. 'Tis bad business and the other judges feel it terribly."[46]

By then the fears that had driven Louis Levy to seek out Davis nine months earlier were being realized. Evidence brought out in Manton's trial deeply implicated Levy; and, although the statute of limitations protected him from criminal indictment, he was subjected to disbarment proceedings in July 1939. The action was brought by the federal government, a more conscientious guardian of legal ethics than the state or local bar associations were.

Levy's personal history was even more tragic than Manton's, for his tastes were more refined, his intelligence more penetrating, his sensibilities more acute. Born in Alabama sixty-two years earlier, he had been elected to Phi Beta Kappa at Yale and had been a founder of the *Law Review* and president of his class at Columbia. By 1910 he was one of the suavest and sharpest lawyers on Wall Street. In 1913 he was closely questioned, but not indicted, by a grand jury investigating his actions in a bankruptcy matter. His firm, Chadbourne, Stanchfield & Levy, was one of the half-dozen best-known law offices in New York, and in the depression year of 1933 his share of the profits was $336,000. During the 1920's Levy had bought Harold Vanderbilt's Palm Beach villa and had cultivated friendships with the great and near great—Lord Duveen, Bernard Berenson, Winston Churchill, Al Smith, Otto Kahn, Dwight Morrow, Walter Chrysler, and Bernard Baruch. He was especially intimate with his Columbia classmate, Manton, whose appointment to the bench in 1916 he had helped engineer.[47]

The main charge against Levy centered on his relations with Manton at the time of *Rogers v. Hill,* the companion case to the stockholders' suit against the American Tobacco Company's stock option plan, *Rogers v. Guaranty Trust.* It involved an attack on the company's regular bonus system, under which President George W. Hill and other executives had awarded themselves more than $10,-000,000, not counting stock options, between 1921 and 1930. A few days before both cases came up in Manton's court in May 1932, the Judge asked Levy, who was representing the tobacco company, to arrange a personal loan of $250,000. Levy turned to Paul Hahn, a vice president of the American Tobacco Company and a former associate in his law firm. Hahn was under obligation to Levy for past favors; moreover, the fate of his bonus rested in Judge Manton's hands. He asked President Alfred Lasker of Lord & Thomas, the advertising concern that handled American Tobacco's $19 million account at a commission of almost $3 million, to advance the sum. Lasker was told that it was to protect some bank loans of the same group of American Tobacco officials who had borrowed, and repaid, $150,000 for similar purposes the year before. The loan was to be secured by National Cellulose stock and was to be made to that company's president, James J. Sullivan. Lasker did not know that Manton was a heavy stockholder in National Cellulose. But he showed no disposition, in any event, to question Hahn, the representative of a $19 million account.

On May 11, one week after the *Rogers* hearings, Levy sent Sullivan to Lasker's firm to pick up a check for $250,000. A month later Judge Manton ruled, for a two-to-one majority, in an opinion written by himself, that the directors of the American Tobacco Company and the officers of the Guaranty Trust Company had acted within the law. Both the special stock option plan and regular bonus system were safe.

Davis was hard pressed, accordingly, to make a convincing case for Levy at his disbarment hearing. The record is sealed, but because of the crisis of confidence in the courts engendered by the Manton case, Judge John C. Knox opened proceedings to reporters at the time. Their accounts reveal a heated exchange between Davis and John T. Cahill, the resourceful United States Attorney who had ripped Manton's defenses apart two months earlier:

DAVIS: I must protest against the cheap charges being bandied about by the District Attorney. I insist that more respect be shown in the handling of this case by a prosecutor who does not understand the dignity of his office.

CAHILL: His Honor will run the court, not you. I will not be bulldozed by your meaningless phrases.

DAVIS: You should learn how to conduct yourself in court.

CAHILL: It is you who should correct your conduct, considering the fact that you have been counsel to Mr. Levy since last September, and yet you appeared as a character witness for Manton.

DAVIS: I am amazed.[48]

At another point, Judge Knox tried to get Davis to accept a strict construction of the Judicial Code, Canon 26 of which prohibits judges from soliciting lawyers even for charitable purposes:

KNOX: What would you think if a judge who has a lawyer's case pending before him asked a lawyer to lend some money to a friend?

DAVIS: I think that Mr. Levy gave the answer . . . when he testified that if the judge was worthy of his office, the lawyer could find nothing wrong with such a request.

KNOX: I think the judge is shaking the lawyer down.

DAVIS: But what can the lawyer do in such a case? In most cases, I believe, the lawyer would make the contribution.

KNOX: But don't you think that if a judge who has a lawyer's case before him asks the lawyer to lend some money to a friend, that the lawyer, if he wishes to comply with the judge's request, should have it understood that the judge had disqualified himself by such a request?

DAVIS: That is the safe position to take.

KNOX: I think it is the ethical position.[49]

Davis left the hearing with mixed feelings. He was "crushed" by Cahill's attack on himself and was worried by the implications of Judge Knox's emphasis on ethics. Yet he also believed that the evidence failed to sustain the charges. A note from Lloyd Paul Stryker, soon to become the most famous trial lawyer of the era, was encouraging: "Will you permit me to express my humble admiration for your handling of the Levy case and particularly for your summing up. I cannot see how you can have other than a favorable outcome unless your client is to be convicted upon sheer suspicion." [50]

Davis' concern about Judge Knox turned out to be warranted. In an indignant opinion which rode roughshod over Davis' argument and even alluded to Levy's "improper" conduct in the bankruptcy matter in 1913, Judge Knox barred Levy from practice in the federal courts:

> Trained lawyer that he is . . . he should have appreciated instantly that his dealings with Manton had been such that, aside from any consideration of venality, they might well be calculated to warp or bias Manton's judgement and prevent him from having the impartiality of mind that was required for the proper performance of his judicial duties. See 26 of Judicial Ethics. . . . Levy, in mind, heart and action, was venal and corrupt. [51]

"I feel I have done all I could do, and am not worrying about it," Davis said in a note to Frank Polk. "I now think, Mr. Polk, that I have served my time at defending lawyers and judges." [52]

Although laymen continued to misinterpret Davis' role in all these proceedings, both bar and bench applauded him for faithfully fulfilling the advocate's duty, as Hugh Macmillan once phrased it, "to present to the Court all that can be said on behalf of his client's case, all that his client would have said for himself." In time, even Felix Frankfurter came to esteem Davis for his services in these and many other matters. "The biggest debt we all owe you," he wrote near the end of Davis' life, "is the debt that you have paid to our great profession. . . . As law teacher and as judge I have often referred to you as one of the finest exemplars of what Elihu Root called 'the public profession of the law.' " [53]

CHAPTER 20

Morgan and the
Pecora Investigation

The Committee . . . succeeded only in proving that we were quite sol-vent and had been conducting a high-class business.

JOHN W. DAVIS

For fourteen weeks in the spring of 1933 Davis sat at the side of his friends and clients, the Morgan partners, during the most far-reaching investigation of finance capitalism since the Pujo committee hearings of 1912. Convinced that the Senate banking and currency committee's investigators aimed to slander his clients and to pry maliciously into their affairs, Davis assumed at the outset that the probe would be a "witch-hunt" and concluded at its end that it had been "a melancholy farce." He tried to prevent it from broadening into a general investigation of private banking. He fought to keep the internal affairs of the Morgan firm confidential. He coached J. P. Morgan and other partners on how to comport themselves on the witness stand. And he issued public statements to correct the often misleading impressions created by the committee's chief counsel, Ferdinand Pecora.

« I »

President Herbert Hoover had long believed that the securities market should be regulated and that investment and commercial banking should be separated. As he wrote near the end of his term, "I have time and again warned, asked and urged" that the banking system be reorganized. "Failure means a new form of the Middle Ages."

He feared, however, that exposure of the financial world's "filth" would destroy business confidence further, and until February 1932 he resisted demands of conservatives and progressives of both parties for a full-scale investigation. Only after receiving reports that prominent Democratic speculators were planning to discredit his Administration by unsettling the market through bear raids did he call for a limited investigation. "[Men] are not justified in deliberately making a profit from the losses of other people," the President told a group of bankers —including the Morgan partner Thomas W. Lamont—who were trying to head off the inquiry.[1]

Hearings that spring failed to uncover a conspiracy to drive the market down. Nevertheless, a five-man subcommittee of the Senate banking and currency committee continued the investigation. By January 1933 the flagrantly unethical practices of numerous pool and market operators had been spread on the public record, and Goldman, Sachs & Co. stood revealed as having abused the interests of both its stockholders and investors. Even so, Senate conservatives were reluctant to pursue the inquiry with vigor. They imposed tight restrictions on the subcommittee's first counsel, and they clashed bitterly with his successor, who resigned after one week. On January 24, 1933, Ferdinand Pecora, a fifty-three-year-old former Chief Assistant District Attorney of New York County, took the post, on the recommendation of Bainbridge Colby and of Davis' partner Frank Polk, among others.[2]

A sturdy, large-jawed Sicilian immigrant with alert black eyes, swarthy complexion, and thick, curly hair streaked with gray, Pecora was preeminently a moralist. "With him the prime consideration is an ethical one," said the District Attorney under whom he had served for almost a decade. "Once convinced of the righteousness of his cause he is . . . unyielding." A fervent "Bull Mooser" in 1912, Pecora had refused to follow Theodore Roosevelt back into the Republican party four years later. Several times in the 1920's he rejected offers from Wall Street law firms, and always he resisted opportunities to supplement his small salary by outside practice. When he left office in 1930 after Tammany ignored the bar's urgent recommendation to appoint him District Attorney, his cash assets were $525. He accepted the $225-a-month position as counsel on the understanding that he would simply complete the probe and submit a report before the change of administration in March.[3]

Although Pecora was good-humored to the point that he seemed bland, his "friendly" questioning and thorough preparation had brought convictions in 80 per cent of his cases, most of which involved concealment and obstruction. More important, his investigations of the Police Department, the bail bond business, the Office of the State Comptroller, and the failure of the City Trust Company had all led to corrective legislation. Moving now to a wider front, he asked for greater latitude. "I do not want to moor my mind to any predispositions," he explained. "I want to keep free to follow any leads that may develop, so that we may get a comprehensive picture." [4]

In truth, Pecora was filled with progressive preconceptions. He disdained the acquisition of wealth through manipulation. He believed that holding companies served mainly to generate artificial profits. He regarded tax loopholes as antidemocratic. And he agreed with the Pujo committee report of 1912, that there existed a "well-defined identity and community of interest between a few leaders of finance," and that this was responsible for the "concentration of the control of credit and money in the hands of a few men, of which J P Morgan & Co. are the recognized leaders." To Davis' dismay, Pecora also believed that considerations of privacy were no bar to disclosure of facts bearing on the public interest. Like many men of certain purpose, he was quite capable of bending his means to his ends; his instinct for the sensational was sure and quick.[5]

Pecora first investigated the securities operations of Samuel Insull, the utilities magnate. He brought out so many unethical practices by Insull's principal bankers, Halsey, Stuart & Co., that Harold L. Stuart himself recommended enactment of a full-disclosure law to protect future investors. Pecora then examined the National City Co. and its security affiliate, the National City Bank of New York, the second largest bank in the world. The operations of these two institutions were so scandalous that they staggered the imagination of even the financial community; and though the gulf between moral and statutory law enabled their officers to escape the penitentiary, Charles E. Mitchell, chairman of the board of both institutions, was eventually assessed more than $1 million in back taxes.[6]

The exposure of the National City group and the election of Franklin D. Roosevelt as President in 1932 led to a broadening of the hearings. Roosevelt condemned the "unscrupulous money changers" who stood "indicted in the court of public opinion, rejected in the hearts and minds of men" in his inaugural address; then, scarcely a week later, the new chairman of the Senate banking and currency committee, seventy-five-year-old Duncan U. Fletcher of Florida, announced that the President had asked him to explore "all the ramifications of bad banking" and had alerted the Attorney General for possible violations of federal law. Soon afterwards, Pecora made arrangements to investigate private bankers. These, he explained, were men "who make their own rules and are not subject to examination . . . by public authority." He turned first to the Morgan firm, the most renowned private banking house in the world.[7]

« II »

Ever since his service in Congress, Davis had been cynical about congressional investigations. As he remarked at the time of Teapot Dome, "there will always be on committees . . . some persons whose daily prayer will be, 'Lord, let the limelight shine on me, just for the day.' " He now took the same attitude. He believed sincerely that private banks should be immune from public scrutiny or control regardless of their economic power, and as counsel to the Morgan firm he himself had drafted the New York State statute that exempted private banks from state supervision. A decade of close association with the House of Morgan had reinforced this conviction; by 1933 Davis' belief in the integrity of the Morgan partners was absolute, his confidence in the soundness of their practices unshakable. Furthermore, he was chary of the calls for sweeping reforms that had been sparked by the inquiry. He had earlier accused the Hoover administration of following "the road to socialism at a rate never equalled in time of peace by any of its predecessors"; and the day after Roosevelt's inauguration he had called on the Democrats to renew their commitment to individualism and constitutional restraints on arbitrary political power. Clearly, the rights of privacy and economic liberty took precedence in his mind over the moral turpitude and concentration of economic power already disclosed by the banking and currency committee investigation. Above and beyond all considerations of policy and philosophy, however, was Davis' dedication to the case at hand. Just as he had defended Louis Levy to the limit of the law, so was he now prepared to protect the Morgan partners from governmental encroachment and from the populist animus that their prestige, the mood of the times, and the slightest revelation of irregular conduct were sure to engender.[8]

On March 22, Davis and Thomas W. Lamont, the effective head of the Morgan firm, conferred with Pecora. They met in the committee counsel's drab, rented office at 285 Madison Avenue. An able, informed, and supple man who possessed a flair for public relations, Lamont was less defensive than Davis about the firm's rights, less disposed, in particular, to hold Pecora to the precise terms of his mandate. He saw no reason why private banks should not be examined, and he was later to tell Roosevelt that there was "not one single item in our whole business" that the partners were unwilling to reveal to the committee. On Davis' advice, however, Lamont refused to give Pecora a statement of the firm's capital. The banker also acquiesced in Davis' demurral to proposals that the partners answer any question Pecora might ask and that the committee staff be permitted to examine the company's records. "I stated distinctly," Davis wrote in a memorandum after the meeting, that the inquiry "was not directed to the investigation of investment bankers as such but to their dealings in securities." The proper procedure was for Pecora to request specific information; if it fell within the scope of the inquiry, the firm "would be glad to furnish it." [9]

Two days later, Davis balked at Pecora's request for the Morgan firm's balance sheets for the preceding five years. ("Told him I was very chilly to that suggestion.") Not only did Davis believe that the request exceeded the committee's authorization, he regarded it as an unconstitutional inquiry into the private affairs of a citizen.* Following a third disagreement, Pecora returned to Washington, where Senator Fletcher instructed him to draft a sweeping resolution, quickly approved by the Senate, empowering the committee to investigate all phases of the banking and security businesses. Prodded by Senator James Couzens of Michigan, a liberal, a former industrialist, and one of the few committee members prepared to treat Morgan as a peer, Pecora told reporters that the resolution had been prompted by the Morgan firm's refusal to answer numerous questions. [10]

This drove Davis to protest to Fletcher that Pecora's statement was calculated to mislead the public; the Morgan firm was preparing a mass of data at that very moment, he pointed out. Conceding that he had told Pecora that many of the questions exceeded both the scope of the investigation and Congress' right to inquire into the private affairs of citizens, he noted that he had assumed that his remarks had been entirely professional and confidential. He then issued his first press

---

* Davis cited three cases in support of this position: *Kilbourn v. Thompson,* 103 U.S. 168 (1880); *Sinclair v. United States,* 279 U.S. 263 (1929); and *McGrain v. Daughterty,* 273 U.S. 135 (1927).

statement: "The impression given that the firm of J P Morgan & Company had refused to cooperate . . . is entirely erroneous. . . . There is no disposition to decline to answer any pertinent inquiries." [11]

Pecora replied in kind. He reminded Davis that he, Davis, had reserved judgment on seven of twenty-three questions and had declined "unqualifiedly" to reveal the firm's capital structure. He added that he himself had not felt then and did not feel now that their discussion was "entirely professional and confidential." [12]

Tension eased temporarily following adoption of the Senate resolution to investigate the inner fastnesses of private banking houses. Davis arranged for the committee's accountants (mainly personal friends of Pecora's, who were working for one-fourth their regular salaries) to examine the firm's files in a comfortable room, and he had a large force of office workers prepare the complex schedules and reports the committee counsel was requesting by the score. In mid-April, a few days after Lamont assured the President that "none of us is holding out on the Committee," Pecora announced that the firm was cooperating fully. Beneath the surface, however, Davis and the Morgan partners were fuming over Pecora's contention that the names of borrowers and depositors were pertinent to the committee's purposes. Persons dealing with bankers regard their relations as confidential, Davis protested; "to disclose their names would be a breach of confidence." Two weeks later, his plea for secrecy having been rejected, Davis refused to let Pecora's investigators work at night because "it would not expedite the conclusion of your inquiry, and would be an excessive strain on the members of my firm and of J P Morgan & Company." [13]

« III »

A few minutes before ten o'clock on Tuesday morning, May 23, guards cleared a passage at the door of the old Senate Caucus Room in the Capitol. As flashbulbs popped and a murmur swept through the overflow crowd, J. P. Morgan strode into the spacious, marble-pilastered chamber. He was flanked by Davis and Thomas W. Lamont, and was followed by several bodyguards. Most of the half-dozen or so Senators present greeted the sixty-year-old banker deferentially. A massive man, Morgan possessed most of his late father's features, including the bulbous nose, in some refinement. He was more dominating than domineering, and was a good listener and a congenial companion; his intimates, including Davis, called him Jack. Like his father, whose memory he revered, he was a devout and active churchman. And like him, he prized character, by which he meant honesty in business relations, above intelligence. He had some bookish and artistic interests, but his mind was conventional and his social and political horizons were limited. Although less grimly masterful than his father, he quite equaled him in power of decision.[14]

Davis was painfully conscious of the public reaction to the first Morgan's overbearing arrogance at the Pujo committee hearings, two decades earlier. Determined to avoid a repetition, he held the first of a series of coaching sessions for the partners in their $2000-a-day rooms in the Carlton Hotel the night before Morgan took the stand. Before each session he would ask them penetrating questions, warn them against being caught off guard, and urge them not to be clever, irritable, or haughty. "I lined up the partners and held school every day," he recalled with a chuckle.[15]

Morgan began his testimony with a self-composed homily on private banking which bore Davis' editorial stamp. His attitude, so Pecora later wrote, was that of a man who had no guilty secrets to hide and whose pride in his firm was deep and genuine. "We have never been satisfied with simply keeping within the law," Morgan explained, "but have constantly sought so to act that we might fully observe the professional code, and so maintain the credit and reputation which has been handed down to us from our predecessors." He observed that private banks were able to assist in industrial development in a way that incorporated banks were sometimes precluded from doing because of their obligation to their stockholders. He also noted that for similar reasons private banks were free to play a constructive role in times of financial crisis. Morgan conceded that not all private banks had observed the professional code faithfully, and he admitted that his own firm had sometimes erred: "Since we have no more power of knowing the future than any other men, we have made many mistakes . . . , but our mistakes have been errors of judgment and not of principle." He further defended his partners' acceptance of directorships on corporate boards. "I cannot remember any partner of the house taking a directorship except at the earnest request of the board of directors of the company in question," he said, as Pecora's protuberant lower jaw dropped in disbelief; corporate directors often needed a financial expert in whom they had confidence. He added that whatever power a private banker possessed came from confidence in his character and credit as a man, not his financial resources. He closed with a declaration of faith: "I state without hesitation that I consider the private banker a national asset and not a national danger." [16]

Morgan was so nervous under interrogation that he proved curiously appealing. He smiled at the slightest provocation, called Pecora "Sir," and refrained from fencing even when the committee counsel pointed his big black cigar at him. Repeatedly, he turned to Davis for advice and to Lamont for information. Explaining that he had been in semi-retirement for some years, he confessed that he was almost totally ignorant of his own income taxes, the firm's internal operations, and many of its key transactions. Once, almost poignantly, he asked that his testimony be revised: "I should like it if the stuttering part were cut out of my answer to that question. I am not used to this form of examination, Mr. Pecora, and I do not get my words quite straight always." [17] Not until late in the day did Morgan show irritation or display determination.

Off the stand, Morgan relaxed. His great body often shook with mirth over the friendly sallies of Kentucky's Senator Alben Barkley, and sometimes he fell asleep in his chair as the witnesses droned on in the scorching heat. Once, he awakened with a start to wonder aloud what year it was. He hesitated momentarily when a Senator suggested that they all remove their coats, then rose ponderously, took off his light gray jacket, and exposed a pair of white galluses. He asked a guard if he carried his gun for protection against the Senators. He even kept his aplomb when a circus press agent plopped a twenty-one-inch-tall midget on his lap. He jiggled the midget on his knee, complimented her on her pretty hat, and then put her down with a forced smile as Davis and almost everyone else leaned back in relief.[18]

The banker's disciplined geniality achieved Davis' purpose. Edwin C. Hill, then a Hearst reporter, dashed off a couple of pieces bristling with invidious comparisons of Morgan, the new "Lorenzo the Magnificent," and Pecora, "the Sicilian immigrant boy." (Ordered to reverse himself by the master at San Simeon, Hill recast Pecora in the hero's role by the end of the week.) H. L. Mencken assured his readers that, when the excitement was over, "J P Morgan & Company will still be J P Morgan & Company." And Will Rogers predicted a brilliant future for the sixty-five year old banker: "I liked this Morgan. You would like him too. You couldn't help it. I am not speaking of his 'racket.' I am speaking of the man. These Senators will be banking with him before this thing ends. . . . I can see the makings in him of a regular guy. He has the money, he has the brains, and, above all, he has the personality. If he will devote (we will say just the afternoons) of his life to public service, or philanthropy of some sort, he will die happy and loved." Only *The Nation* dissented. "I liked [Morgan] . . . better in the old 'go-to-hell' role," wrote its special correspondent. "If we must have financial barons, let them maintain a baronial dignity." (Had he known what the banker was saying in private, he would have been gratified. Pecora, grumbled Morgan, "has the manner and the manners of a prosecuting attorney who is trying to convict a horse thief." As for the Senators, some of them reminded him of "sex-suppressed old maids who think everybody is trying to seduce them.") [19]

Meanwhile, Davis fought a long, losing battle for his clients. He implied that Pecora repeated questions for shock effect and that he was doubling as a witness. He flashed angrily when Pecora accused him and his clients of being uncooperative. He tried to prevent examination of the firm's partnership agreements—agreements which some of the partners themselves had never seen. The articles, he said, were "purely a matter between the partners themselves," were devoid of public interest, and had no bearing on the work of the committee. "It was like asking Morgan & Co. to bare its soul," said Pecora of the unrolling in executive session of the parchment document on which the agreements were inscribed by hand. The senior partner was revealed to have absolute authority to decide any disputes, order any partner to withdraw or retire, distribute undivided profits, and dissolve the entire firm at his pleasure.[20]

The most heated exchanges occurred between Pecora and Senator Carter Glass of Virginia. The former Secretary of the Treasury was preoccupied with his own banking bill and had attended none of the executive sessions at which Pecora had outlined his strategy. Furthermore, he opposed the investigation on principle. Periodically, his face contorted in anger and his small voice rasping like a hacksaw, he would straighten himself up to remonstrate with the committee counsel. He accused Pecora of "badgering" Morgan, of failing to consult him, Glass, and of exceeding his authority. In the cloakroom he came close to blows with Senator Couzens, Pecora's protector. He also interposed procedural objections to Pecora's efforts to pursue any lead, any minor detail, that might fit into an as yet undiscovered pattern. "I do not intend to see any injustice done to the house of Morgan," he explained; "that is my attitude." Provoked by Pecora's retort that he had not sought the assignment and that his salary furnished no incentive to continue, Glass snapped that he could not imagine that he was working for $225 a month. "Far from it." [21]

Even Glass' friends were stunned. Old Washington hands agreed that Glass thought he was standing for justice, but they also felt that he was moved by personal pique. "He took precisely the same attitude last spring, and made just as sarcastic comments during the stock exchange investigation—and for much the same reason," *Business Week* noted. "He wanted action on his banking reform bill and he felt the time of the committee was being wasted for a Roman holiday. . . . Glass is, and always has been, intolerant of anything that seemed to interfere with his particular object at the moment." Furthermore, two of the Morgan partners had been assistants to him when he was Secretary of the Treasury, and the spectacle of "this young Italian immigrant heckling" their beloved senior irritated him thoroughly.[22]

Whatever his motives, Glass had a substantial point. Pecora himself concluded that J P Morgan & Co. "was a conservative rather than a speculative firm," that it had rarely engaged in "flighty ventures," and that the investigation "elicited no such glaring abuses" as characterized the operations of many other banks and financiers. Yet Pecora did uncover—and unfairly exploit—some startling facts and questionable transactions.[23]

The most sensational revelation was that the twenty Morgan partners had paid a total of only $48,000 in income taxes in 1930 and nothing at all in 1931 and 1932. Morgan himself was ignorant of the details. "I do not know anything about income tax questions at all, sir," he said. He then turned his great hulk around in his chair, and pointed to "my clark," Office Manager Leonhard A. Keyes. But instead of calling Keyes to the stand, as Glass and Davis suggested, Pecora shifted the questioning to another line. Late that afternoon, on Davis' urgent advice, Morgan made his lordliest statement of the hearing: "I said that Mr. Keyes was here and had a full explanation, and I would like now to ask that the committee decide that the question, in fairness to us, must be answered, and that Mr. Keyes be asked to testify." Reluctantly, Pecora called Keyes to the stand. The office manager then explained that the decline in the value of the firm's securities had virtually wiped out profits each year. Nevertheless, even the pro-Morgan *New York Times* headlined the disclosure, but not the explanation:

MORGAN PAID NO INCOME TAX
FOR THE YEARS 1931 AND 1932
NEITHER DID HIS PARTNERS [24]

Not until the last day of the hearing, two weeks later, did Morgan point out, in a statement prepared by Davis, that he and the other partners had paid more than $22 million in income taxes from 1927 through 1929. By then, of course, the banker had already been convicted by the man in the street. And though most editorials emphasized that the law was at fault, few people read the editorials. " 'Morgan Partners Pay no Income Tax,' is headlined all over the country, and thousands of good citizens shake their heads over such criminality," the New York *Evening Post* protested. "It is not criminality. Mr. Pecora only makes it seem so." Everyone in banking circles, *Business Week* added, "knew . . . that if the Morgans had not written off enough losses to prevent income tax payments in the years just past, they were just foolish." [25]

Still, the Morgan firm had come perilously close to crossing the thin line between tax avoidance and tax evasion. Over the angry protests of Glass, Pecora forced the disclosure that S. Parker Gilbert, one of Glass' former assistants in the Treasury Department, had been taken into partnership on January 2, 1931, rather than on December 31, 1930, as would have been normal. This enabled the firm to show a capital loss of $21 million for 1931 and to carry it over the two following years.[26]

Internal Revenue agents eventually conceded the legality of this "expedient," as the committee report termed it. But Thomas W. Lamont and his son Thomas S., a junior partner, were not so fortunate; both paid back taxes and deficiency penalties on the basis of facts that came out in the inquiry. Moreover, young Lamont's case provoked another hot exchange between Davis and Pecora and produced a further broadening of the inquiry.[27]

« IV »

On June 2, Pecora began to ask the younger Lamont about his "sale" of securities to his wife on December 30, 1930, for money "borrowed" from himself, and her "resale" of the securities to him three months later. At issue was a $114,000 capital loss. Davis immediately interjected that the committee had no right to inquire into the private transactions of individuals. "I submit it is not fair play." Pecora then asked if Lamont claimed that he could not answer the question, and Davis retorted that he was "not called on to claim."

MR. PECORA: Well, I think the witness is. I do not think you are called upon, as a matter of fact, to represent this witness before this committee with the standing of counsel that usually is accorded in a court. . . .

MR. DAVIS: I am perfectly within my rights, Mr. Pecora. I am perfectly
within my rights, which I know quite as well as you know,
and I am submitting that this is not an orderly procedure
before this committee.

Senator Fletcher then remarked that both Davis and Pecora were
within their rights, and Lamont was excused.[28]

While rumors spread that "powerful" interests were blocking the inquiry, Davis and Pecora thrashed out the authority question before the
full committee in executive session. If they went into income taxes,
Davis warned, they would "sit until the snow flies"; more important,
neither the statute nor the resolution under which the committee was
operating permitted an inquiry into personal taxes. Apparently persuaded by Davis' last point, Fletcher decided to seek additional authority. Even Senators friendly to the Morgan interests then approved
a resolution authorizing investigation of virtually any aspect of the
sale, exchange, purchase, or borrowing of securities.[29]

Davis opened the hearing on June 9, the final day of the Morgan
phase, with an unusual personal statement. He began by observing
that his objection to inquiring into personal income taxes had been
given a full and courteous hearing in executive session. "I made that
objection on my own personal responsibility as counsel because I have
got the old-fashioned idea that every man who asserts his rights serves
both himself and the country." However, he continued, his clients had
overruled him because of their "sincere desire" to furnish the committee whatever information it might want. "That is our attitude now.
. . . I must ask the committee not to require me as a lawyer to confess
error, nor to admit that I do not still entertain the legal opinions I
have heretofore expressed." [30]

Young Lamont then took the stand in a vain effort to explain away
his dealings with his wife. He began with a statement, prepared on
Davis' suggestion, in which he asserted that the transactions had saved
him and his wife only $2035 in tax payments. Pecora cast so much
doubt on the bona fide quality of the sale and resale, however, that
even Glass slumped back in silence, his eyes barely above the level of
the long walnut table top. At the end, Pecora dryly announced that
the committee's accountant had computed that the Lamonts had actually saved $20,365. "Now, do you want to check up on that, or have
someone else do it for you?" [31]

Davis countered with a two-page statement full of citations supporting the taxpayer's right to use any legal device, including sales to rela-

tives, to reduce his tax liability. "These well-established principles of law make it clear that . . . Mr. Thomas S. Lamont . . . was fully within his rights and not subject to any justifiable criticism." Struggling to control himself, Pecora replied that every lawyer knew that "any legal opinion by Mr. Davis is always entitled to respect," but that the real question at law is "the bona fides of the transaction, not the mere form." [32]

Eleven months later the Internal Revenue Service ordered Lamont to pay back taxes and interest. Within a year, other deficiency assessments and penalties exceeding $2 million had been levied as a direct result of facts brought out by the $250,000 investigation. Many millions more flowed into the Treasury from frightened individuals who amended their returns voluntarily.[33]

Manifestly, the foray into tax evasion had been diversionary. As a thoughtful editorial in *Business Week* pointed out, the inquiry's underlying purpose was not to discover which players cheated:

> The real object is to gather every scrap of available knowledge in order to formulate an intelligent judgment as to whether the rules of the game need revision. That is what raises the proceedings to a dignity above that of a mere spectacle.[34]

Although the pursuit of such "scraps" had resulted in some significant exposures, it also led to the most distorted revelation of the entire proceeding—the Morgan firm's offer of common stock in three holding companies to a select list of friends and customers.

« V »

Through most of the 1920's the Morgan firm had refrained from organizing new companies and selling equity securities. But in 1929, as the speculative mania reached its height, it arranged to launch the United Corporation, the Allegheny Corporation, and Standard Brands, Inc. United, a holding company superimposed on holding companies, controlled 38 per cent of the electric power distributed in twelve populous states east of the Mississippi. Its books were kept by J P Morgan & Co., its directors were, with one exception, members of the Morgan firm or its affiliates, and it had no staff of consequence. Neither did it have a productive function. With important variations, the same pattern characterized the Allegheny Corporation and Standard Brands, the one in railroads, the other in foods.[35]

J P Morgan & Co. was primarily interested in establishing a sound basis for secured bond issues as a public investment. The firm had never sold stock, had no distributive system to handle its sale, and saw no reason to enter a new kind of business by forming underwriting and selling groups. So it decided to offer its regular customers and a few other well-known investors an opportunity to become, in effect, the underwriting group for the bulk of the stock in the three corporations. The five hundred individuals selected, explained the partners, were "people that we know intimately, that we believe have enough knowledge of business and general conditions to know exactly what they are buying." Each was given an option to buy a specified amount of the stock at the same price the firm had paid. It was known that the stock would go on public sale at a considerably higher figure, and it was assumed that it would rise rapidly thereafter because of the prestige of the Morgan name. But the firm expected to make its real profit on the sale of the three corporations' bonds.[36]

The "insiders list," as reporters dubbed the five hundred names, fell into four broad categories: rich private investors; the managers and directors of the nation's foremost banks and corporations; friends and associates of the Morgan partners, such as Charles A. Lindbergh, Davis himself, and one of the firm's clerks; and men prominent in public life —Senator William Gibbs McAdoo, Secretary of the Treasury William H. Woodin, Supreme Court Justice Owen J. Roberts, former Secretary of War Newton D. Baker, General John J. Pershing, and former President Coolidge. The implication of the news stories beneath the headlines was clear: the millionaires and influential businessmen on the list could be expected to deposit their own or their companies' funds with J P Morgan & Co.; the public men could be expected to take a kindly view of the firm's exemption from regulation. "We speak not here of the . . . ignorance and unfounded suspicion" but rather of "gross impropriety," *The New York Times* declared:

> Here was a firm of bankers, perhaps the most famous and powerful in the whole world, which was certainly under no necessity of practicing the small arts of petty traders.[37]

Davis was so infuriated by the *Times'* "attempt to blacken the names of innocent men, to arouse distrust of public officers, and to increase the general unrest," that he dictated a long protest (which he did not send) to Adolph S. Ochs. The editorial, he asserted, could not have been written if the writer had known the full facts: None of the public men on the list was in office at the time the stock was offered to him; the Morgan partners had simply "looked about for those who were willing to divide with them the burden and share in whatever profit or loss the investment might bring." [38]

He was substantially right. Most of the public men and small investors on the list were personal friends of the Morgan partners. (Had the firm's objective been legislative influence, it would surely have selected public men of greater real power than those on the list.) McAdoo had grown up across the street from one of the partners; Lindbergh was Dwight Morrow's son-in-law; Coolidge was Morrow's classmate; others were friends of one or another partner. The popular historian John Brooks summed it up:

> There had been nothing in the least exceptional about the whole operation. . . . What it [J P Morgan & Co.] had done was to use its friends and clients as middlemen in the process of achieving the public distribution of the stock necessary to qualify it for listing on the Stock Exchange. Assuming that the distribution was to be undertaken in the first place by a firm that did not sell stock directly to the public, the method used had been a reasonably equitable method. To have distributed the bonanza among widows and orphans would scarcely have been practicable. Pecora knew this, of course. [39]

Pecora's headline-conscious handling of two other aspects of the matter also caused Davis to bristle. First, with a four-day adjournment in the offing, Pecora failed to bring out the fact that Morgan & Co. had disclosed through the New York Stock Exchange the number and price of the Allegheny securities. (In the view of Davis and the Morgan partners, that action absolved the firm of contributing to the speculative orgy that had doubled the price a few days after the stock was offered to the public.) Second, Pecora told the press of a man who had declined as unethical the opportunity to buy stock in the United Corporation, but he failed to reveal that the same man had gratefully accepted an allotment of Allegheny and Standard Brands stock. [40]

Six years later, in conceding the essential soundness of the Morgan firm's operation, Pecora entered a caveat: "The absence of manifest scandal and impropriety [does not] exclude more subtle dangers. . . . [The] truth was far more complex than Mr. Morgan was willing to admit. . . . The bankers were neither a national asset nor a national danger—they were both." Thus the hearings disclosed, among other things, that the Morgan Company and its Philadelphia affiliate,

Drexel and Company, held 20 directorships in 15 banks and trust companies and 126 directorships in 89 corporations. This gave Morgan and Drexel relationships with 537 fellow directors whose connections covered just about every important business in the United States. Yet both J. P. Morgan and George Whitney argued that the assumption that this gave the House of Morgan abnormal influence over the economy was a "popular delusion." [41]

Davis especially resented Pecora's effort to establish his thesis that private banks should be regulated by delving into the firm's internal affairs. Nowhere was the case for exposure more forcefully stated than in the conservative periodical *Business Week*. Investment banking, it pointed out in an editorial entitled "No Banking Is Private," was the wellspring of economic growth. "The investment banker can overexpand some industries at the expense of others; he can starve essential enterprises. He can whip up speculation; he can help subdue it. Through foreign loans he can build international trade, or help strangle it. He can promote world peace, or he can breed and finance wars." This vast array of power was far too great to be entrusted to the consciences of private citizens; anything so intertwined with the nation's well-being was "a proper subject of inquiry." [42]

For Davis, however, the fundamental concern remained the interest of his clients—and properly so. Supported by Carter Glass, who referred to himself ironically at one point as "a paid counsel" for the Morgan firm, he fought hard to prevent disclosure of the names of depositors of more than $100,000, bankers who had borrowed heavily from the firm, and purchasers of securities floated by J P Morgan & Co.

MR. DAVIS: . . . . And we earnestly hope that the committee will consider . . . the rights of privacy which every individual who as a birthright is entitled to enjoy. . . . That is our position.

MR. MORGAN: I object to [disclosure of the depositors' names] . . . because of the breach of confidence which—I object to it because of the fact that our relations with our clients are much more confidential, in my opinion, than the relations with an incorporated bank can be. . . .

Davis again wanted to resort to the courts, but the Morgan partners continued to fear charges of obstructionism. The ensuing interrogation brought out enough about the firm's structure and operations to cause Glass' own newspaper to conclude that the firm's power was "a threat to democratic government" even when not misused. The *World-Tele-gram*, which also conceded that the House of Morgan had committed "no crude crime against the law," grasped the essence of the matter:

> There was the far deeper, more dangerous offense of what Lord Bryce well calls "the submarine warfare which wealth can wage" . . . because of its social predominance and prestige. Power, great wealth, and high respectability confer privileges which plain folks should not question —there is the unspoken Morgan thesis, in all its simplicity and menace.[43]

« VI »

Understandably, Davis' view of the entire inquiry remained colored by his clients' ordeal. He admitted that a "few loose shingles" had been turned up and that the Morgan partners had made "mistakes of judgment here and there perhaps." But otherwise he had nothing but gentlemanly scorn for the "deliberate effort" of the committee and its "hired counsel" to "hunt headlines" and "cast asparagus on us." He took pleasure in reports of disappointment in high quarters (the White House) that "the show turned out to be a 'flop.' " He wrote that all the Morgan partners had "performed magnificently," that the firm had covered itself with glory, and that "Jack in particular" was stronger in the public's estimation than he had ever been. He also believed that sooner or later the public would realize that the preferred list was entirely legitimate and that "the effort to exploit it was one purely for headline purposes." His deepest regret was that the Morgan partners had not allowed him to test the power of the committee in the courts.[44]

Obviously, Davis had been too close to his client-friends, too exercised by Pecora's clever maneuvers, too sensitive to the right of privacy, to put the hearing as a whole in perspective. His most reflective remark was that, although the inquiry "ventilated some things that should have been ventilated," it did not make recovery from the Depression any easier. Allen Wardwell was considerably more philosophical. "When you're close to people under attack," Wardwell said long afterwards, "you sympathize with them a good deal. . . . [They] were being tried under a new code . . . for what they had done under another code." Congress had a right to institute new policies, but it should not have held up to ridicule men who operated under other policies. "It's an *ex post facto* trial." Nevertheless, "some of the changes" that resulted from Pecora's inquiry "were desirable." [45]

Despite his continued invocation of the Jeffersonian rhetoric against "privilege," Davis also failed to perceive the philosophical implications of the concentration of unregulated private economic power. He never addressed himself to *Business Week's* contention that no banking was private, never spoke to Walter Lippmann's observation that the possession of enormous economic power by private individuals who are not publicly accountable "is in principle irreconcilable with any sound conception of a democratic State." Not even an appeal by the distinguished Jeffersonian historian William E. Dodd, then Ambassador to Germany, moved him to reflect on the problem in all its complexity. "One does not need to be a Jeffersonian to understand that [Alexander] Hamilton's granting of special advantages . . . set bad precedents which have been followed till the present day," Dodd wrote from Berlin that summer; Hamilton had "assumed that successful business must have rake-offs," and he had failed, consequently, to "emphasize the great fact that banking is a high public trust and its managers should be held accountable just as public officials [are]." Avowing that he remained a Jeffersonian, Davis replied simply that the Morgan partners had emerged "with no stain on their escutcheon." [46]

For all the strain and tension, the inquiry had strengthened certain personal ties. "We know ourselves too well . . . ," Davis wrote Carter Glass the day after returning to New York, "for either of us to imagine that you would accept or that I would employ the language of flattery." Nevertheless, he wanted the Virginia Senator to realize that he had left Washington with renewed admiration for his courage, independence, and devotion to the public service. That same day Davis received one of his most treasured testimonials—a letter signed by J. P. Morgan and thirteen of his partners:

> Words are entirely insufficient to express our deep sense of gratitude to you and your associates through these past three months of work and strain. Without your wisdom and sympathetic interests we should have been at a loss how to prepare for the examination before the Senate Committee; without your great legal ability we should not have known how, or to what extent it was wise, to defend our rights against the attacks of the Counsel for the Committee. For this and for the tireless work of yourself and all your associates, we wish to express our heartfelt thanks and our true gratitude. [47]

CHAPTER 21

The New Deal and
the Liberty League

The free competitive system . . . has raised human productivity and with it the general standard of human living more rapidly than any other that has ever existed. . . . What is needed for the better functioning of this system is not less, but greater freedom; not more, but fewer restraints.

JOHN W. DAVIS, 1935

« I »

Long before the coming of the New Deal, Davis had reaffirmed the philosophy of his early manhood in almost every particular save opposition to the centralization of private financial and industrial power. "Little by little," he wrote even before Herbert Hoover's inauguration in March 1929, "paternalism fastens its grasp upon the country, and little by little the practice of local self-government fades away. Somewhere, sometime, a halt must be called. Baptize a scheme, even the most fantastic, with a high sounding and attractive title, and it will elicit the public support." [1]

President Hoover's indecisive efforts to combat the Great Depression reinforced Davis' anti-paternalism rather than modifying it. Nothing —not the revelation of corruption in the banking and securities industries, not the specter of twelve million or more unemployed walking the streets, not the inability of the states and municipalities to give them relief, not even the privations suffered by his friends and relatives—could wrench Davis from the conviction that Washington should stand more firmly than ever before on the doctrine of limited powers. Except for the President's support of a national sales tax, virtually the entire Hoover program, from the Federal Farm Board through the Reconstruction Finance Corporation to the paltry appropriation for relief in the summer of 1932, was anathema to Davis. He sensed that the hapless President was breaking with tradition, and when Walter Lippmann later argued that Hoover had sown the seeds of the New Deal, Davis seconded the thesis, but with a caveat:

> I think that Hoover did make an unprecedented departure when he assumed that the National Government is charged with the responsibility of the successful operation of the country's economics and the maintenance of a satisfactory standard of life for all classes in the nation. I do not believe that doctrine myself, first in point of right and second in point of power and capacity. Nothing but mischief, to my way of thinking, can come from any government attempting tasks which lie beyond its power to accomplish. This is one of them.[2]

Davis was neither unaware of nor insensitive to the misery that stalked the land. Almost every mail brought a poignant account of human suffering. A seventy-six-year-old Clarksburg friend wrote that he was "sick, out of work, clothes and shoes, with very little grub to last the month through." James M. Beck sought inside information about Chase National, where his stock had sunk to one-ninth its pre-Crash value. The national secretary of Phi Beta Kappa asked Davis to find work for a penniless member of the Hamilton College chapter. Izzeta Jewel Brown, seconder of Davis' presidential nominations in 1920 and 1924 and now a welfare worker in Schenectady, implored him to call for federal action: "I am brought into daily contact with so much . . . suffering that I am praying some industrial or governmental reform may materialize." [3]

Even worse was the trek of supplicants to Davis' office. It was so bad for a while, he reported, that he dreaded going in each morning to meet the young men "who vainly hoped I could help them to get jobs, and listen to the various tales of woe of our clients." All that one could do was wait it out:

> It is a tribute to the adaptability of the human animal, however, that sooner or later we get used to a mournful as well as to a cheerful atmosphere, and I now find myself growing quite callous and prepared to see it through.[4]

Davis often handed out $25 or $50 and sometimes more for "old times' sake." It is doubtful, indeed, that he ever turned down an old friend or acquaintance who approached him directly. He also contributed modestly to various relief committees and other organized charities. Yet he seems not to have made any truly substantial contributions. "Is it right to be 'hard-boiled'?" he asked his sister Emma. "I don't know, but I do hate to be imposed upon & what I have saved has so shrunken in value that I feel even poorer perhaps than I am." In part, his failure to give more reflected the decline in the income from his practice—to about $250,000—and an accompanying increase in his taxes. "One runs like a squirrel in a cage," he complained, ". . . for the doubtful privilege of trying to remain in statu quo." His attitude was further conditioned by his Calvinistic acceptance of human hardship and his simple faith in the power of the economy to restore itself in time. "We always have lived through it, and I suppose we will again." At any rate, he grumbled far more about taxes and the federal budget than he commented on the unemployed: "Here we are with a government deficit that promises to run to a billion dollars before the year is out. . . . There is no way in which any government . . . can save men from the consequences of their own mistakes. I am not sure that there ought to be. Nature and nature's laws make no such effort. Why should men be wiser? The homely virtues of industry, thrift and prudent saving are as necessary for continued commercial health as they ever were, and we will have to get back to that basis." [5]

Rarely was Davis' commitment to laissez-faire more starkly exposed than at the Jackson Day Dinner in Washington in January 1932, where he shared the podium with Al Smith and James M. Cox. In an electrifying call for warlike measures, Smith ridiculed Hoover's insistence that the states handle relief. Neither the states, nor the municipalities, nor private charities could cope with the problem, Smith declared; New York City alone had several hundred thousand unemployed. Yet, in spite of $20 million in private gifts, $10 million in appropriations by the city, and $8 million in appropriations by the state, the need for relief was greater than ever:

> We must absolutely forget politics and we must regard the United States to be in a state of war. It is a war against unemployment, disease and malnutrition. The results growing out of this business depression are creating greater havoc with the family life of America than did the actual operation of the war, and we must resort to extraordinary means in order to bring about a solution.

It was imperative, said Smith, in words that could have been written by John Maynard Keynes, that Washington revive confidence, reduce unemployment, and restore purchasing power through a permanent federal works program financed by Liberty Bonds. "If it was good business to issue them for the destruction of property . . . during the World War, what's wrong with issuing them to save lives?" [6]

Neither Smith's hard look at the record nor his bold demand for a massive federal relief program modified Davis' views in the slightest. President Hoover, he told an unenthusiastic audience which applauded politely at the end, was interfering with the "inexorable" laws of supply and demand. The error of the Republicans was their apparent determination "to spend all we had and as much more as we could borrow. . . . This was the new economics of the new economic era. . . . Republican teaching to the contrary notwithstanding, governments do not yet control the sunshine or the rain." The party of Jefferson and Jackson should eschew taxing the few for the benefit of the many, and should resume its rightful place as "the militant champion of local self-government." [7]

« II »

Davis went out to the Democratic Convention in Chicago that June as a delegate-at-large. He insisted that he be free to support whomever he chose, and he hoped vaguely to influence the adoption of a conservative platform and the nomination of a conservative candidate. His portfolio was light. He served on no committee, controlled no delegates, and had no voice in the real centers of power. Yet, in a remarkable display of respect for his character and affection for his personality, the delegates gave him one of the most moving ovations of the entire convention when he spoke for the election of Jouett Shouse, the candidate of Al Smith and John J. Raskob, for permanent chairman. [8]

Davis believed, and always had believed, that Franklin D. Roosevelt was too unpredictable to make a good president. "If that man is elected," he said, "he will ruin the United States." But neither did he think that Smith should be renominated. His first choice was Newton D. Baker, though he would have settled happily for the industrialist Owen D. Young or for either of two prominent states' rightists, Albert C. Ritchie of Maryland and Harry F. Byrd of Virginia. He seems to have taken part in a movement to prepare the way for Baker by deadlocking the convention; and to that end he spoke against the Roosevelt forces' effort to abrogate the two-thirds rule. He also cast four votes for Smith in a holding action. [9]

Following Roosevelt's nomination, Davis endorsed him. He also supported the ticket that fall, speaking not so much for F.D.R. as against the "panic-folly" of the Republicans and the "pernicious doctrine" that prosperity depended not upon the strength of the American people's "own right arm and the vigor of their own stout hearts and the shelter of just and equal laws," but upon government favors. Meanwhile, he criticized Smith privately for sulking.[10]

As the campaign progressed, Davis seemed to sense that Roosevelt would break with laissez-faire after the election. He wrote that F.D.R. was not a radical and would have a hard time becoming one. "He is more of the liberal type, and that gives me no offense." Nevertheless, he was in danger of being tagged a radical because of his association with certain of the party's Western elements. "All the government can do is to take off the shackles and give the energies of men free play," Davis warned; were it not for the anchorage afforded by the Constitution, they might be overwhelmed by strange experiments. The party had picked up a "hot poker," and the "angel Gabriel and all his hosts could not perform the miracles for which the country is longing." [11]

Although he had no contact with Roosevelt between the election and the inauguration, Davis drew up a series of policy recommendations at the request of Daniel C. Roper, Secretary of Commerce designate. They differed little from much of the party platform and many of F.D.R.'s campaign speeches: The budget should be balanced, though "it takes the hair off." The soldier's bonus must be resisted, regardless of "Congressional cowardliness." The Hawley-Smoot tariff had to be reduced, even if every manufacturer in the country cried "bloody murder." The war debts should not be canceled "until the last ounce of diplomatic or commercial advantage has been squeezed out." [12]

The dramatic first phase of the New Deal filled Davis with awe, bemusement, and forebodings. "The last eight months," he wrote an Australian friend in November 1933, "have been an odd mixture of wisdom and folly, success and failure, hope and despair." The closing of the banks, the veto of the bonus, and the start of repeal were eminently to the good. Even the National Industrial Recovery Act was grounded on two perfectly sound ideas: first, industry should absorb as many unemployed workers as possible; second, the antitrust laws should be suspended to permit industry to diminish "the wastes of competition" by forming trade agreements. Unfortunately, these objectives "became enmeshed . . . in a wild reach for governmental power and a dream of a regimented economy under the control of a super state." The result staggered the imagination:

Labor was taken up into a high mountain and shown all the kingdoms
of the earth and told that at last the day of unionization had come.
Wages were raised in advance of any supporting profits, and the
N.I.R.A. . . . . advocated things little short of a universal reign of terror.
Parades were organized and a general hoop-la started on the theory
that prosperity could be brought back by the same sort of incantations
Navajo Indians resort to when they pray for rain.[13]

As for the rest of the early New Deal, Davis saw no good and much
evil. The Agricultural Adjustment Act was "a bribe" to farmers. (Will
Rogers, he said, was right: the only practical relief was to relieve them
of being farmers.) The Federal Deposit Insurance Corporation made
solvent banks liable for the actions "of their improvident brothers."
Devaluation of the dollar was wrong, the repeal of the gold clause "of
doubtful morality." The expenditure of vast sums for public works
would force the Treasury to resort to the printing press; it would have
been better to have adopted the English dole system. Senator Hugo
Black's proposal to spread employment by legislating the six-hour day
was just as bad. "I have always believed and still do that no man
should work less than eight hours a day." [14]

Beyond these specifics lay Davis' conviction that, no matter how humane the end or grave the emergency, there should be no deviation
from the principles Jefferson had laid down a century and a half earlier: a government of delegated powers strictly observed; local self-
government in fullest vigor; taxation for revenue only; equal rights to
all and special privilege to none. "I take my Democracy straight from
Jefferson. I was raised to revere him and since coming to manhood, I
have increased my regard." The Roosevelt administration had "thrown
the fundamentals out the window," but he himself proposed "to die in
the faith" by which he had been guided for sixty years.[15]

All through that first fall and winter, Davis was torn between loyalty to party and an urge to speak against F.D.R.'s "violently insane"
policies. What should he do? "Jump off the wagon or hold on, sit
tight, shut one's eyes and wait for the inevitable crash?" Finally, late in
February 1934, he pounced upon an assertion by Secretary of Agriculture Henry A. Wallace, that the short-run resolution of the farm crisis
necessitated some controls. "Who are the men that you would set to
rule over us?" Davis asked in a public statement. "This proposed regi-
mentation threatens . . . that personal liberty which Americans . . .
have been taught hitherto to hold as the most precious of earthly possessions." The law of supply and demand could not be regulated by

governments. "Wisdom . . . consists in discovering the natural laws and following them, not in devising hasty expedients whereby they may be circumvented." Sometime later a young associate asked if he were still a Democrat. "Yes, goddam it," Davis replied, in a rare outburst, "*Very still!*" [16]

Thereafter Davis' criticism increased in tempo. Some of it was well-considered technically, for many New Deal laws had been hastily and loosely framed. Yet most of his non-legal comments were chillingly insensitive. He said that the "chosen goal" of all New Dealers was to employ thousands of Americans at public expense. He declared that it was absurd to propose that incomes be limited to $50,000 a year, for the New Deal tax program had already reduced them to that level. Not once, furthermore, did he speak understandingly of the poverty, malnutrition, and despair that pervaded the nation. Nor did he ever show any awareness that the political centralization he so persistently lamented was simply the logical response to the financial and industrial centralization he so consistently ignored. The end product of a technology not even envisioned in Jefferson's time, it was the national corporations on whose boards Davis sat, far more than Hoover, Roosevelt, or even the intellectuals, that set in motion the subversion of states' rights and so many of the other ancient principles Davis called "natural." Encouraged, nevertheless, by the anti-New Deal press, the superficial comments of his friends and clients, and his own unswerving faith in fundamentals, he came close to opposing any change at all. Asked what he would have done had he been President, he invariably replied: "I would have followed scrupulously the platform adopted by the Democratic Party at Chicago in 1932,* probably the best platform the party ever put out." [17]

In July 1934, still insisting that he was a liberal and that the New Dealers were radicals, Davis went down to Jefferson's University of Virginia to deliver a heartfelt address, "The Old Order," in the shadow of Monticello. In a transparent effort to be fair, he admitted that the New Deal had done some good and that he shared the general admiration for Roosevelt's "energy, promptitude and driving

---

* This internally inconsistent document called for reducing federal expenditures by at least 25 per cent, balancing the budget, and recovering "economic liberty." But it also called for extension of relief and public works, subsidization of low-interest mortgages, crop control, "continuous responsibility of government for human welfare," and a host of regulatory measures later instituted by the New Deal.

power." He also conceded (without referring to the Pecora investigation) that many business leaders had violated their trust: "Men in private station, drunk with desire for easy money, cast off all self-restraint and forgot the rules of prudence, and some the demands of honor also." But the corpus of the address was a brief-like, yet sometimes philosophic, defense of capitalism, laissez-faire, and constitutionalism. Davis implied that the New Dealers sought to destroy capitalism. He misrepresented the relief problem. He blamed the Depression on the failures of men rather than on structural weaknesses in the economy. He equated laissez-faire with an ultra-idealistic form of individualism. He decried social and economic planning. And he deplored the growth of administrative law. Finally, in several passages of extraordinarily moving eloquence, he called for strict observance of constitutional restraints:

> Is the basic American doctrine of a limitation on the powers of government fundamentally unsound? Is it or is it not true, to borrow Lieber's lofty phrase, that man is too feeble to wield unlimited power, too noble to submit to it? Was Jefferson right or wrong when he wrote in the Kentucky resolutions: "In questions of power let no more be said of confidence in man, but bind him down from mischief by the chains of the Constitution?" Is it essential, as Montesquieu thought, that, in order to escape tyranny, the executive, legislative and judicial powers, or any two of them, must never be centered in the same hands? Is it or is it not imperative to the preservation of the Union that the spheres of the State and Federal Governments shall be plainly marked out and rigidly observed? Is or is not the Constitution a law for rulers and people in peace and war alike? Is it or is it not a breach of constitutional duty as well as an invasion of constitutional right to spend money raised by Federal taxation for objects wholly foreign to the powers granted to the Federal Government? Does the binding power of an oath to support the Constitution cease when some ostensible public good may be attained by its evasion? . . .
> Every government of whatever kind professes always to be acting only for the public good. The bloodiest tyrants in history claimed no less. The limitations which our Constitutions seek to impose, however, are not intended to prevent Government and its agents from doing those things which no one could wish to do on any pretext, but rather to fix the bounds which can not be exceeded even by conscious rectitude and righteous purpose. If these bounds can be overpassed at will by the mere magic of the grand, omnific word "emergency," surely they are made of gossamer.[18]

The address evoked a thunderous endorsement by the anti-New Deal press. One Republican newspaper declared that bureaucracy had seldom met with such an "intelligently scathing renunciation." The independent Washington *Post* commented that it took great courage for a prominent Democrat to attack his own party for jettisoning most of its historical principles. *The New York Times* was even more commendatory. Among the handful of pro-New Deal editors not yet silenced by their publishers, however, the reaction was different. Most pointed out that Davis had failed to offer a single constructive alternative, and a few contended that only his literary polish had distinguished the speech from Coolidge's materialistic defenses of the high business order. Liberal intellectuals were especially dismayed by the logical inconsistency inherent in Davis' severe strictures against governmental power and his broad acceptance of business power. As Harry Elmer Barnes acidly observed, "Mr. Davis says nothing about what has happened to private power in the hands of his powerful clients, and he would not have to read Berle and Means' work on 'The Modern Corporation and Private Property' to find out." [19]

« III »

Back in New York, at almost the same time Davis was speaking in Virginia, John J. Raskob, patron of Al Smith and a director of the General Motors Corporation and of E. I. du Pont de Nemours & Co., was conferring with his sometime lieutenant, Jouett Shouse. Raskob urged Shouse to propose to Davis that they form an organization to encourage people, as he phrased it, to work, get rich, and expose the fallacy of communism. Following Davis' return from Virginia, he engaged in extended conversations with the three du Pont brothers and Alfred Sloan, Jr., of General Motors. Then, in late August, Shouse announced the formation of the American Liberty League, so named at Davis' suggestion. The League's purposes, said Shouse, were to defend and uphold the Constitution and to help the Administration by opposing "dangerous" legislation. He and two New York Republicans, Representative James W. Wadsworth and former Governor Nathan Miller, the corporation lawyer and director of the United States Steel Corporation, joined Davis and Al Smith on the executive committee.[20]

Despite private assurances by Shouse that it was to be a positive, nonpartisan force, President Roosevelt quickly grasped the League's essence. "An organization that only advocates two or three out of the Ten Commandments," he said on August 24, ". . . would have certain shortcomings." In its concern for property, the League ignored the government's duty to help the unemployed. "For people who want to keep themselves from starvation, keep a roof over their heads, lead decent lives, have proper educational standards, those [other Commandments] are the concern of government." Furthermore, the League failed to mention the need to protect individuals against elements "that seek to enrich or advance themselves at the expense of their fellow-citizens." What about the Commandment, " 'Thou shalt love thy neighbor as thyself' "? A few days later, thinking more of Smith than of Davis, to whom he rarely referred, F.D.R. gleefully noted that the League had already been labeled the "I can't take it club." He did not believe in that definition of liberty, he added in a Fireside Chat, under which "a free people were being gradually regimented into the service of the privileged few." [21]

The American Civil Liberties Union was equally cynical. How far did the Liberty League plan to go in protecting the constitutional rights of radical and liberal minorities? asked Arthur Garfield Hays in an open letter to Shouse. "With the exception of Alfred E. Smith, there appear few names among your numbers of men who have been conspicuous in fighting for the rights of individuals, particularly workers." [22]

Week after week that autumn, the League's executive committee met in the offices of Davis, Al Smith, or the General Motors Corporation under the driving leadership of Shouse, who drew $54,000 a year as the League's head. Soon the membership rolls bristled with the greatest names in finance, industry, and corporate law. Yet only a few made heavy contributions, and in 1935 the du Ponts underwrote 30 per cent of the operating costs. Of the half-million dollars the organization spent in 1936 to attack Roosevelt and to persuade the country that private industry would resolve the unemployment problem, "if given a chance," two-thirds was contributed by thirty individuals. Some five million copies of 135 pamphlets, including two reprints of speeches by Davis, went out from the League's thirty-one-room headquarters in the National Press Building in Washington. Millions of reprints of 200,000 other items were sent to 7500 libraries, tens of thousands of professors, teachers, and other professional men, and to every member of Congress. Most important of all, the anti-New Deal publishing and broadcasting industries treated the League's releases as straight news stories and gave the organization's speakers uncounted columns of free space and hours of radio time. [23]

Meanwhile, Davis surmounted the inhibitions that made him reluctant even to solicit for charities. He asked a select group of prominent men to join the League. He seems to have brought in about half the Morgan firm, several of his own partners, and Elihu Root, among others. (Frank Polk and Allen Wardwell remained aloof from the organization, as did Newton D. Baker.) Invariably, Davis' letters of invitation made the same points: He had been watching with apprehension the spread of doctrines at variance with what he had been taught to regard as the fundamental principles of American life and government; he felt sufficiently gloomy to assist in the formation of the League. Sometimes he added a paragraph on his personal credo:

> I believe in the Constitution of the United States; I believe in the division of powers that it makes. . . . I believe in the right of private property, the sanctity and binding power of contracts; the duty of self-help. I am opposed to confiscatory taxation, wasteful expenditure, socialized industry and a planned economy controlled and directed by government functionaries. I believe these things to be inimical to human liberty and destructive of American ideals.[24]

Many of the replies overflowed with enthusiasm. As the former president of Union College wrote, the inevitable effect of such an organization would be a "cleaning out of the reds and near reds in places of influence in Washington." Others, however, were more reserved. Former B. & O. President Daniel Willard, who had said to a congressional committee that he "would steal to eat," was beset by conflicting loyalties. "Roosevelt is President of my country," he explained, "and I must assume that he is sincerely desirous of bringing about the things that I would also like to see brought about." Pressed by the du Ponts, Willard joined.[25]

A few respondents were openly hostile. Former Supreme Court Justice John H. Clarke replied, in unconcealed irritation, that most of the New Deal was necessary to avert revolution. The old order, he added in a thinly veiled reference to Davis' Virginia speech, would have ruined the country, Constitution and all:

> Frankly, my dear Mr. Davis, I do not regard my constitutional rights as in peril and I prefer to face the future with power where it now is rather than in a control dominated by men such as recent disclosures prove our bankers to be, or to have been, or such as you and I know from the practice of our profession dominate big business.[26]

Even the Texas cotton broker William L. Clayton, one of the League's original members, warned Davis of myopia: "The voice of conservatism . . . will not carry very far unless accompanied by a frank recognition that the seeds of our present economic distress and social unrest were sown in the sins of people who, as a class, will be associated in the public mind as supporters of the League." Clayton felt that they should seek the support only of those who were willing to fight against abuses in commerce, finance, or government as well as against the subversive practices of radicals.[27]

The League never did reach that group. Most moderate liberals agreed with the *New Republic,* that what the organization stood for was "Liberty for Millionaires," and the man in the street seems to have accepted the assertion of Davis' old friend Senator Joseph T. Robinson, that the League would bring a return to the days when "hungry and abandoned men in the cities were searching garbage pails for waste scraps." [28]

A letter from an Ohio Democrat who wrote that he had voted for Davis in 1924 despite a feeling that his campaign speeches had "chilled rather than enthused" was especially nettling. Now, the Ohioan went on, Davis had joined Al Smith and Carter Glass in trying to stop the "star of hope," Franklin D. Roosevelt:

> You have joined the so-called "American Liberty League," the principle of which, as stated, is to insure "property rights." That has been the cry and slogan of Feudal dynasties of all history. Never a word about "human rights." Your "principle" is the protection of Property and Profits.[29]

Usually Davis replied to such letters with a sentence or two, if he replied at all. But he answered this one at length. "You write that I make poor campaign speeches," he said with a tinge of humor. " [You] are right and you have probably not heard the worst of them." He passed over the writer's assertion that New Deal agencies bolstered capitalism by preventing businessmen from systematically mulcting the public; he also ignored his contention that profits would return only after purchasing power had been restored. Instead, he concentrated on the charge that the League put property rights above human rights: "The two are not antagonistic, but parts of one and the same thing going to make up the bundle of rights which constitute American liberty. History furnishes no instance where the right of man to acquire and hold property has been taken away without the complete destruction of liberty in all its forms." [30]

What Davis' identification of property with freedom omitted, of course, was the requirement, set forth by Cooley, Dillon, and many others, that property must be widely possessed in order to be secure. As the historian Benjamin R. Twiss remarked of the identical contention of another Liberty Leaguer, Raoul Desvernine, "he recognized no degrees or differences between property held for individual use and absentee ownership and control of tremendous equities in the means to production, with its attendant power over the lives and property of others." [31]

As Davis' belief in the righteousness of the cause hardened, the social and economic themes became as prominent in his correspondence as the constitutional theme. "If this concatenated crowd of cacophonous cuckoos that have usurped the livery of Democracy in which to serve the devil of Socialism have their way much longer, there will not be much left for anybody." His only regret, he said, was that he could not give all his time to warning the American people of the danger that enveloped them; were Eleanor Roosevelt his wife, he would put her over his knee and spank her every night. The real villain was "the sincere though soft and mistaken intellectual," not the subversive agitator:

> The mental processes of the genus "reformer" have a curious uniformity. First, an idea of which the reformer believes himself to be the only, first, true, and original inventor. . . . Second, a bureau which the reformer is perfectly willing, if called upon, to man, conduct, and inspire. Third, money—and lots of it—which it is the duty of somebody else to find and furnish for the reformer's laudable purpose.[32]

Occasionally a reflective note crept in. Once Davis conceded that the United States was not "*yet* . . . a socialistic or fascist or communistic . . community." He also cautioned a cousin in the spring of 1936 that it would "not do for two of us who have reached the ripe age of sixty-three to take things too seriously. . . . [The] country will last out our time, and, if it is determined to go to the devil (as I think it is) nothing we can do . . . will greatly affect the result." But such comments were extremely rare.[33]

« IV »

Many eminent lawyers shared Davis' views, and in December 1934 the American Bar Association put him on the air for a fifteen-minute address, "Fundamental Aspects of the New Deal from a Lawyer's Viewpoint." Once again the central theme was the limitation of power; and once again the sub-themes revealed the close connection between Davis' constitutionalism and his social and economic philosophy:

> If within the term "New Deal" there is embraced everything that has come out of Washington in these last two years, then clearly it is a trademark for many wholly different kinds of merchandise—some good, some bad, some better, some worse, having no common likeness except that they come from the same factory. . . . I have never taken the slightest stock in the idea that the American people in 1933, or at any other time in these hard years, were ripe for revolution. . . . The wish must be father to the thought with many of those who say such things. . . . There will be no revolution in this country unless demagogues incite it. That we were ready and willing in 1933 to try experiments there is no doubt; and ready and willing also to give experiments a chance before condemning them. . . . The Government set up for us at Washington is not and was never intended to be an eleemosynary institution or a foundation for miscellaneous charities. It was not designed as a universal parent or an earthly Providence. . . . I do not know of any shelter whatever in the fundamental law of the land, written or unwritten, express or implied, for many of the activities in which the Federal Government is now engaged.[34]

As the New Deal continued its drive to restore and reform the economy by federal action, the corporate bar became increasingly restive. Finally, in the summer of 1935, Davis joined several corporation lawyers in organizing the Liberty League's most controversial adjunct, the Lawyers' Vigilance Committee. Conceived and led by Raoul Desvernine, later president of the Crucible Steel Company, the fifty-eight-man group was a veritable *Who's Who* of the upper reaches of the corporate bar. Three past presidents of the American Bar Association—Davis, Joseph B. Ely, and George W. Wickersham—graced the membership list, along with Joseph M. Proskauer, Frederick R. Coudert, Jr., James M. Beck, and a host of less well-known men. The Committee's announced purposes were to issue reports on the constitutionality of legislation not yet reviewed by the Supreme Court and to supply counsel for "the little man" in test cases.[35]

On September 5, 1935, the Vigilance Committee "ruled," in its first report, that the National Labor Relations (Wagner) Act of 1935, which guaranteed workers the right to be represented by organizations of their choice, was unconstitutional. Although plausible enough on its face, on close examination the report proved to be blandly indifferent to the development of constitutional law over a century and a quarter of time. No description of social evil, such as Davis had written into his child labor brief of 1918, intruded on its uncompromising defense of the Constitution as framed in a pre-industrial society; no indictment of the repression of labor, such as Davis had leveled against the United States Steel Corporation in 1917, marred its measured recital of legal abstractions; no recognition of the changing nature of contractual obligations, such as Davis had written into his defense of workmen's compensation in 1911, softened its literal construction of the Founding Fathers' great work. Instead, in phrases that Davis endorsed as "well composed" and as expressed with "due reserve," it aridly contended that the Wagner Act embodied an improper use of the commerce clause and violated the right of contract. A defiant statement by the report's principal author, Earl F. Reed, chief counsel of the Weirton Steel Company, accompanied its release: "When a lawyer tells a client that a law is unconstitutional, it is then a nullity and he need no longer obey the law." [36]

The reaction was immediate, bitter, and sardonic. Secretary of the Interior Harold Ickes dismissed Davis and Beck as "vestal virgin guardians of the Constitution," and charged "Chief Justice Shouse and his fifty-seven varieties of associate justices" with "gross impertinence and flagrant impropriety." American Federation of Labor President William Green asked why there was no minority opinion. A Textile Workers official, whose union was struggling for the rights guaranteed by the Wagner Act at that very moment, asserted that the notion that a lawyer can set aside the law was "so preposterous and so arrogant that it must tear from our big corporation lawyers the last shred of suspicion of genuine public interest." *The Nation* charged that the Lawyers' Committee should be indicted for conspiracy as "an organized body dedicated to inciting the public to disobey the law." Davis' friend Charles Burlingham was no less exercised. The "mechanicians" behind the project, he said in a letter to *The New York Times,* have nothing less in mind than "creating a public opinion, real or fictitious, which ultimately may reach the 'nine old men.' " [37]

One of the most devastating criticisms came from a former Justice of the North Dakota Supreme Court, Sveinbjorn Johnson. Had it occurred to the "fifty-eight," he asked rhetorically in a heavily italicized article in the *United States Law Journal,* that if the Supreme Court should uphold a law the Committee had pronounced unconstitutional in the newspapers, public confidence in the Court might be shaken? "As a member of a profession of whose past record as sponsor of legal judgment versus mob emotionalism I am genuinely proud, I protest this betrayal of its traditional principles." Many reputable members of the bar, Johnson contended, believed that the Vigilance Committee's conduct should be regarded as contempt of court and dealt with accordingly. The cry, "violation of constitutional rights," had become the stock-in-trade of the corporation lawyer. Why had corporation lawyers not formed a committee when statutes "to take small and helpless children out of coal mines and factories" were being challenged in the courts? This calculated attempt "to prejudice the administration of justice" was not only "an appeal . . . to the mob upon a matter peculiarly within the province of the judiciary," it was an affront to "intellectually honest men" and a violation of "the living spirit" of the Bar Association's canons.[38]

As the attacks mounted through the fall of 1935, a few of the fifty-eight began to reconsider. George Roberts, whose Wall Street firm was representing Wendell Willkie's Commonwealth & Southern Corporation, warned Davis that publication of a report on the Public Utility Holding Company Act "would be regarded as an effort to pull the utilities' chestnuts out of the fire for them." He hoped that Davis would kill the project. But if it were published, his own name should be left off. To mean anything, Roberts explained, the reports "ought not to be briefs but opinions having more of a judicial character and prepared and written by lawyers not then under retainer on the very subject about which they are writing." [39]

Two months later the distinguished Harvard Law School professor Thomas Reed Powell suggested that Davis' signature on a truly dispassionate report would compromise his relations with his client, the Edison Electrical Institute. (Davis had already argued against the Holding Company Act in the lower courts and was expected to take the Institute's case to the Supreme Court.) "Mr. Davis," Powell wrote, "has a mind in pawn to a client. His duty to that client is not to be fair, but to be effective, to present strongly the strength of his side of the case and to minimize the strength of the other side." His "high and supremely competent" service as Solicitor General proved that he could write "a forceful brief against many of the contentions in the report that he is now put in the position of independently supporting"; discerning persons would therefore discount the "professions of intellectual independence made on his behalf by the American Liberty League." [40]

Davis conceded the political, though not the ethical, force of these and other charges. He acquiesced in a decision to withhold publication of the Holding Company Act report; he also agreed, during the presidential campaign of 1936, that release of a brief against the popular Social Security Act would "boomerang." But, as he wrote fellow Liberty Leaguer Thomas C. Haight, who had questioned the propriety of the Wagner Act report even before it was issued, there were larger considerations at stake. If publication "brings on the fight the administration is looking for, must we not accept that consequence and meet it when it comes?" [41]

If proof were lacking that public policy, not law, was the ultimate issue, it came with Davis' opposition to a bill to resolve the constitutional question by amending the Constitution to empower Congress to set hours of labor, fix minimum wages, and regulate production. The bill proved, said Davis, that the New Dealers were "deliberately driving at a substantial change in our form of government." [42]

The one concession Davis did make seems to have inspired a complaint to the American Bar Association's Committee on Professional Ethics and Grievances. Prodded by Haight, Davis suggested to Shouse and Desvernine that the Lawyers' Committee offer free counsel to anyone whose rights were infringed by laws the Committee deemed unconstitutional. He himself made such an offer while in Baltimore to argue the Holding Company Act case, and in mid-October 1935 James M. Beck embellished the offer in a nationwide radio address:

> [If] and when any American citizen, however humble, is without means to defend his constitutional rights in a court of justice, one or more of these lawyers will, without compensation from any source, defend the rights of the individual.

Two days later an official of the Hod Carriers Union in York, Pennsylvania, wired that 500 members of his union were being denied their constitutional right to assemble peaceably. Would the Lawyers' Committee take their case? Shouse announced that the League had the matter under advisement, and nothing further was heard of it. A direct appeal to Davis to endorse the Costigan-Wagner Anti-lynching bill received an even more peremptory burial. Meanwhile, a complaint that Beck's offer of free counsel violated Canons 27 and 28 of the bar's code of ethics was filed with the American Bar Association by an Atlanta attorney. (Canon 27 prohibited solicitation through advertising, Canon 28 the stirring up of litigation).

Quite properly, the Committee on Ethics dismissed the complaint in a formal opinion. Canon 27, it pointed out, was directed against commercialism and was no more applicable to the activities of the Lawyers' Vigilance Committee than it was to those of legal aid societies. As for Canon 28, the fifty-eight's offer of free counsel had been directed exclusively to citizens whose rights were threatened with infringement, and then only "if" they were without funds. A concluding passage alluded to numerous assertions that the Vigilance Committee's advance verdicts had also flouted Canon 20, which prohibited newspaper statements on pending or anticipated legislation. It explained that the issues raised by the New Deal "transcend the range of ethics" and that it was beneficial that those "best versed" in the nation's problems discuss them.[43]

At the time, Davis made light of the charges. "It seems to be considered a great offense in some quarters," he said, "for lawyers to express in public their opinion as to the constitutionality of a law, especially one passed by New Dealers. Joe Proskauer has agreed to defend me in any disbarment proceedings." He also denied that the fifty-eight had aimed to influence the Supreme Court. His main reason for approving the advance opinions, he said, was that they might help prepare the public for later rulings of unconstitutionality by the courts. But aside from insisting, in one letter afterwards, that the reports had contributed to making the nation Constitution-conscious, he rarely mentioned the episode in later life. Like a bad case, it all but faded from memory.[44]

Although Davis' involvement with the Lawyers' Committee compromised his reputation among liberal members of the bar, it strengthened it among those he himself respected. Former District Judge Thomas D. Thacher probably expressed the conservative consensus three years later, in awarding Davis the National Institute of Social Sciences' gold medal for upholding American ideals:

> More recently John Davis and other members of the bar who have asserted against the government and its agencies rights of their clients predicated upon constitutional limitations of power have been publicly criticized and condemned by public officials in high places, who attempt to discredit them in the eyes of the people. If ever such criticism achieves its purposes by destroying the independence and courage of the bar in asserting and maintaining the right of every individual to question the power of government in every court, then, indeed, the integrity of our institutions will be endangered.[45]

By then Davis had resumed the offensive with a sweeping indictment of the New Deal at the annual meeting of the New York State

Bar Association in January 1936. Speaking slowly and with great solemnity to an audience that punctuated almost every statement with applause, he condemned public officials who ignored or treated lightly their oaths to defend the Constitution. He charged that Congress, like the Parlement of Paris in the eighteenth century, was reduced "to registering the edicts of the King." He predicted that its influence would soon "be little more than that of the present Congress of the Soviets, the Reichstag of Germany or the Italian Parliament." He blamed the persistence of the Depression on the government—"a great and cancerous bureaucracy is no substitute for private judgment and initiative nor a cure for its mistakes." And he challenged Walter Lippmann:

> I hear it said, sometimes, that it is useless to battle against the forces of centralization and collectivism; that the tide of the times, the Zeitgeist, is setting in that direction too strongly to be stemmed. . . . I cannot agree. I do not believe that the tide cannot be stemmed.

A closing quotation from Montaigne brought the audience to its feet: " 'I speak truth,' he said, 'not so much as I would, but so much as I dare. And I dare more as I grow older.' " [46]

The pro-Administration press ridiculed both the speech and the laissez-faire philosophy that underlay it. "If Mr. Davis can point to any government on earth that does not seek to foster the economic life of the country—and has survived—he will make a notable contribution to the discussion," the Springfield *Republican* asserted. "It was Thomas Jefferson himself, who declared in his first inaugural: 'The encouragement of agriculture and of commerce as its hand-maid I deem one of the essential principles of our government.' " [47]

From conservatives, however, there came only praise for Davis' "courage, candor and perception." The political currents now swirled furiously around him. He was urged to campaign for Republican presidential candidate Alfred M. Landon, organize a coalition ticket, or run as an independent Democrat. His impulse was to lie low, for he was sure that the New Dealers had succeeded in identifying him and the Liberty League "with large vested interests and the wealthy class." Furthermore, he was not "greatly inspired by Brother Landon"; his tariff policy was too Republican, his farm program too New Dealish. Yet it was imperative that F.D.R. be defeated:

> Roosevelt has done the country politically, materially, and morally— especially morally—harm to an extent that far outweighs any merito

rious action on the other side. ..... I think if reelected he will have a feeling of invulnerability. He will press on from one crazy experiment to another.[48]

All through the spring and summer of 1936, pressure on Davis built up. Al Smith, brooding over the reaction to his red-baiting attack on the New Deal at a Liberty League dinner that winter, was complaining that he stood alone. Roy Roberts, the publisher, was appealing to Davis to stand shoulder to shoulder with the former Governor, and others were doing the same. At last, partly to salve his "conscience," Davis charged, in a nation-wide radio speech on October 21, that the President had dangerously fanned the flames of class feeling, class hatred, and class cupidity. "VERDICT WONDERFUL," Al Smith wired that night. "NOBLY DONE," wrote Walter Lippmann. "That was a fine speech—clear, courageous and full of genuine feeling," said Henry L. Stimson the next morning.[49]

Never, Davis confessed, had he had "so little relish" for making a speech. Determined not to let his political embitterment become personal, he resumed cordial relations with the President after the election. Meanwhile, he kept his sense of humor. In anticipation that the epithet "Morgan's lawyer" would be revived, he had sent the financier an advance copy of the speech. "If the charge is made . . . that *you* wrote [it], I want you to know at first-hand exactly what you did." A few days later Jim Farley made the charge. "Mr. Davis," he announced, "had to choose between his employers and his party." [50]

Although Davis always insisted that the Democratic party had left him rather than he the Democratic party, many of his old friends felt that his rigid views distorted the spirit of Jefferson and ignored the party's historic commitment to the people. A Clarksburg attorney remarked, on returning from a visit to the Davis Polk offices, that "That's the biggest bunch of Republican-Democrats I ever did see." Another West Virginian wrote Davis that, if he thought that Jefferson would have supported Landon, he was "damn glad Old Tom is dead." A third appealed to Davis to break with the du Ponts and his other Liberty League friends. "John, Al Smith and Raskob may tell you that this is not the old Democratic Party, but . . . the rank and file are the same people that were willing to place the laurels on your brow." Hardly less painful was a telegram from a Washington and Lee classmate:

IF YOU WANT TO LEARN WHAT THE NEW DEAL MEANS TO THE AMERICAN PEOPLE, COME DOWN TO VIRGINIA AND MOVE WITH ME IN THE STICKS. YOU CANNOT

LEARN WHILE LIMITiNG YOUR MOVEMENTS AMONG YOUk MILLIONAIRE WALL
STREET CLIENTS.[51]

Davis invariably replied with gentleness and restraint. He wrote his
classmate that he was glad to hear from him and wished only that he
would read the full text of the speech "for old time's sake." He was
equally warm to one of his former assistants in the Solicitor General's
office, who explained that he had meant nothing personal in a recent
attack on Davis' statements. "I have been battered around . . . too
much," Davis assured him, "to get irritated by what is said in political
debate." [52]

The same largeness of spirit characterized Davis' attitude toward
critics whom he did not know personally. In 1936, Francis Pickens
Miller, a future anti-Byrd leader of Virginia, made a devastating commentary on Davis in a book, *The Blessings of Liberty*. Davis, he wrote,
had recently told a college audience that social security was unworthy
of self-respecting men and that the only people who had ever achieved
perfect social security in the United States were the Negro slaves. The
remark, said Miller, was illustrative of Davis' incomparable ignorance
of the realities of life in the American hinterland in the 1930's:

> It justifies the comment that there is another group in America which
> also enjoys the advantages which were the lot of Negro slaves before
> the Civil War and that is the group composed of those corporation
> lawyers who in return for rendering similar services to the industrial
> class enjoy similar security.

Two years after Miller wrote that passage, the Council on Foreign Relations invited him to join its staff. Davis had been president of the
Council from 1921 to 1933 and was still an active member of the
Board of Directors. Miller brought the passage to the Council officials'
attention, and it was shown to Davis. Miller was hired.[53]

CHAPTER 22

Davis Versus the New Deal in the Courts

It seems to be supposed that in times of emergency constitutional limitations fall, and that the existence of an emergency is a matter for legislative determination over which the courts have no control.

JOHN W. DAVIS, 1935

By 1936 the Lawyers' Vigilance Committee had faded into obscurity. The report on the Public Utility Holding Company Act was stillborn, and the brief against the Social Security Act was never distributed. For Davis, however, the campaign to preserve the Constitution against the "planners" and "state socialists" in Washington had barely begun. Seizing every opportunity he was offered and every legal weapon he could muster, he bore into the New Deal through the courts in a half-dozen or more cases. He signed *amicus curiae* briefs against the first Agricultural Adjustment Act and the Bituminous Coal Conservation Act (the "little NRA"). He attacked the Public Utility Holding Company Act of 1935 in a controversial case in the lower courts, then took the fight against the Act to the American Bar Association. He made the principal arguments in Supreme Court tests of the Frazier-Lemke Bankruptcy Act and the National Labor Relations (Wagner-Connery) Act. And he served informally as counsel to opponents of Roosevelt's court-packing plan. As he said again and again, with heartfelt conviction, "If the structure of this Government is to be preserved, the courts must do it; . . . there has been no such bald challenge to the Constitution . . . in American history."

« I »

Franklin D. Roosevelt had come into office determined to prevent further collapse of the debt structure. To this end, the "bank holiday," devaluation of the dollar, the Home Owners' Refinancing Act, and many other early New Deal measures had been directed in whole or in part. The Railroad Transportation Act facilitated reorganization of lines that were on the verge of collapse. The Corporate Bankruptcy Act permitted the scaling down of corporate obligations. And the Farm Credit Act authorized the refinancing of farm mortgages on long terms at low interest rates. Then, in the summer of 1934, just when it seemed that the bankruptcy crisis was resolved, Congress passed the Frazier-Lemke Bankruptcy bill. The most radical of the mortgage-stay measures, it authorized reduction of farm mortgages to the appraised value of the property and provided for a five-year moratorium on foreclosure.[1]

As Davis' old friend Charles Warren noted in a series of lectures at the time, many of these laws were simply the latest development in an expansion of the bankruptcy clause of the Constitution, a development that had begun in 1800 and had been accelerated by every panic and depression thereafter. At first, said Warren, relief was granted only to the creditor, later only to the debtor. But in the first two years of the New Deal, bankruptcy laws finally came to serve "the National interest in general"—to reflect, that is, the growing sentiment that in time of financial distress "it was conservation and not sale and distribution of assets which was needed." [2]

Davis was too exercised by the superficially radical features of most of these laws to perceive their essentially conservative thrust; privately, publicly, and professionally he denounced them as part of a grand design to destroy capitalism in America. But he was moved most of all by the violence they did to his constitutional principles. Not only did he regard them as without warrant by any reasonable reading of the Founding Fathers' work, he feared that they would destroy the moral fabric of the society and create a superstate in the process. As he wrote John J. Parker, after the distinguished Fourth Circuit Judge assailed the emergency doctrine before the American Bar Association in the summer of 1933, "your attack . . . is balm to my soul. . . . [The doctrine] is the very quintessence of despotism—the Trojan horse that will open the gate to any band of heretics." Davis welcomed an opportunity, accordingly, to draw up an opinion on the Frazier-Lemke Farm

Bankruptcy Act for the Association of Life Insurance Presidents in the fall of 1934. (About one-sixth of the $6 billion of farm mortgages was held by the insurance industry.) [3]

This novel measure was almost solely the creation of Representative William Lemke of North Dakota, maverick Republican, sometime ally of the radio priest Father Charles E. Coughlin, and Union party candidate for President of the United States in 1936. Although Lemke had gone East to Yale for his law degree, he remained a powerful orator in the agrarian tradition ("Roosevelt drove the money changers out of the Capitol on March fourth—and they were all back on the ninth"). He subscribed to the international bankers' conspiracy theory of William H. "Coin" Harvey, whose writings had inflamed the Populist revolt of the 1890's. And he shared the sentiment of former Nonpartisan League leader Arthur C. Townley, his long-time ally, that "if you put a lawyer, a banker, and an industrialist in a barrel and roll it downhill, there'll always be a son-of-a-bitch on top." Late in the 1920's, Lemke conceived inflationary and bankruptcy relief programs for the poverty-stricken people of his state, 48 per cent of whom would be on relief by the early 1930's. [4]

His ideas fell on fertile soil. By the end of the Hoover administration, North Dakota's farmers were on the verge of open rebellion, and in February 1933 a convention of the Farm Holiday Association declared war "on the International bankers and lesser money barons." The delegates urged farmers to organize councils of defense to prevent mortgage foreclosures, swore to pay no debts until taxes and mortgages were reduced in proportion to income, and resolved to "retire to our farms, and there barricade ourselves to see the battle through." Meanwhile, the sympathetic Governor threatened to call out the militia to enforce his proclamation against forced sales for non-payment of mortgages. [5]

Lemke went back to Washington for the special session of Congress in the spring of 1933—the "Hundred Days"—confident that his measures would pass. But as it turned out, they proved too radical, too impractical, and too much at variance with Henry Wallace's plan to raise prices by cutting production to appeal to Roosevelt's "Brain Trust"; the North Dakotan was ostracized as "the madman from the sticks," and his bills were buried in committee. Refusing to accept defeat, he buttonholed, cajoled, and threatened his colleagues for four full months during the first regular session; by the deadline in April 1934 he had lined up enough signatures to force discharge of the mortgage moratorium measure. To the Administration's dismay, it then passed the House. In the Senate, where Lemke's fellow North Dakotan, Lynn J. Frazier, sponsored the bill, John Bankhead and others opposed it for fear it would dry up future credit. They amended it to apply only to existing mortgages and would have killed it *in toto* had it not been for the threat of a filibuster by Huey Long.[6]

Roosevelt questioned both the constitutionality and the economic necessity of the measure. He knew that the Farm Credit Act, and especially state stay-laws, had reduced the foreclosure rate to below what it had been in 1927; he had just signed a bill authorizing loans for recovery of properties already foreclosed; and he believed that his commodities-support program would raise prices to the point that foreclosure would become academic. Nevertheless, some of his advisers read a degree of merit into the Frazier-Lemke bill, and, in one of those compromises that made Davis distrust him as a man, he signed the measure. He admitted that it was so "loosely worded" that it would have to be amended, but said that he had "sufficient faith in the honesty of the overwhelming majority of farmers to believe that they will not evade the payment of just debt." [7]

The new law was soon tested. During the early 1920's one William R. Radford of Christian County, Kentucky, had taken out mortgages totaling $9000 on his 170-acre farm, which was then worth at least $18,000. By 1933, Radford was unable even to pay interest or taxes, and, on June 30, 1934, two days after F.D.R. signed the Frazier-Lemke bill, the county court ordered the farm sold. Radford then asked the United States District Court to declare him a bankrupt under the new law. Although the District Judge began hearings in the conviction that the Frazier-Lemke Act was unconstitutional, he gradually concluded that it was not. "I consider . . . some of its provisions unfair to creditors and unwise even as to farmer debtors, for it inevitably closes to them all private sources of long-term credit." But those were matters of policy, and as such "address themselves to Congress—not to the courts." He then appointed a referee who forbade the bank to foreclose for five years, set interest at 1 per cent of the fair market value of the property ($4445), and ordered Radford to pay a reasonable rent starting within six months. Radford was also authorized to pay off the debt in full at the new market value at any time within five years. This judgment was subsequently upheld by the Court of Appeals.[8]

Back in New York, Davis' young associate Paschall Davis, son of Norman Davis, was having difficulty drafting the opinion on the Frazier-Lemke Act for the Association of Life Insurance Presidents. Most of the commentaries in the law reviews seemed to uphold the law on the ground that the due process clause of the Fifth Amendment did not apply, and never had applied, to bankruptcy laws. Moreover, the Supreme Court had already upheld a similar, but much less extreme, Minnesota moratorium law. (Justice Cardozo's concurring opinion in that case had echoed Jefferson's warning that "To lose our country by a scrupulous adherence to written law, would be to lose the law itself, with life, liberty, property and all those who are enjoying them with us, thus absurdly sacrificing the end to the means.") Several times Paschall Davis reported to John W. Davis that he could not make up his mind, only to have the latter reply: "Well, then, work on it some more." John W. especially deplored Hughes' opinion for the Court in the Minnesota case, that although "emergency does not create power, emergency may furnish the occasion for the exercise of power"; conversely, he agreed strongly with Sutherland's cogent refutation of the Chief Justice's opinion on that point, as well as with Sutherland's contention that the Minnesota statute clearly violated the contract clause.* Above and beyond the particular application, of course, was his standing conviction that property rights and personal rights were inseparable—that, as Learned Hand once phrased it, "Just why property itself was not a 'personal right,' nobody took the time to explain." Hence John W.'s instructions to Paschall Davis to continue to work on the opinion.[9]

At this juncture Davis turned to Charles Warren. "I am deep in the mysteries of the Frazier-Lemke bill and need help," he wrote. Warren replied that he had no doubt that the measure was constitutional; he also said that the Circuit Court's decision had been to the point. (A unanimous opinion had dismissed the contention that the Act violated the Fifth and Tenth amendments, had asserted that Congress' power

* *Home Bldg. and Loan Association v. Blaisdell,* 290 U.S. 398 (1934) 733. Cardozo actually said: "A promise exchanged between individuals was not to paralyze the state in its endeavor at times of direful crises to keep its lifeblood flowing." Sutherland said, in part: "The opinion concedes that emergency does not create power, or increase granted power, or remove or diminish restrictions upon power granted or reserved. It then proceeds to say, however, that while emergency does not create power, it may furnish the occasion for the exercise of power. I can only interpret what is said on that subject as meaning that while an emergency does not diminish a restriction upon power it furnishes an occasion for diminishing it; and this, as it seems to me, is merely to say the same thing by the use of another set of words, with the effect of affirming that which has just been denied."

was not confined to the limits of previous use, and had insisted that the emergency be considered regardless of the Act's failure to declare one. It had also affirmed a principle the Supreme Court was becoming loath to recognize during the New Deal—in cases of doubt, acts of legislatures should be upheld.) [10]

Nevertheless, the two Davises and another associate, Edwin F. Blair, concluded that the Frazier-Lemke Act was not a true bankruptcy law and that, in any event, it violated the due process clause of the Fifth Amendment. They incorporated these views in a printed opinion for the Association of Life Insurance Presidents. Then, early in the winter of 1935, Davis' fellow Liberty Leaguer William Marshall Bullitt of Louisville, who had argued the Radford case in the lower courts, asked Davis to associate with him in carrying the case to the Supreme Court. Both Davis and the life insurance presidents, who picked up Davis' $30,000 fee, were amenable.[11]

Shortly, Bullitt and his associate, John E. Tarrant, came up to New York with their brief. They feared that, if they conceded a right to legislate, the Supreme Court would agree with the lower court that the taking of the creditor's property was merely incidental to the exercise of Congress' legitimate power, so they urged Davis to hit the Tenth Amendment (reserved powers of the states) hard. "If it can be shown that this legislation does not come within the Federal power," said one of their letters, "then we would have a situation even stronger than the Child Labor case." Davis needed little persuading. The final version of the new brief asserted that the Frazier-Lemke Act "does not deal with any subject over which power is delegated to Congress, and is, therefore, in contravention of the Tenth Amendment." Significantly, the brief also emphasized Davis' original contention, that the Act was not a true bankruptcy law and that it violated the due process clause of the Fifth Amendment. The authors justified these conclusions on the theory (controverted by Warren's national interest thesis) that the recognized purpose of bankruptcy proceedings was to distribute a debtor's property in return for discharge of his debts. In their view, this made the Frazier-Lemke Act, which aimed to scale down the farmer's debts while permitting him to retain his assets, alien to established principles of bankruptcy law.[12]

They further contended that the Circuit Court's allusion to the similarity between the Frazier-Lemke Act and the Corporate Bankruptcy Act was wrong: first, because the former Act gave the bankruptcy court no discretionary power to sell; second, because the power to coerce dissenting minorities into acceptance of a composition in corporate bankruptcies had never applied to a single creditor and was generally regarded as auxiliary to bankruptcy proceedings. With equal vigor, they maintained that the scaling-down provision violated the Fifth Amendment and could not be sustained under the emergency doctrine as the Court had done in the Minnesota case.[13]

Two separate briefs for Radford, one written by Congressman Lemke himself, assailed those contentions. In essence, they argued that the power of Congress to deal with bankruptcies was all-inclusive, that the Fifth Amendment did not take away any power delegated to Congress, that the United States was not bound by the English common law prevailing in 1789, and that the Tenth Amendment had no bearing on the case. They further contended that the "emergency doctrine" as invoked by Davis in the eight-hour day case of 1917 (they did not refer to him by name) was applicable.[14]

The Radford briefs were also infused with social philosophy, most of it irrelevant to the law, but all of it deeply moving. Among other things, they pointed out that the same corporations that had fought regulation of railroads, enforcement of the antitrust laws, and state regulation of insurance companies were now hailing the Corporate Reorganization Act as a deliverer while denouncing mortgage relief for farmers.[15]

The omens were not good for Davis when the case came up that spring. On Monday, April 1, the day oral arguments began, the Supreme Court upheld the Railroad Organization Act in a sweeping opinion by Sutherland which ran athwart one of Davis' main theses. "From the beginning," said Sutherland, "the tendency of legislation and of judicial interpretation has been uniformly in the direction of progressive liberalization . . . of the bankruptcy power." Then, in Richmond the next day, the Fourth Circuit Court of Appeals upheld the Frazier-Lemke Act in another case.[16]

Such fears as Davis may have had vanished in the afterglow of his own performance and the dense smoke given off by his opponent, Edwin A. Krauthoff of Chicago. Davis glided over the rough spots so gracefully that he was not asked a question. ("Everytime I hear you," wrote Newton D. Baker, who sat through the argument enraptured, "I make up my mind to come as near imitating you as I can.") But Krauthoff was interrupted so frequently and interrogated so fiercely

("You address an argument which this Court could not consider with any self-respect," said McReynolds at one point) that he submitted an additional brief covering a half-dozen or more questions.[17]

Eight weeks later Justice Brandeis overturned the Frazier-Lemke Act for a unanimous Court. In a sharply worded opinion which lifted intact a key phrase in Davis' brief, Brandeis declared that the Act violated the Fifth Amendment, that there was no analogy to the Railroad and Corporate Bankruptcy acts, and that the Minnesota Moratorium law was distinguishable because it did not permanently deprive the creditor of his property. Contrary to Davis' contention, Brandeis also held (as Warren had done in his lectures) that "discharge of the debtor has come to be an object of no less concern than the distribution of his property." He insisted, however, that in relieving the debtor the government was obligated to reimburse the creditor.[18]

Delighted by the outcome, Davis wrote that it was "a —— good opinion." He also sent Bullitt a heady wire:

YOU ARE A PRETTY GOOD LAWYER, ARE'T YOU. SO IS TARRANT.[19]

Lemke immediately urged farmers to organize to prevent state stay-laws from lapsing in the event that a good crop ended the emergency. He also laid plans to drive through a bill to issue $3 million in new currency to refinance farm mortgages and "save a million farmers from the wreckage." Meanwhile, the insurance industry reacted with restraint. Most companies had been uneasy about foreclosing ever since farmers had systematically disrupted forced sales in the winter and spring of 1933; now, industry leaders announced that they would push refinancing rather than foreclosure. "We have no intention of stepping into the villain's role," one company president said. "We shall cooperate with the farmer. He is doing . . . as well as he can in the circumstances, and we shall be patient with him while he is working out his problems." [20]

Three months later, Congress enacted Lemke's new bill, the principal feature of which was to allow farmers in dire straits to retain possession of their property for three years on payment of a court-determined rent. It did not provide for scaling down mortgages, yet Davis held that it, too, was extreme. "I have no doubt it is just as bad as [the judge] says," he remarked when a District Court struck it down. Never, he added in a general commentary on the New Deal, had he been so disgusted. "If this be Democracy, my forty years of consistent service to the Democratic Party have been worse than wasted." [21]

In Boston, at about the same time, Charles Warren revised his lectures for publication. He still held firmly to the proposition that the rights of debtors and creditors alike were subject to Congress' power to act for the national interest under the bankruptcy clause. He also denied that "the mere fact" that the Frazier-Lemke law retroactively affected the rights of creditors would have made it invalid under the Fifth Amendment had the reduction been in the interest of all parties. He now conceded, however, that its "very extreme" provisions undoubtedly warranted the decision striking the law down.[22]

« II »

The New Dealers had been too ambivalent about the Frazier-Lemke Act to condemn Davis for arguing against it; in fact, the government had not even bothered to submit an *amicus curiae* brief. By the time Davis was through assailing the Public Utility Holding Company Act of 1935, however, they had designated him "Public Enemy Number One," "T.R.B." had "exposed" him in the pages of the *New Republic,* and Arthur Krock had gently chastised him for collaborating in what he dubbed a "back-door" case.[23]

Behind the New Deal's drive to restructure the electric power industry was the same belief in the anti-democratic character of centralized economic power that had made Davis an antimonopolist in 1900 and a mild Wilsonian in 1912. Many of the thirteen holding aggregations which controlled three-fourths of the industry in 1932 had been formed for legitimate economic reasons. But in the speculative orgy of the 1920's, holding company had been piled upon holding company to the sixth and seventh tier in a frenetic effort to evade state regulation of rates and to create windfalls for insiders through write-ups and other economically unproductive practices.[24]

Two exhaustive investigations, one begun by the Federal Trade Commission in 1928, the other by the House Interstate Commerce Committee in 1930, had mercilessly exposed widespread perversions of trust by industry leaders. They were shown to have watered stock, falsified accounts, mulcted subsidiaries, paid dividends out of capital, and forced the real operating companies to lend them money. "It is not easy to . . . adequately characterize [their abuses] . . . without the appearance of undue severity," the FTC reported. "Nevertheless, the use of words such as fraud, deceit, misrepresentation, dishonesty . . . and oppression are the only suitable terms to apply." As Wendell Willkie, whose Commonwealth & Southern was relatively clean, later admitted, it had been "a crazy period when men went crazy and did a lot of foolish things." [25]

Roosevelt had wanted to wipe all but one tier of the holding companies off the corporate map. The holding company, he said in his message transmitting Harold Ickes' National Power Policy Committee report to Congress, was an invention which gave "a few corporate insiders unwarranted and intolerable powers over other people's money." It had destroyed local control by substituting absentee management, and it had created "what has justly been called a system of private socialism . . . inimical to the welfare of a free people." Most Congressmen agreed with the President, and had it not been for an unparalleled counteroffensive by the utility industry, a true "death" bill would doubtless have been enacted. But in a campaign that cost over a million dollars, the industry reportedly sent more lobbyists to Capitol Hill than there were Congressmen, jammed the telegraph wires with protests (thousands of bogus messages were dispatched with the connivance of at least one Western Union official), and indulged in numerous other manipulative techniques in a shameless effort to persuade the public that the Administration aimed to institute socialism rather than destroy monopoly and restore competition. "The kid-glove stage has passed," snarled New Jersey utility magnate Thomas N. McCarter, as he fanned rumors about Roosevelt's "mental condition" with allusions to what he called the President's "obsession." [26]

The fusillade failed of its objective in the Senate. "I knew that the 'wrecking crew' of Wall Street was . . . responsible for the thirty thousand requests . . . on my desk," Harry S Truman recalled. "I burned them all." Others did or said the same, and on June 11, 1935, the Senate approved the Administration bill's most controversial feature, the so-called "death sentence" clause, by a margin of one vote. In the House, however, pressure from constituents who had been told their investments in operating companies were imperiled broke the Administration's lines, and for a while prospects were so bleak that Felix Frankfurter advised the President to hold the bill over. ("Felix sounds just like John W. Davis," F.D.R. grumbled.) Eventually, a compromise proposed by Frankfurter himself was worked out, and on August 26 the Holding Company Act became the law of the land.[27]

Neither the bill signed by the President nor any of its earlier versions posed a threat to capitalism, the operating companies, or more than a few handfuls of investment-speculators. It empowered the Securities and Exchange Commission to regulate holding companies with sufficient rigor as to stamp out the abuses that had prompted the bill's passage, and it gave the Federal Power Commission authority over all operating companies engaged in interstate transmission. But it did not destroy, nor did it even propose to destroy, all holding companies. It recognized the economic value of limited integration, and, though it set one tier as the ideal, it authorized more than one where efficiency and economy of operation could be shown. Holding companies were given five years to prepare and submit simplified plans for reorganization. As A. J. G. Priest, who helped prepare the industry's main suit against the Act, concluded years later in his monumental work on utility regulation, the measure was eminently in the public interest; its authors "earned the gratitude of the Republic and also of many operating company executives who were manumitted from holding-company controls not always suffused with sweetness and light." ("I didn't think that at the time," Priest recalled privately, "but one views things more objectively in retrospect.") [28]

The Holding Company Act thrust hard toward much that Davis had always believed in—decentralization, economy, efficiency, honesty, antimonopoly, and diffusion of ownership. But for the same anti-statist reasons that had impelled him to reaffirm the laissez-faire philosophy of his pre-congressional years in the 1920's, to call the Hoover administration socialistic in the 1930's, and to help form the Liberty League in 1934, he opposed the Act. In so doing he in effect repudiated a dozen or more of his great arguments as Solicitor General. He also fell back on the simple interpretation of the commerce clause in his 1906 address to the West Virginia Bar Association, an interpretation which he had conceded in 1918 had already been superseded. "If that Bill is constitutional," he wrote Newton D. Baker, "then, in the language of Mr. Shakespeare, I am 'a soused gurnet.'" Obviously, he added in a letter to another friend, the measure's authors "felt no concern whatever as to the scope of Federal power." [29]

Hardly had the Holding Company Act become law than the trustees in bankruptcy of the American States Public Service Company contrived a means of testing it that would give the utility industry, as Arthur Krock wrote in disgust, "the best possible break." On September 16, James Piper, counsel for the trustees, asked District Judge William C. Coleman in Baltimore whether his clients should register with the Securities and Exchange Commission. By prearrangement, Ralph B. Buell, attorney for a number of American States bondholders organized as Burco, Inc., informed the Judge that the group he represented would profit most by immediate liquidation of American States and that this would be facilitated if the Holding Company Act were upheld. (Buell's firm, it later came out, was also counsel for International Utilities Corporation, which had an interest in having the Act struck down. Furthermore, Buell, upon whom the weight of defending the constitutionality of this monumental Act would fall, had opposed its passage just a few weeks earlier.) [30]

This was an *ex parte* proceeding and would normally have remained such. The Judge could have directed the trustees to register, or he could have advised them to run the risk of penalty in the expectation that the Supreme Court would overturn the Act. But Judge Coleman, a Harvard-trained appointee of President Coolidge, was a fervent anti-New Dealer. He replied that he too regarded the Holding Company Act as unconstitutional, and he agreed to entertain a formal suit on its constitutionality on September 27.[31]

In New York, meanwhile, the Edison Electrical Institute announced that it had retained Davis, Newton D. Baker, James M. Beck, and Forney Johnston to test the constitutionality of the Holding Company Act and other New Deal laws based on "a theory of state socialism . . . inimical to the rights of the American people." Piper then went to New York to ask Davis to come in as *amicus curiae*. Davis was too keenly aware that the real issues were usually fought out by the adversary parties to accept. However, he indicated that he would argue the case if one of the bankrupt company's bondholders asked him to represent him as a true party.[32]

Piper rushed back to Baltimore to find Davis a client. At the last minute the broker friend of another broker friend turned up a Baltimore dentist named Ferd Lautenbach, who held $2500 worth of American State securities. Dr. Lautenbach was told, so he later testified, that "they wanted to reorganize the company"; also, "something about a Mr. Davis being in town representing the company." He was not told that Davis was to represent him personally. Nor had Davis himself been fully informed by Piper. Surprised and embarrassed by the dentist's revelations in court, Davis rose to his feet, said that there had possibly been a misunderstanding, and asked if Dr. Lautenbach wanted to be represented by him. Lautenbach replied that he did, and the matter was closed as far as the court, though not the liberal press, was concerned.[33]

New Deal attorneys had expected the Holding Company Act to be challenged sometime after it became effective in December. They were outraged, consequently, when Judge Coleman informed the government of the hearing in Baltimore after everything was arranged. The government was ready for a test case, snapped Chairman James M. Landis of the SEC, but not a "sham" one. Even Arthur Krock, the normally anti-New Deal columnist of *The New York Times,* was shocked. By its "clever technical" maneuvers, he wrote, the utility industry had brought in Davis, a lawyer of great learning and ability, and had confined the government to an *amicus* role on the suffrance of Burco, Inc. This meant, as SEC counsel John J. Burns and his associates, Ben V. Cohen and Thomas G. "Tommy the Cork" Corcoran, bitterly protested when the hearing opened, that the government could make no motion, could enter no appeal, and could appear as *amicus curiae* in a higher court only if Buell continued to represent Burco. As they also complained, the issue was premature, the trustees not being liable for non-registration until after December 1. Furthermore, said Corcoran, in a fruitless plea for a thirty-day postponement, there had been "professional impropriety" and "collusion," Burco having more interest in cooperating with Davis' real client, the Edison Electrical Institute, than in winning a true adversary proceeding. Burns added that the government had been "railroaded" into a "cooked up" case.[34]

The instant Burns finished, Davis jumped up, his face flushed deep red and his voice edged with passion. The assertion, he virtually shouted, "would have been offensive to the dignity of a police court in Massachusetts. [Burns was a former Massachusetts magistrate.] They stoop to seize a handful of mud . . . and think by throwing it at the litigants and their counsel that in some way they can influence the action . . . of this court. I say it is an unworthy, an undignified and a contemptible presentation. God save the Securities and Exchange Commission and the people of the United States!" He then asked that the charges against himself be embodied in the permanent record "as an example of what a brief should not be." [35]

For two hours the next day, and again in a formal brief the following week, Davis attacked the Holding Company Act on every conceivable count. He called it "unreasonable and capricious," said that it was "shot through with power of the most arbitrary and unreasonable character," and declared that "no more pernicious doctrine was ever hatched or promulgated in the lives of this great free people" than the one behind the authorization to the Securities and Exchange Commission to close the mails to companies that failed to comply with the Act's provisions. The Act, he asserted, violated both the commerce and due process clauses. He further contended that the notion that the government had been deprived of a proper role in the suit was absurd; the government had not been a party in the *Dred Scott* case and had recently accepted *amicus curiae* roles in the gold-clause suits.[36]

To compound matters, the court heard no oral defense of the Act itself. Buell failed to raise the constitutional issue in his sixty-five-minute argument for Burco, and Burns spent his entire time trying to prove that the court had no right to convert the case into a constitutional test. Four weeks later a blistering brief signed by Burns, Cohen, and Corcoran asked dismissal on grounds of "collusive" cooperation: "The inference is inescapable that the interest of Burco, Inc., in supporting the act is negligible compared with its interests in cooperating in the arrangement of a test case suitable to the Edison Electrical Institute." The brief also asserted that cross-examination had elicited clear testimony that the parties had conferred and collaborated in closing the pleadings before the government was even notified of the pending proceedings. A second brief argued the constitutional question.[37]

All Burns, Cohen, and Corcoran managed to do was infuriate Judge Coleman. In an impassioned, 20,000-word opinion which echoed many of Davis' contentions, Coleman declared that Congress had "flagrantly exceeded its lawful power" and had produced a law so "grossly arbitrary, unreasonable and capricious" that he had no recourse but to rule it unconstitutional. He also chastised the government attorneys:

> It is not forbidden "collusion" for the parties to a case, by agreement, to put it in such shape that the rights and obligations of the parties can be the more readily determined by the court, especially when matters of public moment are involved requiring speedy settlement, regardless of an adverse effect upon the Government's interests. . . . What has been said applies equally to the status of . . . Ferd Lautenbach, and his counsel. The attempt on the part of counsel for the Government and for the Securities and Exchange Commission to disparage the motives of both intervenors and their counsel is not only baseless, but unworthy of any representative of any branch of our Government.

On Wall Street the next day, utility stocks rose between one and three points. Significantly, however, a few of the industry's more responsible

spokesmen tempered their elation with hope that a "new and constitutional" bill could be drafted in order to prevent the recurrence of
abuses.[38]

Less than three months later, Davis was in Charlotte, North Carolina, arguing the appeal in the Fourth Circuit. After denouncing the
Act as "vicious" and as "the last word in federal tyranny," he told the
court that it had never before been forced to rule on a law on which
the brand of unconstitutionality was more strongly imprinted. Although the court rejected this sweeping rhetoric decisively, it did find
the Act unconstitutional insofar as it applied to the reorganization of a
debtor not engaged in interstate commerce; otherwise its provisions
stood.[39]

Late in March Davis' crusade against the Holding Company Act suffered another setback when the Supreme Court refused to hear an appeal. Presumably, the refusal was influenced by Solicitor General Stanley Reed's plea that pending suits would offer a test "in which the
government has had an opportunity to share and in which the act is
applied to the kind of typical holding situations which Congress had
in mind at its enactment." [40]

The denial of certiorari, reflected Arthur Krock, was morally useful.
There was no law against the Supreme Court proceeding on a "thin
foundation"; nor was there a law against the kind of "circumvention"
the utility company's lawyers had resorted to in Baltimore. Nevertheless, it would have been "imprudent as well as unfair" to have tried
such a grave and basic issue under such unworthy circumstances. At
the very least, the Supreme Court was obligated to "uphold the highest standards of equitable procedures." [41]

Davis was too defensive of his own role, too convinced, as he said in
remarks to the American Bar Association in August, that the Holding
Company Act was "the gravest threat to the liberties of American citizens that has emanated from . . . Congress in my lifetime," to credit
the question raised by Krock. He simply saw no reason, as one of his
associates later wrote, why the government, but not private litigants,
should be given the advantage of picking and choosing test cases.
"Who told you that there was anything unusual about a decision on
the unconstitutionality of an Act of Congress without the Government
or any of its agencies being formal parties to the suit"? Davis asked
Krock. "Whoever did certainly did not know his onions." The columnist replied that he would not venture to debate legal points with

the greatest lawyer in the United States; nevertheless, the brief time afforded the government to prepare for the slight participation it was permitted made it right to call it a "back-door" affair.[42]

That was the only time in thirty years that Krock ever questioned Davis' legal ethics.

« III »

By then Davis was representing the Associated Press against the National Labor Relations Board in one of the few cases in which he changed the thrust of his argument partly because of pressure from a client. At stake was the umbrella over organizing activities and collective bargaining raised by the Wagner Act.[43]

Through all his years on Wall Street Davis remained pro-labor in the abstract. He continued to be proud of his role in framing the Clayton Act, and he pronounced himself a "labor sympathizer" even as he criticized President Roosevelt's failure to invoke federal power against the sit-down strikers in 1937. He believed, of course, that the New Deal "leaned too far in the direction of giving labor monopolistic power," and he was to rejoice when President Truman asked Congress to draft striking trainmen in 1946. Yet even then he warned that it would be "equally fatal to swing the pendulum all the way to the other side." [44]

For all his good will and essential humanity, however, Davis had consistently opposed efforts to redress the imbalance between labor and management during the 1920's and 1930's. His personal letters and public statements are devoid of criticism of the corporate world's sustained offensive against labor through the period—an offensive which foreclosed free speech in company towns, perpetuated child labor in mining and textiles, and prevented most steel, rubber, electrical, and automobile workers from organizing until the late 1930's. (General Motors alone spent $839,764 on labor spies between 1934 and 1936.) As in his presidential campaign, Davis seemed unaware that management's power to intimidate and suppress made government support of organization and collective bargaining the only way to achieve in reality the rights of labor he endorsed in theory. In 1928 he ignored a plea by William Green to support the American Federation of Labor's anti-injunction campaign; in 1932 he disapproved of the Norris–La Guardia Anti-injunction Act; and in 1933 he deplored the pro-labor provisions of the NIRA.[45]

The Associated Press, observed *Fortune* in an otherwise laudatory article on that organization the month Davis argued the case in the Supreme Court, had been "steadily reactionary" in its labor relations. It had refused to bargain with its telegraphers, much less with its news and editorial employees, and in the fall of 1935 it summarily fired Morris Watson, a reporter who headed the American Newspaper Guild's Associated Press unit in New York. A thin, sallow man who had been gassed and wounded in World War I and had spent several years in a rehabilitation center before joining the AP in 1928, Watson was known as "a hard guy to work with." But he was also one of the organization's crack newsmen and had been assigned to some of the biggest stories of the day. His $73.75 weekly wage was only a dollar and a quarter off the maximum. "You are the best reporter we have," the assistant general manager told him a year or so before his dismissal.[46]

About eight months after he had organized the New York office in November 1933, Watson asked General Manager Kent Cooper to recognize the Guild. Cooper replied that he would quit his job before bargaining with "an outsider"; however, he did put the New York office on a five-day week. The assistant general manager then transferred Watson to the Southern wire, a position, so the reporter complained, for which he was unfitted by temperament or experience. Despite his discontent, he twice won commendations from local Associated Press offices for his writing of headlines in the new assignment.[47]

On October 7, 1935, Cooper arbitrarily restored the five-and-a-half-day week. Two days later Watson won almost unanimous approval by the Guild local of a resolution for collective bargaining under the Wagner Act. The trenchant liberal columnist Heywood Broun, founder and national chairman of the Guild, then asked Cooper to meet with him. Within hours of Broun's request Watson's immediate supervisor placed a five-point indictment of Watson on Cooper's desk. It called him an "agitator," charged him with poor work and dereliction of duty (he had once arranged a replacement while he led a Guild meeting), and recommended his dismissal. Cooper added a notation: "But *solely* on grounds of his work not being on a basis for which he has shown capability." Early that afternoon Watson was discharged. Four days later Cooper explained to Broun that AP employees had always evidenced faith in management and that to force acceptance of a union "would be disruptive of . . . morale." [48]

Soon afterwards, the Guild filed a complaint with the National

Labor Relations Board, stating that Watson had been dismissed for union activities and that the Associated Press had refused to bargain collectively. The AP then went to Davis, who had been under retainer since 1921. In consultation with a senior partner, William Cannon, Davis decided that the AP should apply for a declaratory judgment holding the Wagner Act unconstitutional, and that it should request a preliminary injunction to restrain the NLRB and the Newspaper Guild from interfering with its business. He and Cannon further concluded that the Associated Press' contention that Watson was fired for poor performance rather than union activities was "equivocal" and that the AP should not contest the Guild on that point.[49]

On January 17, 1936, Davis vigorously contended before United States District Judge William Bondy that the Wagner Act was "null and void *in toto.*" His argument paralleled the one set forth in the Liberty League report he had signed four months earlier. He charged that the Act violated the interstate commerce clause, impaired the right of contract, and deprived the Associated Press of property in violation of the due process clause of the Fifth Amendment. He also asserted that it discriminated against minority employees by giving the majority the sole right to elect representatives for collective bargaining. He noted, however, that the constitutional issue did not have to be decided at that time: "If the court holds any serious doubt on that question, you should hold it in status quo while you relieve us . . . by means of the preliminary injunction." [50]

Counsel for the NLRB replied that the Wagner Act was modeled on the Federal Trade Commission legislation and that men like Watson were as much entitled to protection under the Constitution as were corporate interests such as the Associated Press. But the most effective argument came from the noted civil libertarian Morris Ernst, who appeared for the Guild as *amicus curiae.* Ernst charged that the Associated Press had been evasive in responding to the requests for collective bargaining and had "kidded us along in an effort to break the strength of the workers." He further charged that Davis had failed to prove that the AP was threatened with "irreparable damage," an indispensable condition for the issuance of an injunction. Neither, Ernst added, should an injunction be granted if an employer "has not acted in good faith, honor and decency." He then asked Judge Bondy to let Heywood Broun speak for five minutes.[51]

Bondy replied that Ernst himself had narrowed the issue to whether the Associated Press had offered sufficient facts to warrant action. But before the Judge could stop Broun, the columnist was on his feet reading from a paper in his hand: "John W. Davis is asking you for permission for the Associated Press to run a yellow-dog shop." Leaping up, Davis demanded, in a voice quivering with anger, that the remark be stricken. Broun then began to speak again. "But you're arguing economics now," Bondy interrupted. "Doesn't economics belong in a court of law?" Broun asked. "No," the Judge responded, "and it would be better for our government if it would desist from entering into economic problems in which there is so much diversity of opinion." Afterwards Broun went up to the bench and shook hands with Bondy, an old acquaintance.[52]

Six weeks later Broun sent Judge Bondy an extraordinary letter. "Your Honor," he wrote—

> You promised an early decision, accepted briefs, and took the case under advisement. The Guild is making no attempt to influence your decision one way or another but it thinks it has a right to protest against the law's delays and to ask for a speedy ruling.
> The Wagner-Connery Act until invalidated is the law of the land and the delay deprives us of its potential benefits. You did not grant an injunction but you have presented the Associated Press with an easement, a kind of legal laxative which works while you sleep.
> In the event of an adverse decision, we can appeal, but as things stand the Labor Board is not free to proceed, Morris Watson has not got his job and the Associated Press sits just as prettily as if you had already decided in its favor.
> We think we have a reasonable right to protest against this situation. We do protest. We think your Honor should make up your mind.[53]

Davis read a copy of Broun's letter in disbelief. "He might well be held in contempt, but I think that would please him beyond words. He would put on the crown of martyrdom." Three weeks later Judge Bondy ruled that Davis' plea of unconstitutionality was "hardly tenable" and that mere collective bargaining could not possibly "irreparably harm" an employer. Then, on April 24, the trial examiner for the National Labor Relations Board found that Watson had been discharged solely because of his union activities. (At Davis' instance, the Associated Press had again refrained from testifying on Watson's severance, moving instead to dismiss on the ground that the Wagner Act was unconstitutiional.)[54]

Davis planned to repeat in the Court of Appeals the interstate commerce and due process arguments he had made in the hearing before Judge Bondy. But Kent Cooper and the coterie of powerful publishers

who dominated the Associated Press' board had been saying all along
that the real issue was freedom of the press. It was imperative, urged
Cooper, that the news be "unsullied." Could not the First Amendment
be emphasized? asked Colonel Robert McCormick of the Chicago
Tribune. As Frank B. Noyes, president of both the AP and the Washington *Star*, explained to Davis, "We may properly regard an employee as disqualified . . . if we fear that his partisan-ship outruns his
devotion to an unbiased news report." [55]

A small minority of publishers thought this was nonsense. "Unlike
some of you," Arthur Hays Sulzberger of *The New York Times* told
his fellow publishers at a convention that spring, "I am not convinced
that the . . . Administration . . . has or had designs upon freedom of
the press or any other fundamental right of our citizenry." Philip
Stern of the New York *Evening Post* and Philadelphia *Record*, the
first publisher to come to terms with the Guild, was of the same mind:
The "economic security of the profession is essential to its dignity"; the
contract "is an agreement . . . to insure fairness and decency in our relations with the newsroom, to promote machinery for correcting any
unfairness, whether . . . intentional or unintentional." There was,
furthermore, a certain irony in the professed concern for truth by men
such as Colonel McCormick and William Randolph Hearst (who was
a member of the AP, but not a director). The editor of McCormick's
Chicago *Tribune* was under orders, or about to be put under orders,
never to print the name of President Robert M. Hutchins of the University of Chicago. And the editor of Hearst's Chicago *Herald-Examiner* was to confess, after deliberately misquoting a speech by a prominent intellectual that very year, that "we just do what the old man
orders. One week he orders a campaign against rats. The next week he
orders a campaign against dope peddlers. Pretty soon he's gong to
order a campaign against college professors. It's all the bunk, but
orders are orders." Indeed, as Will Irwin observed in a perceptive
partial truth, the Associated Press itself could be misleading:

> A movement in stocks is . . . big news. Widespread misery in a mining
> camp is scarcely news at all. The flare and action of a strike in Paterson is news. The weight of vested power crushing down the union after
> the strike is not news. . . . The agents of this dominant bureau, owning their own point of view, select from the events of the day such
> news as squares with their conservative picture of the world. . . . The
> Associated Press is in bulk a powerful force of reaction.[56]

As a public man, Davis was well aware of the perversion of truth by
the Hearsts, McCormicks, and their like. But he would no doubt have

disagreed with Irwin's more subtle analysis of the Associated Press; indeed, his associate in the case holds that he was absolutely convinced of the AP's dedication to the impartial dissemination of news. He also believed, of course, that the employer had the right to demand whatever he chose of the employee, short of libel. Still, as Cannon explained when the AP's assistant manager, Lloyd Stratton, implored them to emphasize freedom of speech in the appeal, Davis did not think that regulation of employer-employee relations fell under the purview of the First Amendment.[57]

Yet Davis was anxious to oblige the AP. He asked Paschall Davis to work up a First Amendment argument for him to consider. It was a tough assignment. Young Davis found that the handful of Supreme Court decisions on freedom of the press all dealt with prior restraint. On the other hand, he turned up legions of decisions holding that employer-employee relations were *not* interstate commerce and *were* a matter of private contract. He also concluded that it was an open question whether the AP could be defined as "the press," for it was not a publisher. After considerable discussion the two men decided that, if the court could be prevailed on to accept the view that the AP was "the press," they could properly argue that the Wagner Act violated both the First and Fifth amendments. They then appended such an argument to the brief.[58]

Although Davis did press the First Amendment point in his oral argument in the Second Circuit Court of Appeals in late June, he pounded hardest on the interstate commerce clause. "News is manufactured by the open-hearth process," he declared, in an effort to revive the distinction between manufacture and commerce set forth in the *Knight* case of 1895; only after it was shaped by editorial employees did it enter the stream of commerce. ("Many readers of the Associated Press have doubtless long suspected them of manufacturing news," quipped one of the Guild's attorneys, "but I never expected the company's learned attorney to so admit in open court.") Morris Ernst then tore into Davis' contention that the Associated Press was a nonprofit organization and therefore immune from the commerce clause. "It is quite clear," said Ernst, "that . . . [it] is not an eleemosynary institution, but . . . a business association through which member newspapers make greater profits through decreased costs. Assessments vary in the same manner as dividends." [59]

Thereafter Davis' difficulties mounted. Later that month the Court of Appeals found unanimously against the Associated Press, and all summer long Cooper and Stratton tried to prevail on Davis to emphasize freedom of the press when he went to the Supreme Court. For months Davis resisted. As he wrote to one of his assistants from England, newspapermen were not engaged in interstate commerce, and the master-servant relationship was not within the power of Congress to regulate, except possibly in the case of railroads. "We will win on these points when we get to the Supreme Court. We will not win on the 'unsullied news' doctrine put forth by Cooper and Stratton. . . . Their argument rests on too narrow a ground. We stand for the right to hire & fire on any grounds deemed adequate by the employer. And we deny the right of the Federal Government to inquire whether this ground or that is sufficient." He then added a passage which he implicitly repudiated when he got into court.:

> If they as employers are interested in "impartial news," another employer may make an argument no weaker & no stronger for a similar integrity in his commodity or service. All this of course you know as well as I & I thought we had convinced Bros. Cooper & Stratton to this effect.[60]

Although Cooper deferred "humbly" to Davis, Stratton continued to fight. On receiving a draft of the brief in September, he urged Cannon to relegate the points on interstate commerce to the end and put those on freedom of the press and freedom of contract first. Wearily, Cannon had Frank Polk's son reply, "Mr. Davis himself," wrote young Polk, "outlined the argument. . . . [The] fifth and first amendment arguments, though important, are secondary." Nevertheless, Cooper and Stratton had carried their objective partially, for inclusion of the First Amendment point, no matter where placed, enabled the AP to dramatize the case in its wire stories on the briefs as a conflict over freedom of speech. (The real issue, said Morris Ernst in his *amicus* brief for the Guild, was "whose prejudices shall color the news?" This point was recognized implicitly in Davis' statement in his brief that the AP was contending for the right to "print the news it wants as it wants to.")[61]

On February 8, 1937, as Davis boarded the train for Washington, where the hearing was to open the next day, he startled Paschall Davis by saying that he believed that they would actually win the case on freedom of the press. It was quite possible, he explained, that the Jones & Laughlin Steel Corporation might lose the companion case on the commerce clause and Fifth Amendment arguments; but of all the Wagner Act appellants, the AP alone was in a position to invoke a

First Amendment argument. How much this reversal of emphasis reflected Davis' fear that Roosevelt's implied threat to pack the Supreme Court might swing the high tribunal away from *stare decisis,* and how much to a veteran's instinct for the situation, his young associate could not say; he insisted, however, that the pressure of the Associated Press and the publishers was inconsequential.[62]

As Davis walked from the Carlton Hotel on Sixteenth Street to the Supreme Court Building late the following morning, he turned to Paschall Davis and asked, "Who said, 'Let me write the songs of a nation and I care not who writes its laws'?" The associate did not know. Some minutes later they entered a chamber so packed with publishers and government officials that folding chairs had to be set up.[63]

Davis began his oral argument by again denying that news and editorial employees were in interstate commerce. "These editorial employees are engaged—in the court below I used the phrase 'in manufacture of news,' and the double implication of that word caused me some embarrassment. Therefore I do not use that phrase here. They are engaged in the production of news . . . as truly a productive energy as that of the roller in the steel mill." He then charged that the Wagner Act sought to make the closed shop universal and compulsory and that the National Labor Relations Board was serving that objective by finding that "the flow of commerce" put almost all industry into interstate commerce. The Board's decisions, he said, leave only one conclusion: "the word 'flow' is to them the grand omnific word that disposes of all their doubts and controversies." The reasoning in the *Schecter* and *Carter* cases, he declared, "dooms this statute beyond all reasonable hope of recovery." After hammering further the proposition that the Act violated the due process clause of the Fifth Amendment, he gulped a glass of water in a long, dramatic pause: "And now we come to the freedom of the press, . . . perhaps the most important subject I have to present on this argument." [64]

"I assert," Davis said, " [that] this act . . . is a direct, palpable, undisguised attack upon the freedom of the press." It was possible, he conceded, to overstate the point on the commerce clause, and perhaps he had done so. But it was of no moment, for the First Amendment argument transcended all others. "As the great Montesquieu observed," he said as his voice rose almost to a shout, " 'Let me write the songs of a nation, and I care not who writes its laws.' " (The name had come to him a few moments earlier.) Morris Watson "may have a heart as pure as Galahad and be as wise as Solomon, but if he is forced upon us by law to formulate and write what we must publish, we are no longer free insofar as the outgivings of the Associated Press are concerned":

> I submit that whatever may be said of this Act, whether it is as fatally inclusive as I contend, or whether there is a field where its operation may lawfully be effective, if there is one field which, under the Constitution of the United States, escapes congressional intrusion, that field is the freedom of the press, which the order entered here clearly and directly invades.[65]

The best Davis' friends could say afterward, wrote Heywood Broun in a slashing attack on what he termed Davis' "bravura stuff" and "stock-company dramatics," was that he had been "smooth." Even neutral observers felt that young Charles E. Wysanski, Jr., who had shared the government's time with Charles Fahey, had overpowered him. Reeling off citation after citation without glancing at a single note, Wyzanski had riddled the notion that the Associated Press was not a profit-making business. He had also shredded Davis' construction of the commerce clause, standing partly on the *Pipe Line* cases which Davis himself had argued so brilliantly as Solicitor General in 1913. Fahey closed for the government by arguing what Davis had so long maintained in private—that freedom of the press was extraneous to the question before the Court.[66]

The opinions compounded the irony. Justice Roberts, speaking for himself and the four civil libertarians, Brandeis, Cardozo, Hughes, and Stone, called Davis' First Amendment argument an "unsound generalization" utterly lacking in relevance; he also held that the Associated Press was patently an instrumentality of businesses whose operations involved constant use of the channels of interstate commerce. But Justice Sutherland found the freedom of press issue fundamental in a dissent joined by the three other most anti-civil libertarian men on the Court—Butler, McReynolds, and Van Devanter. In language that echoed Davis' argument in places, and which was to contribute to later freedom-of-speech cases, Sutherland declared that First Amendment liberties were so precious that they were guaranteed without qualification, including due process.[67]

By then Davis had become completely convinced that the First Amendment question was central. "I had the shock of my life," he said when the decision came down. "I really thought . . . I could carry them on the freedom of the press." Publicly, he used the defeat, so painful to him, to rebuke Roosevelt by implication for his court-packing proposal and for his derogatory allusions to the bench:

> When a majority of the Supreme Court has spoken on a constitutional question, it is the duty of every citizen to accept the result. That is the sort of government we have. It is the sort of government we ought to have.
>
> A lawyer may feel disappointed when his arguments are not accepted. . . . But when the court has spoken, that is the end of the matter so far as the legal aspect is concerned.[68]

« IV »

On February 5, 1937, just two and a half months before the Supreme Court upheld the Wagner Act in the *Associated Press* and *Jones & Laughlin* decisions, President Roosevelt had submitted his ill-fated court-packing bill to Congress. Although not without redeeming features, the bill in essence was a thinly disguised proposal to circumvent the conservative majority on the Court by adding one Justice for each Justice who failed to retire on reaching the age of seventy (up to six in all). Nothing Roosevelt ever did infuriated Davis more. Terming it a direct attempt to influence the Court's opinions, he denounced it as the "rawest attack on our system of government in my lifetime." He was sorely tempted by the Columbia Broadcasting System's offer of a half-hour of prime time to rebut the President. But, "bursting for utterance" though he was, he wisely decided to let the Democrats in Congress carry the fight—"the authorities in Washington would like nothing better than to say that the opposition to the scheme comes from the registered opponents of Roosevelt—*of whom I am which* and no apologies for it!"[69]

Privately, Davis spared no effort to spur the bill's opponents. He drafted a statement for a group of attorneys to sign and publish. He assigned a young associate to assist a special committee of the American Bar Association. He counseled Walter Lippmann. And he sent Senator Walter George and Representative Samuel B. Pettengill a series of memoranda designed to show that "in spite of all the talk about divisions of opinion in the Court . . . and the unhappy phrases used by some of the dissenting Justices" the Court was a unit on fundamentals. One memorandum listed those cases in which the Court had vindicated the rights of labor. ("To speak of it as an 'anti-Labor' court in the light of these cases is nothing short of fantastic.") Another summarized cases upholding the rights of Negroes. A third collated instances of the invasion of the independence of the judiciary by the Stuarts as culled from a moving article, "The Kings and the Courts," by a young associate, Luke W. Finlay.[70]

Davis also challenged some of the more worthy aspects of the President's package. He objected especially to a proposal, prompted in no small measure by criticism of his own utility case in Baltimore, to make the Attorney General a party of right in any case involving a constitutional question. This, he protested, was both unnecessary and dangerous: unnecessary because the Attorney General could appear anyway by leave of the Court; dangerous because there would be a constant appeal to "consider the convenience of the Attorney General rather than the rights of the litigants." [71]

By the time Davis wrote the last of his memoranda, the question was almost moot. F.D.R.'s deviousness had angered even his staunchest supporters, and Congress was prepared only to save a little presidential face with a watered-down measure. More important, Justice Roberts had defected from the anti-New Deal faction and had turned it into a minority. In a series of five-to-four rulings that spring, the Court had upheld a Washington minimum wage law, the second Frazier-Lemke Act, and the Social Security Act. Then, on April 12, the day of the *Associated Press* decision, the Court sustained the Wagner Act in the more far-reaching *Jones & Laughlin* case.[72]

Shocked as he was by the implications of the decisions to constitutional law as he understood it, Davis kept his sense of humor. Under the signature "Hamlet," he penned a lament to his old friend Justice McReynolds:

> Alas, poor Stare Decisis! I knew him well Horatio: a fellow of infinite jest, of most excellent fancy. He hath borne me on his back a thousand times; and now, how abhorred in my imagination it is! my gorge rises at it.

Yet there was compensation. "It seems to me," Davis reflected, "that yesterday's work knocks the last prop out from under . . . [the President's] court-packing argument.[73]

BOOK IV

Elder Statesman of the Law

CHAPTER 23

The Complete Man

Personal liberty is the doctrine of self-restraint.   JOHN W. DAVIS

« I »

Despite his brooding concern for the fate of the nation, Davis remained a contented man in his private life. The grace and charm, the empathy and sensitivity, the exquisite sense of occasion—all the qualities that had prompted George V to call him "the most perfect gentleman" he had ever met—became even more refined as his self-confidence deepened and his early aspirations for security, comfort, and professional eminence were fulfilled. Intimates and acquaintances alike were struck by how his "rare and wondrous" faculty for making others feel greater than they really were would lift everyone's spirits the moment he walked into a room. "I remember so vividly what he did for me," one of his daughter's house guests recalled. "After a weekend with him I felt so beautiful, so charming, so witty, so intelligent—all the things I couldn't possibly be." [1]

In 1923 Davis had bought a small estate consisting of a house, servants' cottage, outbuildings, and five acres of land in Locust Valley, Long Island, near the place he and Nell had been renting a couple of miles out from Glen Cove. The main house was a rambling, broad-shingled, pseudo-Tudor structure of twelve or so rooms, later expanded to sixteen. It was situated on a knoll overlooking St. John's of Lattingtown Episcopal Church, and from the third floor the Sound was visible. In time Davis bought ten acres of adjacent field which Nell converted into an attractive garden-park with the help of an architect. She laid out a circular rock garden, followed a year or two later by an herb garden, a tea house, and an avenue of hawthorns with one enclosed paved garden and another encircled by peonies and lilacs. Several strategically planted groves of white pines filled out the composition.[2]

From November through April the Davises resided in a capacious, seventh-floor apartment on the corner of East 88th Street and Fifth Avenue, across from Central Park. They also maintained what he liked to call a "guest proof" five-room cottage at Yeamans Hall, South Carolina, a club-type development a few miles north of Charleston. Yeamans Hall had been the seat of one of the Carolina Governors in the days of the Lord Proprietors. The Olmsted firm planned the landscaping in the early 1920's, and members and their guests were comfortably housed in a clubhouse and some forty picturesquely sited neo-Colonial cottages. The 1000 acres or more were resplendent with broad vistas and sunny glades framed by groves of giant oaks and silver gray curtains of Spanish moss, all partly surrounded by a sheltered tidal river. A well laid out and not too strenuous golf course, together with rambling woodland paths, gave ample opportunity for exercise. The winter months were usually gentle, the early spring idyllic. In this congenial atmosphere Davis, who was prone to pneumonia and under orders from his doctor to avoid the cold season in New York, sojourned annually for a number of weeks for more than twenty years.[3]

Davis' extraordinary power of concentration drained his reserves so much that his card games, conversation, vacations, and trips abroad were all directed to the single aim of total relaxation. He even refused to apply his analytical powers to bridge, holding steadfastly to the "Davis Intuitional System"—so named when Ely Culbertson asked in astonishment what method he was using in a shipboard game. He relished most his fierce cribbage and backgammon battles with J. P. Morgan at a nickel a game. Once, when Morgan ran up a seven-game winning streak, the financier growled to Davis' butler that his wages were in danger. Another time Davis ended the evening with a long string of victories and demanded that Morgan, who was out of pocket change, give him an I.O.U. Davis' use of alcohol was temperate and regular in the manner of everything else. He refused to buy liquor during Prohibition, but his friends kept his closet stocked, and he usually had one martini or a bourbon before dinner. He also smoked three cigars and several pipefuls of tobacco a day, partly, he jokingly said, to give the impression of being wise while thinking of something to say to his clients. His all-purpose servant, Charles Hanson, whom he had brought over from England in 1923, saw to it that the routine was inviolate. An efficient, solicitous, omnipresent man who possessed the bearing of Morgan himself, Hanson could make a production out of serving a glass of water. Davis he deemed the perfect master. "They say no man is a hero to his valet," he once wrote him, "but I can give the lie to that." [4]

For a while after settling in Locust Valley, Davis thought he might keep a horse, but Nell vetoed the idea. On hot summer evenings he would go down to the Sound, swim backstroke for a few moments, and return refreshed. Toward golf he was ambivalent. He played partly on his physician's instructions, mainly for the companionship. On missing a stroke he would sometimes sing out "The Old Gray Mare ain't what she used to be"; and once, after his ball landed in a trap, he boomed forth all the words of the hymn, "Rescue the Perishing." [5]

Only fishing came close to being a passion. In 1938 Davis realized a long-term ambition by hooking and landing a savage, 130-pound tarpon off the coast of Florida. The challenge mastered, he let several others escape because he found no "fun in killing for killing's sake." Usually he fished for salmon in Canada, where he, Edwin S. S. Sunderland, Henry Alexander of Morgan Guaranty, and several others kept a camp on the Sebatis River in New Brunswick. There, as to every place else, he brought his special *joie de vivre*. Often he would put down his rod early, loll on the bank, and bring belly laughs to his companions by reading Damon Runyon aloud. And always around the fire at night he would regale them from his endless fund of stories. If he personalized at all, it was usually to cast himself as the anti-hero. Once, after reflecting on the number of people who had shaken his hand since the presidential campaign of 1924, he wryly concluded: "If everybody who says so actually voted for me, I would have been elected." [6]

His repartee, always sharp, became exceptionally well honed as his self-assurance grew, and several times in the 1920's and 1930's he put down Charles Evans Hughes. At one luncheon or dinner, Hughes, in a rare expansive mood, related how a group of undertakers had petitioned him on a matter during his governorship of New York. That was the first time, said Hughes, that he had ever heard of the undertakers' vote. "Have any of you gentlemen ever run into it?" Dryly, Davis responded: "Yes, I did in 1924!" [7]

Davis always enjoyed the forced leisure of long train trips and, especially, ocean crossings. Six months after the Pecora investigation in 1933, J. P. Morgan took the Davises on a "glorious" 6800-mile voyage on the *Corsair* through the Caribbean and out to the Galapagos Islands in the Pacific. Eighteen months later Davis and Nell went through the Mediterranean and Aegean on their own, stopping to see Delphi, the ruins of Troy, the palace of King Minos in Crete, and other ancient wonders which had always fascinated him. Occasionally they went to Paris, though it held little appeal for him. ("Having seen all the sights, it now bores me to death, especially since I cannot carry on a French conversation.") Once Nell went to Switzerland while he shot grouse with Morgan on the Scottish moors. But it was to England and their old friends from the ambassadorial years that they gravitated. ("When I smell those smoky streets of London," he said, "I snort like an old fire horse turned out to pasture.") He had several pleasant audiences with George V and later with Edward VIII, whose interests he represented in the United States. His affection for Edward was almost fatherly, and he was so shaken by his abdication that he termed it the greatest personal tragedy he had ever known.[8]

As he grew older, Davis fed more and more on the companionship of his peers. He always surrounded himself with congenial lunch partners, often opposing counsel. (During the Associated Press hearing in Washington he included Morris Ernst, to the consternation of Guild officials.) For years he belonged to The Round Table, a semi-formal group which met regularly at the Knickerbocker Club and numbered Nicholas Murray Butler, William Lyon Phelps, Learned Hand, Thomas S. Lamont, and William Church Osborn among its regulars. Davis was the center, and after his death the group lost its vitality. "As a raconteur, as an intimate with the treasures of culture, as a troubadour," wrote one of its members near the end, "you are without a rival —the companion supreme." Davis also belonged to a dinner club composed of the Hand cousins, Judges Thomas Swan and Samuel Seabury, Charles Burlingham, Whitney North Seymour, and his partners Wardwell and Chandler. They met at the Century Association four times a year and usually discussed law and the state of the nation. To this group, as to the Round Table, Davis brought the same bonhomie, the same bubbling wit, that made his partners' eyes glow with warmth whenever his name was mentioned.[9]

Time served only to strengthen his affection for Nell; rarely were they separated voluntarily except for his two weeks of salmon fishing in Canada. They kept a box at the Philharmonic, and she continued to grace his table at the small formal dinner parties that were their main form of entertaining. They remained highly selective, hardly

ever receiving clients, political acquaintances, or even the younger
partners. Nell never lost her almost coldly formal air, but neither did
she lose her keen social sense and quick social smile. She regretted that
she was no longer as integral to his work as she had been in London,
and she absorbed herself in raising prize roses, in refurbishing the
house and apartment, and in collecting antiques. Her neuralgia became increasingly painful, and in the late 1930's and early 1940's she
underwent two complicated operations; at the same time her general
health deteriorated. "It is hard to see her slipping away from me," he
said. He indulged her constantly, and she reciprocated as best she
could. Just before one of her operations, she wrote him:

> Dear Lover,
>   Tonight I can tell you only this. My years with you have brought
> me nothing but happiness. You have been the noblest man and the
> most perfect husband any woman ever had.
>   Your adoring Nell.

On July 13, 1943, she died. During the funeral service Davis stiffened perceptibly at one point, but otherwise he maintained his iron
discipline. Afterwards he declined to visit Clarksburg. "Three-fourths
of those I happen to meet would feel it their duty to express some
words of condolence. I don't think I could stick it out." [10]
Financial security enabled Davis to satisfy his generous impulses in a
modest way. Although his taxes were never as high as he complained
they were, they did prevent him from acquiring a substantial fortune.
He abandoned his hope of endowing a law chair at Washington and
Lee, but he lavished gifts on his relatives. Worried that the trust fund
he had set up for his sister Emma in the early 1920's was inadequate,
he supplemented her income to the point that she pleaded with him
to stop. "It is not right to feel that any one is as perfect as I believe
you to be. . . . You are just what I used to think you to be when we
were children—my ideal. If you have any faults . . . , they only add
to my admiration." [11]
Children felt Davis' instinctive warmth, and they unfailingly sought
him out. Among his papers are dozens of letters, some in childish
scrawls, from grandnieces and grandnephews, from Hanson's child,
and from his daughter Julia's wards, thanking him for gifts ranging
from dolls and fire engines to tuition for college. He took special interest in the two sons of Carl Vance, his cousin and former campaign
manager. Vance had died when the boys were small, and Davis stood

in loco parentis to them throughout their youth. They were often in and out of his house and apartment, and Cyrus, who later became Deputy Secretary of Defense, remembered vividly how Davis would discuss books with them and ask their opinion on legal questions. Only once, in a letter to the widow of an old friend, did Davis reveal how much he himself longed for grandchildren. He would give all he possessed, he wrote her, to have some of his own.[12]

« II »

The house in Locust Valley suited Davis perfectly. He loved the large, oak-paneled living room, so reminiscent of English houses, and he felt secure, comfortable, and immovable in his big study on the top floor. He named the place Mattapan, from an Indian word meaning "I sit down." Rainy Sundays were his favorite days. He would say "Thank God, I don't have to play golf," then stay home from church and seclude himself in his study until the current dog brought up a note announcing a meal. There, seated in an easy chair overlooking the Sound, he did much of his serious reading. "He was a great reader," his intimate friend and partner Sunderland recalled with awe. "He read after campaign speeches. He read when fishing salmon. He always read for an hour or more before sleep. He never wasted a moment. This gave him a great facility in speaking extemporaneously. When I would ask him how he fastened on one or another quotation he would say, 'I just opened a bin in my granary.'"[13]

Davis was enamored of history, especially biography, and there was probably not a single English historian of note whose works he had not read. He was also intimate with the ancients, Greek and Roman, and he drew great comfort from Epictetus and other Stoic philosophers. In literature his taste ran to the English romantic poets and nineteenth-century novelists. He seems also to have read most nineteenth-century American poets and writers, and he regarded the apostrophe to liberty in Henry George's *Progress and Poverty* as one of the finest pieces of rhetoric in the language. He had considerable interest in science (he subscribed to *Scientific American*) and great curiosity about anatomy and histology, as well as botany. He disliked contemporary American literature, though he thought that Margaret Mitchell deserved the Nobel Prize for *Gone With the Wind*. "The characters come alive," he said; "that's the real test of fiction." He called Bruce Barton's *The Man Nobody Knows* "a vivid, compelling portrait" which he hoped would be widely read. Yet he could also write Walter Lippmann, presumably on greater reflection than he gave Barton's work, that *The Good Society* afforded all the delight "one feels in finding his own thoughts expressed in language more clear and convincing than he could hope himself to command." He searched the classics for adages, and he carried many through life. One of his favorites was from Dr. Johnson: "Let every man make an honest man of himself; he will be sure there will be one rascal the less." Another was from Epictetus: "If a great bear appear, I will fight a greater fight." [14]

Religion remained a perversely engaging intellectual interest. As a widower in Washington, Davis had attended church regularly, and he had even gone once to a revival meeting conducted by Billy Sunday. ("There is no touch of the divine afflatus about him," he reported.) Following his marriage to Nell, an Episcopalian, he took the path of least resistance, as he phrased it, and identified with her church. He also maintained a tenuous relationship with the Brick Presbyterian Church after they moved to New York, in part because of his respect for the Rev. Paul Austin Wolfe. Sometimes he listened to Harry Emerson Fosdick on the radio. "Lord, how refreshing to hear a man in the pulpit who has something to say. I could almost forgive the extempore prayers . . . for the sake of it." [15]

In 1931 Davis became a vestryman of St. John's of Lattingtown. But, as he emphasized to an old college friend who professed to have been hoping all his life that Davis would be saved so that they could sing together in the celestial choir, no theological commitment accompanied the position; he carried his religion in his wife's name, he explained, and when her church was looking about for a person "of preeminent piety, high moral reputation, and sound financial judgment," it naturally selected him. What could he do but accept? Thirteen years later a question arose over his not having been baptized, and he resigned.[16]

The problem, Davis confided to Thomas W. Lamont in 1946, was that the cement poured in more than a half-century earlier in Clarksburg had failed to set. "Not so long ago I got a copy of the Westminster Shorter Catechism . . . and sat down . . . to strike out so much as I affirmatively disbelieved, though sparing the doubtfuls and unprovens. When I finished the paper looked like nothing so much as a draft of a proposed public statement by J. P. M. & Co. after it had been censored by yourself." The first passage to go was the major premise that all mankind sinned and fell from grace with Adam. "As a small boy I resented having my fate linked with so remote and disreputable an ancestor. Persuaded as I now am of his wholly mythical character, I resent it even more." Sometime later he confessed to a classmate that he had no belief whatever in a dispensing Providence. "I think the Universe is ruled by immutable laws that are not set aside for the hurt or benefit of any individual. Indeed I should not want to live in a world where special favors were handed out." [17]

Nevertheless, Davis approved the conservative force of organized religion so strongly that he insisted that the churches' contribution to public order was warrant enough for exempting them from taxation: "The chief concern of the State is public order; the chief ally of the State in securing it is unquestionably the church." He agreed with John Foster Dulles, with whom he maintained a cordial relationship over the years, that the primary duty of Christians was to preserve in themselves and inculcate in others the spiritual qualities of Christ. "Religion," he wrote Dulles, "is, and must always be, personal. . . . Unless the Church can act upon the individual its corporate activities are of little worth." Yet he regretted (paradoxically, as he admitted) the transfer to the state of the church's historic functions of healing the sick, teaching the young, and succoring the poor. As Catholicism's political conservatism became more manifest after World War II, Davis came to view the Catholic Church as an ideological ally. He supported the decision of his partner Porter Chandler to become a counsel to the Archdiocese of New York. And he encouraged Chandler to handle *Everson v. Board of Education,* the case in which New Jersey's subsidization of transportation of children to parochial and other private schools was upheld. "Take it," he told him; "you should win easily." To his Australian friend Herbert Brookes, Davis explained his outlook at length:

> Nor am I as much concerned about our Catholic friends and neighbors as you seem to be. They are strong in this country, and growing. But it will be a long time before they "take over" the country. It is easy to say that their methods and motives do not change at all from age to age. But I think they do change from country to country. There is little parallelism between the Roman Catholic church . . . in Spain and the Roman Catholic church in the United States. . . . For years they have aspired to special finance from the state for the parochial schools, to match funds which are given to the public schools. I think they are further away from this than ever.

He added that American Catholics constituted the nation's strongest organized opposition to socialism and communism. "This I mark down to their credit." [18]

Davis also had a scholar's knowledge of the Bible in both the King
James and Douay versions and a more than passing familiarity with
the Koran, Talmud, Book of Mormon, and other religious works.
Among his papers is the following order to a bookseller:

> Bhagavadgita
> Laws of Manu   Texts of Taoism
> Upanishads   The Gatakamala
> Texts of Confucianism   Dialogues of the Buddha

He laced his correspondence and speeches with biblical allusions, and
he engaged in numerous exchanges with friends, especially the de-
voutly Catholic Porter Chandlers, over abstruse points of interpretation and translation. He once wagered a dollar with Mrs. Chandler,
herself an expert in biblical criticism, that she could find nothing in
the Bible condemning polygamy unequivocally. After consulting with
eminent Catholic theologians, she conceded defeat. To her surprise, he
then went to a shelf, pulled down the Book of Mormon, opened it to
Jacob 2:27, and showed her that, conversely, the Book of Mormon *did*
disapprove it:

> Wherefore, my brethren, hear me, and hearken to the word of the
> Lord: For there shall not any man among you have save it be one wife;
> and concubines he shall have none.

Dazzled on another occasion by his mastery of the comparative zoology
of Isaiah, Mrs. Chandler wrote in mock seriousness that if all Protestants possessed Davis' vast erudition Rome might be prevailed on to
revise its views on individual interpretation of the Scriptures.[19]

« I I I »

For twenty-seven years Davis' conviction, as expressed to the president of Washington and Lee at the end of World War II, that "we
can afford to stick to 'whatever things are true' a long time yet," governed his conduct as a member of his alma mater's board of trustees.
One of those "things" was academic freedom. A first, and inconclusive,
test arose back in 1926, when a bright young professor of criminal law
gave his class a breezily phrased examination on five hypothetical cases
involving sexual or unusually gruesome incidents. Appalled by such
"rot," one of the resident trustees sent Davis a copy of the examination. "This strikes me as the Harvard method carried to its ultimate

limit," Davis replied. "I would be glad to have any further samples." Davis was detained in New York when the board voted to give the professor a terminal contract that June. With his usual kindliness, however, he recommended the professor for a position in the National City Bank the following year.[20]

Five years later, the desire of a fellow board member to endow a chair of Bible with $25,000 produced a considerably more awkward situation. The prospective donor stipulated that the occupant must "hold to, acknowledge, teach and inculcate the Christian religion as being above all others the true religion," and that he be "conservative, and not liberal or radical" in his interpretation of the Holy Scriptures. He further stipulated that the occupant must be removed if he "teach contrary" to those views. Davis agreed with the president of the university, Francis P. Gaines, that the gift had to be refused, and he drew up a statement of principles couched in jurisdictional terms. The board's absolute discretion to remove a professor, he asserted, should not be compromised; no donor of a chair had the right "to limit the academic freedom of the occupant either as to the substance, the scope, or the matter of his teaching." [21]

How far Davis would have defended freedom as an absolute right of students and faculty is conjectural, for Washington and Lee never produced a hard case. Assuredly, he fretted over reports of rampant New Dealism on campus. He wrote that he was particularly shocked to hear that some members of the law faculty approved of Roosevelt's court-packing scheme, and he questioned whether a trustee could do his duty sitting in remote seclusion. In the only specific matter that came before him, however, he stood firmly for freedom.[22]

In March 1935, one of Davis' classmates reported that Lucy Mason, an intimate of Secretary of Labor Frances Perkins, and Secretary of Agriculture Henry A. Wallace had been invited to speak at Washington and Lee, also that permission had been granted interested students to form a chapter of the left-wing League of Industrial Democracy. "Ye Gods—in the name of . . . the conservative University that we know," wrote the classmate, "I protest." Meanwhile Newton D. Baker, one of Davis' fellow trustees, dismissed the complaint with the remark that the real trouble was "professors who lack manners and intellectual humility rather than . . . professors who have dangerous notions." [23]

Before Davis could reply to the original protest, President Gaines reported that Miss Mason's speech had been entirely innocuous and that the invitation to Wallace had been extended at the instance of Davis' old friend, Edward A. O'Neal, president of the American Farm Bureau and an 1898 graduate of the university. He added that the League of Industrial Democracy had chapters on 124 other campuses and that a ban would have brought unfavorable publicity. "We advised these young men that we would not tolerate . . . any student propaganda subversive to our basic forms of government. . . . Within these restrictions the students have a right, we feel, to discuss any political theories." [24]

Davis endorsed Gaines' position emphatically. "Firm as I am in my own individualistic convictions," he wrote the classmate who had raised the issue, "I do not believe in tying down the safety valve. Let these boys alone and let them listen to nonsense and they will know it when they see it." He appended a quotation from Jefferson:

> . . . truth is great and will prevail if she is left to herself; that she is the proper and sufficient antagonist to error, and has nothing to fear from the conflict unless by human interposition disarmed of her natural weapons, free argument and debate; errors ceasing to be dangerous when it is permitted freely to contradict them. [25]

That same year, 1937, brought a test of an entirely different kind of principle—federal aid to private institutions. Following destruction of the law building and library by fire in 1934, Gaines and a majority of the board decided to apply for a PWA grant. The decision saddened and frustrated Davis. "I do not know of any theory which justifies the Federal Government in thus dispersing money . . . ," he wrote Gaines. "I have pretty distinct ideas as to the things the Federal Government can and cannot do within its constitutional powers. For much of this I have my training at Washington & Lee to thank. . . . Believing as I do . . . how can I in conscience . . . vote for its acceptance?" That was the only important difference Davis and Gaines had in seventeen years of close association. [26]

Davis repeatedly proposed that the terms of board members be limited to ten years. This had been a pet project of Gaines' predecessor, Dr. Henry Louis Smith, a crusty, dominant man who had been thwarted for years by what he called the "ultra-conservatism and . . . childish vanity" of even the better board members. Smith's special burden was the provincialism of local trustees:

> The town of Lexington simply cannot generate or build up suitable men for such a task. It is too brimful of and dominated by village views and sects and groups and standards of judgment. An institution

like W. and L. is and should be inter-church, inter-state, inter-party, and all-American. A tiny ultra-patriotic group of little-business, home-grown, home-loyal, utterly sectarian villagers can neither visualize, long-for, manage, or build up a 20th century inter-state institution. They will instinctively feel hostile toward plans and people that are different from OURS and US.

Davis was understanding, although he never criticized the Lexington group so directly.[27]

Actually, Davis had been responsible for Gaines' appointment. On President Smith's retirement in 1930, Davis had insisted that they bring in a broad-gauged man to succeed him; and, in a rare exercise of power, he had swung the board behind Gaines, who was then president of Wake Forest. A cultured gentleman, polished orator, and idolator of Robert E. Lee, Gaines had turned down the presidency of the University of Minnesota shortly before going to Washington and Lee. Davis explained that he wanted him because he was imbued with "the cultural view of education and [was] quite averse to putting Washington and Lee in competition with technical schools." He also wanted him because, as a Baptist, his appointment would halt the tendency to "Presbyterianize" the institution and would give an "outward and visible demonstration" of the absence of sectarian bias.[28]

Davis never regretted the choice. He often stayed with Gaines, whom he called "Boss," during visits to Virginia for board meetings. He brought him into the The Round Table in New York, sponsored his election to the Carnegie Endowment, and made a special trip to Lexington in 1936, when Gaines was weighing an offer from Tulane. He also supported his decision to hold down enrollment, de-emphasize athletics, and let the engineering school die. As he remarked in the mid-1930's, when the Washington and Lee president criticized Duke for hiring the highest paid football coach in the South, "Gaines is right—as usual." Davis recognized, nevertheless, that Washington and Lee lacked the verve, resources, and intellectual distinction of its Northern counterparts, and he consoled himself in the faith that it was unexcelled in character-building: "Either a university contributes to this end, or it has no real reason for existence. I think Washington and Lee meets this test." [29]

Through all these years Washington and Lee's chronic shortage of funds sapped Davis' trusteeship of much of its gratification. Both he and Baker were too sensitive, too unwilling to impose themselves, to be good fund-raisers, and no one else had the necessary stature and connections. In 1932, when the Depression forced a reduction in the instructional budget, Davis urged that any cut be treated as temporary. Sixteen years later he was badly shaken when the American Bar Association warned that the Law School might be dropped from the approved list unless it raised salaries substantially. "Is it possible," an Association official asked the dean in 1948, "that the salary scale . . . is as low as it appears to be?" Washington and Lee should be able to pay at least $7500 for first-class, full-time, law professors. There was little Davis could say when the report was forwarded to him other than that they would pay at the top if they had the money and that he hoped they could find "some middle ground."[30]

Government subvention was not that "middle ground," even though individual scholarships under the G. I. Bill were then proving decisively that federal aid did not necessarily destroy freedom. To the end of his trusteeship, Davis insisted that federal control was certain to follow subsidization in any form. Never did he express this faith more eloquently than in an address in 1939 to the Regents of the State University of New York:

> It is precisely because I dread an impairment of this independence and diversity that I deplore the possible retreat of privately endowed colleges and universities before their tax-supported rivals. It is precisely because of this that I dread each advance by the Federal Government into the field of public education.[31]

For more than a decade Davis tried to resign from the board. The long trip to Lexington became more arduous each year, and often he was detained in New York by court cases. His isolation also gave him a sense of frustration. "My conscience pricks me with a sense of obligations undischarged," he complained. Always, however, President Gaines, the dean of the Law School, and the other trustees protested so strenuously that he would agree to stay on. As Gaines said a half-dozen or more times, Davis' "sanity of judgment, tolerance of view, and allegiance to the fundamental and . . . unchanging purposes of the school" were too precious to lose. In 1940 the board elected Davis Rector of the University, but he declined to serve. Five years later he wrote that all that kept him on the board was the opportunity the meetings gave him to see his dear friend and classmate Hale Houston, professor of engineering and his "only anchor" to Lexington. Finally, in 1949, the year he inaugurated the lectures in honor of his old law professor, John Randolph Tucker, Davis resigned. "When a man can no longer fulfill duties for which he has pledged himself, he ought in fairness and honesty to quit." He was then made Trustee Emeritus. Three years earlier, in gratitude for his service to the judiciary, a group of New York State judges had established the John W. Davis Prize for excellence in the Washington and Lee Law School. After his death, the board named a dormitory in his honor.[32]

CHAPTER 24

Leader of
the Appellate Bar

In the heart of every lawyer worthy of the name there burns a deep ambition so to bear himself that the profession may be stronger by reason of his passage through its ranks and that he may leave the Law itself a better instrument of human justice than he found it.

JOHN W. DAVIS,
"THOMAS JEFFERSON, ATTORNEY-AT-LAW"

To the end of his life, advocacy was John W. Davis' pleasure, passion, and genius. Three times or more in the 1920's and 1930's he rejected overtures to become a college president. "I am first and last a lawyer," he explained on being asked to succeed Edwin A. Alderman at the University of Virginia in 1932. "When I have strayed . . . into other paths, I have always come back with a sense of relief. . . . The cobbler should stick to his last." Reports that President Hoover might appoint Davis to Justice Edward T. Sanford's seat on the Supreme Court two years earlier had been hardly more inviting. "I really do not know what I would do . . . , but I hope I will not be called on to confront the possibility. I am quite happy at the Bar, happier I think than I would be on the Bench." [1]

« I »

From his opening statement in the *Pipe Line* cases in 1913 to his second argument in the segregation suit of 1954, Davis' appellate techniques changed in no essential. Age and experience strengthened his confidence and eased his preparation; rarely after he left the solicitor generalship did he work night after night on a single case. So great was his capacity for total absorption, however, that a decade after his death his partners were still speaking in awe of his ability to master the record within a few hours. "I think about nothing else," he explained. "Even the notion that I ought to be thinking about something else is in itself a distraction." [2]

His mind filled only with the germane, Davis would carry into court a batch of notecards containing a skeletal outline of his argument, a selective list of citations, a few pithy phrases or sentences, and some quotations drawn from memory but checked in *Bartlett's*. ("Lawyers couldn't survive without Shakespeare and the Bible," he said.) An associate would then spread out the record and briefs on the counsel table. Davis would shake hands with his opponent with a cordial smile and sometimes engage in a sally while waiting for the preliminaries to end. But mostly he would sit in silence, his lips taut and his fingers softly tapping the table. Once, in the 1940's, a young government attorney who had been so unnerved by the prospect of facing Davis that he had arisen after a sleepless night to practice his argument before a mirror, asked him if he were ill. "Oh, I'm just a little nervous," Davis replied. "I've been coming into court for fifty-two years and I'm always scared to death until the proceedings begin." The instant he rose to his feet the confidence would surge. "Throughout the courtroom," Felix Frankfurter recalled, "the murmurs would cease and the court would sit back in anticipation of a superb performance." [3]

Davis was too modest—really too self-disciplined—to talk much about his performances or techniques. Usually he brushed off queries with a few impersonal generalizations about hard work and thorough preparation. If pressed he would offer two maxims, one from Jefferson, the other from Webster: "Never use two words where one will do." "The power of clear statement is the great power at the bar." Beyond that he rarely went. There was so much to do in the present and future, he would explain when asked to write his reminiscences, that he simply had no time. More to the point, he had neither the instinct for self-advertising nor the need for self-justification. He also doubted that he had much to say. "Various legal autobiographies contain crushing illustrations of the author's demolition of a witness on cross-examination. I may have had such an experience but I have no present recollection of it." [4]

Only once did Davis' resolve to let the record speak for itself weaken. In the fall of 1940, before the Association of the Bar, he delivered a paper, "The Argument of an Appeal," which is still regarded as the definitive statement of the master, though it contained not a single self-serving allusion. The paper was rife with shrewd observations about lawyers, judges, and the decisional process. It extolled the adversary system and paid due obeisance to the quest for truth and justice. But above all it described with extraordinary urbanity those techniques best calculated to satisfy the psychological and intellectual needs of the court.

Davis began with an engaging commentary on the ideal brief, then quoted Coke and others in defense of oral argument. He drew especially on the assertion of John F. Dillon, the railroad lawyer, that "mistakes, errors, fallacies and flaws elude us in spite of ourselves unless the case is pounded and hammered at the bar." Most judges, said Davis, would agree with that statement, provided the oral argument was "inspired . . . with a single and sincere desire to be helpful to the court." Then, disclaiming special fitness for the task, he set forth a decalogue.

The first—the cardinal—rule was to change places with the judge. "To adapt yourself to his methods of reasoning is not artful, it is simply elementary psychology; as is also the maxim not to tire or irritate the mind you are seeking to persuade." The advocate should always make himself heard, and should never speak in monotones. After stating the nature of the case, he should give its history insofar as it bore on the court's jurisdiction. Judges were curious to know whose judicial work was under review, for, like other men, they also judged each other. The facts, which came next, were more often than not the argument itself in appellate cases; it was imperative that they be set forth chronologically, with candor, clarity, and without "purple passages."

When the facts were brought out properly, Davis continued, the legal questions often proved so elementary that the advocate need do little more than allude to the applicable precedents. Yet the law could also be so unsettled as to require additional exposition in order to show how the facts supported a particular interpretation:

> It may be that in these days of what is apparently waning health on the part of our old friend *Stare Decisis,* one can rely less than heretofore upon the assertion that the case at bar is governed by such-and-such a case, volume and page. Even the shadow of a long succession of governing cases may not be adequate shelter. In any event the advocate must be prepared to meet any challenge to the doctrine of the cases on

which he relies and to support by original reasoning. Barren citation is
a broken reed. What virtue it retains can be left for the brief.

The fifth point—"Go for the jugular vein"—was especially revealing
of Davis' own arguments. There was always a temptation to "let no
guilty point escape," in the hope that if one hook broke, another might
hold. But, he warned, oral argument allowed little time for such diversion. Thus, John G. Johnson (the man who had said in 1916 that
there was no more concise appellate lawyer than Davis himself) normally spoke to a single point, often for only twenty minutes but always with compelling force. "When he had concluded it was difficult
for his adversary to persuade the court that there was anything else
worthy to be considered. This is the quintessence of the advocate's
art."

There followed a point all the more interesting because of the tendency of appellate courts to let Davis himself escape without interrogation. "Rejoice when the court asks a question . . . rejoice!" Why? Because it affords an opportunity to penetrate the court's mind. Answer
with a bold negative if the question warranted; make a concession if it
called for one. But no matter how embarrassing or disconcerting the
question, answer it at once. Recognize, furthermore, that questions
were not designed to fluster; the judge was seeking help, that was all.
Chief Justice John H. Denison of the Supreme Court of Colorado
summed it up well:

> A perfect argument would need no interruption and a perfect Judge
> would never interrupt it; but we are not perfect. . . . The Judge knows
> where his doubts lie, at which point he wishes to be enlightened; it is
> he whose mind at last must be made up . . . and he must take his own
> course of thought to accomplish it.

The four last points described Davis' own methods almost literally,
although they too were impersonally phrased:

7. Read sparingly and only from necessity.
8. Avoid personalities.
9. Know your record from cover to cover.
10. Sit down.

There was something about a piece of paper interposed between
speaker and listener, Davis explained, that walls off the mind of the

latter "as if it were a boiler-plate." An occasional pithy and pertinent sentence, yes; pages or paragraphs, no! A cognate fault was the tedious recital, usually beginning with "That was a case where," of the facts of decisions that supported or were distinguishable from the case being argued. "What the advocate needs most of all is that his facts and his alone should stand out stark, simple, unique, clear."

Personalities? It was hard to avoid them, yet it was imperative to do so. To criticize a lower court harshly was to risk offending the judiciary's *esprit de corps.* To denounce opposing litigants was to invite sympathy for them. To argue with opposing counsel was to impose upon the court the burden of restoring order. "Such things can irritate, they can never persuade." As for the ninth point, knowledge of the record, it was the *sine qua non* of all effective argument, and probably should have headed the list:

> At any moment you may be called on to correct some misstatement of your adversary; and at any moment you may confront a question from the court which, if you are able to answer by an apt reference to the record or with a firm reliance on a well-furnished memory, will increase the confidence with which the court will listen to what else you may have to say.

To his audience's great delight, Davis added that there was just one thing to do once the essentials were covered: "siddown!" The allotment of so many minutes was not "a contract with the court to listen for that length of time"; on the contrary, "a benevolent smile overspreads the faces on the bench and a sigh of relief and gratification arises from . . . the bar" when one stopped before the expiration of time. "Earn these exhibitions of gratitude whenever you decently can, and leave the rest . . . to the judges on high Olympus."

A coda followed. He was painfully conscious, Davis said, that he had offered nothing new; the process of appeal was too ancient, its essentials too unchanging:

> The need . . . arises from the innate realization of mankind that the human intellect and human justice are frail at their best. It is necessary therefore to measure one man's mind against another in order to purge the final result, so far as may be, of all passion, prejudice or infirmity. It is the effort to realize the maximum of justice in human relations; and to keep firm and stable the foundations on which all ordered society rests.

For the lawyer, as Chancellor D'Aguesseau so eloquently said, belonged to an order "as old as the magistracy, as noble as virtue, as necessary as justice." [5]

« II »

For all its luminous force, "The Argument of an Appeal" was a pale commentary on the qualities that made Davis himself a supreme appellate lawyer. As his partners Brownell and Carson remark, he "combined speed, concentration, and force blended with a grace peculiar to . . . [him], and not all the clues to the combination appear in his celebrated lecture." Davis' oral arguments in the 1920's, 1930's, and early 1940's were models of near-perfection—more polished, even, than those that had made him the greatest Solicitor General in history. "The artistry, the seductiveness, the punctiliousness!" exclaimed Columbia's Herbert Wechsler. "My God, how I would have liked to have made that argument," A. J. G. Priest used to say. "Come on Stone," Justice Harlan Stone said to himself while listening to Davis and George Wharton Pepper duel in the 1930's, "nothing can be this clear." [6]

Nevertheless, it was the sum of Davis' qualities, many preeminently personal, that gave him his almost unmatched reputation. Even Learned Hand and Felix Frankfurter, who questioned his intellectual depth, were enchanted by his courtroom personality. "He was delightful and engaging," Hand recalled. "He had a way of stating differences that left no record of ill feeling. . . . He had no sign of passion. He was a selfless man." Long before he himself went on the bench in 1939, remarked Frankfurter, Davis' grace, charm and distinction had made him a living tradition. "He was the most courtly, gracious man I have ever known," said Chief Judge David Pine of the United States District Court for the District of Columbia. "I never saw him steal the spotlight. He was just a little withdrawn." [7]

Davis' mere presence could exert a subtle influence on a court. "He treated me as an equal," said Pine, in words that cast a penetrating light on the awe in which even federal judges held him. Once, in the 1930's or 1940's, Davis and Beryl H. Levy appeared on opposite sides in a corporate case being tried by a Davis Polk junior partner. Davis' main function, Levy recalled, seemed to be to lend the dignity of his presence to the side of his firm's client. "His soft-spoken manners, his white hair, his erect posture, his courtly manners, his absence of pretension: all were deeply impressive." The judge was extremely courteous, almost deferential, toward him in conferences in his chambers, and Davis' quick, "No, we can't do that," foreclosed further discussion. Davis was well aware of this commanding power. In the mid-1940's he and Ralph M. Carson were arguing an appeal in the Second Circuit before Augustus Hand, Charles Clark, and Thomas Swan or Jerome Frank. No sooner had Davis completed his opening statement than his adversary impugned his good faith and truthfulness. Outraged, Carson scrawled an indignant reply for Davis to use in rebuttal. Davis glanced at the note, then pushed it aside: "Let it alone! Nobody can hurt me in this Court!" [8]

Theodore Kiendl, who shared many of Davis' most important cases, was especially impressed by his ability to convert the bench into a receptive audience. Even tough-minded jurists had to fight off his seductive charm. "He was like Caruso singing, and the bar and the bench just sat there enraptured," one of Frankfurter's law clerks recalled. Learned Hand admitted as much. "I do not like to have John W. Davis come into my courtroom . . . ," he confided to Joseph M. Proskauer. "I am so fascinated by his eloquence and charm that I always fear that I am going to decide in his favor irrespective of the merits of the case." Another judge said that he always closed his mind to Davis' argument for a full week so that the magic of his voice might subside before he grappled with the case. Holmes was even more graphic. He had to pay extremely close attention when Davis argued, he once told John Lord O'Brian; "otherwise he skims over the thin ice before I know it." [9]

Even the Supreme Court could be defensive of Davis' interests. It tended to be gentle when it did interrogate him; and though it testily put down his opponent on two or three occasions for quoting Davis' briefs as Solicitor General against him, it seems never to have admonished Davis for the same tactic. Almost alone, Chief Justice Hughes failed to defer to him. He once asked Davis to remove a pencil from behind his ear. And though he never cut him off in the middle of the word "if," as he supposedly did to another prominent New York attorney, he always called time on him as promptly as on everyone else. Davis, who did not really like Hughes, gave as much as he took. "Mr. Chief Justice," he asked one afternoon in the 1930's as the clock ran down, "may I trouble you to tell me how much time I have left?" "A minute and a half," Hughes replied. Davis paused momentarily, then, bowing low in the Castilian manner with his right arm making a great

arc, announced: "I present the Court with the minute and a half."
Tersely, Hughes called up the next case.[10]

Yet it was more than the euphonious language and the authoritative
baritone voice, the stately presence and the unsurpassed mastery of
case law that set Davis off from the handful of advocates to whom he
was most often compared—John G. Johnson, George Wharton Pepper, Robert Jackson, and Hughes himself. Each was a stylist in his own
right, each had special qualities of his own. None, however, equaled
Davis in the ability to simplify complex matters with a few pithy Anglo-Saxon phrases devoid of adjectives and drained of all emotion.
Davis had the "precision of cold steel," A. J. G. Priest remarked. His
faculty for uncovering and explaining the essential point, said Judge
Pine, made him "the greatest lawyer I ever knew." Learned Hand was
more measured. Although he ranked Davis below Hughes intellectually, he felt that Davis deserved his place at the head of the forensic
bar. "He made the best kind of presentation I ever saw . . . because
he would create a bias in his favor by the brevity of his statement." Arthur Krock's appraisal differed little. Davis' power of expression, he
said, was so superb, his choice of words so perfect, that he simply did
not need adjectives. "I never heard a lawyer argue as persuasively as
he." In a suit over a contested will in the mid-1930's, Davis' opponent,
former Governor Nathan Miller, argued for more than an hour that
funds left for charitable and scientific purposes could be invested for
private gain. When Miller had finished, Davis rose and said, "If my
opponent were not so distinguished, I would hand your honors the
will and sit down." He then won the case with a fifteen-minute statement in which he assured the court that, since it had sustained a fight
"for the advancement of Christ's kingdom on earth" in another suit,
it would have no difficulty upholding the bequests under review.[11]

Davis depended heavily on, and drew enormous confidence from,
full and proper presentation of facts. He encouraged his partners and
associates to utilize every legitimate means, documentary and oral, to
ferret them out; and under his leadership the firm always capitalized
on the resources of pre-trial examination and documentary disclosure
to present and develop them further. Erwin Griswold, former dean of
the Harvard Law School and Solicitor General in both the Johnson
and the Nixon administrations, termed Davis the "best expositor of
facts" in his experience. Cardozo reported that, in an argument Davis
made before the New York Court of Appeals in 1930, every judge on
the bench was against him when he began to speak on the facts, and

every one was in agreement with him by the time he was through. But the most personally gratifying victory was won against Davis' close friend, Joseph M. Proskauer. Proskauer made a fiery argument on a brief laden with distortions. Fact by fact, Davis then tore his argument to shreds, shaking Proskauer so badly that he appealed to the court for five extra minutes to reply. Before the court could respond, Davis interjected: "Don't worry, Joe, I'll give you more than five minutes." [12]

In another memorable case, Davis' clients were charged with manipulating the stock of a certain corporation and wrongfully acquiring control. "I wondered how Davis would meet his opponents," an observer wrote:

> He never cited a single authority, because the case turned on the facts, not on the law. Davis began with a casual unhurried calmness that might have disarmed his adversary. He made an analysis of the complaint of the plaintiff, pointed out the true inwardness of the case; showed who was protesting and why and why they had no standing in court and had misconceived their remedy, if they had one. Piece by piece he ripped the plaintiff's case apart and when he had finished the plaintiff was without standing in the court and the court later so held. Davis had a smoothness of delivery, a quiet ease of presentation that disarms hostility or criticism. . . . He is without fear or resentment or any quality of pugnacious or hostile opposition in his manner of speech. You can't help but listen. And he is crystal clear.[13]

Davis also followed faithfully his own admonition to limit citations. As early as 1916 he had decried the multiplication of precedents because of their tendency to obscure the grounds of decision as among alternative principles. A quarter-century later, in delivering "The Argument of An Appeal," he noted that a "horrible example" of excessive citation—a brief listing 304 cases—had crossed his desk within the month. One of the authors of that brief, Frederick Bernays Wiener, was in the audience, and after Davis had finished speaking Wiener sought him out:

WIENER: I'm sorry you didn't like our brief.
DAVIS: Well, I did think you cited too many cases.
WIENER: If I were inclined to be critical of your production, I should say that you cited too few cases.
DAVIS: Had it occurred to you that we had too few cases which we could cite?

Weiner went on to win the case, and a decade later Davis wrote the foreword for his book, *Effective Appellate Advocacy . . . Including*

Examples of Winning Briefs and Oral Arguments. One of those "examples" was the one mentioned above.[14]

Most men who knew the Supreme Court in the 1920's ranked Davis with Hughes as the ablest advocate of the era. Felix Frankfurter was almost alone in praising him faintly. Despite his later affection and respect for Davis, Frankfurter deplored his lack of depth: "He was like Tennyson. He saw only surfaces which he painted delicately. Hughes had more power, Davis more charm." Newton D. Baker, himself a sparkling adornment of the appellate bar, felt differently. "Do you know," he once said to a banker who asked if Davis was as great a man as he appeared to be, "if I could change my own mental equipment for that of any man I have ever known, I would unhesitatingly select John W. Davis." [15]

Many lawyers, including Wiener and Morris Ernst, regarded Davis as a sounder advocate than Hughes. "Hughes was a man with an automatic bludgeon," said Wiener, "Davis a man with a rapier." One of Hughes' former partners elaborated a little; the difference between the two, he wrote, was that Hughes knew "all there was to know about the case, Davis all he needed to know." Chief Justice Taft was of the same mind. Hughes and Davis were the two leading counsel before the Court, he confided to one of his sons in 1928. "Davis is the more graceful of the two and is rather wiser in not pressing too hard on an issue that is marginal. Hughes is thorough and seems to think it is his duty . . . not to omit anything." As a result, Hughes often detracted from his strong point. The only other advocate comparable to either, Taft added, was the late Charles Choate of Boston.[16]

Justice Stanley F. Reed insisted that Hughes was not in the same class with Davis. "There were two preeminent advocates, John W. Davis and George Wharton Pepper. And that includes Charles Evans Hughes!" As between Davis and Pepper, Davis was the "more reasoned." Justice Hugo Black, who never heard Hughes, felt that Davis and Robert Jackson were the finest advocates in his experience. Reluctant to rate one above the other, he said simply that both were "great." [17]

« III »

Had Davis' sense of responsibility been less acute or his desire for the respect of the bar less strong, he would surely have spent his leisure reading, fishing, attending concerts, visiting in England, and relaxing at Yeamans Hall. Pulled constantly by competing demands and consumed always by the case at hand, he longed to escape the burdens of office in legal and other organizations. When, for example, he was elected president of the Association of the Bar of the City of New York in 1931, he termed the honor the latest of his "embarrassments" and half-seriously complained that it would cut deeply into time that might be better spent "earning necessary shekels." But, partly out of pride and largely out of duty, he accepted. For, as he said over and over again in one form or another, no American lawyer "has fully met the rightful demands of his profession until he was made himself an active member of his local, state and national bar associations." 18

Davis' lack of an urge to reform made his offices doubly onerous. "I should like to know . . . just how vigorous you expect your committee to be," he wrote the president of the American Bar Association on being named chairman of the Committee on Legal Education in 1925. Always, of course, Davis read, digested, and edited the drafts of the reports to which his name was attached. Yet the innovative proposals were invariably made and the arduous detailed work invariably done by others. Never, apparently, did he initiate an important reform, and rarely did he push one already under way. He would let the momentum generated by others carry the project to the point of real friction, then back off or arrange a compromise. This worked well on routine or minor matters. But on issues of moment, such as the Seabury investigation of Major James J. "Jimmy" Walker, it led to irresolution.19

George Martin, who studied the Association of the Bar's records intensively for his history of that organization, reports that when he began his research he anticipated that Davis would emerge as one of the "heroes" of the book.

> But he really didn't suffer . . . much for the Association or the kind of reforms it was trying to push. In this he seems to be very like Joseph Hodges Choate . . . who also was a brilliant advocate, a charming man, and should have been a great president . . . but was not. Charles Evans Hughes was always moving projects forward, dismantling obstacles with a phone call, a memorandum, or merely an "I'll take care of that." Later . . . C. C. Burlingham left the same sort of footprints on the minutes, and still later . . . the chief prints were those of Harrison Tweed and Bethuel M. Webster. . . . Davis was constantly giving speeches at the Association, writing memorials of its members, and serving on occasion as an honorary member of special committees. But the real work of the Association was being done by others—even in the period when Davis was its president.

Martin added that Davis never played a leading role in any of the Association's crusades: The fight over the socialists in the 1920's had

been led by Hughes, that over municipal corruption in the early
1930's by Burlingham, that over reorganization of the Association in
the 1940's by Tweed, and that over court reform in the 1950's by
Tweed, Webster, Seymour, Loeb, Klots, and others.[20]

Reluctant, nevertheless, to dismiss Davis, Martin sought out the Association's executive secretary, Paul B. De Witt. "Why," he asked,
"hadn't [Davis] done more, hadn't been more effective?" De Witt
thought a moment, then replied: "I think he was more interested in
his practice." Harrison Tweed agreed. Davis' role, he said, was honorable but relatively inactive, always in support rather than in the lead.
Somewhat hesitantly, Tweed volunteered that Davis had little knowledge of the needs and feelings of the people and would probably have
done even less for the country than Coolidge had he been elected President. What, then, made him great? asked Martin. This time Tweed
responded with a smile: "Well, he had more charm than any man in
the world, and he was a helluva good lawyer." [21]

As that last remark suggests, Tweed and almost everyone else Davis
ever touched adored him. "He was such a beautiful man," recalled the
wife of a Georgia attorney who met him just once. "To be with him
was to be uplifted," a dozen others remarked; one had to be present to
appreciate the "infectious gaiety" he instilled in the most prosaic occasion. As a young Kansas lawyer who worked closely with him on a suit
near the end of Davis' life concluded, "his greatness as an advocate was
only an adjunct of his greatness as a human being." Lloyd Paul Stryker summed it up:

> In my heart what makes him live was his gentle kindliness and unfail-
> ing sympathy, his gift of humor and his flashing wit, the ability to
> laugh with and not at his fellow men, his invariable simplicity, his
> human understanding, his patience to listen to those less gifted and less
> wise, his readiness to help those who had no justifiable claim upon his
> time, his unaffected modesty.[22]

Actually, Davis' ceremonial addresses cost him heavily. "Such
things," he once said, "come forth with me by prayer and fasting, and
I am sure I agonize over preparation out of all proportion to the results obtained." Furthermore, he put in a great amount of time simply
attending the committee meetings of the dozen or more organizations
in which he was active. More important, as Martin also suggests,
Davis' contribution of time and energy to the defense of men such as
Macintosh and Kresel was an enormous contribution in its own right

—one that perhaps offset the more active committee work of lesser men. Nevertheless, the harsher truth remains: Not only did Davis fail to use his vast prestige to encourage reform of either the law or the legal profession, he also opposed and frequently denounced those who did. "I am getting very tired of lawyers who rise in public and criticize their profession," he complained. "It is this which gives so funereal a tone to much of the reported proceedings of our bar associations. . . . We view with alarm . . . far more often than we point with pride." 23

Once, in a rare concession to the reformers, Davis termed ambulance chasing and bankruptcy proceedings "ugly and cancerous sores" and called on the New York State Bar Association to cut them out "with the most ruthless surgery." Characteristically, however, he blamed men rather than institutions, and passed over proposals to replace the accident liability system with no-fault insurance. He also hastened to rise to the defense of the legal profession as a whole. Denying that lawyers were greedy, judges legalistic, and the law itself behind the times, he asserted that "the public should be assured . . . that the Bar . . . is composed in the main of honest and upright men, earnestly devoted to the welfare of their clients, not forgetful of the high responsibilities incumbent upon them . . . , and ready now as . . . in all times past to defend at no matter what cost to themselves the essential liberties of their fellow citizens." Or, as he put it in one of his lighter moments:

> The lawyer's a man of sorrow, and acquainted with grief;
>   Among all the sinners, he's considered the chief.
> His friends all admire him when he conquers for them;
>   When he chances to lose, they're quick to condemn.
> They say, "Ah! He is bought!" if he loses a case;
>   They say, "Ah! He is crooked!" if he wins in the race.
> If he charges big fees, they say he's a grafter;
>   If he charges small fees, "He's not worth going after."
> If he joins the church, "it's for an effect;"
>   If he doesn't join, "He's as wicked as heck."
> But here is one fact we all must admit:
>   When we get into trouble, our lawyer is IT.24

This tendency to affirm and exalt pervaded almost all Davis' speeches and commentaries. "There are not many lawyers of whom it can be said that they are deaf to the cry of the needy," he declared in one of his annual appeals for support of the Legal Aid Society. "May we not claim," he said in another speech, "that the common rules by which our governmental and civic order is controlled have been justified in the event?" The law, he wrote in a little essay on vocations, is "a profession, not a business, . . . [one whose] members shall serve all men who call upon them . . . putting first the duty to serve and last of all the compensation to be earned thereby." The legal profession, he told the Association of the Bar on its seventy-fifth anniversary, "makes demands upon the person and character of its members second to no other calling. . . . Uprightness, honor, industry, integrity, candor to courts, courtesy to colleagues, loyalty to clients—these are its familiar and constant demands." [25]

Behind those partial truths lay Davis' consuming need to believe that his life's work was in truth idealistic—that the law was literally "the science of human rights and remedies," and that its practice was in fact "an avenue for service and not a means for private gain." Behind them also was the conviction, perhaps just the hope, that to state and restate the ideal was to inspire men to rise to it. No one who has marked the hortatory passages in even his most ephemeral talks can fail to sense this; no one who has read his account of the lawyers of Louis XVI—Malesherbes, Tronchet, and De Seze—of those men who chose, as he phrased it, "the path of duty and of moral danger," can but be himself moved.[26]

« IV »

To the end of his life Davis continued to decry almost all movements for substantive change, whether in the law, society, or politics. "Is it not true," he remarked rhetorically, "that the Americans as a whole are obstinately conservative in things which touch the *ritual* of government but follow blindly innovations that reach matters far more serious?" Having no complaint against the American economic system (except as government intervention inhibited its "free" functioning), he had no quarrel with the legal order which reflected it. Having no reservations about the immutability of the first principles revealed to him in his youth, he had no reason to challenge their relevance to modern society. John Randolph Tucker, he continued to maintain, had laid it all out at Washington and Lee: "As to what is law, I hark back to the definition my old teacher . . . used to give us: 'Law is a rule of conduct prescribed by the supreme legislative power in the state enjoining what is right and prohibiting what is wrong.' " * [27]

---

* This definition, as I pointed out in Chapter 2, is almost an exact quotation from Blackstone. Compare it to the statement of Felix Cohen: "It is the

Davis never concealed his unfamiliarity with the new jurisprudence. With characteristic candor, he said at least three or four times that, as a lawyer "nurtured in the chaste simplicities of the common law," he simply did not think in abstract terms. Near the end of his career he was invited to deliver the Cardozo Lecture at New York University. Unable to settle on a suitable topic and unwilling to exploit an audience's time in light-minded discourse, he declined the invitation with the remark: "I've never had any interest in the philosophy of law." [28]

This admission confirmed what those who knew and revered Davis had long known—he was almost totally without sham. But it also pointed up what a few of his intimates reluctantly conceded: he was an extraordinarily rigid man philosophically, one who seemed to exemplify the inhibiting influence of the legal profession described by the English essayist Hamerton. "Lawyers whose heart is in their work," he wrote, "are invariably men of superior ability, which proves that there is something in it which affords gratification to the intellectual powers. However . . . they get the habit of employing the whole strength and energy of their minds for especial and temporary ends, the purpose being the service of the client, certainly not the revelation of pure truth." [29]

There is a sense, of course, in which that commentary fails utterly to apply to Davis. Again and again he astounded friends and acquaintances by the breadth of his knowledge; over and over he edified the court and frustrated his opponent with an obscure but pertinent classical allusion. Indeed, his moving paper "The Lawyers of Louis XVI" was actually written from French sources which he translated himself. Curious to know more than English histories related of the men who defended the King at the trial that sent him to the guillotine in January 1793, Davis delved deeply into French accounts. The more he read of this poignant episode, one of the most dramatic and moving of the entire Revolution, the more impressed he became by the courage of the King's attorneys. The story of their devotion to the ideals of the legal profession, he concluded, should be known to American lawyers, and in thirty-eight pages of graceful, yet graphic and forceful prose, he told it:

great disservice of the classical conception of law that it hides from judicial eyes the ethical character of every judicial question, and thus serves to perpetuate class prejudices and uncritical moral assumptions which could not survive the sunlight of free ethical controversy." *The Legal Conscience: The Selected Papers of Felix Cohen* (New Haven, 1960), 67.

Now the trial was over; now Louis was dead; and Malesherbes, then seventy-two years of age, was free to go back to the home he loved, there to spend his declining years.[30]

Nevertheless, Davis' intellectual interests served more to reinforce and hone his mind than to liberate it. His attachment to the received wisdom of his formative years was so firm, his belief in fixed principles so unshakable, that he would doubtless have remained a formalist had he never studied law. For, as his whole intellectual being suggests, he lacked the flexibility, the power of imagination, that makes constructive critics of many men and original thinkers of a few. Morris Ernst, who idealized him in many ways, captured this in words strikingly similar to those of one of Davis' partners. "John W. Davis," said Ernst, "had remarkable precision, logic, memory and work habits. But he was not inventive. His mind rarely leaped." [31]

Modest man that he was, Davis would have agreed; in fact, he said as much several times. But he would have surely challenged the implication that he should have moved beyond the fundamentals of his early training. "I have never altered my convictions," he said near the end of his life. "Every principle I stood for when I first entered practice and politics I still stand for"—by which he meant laissez-faire, minimal taxes, states' rights, survival of the fittest, and an almost literal acceptance of the Constitution as written in 1787 and formally amended thereafter.[32]

Except for applied science, Davis scorned virtually all that was new or reformist, all that was innovative or creative, in twentieth-century society. He disliked contemporary music and architecture, termed modern painting "base and obscene," and put down *For Whom the Bell Tolls* half finished. He resented the rise of the social sciences so much that he could ill-conceal his delight in someone's remark: "What does social science require therefore? I think it requires to be dethroned." But he took greatest offense at the sweeping, sometimes penetrating, yet often shallow critique of American jurisprudence by the "legal realists," that school of scholars and analysts inspired, but not endorsed, by Holmes and Pound.* [33]

---

* The historical impact of the legal realists, the most important of whom originally were Karl N. Llewellyn, Underhill Moore, Herman Oliphant, Jerome Frank, Thomas Reed Powell, Thurman Arnold, and Felix S. Cohen, has probably been most fairly assessed by Edward A. Purcell, Jr., writing in the *American Historical Review* in December 1969. Purcell concludes: "While ignoring some of its more extreme theoretical tendencies, the profes-

Davis had no more sympathy in his maturity for Pound's original strictures against the mechanical jurisprudence on which he himself had been nurtured than he had had when they were first uttered in 1908. The ultimate end of law, said Pound, was the administration of justice:

> Law is not scientific for the sake of science. . . . It must be judged by the results it achieves, not by the niceties of its internal structure; it must be valued by the extent to which it meets its end, not by the beauty of its logical processes or the strictness with which its rules proceed from the dogmas it takes for its foundation.

For Davis, however, the notion that law was less than an absolute remained the ultimate heresy. By 1936, partly because dissenting opinions implied that the law was not based on absolutes (or at least that the dissenter had not uncovered them), he was even writing that he would prohibit their publication if he could. "They are nearly always intemperate, . . . are inclined to over-statement . . . [and] disturb the public." This position put him at the other end of the spectrum from Hughes. Said the Chief Justice: "A dissent in a court of last resort is an appeal to the brooding spirit of the law, to the intelligence of a future day, when a later decision may possibly correct the error into which the dissenting judge believes the court to have been betrayed." [34]

Davis was also impatient with the realists' contention that neither the Constitution nor the common law could serve the complex and changing demands of industrial society without continual reinterpretation. Hence, in part, his insistence that, except for obvious misconstructions of the original statute, *stare decisis* was, or should be, the inviolable principle of pleading and judging. As he said with emphasis in a memorial to Justice McReynolds, "the rule of *stare decisis* was to him something more than an essential fetish deserving of a passing

sion generally accepted many of the ideas associated with legal realism. That movement helped establish the importance of factual research in law, the necessity of empirical studies of the legal process, the legitimacy of a more flexible constitutional interpretation, and the acceptance of a pragmatic, operational concept of law. In spite of the problems the realists presented, both philosophically and legally, they were pointing toward the future by suggesting fruitful courses of study and more useful methods of analysis. The alliance the realists helped forge between legal theory and empirical analysis fortified the trend toward sociological jurisprudence that had begun forty years before and that was to become a commonly accepted part of American law in the years after the Second World War."

bow. When a doctrine once had been firmly established, whether in the field of public or private right, he was content to abide by it until it was changed by the law-making power." More commonly, Davis justified *stare decisis* with a homely illustration. "Here comes a client to me who says that he has need of advice," he half humorously wrote the editor of the *Hartford Courant* in 1942:

> He may even be willing to pay a modest fee for the lawyers' opinion. The lawyer reads the decisions of the Supreme Court of the United States and says that the law has been settled so and so. . . . The next week the Court says the law . . . is exactly to the contrary. This is hard on the lawyer and may be even harder on the client. . . . He ceases to employ lawyers and goes down and throws dice with the copper on the corner. He may do worse than this. He may go and ask some editor about it.[35]

Only once or twice during his half-century at the bar did Davis speak tolerantly, much less understandingly, of reinterpretation. In 1932, in a charming address at the cornerstone ceremony for the Supreme Court building, he said almost parenthetically that "there will arise again and yet again the challenging question whether old words have taken on new meaning in the light of changing facts, or whether new facts must find their proper setting in the frame of the ancient words. It cannot be otherwise in the expanding life of an advancing people." He also denied, in another speech, that the Constitution was a "straitjacket, cramping and binding" the body politic:

> This is the shout of every discontented radical who can find no good in any man's work but his own; of every envious idler who would charge his own shortcomings to the roof that shelters him; and of every perfervid and short-sighted reformer who in his blind haste to reach his desired goal would break without remorse through every barrier of principle or prudence that lies in his way.

The truth was, he insisted, that "we can amend the Constitution whenever we choose." Yet the amending process should not be used lightly: "Great and solemn documents must be held above the passing gusts of momentary sentiment. Constant meddling with the foundation will surely bring any building to the ground." [36]

Clearly, Davis wanted few substantive changes at all. Invoking the epigram "Striving to better, oft we harm what is well," he opposed almost every proposed reform of his era, from abolition of child labor to equal rights for women. He even had scant enthusiasm for the American Law Institute's monumental effort to codify the common law, though he sat on the Institute's council.* "Highly trained and efficient judges," he insisted, "can do more than any revision of statutes or rules [can] to promote the administration of justice." [37]

Davis also deplored the creation of administrative law by regulatory commissions. Condemning it as "so-called law . . . which no layman can discover, and no lawyer can keep pace with," he challenged in particular its underlying rationale—the notion, as he termed it, that the primary function of government was to nurse the economy. Assuredly, he continued to hold that "the greatest care of the State should be the individual liberty of the citizens." (Near the end of his life he would again rise to the defense of the right of conscience in the case of J. Robert Oppenheimer.) Yet his central concern remained the freedom of the entrepreneur, not the excesses of the government's loyalty program nor the failure of society to give poor whites and blacks of all classes equal justice under law. Thus it was against the expansion of the commerce and general welfare clauses that he most often and most feelingly declaimed—against the former because of the power it gave government to regulate the economy; against the latter because of its justification, among many other things, of Congress' penchant for "scattering money for anything that struck its fancy." Not once in hundreds of commentaries did he inveigh against that body of judge-made law which by 1898 had written laissez-faire economic theory and vested property rights into the Fourteenth Amendment to a degree that the corporations' most ardent proponents had hardly dreamed of when the Amendment was framed in 1866 to secure the rights of ex-slaves.[38]

Davis also abhorred the theory that law was an integral component of political science and should be studied as such. He fulminated against the tendency of Harvard, Yale, and a few other law schools in which the legal realists' influence was strong to introduce courses in public policy and the sociology of law. He even questioned the wisdom of spending course time on general jurisprudence. He had no objection to jurisprudence as such, he explained, "but when a client comes to ask what are the rules by which his conduct is to be weighed

---

* The legal realists also questioned the wisdom of the Institute's Restatement, though for different reasons. As Felix Cohen put it, "the more intelligent of our younger teachers and students are not interested in 'restating' the dogmas of legal theology." See Wilfrid E. Rumble, Jr., *American Legal Realism* (Ithaca, 1968), 156–57, for background.

or governed he will not be much helped by a dissertation on the Pandects of Justinian." [39]

In reality, the waters ran deeper. Davis was willing to give the beginning student a "map of the legal field," and if it included a general survey of jurisprudence, well enough. What he resented was Holmes' contention that it was necessary to grasp what the law was in the process of becoming, that, as Eugene V. Rostow, one of the later, more moderate realists, phrased it,

> . . . the lawyer had to understand and consider the ideas playing in the formation of law—the pressures for social change in many areas, from banking and bankruptcy to labor law and the law of torts. He had to master all the sciences of society, from anthropology to statistics. [40]

Davis' comments on such propositions were sharp and frequent: "Surely it never entered the minds of the founders that the law could ever degenerate, as the German school would have it, into 'a perpetual flux of speculative ideas.' " Law is not something "drawn from the circumambient atmosphere or the social urge generated in a scholar's head." The purpose of a law school is to teach what the law is, not what it should be. "Harvard . . . has reached a point in legal nihilism which even they are beginning to worry about. It is a patriotic service to counter these doctrines when and wherever one may." Finally, in utter exasperation, he attacked the legal realist's personal motivation:

> There is a terrible accounting due from these la-d-la professors who have been teaching the youth of the country that whatever is is wrong. I believe that most of them, consciously or unconsciously, were moved by motives of envy rather than anything else. Lacking the courage to strike out for themselves, they have lingered on academic salaries where they could criticize without restraint and blame without responsibility. [41]

Davis' attachment to precedent put him in tacit disagreement with his partner Wardwell, who held that the memorization of cases was not crucial to legal education. "We got a point of view [at Harvard]," Wardwell recalled. "You can see it today. I know many good lawyers who can remember cases. John W. Davis . . . has a pretty good memory that way. However, I know plenty of good [Harvard] lawyers who can't remember any cases, but they know how to attack a problem." Neither could Davis have accepted the legal realism implicit in Wardwell's reflective remark that the New York bar should have "foreseen" some of the changes in the relations between business and government and "should have been a little more progressive about them." * Yet, with the modesty that was his abiding charm, Davis conceded that in spite of the "wild men" among their teachers, recent Harvard and Yale graduates did so much better work than he could have done at their age that he was "a bit ashamed" of himself.[42]

Davis regularly advised young men to study law at Harvard, Yale, Michigan, or the University of Virginia (he had an unexplained bias against Columbia) because the numerous alumni of those schools on Wall Street made it easier to get a job. Occasionally he recommended Washington and Lee, and sometimes he suggested that it made little difference where one went:

> What a man does for himself is far more important than what any school can do for him. If you should go to a night school and work hard you could come out quite as good a lawyer as if you went to a school that could give you more help. After all, there are only two classes of lawyers in the world—those who work and those who do not.[43]

When asked to describe the ideal pre-law curriculum, Davis frequently replied: "First, English; second, English; third, English." More often he listed most of the subjects he himself had taken—Latin, logic, a modern language, history, mathematics, physics, chemistry, and physiology. He always added accounting, and he invariably excluded, often with a negative comment, economics, sociology, psychology, and political science. He also counseled against general jurisprudence on the undergraduate level because "a little learning" for the lay mind was always dangerous.[44]

As chairman for twenty years of the relatively inactive New York State Joint Committee on Legal Education, Davis took a middle course on raising standards for admission to law school. He strongly endorsed a proposal, recommended by the American Bar Association

---

* Many Wall Street lawyers shared Wardwell's view of the need to reform corporate law. In 1949, for example, the distinguished Cravath partner Robert T. Swaine warned that "it behooves all of us who render 'specialized service to business and finance' to seek such solutions of the legal problems of our clients as are compatible with changing social concepts and as will avoid the abuses of economic power to which our profession too often contributed in past decades." *Impact of Big Business on the Profession: An Answer to Critics of the Modern Bar*, 35 A.B.A.J. 89, 171 (1949).

during his presidency, to require two years of college. Following adoption of the two-year requirement by New York in 1927, he pronounced
it "enough for the present" and discouraged efforts of college officials
and law school deans to increase it. The additional courses, he gently
admonished Dean Arthur T. Vanderbilt of New York University Law
School, were likely to be taken in the social sciences, and "a great deal
of what is thought science in economics, sociology and psychology does
not fall under that head." If a man wanted knowledge of those subjects, he could acquire it by general reading. He further held—and in
this his essential democracy contrasted sharply with those elitist leaders
of the corporate bar who wanted to restrict admission of lower class
Jews to the urban bar—that to stretch the undergraduate requirement
to four years would subject poor boys to unnecessary hardship.[45]

On balance, Davis' uncompromising defense of *stare decisis* and his
biting comments on theoreticians were probably more extreme than
he intended them to be. They also gave a distorted impression of his
own techniques as a lawyer. Until the New Deal, certainly, his handling of constitutional questions in court was more flexible than his
hastily dictated letters would suggest. He believed that McReynolds'
application of *stare decisis* tended to be too automatic, and he himself
used the concept with considerable sophistication. Where judicial interpretations varied and the exact boundary of *stare decisis* was in
doubt, he invariably discussed the proper application in terms of semantics, legislative history, and public policy. In case after case, furthermore, he faced competing rules independently of the problem of
controlling facts. Almost always his procedure was to emphasize the
reasoning behind the rule he relied on and then to go into considerations of policy—a practical application of what the realists called "rule
skepticism." His practice of "fact-skepticism," another of the realists'
imperatives, was heavily dependent on economic data (it was his realization of the importance of such data that caused him to urge the inclusion of accounting, though not economics, in the pre-law curriculum). Indeed, Judge Jerome Frank, the leading realist writer on the
subject, was so impressed by Davis Polk's observance of "fact-skepticism" that he once remarked that he supposed the firm *concentrated*
on establishing the facts. Had Davis himself not practiced in this manner, and had he not also been perceptive, rational, and flexible in
court, he would not have earned the appellation, Leader of the Appellate Bar.[46]

CHAPTER 25

War and Peace

And when the fierce struggle is ended
And he pauses to count the cost,
What is it the Victor will garner
To pay for the things he has lost?

The hate of unnumbered millions
Who forever and a day
Will turn with contempt and loathing
When a German comes their way.

JOHN W. DAVIS, 1941

« I »

Davis was too nonpartisan and too internationalistic to let his antipathy for the New Deal warp his judgment of President Roosevelt's conduct of foreign affairs. Except for F.D.R.'s aversion to British and French colonialism, their views on foreign policy were identical; from the Reciprocal Trade Agreements Act of 1934 to the decision to create the United Nations a decade later, Davis supported Roosevelt with scarcely a reservation. "I was all with him," he said on his death. "I heartily approved and greatly admired the wisdom, courage, and vigor of his foreign policy." [1]

The overarching consideration for Davis was distrust of Germany and love of England; the German State epitomized force and lawlessness, the British Commonwealth reason and the reign of law. He had more fear of Germany than of Russia, more concern for the security of Britain, including her empire, than for any country save his own. He always insisted that Germany had been the principal aggressor in World War I, and he had brusquely dismissed proposals to repeal the war guilt clause of the Treaty of Versailles in the 1920's. He also continued

to believe that the United States had gone to war in 1917 for one reason alone—the preservation of civilization. He felt that the revisionist
historians' attempt to read commercial influences into Woodrow Wilson's resort to war was an insult to the President's memory, the Nye
committee's "calculated effort to misrepresent the reasons" for Wilson's
action "one of the most amazing events" of his lifetime. The House of
Morgan, said Davis, in a statement he and Allen Wardwell drew up
for the Morgan partners in early 1936, realized that a German victory
would have destroyed the freedom of the rest of the world. Indeed,
President Wilson's war message had "exactly expressed" Morgan's own
feelings; hence the firm's resolve to do all in its power to help the Allies win the war.[2]

Davis' conviction that mankind's last best hope lay in international
cooperation was almost as deeply rooted as his Anglophilia. Assuredly,
he had no utopian illusions. He believed that the chief value of the
World Court was symbolic, and he was unsympathetic to unilateral
disarmament. But he also believed, as he admonished Joseph T. Robinson and several other Senators during debates over American membership in the World Court in the 1920's and early 1930's, that the
United States should give just a little. An agreement to submit disputes in advance, he pointed out, was no more open to constitutional
objection than one to submit to a tribunal organized after a dispute
had arisen.[3]

From his return from the Court of St. James's to his death in 1955,
Davis invested himself in the moderate peace and internationalist
movements. He sat on the boards of the Carnegie Endowment, the
American Foundation, and the League of Nations Association, was almost continuously a member of one or another bar association's committee on international law, and served as president of the Council on
Foreign Relations for twelve years and as a director for as many more.
In none of these groups was he a driving or initiating force. But he attended meetings faithfully, gave his name freely, and was valued for
his wise counsel. As Hamilton Fish Armstrong recalled of Davis' presidency of the Council on Foreign Relations, Davis accepted routine
recommendations as a matter of course, but took a stand on important
issues. "He was self-contained and when he disagreed with someone
was apt to do so in a restrained, if ironical manner." He was also
generous with his time.[4]

The last vestige of Davis' hope for permanent peace was shattered
when Hitler's columns and Mussolini's legions stamped their iron

heels on Czechoslovakia and Albania in the spring of 1939. "For twenty years," he sadly reflected, "many of us have been working and striving for a regime of international peace. Yet here we are in a world dominated by power politics once more." No longer could men of good will within the totalitarian states speak for the peace movement; should peace leaders in the democracies therefore lie low lest the dictators construe their pleas as weakness or timidity? [5]

Yet not until he sensed that England was imperiled did Davis conclude that fascism would have to be crushed by armed force. He was appalled by Hitler's persecution of Jews. "If those responsible . . . had a single neck, it would be a pleasure to swing the axe," he said in 1938. But he surmised that protests by Americans would backfire, and after participating in one mass rally, he remained silent. As for the Spanish Revolution, his few comments were of the "plague on both your houses" variety. He read no moral issue into the advantage the Neutrality Acts gave Franco, and he tartly rejected a request to support an appeal for removal of the arms embargo with the observation that he was "not disposed to petition the government on foreign affairs." Meanwhile, he privately endorsed Britain's equivocal Ethiopian policy on the theory that firmness might provoke a general war. And, though he seems to have had doubts himself, he did not dispute the contention of his conservative English friends that Britain needed to buy time at Munich and that, as one of them phrased it, war over Czechoslovakia would have been utterly wrong because creation of that nation in 1919 had been an experiment. But on being advised in the early summer of 1939 that Britain would retaliate if Hitler struck again, Davis grimly approved.[6]

For several months after Hitler's panzers had rolled over Poland, in September of 1939, Davis' economic orthodoxy inhibited his conception of the United States' potential role. Seven years of New Dealism, he explained to Lord Midleton, had piled up an enormous debt, weakened credit, imposed debilitating taxes, and taken the nation far down the road to socialism. "Now, if on top of all this, there comes a war with its vast expenditures and its inevitable expansion of governmental power, how can we hope ever to return to a free economy? In short, if victors abroad may we not be losers at home?" [7]

The Battle of Britain changed everything for Davis. Nothing, not even the charming talks he had made every year as head of the English-Speaking Union, more revealed his love of England than his anguished comments during the dreary winter of 1940–41: "Every bomb cast on London is a dagger through my heart." "I cannot bear to think of the destruction the barbarians are creating." "Where in all history is there a finer exhibition of physical and moral courage?" "Day by day my wonder and admiration for the fight England is putting up grows greater." [8]

Actually, Davis had concluded in the spring of 1940 that Britain was fighting America's war. On May 14, just a few weeks before the fall of France, he pronounced the war "a basic struggle between right and wrong" in an address to fifteen hundred members of the English-Speaking Union at the Waldorf-Astoria. Congress, he declared to wave on wave of applause, should rise to the crisis. Two weeks later he joined William Allen White's Committee to Defend America by Aiding the Allies. Then, after supporting rearmament and the renewal of the Selective Service Act that fall, he appealed with great fervor for lend-lease at a Committee to Defend America meeting in February 1941. Regardless of race or creed, he asserted, Americans "dislike, abominate, hate and despise Adolf Hitler and his . . . water boy, Benito Mussolini." They knew that Hitler aimed to make the German people lords and masters of the world, and they were determined that his "hateful system" should not find a foothold in the Western Hemisphere. They also knew that the English were fighting on behalf of free men everywhere and that aid to Britain was "the surest protection to ourselves . . . and to the preservation of a world in which we wish to live ourselves and hope to leave to our children." Admitting that he had opposed Roosevelt in the past because of his arrogation of power, he insisted that foreign policy was a special case. Even if the lend-lease bill failed to pass, the President "could use the great and awful power of his office . . . to bring us into war. . . . In times of foreign crisis he, and he alone, carries the burden and owes the duty of leadership." [9]

« II »

Whether Davis would have called for an American declaration of war against Germany had Hitler not acted first is uncertain. In April 1941 he rejected a request that he petition the President to order convoys for American ships carrying supplies to Britain. But in May, in a gesture that drew a warm telegram from Roosevelt, he joined Al Smith and James M. Cox in endorsing the President's proclamation of an unlimited national emergency. The situation, said Davis, was like that in Rome when one leader was given the power to protect the republic. Five weeks before Pearl Harbor, he told an old friend that if it took war to stop Hitler, he favored war.[10]

Proudly, Davis watched some eighty partners, associates, and clerks leave for the service during the war. He joked about "the load on elderly gents like myself," saying that he had not done so much of his own research since he had come to Wall Street. More seriously, he complained that it was difficult to relate his practice to the war effort. How he wished, he said in letters to the men overseas, that he might take part. All he could do, he lamented, was speak at war bond rallies and draw such comfort as he could from the realization that civilian activity was the foundation of the military effort.[11]

As Allied strength slowly built up on the British Isles and in the Mediterranean in 1943, Davis reflected increasingly on the presidential succession and the postwar world. In 1940, he had supported Wendell Willkie wholeheartedly, despite Willkie's warmongering charges against Roosevelt in the last month of the campaign. The Indianan, he surmised, was "a man of great capacity and lofty purpose" who had made some rash statements under the pressure of events. Willkie's subsequent crusade for a bipartisan foreign policy confirmed Davis' view that he was a man of parts and courage, and he hoped fervently that he would win the presidency in 1944 and take the United States into a revitalized League of Nations. Disappointed by Willkie's defeat in the Wisconsin Republican primary early in 1944, Davis voted for Thomas E. Dewey that fall, but only because he would not support "the Archangel Michael attended by all his angels for a fourth term." [12]

The economic realities of the impending peace gave Davis considerable intellectual difficulty. He had accepted heavy taxation during the war with only minor grumbling. "I do not complain, because if we can pull out of this thing the Government can have all I own. Of course, when I listen to some of the starry-eyed like Henry Wallace I conclude they will have it all anyhow." But he was cool to suggestions that the United States rehabilitate Europe at the end of hostilities; America's own burdens would be too heavy, he explained to Hamilton Fish Armstrong. Consequently, he failed to add his voice to the mobilization of sentiment that made possible the crucial loan to Britain in 1946. On such root-conservative matters as the confiscation of enemy property, however, he did contribute to the debate and, indirectly, to the formulation of policy.[13]

Davis believed as strongly as ever that international trade was indispensable to world prosperity and peace, and that property rights were indispensable to trade. In 1943 he advised John Foster Dulles on the draft of a resolution for the American Bar Association which urged the American government to abstain from confiscating property of nationals of enemy or enemy-occupied countries. Two years later, for the Council on Foreign Relations, he reconciled the conflicting views of fourteen lawyers into a thoughtful report on the settlement of postwar property rights.[14]

He admitted that the amorphous character of international law made the report's conclusions tenuous at best. "I do not know what . . . [international law] is," he wrote one mild critic. "You do not know what it is. And who does know? . . . I suppose . . . so far as it has any mandate, it rests upon the innate ideas of right and justice entertained by a majority of mankind." Nevertheless, given the Allies' resolve to exact reparations from Germany, the committee had had little alternative but to assume that a victorious nation's right to impose reparations was recognized by international law. This did not include sanction to "sack a city or loot at pleasure." Neither did it include authorization to confiscate the property of enemy aliens; indeed, he regarded the Alien Property Custodian's decision to license German patents to American companies as a gross violation of private property rights. "Whether those patents are held in trust for the German owners on the principle of non-confiscation or whether they belong to the United States by right of seizure, there is no reason . . . for donating them to individual private users without just compensation for their use." [15]

Davis further believed that governments could not expropriate or assign property held by their nationals in other countries. He pointed out that American courts had refused to recognize Soviet decrees claiming title to former Russian citizens' property in the United States, and he thought it unlikely that the United States government would agree to accept the American property of German citizens as payment of reparations. "It all harks back, does it not, to our theory—somewhat different in this respect from Roman law—that the laws of every sovereign have territorial extent only?" He conceded, however, that several recent court decisions seemed "to fire across the bows" of those doctrines.[16]

The postwar trials of Nazi war criminals similarly affronted Davis' legal conscience. He resented the effort to cover political retribution, as he believed it to be, with a mask of law. And though he said little in his letters about Nuremberg, he strongly seconded Charles Warren's assertion that punishment of war criminals "must be a matter of policy by the victors in the war, and not a matter of law, either international or domestic." (Neither he nor Warren seems to have realized that the only novel charge in the main Nuremberg indictment was that of aggressive war, and that no one was sentenced to death solely on that count. The other two charges, violation of the laws of war and inhumane acts against civilians, had long been recognized in international law.) [17]

Davis also suffered a fleeting fear that the United States had violated moral law, if not the rules of war, by unleashing atomic weapons. "Immediately after Hiroshima and Nagasaki," he reported, "I wondered whether we were justified in killing so many non-combatants at a single blow . . . when the game seemed to be about over anyhow." However, he added, his uneasiness had been soon allayed by a graphic report on the "sadistic cruelty" of the Japanese.[18]

Memories of the bitter struggle over the League of Nations in 1919 weighed heavily on Davis all through the war. Reluctant to incite the old anti-League forces, he believed until well into 1944 that the internationalists should act with circumspection. The best tactic, he warned John Foster Dulles, was to focus on the general rather than the specific. Only because "you ask for it," he told him in April, would he sign the Federal Council of Churches' declaration of support for a new, League-like organization. By the fall of 1944, however, Davis was ready to confront the isolationists then rallying around Senator Robert A. Taft of Ohio. Just before the election in November, he joined Professors Philip C. Jessup, James T. Shotwell, Quincy Wright, and others in a long, uncompromising endorsement of the proposal to create the United Nations.[19]

This group took particular exception to the view that it would be unconstitutional to delegate the war-making power to the Security Council. They noted that presidential action had preceded congressional action in the Mexican, Civil, Spanish-American, and First World wars (World War II was not mentioned), and they argued that the prerogatives of Congress would be better protected by going through the Security Council: the public debate preceding decision would create an awareness in Congress "which has sometimes been lacking in the past"; should extensive force be necessary, the President "could hardly avoid laying the whole matter before Congress." [20]

Isolation, Davis declared in a radio address the next month, could not guarantee security; it was imperative, therefore, that the United Nations be authorized to use force. "It is cheap insurance if it will work. It can never work unless America joins in the effort. . . . The decision before us is the acid test of our sincerity in all our many peace-loving protestations." Three weeks later he urged all internationalists to combine forces against the opposition. Then, in February 1945, he, Shotwell, and the others warned that abandonment of the old League of Nations mandate system "might imply a step toward division of the world into several great power zones of exclusive domination." Changes in the status of mandates should not be merely the province of a small coterie of great powers directly interested in their disposition; the United States, in particular, should set an example by refraining from outright acquisition of Japan's former mandates.[21]

So strongly did Davis feel that he even took to the air to call for a permanent United Nations Commission on Human Rights. He especially wanted the United Nations to foster reduction of trade barriers, stabilization of currency, and creation of a world bank; and he shared the disappointment of his friend A. Willis Robertson of Virginia, one of the strongest internationalist voices in the House, over Senator Arthur Vandenberg's initial refusal to support the proposed program. Still, there was much to be heartened about. "How true it is," he remarked in the spring of 1947, ". . . that history has vindicated Wilson and blasted his opponents. If there had never been a League of Nations there would not today be a United Nations." [22]

Meanwhile, Davis gave short shrift to the movements for world federalism or political and military union of Britain, France, and the United States. "How anybody can follow the will-o-the-wisp of a world government or super-state in the present posture of world affairs beggars my imagination," he said; if the United Nations proved unworkable, why should one think that it could be supplanted by a more formal organization? The proposal to create a military union of Atlantic powers on the assumption that "the U.N. cannot stop the cold war and cannot get Russia back on her own ground without a shooting war" was hardly better. To support it over the United Nations, Davis gently remonstrated with Will Clayton, would be "to throw in the sponge." [23]

« III »

For some time after Roosevelt's death in April 1945, Davis was ambivalent toward the Truman administration. Sizing up the new Presi-

dent as a man of good impulses but "without large capacity," who
wanted "to do right if he can be shown it," he half-persuaded himself
that he would give the country the conservative government essential,
as Davis believed, to the revival of private and public morality. He
commented favorably on Truman's disposition "to demobilize the artificial controls built up by the War and to restore the power that has
been filched from Congress," and he dismissed the liberalism of his
first major domestic message as merely "a collection of all the unfin-
ished business on his desk." As the months passed, however, Davis
began to fret over Truman's emerging liberalism. Despite the drastic
and instantaneous inflation sparked by the premature end of price
controls in June 1946, he agreed with Taft that the controls should
have been removed right after V-J Day. He fumed over Truman's tendency to tie the New York Democratic party to "the CIO-PAC-XYZ
Kite." And he insisted that the President's civil rights program, including the anti-lynching bill, was unconstitutional; alternately, he blamed
it on Truman's effort "to re-assemble the rather miscellaneous cohorts
who followed Roosevelt" and on the capture of the President by "the
Northern Liberals." [24]

The renomination of Thomas E. Dewey in 1948 was equally depressing. Disgusted by "the smugness and ineptitute" of Dewey's campaign,
Davis would have voted Democratic for the first time since 1932 had
Truman not sent Chief Justice Fred M. Vinson to Moscow on a special
mission a few weeks before the election. "That seemed . . . so irresponsible a gesture and so obviously intended to detach some of Wallace's
pro-Russian following that I could not stick it out." As for Truman's
dramatic victory, the blame lay with "the 'gimme' boys"—the labor
unions, the Jewish voters in New York, and the "negro blocs . . . attracted by the President's so-called Civil Rights' Program." Yet no
more than before could Davis repress his sense of humor. Late in the
morning on the day after the election he stopped by the open office
door of Theodore Kiendl, who had supported Dewey with smoulder-
ing passion. Smiling benignly, he raised his thumb to his nose, bowed
low, and walked rapidly away.[25]

Not until Davis concluded that Truman was serious in his liberalism did Davis give up hope for the President and the Democrats. He
refused for sentimental reasons to join the Republican party. But in
1950 he flirted briefly with a Liberty-League-like organization, the Citizens' Political Committee, supported by right-wing New Jersey Senator Albert W. Hawkes. The Committee hoped to create a formal alliance of conservative Southern Democrats and Northern Republicans

by making a joint presidential nomination in 1952, and it engaged the passing interest of John J. Raskob, James F. Byrnes, and Louisiana demagogue Leander Perez. With the reaction against the Liberty League a decade and a half earlier still on his mind, Davis warned, in signing a letter of solicitation, that the names of financial sponsors should be kept confidential. As it turned out, key Republican Senators failed to warm to the merger proposal, and Davis was once again without a political home. "Like yourself," he commiserated with Harry Byrd, "I am and remain a Jefferson-Jackson democrat. . . . I have nothing but contempt for those who 'have stolen the livery of heaven to serve the devil.' In my darker moments I reflect with bitterness on the possibility that in my few remaining years I can probably cast only protest votes." [26]

Even on Europe, Davis' and Truman's views were not quite identical. Davis inclined to blame the Cold War more on the Russian than the communist mentality: " [The Russians] have the same secrecy, the same distrust of foreigners, the same ambition for expansion they had under the Czars. The Russian will remain a Russian still." It was possible, he wrote, that the communists genuinely feared attack by the capitalists and were thus animated by desire "to insure a future security by building up a *cordon sanitaire* of satellite states." It was also possible that they really did want to promote world revolution on the old Lenin-Trotsky thesis. But whatever their reasons, they were clearly the main obstruction to peace. It was well that Secretary of State Byrnes and Senator Vandenberg had served notice "that we are getting fed up." [27]

Accordingly, Davis approved rearmament of Germany, military aid to Greece and Turkey, and containment as posited by George Kennan under the pseudonym "Mr. X." He also gave his name to the Citizens' Committee for the Marshall Plan, though with slight enthusiasm. He supported it, he explained privately, because, even if the United States wanted to retreat, she had gone too far to do so. "But I read a booklet the other night by Henry Hazlitt, 'Will Dollars Save the World?' which shook me considerably." By 1950, when proposals to recognize and subsidize Franco Spain came to a head, he had had enough. "Recognition is one thing and subsidies . . . another. I grow weary of pouring good American money down foreign rat holes." [28]

Davis also disapproved of Truman's Palestine policy. He himself had always regarded Zionism as a tragedy. "I can imagine no greater misfortune for the Jews . . . in America," he said at the end of the war "than to set up a national Jewish state with the resulting chance . . . of a divided allegiance." He took heart at Truman's reluctance to support the proposed new nation in the fall of 1945, and he would have accepted the President's request that he head an Anglo-American inquiry into the Arab-Jewish disorders had his physician not vetoed the project. He was thoroughly disgusted, consequently, when Truman reversed himself under domestic political pressures and put the United States behind Israel. The President, he said, was simply pandering to the "so-called Jewish vote in the city of New York." [29]

Yet Davis himself was barren of a solution. He shared the Jewish people's resentment of their persecution "so far as a gentile can," and he felt that the United States should admit a token quota of displaced persons. But he declined to join a committee to liberalize the immigration laws, and he disapproved of accepting refugees in large numbers. "I cannot say that I want them out in the swamp, but in the language of the scripture: 'Not for thy sake, O Israel, but for My name have I done this thing.' " [30]

« IV »

Davis believed that the oscillations in the Truman-Acheson Far Eastern policy were as indefensible as those in the Palestine policy. He thought for a while that Chiang Kai-Shek's government might prove viable, and he endorsed aid to the Generalissimo as late as the fall of 1947. But as the evidence mounted that not even a massive injection of American men and money could save Chiang's mainland forces, Davis backed off. He approved of the plan, drawn up in 1947 by the Joint Chiefs of Staff under Dwight D. Eisenhower, to disengage and let the Chinese Revolution run its course. And from the winter of 1948–49 to his death six years later, he held more or less consistently to the view that the United States' only obligations in the Far East were to Japan and the Philippines.[31]

Unlike the liberal-realists, who perceived that independence movements were the wave of the future, Davis based his opposition to American involvement in Asia on what might be called a conservative-realist assessment of American capabilities. His unwavering faith in the "civilizing" force of colonialism, especially in its British version, gave him little sympathy for the resolve of the Indians, Malayans, and Indo-Chinese to break their Western yokes. "That was certainly a foolish speech of Mr. Justice Douglas, urging us to go all out against colonialism and support any revolutionary movement," he remarked in 1952. Yet, at root, Davis was so skeptical of the United States' ability "to lighten the dark places of the world without injury," so fearful that containment in the Far East would bankrupt the nation, that he opposed all aid to Asia, including Point Four.[32]

Distressed by rumors that Truman was going to warn the Chinese communists against seizing Formosa early in 1950, Davis unburdened himself to Lord Astor. For the United States to support Chiang on his island fiefdom, he prophetically wrote, "would embark us on a course of which no man is wise enough to see the end." The American people had neither the strength nor the will to carry through "any military adventures by this country in China or its outlying islands." [33]

True to this logic, Davis deplored the decision to resist the invasion of South Korea in June 1950. He and Ambassador Lewis Douglas happened to be guests of the Astors at Cliveden when the communists struck. Truman telephoned, and both men advised the President against intervening. "Poor humanity!" Davis remarked to Douglas. "Is it doomed to go 'round and round' the military treadmill?" Once again the United States had underrated its adversaries. "When will we cease to permit our diplomatic involvement to outrun our available force?" Formosa was especially puzzling:

> Our original attitude between Chiang and the Communists was "to let the dust settle," withdraw aid from Chiang and not take sides. When Chiang went to Formosa we announced that we had no further interest in the matter. When the Korean affair broke out we announced that we had stationed our Asiatic Fleet between Formosa and the mainland to bar any invasion of Formosa. . . . Now, if you know what our Formosan policy is, I wish . . . you would give me some enlightenment.[34]

Davis' letters are silent on the heady decision to change objectives from the expulsion of the North Korean communists to the unification of all Korea during MacArthur's drive to the Yalu in the fall of 1950. But by the summer of 1951 he was writing that, although he still deemed "the Korean adventure" a mistake, the Administration should "quit advertising that . . . [our policy] is dictated by caution rather than a hope of victory." Five months later, he concluded that time had amply proved that the war was a blunder. He refused to sign a public letter defending Dean Acheson against the smears of the Taft-McCarthy wing of the Republican party, although he sympathized with the Secretary of State and deplored the attacks on him. He was not sure, he explained, what the Secretary's policies really were; only if the phrase "extraordinarily skillful handling of international affairs" were deleted from the letter would he lend his name.[35]

Davis' last written comment on Far Eastern affairs was dated June 23, 1954. Musing over the fall of the French at Dien Bien Phu and the earlier calls of Vice President Richard M. Nixon and Admiral Arthur W. Radford for American intervention, he said: "But when you ask 'where do we go from here,' I answer at once, 'we don't go to Indo-China, or Southeast Asia.' I am appalled by the mere suggestion." [36]

« V »

For many months in late 1951 and early 1952, Davis had feared that the appetite for power would impel Truman to run for re-election. He never forgot what Admiral Cary Grayson, the personal physician of Theodore Roosevelt, William Howard Taft, and Woodrow Wilson, once said to him: "I walked out of the White House with three of them and not one of the three wanted to go." He believed, moreover, that 'if Truman stood for a new term the twelve million people on the federal payroll would make him a dangerous contender.[37]

Yet he also felt that the nomination of Robert Taft would be disastrous, partly because the Ohioan could not win the independent vote. "The Taft machine conceives that the Republicans are still a majority party and can win on their own strength for any nominee. They are wrong." He regarded the Senator as an honest, courageous man of considerable ability who had the "unhappy faculty of saying the wrong thing at the right time," and he was inclined to agree with those who said that he " 'has the best mind in the Senate until he makes it up.' " [38]

Conversely, Davis had no use for the argument, made most insistently by Taft's supporters, that Eisenhower's services to the North Atlantic Treaty Organization were too valuable to lose. The obvious answer to that, he said, was that he would have "ten times the influence and power" as President. Neither did Davis take exception, as he had done in 1948, to the prospect of a military man in the White House. Eisenhower's outlook, he concluded on reflection, was so patently civilian, his world view so clearly internationalist, that it was absurd to stand any longer on abstract fear of militarism.[39]

Although Davis said that he "would walk forty miles on frozen ground" to make Senator Harry F. Byrd President, he was pleased at

first by the Democrats' nomination of Adlai E. Stevenson; the Governor's character was "superb," his speeches "extraordinary." He was disappointed, however, by Stevenson's criticism of the Taft-Hartley Act
and by his failure to dissent from Truman's assertion that the Democratic party had to run on the record of the Roosevelt and Truman
administrations. On October 22, following a meeting with Eisenhower,
Davis announced that he regarded the General as better equipped
than any living American to handle the critical military and diplomatic problems of the times. He added that "the proven facts of widespread corruption, of carelessness, complacency and favoritism in governmental circles demand a change." [40]

The Davis' faith in Eisenhower was soon justified in part. Not only did
the General give the country a conservative government, he extricated
the United States from Korea, rejected the counsel of Radford and
Nixon on Indochina, and let Senator Joseph McCarthy destroy himself
(though not without tragic damage to the Far Eastern Division of the
State Department). In addition, Eisenhower leaned heavily on Davis
during the crisis over Senator John Bricker's proposal to limit the treaty-
making power and the President's authority to make Executive
agreements.[41]

The original version of the Bricker amendment proposed, first, to
invalidate all treaties affecting matters constitutionally reserved to the
states in the absence of specific approval by the forty-eight states, and,
second, to give Congress the power to regulate and to approve or disapprove all Executive agreements with foreign nations. Among its
more than sixty sponsors in the Senate were numerous Republican internationalists and several Democratic internationalists as well. But the
real thrust came from ultraconservative isolationists or states' rightists
in both parties—from Democrats McCarran, Byrd, Eastland, George,
and McClellan, and from Republicans Dirksen, Goldwater, Jenner,
Mundt, McCarthy, and, until his death in July 1953, Taft. Almost all
subscribed to the "conspiracy" or "sell-out" theory of Yalta, and they
were determined to forestall a repetition of that "tragedy." (The
amendment would not really have applied to Yalta, which was a political settlement rather than an Executive agreement; nor would it have
prevented Truman's decision to fight in Korea, the Kennedy-Johnson
intervention in Vietnam, or the Nixon invasion of Cambodia.) They
were equally determined, in Bricker's words, to prevent the imposition
of "socialism by treaty." The Southerners, in particular, wanted to destroy all possibility of adherence to the United Nations Covenant on

Human Rights—essentially the creation of Eleanor Roosevelt—
because of the Covenant's implications to the maltreatment of Negroes
in the United States.[42]

The amendment had surprisingly strong support in normally sophisticated Eastern circles. Ten days after Eisenhower's inauguration, for
example, the New York State Bar Association rejected the recommendation of a committee headed by former Attorney General William D.
Mitchell, and including Davis in its membership, that the Association
oppose the amendment. That summer the committee came back with
a second, and sharper, report. It pointed out that the amendment
would require congressional approval of even the most routine battle-
field agreements. It noted that formal treaties were invalid if they violated the Constitution, and that it was therefore absurd to require
state ratification. And it emphasized that the Eisenhower administration had already declared that it would not become a party to the
Covenant on Human Rights. This report was also rejected.[43]

In the autumn of 1953, the Association of the Bar of the City of
New York, the only bar association in the country to oppose the
Bricker amendment, formed a special committee under the joint chairmanship of Davis, General Lucius Clay, and Professor Edward S. Corwin of Princeton, the nation's most eminent authority on the Constitution. The committee concluded that the amendment would make the
United States' procedure for carrying out treaty obligations "the most
cumbersome in the world," would deprive the federal government of
authority to act on narcotic or navigation matters, and would preclude
such emergency actions as the Berlin airlift. The report, which went to
Eisenhower in December, influenced the President profoundly. "I
deeply respected" Davis and Corwin, he said in his memoirs; they
showed that the amendment's proposed changes were "both unnecessary and harmful." [44]

At the time, however, the President was groping desperately for a
compromise formula. Privately, he was furious. He denounced Bricker's proposal as "senseless and plain damaging to the prestige of the
United States." He also dismissed Frank E. Holman, a past president
of the American Bar Association and a vehement opponent of the Covenant on Human Rights, as a man bravely determined "to save the
United States from Eleanor Roosevelt." Nevertheless, as Vice President
Nixon warned, the amendment had enormous public support. "You
take a fellow like Lyndon Johnson," said Nixon. "He says he doesn't
think it's [the amendment is] wise at all, but he's going to vote for it

. . . 'Because all my people in Texas want it.' " In these circumstances, Eisenhower temporarily concluded that he could not "combat the almost hysterical attitude of so many people." [45]

In mid-January of 1954, Eisenhower appealed to lawyer-banker-statesman John J. McCloy. After explaining that he shared McCloy's belief that no amendment was necessary, he noted that a great many Americans had "absorbed the idea that Mr. Roosevelt [had] exceeded his powers during the World War." They were also convinced, he wrote, that the United Nations Charter gave international bodies the right to intervene in the internal affairs of the United States. Could they not allay these fears through an amendment which would be "nothing more than a reaffirmation of the supremacy of our Constitution?" The President then asked Davis, through McCloy, for a new formula.[46]

Davis responded on January 12 with a three-page, single-spaced assault on both the Bricker amendment and the proposed substitutes. He was unable, he said in conclusion, to suggest an acceptable alternative:

> Our present method for the making of treaties has worked without injury to the country for 160 years. Those who would change it find support only in imagining hypothetical dangers. But solely to calm their fears it would be, as it seems to me, an act of folly to hamper the power of the nation to reach by negotiation with foreign powers the solution of great and present problems. By way of illustration, if the atomic crisis is to be solved by general agreement, the difficulty in so doing would be measurably increased in my opinion by any of the proposed amendments which I have seen.

He added that he hoped "all proposals to modify the existing machinery" would fail.[47]

The impact of Davis' letter cannot be measured. All that is certain is that shortly after receiving it Eisenhower abandoned his search for a compromise. "We refused," the President said, "to take anything that in reality would change the substance of the Constitution as it stood." Six weeks later, Bricker's revised version having been decisively defeated for lack of Administration support, a substitute measure by Senator Walter George failed by one vote to win the necessary two-thirds majority.[48]

« CHAPTER 26 »

The Cold War and the Law:
Hiss and Oppenheimer

For this, brethren of the Bar, is our supreme function—to be sleepless sentinels on the ramparts of human liberty and there to sound the alarm whenever an enemy appears.

JOHN W. DAVIS, 1946

During all these years, the national hysteria over internal security was raising one First Amendment or due process question after another. Notwithstanding Davis' deep concern for personal freedom, his acceptance of infringements on political liberty went considerably beyond Holmes' "clear and present danger" dictum and far beyond Jefferson's near absolutes. "With all the enthusiasm I feel for civil liberties," he explained, in supporting an alien detention bill on the eve of World War II, "we must avoid letting ourselves be over-persuaded by the extremists." Unlike many other leaders of the bench and bar, however, Davis never let the dictates of security completely obscure the conditions of freedom, especially when the fate of an individual engaged his personal interest. On several of the constitutional controversies of the era he took the libertarian position, and in two of the most tragic episodes of all—the Hiss and Oppenheimer cases—he set a high example of devotion to the lawyer's ideal.[1]

« I »

Davis' infrequent public stands and few private comments on the
great civil liberties issues of the times make the degree of his commitment difficult to assess. Although his friends report that he was utterly
contemptuous of Senator Joseph McCarthy, his personal letters contain hardly any allusions to McCarthyism, and his public statements
none whatever. Almost always, moreover, his remarks on civil liberties
lacked the urgency, the almost apocalyptic quality, of his strictures
against government intervention in the economy. Most were prompted
by requests to sign public letters and *amicus* briefs or to approve bar
association reports, and often they comprised no more than a sentence
or phrase. As a member of the County Lawyers Association's committee on civil rights, for example, he was asked, in the winter of
1939, to review a memorandum on a state senate bill authorizing suppression of any public utterance deemed offensive to racial or religious
groups. "It would be difficult," said Chairman Paul Windels, "to conceive of a more . . . sweeping, dangerous [and] intolerant statute."
Davis replied in three words: "I entirely agree." [2]

A memorandum on wire-tapping drew very little attention.
During the New York State Constitutional Convention of 1938, liberal
Democrats had fought to restrict the admission of evidence gleaned
from wire-tapping. But Thomas E. Dewey, then in his racket-busting
phase, helped force through a provision which permitted the use of evidence gained through illegal wire-tapping. This was a virtual invitation to private detectives to indulge in an orgy of "bugging." Terming
electronic eavesdropping an "unconscionable" violation of the right of
privacy, Governor Herbert H. Lehman gave top priority in January
1939 to a bill, sponsored by Assemblyman Robert F. Wagner, later
Mayor of New York, to prohibit the admission of unauthorized evidence. Davis seems not to have followed the controversy. But when
William D. Mitchell recommended endorsement of an alternative measure which would restrict wire-tapping by state officials but would
allow introduction of evidence obtained through wire-tapping by private individuals without court approval, he concurred in a few words. [3]

A year later, Charles Burlingham, that "Peck's bad boy of the bar"
who badgered Davis for almost thirty years, enlisted his active support
against a congressional bill to deport Harry R. Bridges, the Austra-
lian-born longshoremen's leader and fellow-traveler. The measure, said
Burlingham, was a clear "deprivation of due process" and possibly a

bill of attainder as well. Would Davis sign a letter to Senator Lewis B. Schwellenbach of Washington asserting that no action of Congress had ever singled out an individual for deportation? Replying that, although Bridges "may be and probably is a 'syncopated son-of-a-sea cock,' " he opposed any bill to punish a single person, Davis joined Thomas D. Thacher in signing Burlingham's letter. Then, on his own initiative, he wrote Schwellenbach that, contrary to the measure's proponents, Holmes' opinion in *Tiaco v. Forbes* did not exclude deportation proceedings from the restraints imposed by the Bill of Rights. Once an alien has been admitted, Davis declared, he was entitled to the protection of the Constitution and could be deported, if at all, only after a fair hearing:

> The precedent which this Bill would set for Congressional action directed towards a single individual, no matter how obnoxious, is so shocking . . . that the Bill stands condemned on the merits, regardless of any questions of power.[4]

That was the last time Davis actively defended civil liberties for almost a decade. In 1942 he rejected a plea to support an attack by the American Civil Liberties Union on the indictment of twenty-eight radicals for sedition. (Most of the statements for which they were charged had been made before the United States entered the war.) In 1943 he turned down a request by Arthur Garfield Hays, the ACLU's general counsel, to sign an *amicus* brief in behalf of three Japanese-American evacuees from the West Coast. Then, a few months after VJ Day, he inadvertently encouraged the House Un-American Activities Committee to go far beyond the kind of fishing expedition he had accused Ferdinand Pecora of launching during the investigation of the House of Morgan twelve years earlier.[5]

Asked by Congressman Karl Mundt, the right-wing South Dakotan, to suggest standards of Americanism for the committee, Davis replied that the committee's activities "might properly be directed to ventilating" any challenge to the Preamble to the Declaration of Independence, the Constitution proper, or the Bill of Rights. "The fact that men have the right to speak or write as they please does not exempt their speech or writing from the field of your inquiry." The committee was fully within its rights in investigating "those movements essentially disloyal in character which are designed to weaken the allegiance of their members to the United States or to favor some foreign sovereignty." [6]

To Davis' mild embarrassment, Mundt quoted his letter at length on the floor of the House in May 1946. "If any one man in America has set the standards for this committee," the South Dakotan declared, in a burst of hyperbole aimed at the left-wing New Yorker Vito Marcantonio, "it is Mr. John W. Davis"; the committee has tried to carry out his recommendation "faithfully, full, and well." [7]

Davis had suggested no standards of procedure, had issued no warning against witch-hunting, and had made no mention of defamation of character. He had simply assumed, apparently, that the committee would be properly solicitous of the Bill of Rights. "I myself agree with most of what you said," Corliss Lamont, then under citation for contempt of Congress, plaintively wrote Davis, after reading Mundt's remarks in the *Congressional Record*. But the truth was that the new committee had been "just about as bad as the old Dies Committee in violating Constitutional procedures and functioning as a Smear Committee rather than a truly investigatory one." It had been especially unscrupulous in invoking the opprobrious term "un-American." He added that the committee was now claiming Davis' backing in its drive for additional appropriations. [8]

Davis replied that, although he had not known that the letter would be given the importance Mundt ascribed to it, he had no desire "to retract or modify" it. He added that he had not "kept up" with the committee and had no idea what it was doing. [9]

The fact was that Davis had even less sympathy for Lamont, a radical humanist, professor of philosophy, and son of the Morgan partner, than for most opponents of the status quo; Lamont, he believed, had "asked for it." Assuredly, Davis remained strongly opposed in principle to guilt by association, loyalty oaths, and many of the other perversions of liberty that fell under the rubric of "McCarthyism." Unlike the welfare state, however, none of these matters weighed heavily enough to move him publicly or consume him privately. In 1947, to be sure, he told John Lord O'Brian that O'Brian's pamphlet decrying loyalty tests and guilt by association was "sound as a nut" and should be taken to heart by the proponents of what later became the Mundt-Nixon Act. Four years later he congratulated the Harvard English professor Howard Mumford Jones on his article on loyalty oaths in the *American Scholar*. "I am glad that you took a shot at the absurd resolution adopted by the American Bar Association requiring from lawyers periodical oaths of non-membership in the Communist party." But not until his association with the Carnegie Endowment involved

him with Alger Hiss in a personal way did he move to stay the corro-
sion of those principles which he insisted to his death made him "a
Jeffersonian Democrat, defiant and unashamed." 10

In December 1948 Davis had again rejected an appeal from Arthur
Garfield Hays, this one to sign an *amicus* brief attacking the procedural aspects of President Truman's loyalty program. "While the
American Civil Liberties Union has recognized the right of the Government to require loyalty from public servants," Hays explained, "we
have challenged the Executive Order as lacking in due process, by its
authorizing the blacklisting of organizations without notice or charges
or a hearing, and because implicit in the program is the principle of
guilt by association." Davis replied that he agreed with Hays in principle, but was reluctant to sign because of his standing "repugnance to
briefs *amicus curiae* where the question is being fairly presented by
counsel in the case." 11

Ten months later, Davis gave short shrift to Burlingham's request
that he sign a Civil Liberties Union letter asserting that the virtual
outlawing of the Communist party by the Smith Act was unconstitutional. Then, after Learned Hand drastically narrowed the application
of the "clear and present danger" doctrine in affirming District Judge
Harold Medina's ruling that the Act was constitutional in the trial of
eleven top Communist party functionaries, Davis dismissed Burlingham's suggestion that he argue the Communists' appeal in the Supreme
Court. "If the Commies had any sense," Burlingham wrote him, "they
would try to get conservative lawyers to argue their cases. I had got
this off several times to Roger Baldwin, and once he did call my bluff
and now this other friend has done so, and I told him that the best
man in the United States for them was a fellow named Davis, John
W." Davis, who was often irritated by Burlingham's insistent enthusi-
asms, was unmoved. Dryly, he replied: "I do not want to argue the
'Commie' case; Learned Hand's remarks on the constitutionality of
the Smith Act are quite sufficient for me." 12

A request to sign an *amicus curiae* brief on behalf of the convicted
Communists' lawyers received the same treatment. Sentenced by Judge
Medina to up to six months for their blatant obstructionism during
the trial (presumably, they had hoped to provoke Medina into reversible error), the lawyers were requesting a stay of sentence pending the
appeal by their clients. The *amicus* brief, which was drafted for the
ACLU by Wall Street lawyer Osmand K. Fraenkel, disclaimed sympathy with communist doctrines. It also said that its signers believed

that the lawyers "merited" punishment for their behavior. But it questioned the severity of the sentences, and it implied that Judge Medina had acted arbitrarily:

> Whether the procedure of summary punishment without hearing on such a charge comports with due process presents a question so serious that we believe appellants should not be imprisoned while that question is being considered on appeal.

The brief further declared that the convicted Communists' right of appeal would be gravely compromised if their lawyers were imprisoned while the appeals were pending.[13]

Davis had no interest in signing. "It does not seem to me," he wrote Fraenkel, "that any privileges of the bar have been invaded by the action of Judge Medina, and I think he was quite within his judicial rights in imposing punishment for contempt committed in the presence of the Court." He added that he disliked *amicus* briefs anyhow. The Supreme Court subsequently confirmed Davis' judgment, but only over the impassioned protests of Justices Frankfurter and Black. "The Judge [Medina]," Frankfurter complained in dissent, "acted as the prosecuting witness; he thought of himself as such. His self-concern pervades the record; it could not humanly have been excluded from his judgment of contempt." Black's dissent was even more anguished.[14]

Meanwhile, Davis agreed to serve as a sponsor of a dinner honoring Judge Medina for his long and harrowing ordeal. Burlingham, who continued to badger Davis, was incredulous. "We don't understand how you got into a Medina galère," he wrote him after talking with two other past presidents of the Association of the Bar, Thomas D. Thacher and Harrison Tweed. "Almost every lawyer I have seen is shocked that a Tribute Dinner should be given a judge for his behavior in the trial of a case, especially when that case is now on appeal." Would Davis not advise Medina that it would be the better part of wisdom for him to decline to be honored? Davis explained that it had been "yesterday," when he had given his name. "What's done is done." (Medina subsequently called off the dinner at the suggestion of Burlingham and others.) [15]

Late in August that same year, 1950, former Attorney General Francis Biddle appealed to Davis by telegram to endorse a statement against the McCarran Internal Security Bill.

BELIEVE GREAT GOOD COULD BE ACCOMPLISHED BY YOUR NAME ASSOCIATED WITH OTHER OUTSTANDING LEGAL AUTHORITIES.

He suggested that an alternative measure, sponsored by Senators Scott Lucas, Estes Kefauver, Frank Graham, and others, be supported instead:

> [The McCarran bill] WILL DO IRREVOCABLE HARM TO INDIVIDUAL LIBERTIES IN VIOLATION OF BILL OF RIGHTS WITHOUT EFFECTIVELY COMBATTING COMMUNIST EFFORTS TO UNDERMINE OUR NATIONAL SECURITY. SUCH INDISCRIMINATE LEGISLATION HIGHLY UN-AMERICAN. WILL INCREASE PRESENT OBSESSION OF FEAR WHICH IS HARMING NATIONAL MORALE.

Davis did not reply. However, he did join twelve other lawyers in a public letter defending former New York City Judge Dorothy Kenyon against charges of "communist activities" by Senator Joseph McCarthy.[16]

Meanwhile, Gus Hall, one of the convicted Communists, asked Davis to argue for continuation of their bail pending action on their petition to the Supreme Court for review of their convictions. (The Second Circuit had refused to continue bail despite Learned Hand's biting contention in dissent that the substantial constitutional questions raised by the case warranted continuance.) Hall, who was to be refused counsel by twenty-three other attorneys, pointed out that the Ninth Circuit had recently ruled in the *Bridges* case that revocation of bail because of a defendant's opposition to government policy was "as novel as it is startling." He hoped that Davis would agree that the issue transcended political differences and that he would come into the case. Politely, Davis pleaded the pressure of other business, adding that he doubted that he could argue successfully that the revocation of bail was not solely within the discretion of the court. (The abuse of discretion by any lower court judge in the federal court system is always reversible, so Davis was really speaking directly to the merits.) [17]

Davis was not alone in failing to fight vigorously for principle throughout a crisis roughly comparable to the one engendered by the South's closing off of internal debate on slavery a century earlier.* As Philip Graham of the Washington *Post*, one of the few forthrightly

---

* I compare McCarthyism to the closure of debate on slavery rather than to the Alien and Sedition Acts of 1798 or the Great Red Scare of 1919 because the latter two episodes, though analogous in many respects, were more short-lived and less far-reaching in effect. The silencing of discussion of slavery within the Old South foreclosed any possibility of nonviolent emancipation; the intimidation of professors, editorial writers, and public men by McCarthyism locked American society into a monolithic interpretation of communism and the Cold War from the mid-1940's to the mid-1960's.

anti-McCarthy publishers in the nation, charged, virtually the entire leadership of the American bar was remiss. "I feel," said Graham in a speech to the Association of the Bar of the City of New York in late 1951, "that the legal profession has substantially failed to meet its proper obligations of supporting individual freedom."

> By and large, the attitudes of the bar have indicated silent acquiescence in, and even occasionally affirmative support for, innovations affecting personal freedom that would have raised the collective hairs of this Association straight on end not many years ago.
>
> « »
> Over thirty years ago this Association raised its voice against the expulsion of the Socialist legislators at Albany. One of your most eminent members, Mr. Charles Evans Hughes, added to the literature of liberty when he reminded the Legislature for this Association that "it is the essence of the institution of liberty that it be recognized that guilt is personal and cannot be attributed to the holding of opinion or to mere intent in the absence of overt acts."
> It is to the shame of this great profession that [today] others have largely provided the leadership and taken the blows in defense of those Constitutional rights of which you should be especial guardians. . . .[18]

There was a sense, writes George Martin in his authoritative history of the Association of the Bar, in which Graham's indictment was fair. "At the Association's seventy-fifth anniversary meeting, held in 1946, John W. Davis had described the 'supreme function' of lawyers 'to be sleepless sentinels on the ramparts of human liberty and there to sound the alarm whenever an enemy appears. What duty,' he asked, 'could be more transcendent and sublime? What cause more holy?' But when, only five years later, the enemy was at the gates, many, like Graham, asked, 'Where are the lawyers?' What was needed was another Charles Evans Hughes, a leader of courage and of political as well as professional stature; for the latter alone . . . would not have been enough. But those who had the courage had not the stature; and of the few who had the stature, apparently not one had the courage." [19]

Patently, Davis' silence had little to do with courage; he had defied or ignored public passions in the past, and he would do so again in the few years of life that remained. Rather, it was a function of his congenital distrust of reformers and "agitators" and of his extreme reluctance to put himself forward. So intensely did he abhor radicalism in all spheres except the religious that he blinded himself at times to the perversions of liberty inherent in the crusade to extirpate it. Only during the New Deal had he engaged in moderately sustained public protest, and then he had done so at heavy emotional cost and only because he believed that his political and economic philosophy was being subverted. Otherwise he had made few public statements not incumbent upon him as an official of organizations such as the League of Nations Association and the Council on Foreign Relations. His natural inclination toward reticence and against self-serving publicity was strengthened in this instance by his conviction that communism was a domestic threat and by his loathing of the communists' demonstrable use of liberty to destroy liberty. This was unfortunate, for it exposed him to charges that he was more devoted to property rights than to civil liberties. As Martin reports, many disenchanted younger members of the Association of the Bar came to regard Davis as "a liberal Democrat with a broad view of the world who had grown, after forty years on Wall Street, into an ultra-conservative Republican unable to see beyond the corporate interests he represented." [20]

Yet, as Martin also suggests, this view was somewhat unfair to Davis and to certain of his partners. Theodore Kiendl was to represent former Senator William Benton in his libel suit against Senator Joseph McCarthy. Allen Wardwell, who contributed privately to Owen Lattimore's defense fund, was to lead an abortive movement within the Association of the Bar to declare Senator McCarran's lieutenant, Robert Morris, unfit for a Municipal Court judgeship. At the moment Graham leveled his indictment, moreover, Davis Polk was representing the Institute of Pacific Relations, the scholarly organization that McCarran's subcommittee virtually destroyed during an eighteen-month-long investigation. Furthermore, Davis had already comported himself with decency and sensitivity in the Hiss case and would end his career as one of Dr. J. Robert Oppenheimer's attorneys.[21]

« II »

On December 9, 1946, Alger Hiss had been unanimously elected President of the Carnegie Endowment on the recommendation of a three-man committee of trustees, composed of Davis, Arthur Ballantine, and Eliot Wadsworth. The forty-two-year-old State Department officer had first been suggested to Davis by John Foster Dulles, who had agreed to become chairman of the board if he were given a working president. Dulles had been so impressed by Hiss' performance at the San Francisco Conference of the United Nations in the fall of 1945

that he had sounded him out on his own before mentioning him to
Davis. The Davis committee discussed about ten men, but its interest
centered exclusively on Hiss after one or two other prospects proved
unavailable. As Dulles later explained, Hiss displayed a "quick grasp"
of the Endowment's problems and was strongly recommended by Secretary of State James F. Byrnes, Senator Arthur Vandenberg, and
many other prominent men. "I am more than ever convinced," Dulles
wrote Davis early in 1946, "that he would be ideal for the job." [22]

Shortly after Hiss' election, two persistent anti-communists, Alfred
Kohlberg and Larry Davidow, advised Dulles that Hiss had probably
had communist connections during the New Deal. Neither informant
had any hard information, and when Hiss categorically denied that he
had been either a communist or a fellow-traveler, Dulles dropped the
matter. "I gained the impression," he later testified, "that [Hiss] . . .
had satisfied the F.B.I. on that point." The following winter, Representative Walter Judd of Minnesota, one of the most insistent of those
who charged that the State Department had "sold out" Nationalist
China, repeated the allegations against Hiss. A second inquiry by
Dulles drew the admission from Hiss that he had been exposed to casual association with communists as a New York attorney and as an official in the Department of Agriculture in the 1930's. Again, however,
he denied that he had been a communist or fellow-traveler, and again
the State Department affirmed his loyalty. Dulles had then placed the
record before Davis and Ballantine. "[It] was their common feeling,"
Dulles said, "that there was no basis for any Endowment Action."
(Security officers reported, among other things, that Hiss was regarded
as more conservative than many State Department officials. Meanwhile, as Dulles himself emphasized to Judd, Hiss was urging the Endowment to endorse the Marshall Plan, "the phase of our foreign policy
which the Communists are fighting most bitterly.") [23]

Six months later, on August 3, 1948, the Hiss affair became a *cause
célèbre* when *Time* editor Whittaker Chambers told the House Un-
American Activities Committee that he had known Hiss as a member of
the communist underground in Washington in the 1930's. Hiss' colleagues on the Carnegie Corporation advised him to ignore the
charges, saying that the Un-American Activities Committee was discredited and had no real public support. (Its allegations against Dr.
Edward Condon, Director of the National Bureau of Standards, had
been decisively disproved just two weeks earlier.) Nevertheless, Hiss
decided that he should appear before the Committee as "a matter of

principle." That same afternoon he asked the Committee by telegram for permission to deny Chambers' charges under oath. From Philadelphia, where he went on Endowment business the next day, he informed John Foster Dulles of his plans by telephone. Dulles suggested that he "think back" carefully to Depression days, when many young men had been so outraged that they had taken extreme positions and had associated with "all kinds of people." Hiss regarded this as "avuncular advice" at the time, but he later concluded that Dulles had probably meant to encourage him to "minimize" the scope of his denials.[24]

There followed the familiar story of Hiss' denial that he had been a communist or had known a man named Whittaker Chambers, of Chambers' elaboration of his relations with Hiss, and of Congressman Richard Nixon's insistence within the Committee that it continue the investigation. Unknown to Hiss, Nixon was encouraged in his resolve to pursue the matter by Dulles and his brother, Allen. On the night of August 11, at Nixon's request, the Dulles brothers had reviewed Hiss' and Chambers' conflicting testimony at the Hotel Roosevelt in new York, where John Foster maintained a suite in the Dewey presidential campaign headquarters. "There's no question about it," said John Foster. "It's almost impossible to believe, but Chambers knows Hiss." Years later, after his dismissal of several Foreign Service officers* on flimsy grounds while he was Secretary of State had made Dulles defensive of his own reputation for fairness, he expanded on the incident: "Dick had gotten a lot of evidence, but it was clear he did not want to proceed with Hiss until people like myself had agreed that he really had got a case. . . . He did not want to jeopardize a person's right. . . . Dick wanted to be careful about hurting reputations. . . . I formed a very high judgment of the sense of responsibility under which he operated." Subsequently, Committee Chairman J. Parnell Thomas, who was later convicted of padding his own payroll, reported that the Republican National Committee urged him "to set up the spy hearings" during the presidential campaign that fall "in order to put the heat on Harry Truman." [25]

Meanwhile, Hiss continued to confide in Dulles, who never informed him of the meeting with Nixon at the Roosevelt. Sometime between Dulles' session with Nixon on August 11 and Hiss' second appearance before the Committee on August 16, Hiss told Dulles that he wanted to seek out Chambers, see whether he had known him, and

---

* Notably, John Carter Vincent and John Paton Davies.

find out what could motivate him. Dulles responded that the Committee had "seized itself" of the matter and that Hiss would be ill-advised to proceed on his own. Then, following Hiss' identification of Chambers, on August 17, as a man he had known as "George Crosley," he and Dulles discussed the possibility of Hiss' resigning as president of the Endowment.[26]

Dulles' account of this discussion, in a statement he prepared for the Endowment on December 27, differs somewhat from his subsequent testimony at Hiss' perjury trials. It is clear, however, that Dulles, without consulting Davis or any other trustee, indicated to Hiss that he felt that he should resign. "I . . . told him," one account reads, "that while I was confident that the Trustees would not themselves want to . . . imply judgment against him or be prejudicial to him . . . , I thought that [he] . . . should voluntarily . . . relieve the Endowment of embarrassment." * Hiss' lawyer had already warned him that a premature resignation would damage his position, so he replied that he would like to stay on until the hearings were completed. He added that he too was anxious to avoid "embarrassing" the Endowment, and that he would offer his resignation at an appropriate date. Reluctantly, Dulles acquiesced, but only, so he later said, after relieving Hiss of all duties. (Actually, Dulles did *not* relieve him of his duties in the

* Richard D. Challener reports that, early in September, Nixon sent Dulles a four-page, single-spaced letter remarkable for its factual tone and straightforward marshaling of evidence. It focused on the points in Hiss' testimony that would prove weakest at his trials, and it concluded that, "at the very least, Hiss deliberately misled the committee in several important respects." Dulles, who expected to become Secretary of State under Thomas E. Dewey, was already facing hostile questions about Hiss from newspapermen. Yet Hiss had strong support from many trustees, including General Dwight D. Eisenhower. Dulles also recognized that it would be "precipitate," and probably not even possible under Endowment by-laws, to take formal action at that time. He appealed, in effect, to Nixon for forbearance and embarked for the UN meeting in Paris, leaving only a vague statement behind. He gave no guidance to Davis, who acted as chairman in his absence, and he responded cryptically to James T. Shotwell's reports. On November 10, for example, Shotwell wrote Dulles: "Alger is . . . spending practically full time at the office, allowing himself only one or two days now and then to consult with lawyers. But this means . . . poor preparation for a trial. . . . Chambers . . . is strongly backed by Henry Luce. . . . The evidence points to paranoia, for Chambers evidently believes what he says and he says different things, each with the same intense earnestness. He has now expressed himself as of the opinion that Alger will 'persecute' him." (Copy in Davis Papers.) Challener, "New Light on a Turning Point in U.S. History," *University: A Princeton Quarterly,* LVI (Spring 1973), 30–31.

sense his statement implied. He assigned James T. Shotwell administrative direction of the Endowment with the understanding that Hiss
would, "for the time being, be unable to devote continuous time and
attention [to it]." Hiss continued, however, to perform many of his
duties until the eve of his indictment.) [27]

On August 27, Chambers declared on a national radio program,
"Meet the Press," that Alger Hiss "was a communist and may be [one]
now." A month later to the day, Hiss filed a libel suit against Chambers in Baltimore. Davis, who was fond of Hiss, a sensitive man of civilized tastes and quiet charm, followed the suit closely and even corresponded with Hiss' attorney. Hiss himself was reluctant, as he
remembered a quarter of a century later, to consult such a busy and
important man as Davis on a personal matter. "He was a great, noble
and lovable man. I not only admired and revered John W. Davis, but
loved him and cherished the limited opportunities I had . . . to be
with him." Not until after a federal grand jury had subpoenaed Hiss,
in early December, and Chambers had produced four documents in
Hiss' handwriting, did he seek out Davis, who was then acting chairman of the Endowment in Dulles' absence in Europe.[28]

Davis told Hiss, as he was to tell others, that the handwritten materials actually strengthened his belief in Hiss' innocence. No one of
Hiss' intelligence, he said, would be "so stupid," were he in fact a spy,
as to give papers in his own hand to a confederate. He suggested that
Hiss ask former Secretary of War Robert P. Patterson to represent
him.* He also advised him not to testify before the grand jury, on the
ground that he never let his own clients do so, regardless of the merits,
because what they said might be distorted and used against them. Hiss
replied that he felt that he had to testify, and Davis seemed to understand. "I think," Hiss mused many years later, "that he respected the
fact that I must take that position as a matter of principle." After observing that he was proud of the regard Davis seemed to have for him
and was honored by the time he had given him when he urgently
needed advice, he added: "I have never regretted my brash disregard
of the great lawyer's sage advice based on his many years of
experience." [29]

On Sunday, December 12, 1948, three days before the grand jury in-

* Patterson felt that he could not take the case. Meanwhile, Felix Frankfurter sent word to Hiss that he should get a criminal lawyer. Philip Jessup,
an Endowment trustee, then suggested Davis' friend Lloyd Paul Stryker, who
willingly agreed to serve.

dicted him for perjury, Hiss decided to submit his resignation as president of the Endowment. Although he did not expect to be indicted, the regular board meeting on the thirteenth seemed a proper time to fulfill his earlier promise to Dulles to "relieve the Endowment of embarrassment." On Sunday night the trustees met at the Beekman Hotel for a preliminary dinner session at which, by custom, the hard decisions were made. Hiss ate with them, then excused himself to draft his resignation. Harvey Bundy, father of McGeorge and William P., and "a lovely man," in Hiss' description, helped him with the draft. The letter was then sent in to Davis, who was presiding because Dulles was still abroad. It soon became evident that the discussion would be long and acrimonious, and President Henry R. Wriston of Brown University went out to suggest to Hiss, "as an act of humanity," that he not wait until its end.[30]

Tempers flared early and often, and at times only Davis' skill, grace, and courtesy preserved the amenities. William Marshall Bullitt, the Louisville attorney who had brought Davis into the Frazier-Lemke Act case in 1935, made the first long statement. A small man with a shiny bald head, thick glasses, and the manner of a zealot, Bullitt was obsessed by the fear that the United Nations Commission on Human Rights (the Endowment's energies were directed toward strengthening the UN) was going to impose "pure communism" on the United States. Six months later, at Hiss' first trial, the presiding judge would reprimand him for sitting in the press section and distributing a printed diatribe against Hiss. Now, in what Henry Wriston remembered as a "tirade," Bullitt demanded Hiss' instant dismissal. Dr. Edward L. Ryerson, a steel company executive, countered by insisting that they reject Hiss' resignation categorically. Meanwhile, Wriston, Philip Reed, and David Rockefeller, all of whom would be among the last to be polled, said, *sotto voce,* that Hiss had no financial assets and should be given a leave of absence with pay in order to defend himself in the event that he were indicted. Thomas J. Watson of International Business Machines, whom Davis regarded as one of the two vainest men of his acquaintance, indignantly added that Hiss had damaged his (Watson's) reputation. Arthur Ballantine, a corporation lawyer, then joined Bullitt and Watson in demanding immediate, unqualified acceptance of the resignation.[31]

As Davis slowly polled each of the nineteen trustees present, support developed among Bundy and others for the Wriston-Reed-Rockefeller contention that prudence and justice demanded that Hiss be given a leave of absence with pay and that a decision on the resignation be deferred. Afterwards, to the surprise of all and the relief of many, Thomas J. Watson rose to announce that he was switching his support to the Wriston group's proposal; his original remarks, he confessed, had been egocentric. By then Davis had quietly revealed that he also favored a leave of absence with pay, and after further discussion he persuaded the entire board to endorse it. Even Bullitt was satisfied for the moment. "Your handling of everybody was a masterpiece," he wrote Davis the day after Hiss' indictment. "To compose Ballantine and me with Dr. Ryerson was a feat!" [32]

Davis reacted with his usual modesty and restraint. He told Bullitt that he was well-satisfied with the middle course, and he urged a Philadelphia trustee of the Endowment to ignore a blast in Walter Annenberg's *Inquirer* against their "kid-glove" handling of Hiss. Three years later, in testifying before a congressional committee, Davis glossed over both the controversy and his own leadership. "There was a feeling . . . which I personally thoroughly shared," he said, "that to accept his [Hiss'] resignation and deprive him of the presidency instanter would be a pre-judgment of his case, and we had no right to do that." [33]

Davis never lost his faith in Hiss. He served as a character witness at both his trials, and he maintained to the end of his life that Hiss had been framed:

> I never believed and do not now believe that he was guilty as charged. Among the documents which Chambers produced were four desk memoranda written in Hiss' own hand, along with typewritten documents. Now, if Hiss was in a conspiracy to deliver documents to Chambers certainly he would not have turned over these autographed specimens when he so easily could have turned to his secretary and had a copy made. This phase of the matter convinces me that some person was systematically plundering Hiss' desk. To my mind it tends to disprove that Hiss, himself, was the transmitter of the documents. I am bound to say, however, that partly by over-confidence, and partly by reason of some intellectual arrogance, he handled his side of the matter in very maladroit fashion. I feel that the whole story has not yet been told.[34]

Davis made his last public reference to the case in 1952. Early in the presidential campaign, Senator Everett Dirksen and numerous second-echelon Republicans began to assail Adlai Stevenson for testifying as a character witness for Hiss. R. Keith Kane of Cadwalader, Wickersham & Taft then drew up a vigorous defense of Stevenson which was signed by twenty-one prominent attorneys, including both Eisenhower and Stevenson supporters. Among the signatories were Davis, Burlingham,

General William J. "Wild Bill" Donovan, and Dulles' own law partner, Eustace Seligman. "In our view as lawyers," said their statement,
"the Governor acted properly in this matter and did what any good
citizen should have done under the circumstances." * The signers
hoped that they would not have to publish the statement despite the
Republican drive to link Hiss to Stevenson. But on October 13 Nixon
forced their hand by declaring that Stevenson's lack of judgment in
testifying for Hiss "disqualified" him from the Presidency.[35]

Unabashed when the Kane group published their rebuke, Nixon repeated and embellished the indictment. He charged in one speech that
Stevenson was a "dupe" and declared in another that he had gone
"down the line for the archtraitor of our generation." He also explained the reason for Stevenson's comportment: "He is a graduate of
Dean Acheson's spineless school of diplomacy which cost the free
world 600,000,000 former allies in . . . seven years of Trumanism."
The Democratic candidate replied in characteristic vein. "The brash
and patronizing young man who aspires to the Vice Presidency [says]
. . . that I exercised bad judgment in stating honestly what I had
heard from others about Hiss' reputation. . . . I hope and pray that
his standards of 'judgment' never prevail in our courts." Stevenson
added that both Eisenhower and Dulles,† as trustees of the Carnegie

---

* Among the other public men who testified to Hiss' high reputation at the
time they were associated with him were Justices Felix Frankfurter and Stanley F. Reed, Judges Calvert Magruder and Charles Wyzanski, Assistant Secretary of State Francis B. Sayre, Rear Admiral Arthur J. Hepburn, Ambassador Philip Jessup, and Gerard Swope, Jr., counsel to the International
General Electric Company.

James T. Shotwell solicited statements for the Endowment from several
other persons, including Eleanor Roosevelt, Joseph C. Grew, Benjamin
Cohen, Clark M. Eichelberger, and former Senator Gerald Nye. All wrote
that they had never observed any communist sympathies in Hiss, and all expressed confidence in his complete loyalty. The longest and most interesting
statement was made by Mrs. Roosevelt, whom Hiss did not ask to testify at
either of his trials. She had first worked with him at the United Nations
meeting in London in January 1946. Mrs. Roosevelt wrote, in part: "People
who are sympathetic with Communists show certain tendencies. One is to
make certain kinds of excuses. The other way to tell is by their actions during the time between the [Soviet-German] alliance and the invasion [of Po-
land] by the Germans. Those people were justifying their changes in opinion. As far as I know I never heard Mr. Hiss whisper a suggestion or
argument that would indicate sympathy with Communism, and I am very
watchful of these things. I know the earmarks so well. I feel it is entirely
safe to say this is an incredible accusation." (Copy in Davis Papers.)

† On February 17, 1949, Dulles had presided over an executive committee
meeting of the board which extended Hiss' leave of absence until May 5.

Endowment, had acquiesced in the decision to grant Hiss a leave of
absence.[36]

Eisenhower said nothing. But Dulles replied that Stevenson's faith
in Hiss had outlasted his own. "I was approached . . . to be a character witness. I refused. Instead, I became a witness for the prosecution."
(According to Hiss, Dulles was not asked to be a character witness.)
He then addressed Stevenson's assertion that he had been chairman of
the board at the time of Hiss' election. "That is not true. I was elected
chairman at the same meeting at which Hiss was elected president and
I did not even attend that meeting." Seventeen years later Henry R.
Wriston was still outraged. Dulles, he said, "had told the truth in a
way to deceive." [37]

In December 1952, Davis had been annoyed by Dulles' false implication, in his statement for the Endowment, that the search committee
of 1946 had turned to Hiss only after three other men had declined
the presidency. Now, in Wriston's words, Davis "was furious" over
Dulles' implied suggestion that he (Dulles) had had no part in the
selection of Hiss. Nevertheless, Davis was too close to Dulles, and too
averse to controversy, to issue a corrective statement. Not until a
month after the election did he clarify Dulles' role, and then he did so
in the gentlest possible manner. "The first person who mentioned him
[Hiss] to me was Mr. Dulles," he said to a House Committee investigating tax-exempt foundations:

> Mr. Dulles was the prospective chairman, and naturally the committee
> wanted his advice and any assistance he could give. He mentioned Mr.
> Hiss and spoke of having encountered him in this, that, or the other
> international affair, and recommended we look him over which we
> did.[38]

« III »

Despite the debilities of old age, Davis responded up to the limits of
his power to the next request that he defend an individual in a matter
of urgent public concern. In March 1954, a few weeks before Davis'
eighty-first birthday, Lloyd K. Garrison of Paul, Weiss, Rifkind, Whar-

---

Dulles told Davis that he was "sympathetic from Hiss' standpoint with
postponing decisive action." He also wrote Philip Jessup that they should
not take any action "that presumes Alger Hiss to be guilty." But he also
believed, reports Challener, that they should begin to search, informally, for
a successor to Hiss.

ton & Garrison asked him to serve as chief counsel to Dr. J. Robert
Oppenheimer in a security clearance hearing before the Personnel Security Board of the Atomic Energy Commission. At the time, Oppenheimer was director of the Institute for Advanced Studies at Princeton
and a consultant to the Atomic Energy Commission.[39]

Dr. Oppenheimer's leadership of the atomic bomb project at Los
Alamos during World War II had made him the most famous scientist
in America, excepting only Albert Einstein. General Leslie R. Groves,
commander of the Manhattan District, termed his role in the development of the bomb indispensable, and President Truman declared that
the program's success was attributable to him "more than [to] any
other one man." Much of the scientific community echoed those judgments, and on Oppenheimer's appointment to the nine-man General
Advisory Committee to the AEC in 1947, he was unanimously elected
chairman. Several times during his five-year tenure he tried to resign
the chairmanship, but as one of his colleagues said, "He was so naturally a leader . . . that it was impossible to imagine that he should not
be in the chair." Before joining the GAC he had played a major role
in formulating the so-called Baruch Plan for international control of
atomic weapons; and on March 7, 1947, the same day J. Edgar Hoover
sent the AEC a summary of his FBI file, Oppenheimer had, on his
own initiative, flown from San Francisco to New York to warn Baruch's successor at the United Nations against compromises "which
would put the United States in a very dangerous position of not really
knowing what was going on in Russia." Yet, like so many of the scientists who had worked on the atom bomb, Oppenheimer was also tor-
mented by the ultimate moral question. "Mr. President," he once
blurted out to Truman, "I have blood on my hands." [40]

During his five years on the General Advisory Committee, Oppenheimer's views on policy were often in conflict with those of Rear Admiral Lewis L. Strauss, then a member of the five-man Atomic Energy
Commission and later its chairman. Strauss was an able former businessman, a dedicated public servant, and a relentless cold warrior with
a passion for security. He disapproved of Oppenheimer's desire to exchange atomic secrets with Great Britain, and he resisted his proposal
to ship certain radioactive materials abroad. Once, in a discussion on
isotopes, Oppenheimer ruthlessly exposed Strauss' ignorance before a
congressional committee. More important, probably, Strauss deplored
the physicist's opposition to the production of a hydrogen bomb in
1949. As Oppenheimer later explained, "I felt, perhaps quite wrongly,

that having played an active part in promoting a revolution in warfare, I needed to be as responsible as I could with regard to what came of this revolution." Five other members of the nine-man General Advisory Committee, including Dr. James B. Conant, author of the majority recommendation against the H-bomb, shared Oppenheimer's fear that the project would encourage a limitless and possibly catastrophic arms race. Two others, Enrico Fermi and I. I. Rabi, opposed production so fervently that they submitted a separate recommendation couched essentially in ethical terms. Only Dr. Glenn Seaborg, the youngest member of the committee, supported the project, and he did so in anguish. "Although I deplore the prospects of our country putting a tremendous effort into this," he wrote Oppenheimer, in a letter in which he implied that he might change his mind were he able to attend the crucial meeting and participate in the debate, "I must confess that I have been unable to come to the conclusion that we should not. . . ." [41]

Many of Oppenheimer's judges would later insist that the H-bomb controversy had no bearing on their decision to deny him security clearance. Indeed, President Eisenhower was so sensitive to charges that the case turned on that issue that he suggested in his memoirs that Dr. Oppenheimer's stand might have been an act of "conscience" similar to his own assertion, made *before* Hiroshima, that it was "completely unnecessary" to drop the atomic bomb because Japan was already "seeking some way to surrender." But, as Philip M. Stern shows in his penetrating study of the Oppenheimer case, the H-bomb controversy figured crucially in the original charges and perhaps decisively in the subsequent proceedings. By opposing the thermonuclear program in its early stages, Oppenheimer had made powerful enemies in Congress, in the Pentagon, and in the Truman White House. (Two other opponents of the H-bomb, Dr. Conant and Lee DuBridge, were not reappointed to the GAC in 1952, partly on the recommendation of Admiral Sidney Souers, Truman's adviser on security matters.) In addition, Oppenheimer had incurred the enmity of Hungarian-born Dr. Edward Teller, father of the H-bomb and as uncompromising a cold warrior as Admiral Strauss. [42]

Until 1936, Robert Oppenheimer had been a political innocent; he had never owned a radio and had rarely even read a newspaper. But in that year the anti-Franco forces in Spain engaged his sympathies, and from then until 1942 he was an avowed fellow-traveler. His brother joined the Communist party, and he himself married the communist widow of a party member and contributed liberally to communist and anti-Fascist causes. "I became a real leftwinger, joined the teachers' union, had lots of Communist friends," he told a *Time* reporter in 1948. "It was what most people do in college or late high school. The Thomas [House Un-American Activities] Committee doesn't like this, but I'm not ashamed of it. . . . Most of what I believed then now seems complete nonsense, but it was an essential part of becoming a whole man." [43]

The Nazi-Soviet Pact of 1939 prompted Oppenheimer to begin to rethink his communist commitments, and during the next three years his support of front organizations virtually stopped. By 1947, when he went on the GAC, he had long since selectively disclosed his past to an endless string of government investigators. Yet, like many men under external pressure to reveal everything and under internal pressure to protect their friends as well as themselves, he had also made up what he later called a "cock and bull story" about his relations with Haakon Chevalier, a French communist intellectual he had known at Berkeley.[44]

It was the Chevalier incident that would enable Oppenheimer's prosecutor to put the most quoted phrase of the hearing, "a tissue of lies," into the physicist's mouth; and those words, together with Oppenheimer's failure to sever completely his social relations with his brother and a few old friends and former students, would constitute the most damaging evidence against him. But as Dr. Ward V. Evans of the Personnel Security Board was to point out in his formal opinion, "What he had said was not a tissue of lies; there was only one lie." Dr. Henry DeWolf Smyth, alone among the five members of the AEC who passed final judgment, would manage to view Oppenheimer in the fullness of time and in the context of a complete human being. Wrote Smyth: "He sees his brother [who left the party in 1941] . . . not 'much more than once a year.' " He ran into two other former communists while returning from the barber in Princeton. He occasionally saw a few others at professional meetings. "The Chevalier incident involved temporary concealment of an espionage attempt and admitted lying, and is inexcusable. But that was 11 years ago." Chevalier visited Oppenheimer in Princeton en route to France in 1950, and Oppenheimer visited him and his new wife in Paris in December 1953. They had dinner together and met with André Malraux, General de Gaulle's anti-communist adviser whose works Chevalier was translating. "I find nothing . . . to substantiate the charge that Dr. Oppenheimer has had a 'persistent and continuing' association with subversive individuals. These are nothing more than occasional incidents in a complex life, and they were not sought by Dr. Oppenheimer." [45]

In November 1953, William L. Borden, former staff director of the Joint Congressional Atomic Committee and a fanatical proponent of the H-bomb, sent J. Edgar Hoover a long and portentous letter. The letter dilated on Oppenheimer's radical past, accused him of giving false information to the Federal Bureau of Investigation, and charged that his opposition to the hydrogen bomb had been communist-inspired. "More probably than not," Borden concluded, " [Oppenheimer] . . . has . . . been functioning as an espionage agent. . . ." Hoover sent the letter and a bulging file on Oppenheimer to President Eisenhower, and copies to Admiral Strauss, who was by then chairman of the AEC. Eisenhower, who had come into office pledged to drive the subversives out of government, told Strauss on December 3 that a "blank wall" should be placed between Oppenheimer and any sensitive information until a hearing could be held. That night the President wrote in his diary:

> It is reported to me that this same information, or at least the vast bulk of it, has been constantly reviewed and re-examined over a number of years, and that the over-all conclusion has always been that there is no evidence that implies disloyalty on the part of Dr. Oppenheimer. However, this does not mean that he might not be a security risk.[46]

Late in December, Strauss called Oppenheimer into his office. The physicist left the meeting an hour or so later with the option of resigning as a consultant or undergoing a formal hearing. "I can't believe what is happening to me," he said in anguish that evening. The consultant's post meant relatively little, for his services had been used only twice since he had gone off the General Advisory Committee in 1952. But, as he wrote Strauss the next day, to resign without a hearing "would mean that I accept and concur in the view that I am not fit to serve this Government, that I have now served for some 12 years. This I cannot do." A few days later, Kenneth D. Nichols, a retired army officer and the general manager of the AEC, sent him a statement of twenty-four charges. As Stern notes, twenty-three of them dealt with events which had occurred before 1947, when the AEC had reviewed Oppenheimer's file and had granted him security clearance. The twenty-fourth asserted, at considerable length, that his opposition to the H-bomb had "definitely slowed down its development." [47]

In early January of 1954, on the recommendation of John Lord O'Brian, Oppenheimer went to Lloyd K. Garrison for counsel. Garrison was the great-grandson of William Lloyd Garrison, the abolitionist, and a gentle, self-effacing reformer and civic leader in his own right. He had long been a director of the National Urban League and the American Civil Liberties Union, had served briefly as chairman of the National Labor Relations Board, and had been dean of the University of Wisconsin Law School. As a trustee of the Institute for Advanced Studies at Princeton, he had developed considerable affection and great respect for Oppenheimer. He agreed to handle the preliminary aspects of the case, but suggested that they bring in a man of towering national reputation as chief counsel.[48]

Garrison later explained why they needed such a figure. "In the atmosphere of those days, in which public accusation of associations, no matter how far back in time, with Communists or Communist-supported causes, was enough to ruin any man's career, even liberally-minded lawyers were hesitant to involve themselves in the defense of persons so accused." What Oppenheimer needed was "a statesman and a patriot, a symbol of all that was highest in the profession"—a man who would carry great weight with both the review board and the public.[49]

"I had long looked up to [Davis] . . . as an advocate of incomparable ability and as a man of courage and honor," Garrison added. "He was by now old and frail, but his intellectual powers were as vigorous as ever." The two men discussed the case at length, after which Davis read both the charges and Garrison's reply. Davis agreed to become chief counsel if the Personnel Security Board, headed by former Secretary of the Army Gordon Gray, would hold the hearings in New York. He was too weak, he explained to shuttle between New York and Washington. His decision to enter the case, as Garrison recalled, was grounded on the simple conviction that Oppenheimer had been wronged: "I don't think that he was at all influenced by the larger issue. He was concerned with Oppenheimer the individual, not with high policy or the security program as a whole." [50]

To Garrison's dismay, the Atomic Energy Commission refused, in the first of several uncooperative actions, to set the hearings in New York. Garrison therefore acted as Oppenheimer's chief counsel throughout the sessions, which began in April, shortly after Senator Joseph McCarthy informed the nation that there had been an eighteen-month "deliberate delay" in the development of the H-bomb because of communists within the government. (On announcement of the hearing and the earlier suspension of Oppenheimer's security clearance, McCarthy pronounced the suspension "long overdue" and credited it to Strauss. He added that he and Senator Mundt had called off an investigation of their own on assurances from the White House that the physicist's record would be explored in detail.) Garrison made the oral argument; his partner, Samuel J. Silverman, handled much of the questioning of the forty witnesses. "There is more than Dr. Oppenheimer on trial in this room," Garrison said near the end of an often eloquent two-hour presentation on May 6. "The Government of the United States is . . . on trial also. . . . There is an anxiety abroad that these security procedures will be applied artifically . . . like some monolithic . . . machine. . . . America must not devour her own children . . . , must not devour the best and the most gifted of our citizens in . . . mechanical application of security procedures." [51]

On June 1 the Gray Board ruled, with Dr. Evans dissenting, that, although Dr. Oppenheimer had not been "disloyal" and had in fact displayed "a high degree of discretion" and an "unusual ability" to keep vital secrets to himself, he was, nonetheless, a security risk. The Board further found that "he did not show the enthusiastic support for the [H-bomb] program which might have been expected of the chief atomic adviser to the Government under the circumstances," that his failure "to communicate . . . abandonment" of his earlier opposition "undoubtedly had an effect upon other scientists," that "he may have . . . [exercised] highly persuasive influence in matters in which his convictions were not necessarily a reflection of technical judgment," and that, "whatever his motivation, the security interests of the United States were affected." [52]

Davis then joined Garrison in a long letter to General Nichols, protesting his refusal to allow oral argument on the appeal before the AEC. ("As a member of the bar," a Maryland attorney wrote Davis on reading of his involvement, "I am shocked to note that you are associated with Mr. Garrison in defending J. Robert Oppenheimer. . . . In view of the present frightful situation as regards world Communism, just how can you in good conscience . . . be associated in such an affair?") In strong but politely phrased language, the Garrison-Davis letter deplored the unfair procedures imposed upon the Gray Board by the Atomic Energy Commission—among them the withholding of pertinent documents until it was too late to prepare a proper defense. As Garrison later observed to Davis, he and his associates all felt "profoundly . . . not just the tricks of the clever cross-examiner but the deeper implications of the use and misuse of the FBI files, the effect on the judging body of their immersion in a secret dossier, and the broader question of the propriety and effectiveness of any proceeding of this character cast in quasi-judicial trappings but so different from a genuine trial." [53]

By then Davis was so disgusted by the Gray Board's finding that he contemplated defying his physician and making the trip to Washington to argue the appeal orally if General Nichols would relent. But Nichols, a narrow authoritarian who had long harbored a grudge against Oppenheimer, held firm despite a second request by telegram. Garrison then drew up another letter to Nichols. Davis suggested that they use the phrase, "government monastery," but Garrison regretfully declined to include it because he feared that the Catholic member of the AEC, Thomas E. Murray, might not "relish" it. "We asked you to reconsider your decision about oral argument," the letter explained, "not because of Dr. Oppenheimer's prominence but because such argument is one of the most important means of arriving at a clear understanding of voluminous and complex records." Meanwhile, Davis reviewed and signed a new brief which had been put together by the Garrison group, working frenetically under another close deadline. (Davis' support," recalled Garrison, "was a great tonic for all of us.") The brief said, in summary:

> Dr. Oppenheimer is unquestionably loyal, and the Board has so found.
>
> He is discreet, and the Board has so found.
>
> He has rendered great public service, and the Board has so found.
>
> His position in the hydrogen bomb controversy was his honest view, based on his judgment of the interests of the country and the good of humanity; there was not the slightest motivation of disloyalty, and the Board has so found.
>
> Lack of enthusiasm for a program in which a scientist does not believe, or lack of unqualified commitment to a single strategic theory, is not an admissible consideration in determining whether a man is a security risk.[54]

A few days later General Nichols forwarded the Board's findings to the full Commission, along with his own recommendation that Dr. Oppenheimer's security clearance not be restored. Although Nichols hinged his recommendation on the physicist's lack of "veracity" and "past" and "continued" communist associations, he echoed the Gray

Board's indictment of Oppenheimer's failure to support the thermonuclear project enthusiastically.[55]

On June 29, 1954, shortly after the Army-McCarthy hearings ended, Admiral Strauss and three of his four colleauges found Dr. Oppenheimer to be a security risk. Each commissioner maintained, in one form or another (there were three concurring opinions), that he had not been influenced by the emphasis of the Gray Board and General Nichols on Oppenheimer's lack of enthusiasm for the hydrogen bomb project. It seems likely, however, that Eisenhower's friendly biographer, Herbert S. Parmet, has come close to capturing the larger truth:

> The price for public confidence meant getting rid of Oppenheimer, just as surely as it had led to the separation . . . of John Carter Vincent and would, at the end of 1954, lead to the retirement of a constant McCarthy target within the State Department, John Paton Davies.[56]

Davis' own comments were sparing but sharp: "I am appalled by the result." The ruling was "not only unjust," it was "silly." [57]

Nine years later, on November 22, 1963, the nation's morning newspapers announced that on December 2 President John F. Kennedy would present the $50,000 Enrico Fermi award to Dr. J. Robert Oppenheimer for "his outstanding contribution to theoretical physics and his scientific and administrative leadership." That afternoon Kennedy was shot dead in Dallas. Ten days later, Lyndon B. Johnson received Dr. Oppenheimer at the White House.

"One of President Kennedy's most important acts was to sign [this] award," Johnson said to the scientist.

"I think it is just possible, Mr. President," Oppenheimer replied, "that it has taken some charity and some courage for you to make this award today." [58]

CHAPTER 27

Steel, Labor, and Harry S Truman

*The Founders of this Nation entrusted the lawmaking power to the
Congress alone in both good and bad times. It would do no good to
recall the historical events, the fears of power and the hopes for freedom that lay behind their choice.*

JUSTICE HUGO L. BLACK

On May 12, 1952, less than a month after his seventy-ninth birthday,
Davis reached the summit of his appellate career. In an eighty-seven-
minute argument before an overflow audience in the Supreme Court,
he charged that President Harry S Truman had flagrantly breached
the Constitution of the United States when he had seized the steel industry in order to avert a nationwide strike. Truman's action, Davis
declared, in words as heartfelt as any he had ever uttered, was not only
a "usurpation" of power, not only a deed "without parallel in American
history," but "a reassertion of the kingly prerogative, the struggle
against which illumines all the pages of Anglo-Saxon history." [1]

« I »

Late in December 1951, contract talks between the United Steelworkers and the major steel producers had ground to a halt. At the
time, American and North Korean troops were locked in an artillery
duel in Korea, peace negotiaions were bogged down at Panmunjom,
and the cost of living was up roughly 12 per cent since the start of the
Korean War eighteen months earlier. Steelworkers' wages had risen

13.5 per cent and were at $1.80 an hour, while automobile workers were making $1.99 and coal miners $2.34 an hour. Net profits in steel were running about 15 per cent below those of 1950, but were still far above all previous levels. (Between 1945 and 1950, profits after taxes had increased 219 per cent, gross hourly earnings 60 per cent.) On November 22, 1951, the union had submitted twenty-two demands, among them a 15-cent wage increase, six paid holidays, overtime for Saturdays and Sundays, the union shop, and a guaranteed annual wage of $3000.[2]

The industry resolved to stand firm unless the Office of Price Stabilization granted a price increase. Eugene G. Grace of Bethlehem Steel announced that his company would have "no offer to make," and Benjamin F. Fairless of United States Steel indicated that his company had little hope of a voluntary settlement. They bargained only desultorily. His patience worn thin, Philip Murray, president of both the Steelworkers Union and the parent Congress of Industrial Organizations, called Fairless "an ordinary liar." (Fairless later admitted that there had been "a series of mistakes by all of us.") Meanwhile, industry leaders pushed for "price relief" in private talks with officials of the Office of Price Stabilization.[3]

The Administration was utterly unsympathetic. OPS regulations authorized price increases only after profits, before taxes, had fallen below 85 per cent of the average for the base years 1946–49, and three separate reports by government economists concluded that the industry could easily absorb "any remotely reasonable wage increase" under that formula. The steel companies, said Economic Stabilizer Roger S. Putman to Fairless, would have to bargain with their "own money." [4]

Murray's anger over the industry's failure to negotiate in good faith was heightened by warnings from the White House against disruption of the stabilization program. On December 18, Murray had the Steelworkers' Policy Committee schedule a shutdown for midnight, December 31. He also had the committee bind him to accept no government recommendation for a settlement without the approval of a special 3000-delegate convention. This prompted Truman, who had invoked the Taft-Hartley Act a dozen or so times previously, to order government lawyers to draw up a Taft-Hartley injunction. Under this threat, Murray had the binding resolution rescinded, though the strike deadline held. The President then buried the injunction.[5]

Truman was determined both to hold the line in prices and to prevent the slightest interruption in war production (there was about a thirty-day supply of steel on hand). He thought briefly of seizure but dropped the idea when his legal advisers said that they doubted existence of "a sound legal basis" for such action. He then referred the dispute to the Wage Stabilization Board, a procedure authorized by Title V of the Defense Production Act of 1950. Hopeful that the WSB would link wage recommendations to price increases, management agreed to cooperate. But labor balked. Only after Truman again threatened to invoke Taft-Hartley did the union postpone the strike, first to January 3, then to February 4. The President's decision to work through the WSB seemed sound at the time. The Taft-Hartley Act had been designed primarily for peacetime disputes. But the Wage Stabilization Board, as Truman later emphasized, had been established especially for defense industries and had been reaffirmed by Congress within the year. Furthermore, as one authority notes, Taft-Hartley provided no means for recommending a basis of settlement:

> Not to have used the WSB procedure would have amounted to a reversal of a previous decision, an overriding of the opinions of most of the industrial relations experts who had been consulted, and the repudiation of a tacit guarantee to labor.[6]

Although Davis did not enter the controversy directly until March 31, 1952, the industry's refusal to bargain seriously during the fall may have been influenced by an opinion he had given the Republic Steel Corporation during the steel strike of 1949. At that time, Attorney General Tom C. Clark had advised the President that he could seize property during national emergencies. Fearful that Truman might act, Republic officials had gone to Davis. Did the President actually possess such power? they asked.[7]

In an eleven-page, single-spaced formal opinion which staked out the strict constructionist ground he was later to stand on in oral argument, Davis had replied that he did not. No federal official, he declared, "has any power whatever except those derived either from an Act of Congress or directly from the Constitution itself. The existence of a national emergency may furnish the occasion for exercising a power which already exists under the Constitution or the laws; but the declaration of such an emergency cannot create the power itself." He further asserted that a seizure provision in the Selective Service Act of 1948 was meant to apply to factory owners who refused to give government orders priority, "certainly not" to the parties in labor disputes.[8]

Davis conceded that the theory that the Executive possesses "a broad

LEFT: The Davises attend a polo match

BELOW: "Mattapan," the Davis residence at Locust Valley, Long Island

Davis and his running mate, Governor Charles W. Bryan

Davis and his "distinctly unfriendly" riv William G. McAdoo

Davis in Clarksburg, August 1924

President Calvin Coolidge

anklin D. Roosevelt, Davis, and Al Smith at
Hyde Park

Robert M. LaFollette

Davis denounces the Ku Klux Klan

Professor Felix Frankfurter

Ferdinand Pecora, Carter Glass (wearing hat), and J. P. Morgan

Pecora and Davis confer

Davis counsels Morgan during the Pecora inquiry, May 1933

The Davises and Morgan aboard the *Corso*

Charles Evans Hughes

Rosika Schwimmer, Douglas Clyde Macintosh,
and Marie Averill Bland

Davis and Isador J. Kresel

Nicholas Murray Butler and Charles C.
Burlingham

Theodore Kiendl and Davis refuse to discuss the steel case Solicitor General Philip B. Perlma

Alger Hiss   Dr. J. Robert Oppenheimer

...is and Thurgood Marshall confer before arguing the school segregation case

Davis, before a House committee, testifies to Dulles' role in the selection of Hiss as president of the Carnegie Endowment

...indsay Almond, Attorney General of Virginia, Davis, and T. Justin Moore, chief counsel for Virginia

Governor James F. Byrnes presents a scroll of appreciation to Davis

LEFT: Davis in his office, n the end. The picture is of L Chief Justice Reading.

BELOW: Davis at the fish camp on the Sebatis Rive New Brunswick

and undefined inherent power to do almost anything which he conceives in the public interest . . . enjoys certain currency in some quarters." He insisted, however, that it had no foundation in law. For, unlike the powers of Congress, the powers of the President "are carefully and specifically enumerated, and there is no catch-all or general grant of authority to him." Even the constitutional admonition to execute the laws meant merely that the President was obligated to see that acts of Congress were faithfully carried out.[9]

Finally, Davis denied that seizure could be justified under the "so-called 'war powers.'" In the first place, the philosophy behind those powers was "alien to the spirit of the Constitution"; in the second, the nation was not then at war. Besides, the Taft-Hartley Act provided the means to resolve the dispute. Once Congress acted in a specific field, there was "even less reason than might otherwise exist for arguing that the matter may be dealt with under the vague theory of 'implied powers' of the Executive." [10]

« II »

For fourteen days in January and February, industry and union witnesses testified before a special six-man panel of the Wage Stabilization Board. Spokesmen for industry charged that the union's demands would necessitate price rises of from $5 to $15 a ton, predicted that elimination of the ten-cent wage differential in the South would lead to "totalitarianism," and labeled the guaranteed annual wage a form of unemployment insurance. Workers, they said, should put aside $15 a week (about a quarter of their take-home pay) for slack periods. They also spoke darkly of "communism" and asserted that the economic condition of no class in America, excluding the professional class, had deteriorated as much as had that of the managerial class. (Murray asked if that included Eugene Grace, whose salary alone was $438,000 in 1950.) At the same time, the industry refused to disclose to the Office of Price Stabilization its actual costs.[11]

Union economists countered that 60 per cent of all steelworkers made less than the minimum standard of "decency" set by the Department of Labor. But they were so confident that labor's failure to share proportionately in the extraordinary postwar profits made their case airtight that they were generally restrained. To give the WSB time to study the evidence, they agreed to defer the strike until March 23. In so doing, however, they made it plain that they regarded the eighty-two-day delay as the moral equivalent of a Taft-Hartley injunction's eighty-day "cooling off" period.[12]

On March 20, over the angry dissent of its industry members, the WSB recommended a twelve-and-a-half-cent increase retroactive to January 1, with two increases of two and a half cents to follow at six-month intervals. The Board also recommended the union shop, company incentive systems, paid holidays, time-and-a-quarter for Sundays, and a three-week vacation after twenty-five years. The total cost was estimated at between $5.50 and $6.50 a ton. This could have been absorbed under the original OPS regulations, though only by cutting profits drastically. Under the terms of the Capehart amendment to the Defense Production Act, however, the industry was authorized to increase prices by about $2.75 to cover war-induced costs. Truman eventually raised this to $4.50, but not until after Mobilization Director Charles E. Wilson had resigned in protest over the President's failure to stand on an offer of $5 which he (Wilson) had made in private negotiations, purportedly with Truman's acquiescence.[13]

Meanwhile Clarence Randall announced, for the eight or more companies involved, that the proposed package would cost $12 a ton. The United Steelworkers' secretary-treasurer, David J. McDonald, promptly added to the tension by declaring that Truman was "a rather friendly gentleman" and that labor would have faced a no-strike injunction if "a Bob Taft or some other reactionary President sat in the White House." (On March 29, two days after McDonald's remark and considerably in advance of the date he had set, Truman announced that he would not run for another term.) [14]

By then the union had agreed to a fourth postponement, to April 9, ninety-nine days beyond the deadline first set in December. The Republic Steel Corporation, which was alarmed by talk of seizure, had also asked Davis to update his opinion of October 1949 in the light of legislation enacted since the beginning of the Korean War.[15]

Davis again advised Republic that the President had no seizure powers in labor disputes. He further contended that the Defense Production Act of 1950 had reaffirmed Congress' intent that he should have none, and that Title II was a power to condemn by way of eminent domain. "Such a power is indeed a drastic one to exercise in . . . a labor dispute; and it is my opinion that . . . the language . . . precludes its application in such cases." He further noted that Title V referred specifically to labor disputes without authorizing seizure, and also that it authorized the President "to initiate voluntary conferences" (the WSB procedure, though Davis did not so call it). Adding that Congress had provided that there should be no action inconsistent with the Taft-Hartley Act or other applicable laws, he concluded that the President had neither "statutory authority" nor "undefined inherent powers" to seize the mills.[16]

Despite the quickening sense of crisis, hope for a settlement rose temporarily. The day after Davis sent his opinion to Republic Steel, Fairless gave Office of Price Stabilization Director Ellis Arnall the cost figures the OPS had been requesting for three months. On Wednesday, April 2, several small companies accepted the WSB recommendations. And on Thursday, Kaiser, the industry's most enlightened employer, followed suit. That same day, however, the industry as a whole countered with an offer of less than half the WSB package. This the union brushed aside contemptuously. Then, on Sunday night, April 6, Fairless attacked the Board's recommendations and urged the union to compromise. Speaking on U. S. Steel's "Theatre of the Air" program, he ignored Arnall's offer of a $4.50 price increase and baldly stated that the government had proposed no relief beyond the $2.75 authorized by the Capehart formula. He also condemned the union shop and added that it was hard to believe that the government would actually seize the mills.[17]

By Monday, April 7, the situation was desperate. The steelworkers were scheduled to walk out at 12:01 a.m. Wednesday, and neither side was disposed to make the slightest compromise. At three o'clock that afternoon, the President met with the Defense Mobilization Board and his principal advisers. Among them were Secretary of State Dean Acheson, Secretary of Defense Robert Lovett, and Gordon Dean of the Atomic Energy Commission. Lovett and some of the others felt that the President should invoke the Taft-Hartley Act rather than resort to seizure, but they did not push him. All deplored the impending strike, and all asserted that a prolonged work stoppage would have a disastrous impact upon the war and foreign commitments generally. Yet, judging by the affidavits they later filed, none made a truly compelling case for the existence of an emergency. Between assertions that the slightest stoppage would impede the war effort, their statements were strewn with adjectives such as "prolonged," "protracted," and "eventual." This meant (assuming that the Administration's real, but publicly unspoken, fears of Russian intervention in Korea were groundless) that the more time-consuming seizure provisions of the Selective Service Act might have been invoked to assure the flow of critical items. But in his mood of the moment, Truman was willing to allow no stoppage at all. Furthermore, Department of Justice lawyers had advised against relying on the Selective Service Act, presumably for the same reasons Davis had counseled Republic Steel that it was not applicable. Significantly, however, they had concluded that full seizure could be justified under the inherent power doctrine.[18]

Late Tuesday afternoon, April 8, Truman and Dr. John R. Steelman, Mobilization Director Wilson's replacement, met with Secretary of Commerce Charles Sawyer. The President explained that he was going to seize the steel industry in Sawyer's name, adding that it was the dirtiest job he had ever given anyone. Sawyer, a self-styled "conservative" Democrat, asked if he would have a free hand. Steelman assured him that no *"real"* commitments had been made to either side, but implied that Murray had been given some encouragement. "Mr. President," Sawyer then said, "this job will be tough enough as it is and I hope that your talk tonight will not make it any tougher." [19]

At 10:30 that night Truman went on television and radio to announce his decision to seize the industry. Early in the evening he had contemplated combining seizure with appointment of a Taft-Hartley board of inquiry, but when a union official reported at 8:00 p.m. that an uncontrollable wildcat strike would surely follow, he had dropped the idea. Now, beginning on a somber note, he warned that work stoppage would soon create a shortage of ammunition, delay the atomic energy program, and halt the production of airplane engines; the resultant failure of strength might enable "the forces of aggression . . . [to] break out in renewed violence and bloodshed" in many parts of the world. He further emphasized the need to prevent a runaway inflation and insisted that the WSB recommendations would "simply" enable the steel workers to catch up with other wage earners.[20]

About half way through, Truman lapsed into his old "give-'em-hell" oratory. "I think [the company managers] . . . are raising all this hullabaloo in an attempt to force the Government to give them a big boost in prices." Using *before*-tax figures, he added that a $3.00-per-ton increase would give the companies a profit of $17 or $18, and he compared that to the $11 they had made in the three years immediately preceeding the Korean War. "The plain fact is—though most people don't realize it—the steel industry has never been so profitable as it is today—at least not since the 'profiteering' days of World War I." And yet, he continued, the steel companies were demanding an increase of $12 a ton for a profit of $26 or $27 a ton. "That's about the most outrageous thing I ever heard of. . . . They want to double their money on the deal." [21]

In New York that very afternoon, industry leaders had persuaded themselves that seizure was "so monstrous" that it was inconceivable. Listening to the President that night, they were dumbstruck by his action and outraged by his three-quarters truths. "I felt physically ill," Clarence Randall recalled. "It seemed to me that all that I had learned of government from school days on, all that I had believed in with respect to the balance of powers . . . had suddenly been swept away. One man had coldly announced that his will was supreme, as Caesar had done, and Mussolini and Hitler." [22]

Twenty-four hours later Randall went on the air to reply in kind for the industry:

> . . . It is Harry S Truman, the man, who last night so far transgressed his oath of office, so far abused the power which is temporarily his, that he must now stand and take it.
> . . . He has seized the steel plants of the nation, the private property of one million people . . . without the slightest shadow of legal right. No law passed by the Congress gave him this power. He knows this.
> . . . I say, my friends, that the Constitution was adopted by our forefathers to prevent tyranny, not to create it. . . .
> . . . This evil deed, without precedent in American history, discharges a political debt to the C.I.O. Phil Murray now gives Harry S Truman a receipt marked, "paid in full." [23]

Struggling to control himself, Randall pointed out that steelworkers' wages had risen 13.5 per cent since the outbreak of war, the cost of living only 11 per cent. He then charged that the "so-called" public members of the WSB had been on labor's payroll. (Actually, as professional arbitrators in past disputes, they had been paid *jointly* by labor and industry.) Finally, Randall returned to the President. "But for downright distortion of fact, Harry Truman was at his magnificent best. . . . He tossed off vast figures of profits without telling the American people that he meant profits before taxes." [24]

Within weeks, fourteen separate resolutions to impeach Truman were introduced in Congress. The American Association of Newspaper Publishers and the United States Chamber of Commerce censured the President. Senator Bricker declared that Truman's action was "smacking of totalitarian philosophy." Lyndon B. Johnson said that the seizure showed a trend toward dictatorship. Pat McCarran announced that "we have lost the democracy that we have long loved." And Sena-

tor Joseph McCarthy blamed everything on the Council of Economic
Advisers' chairman, Leon Keyserling, whose wife, he said, was a communist. Meanwhile, Senator Taft launched his campaign for the presidential nomination with a slashing, yet thoughtful, attack similar to
the opinion Davis had given Republic Steel on March 31. Almost
alone, Wayne Morse, Herbert Lehman, and Hubert Humphrey defended the President. A Gallup Poll showed that 43 per cent of the
public disapproved of the seizure and 35 per cent approved. Among
manual workers, 40 per cent approved and 37 per cent disapproved.[25]

Shocked by the force of the reaction, Truman sent a measured message to Congress. He explained that, although government operation
of the mills was "thoroughly distasteful," the alternatives appeared to
be so much worse that he could not accept them. He added that Congress had the power to supersede his order, and he invited it to pass
remedial legislation. But in spite of the impeachment resolutions and
all the rest, Congress failed to act, nor did it respond to a second presidential request twelve days later. Not until after the Supreme Court
had heard and decided the case did both houses adopt a resolution,
proposed by Senator Harry F. Byrd, asking the President to invoke the
Taft-Hartley law.[26]

« III »

Twelve hours after the President announced the seizure, attorneys
for the industry asked the Federal District Court for the District of
Columbia to issue a temporary restraining order on the ground that
the government planned to raise wages and cram the union shop
down the industry's throat. Undaunted by Judge Alexander Holtzoff's
ruling that they had failed to show the likelihood of "irreparable damage," they came back the next day with motions for temporary and
permanent injunctions. This time Judge David A. Pine, former confidential clerk to James Clark McReynolds and an old acquaintance of
Davis, presided. Pine was a strict constructionist and a no-nonsense
craftsman who had been briefly in the headlines in 1945 for finding
the "Hollywood Ten" guilty of contempt. Although he seemed anxious to hear the motions, he dutifully disclosed that his wife owned
about a thousand dollars worth of Bethlehem stock. "Now," he said,
"if you wish to make any point of that . . . , this is the time to do
it." [27]

By April 24, when trial on the merits began, Davis Polk had entered the case as counsel for U. S. Steel. By then, too, Truman had already had Secretary Sawyer announce that he planned to grant some wage increases. This, the first of several blunders by the government, gave point to the companies' contention that irreparable damage was inevitable. Three times during the two-day hearing Judge Pine asked Assistant Attorney General Holmes Baldridge for an assurance that no changes would be made while the suit was still in the courts. But Solicitor General Philip Perlman, the Acting Attorney General, refused to let Baldridge give it. Only under pressure from Sawyer and the President did Perlman finally yield, and by the time he did so Judge Pine was already writing his opinion.[28]

Actually, Pine's determination to rule on the seizure itself made the matter academic. He was astounded when Davis' partner Kiendl insisted that all he wanted was a preliminary injunction against changing the conditions of employment. (Kiendl's brief did charge that the seizure itself was unconstitutional.) "I can't understand Mr. Kiendl's position," Pine said, turning to the other lawyers. "[He] asks me to find the Act illegal, and yet he wants to continue the illegality." Unsatisfied by Kiendl's explanation that he hoped merely to raise enough doubt about the legality of seizure to assure issuance of a temporary injunction on the conditions of employment, Pine replied that he had quite enough "patience" to hear out the ultimate question.[29]

Ordinarily, Kiendl's tactics would have been correct. Under what Paul Freund calls the "time-honored practice in equity on applications for temporary injunctions," Pine should have left the government in possession, while enjoining a grant of wage increases pending a factual determination of irreparable harm at a final hearing. Pine was so outraged by the seizure, however, that he insisted on ruling on a permanent injunction.[30]

As the hearing proceeded, Pine drove Assistant Attorney General Baldridge deeper and deeper into a hole. To the Judge's disgust, Baldridge tried to stand on the theory Davis had rejected in his two opinions for Republic Steel—that the President was empowered to take emergency action without statutory sanction:

THE COURT: If the emergency is great, it [the President's power] is unlimited, is it?

MR. BALDRIDGE: I suppose if you carry it to its logical conclusion, that is true. . . .

THE COURT: And that the Executive determines the emergencies and
              the courts cannot even review whether it is an emer-
              gency.
MR. BALDRIDGE: That is correct. . . .[31]

The more Baldridge talked, the deeper he sank. He declared at one
point that the Constitution imposed no limit on the powers of the
President. ("I have never heard that view expressed in any authoritative opinion of any court," Pine snapped.) He said at another that the
long history of Executive actions proved that Congress assumed the existence of an inherent power. ("I think that argument is something
like my suit," an industry attorney interjected. "I could not get a taxi-
cab at noon and it is all wet.") Relentlessly, Judge Pine pressed the be-
leaguered government counsel. "You are arguing for expediency. Isn't
that it?" "Well," Baldridge replied as a great gasp shook the courtroom, "you might call it that, if you like. But we say it is expediency
backed by power." [32]

Even Truman was sobered by Baldridge's extravagant claim. Earlier, the President had told reporters that "a lot of hooey" was being
handed out about the case. He had also come close to denying any
limitation whatever on the Executive's emergency powers: "There are
a lot of Presidents who have had to make decisions in emergencies . . .
but you will find it made the Republic better." But now he tried to
undo the damage. He sent a carefully phrased public letter explaining
his position to Charles S. "Casey" Jones, the World War I aviator. He
pointedly told Hubert Humphrey that he was "a constitutional President," after which the Minnesota Senator announced that Baldridge's
argument was bad law and a great disservice to the President. Finally,
Truman had Baldridge submit a supplemental memorandum to Judge
Pine:

> At no time have we urged any view that the President possesses power
> outside the Constitution, and our brief, filed with the court, is clear on
> that point. On the contrary, we have urged that the President must act
> within the Constitution, specifically Article II. . . . If the court under-
> stood us to say more, we respectfully ask that this memorandum be ac-
> cepted as the accurate statement of our views.[33]

The clarification came too late, and it would not have influenced
Pine in any event. On April 29, in a courtroom jammed with newspapermen poised to run for the telephone, Pine declared that he was un-

willing simply to enjoin changes of working conditions, as Kiendl had requested. Matters, he insisted, were in a "materially different posture" than they had been when the industry was first seized, and he could not confine his order to a temporary restraining order because of its "stultifying" implications. The damages to the companies were irreparable in "fact," and the "wrongful" actions should not be allowed to stand. Manifestly, the government's contention required discussion "of the fundamental principles of constitutional government, which I have always understood are immutable." [34]

Only one sentence in the 4000-word opinion referred to the Taft-Hartley Act: the government, said Pine, presupposes that the Act "is inadequate when it has not yet been tried, and is the statute provided by Congress to meet just such an emergency." Otherwise, in words that the New York *Herald Tribune* declared rang "with the defiant note with which justice . . . has dared in great epochs of freedom to oppose deeds not sanctioned by law," he repudiated the concept of inherent powers and ordered the properties returned to the companies. Never before had an administrative action of a President been enjoined.[35]

Within the hour the steelworkers struck. "This is a fight between U.S. Steel and the U.S.A.," a union official announced. "We're going to find out which is the biggest." The sentiment was hardly unanimous. Secretary Sawyer urged Truman to resort to the Taft-Hartley Act. The Senate judiciary committee approved, without public hearings, a resolution for a constitutional amendment against seizure of private property. The House labor committee recommended that the Wage Stabilization Board be abolished. And the press made Judge Pine an instant hero. Even the American Civil Liberties Union, a perennial critic of the steel industry's long, violent, and often unlawful repression of labor, endorsed Pine's decision.[36]

The day after the decision Perlman himself went into the Court of Appeals to plead for a stay. His voice throbbing with passion, he shouted that the seizure was "for the benefit of all the people" and that its reinstitution would "get those men . . . back before the furnaces get cold." At 6:50 that evening, by a five-to-four majority, the Court of Appeals stayed Pine's order. On the following day, by a similar majority, it rejected the industry's request that changes in working conditions be prohibited during the stay. Philip Murray, who was so wrought up that he told the White House he would go to jail if necessary to gain justice, then called off the strike after being promised that the government would institute a cost-of-living increase. Twenty-

four hours later the Supreme Court agreed to hear the case and ordered Sawyer not to change the conditions of employment.[37]

« IV »

Davis had taken no active part in the proceedings since submitting
his opinion to Republic Steel on March 31. Rarely, however, had he
been so certain that one party to a suit was more wrong in law, in
principle, and in policy. "There is not the slightest doubt," he wrote
privately, "that the President's action . . . is without legal warrant—
constitutional or statutory. It is an act of pure usurpation and I
should hope that Congress as well as the courts would so declare." He
was delighted, accordingly, when the industry's corps of attorneys
asked him to make the sole oral argument. "I had some very able colleagues who stepped aside," he graciously explained; besides, "multiple
arguments . . . are always dangerous." [38]

News of Davis' involvement cheered a meeting of the Department of
Commerce's Council of Economic Advisers down at the Homestead in
Hot Springs, Virginia, where Davis had made his decision to go to
Wall Street thirty-two years earlier. He had many admirers and well-
wishers "among this very interesting and cordial group," reported his
partner Sunderland. Charles Wilson of General Motors was "praying"
for him. Others, including the dean of the Harvard Business School,
were similarly moved. Meanwhile, the Railroad Brotherhoods drew up
an *amicus* brief opposing the seizure.[39]

Back in New York, Porter Chandler and a half-dozen assistants
began to work almost around the clock, recasting their brief (they
were representing U. S. Steel) for the Supreme Court. At midnight
they would send out for coffee and sandwiches, then, too weary to go
on, they would rush the completed sections to the printer between
2:30 and 4:00 a.m. Four or five hours later they would begin the process anew, until, four days after they had begun, they had produced a
persuasive and lucid 175-page document. It included a discourse on
the *Ship Money* and other English precedents, which Judge Pine had
dismissed as irrelevant when Kiendl had dilated on them. But it bore
most sharply on the government's failure to invoke the Taft-Hartley
law and its reliance upon "the nebulous theory of a 'broad residuum
of powers' in the President and of his 'aggregate' of powers." Interruption of the production of steel for the Korean War, it emphasized, in a
section headed "What This Case Does *Not* Involve," was in no sense

the issue; the means to meet "those vital needs . . . were available . . . and are available" in the Taft-Hartley Act. Neither did the case involve the merits of the wage issue. "The sole issue . . . is whether Mr. Sawyer may seize private property, impose by administrative fiat his own settlement of a labor dispute, and proceed to confiscate private property. . . ." [40]

Davis did not participate in the drafting, although he read the proofs carefully and sometimes suggested minor changes. Mainly he sat in his office, reading cases and jotting down points to emphasize in his oral argument. Once he went to the firm's library, drew several volumes off the shelves, and sat down at a long table to peruse them. "We were so thrilled," one of the librarians recalled. "Mr. Davis hadn't done that in years, and some of the senior partners had never done it." Davis also spent much time fencing with the string of company attorneys who wrote, telephoned, and sought him out in his office. "He fended them off without offense," Sunderland said; "he maintained his independence." [41]

Davis' oral argument before the Supreme Court on May 12 was his one hundred and thirty-eighth since he had first addressed that tribunal in the *Pipe Line* cases on October 13, 1913. He spoke vigorously, if a little less rapidly than in the past, used few dramatic gestures, and held his reading glasses in his right hand except when referring to a large loose-leaf notebook in front of him. For emphasis, he would lower rather than raise, his voice. As one reporter noted, his sturdy figure seemed "to personify the spirit of constitutionalism, his voice . . . that of history itself." [42]

For fifteen minutes, with all the lucidity of old, Davis stated the facts. He then surveyed the history of property seizures. His conclusion, he said in the deep, dispassionate tone that lent his utterances a kind of unofficial authority, was that the seizure power was drawn from legislative sources and had been granted grudgingly for limited periods with clear safeguards. It was true that the Court had ruled in the *Russell* case of 1871 that private property could be seized in instances of extreme necessity. It had specified, however, that "the public danger must be immediate, imminent, and impending, and the emergency . . . such as will not admit of delay or a resort to any other source of supply." He did not know how "the English language could provide a better catalogue of adjectives" to specify the requirements of emergency. Never, he added, had there been a seizure of property when an existing statute provided an alternative.[43]

Davis hammered hard on Truman's failure to invoke Taft-Hartley, asserting that the Act's provision for an eighty-day stay ruled out justification of the seizure under the *Russell* or any other doctrine. The President did not have to use the Act; he could resort to it or not, as he wished. But the fact of its existence removed the option of seizure. As for the contention that the time lost in getting a Taft-Hartley injunction would have impeded the war effort, the record showed that in one recent longshoremen's strike the injunction had been issued on the fourth day; "neither the military nor the economic structure of the country would have fallen" had a similar delay occurred in the steel case.[44]

Davis also scorned the government's claim that the industry could sue for damages after the seizure. "That is a gesture so generous it is quite appealing," but the Department of Justice "cannot give to the court what the court is forbidden to entertain." Then, speaking from the depths of the conviction instilled in his father by Judge Brockenbrough almost a full century earlier and nurtured in himself by both his father and Dean John Randolph Tucker forty years after that, he expressed astonishment at the government's statement that Judge Pine's reliance upon "immutable principles" embodied "a discredited technique of constitutional interpretation."

> Is it or is it not an immutable principle that our Government is one of limited powers? Is it or is it not an immutable principle that we have a . . . tripartite system of legislation, execution and judgment? Is it or is it not an immutable principle that the powers of government are based on a government of laws and are not based on a government of men? You cannot dispose of those immutable principles merely by a seizure of this kind.

As he neared the end of his eighty-seven-minute argument, Davis tossed his notebook on the table, fastened his eyes on the high coffered ceiling, and averred in low somber tones that Jefferson had summed up in one sentence the theory that the occupants of public office are servants of the people—"In questions of power, let no more be said of confidence in man, but bind him down from mischief by the chains of the Constitution."[45]

Seldom, wrote Chalmers Roberts of the Washington *Post,* "has a courtroom sat in such silent admiration for a lawyer at the bar."[46]

There had been only one untoward interruption. How, asked Justice Frankfurter, did Davis square his assertion that President Truman had no right to seize the steel industry with his contention in the *Midwest Oil* case of 1915 that former President Taft had possessed power to remove public lands from entry without statutory authority? The courts, Davis' brief as Solicitor General had said in defense of Taft, should

> avoid a slavish formalism which can only serve to ossify the Government. . . . The Executive may be under a grave constitutional duty to act for the national protection in situations not covered by the acts of Congress, and in which, even, it may not be said that his action is the direct expression of any particular one of the independent powers which are granted to him specifically by the Constitution. . . . Being for the public benefit . . . [such] acts have seldom been challenged in the courts.[47]

Davis replied simply that he had taken "a somewhat rather broad ground." Then, after a momentary pause, he drew a chuckle from the bench by quoting the note Justice Day had written him at the time: "And you, a Jeffersonian Democrat, have done this thing." Only Truman's intimate friend and appointee, Chief Justice Vinson, followed up. "Mr. Davis confesses," he remarked with a smile, "that he had certain ambitions that perhaps he attributes to the present Solicitor General." [48]

Perlman, who followed for the government, stood in striking physical contrast to Davis. A homely man whose few wisps of dark hair curved gently up from his shining head, he wore a bulging cutaway and striped trousers which reached to the floor and were too large all around. Yet he was an effective, if unpolished, advocate; in five years as Solicitor General he had won forty-five cases and lost only ten. Now, at the age of sixty-two, he faced the heaviest odds of his career, and he knew it. His only hope was to convince the Court that the crisis was so grave, the statutory options so ineffectual, that the President had had no recourse but to fall back on his residual powers.[49]

The Court, said Perlman in opening, had just listened to an eloquent argument, one designed to turn its mind from the facts in the case and from the reasons for the President's action:

> Very little if anything was said . . . about the condition in the world today, about the struggle in which this nation is engaged, and practically nothing at all about the necessity, the vital necessity, to keep the plants . . . in operation without interruption of any kind. And it is argued that your Honors should practically ignore that situation and

pass on some Constitutional interpretation of the powers that the President exercised.

Any suspension of production, Perlman insisted, would have imperiled the nation's security; to preserve it the President had resorted to both his residual powers and those conferred upon him by Congress.[50]

That was one of the few sustained statements Perlman managed to make. Justices Frankfurter, Black, Douglas, Jackson, and Reed interrupted him so often that the Chief Justice complained that the Solicitor General "bounced around" so much that he never completed a subject, and Perlman himself implored the bench to "let me finish." Meanwhile, the Justices demanded that he specify the statutes justifying the seizure. "I'm relying on every single law . . . ," he started to say. "That doesn't help me," Douglas snapped. "Would you mind sometime giving me just one single law this seizure helped to enforce?" Truman's friend, Sherman Minton, tried to help with a soft question or two, only to be jumped upon by Frankfurter. Even Davis' sympathies were engaged. "My heart bled for Perlman," he said afterwards. "They gave him a terrible time." [51]

Through a forty-minute extension of time on Tuesday, the Solicitor General tried hard to persuade the Court that the Taft-Hartley Act had not been bypassed deliberately. The President, he contended, had the choice of invoking it on January 1 or of asking the union to refrain voluntarily from striking while the WSB drew up recommendations. The second course had seemed to be more in the public interest at the time, but now management was saying that he should have used Taft-Hartley. "They didn't say that in December." Frankfurter then asked why the government had failed to requisition facilities under the terms of the Defense Production Act. Perlman replied that this would have necessitated condemnation suits in every Judicial District in the United States; perhaps, he gently added, the Justice had confused the Defense Production Act with the Selective Service law. Near the end of Perlman's long ordeal, Frankfurter and Jackson pounced upon him for denying on Monday that the President had acted under his war powers and asserting on Tuesday that "we are at war" and that seizure was essential to the war effort.[52]

In an extraordinary display of confidence, Davis used only ten of his more than sixty allotted minutes for rebuttal. First, he underscored his conclusion that Title V of the Defense Production Act forbade procedures inconsistent with the Taft-Hartley Act in labor disputes. Next,

he defended the "irreparable damage" thesis by emphasizing that seizure, and especially the announced plan to raise wages, had compromised the companies' relations with their employees. Finally, he
heaped scorn on Perlman's contention that the companies were treating the matter as a normal suit: "We are asking the court to treat it as
an abnormal case . . . without parallel in American history." [53]

«   V   »

A minute or two after the Court convened on Monday, June 2, less
than three weeks later, Chief Justice Vinson solemnly announced that
routine business would wait on the reading of the opinions in the steel
seizure case. Justice Black then put on his thick horn-rimmed glasses
and began to read in his resonant Alabama half-drawl. At the end of a
seven-and-a-half-page opinion remarkable for its paucity of citations
and its failure to examine the actual development of the emergency
and implied powers doctrines over a hundred and sixty years of constitutional interpretation, he pronounced the seizure unconstitutional for
a six-to-three majority. After observing that prior cases had "cast
doubt" on the right to recover damages for "unlawful" takings, he
pointed out that Congress, in framing the Taft-Hartley Act, had explicitly rejected seizure. He also noted that the President had failed to
root his order in the seizure provisions of either the Defense Production Act or the Selective Service Act. But he thrust hardest in support
of the proposition that no emergency, not even one created by war,
could alter the fact that Article I vested the lawmaking power exclusively in Congress:

> The Founders of the Nation entrusted the lawmaking power to Con-
> gress alone in both good and bad times. It would do no good to recall
> the historical events, the fears of power and the hopes for freedom that
> lay behind their choice. Such a review could but confirm our holding
> that this seizure order cannot stand.[54]

Four other Justices, Frankfurter, Douglas, Jackson, and Burton, concurred in both the judgment and Black's opinion, though all amplified or qualified his words in statements of their own. A sixth, Clark,
concurred in the judgment but not the opinion. Chief Justice Vinson entered a vehement, forty-four-page dissent in which Justices Reed and
Minton concurred.[55]

For a full hour, his voice frequently rising and his words often dripping sarcasm, Vinson echoed the government's contentions on point after point. He cited Marshall's warning that the Constitution must be "adapted to the various crises of human affairs," reviewed the long history of independent Executive actions, and derided the majority's "messenger boy" concept of the presidency. The Chief Justice even read at length from Davis' "excellent" brief in the *Midwest Oil* case. He also chided Justice Jackson for his defense, while Attorney General, of President Roosevelt's seizure of the North American Aviation Company plant six months before Pearl Harbor. Jackson, he said, to a burst of laughter up and down the bench, stated his opinion as vigorously and as forcefully at that time "as he ordinarily does now." [56]

Contrary to the popular impression at the time, the majority had not really upheld Judge Pine's and Davis' sweeping rejection of the doctrine of implied powers. Only Justice Douglas accepted Black's literal construction of the separation of powers without qualification. Frankfurter insisted that enforcement was "more complicated and flexible" than Black allowed; and in a long concurring opinion which rebuked the Chief Justice for quoting Davis' *Midwest Oil* brief, given the "well-known astigmatism of advocates," he left the matter of implied powers suspended. Justice Burton also affirmed the implied powers doctrine, but he agreed with Frankfurter that Congress' express refusal to write seizure provisions into the Taft-Hartley Act was controlling in this case. Justice Clark echoed the opinion that he, as Attorney General, had given Truman in 1949. The President, he insisted, possessed "extensive" authority in times of crisis, and it made no difference whether it was called "residual," "inherent," "moral," "implied," "aggregate," "emergency," or otherwise. Nevertheless, the fact that Congress had laid down specific seizure provisions in the Selective Service Act, to say nothing of the mediation procedures of the Taft-Hartley law, made it mandatory for the President to "follow" them.[57]

Only Justice Jackson seemed to perceive the true subtlety and complexity of the issue. In a long, graceful essay which went far beyond Black's mechanistic approach to the separation of powers, he contended, in John P. Roche's persuasive analysis, that "the critical point was not that presidential autonomy violated the principle of the separation of powers, but that irresponsible presidential autonomy . . . did breach a basic principle of American constitutionalism: that the actions of the executive must be based on community consensus." Had Congress and the public agreed with the President that the emergency was real, urgent, and grave, then the long line of precedents upholding the inherent power doctrine would have been controlling. But there had been nothing remotely approaching a consensus on that point. Jackson then warned that the Court should be the last, rather than the first, to sanction the growth of presidential power: "With all its defects, delays and inconveniences, men have discovered no technique for long preserving free government except that the Executive be under the law, and the law be made by parliamentary deliberations." [58]

Yet Jackson, like Douglas and Frankfurter, made it clear that he did not regard Harry S Truman as an incipient dictator. (Douglas had called him "a kindly President," and Frankfurter had said that it was "absurd to see a dictator in a representative product of the sturdy democratic traditions of the Mississippi Valley.") He had no fear, said Jackson, that Truman would "plunge us straight-way into dictatorship"; the real concern was the gradual accretion of Executive power.[59]

Any possibility that the case would become a landmark in the traditional sense of that term was destroyed by the austere simplicity of Justice Black's majority opinion and the extraordinary diversity of the concurring opinions. Edward S. Corwin was so disgusted that he subtitled an article on the case "A Judicial Brick Without Straw." It would go down, he asserted, "as an outstanding example of the *sic volo, sic jubeo* frame of mind into which the Court is occasionally maneuvered by the public context of [a] . . . case." Paul Freund suggested that the case should never have reached the Supreme Court, and that the Court should not have decided on the validity of the seizure in the posture in which it did reach the Court. Another scholar predicted that the majority's evasion of the question of the existence of a national emergency, coupled with its failure to recognize the existence of a conflict among statutory powers, would confine the decision "to its very special facts." What had happened, Corwin contended, was that the Court had come to the right conclusion for the wrong reasons; only Clark, guided by Marshall's opinion in *Little v. Barreme*, had had the "courage" to pursue to its logical end the line of reasoning suggested by Frankfurter, Jackson, and Burton in their references to the Taft-Hartley Act.[60]

Still, there was no stripping the case of the symbolic importance that Davis, Judge Pine, and Justices Black and Douglas had read into it. The Court, said *Time,* in a generalization which captured the mood of the nation, "decided that the President of the U. S. has no powers other than those named in the Constitution or derived from acts of Congress." Even Paul Freund agreed in part: The suit echoed "the ancient voices of Bracton and Coke proclaiming that not even the King is above the law; and this principle is so greatly to be cherished that perhaps its reassertion is never untimely." [61]

Davis himself never commented on the subtleties of the case. He believed that the decision should have been unanimous, and he scarcely concealed his contempt for the dissenters. "I really do not see how any man who has a certificate for admission to the bar could write an opinion sustaining the President's action." Most of the Justices' minds, he surmised, were made up before they heard the arguments.[62]

Meanwhile, he quietly enjoyed the congratulatory messages piled high on his desk. "I'm proud of you," Charles Burlingham wrote. "We all are. . . . How wise Steel was to have but one lawyer and that one you." From Boston came a report that Charles Wyzanski, the brilliant federal judge who, as a young government attorney in 1937, had defeated Davis in the *Associated Press* case, was gratified by Davis' "magnificent performance." Learned Hand was also impressed. At breakfast the day after Davis' argument, so the Judge wrote in his almost indecipherable scrawl, his wife had held up a copy of the *Herald Tribune* showing a photograph of Davis striding through the plaza of the Supreme Court building and said: "There, now that's the picture of a really distinguished man." [63]

Davis took the plaudits lightly. "The most I can say is what Joffre said after the battle of the Marne, that he did not know who won it, he only knew who would have been blamed if it had been lost." The only thing that got his "goat," he feigned to protest, were the newspapers' repeated references to his age; "the final blow fell when one of them spoke of me as 'venerable.' " He even refused to allow his oral argument to be printed because the stenographic transcript was so garbled that he feared that it would put down more or less than he actually said. "So my oral argument vanishes, as most oral deliverances should, into the limbo of the past." [64]

To Eleanor Belmont alone—the "heart" of his old age—did he intimate how strongly he felt: "I had given (and been paid for) two formal written opinions that the president had no power of seizure. I think those opinions had something to do with the resistance the steel companies put up. So I *had* to win." [65]

CHAPTER 28

The Segregation Case
of 1954

Somewhere, sometime, to every principle comes a moment of repose when it has been so often announced, so confidently relied upon, so long continued, that it passes the limits of judicial discretion and disturbance.

JOHN W. DAVIS IN THE UNITED STATES
SUPREME COURT, DECEMBER 7, 1953

Nine months before the steel seizure case, Governor James F. Byrnes of South Carolina had come up to New York to confer with Davis. The former Secretary of State and onetime Supreme Court Justice had served with Davis in Congress forty years earlier and had long regarded him as "the ablest constitutional lawyer" of his time. He asked him to defend South Carolina in the appeal to the Supreme Court in a school desegregation suit brought by the National Association for the Advancement of Colored People. Byrnes was determined to prevent "the politicians in Washington and the Negro agitators in South Carolina" from disrupting "the Southern way of life," and he had sworn to abandon the public school system rather than allow the races to mix. He was confident, however, that the Supreme Court would affirm the fifty-five-year-old "separate but equal" doctrine, and he impressed upon Davis the extraordinary effort he was then making to raise Negro school facilities to the same level as those of white schools. Davis listened receptively, perused the record after Byrnes left, and agreed to take the case a few days later. He was confident that they would win, and he refused to accept a retainer.[1]

Davis' commitment to what many sophisticated observers had already pronounced a lost cause distressed a number of his partners. Many of them opposed segregation, and some had long supported Negro causes. As tactfully as they could, several senior partners suggested that Davis withdraw. His daughter added her voice to theirs, but to no avail. As one of his friends said, "he simply didn't give a damn what people thought." And even if he had cared, he was so convinced that South Carolina was right and the Negro plaintiffs were wrong that he would have felt duty-bound to honor Byrnes' request. "Mr. Davis was a Southerner," his chief assistant recalled. "This was one case he was personally involved in. Normally he seldom changed a brief; this time he wrote much of it." [2]

« I »

The suit's origins went back to 1948, when the parents of Harry Briggs, Jr., and several other Negro children in the low-country county of Clarendon had asked the United States District Court to require school officials to supply school buses. They had been emboldened to act by the Truman administration's civil rights rhetoric, the course of judicial decisions elsewhere, and, especially, the favorable rulings handed down by District Judge J. Waties Waring in two recent civil rights cases.

President Roosevelt had reluctantly appointed Judge Waring to the bench in 1942, at the instance of Senators Burnet Maybank and Ellison "Cotton Ed" Smith, the foul-speaking racist whom F.D.R. had tried to purge from the Senate in 1938. Soon after his confirmation, the sixty-two-year-old Charleston aristocrat's own white supremacist views began to change. He insisted that blacks be treated with dignity in court, refused to let whites call black witnesses by their first names, and integrated the jury box, the spectators' section, and the restaurants in which the jurors ate. Even his bitterest editorial critic, the Charleston *News and Courier,* would concede on his retirement that, aside from his "crusading" on race, he had comported himself with "judicial dignity, intelligence, and ability." In his first case with racial overtones, Waring sent a white man to the penitentiary for keeping a black youth in peonage. ("The man ought to have been sent to jail," a white South Carolinian wrote the Judge afterwards, adding, inferentially, that he and his friends would not have had the courage to find

him guilty, had they been in the Judge's place.) Then, in 1945, Waring ruled that Negro teachers had to be put on the same salary schedule as white teachers. Thurgood Marshall, the attorney for the National Association for the Advancement of Colored People, was astounded. He had expected the "usual legal head-whipping," Marshall
recalled, but "it turned out to be the only case I ever tried with my
mouth hanging open half of the time." As Waring mused years later,
"By becoming a judge, I gradually attained a passion for justice."

Many white South Carolinians had endorsed the teachers-pay decision. The *News and Courier* expressed gratification that "evasion, double dealing and trickery" would have to stop, and the College of
Charleston gave the Judge an honorary degree that June. Two years
later the good will began to dissipate when Waring ruled that South
Carolina's all-white Democratic party was unconstitutional. ("Negroes
have thanked me for giving them the right to vote," he remarked
shortly before his death, "but my colleagues in the law know that I
gave them nothing. The right to vote belonged to them as much as to
me.") Immediately after that decision, Judge Waring ruled that South
Carolina must offer blacks law school facilities equal to those of whites
at the University of South Carolina, *"or furnish none to anyone."* (Italics his.) Although many fair-minded whites around the state endorsed
both decisions openly, a widening group of old Charleston friends
began to snub the Judge and his family.

Determined to circumvent the all-white primary decision, the Democratic leadership transformed the state party into a private club in the
spring of 1948; members were required, among other things, to take a
loyalty oath affirming their belief in, and support of, "the social, religious and educational separation of the races." A number of liberal
white Southerners protested privately to Judge Waring. "Thanks to
men like [Governor Strom] Thurmond, the South has become a
stench in the nostrils of the civilized world," wrote one Virginian. Others, native-born South Carolinians, said as much or more. The party
leadership retreated only slightly, and in July Waring struck down the
new rules and threatened with imprisonment anyone who violated his
order to keep the party open. "It is a pity and a shame," the Judge
said in court afterwards, "when a Federal Judge has to tell you how to
act like an American citizen." This prompted Representative Mendel
Rivers to call Waring a "monster" with "lemon juice flowing in his
frigid and calculating veins," and Representative W. J. B. Dorn to call

for his impeachment. Yet a residue of good will, most of it silent, remained. As a white woman from upstate wrote privately, "Thank God South Carolina can still produce a Judge Waring."

Nevertheless, the ostracism of the Judge, which had begun among a small group when he divorced his wife of thirty-two years in 1945, continued to increase.* Even his daughter, who visited him that summer, found that she and her father were "utter strangers to the rest of the people." Goaded by editorial criticism and by abusive telephone calls, day and night, Waring declared, in a speech before the New York Lawyers Guild in October, that "the South should not be left alone to deal with racial problems in its own way." Two weeks later, after ignoring a request by the Ku Klux Klan that he modify his injunction against discrimination in the Democratic party, Judge Waring reaffirmed it, to the gratification of the White House. "I wish," wrote President Truman, that "we had more Federal judges like you." Thereafter, Waring's off-the-bench statements became increasingly biting and unjudicial.

The Judge's new wife, a vivacious, outspoken Northerner who had at first charmed many of Waring's friends, exacerbated the situation. Encouraging him to sharpen his developing understanding of the race problem, she introduced him to W. J. Cash's *Mind of the South* and Gunnar Myrdal's *American Dilemma*. "I couldn't take it at first," he said years later. "I used to say it wasn't true, it couldn't be. I'd put the books down so troubled that I couldn't look at them." After their ostracism had become more or less total, Mrs. Waring persuaded the Judge to visit blacks socially and to receive them in their home. Then, in January 1950, at a meeting of the black branch of the Charleston YWCA, she proclaimed that white Southerners in general were "a sick, confused, and decadent people . . . full of pride and . . . morally weak and low." She added that South Carolina was a "Dixiecrat Gestapo." A month later the Judge told a Negro audience in a Harlem church: "We don't have a Negro problem in the South; we have a White problem." Soon afterwards, a cross was burned on the Warings'

* There is a continuing debate over how much Judge Waring's liberal racial views resulted from the influence of his second wife, how much his ostracism was caused by his divorce, and how much the ostracism reflected a natural reaction to Mrs. Waring's harsh statements about white Southerners. This matter has been thoroughly explored by Robert L. Terry in a doctoral dissertation, "J. Waties Waring, Spokesman for Racial Justice in the New South" (University of Utah, 1970), and the facts and their chronology seem to be as I have set them forth here.

lawn, a chunk of concrete was thrown through their front window, and 20,000 South Carolinians signed a petition for the Judge's impeachment. The obscene phone calls mounted, Mrs. Waring was jostled when strolling on the sidewalks, and drug-store gangs shouted "prostitute" and other epithets as she passed by. Firm in the conviction that they were morally right, the Warings continued to denounce white supremacists in speeches and interviews.[3]

In May 1950, the parents of Harry Briggs and the other black children returned to court to demand that Negro schools in District 22 of Clarendon County be raised to the same level as white schools. Although conditions had improved since 1940, when the annual per capita outlay had been $6.25 for each white child and $0.66 for each black child, inequality still pervaded the entire school system. There were 80 Negro high schools and 301 white high schools in the state. These serviced a school-age population that was 42 per cent black. Five white public institutions of higher learning received $4,500,000 in operating funds, the lone black agricultural and mechanical college only $600,-000. In Clarendon County, where black pupils outnumbered whites by three to one, 59 per cent of the funds went to the white schools. In District 22, which had 298 whites and 2259 blacks, the disparity was even worse.[4]

Shortly before the equalization suit was scheduled to come before Judge Waring's court, the NAACP altered its strategy. Heartened by the Supreme Court's June 1950 ruling, in *Sweatt v. Painter,* that the University of Texas must integrate its law school, it had Briggs expand the suit to include an attack on segregation *per se.* By November 17, the day of the pre-trial conference, Waring also had decided that the time had come for a frontal attack on segregation. All of his previous decisions had been firmly grounded on precedents set by higher courts; what had distinguished his judicial performance to that point had simply been the forcefulness of his opinions and his insistence that his rulings not be evaded. As he had explained to a magazine writer that January, however, he had gradually come to perceive the "illogicalities" in segregation, and "suddenly the whole . . . system appeared absurd." He now informed Thurgood Marshall that his pleadings only "partially raised the issue"; the NAACP, he said, should bring in a new suit, directly challenging the "separate but equal" doctrine and raising the "issue for all time as to whether a state can segregate by race in its schools." This Marshall did.[5]

Governor-elect Byrnes then prepared, as he frankly confessed, to

forestall an unfavorable ruling by overcoming "a hundred years of neglect" of Negro education through a massive injection of funds. "Except for the professional agitators," he declared in his inaugural address in January 1951, "what the colored people want, and what they
are entitled to, is equal facilities in their schools." That spring, the legislature authorized a $75 million bond issue. It also honored the Gov-
ernor's request for strong anti-Ku Klux Klan legislation and a series of
"preparedness" measures authorizing lease or sale of the public schools
in the event the courts struck down segregation.[6]

Late in May, a three-judge District Court, headed by Circuit Judge
John J. Parker and including Judge Waring, heard oral argument in
the *Briggs* case. Parker, who was senior Circuit Judge in the United
States and the most respected jurist in the South, was cut of the same
legal cloth as Davis. As the *New Republic* said in a commentary
(probably written by Felix Frankfurter) on President Hoover's nomination of Parker to the Supreme Court in 1930, his opinions were "decisive and solid," "state the existing law carefully," and show "considerable . . . power in presenting a mass of material in clear and orderly
fashion." But they failed to display "a spark of inspiration," were
dependent on the reasoning of others, and gave "no evidence as yet of
a power to adjust the law to important new conditions." [7]

Parker had favored restriction of Negro suffrage before he went on
the bench, and in 1927 he had upheld the "yellow dog" contract in a
case in which he had little alternative but to uphold it. On these
counts the NAACP and the American Federation of Labor had
mounted a full-scale campaign against his nomination to the Supreme
Court, and the Senate, by a two-vote margin, had refused to confirm
his appointment. More than ability and integrity were necessary, Senator George W. Norris of Nebraska had explained. "Everyone who as-
cends to that holy bench should have in his heart and mind the intention . . . of discarding if necessary the old precedents of barbarous
days and construing the Constitution and the laws in the light of a
modern day." Rising above his bitterness of the moment, Judge Parker
remained on the Court of Appeals for the Fourth Circuit. Although he
never achieved the intellectual distinction of a Learned Hand, his
commanding presence, superb legal craftsmanship, and notable services to the profession on a half-dozen or more fronts gave his judicial
utterances great weight, especially in the South. In time, many men
who had voted against his confirmation came to regret their decision.
Indeed, Judge Waring's decision in the salary equalization case had

merely followed the precedent Parker had boldly established in 1940 in *Alston v. School Board of Norfolk*. In 1947, furthermore, Judge Parker had upheld Waring in the all-white primary case, saying that "The disfranchised can never speak with the same force as those who were able to vote." As Waring himself conceded, Parker was "an extremely able judge who knows the law and follows the law, but quite unwillingly, in the Southern country." [8]

For two days in late May of 1951, Parker, Waring, and District Judge George Bell Timmerman of Columbia, South Carolina, a staunch segregationist, heard a battery of NAACP lawyers argue that Clarendon County's black schools were patently inferior to its white schools and that segregation flouted the Fourteenth Amendment. In eighty years, observed Thurgood Marshall, chief counsel for Briggs *et al.*, the only evidence of the state's "good faith" was "an inferior collection of Negro schools that need $40,000,000 right now to bring them up to white school standards." Relying heavily on the testimony of a half-dozen social scientists, the NAACP attorneys insisted that "scientific evidence" proved that segregation was harmful to black children. Robert McC. Figg, Jr., an able Charleston corporation lawyer, and S. Emory Rogers, a vehement local white supremacist, represented South Carolina. They conceded that the schools were in fact unequal, and they pleaded for "reasonable" time to equalize them. But they grounded their case on the proposition that segregation statutes had long been recognized as "a valid exercise of legislative power." They also went far beyond narrow considerations of law (as the NAACP attorneys had also done) by warning that disruption of the status quo would produce "dangerous tensions and unrest." [9]

On June 23, in flat, judicial language devoid of moral outrage over the injustice his words struck down, Judge Parker held, for himself and Judge Timmerman, that the Negro facilities were unequal. He enjoined the authorities to equalize them "promptly" and to report back within six months. In an analysis that influenced Davis profoundly, he further ruled that segregation was constitutional. Leaning heavily on the "separate but equal" doctrine laid down in *Plessy v. Ferguson* in 1896, he noted that neither the Texas law school decision nor a companion case from Oklahoma, *McLaurin v. Board of Regents,* had overturned that doctrine explicitly. Segregation, he insisted, was a matter of "legislative policy" and the federal courts were "powerless" to interfere with it. Taking judicial notice of "reason and experience," he further asserted that segregation was "the only practical way" for South

Carolina. He also remarked with spirit on the expert witnesses' "doctrinaire disregard of existing conditions," alluded to the "theories advanced by a few sociologists or educators," and observed that it was "late in the day" to contend that segregation violated fundamental constitutional rights. After noting that the testimony of the expert witnesses had been contradictory, he warned, elaborating on Holmes, that judges "have no more right to read their ideas of sociology into the Constitution than their ideas of economics." [10]

Judge Waring, in a sweeping, emotional dissent that was freighted with moral overtones and appeals to conscience, rejected both Parker's findings and his reasoning. The defendants, he pointed out, had first denied the existence of inequalities, then had admitted them after Governor Byrnes had come out for equalization while the suit was already in process. If the "false doctrine and patter called 'separate but equal' " were allowed to stand, thousands of suits over unequal buildings, blackboards, and lighting fixtures would ensue. The court should meet the issue "simply and factually and without fear, sophistry and evasion." The children before it were entitled to their rights "now and not in the future," and he wanted "no part" of the defendants' "maneuver" to convert the suit into another "separate but equal" litigation.

Judge Waring went on to adduce the "fine statements" and controlling principles of the Declaration of Independence and the deeds, words, and attitudes of the Founding Fathers, Abraham Lincoln, and the authors of the Thirteenth, Fourteenth, and Fifteenth amendments. There was no need, he declared, "to pore through voluminous arguments and opinions" to ascertain that the intention of the Fourteenth Amendment was "to remove from Negroes the stigma and status of slavery and to confer upon them full rights as citizens." A modern court, he felt, should follow *Sweatt* and *McLaurin,* not the majority opinion in *Plessy.* Justice Harlan's memorable dissent in the latter case was the "true declaration of the meaning of the Fourteenth Amendment and of the spirit of the American Constitution and the American way of life."

Waring added that the conception of a pure Caucasian race was unreasonable, unscientific, and based upon "unadulterated" prejudice:

> We see the results of all of this warped thinking in the poor underprivileged and frightened attitude of so many Negroes in the southern states; and in the sadistic insistence of the "white supremacists" in declaring that their will must be imposed irrespective of rights of other citizens.

Passing over conflicts in testimony, he averred that the plaintiffs' expert witnesses had proven "beyond a doubt" that the evils of segregation and color prejudice came from early training and that the place to eradicate them was in the first grade. Waring also took judicial notice of "common experience," "our own reasoning," and so forth, but in a way diametrically opposite to that of Parker:

> [It] was clearly apparent, as it should be to any thoughtful person, irrespective of . . . expert testimony, that segregation in education can never produce equality and that it is an evil that must be eradicated. . . . *Segregation is per se inequality.* [Waring's emphasis].

Never before had a federal judge written a formal opinion directly challenging "separate but equal" as applied to schools.[11]

Buoyed by Judge Waring's dissent, Thurgood Marshall appealed to the Supreme Court. Meanwhile, Clarendon officials strove frenetically to equalize physical conditions in the schools. The salaries of Negro teachers were brought up to those of whites, one-room schools were consolidated, a school bus system was instituted, and thousands of dollars were spent for furniture and equipment. In the state as a whole, contracts were let for $5.5 million of Negro school construction as against $2 million for white schools. Then, in January 1952, the Supreme Court remanded the suit to the District Court with instructions to ascertain the degree of progress. (Justices Black and Douglas called the decision to remand "wholly irrelevant to the constitutional questions presented"—the same position Judge Waring had taken.) Ten weeks later Judge Parker found, for a unanimous court, that the school board had "proceeded promptly and in good faith" and that the new school year would see full equalization of facilities. As he finished reading his opinion one of the attorneys in the courtroom turned to Thurgood Marshall and said in a voice that carried up to the bench, "If you show your black ass in Clarendon County again you'll be dead."[12]

The decision had been unanimous only because Waring had retired. Unable to endure the increasing hostility of his old friends any longer, the seventy-one-year-old judge and his wife had gone into self-imposed exile in New York, where he became head of the National Committee Against Discrimination in Housing and vice chairman of the board of the American Civil Liberties Union. In time, he added an honorary degree from Howard University to the LL.D. the College of Charleston had conferred upon him. But his white South Carolina friends never really forgave him, not even in death, sixteen years later. Fewer than a dozen white people heard the rector of St. Michael's Episcopal Church conduct graveside rites for Waring in the city of his birth and ancestry on January 17, 1968; they were joined by some two hundred blacks, who came in a motorcade from St. Matthew's Baptist Church were they had held a memorial service of their own.[13]

« II »

From the moment he read Judge Parker's first opinion after talking with Byrnes in August 1951, Davis voiced the fervent belief that segregation was constitutional. Never, he said again and again, had the precedents been so overwhelmingly on his side. "There is nothing . . . in the Fourteenth Amendment which removes from the states . . . control of the educational process—so long as equal facilities are afforded the children of all races. . . . The Supreme Court has decided the question . . . directly in three cases and by implication in several others." Furthermore, the courts of last resort of twenty-one states, including West Virginia, "to which be honor," had held to the same effect:

> Against this truly formidable array of authority . . . the petitioners . . . have argued it as a question of policy and have undertaken to support their petition by the testimony of some half-dozen anthropologists, psychologists and professors of education, who testify that in their opinion segregation is a bad thing and leads to bad results.

These conclusions were reinforced by his standing opposition to centralism, his reluctance to compromise states' rights even in the interest of individual rights, and by his belief in the right of voluntary association and its unwritten corollary, the right to exclude. They were further reinforced by his literal acceptance of the majority's dictum in *Plessy,* that "if one race be inferior to the other socially, the Constitution of the United States cannot put them on the same plane." [14]

Although Davis shared his father's conviction that Negroes were inherently inferior to whites, he was both tolerant of and paternalistic toward individual blacks. As a young man he had been sympathetic to a Negro attorney who tried, unsuccessfully, to establish a practice in Clarksburg. On his trips home he invariably gave his boyhood playmate, "Billy Coon," a few dollars. Several times he sent letters to railroad officials commending porters and waiters who had served him on

trips. And at least once he sent a small check to a sick Negro acquaintance who appealed for help. Black doormen, waiters, charwomen, and
Supreme Court attendants seemed to sense his concern for the individual in his private relations, and once an aged elevator operator affec-
tionately said to him, as he was shoved into her cage, "We Southerners
got to stick together, Mr. Davis. Yes sir!" [15]

Like many men of his generation, Davis made mildly derogatory
comments about Negroes in passing. ("I am busier than a nigger at
election" was the most common.) But he was never virulent and only
rarely negative. In the 1930's he even gave his name to a fund drive
for Fisk University, at Paul Cravath's instance. When the segregation
suit came up, he remarked to Porter Chandler that "a special place in
hell is reserved for those who started the slave trade." He also said that
Negroes should be allowed to reach their "just level" and that the time
had come for graduate schools to integrate. Unquestionably, he was
sincere in saying that he had the black man's best interest "at heart"
when he declared that full integration would be "the worst thing for
the Negro" and would "set race relations back fifty years." [16]

Yet his heart was really with the white social order. Despite his frequent references in the campaign of 1924 to his argument in the Oklahoma grandfather clause cases of 1915, he privately defended poll
taxes, never criticized the exclusion of blacks from Democratic primaries, and never commented, privately or publicly, on the nation's dual
system of justice.[17]

For a while, in the 1920's and 1930's, Negro leaders had hoped that
Davis would support their drive for equality of opportunity and equal
justice under law. "You do not perhaps know, Mr. Davis, the gratitude
and appreciation in which you are held by millions of colored people," wrote a black former Assistant Attorney General, in a letter of introduction for Walter White of the NAACP in 1929. "The only distinct advance made in the establishment of their constitutional rights
and civil liberties within the last two decades was made by you during
your term as Solicitor-General. . . . They have not forgotten also, the
fine, courageous stand you took in 1924 against the Ku Klux Klan,
and upon other issues dear to their hearts." Davis received White graciously, but he declined to serve on either the NAACP's board of
directors or its legal committee.[18]

He also rejected requests by Roger Baldwin and others that he enter
the notorious Scottsboro case, first at the trial level and then on appeal. The young Negroes' flamboyant counsel, Samuel Leibowitz, im-

plored him in the fall of 1934 to petition the Supreme Court to hear the appeal. Davis' participation, he said, would not only give the defendants "the best possible legal assistance," it would prevent the communists from making further capital of the case and would create among "the decent element in America . . . a favorable sentiment." Davis replied that he was "sympathetic," but that he did not believe that the record, which involved a question of fact, was open to certiorari under the Supreme Court's previous rulings; he would therefore be "embarrassed" to participate.[19]

That seems to have been the last time Davis gave even fleeting consideration to a Negro cause. In 1935, citing states' rights, he turned down Walter White's request that he testify for the Costigan-Wagner anti-lynching bill. Ten years later, in signing the call for defeat of a measure to ban religious or racial discrimination in businesses and unions in New York State, he predicted that the measure would "breed three new injustices for every one it relieves." And in 1948, of course, he bitterly opposed President Truman's civil rights program. In that year he also refused to join Thomas K. Finletter, Harry D. Gideonse, Elmo Roper, and Herbert Bayard Swope in forming a civil rights council under the auspices of Freedom House.[20]

Davis' opposition to state fair employment commissions should have made it clear that his political philosophy was based more on his conservative social values than on the abstraction of states' rights. Nevertheless, many of his friends were surprised by his participation in the segregation case. One of the first to comment was Mrs. Joseph Proskauer. She had just read to her husband, she wrote Davis in October 1951, a newspaper item about James F. Byrnes and school segregation. " 'That *can't* be the former Secretary of State, can it?' Joe said, 'It is, and I want to tell you something that will upset you even more than that—John Davis is going to argue the case for the State of South Carolina in the Supreme Court.' I replied I couldn't believe it & asked him if he would have done it & he said 'No.' " She then admonished Davis directly:

> Perhaps you do not realize what you are going to do in favor of segregation. It is not only that you are such a good lawyer that you will undoubtedly win the case, but the mere fact that you are defending segregation in the South will make many people, now on the fence, say "If John Davis defends South Carolina in this suit perhaps there is something to be said for the case of segregation!"

"Please tell me," she pleaded in conclusion," . . . how you, a believer in democracy, can defend such a cause." [21]

What Mrs. Proskauer had not known was that Davis regarded segregation as wise policy. Replying that he was "pained that you are pained," he set forth the law as he would argue it in the Supreme Court. Near the end of his letter he touched the social issue lightly: "I do not believe that justice demands that public policy must ignore existing facts. Race is a fact; sex is a fact; age is a fact. . . . None of these can be wiped out by waving a legislative wand. . . . Whether segregation is reasonable or not is a question largely affected by numbers and also by the local *mores* of the people. So long as substantial justice is done, I am sure such questions are best decided by the States in which they arise." [22]

The more Davis studied the record, the more he fumed over the social scientists' contention in the District Court that school segregation was psychologically harmful. He concluded that their evidence was self-contradictory, and he dismissed it all with the same contempt he visited upon modern economic theory. "I think," he wrote Robert Figg, his new associate, "I have never read a drearier lot of testimony than that furnished by the so-called educational and psychological experts." [23]

Subsequently, he unburdened himself to Governor Byrnes:

> I do not believe that the only distinction between the races of mankind is to be found in the color of their skins. There are anatomical differences. . . . I have been told, and I think it is true, that a cross-section of the hair of Mongolian races indicates that the hair is cylindrical. A similar cross-section of the hair of the Caucasian races indicates that the hair is elliptical, while a cross-section of the hair of the Negro race shows that it is flatter and more ribbon-like, hence kinky. Is it not conceivable that in addition to anatomical differences there are also differences in the intellectual processes, in tastes and in aptitudes? [24]

Yet even as he exposed the bent of his thought, Davis underscored his conviction that Negro schools should be brought up to white schools physically. "I am quite content with the 'separate but equal' doctrine, with emphasis, however, on the word 'equal.' This you have exemplified by your program . . . in South Carolina and I give you all praise for having instituted it." Then, in a perception that stripped

Byrnes' equalization drive of its idealism, he added: "I think the
N.A.A.C.P. and its followers can congratulate themselves on the stimulus their fight has given to the educational program of the South." [25]

« III »

Davis' contention that all the precedents were on his side seemed
persuasive. The Fourteenth Amendment made no mention of segregation, and Charles Sumner had met rebuff after rebuff in his efforts to
drive school integration measures through Congress following the
Amendment's adoption. Over and against these hard facts, however,
stood other compelling realities. Interpretation of the Constitution
had never been consistently literal; nor had the intent of the enacting
legislature always been accepted as controlling. Through more than a
century and a half of decision-making, the Supreme Court had managed to adapt the Constitution to the felt needs of the nation. Usually
it had done so reluctantly; and often it had failed to admit what it was
doing, for most Justices remained uneasy with broad construction. Yet
more than once the Court's bolder spirits had generalized freely and
openly on the process. As Chief Justice Hughes declared in 1934:

> If by the statement that what the Constitution meant at the time of its
> adoption it means today, it is intended to say that the great clauses of
> the Constitution must be confined to the interpretation which the fram-
> ers, with the conditions and outlook of their time, would have placed
> upon them, the statement carries its own refutation. It was to guard
> against such a narrow conception that Chief Justice Marshall uttered
> the memorable warning—"we must never forget that it is *a constitu-
> tion* we are expounding—a constitution intended to endure for ages to
> come, and consequently to be adapted to the various crises of human
> affairs." [26]

Furthermore, the "separate but equal" dictum was a frail reed in
certain respects. It had been laid down in a transportation case
twenty-eight years after adoption of the Fourteenth Amendment in
1868, and the Court had neither cited it nor ruled directly on school
segregation in two of the three cases upon which Davis was to stand.
Only once, in 1927, had "separate but equal" been explicitly affirmed
in a school case—*Gong Lum v. Rice.* More important, the majority in
Plessy had rationalized the formula with a statement known to be false
when it was uttered: separation does "not necessarily imply the inferiority of either race to the other." [27]

Justice Harlan had clearly perceived the real nature of segregation in his impassioned dissent. "The arbitrary separation of citizens, on the basis of race," said Harlan, in words that took judicial notice of what was common knowledge even in that pre-social-sciences era, ". . . is a badge of servitude wholly inconsistent with . . . the Constitution." The notion that separate accommodations could be equal was "a thin disguise" that "will not mislead anyone, or atone for the wrong this day done." Predicting that the decision would prove "quite as pernicious as *Dred Scott*," he caustically pointed out that most of the state court decisions cited in the majority opinion had been made at a time when race prejudice was, for all practical purposes, the supreme law of the land:

> Those decisions cannot be guides in the era introduced by the recent amendments of the supreme law, which established universal civil freedom . . . , obliterated the race line from our systems of governments, national and state, and placed our free institutions upon the broad and sure foundation of the equality of all men before the law.[28]

Of more immediate importance was the steady movement of the Vinson Court against discrimination. It had all but rejected "separate but equal" by implication in housing, transportation, and higher education cases; and in 1948, when there had been no other way to strike down a racially restrictive covenant, the Kentucky-born Chief Justice had invoked the Fourteenth Amendment. By 1951, the ground for destruction of the citadel itself was so well prepared that insiders would afterwards say that "the office boy could have won the segregation case." As former Justice Tom Clark later observed, to call *Plessy* "established doctrine" in public education after the rulings in *Sweatt* and *McLaurin* was to deal "with shadows rather than substance." Nevertheless, Davis was so anxious to "sound off," was so sure that the Justices would not "eat" their words of 1896, that he was relieved when the Court turned down South Carolina's motion to dismiss the appeal that fall.[29]

News of Davis' involvement produced a considerable volume of mail. Two of the most interesting letters came from businessmen in New York, one a Northerner who kept a hunting preserve in South Carolina, the other a Southern-born graduate of the College of Charleston and the grandson of a Confederate officer. New Yorkers failed to realize, wrote the Northerner, "how happy and contented most of the negroes are. I asked . . . [my superintendent] if he wanted to send his daughter to the white school; he said no. I asked him if he wanted to vote; he said certainly not." The writer added that Davis' participation might help New Yorkers see the light. The perspective of the Southerner was radically different. "I hope you will lose this case," he wrote, "for the sake of our beloved South, as well as for all mankind. Organized, provincial minority segregation is *aggression* on the rights of the rest of America." Davis' Australian friend Sir Herbert Brookes added an international note: "for the . . . good name of the U.S.A. in the world and the absence of hostility of the coloured people of the Far and Middle East, I hope the case goes against you." [30]

Foreign opinion was the last thing Davis thought the Court should consider; and even if he had thought it relevant, his lack of sympathy for the anti-colonial movements abroad would have impelled him to dismiss it. Ignoring charges that communists had inspired the suit, or, conversely, that discrimination fed the Russian propaganda mill, he stood fast on *stare decisis* and "separate but equal." Yet the temptation to speak to the social issue remained great, and he sometimes gave in to it. Comforted by reports that most Negroes wanted separate schools, he usually asserted that segregation was in the "best interest" of both races—but especially the black. To Walter White he elucidated a little more fully: "I think there is a genuine distinction to be drawn in policy between the immature children in the primary schools and the more mature individuals who attend graduate schools. . . . Meantime we should both feel satisfaction in the genuine efforts . . . being made to bring about equality in the schools." [31]

« IV »

When, against this background, Thurgood Marshall, in the late summer of 1952, submitted a brief fairly glistening with statements by social scientists, Davis threw up his hands in despair. "I can only say that if that sort of 'fluff' can move any court, God save the state!" In a sense, his disgust was justifiable. One of the expert witnesses cited by the NAACP had conceded, in the lower court, that the commingling of the races did give rise to frustrations and aggressions. Another, Dr. Kenneth Clark, drew misleading conclusions from the extraordinarily tenuous research on which he grounded some of his testimony. Others merely expressed opinions based on secondary sources rather than on direct observation of black children in segregated and nonsegregated schools. As the eminent legal philosopher Edmund Cahn afterwards commented, "I would not have the constitutional rights of Negroes— or of other Americans—rest on any such flimsy foundation as some of the scientific demonstrations in these records." * In a tack which veered diametrically from Davis', however, Cahn emphasized that the moral factors involved in racial segregation were "exceedingly ancient"; indeed, the fact that "official humiliation of innocent, law-abiding citizens is psychologically injurious and morally evil" was recognized by Justice Harlan and "many other Americans with responsive consciences" before, during, and after the rise of "separate but equal." [32]

Unwilling to accept battle on Marshall's terms, Davis cast his own brief in traditional form. The right of a state to maintain segregated schools, he insisted, had been so often and so pointedly declared by the highest authorities that it should not be regarded as open to debate. "Only an excess of zeal can explain the present challenge." Twenty-three of the thirty-seven states in the Union when the Fourteenth Amendment was adopted had, or soon made, statutory or constitutional provisions for segregation. Furthermore, "nothing" in the Supreme Court's recent decisions weakened the doctrine laid down in *Plessy*. (The NAACP brief had contended that custom and usage rooted in the slave tradition could not be the yardstick for interpreting the Fourteenth Amendment, that *Gong Lum* had been decided without "full argument and consideration," and that the Court had gone beyond the issue of physical facilities in the Texas and Oklahoma law school cases.) [33]

Despite his own confidence in the precedents, Davis feared that the experts' testimony might swing some of the Court's "wavering brethren." He therefore added a section on public policy, prefaced by a declaration that Judge Parker had correctly held that the testimony related to questions of legislative policy, not constitutional right. The section featured a low-key attack on Kenneth Clark. Professor Clark and his wife, it dryly stated, had also done research which suggested that segregated Southern blacks were somewhat healthier, psychologi-

---

* Cahn added: "It is one thing to use the current scientific findings, however ephemeral they may be, in order to ascertain whether the legislature has acted reasonably in adopting some scheme of social or economic regulation. . . . It would be quite another thing to have our fundamental rights rise, fall, or change along with the latest fashions in psychological literature."

cally speaking, than desegregated Northern blacks. (In Clarendon
County, nine of sixteen black children tested by Clark preferred white
dolls to black dolls. This, said Clark, was "consistent" with the results
of previous tests of more than 300 children. He did not point out that
these tests, which involved 134 black children in segregated schools in
Arkansas and 119 in nonsegregated schools in Massachusetts, showed a
higher percentage of identification with the white dolls in the nonsegregated Northern schools than in the segregated Southern schools.
The plain implication, of course, was that the psychological damage
was attributable to factors other than, and precedent to, school
segregation.) [34]

Davis concluded the section with a long excerpt, shorn of its historical context, from a 1935 article by W. E. B. Du Bois. Inserted because
it seemed to support segregation, it was actually a damning indictment
of that barbarous treatment of Negroes by white Americans (mainly
Northern, in this instance) which the NAACP was striving to overcome. Wherever he observed mixed schools, Du Bois reported, "the
white children, white teachers, and white parents despised and resented the dark child, made mock of it, neglected or bullied it, and literally rendered its life a living hell." * [35]

The brief delighted Governor Byrnes. "I liked your having Clark &
Clark answer Witness Clark," he wrote. He also took satisfaction in
Davis' assertion that the lower court's decision to allow South Carolina
to continue its equalization program indicated that it shared Davis'
and his own view that "separate but equal" was acceptable. "I want
you to know," he said, "that this client is proud of his lawyer." [36]

By then Davis and Figg were in close touch with T. Justin Moore of
Richmond, Virginia, counsel for the Prince Edward County School
Board in a similar suit, and with J. Lindsay Almond, Jr., Attorney
General of Virginia. (As Governor of Virginia in the early 1960's, Al-
mond was to lead the state in abandoning the Byrd organization's pro-
gram of "massive resistance" to desegregation.)

With Davis' acquiescence, Moore prompted Byrnes to persuade Governor Edward F. Arn of Kansas to have a case from Topeka, *Brown v.
Board of Education,* heard along with the South Carolina and Virginia cases. Arn also agreed to instruct his Attorney General to follow

---

* Du Bois' statement in the same article that he would "welcome" a time
when "racial animosities and class lines will be so obliterated that separate
schools will be anachronisms" was not included in Davis' brief. Nor did he
mention it when he quoted Du Bois in oral argument.

the strategy of the South Carolina brief. By a quirk of chronology, the consolidated suit became known as *Brown v. Board of Education of Topeka*.[37]

As the date for the hearing drew near, Davis' emotional commitment continued to deepen. He was gratified by the Court's refusal to let the left-wing National Lawyers Guild submit an *amicus curiae* brief: "They are a crowd of 'pinkos' and self-advertisers [who] . . . like the American Civil Liberties Union, try to horn into every case that arouses public interest." He sent Mrs. Proskauer a copy of his brief and threatened, in jest, to read it to her word for word if she failed to look it over. (Replying to his "somewhat sarcastic note," she said that her husband termed the brief "excellent" and, she was "sorry" to add, he believed that it would carry the Court.) Then, following postponement of the hearing from October 14 to December 9 to allow time for preparation of a parallel case from the District of Columbia, Davis had a day or two of uneasy speculation. What, he asked, did the delay really imply? "Does the Court want to dispose of the question once and for all in every conceivable phase . . . [and] wipe out segregation entirely?" [38]

« V »

Tension ran high as Chief Justice Vinson convened the Supreme Court at noon on Tuesday, December 9, 1952. Three hundred people, almost half of them black, packed the Chamber. Outside the great bronze doors, some four hundred more stood in a line that stretched out through the long marble corridor to the bottom of the white granite steps. Over the entire scene loomed the specter of a brooding, defiant South. The Grand Dragon of the Ku Klux Klan had already sworn that the "American Confederate Army" would march if segregation were abolished. Herman Talmadge had whipped a bill through the Georgia state legislature which would withhold state funds from any school district that desegregated. "As long as I am Governor," he bellowed, "Negroes will not be admitted to white schools." And James F. Byrnes had led white South Carolina to a two-to-one endorsement of an amendment repealing the constitutional provision for a state-supported school system.[39]

Thurgood Marshall, the big, tan-skinned lawyer with large penetrating eyes and sharp, strong features who doubled as chief of staff and field commander of the NAACP's legal arm, was not intimidated.

Night and day since the 1930's he had pleaded for justice for his people in the courts, in speeches to college students, and in discussions with government officials and civic leaders in all forty-eight states. The grandson of a slave, he had been born in 1908 of a schoolteacher and a country club steward and had been educated in segregated public schools and at Lincoln University, the "Black Princeton." ("Son," his father would say, "if anyone ever calls you a nigger, you not only got my permission to fight him—you got my orders to fight him.") Barred from the University of Maryland Law School because of his race, he studied law at Howard, where he finished first in the class and "found out . . . my rights" along the way. Within three years of his graduation, he won a decision in the Maryland Court of Appeals which ordered the University of Maryland Law School to integrate. Meanwhile, he became a special counsel to the NAACP. In 1939, he was appointed chief counsel of its Legal and Educational Fund.[40]

A man of commanding physical and personal presence, Marshall had a good mind, a strong social sense, and the piercing insight of one who had been excluded from the full rights of citizenship by birth and had been threatened by a half-dozen or more mobs over the years. He understood what Edmund Cahn meant when he said that for an advocate to persuade a judge to overturn a settled and established rule of law, he "must convince both [the judge's] . . . mind and his emotions, which together in disassociable blend constitute his sense of injustice"; in oral argument Marshall was quick to thrust for the bench's moral center. When, for example, Davis suggested to the Court that equal, albeit separate, education was in danger of being "thrown away on some fancied question of racial prestige," Marshall replied:

> I understand the South's lawyers to say that it is just a little feeling on the part of Negroes—they don't like segregation. As Mr. Davis said yesterday, the only thing the Negroes are trying to get is prestige.
> Exactly correct. Ever since the Emancipation Proclamation, the Negro has been trying to get what was recognized in *Strauder v. West Virginia* [1880], which is the same status as anybody else regardless of race.[41]

Yet for all the moral indignation that lay below the surface, Marshall tended to be more conversational than oratorical, more reasoned than impassioned, in court; only in rebuttal did he give himself over to fervor. He was determined, as he put it, that no one should ever charge the NAACP with filing a "nigger brief," and he inculcated in his staff the maxim: "Lose your head, lose your case." Anticipating always the worst contingencies, he used academic experts freely. But as Professor Charles Black, Jr., one of those experts, emphasized, "He made the decisions. No votes were taken. He took the responsibility. There was never any doubt who was in charge." Marshall instructed his staff to prepare all briefs with Justice Frankfurter in mind, on the theory that they would then be ready for almost anything; and he prided himself, with good reason, on his ability to respond frankly, fully, and relevantly to the most penetrating questions the bench could put. In 1940, the Court of Appeals for the Fourth Circuit had been so impressed by his attack on salary discrimination against Negro teachers in the Norfolk case that all three judges, headed by Parker, had stepped down from the bench to congratulate him. By 1952, the white primary, segregation on interstate buses, judicially enforceable restrictive covenants, and the exclusion of Negroes from the University of Texas Law School had all been declared unconstitutional in suits argued by him. As *Time* summed it up, "Marshall generally has a running head start on opposing lawyers. . . . [T]he law he made yesterday is today's precedent." [42]

Rarely did Marshall let devotion to cause distort his view of men and events. John W. Davis was and remained his beau ideal. "Davis," he later said, "was the greatest Solicitor General we ever had. You and I will never see a better one. He was a great advocate, the greatest." As a law student, Marshall had often cut classes to watch him perform. "Every time John Davis argued," he recalled, "I'd ask myself, 'Will I ever, ever . . . ?' and every time I had to answer, 'No, never.' " Now, preparing to argue against him for the first time, he could not believe that Davis was animated by anything but states' rights; the worst he would say was that his adversary was "all wrong" on civil rights. Indeed, when a Negro newspaper reported that South Carolina was paying Davis a huge fee, Marshall called the editor and told him to kill the story. "You can't do that to a man like him," he said.[43]

« VI »

To the apprehension of Paul Wilson, the young Assistant Attorney General of Kansas assigned to *Brown v. Board of Education,* that case was docketed first. Wilson had never argued in the Supreme Court; in fact, he had never been in Washington. Moreover, he had no faith in the moral righteousness of his cause, although he was prepared to fulfill his duty to put the best possible face on it. Willingly, he agreed to discuss his proposed argument with Davis and the other South Carolina and Virginia lawyers at the Carlton Hotel the evening before the hearing began. "I think," he said, "that [they] . . . feared that I might concede the invalidity of the Kansas statute or make no argument in its defense."

For several hours, without the slightest hint of impatience, condescension, or superiority, Davis discussed the case with Wilson. He emphasized the kind of questions the Justices were likely to ask, and he suggested reasonable responses. Near the end, to Wilson's abiding pleasure, Davis offered to move his admission to the Supreme Court bar the next day. Twenty years later, Wilson still carried an overriding impression of Davis as a man of gentleness, civility, learning, and poise.[44]

In court on the following afternoon, Davis and Wilson sat next to each other, and several times during Robert L. Carter's argument for the black plaintiffs, Davis passed Wilson notes on points to raise. Then, in spare but forceful language, the young Kansan argued that the Supreme Court of Kansas had upheld the Topeka statute, that decisions of the United States Supreme Court supported the Kansas court's construction, and that even his adversary had conceded that the Negro schools in Topeka were substantially equal to the white schools in facilities. In candid responses to questions from the bench, he also made two important admissions. He told Justice Frankfurter that the consequences of a reversal would "probably not be serious." And he agreed with Justice Burton that changed social and economic conditions might warrant a valid reinterpretation of the Fourteenth Amendment, although he denied that the record disclosed "any such" changes. His duty performed, Wilson then sat back to listen to Marshall and Davis.[45]

Marshall led off in *Briggs v. Elliott* with a long defense of the expert witnesses' contention that segregated schools were degrading and inherently inferior. The notion that segregation was an internal legislative matter, he went on, was "directly contrary to every opinion of this court." Segregation in schools was "no more ingrained . . . than segregation in transportation, and the Court upset that." His passion rising under interrogation, Marshall insisted that segregation was far more destructive psychologically than inadequate facilities were. The "humiliation" the children go through was "not theoretical injury"; it was "actual injury." Furthermore, there already existed a body of law that held that distinctions on the basis of race are "odious and invidious."

The Court fired question after question at Marshall. Justice Frankfurter, in particular, challenged his sociology. "Do you really think," he asked, "it helps us not to recognize that behind this are certain facts of life?" Was it "irrelevant" to recognize that some states have "a vast congregation of Negro population and some don't? . . . Can you escape those sociological facts, Mr. Marshall?" Marshall conceded that he could not, adding that if he could do so the "personal and present rights of these . . . Negroes" would be cast completely aside. Asked by Justice Jackson what impact a favorable ruling would have on American Indians, he proudly retorted: "The trouble with the Indians is that they haven't had the judgment or the wherewithal to bring lawsuits." [46]

Frankfurter and Marshall also engaged in a long colloquy in which the NAACP attorney came close to indicating that he would be willing to accept *de facto* segregation where geography made it reasonable. "You mean we would have gerrymandering of school districts?" snapped the Justice. "I think that nothing would be worse than for this Court . . . to make an abstract declaration that segregation is bad and then have it evaded by tricks." To this Marshall replied that if the lines were drawn "on a natural basis, without regard to race or color, then I think that nobody would have any complaint." Pressed by Frankfurter on black ghettoes, Marshall said that to enclose them would be unreasonable, and thus in violation of the law, once segregation was struck down. He added, in response to a diversionary question on Washington, D.C., that some concentrations, especially of whites in the Northwest, might remain. If children wanted integration, he said, they could move into adjacent districts. "[A]ll we are asking . . . is [that you] take off this state-imposed segregation. It is the state-imposed part of it that affects the individual children. . . . The important thing is to get the principle established." The actual redistricting was "not a matter for judicial determination." Rather, it was one "for legislative determination."

Davis then spoke "to the limit" of his strength for almost an hour. One eloquent passage followed another as he roamed far beyond his brief in an urbane, often moving, and always forceful effort to persuade the Court that social wisdom, no less than the law, was on his side. "One need not have heard Mr. Davis' argument," said Paul Wilson, "to know that a great lawyer was speaking. . . . The esteem of the

Court was reflected in the face of each of the Justices." Davis began on familiar ground. For ninety years, he declared, a "vast body" of court rulings, wise legislation, and learned persons had supported the constitutionality of segregation; manifestly, the policy had been established *under* the Fourteenth Amendment rather than *in violation* of it. He dripped scorn on Dr. Kenneth Clark and the social sciences: "I ran across a sentence the other day which . . . described much of the social science as 'fragmentary expertise based on an examined presupposition.'" He quoted Judge Parker liberally. He dismissed Marshall's contention that segregation was "entirely a legislative policy and does not depend on Constitutional rights." And he spoke rhetorically of "the great national policy" underlying the whole question:

> . . . Is it not a fact that the very strength and fiber of our federal system is local self-government in those matters for which local action is competent? Is it not of all the activities of government the one which most nearly approaches the hearts and minds of people, the question of the education of their young?
>
> Is it not the height of wisdom that the manner in which they shall be conducted should be left to those most immediately affected by it, and that the wishes of the parents, both white and colored, should be ascertained before their children are forced into what may be an unwelcome contact?
>
> I respectfully submit to the Court, there is no reason assigned here why this Court or any other should reverse the findings of ninety years.

As a close student of the arguments observed, the total effect "was almost—almost—irresistible." [47]

After Marshall and Davis, said Wilson, the arguments in the three remaining cases were superfluous. "The personalities of each [had] seemed peculiarly appropriate to the cause that he represented. It [had] seemed a duel between the champion of aristocracy and rationalism on the one hand and populism and humanitarianism on the other." There was, furthermore, an element of poignancy in Davis' involvement—"a great lawyer at the end of his life speaking, however eloquently, in support of a policy that was no longer tolerable in a free country." [48]

"Unless the Supreme Court wants to make the law over," Davis wrote a few days later, "they must rule with me." The majority, he felt certain, would "treat the matter as entirely settled by history and precedent," though a minority might "try to rewrite the law with some high-flying remarks on the iniquity of considering the irrelevant subject of race." But that any "thorough-going" lawyer would do so was unthinkable.[49]

His surmise was not far off—at that moment. On Saturday morning following the last day of the hearing, the Justices had discussed the case in conference. Chief Justice Vinson noted that Congress had declined to bar racial segregation in the District of Columbia schools at the time the Fourteenth Amendment was adopted and that Harlan had avoided referring to public schools in his dissent in *Plessy*. Justices Reed, Frankfurter, Jackson, and Clark all leaned, with Vinson, toward upholding segregation. Some time that winter or spring, however, Justice Clark and probably Justice Reed, though possibly Jackson, switched. By May the Court stood six to three in favor of striking down the segregation statutes. Largely in the hope that an even stronger majority might be formed, the Justices decided to call for reargument on five questions.[50]

What evidence, the Court asked, was there that the Congress that framed the Fourteenth Amendment "contemplated or did not contemplate, understood or did not understand, that it would abolish segregation in public schools?" If none, had the framers nevertheless understood that (a) future Congresses might abolish segregation under Section 5, or (b) that the courts might construe the Amendment as doing the same "in the light of future conditions"? If not, did the judiciary still have the power "to abolish segregation in the public schools?" Could the Court then authorize "gradual" desegregation, and should it also formulate detailed decrees? [51]

Meanwhile, Davis refused to bill South Carolina despite the seventy-five hours he had spent on the suit and the more than four hundred hours his two assistants had put into it. For twenty years, he explained to Byrnes, he had been received with courtesy and kindness by South Carolinians on his annual visits to Yeamans Hall. The case was clearly "a political and social problem," and he was "happy" to assist the state. Deeply moved, the Governor had the legislature pass a resolution of appreciation. Then, in April, as Davis' eightieth birthday approached, Byrnes arranged for a joint session to present to him a handsome silver service on behalf of "the people" of South Carolina.[52]

« VII »

Although Davis was to open reargument in December 1953 by remarking that "there are few invitations less welcome in an advocate's life than to be asked to reargue a case on which he has once spent himself," he had actually seized the opportunity. "I want to participate," he wrote Byrnes that summer, ". . . even if, like Chatham, I must be brought in in a wheelchair." He then asked Byrnes to arrange with the Virginia attorneys and others for him to make the sole argument. The Virginians liked and admired Davis greatly. (One of the pleasant parts of the hearing in 1952 had been the lively cocktail banter at the Carlton Hotel among Davis, T. Justin Moore, and J. Lindsay Almond.) But for reasons of state they declined to honor his request. With wonted grace, Davis accepted the situation.[53]

In mid-June of 1953, the Virginia group went to New York for a strategy conference with Davis and his assistants. Davis opened the session with the portentous observation that Justice Douglas had said, in a new book, that Malaya needed to integrate its Chinese, Indian, Japanese, Australian, and English schoolchildren. The group then addressed the questions posed by the Court. Davis Polk was given the research assignment on the congressional debates on the Fourteenth Amendment and the Civil Rights acts of 1866 and 1877; Moore's firm, that on the ratification process. Seemingly, the conferees agreed that the consistently expansionary construction of the commerce clause over the years provided weighty authority for the proposition that the Court could construe the Constitution differently than the framers had intended, "in the light of future conditions." This meant, said Moore, that if the Court held that it had judicial power to construe the Amendment "so as to abolish segregation of its own force, or . . . by interpretation of the Amendment, that ends the matter."

A few minutes later Davis backed away from that categorical conclusion. The framers of the Fourteenth Amendment, he said on reflection, had "so clearly understood" that it did not apply to schools that it "is not properly within the judicial power . . . to construe the Amendment so as to abolish segregation." Changed conditions might be important in some instances, but not in this one. Accordingly, they decided to contend that conditions had not changed since the 1860's, the "speculative" evidence of the social scientists to the contrary notwithstanding. They also resolved to distinguish the transportation cases. To this end, they noted that "actual discrimination against the Negro" had existed in those cases, but that there was no factual evidence of discrimination in the school cases "if equal facilities are assumed."

Finally, they concluded that if the Court found segregation unconstitutional, they would recommend that the cases be remanded to the lower courts with directions to frame decrees "based on local conditions and practical considerations." The conference closed with a criticism of the three-month-old Eisenhower administration:

> We agreed that the Attorney General of the United States [Herbert Brownell] should not be consulted about this matter, as the present administration seems to be committed to do everything it can to abolish segregation in every form and we could not expect any help from that source. . . .[54]

Late that summer, six young Davis Polk associates began investigation of the legislative history of the Fourteenth Amendment and the Civil Rights Acts in the sweltering humidity of the New York Public Library. After weeks of research, they concluded, just as a task force of historians working on the NAACP brief was to conclude at first, that Congress had not contemplated the abolition of school segregation. These findings were then incorporated in a brief drafted under the direction of Taggart Whipple, a young partner. Whipple was out of sympathy with school segregation, and after Davis' death he would reject a request from the office of the Attorney General of Alabama that Davis Polk handle a matter growing out of the suit. But when Davis asked him to help in the fall of 1953, he applied himself unstintingly. The Virginia group's finding that there was substantial evidence that, in twenty-three of the thirty-seven states that had ratified the Fourteenth Amendment, it was not thought at the time that it outlawed segregated schools was also included in the brief. Finally, the brief asked the Court to take judicial notice, in effect, of Byrnes' threat to destroy his state's public school system if forced to integrate: "Appellants offered no evidence to show that the public school system of South Carolina could survive the abolition of segregation." [55]

The NAACP came in with a consolidated brief which the Davis group charged was a veritable rape of history. On its face, the charge had considerable merit. The historians retained by the NAACP found that the Civil Rights Act of 1866 had been amended in committee so as not to abolish legalized segregation. They also found, initially, that the Fourteenth Amendment had been passed, at least on the surface, merely to give constitutional sanction to the provisions of the Civil Rights Act of 1866. One of the NAACP consultants, the distinguished constitutional historian Alfred H. Kelly, described the dilemma in which this placed them:

I was fa'cing for the first time in my own career the deadly opposition between my professional integrity . . . and my wishes and hopes with respect to a contemporary question of values, of ideals, of policy, of partisanship, and of political objectives.

For a while they thought their only recourse would be to give a general answer, one that evaded the Court's hard questions. But Marshall refused to accept this. "I gotta argue these cases," he protested, "and if I try this approach those fellows will shoot me down in flames." He then explained that they did not have to win the historical argument hands down; all they had to do was present the Court with a face-saving draw. "A nothin' to nothin' score means we win the ball game." [56]

That was just about what Kelly finally gave them. By separating the Fourteenth Amendment from the Civil Rights Act, he and his associates came up with enough evidence to make a plausible case that the Amendment was in truth broadly conceived, that, as they phrased it in the brief, it was intended "to write into the organic law of the United States the principle of absolute and complete equality in broad constitutional language." Seven years later, Kelly explained to the American Historical Association that in reaching this conclusion he had been practicing law, not history:

> The problem we faced was not the historian's discovery of the truth, the whole truth and nothing but the truth; the problem instead was the formulation of an adequate gloss on the fateful events of 1866 sufficient to convince the Court that we had something of a historical case. Never has there been, for me at least, a more dramatic illustration of the difference in function, technique and outlook between lawyer and historian. It is not that we were engaged in formulating lies; there was nothing as crude and naïve as that. But we were using facts, emphasizing facts, bearing down on facts, sliding off facts, quietly ignoring facts, and above all interpreting facts in a way to do what Marshall said we had to do—"get by those boys down there." [57]

By then Kelly had come to believe that the NAACP brief had grasped the essential truth anyway. The political historian Howard K. Beale had also reached that conclusion. In 1957, Kelly disclosed, Beale had told him that, although the Fourteenth Amendment "had not been written specifically to prohibit segregation, he believed that it had indeed been drafted deliberately to effect a revolutionary equality in the Negro's status, the details to be left to the creativity of subsequent generations. [58]

During the hearings on Thurgood Marshall's nomination to the

Supreme Court in 1967, Marshall was charged with "arrogant disregard of elementary legal ethics" for his instructions to Kelly in 1953. Senator Philip Hart of Michigan thereupon put in the record excerpts from a statement Professor Kelly had made to the Committee on the Judiciary in 1962 in support of Marshall's nomination as Circuit Judge. He had made the remarks on "sliding off facts" when preparing the school segregation brief, the Kelly statement said, in order to explain to a group of professional historians the difference between the way lawyers wrote briefs and the way historians wrote history:

> The argument in the brief was not history; it was advocacy. . . .
> Within the ethics of the legal profession, Thurgood Marshall's professional obligations required him to handle his available evidence in this fashion. . . . To imply that because Marshall and his professional associates did not write professional history . . . they were thereby guilty of professional malfeasance, is grossly to misconstrue the *modus operandi* of the legal profession. . . . The brief prepared by the late John W. Davis . . . is, from a technical historical point of view, every bit as far from a balanced constitutional history of Reconstruction as is the NAACP brief. . . . Mr. Davis' brief was not history; it was advocacy. Yet no one has indicted him for having argued his case adequately for his clients. No doubt he would have been open to a charge of professional dereliction and malpractice had he done otherwise.[59]

Meanwhile, Davis' sense of injury was compounded by the government's *amicus curiae* brief for the Negro plaintiffs. President Eisenhower was to fail to give the nation moral leadership after the Court rendered judgment in June 1954 because, as he told one of his staff, "I personally think the decision was wrong." But in the summer of 1953 he gave Attorney General Brownell free rein. Davis never had believed that Brownell would "back down from or modify" the position taken by the Truman administration, yet he was quite unprepared for the final thrust of the Brownell brief. The Attorney General declared that the legislative history of the Fourteenth Amendment was "not conclusive" and that the ratification records were "too scanty and incomplete" to be a reliable basis for modern interpretation. But then, in language remarkably similar to that of the NAACP brief, he concluded that the framing Congress "did understand that the Amendment established the broad constitutional principle of full and complete equality of all persons under the law, and that it forbade all legal distinctions based on race or color." [60]

All through that long summer and fall, Davis' spirits alternately rose and fell. In June, tongue in cheek, he sent Byrnes a copy of a tele-

gram, sent by Marshall, Walter White, and Harry Emerson Fosdick to
Allen Wardwell, soliciting funds for preparation of the NAACP briefs.
Wardwell, he explained, "does not feel that he can contribute. . . . I
send it on the possibility that you might be willing to." (Byrnes, who
was not amused, forwarded it to Senator Harry Byrd with the suggestion that the NAACP's tax-exempt status be examined.) In September,
Davis was cast down by reports that Eisenhower was going to nominate Governor Earl Warren of California to replace Chief Justice Vinson, who had died suddenly. "The President," he confided to Byrnes,
"could go further and do better." But by December he was almost
soaring. "In the language of a famous general," he wrote Justin Moore
on the eve of the hearing, " 'We have got them and they will never get
home.' " [61]

« VIII »

Early on the morning of December 7, 1953, a long line again formed
outside the Supreme Court. This time it was more than two-thirds
black. By ten minutes before noon the ticket-holders were seated inside. A few minutes later Davis' daughter, Julia, was ushered to a seat
beside Mrs. Thurgood Marshall. Soon Davis and Marshall sat down
next to each other at the counsel table, prepared to whisper sallies
and exchange humorous stories as they had done during the first hearing. (Just before his brief had gone to the printer, Marshall had sat up
until early morning striking out the "snide cracks" about Davis that
had been inserted by the younger members of his interracial staff.) At
noon, almost to the second, the red velour draperies behind the bench
parted and Chief Justice Warren and the eight Associate Justices entered.[62]

A plain, large-framed man who conveyed an impression of quiet reserve strength, the new Chief Justice combined the qualities of prag-
matist and idealist. As Attorney General of California he had been a
relentlessly successful and singularly unjoyous prosecutor. "I never
heard a jury bring in a verdict of guilty," he recalled, "but that I felt
sick at the pit of my stomach." As Governor he had appointed able
judges, had struck out against discrimination in state agencies, and
had urged every legislature from 1945 to 1953 to enact fair employment legislation. He had long since come to regret his role in the evac-
uation of Japanese-Americans from California during the war, and in
1948 he had summed up the credo that would guide him for sixteen

years as Chief Justice and stamp his name on an era: "We must insist upon one law for all men. . . . Anything that divides us or limits the opportunities for full American citizenship is injurious to the welfare of all." Now, casting a friendly glance over the courtroom, he seated himself in the Chief's chair and conducted routine business for sixty-five minutes. At 1:05 he called up the five segregation cases.[63]

For more than five hours, spread over three days of argument, attorneys for the plaintiffs contended that segregation was unconstitutional on any ground and in any circumstance and that there was no evidence that Congress had not intended that the Fourteenth Amendment and the Civil Rights Acts should uproot it. The press gave considerable attention to Assistant Attorney General J. Lee Rankin, as the representative of the Eisenhower administration, and, to Davis' disgust, the government counsel went almost as far as the NAACP. Nothing in the legislative history of the Amendment and the Civil Rights measures, declared Rankin, refuted the thesis that Congress had intended to end discrimination in all its forms. Asked by Justice Frankfurter how that interpretation squared with Congress' establishment of segregated schools in the District of Columbia in 1871, Rankin replied that that action did not alter his construction of the Fourteenth Amendment. "You think then," Frankfurter retorted, "that legislation by Congress is like the British Empire, something that is acquired in a fit of absentmindedness." At another point, Rankin disclosed that the Justice Department opposed giving the states indefinite time to desegregate in the event the decision went against them.[64]

Despite the interest in Rankin, the duel between the two dissimilar giants, Marshall and Davis, was again the dramatic highpoint. His big deep voice almost throbbing at times with passion, the black man conceded absolutely nothing. The answer to whether the Court had power to outlaw segregation, he almost thundered, was a "flat yes"; more than that, the Fourteenth Amendment "imposed a duty" upon it to do so. Segregation statutes fell into the same category as the post-Civil War "Black Codes," and it had been to prevent the states from enforcing those codes that the Amendment had come into being. Moreover, the framers had not intended that the states could re-enact them in the future. The question was whether the wishes of South Carolina and Virginia or the provisions of the Constitution should prevail. The defenders of segregation were asking for nothing less than "an inherent determination that the people who were formerly in slavery . . . shall be kept as near that stage as possible. Now is the time . . . that this court should make it clear that that is not what our Constitution stands for." [65]

As Marshall finished, Julia Davis turned to his wife and congratulated her on his performance. "So you are the daughter of Judge Davis," Mrs. Marshall exclaimed. "My husband admires him so much." Davis then stepped to the bar to challenge his forty-five-year-old adversary's contentions. Davis at eighty, reported *Time,* was "a white-maned, majestic figure in immaculate morning attire who looks type-cast for the part. . . . Some of his friends were sorry to hear him, at twilight, singing segregation's old unsweet song. But the popularity of a cause rarely cuts any ice with John W. Davis. . . . In the 29 years since his defeat [for the presidency], Davis has all but faded from popular memory; in his own profession, he is a living legend. Most Davis Polk business never reaches a courtroom at all. But the courtroom is still the showcase of the legal profession, and John W. Davis the acknowledged star of the show." [66]

The "naked question," Davis began, was whether segregation *per se* violated the Fourteenth Amendment. He then heaped ridicule on the historical "fallacies" in the NAACP briefs and scorned the government's finding that the evidence of congressional intent was inconclusive: "After so prolonged a study as has evidently been made, that does seem rather a lame and impotent conclusion." He next drew on Claude Bowers' twenty-five-year-old distortion of Reconstruction, *The Tragic Era,** to excoriate Thaddeus Stevens—"called by historians perhaps the most unlovely character in American history"—for urging confiscation of Southern estates and grants of forty acres to each former slave. Davis also denied that the judiciary was empowered to construe the Fourteenth Amendment differently than its framers intended. If the principle of *stare decisis* were applied, he added, it would be impossible to rule against segregation. Then, drawing back a little, he conceded that precedent was not always controlling. "But," he continued, his voice vibrant with conviction, ". . . somewhere, sometime, to every principle comes a moment of repose when it has been so often announced, so confidently relied upon, so long continued, that it passes the limits of judicial discretion and disturbance."

Near the end, Davis attacked the plaintiffs on their own ground. En-

---

* Probably more than any other general history, Bowers' eminently readable book reinforced the popular notion that Reconstruction was an unmitigated evil. It had been discredited by professional historians for more than a decade at the time Davis used it.

dorsing, in effect, the Sumnerian sociology that had infused the majority opinion in *Plessy*, Davis asserted that the doctrine of "reasonable classification" was enough to uphold segregation even if the principle of *stare decisis* were denied. How, he asked, would "the terrible psychological disaster being wrought" be relieved by putting three whites in a room with twenty-seven blacks?

> . . . it is not racism to recognize that for sixty centuries or more humanity has been discussing questions of race and race tension. Say that we make special provisions for the aboriginal Indian population of this country. It is not racism. Say that twenty-nine states have miscegenation statutes now in force which they believe are of beneficial protection to both races. And what of racial distinctions in our immigration and naturalization laws? . . . It is not necessary to enter into any comparison of faculties or possibilities. You recognize differences which race implants in the human animal.

The Court, he warned, simply could not sit as a "glorified board of education."

As Davis built up to his climax, the emotional strain under which he was laboring became more and more apparent. "Let me say this for the State of South Carolina. It did not come here, as Thad Stevens would have wished, in sackcloth and ashes. . . . It is convinced that the happiness, the progress and the welfare of these children is best promoted in segregated schools." Adding that he hoped his observation would not be treated as a reflection on anybody, he said that he was reminded of Aesop's fable of the dog and the meat: "The dog, with a fine piece of meat in his mouth, crossed a bridge and saw the shadow of the meat in the stream and plunged for it, and lost both substance and shadow."

Only once had the Court interrupted him. Two-thirds of the way through, Justice Jackson asked if Congress might not use the "necessary and proper" clause to abolish school segregation in order to promote equality in other fields. Davis replied that for Congress to "do what the Amendment did not warrant under guise of enforcing the Amendment would be a contradiction in terms." To Frankfurter he added that "to interpret the Amendment as including something that it does not include . . . is to amend the Amendment"; and that, he emphatically declared, "is beyond the power of the Court." [67]

The Court's deference had been an act of respect to the man who had appeared before it more times (140) than any advocate in modern history. Flashes of his old grace, eloquence, and precision had marked many passages, but the sustained brilliance of the first argument had been lacking. His voice, though still sonorous and authoritative, had lost carrying power over the year. "The horn," he explained to the Court, "doesn't blow as loud as it used to." The powerful memory had also begun to fade. "He read from notes much of the time," Thurgood Marshall recalled. "He didn't used to do that. He was over the hill." Once, Davis even stumbled: "I thought I had the exact language," he said, searching in embarrassment for a reference. "I have no feeling," Justice Reed mused years later, "that his argument was outstanding beyond his usual excellence. He marshaled the facts totally; all that I ever heard of. But there was an inevitability about it all. Mr. Davis was following the accepted concept of law as it was." Still, as Alexander Bickel has observed, "No one hearing . . . Davis . . . emphasize how pervasive and how solidly founded the present order was could fail to be sensible to the difficulties encountered in uprooting it."

> Mr. Davis was intimating that the existing order was no longer subject of judicial change, that no principle of its alteration could now be announced. This was to deny the essence of the Court's function, and on the basis of no more than an inadmissibly static view of society. But the suggestion that judicial alteration of so deep-rooted an order of things raises special problems to which the Court must have due regard—that could not be ignored.[68]

« IX »

Three days after the hearing ended, Chief Justice Warren opened the Justices' Saturday morning conference by remarking on the high quality of the arguments. He then said that the Court could not evade the issue but must decide on the constitutionality of segregation. Without referring to the legislative history, he added that the Thirteenth, Fourteenth, and Fifteenth amendments were all clearly designed to make former slaves equal to all others, and that discrimination on the basis of race violated these amendments. He hoped, he said, that segregation could be abolished in a way that would recognize the different conditions in different areas. Justice Reed, a Kentuckian, indicated that he understood Warren's attitude and that he recognized the dynamic character of the Constitution. But he also reminded the Chief Justice that segregated schools had not been barred by the Congress that had framed the amendments. Justice Clark, a Texan, added that the legislative history could not be used, but that he would support

Warren if they took a flexible position on implementation. Justice Black, the third Southerner, was absent from the conference, but he was known to favor striking down the segregation statutes. Both Justice Douglas and Justice Minton also agreed with Warren that official discrimination on the basis of race was intolerable in a modern democratic society, although Douglas said that the legislative history was inconclusive. Justice Burton supported the Chief Justice enthusiastically.

The views of Justices Jackson and Frankfurter were more complicated. After quoting Cardozo to the effect that the Court's work is partly political, Jackson said that the cases before them required a political decision; the problem was how to create a judicial basis for such a decision. He also predicted trouble when white children were sent to colored schools under colored teachers. Frankfurter said flatly that the Fourteenth Amendment "did not . . . purpose to abolish segregation." He further deplored the fact that the Court was the guardian of the due process clause and warned that the Court should not be self-righteous.

Chief Justice Warren decided, probably even before the conference, that he should write the opinion himself and do everything possible to mass the Court behind it. Repeatedly that winter and spring, he discussed the case over lunch with some of his colleagues (Frankfurter and Jackson never joined them, and Black rarely did so). He concluded that the best way to win unanimity was by composing a short, non-rhetorical, unemotional, and non-accusatory opinion. This he did, and on May 12, five days before the decision was rendered, Frankfurter, the last holdout, indicated that he would probably sign it. The Chief Justice, wrote Burton in his diary, had done a "magnificent job"; the impending unanimous opinion was a "major accomplishment for his leadership." [69]

On May 17, 1954, Chief Justice Warren ruled, for a unanimous Court, that segregation based solely on race denied to Negro children equal protection of the laws guaranteed by the Fourteenth Amendment—"even though the physical facilities and other 'tangible' factors of white and Negro schools may be equal." The short, almost starkly simple opinion stated that the historical evidence on the Fourteenth Amendment was "inconclusive" at best; that cases decided immediately after its adoption in 1868 had interpreted it "as proscribing all state-imposed discriminations against the Negro race"; and that " 'separate but equal' had not made its appearance in the Supreme Court until 1896." It also delineated the familiar history of that doctrine. But instead of standing categorically on Justice Harlan's noble statement of controlling principles or pursuing any of several other lines of reasoning open to it, it declared that "modern authority" amply supported the finding that separate educational facilities are "inherently unequal." A long footnote implied that the "modern authority" upon which this epochal reaffirmation of democratic principle was based was a body of social-scientific writing more convincing as a description of the cruel treatment of blacks and the deeply ingrained prejudices of whites than as hard evidence of the specific impact of school segregation.* The allusion was as regrettable as it was superfluous, for it diverted attention from the fact that the decision had really turned on the growing consensus of sensitive white Americans that segregation was morally wrong—a consensus based on the same kind of personal observation, the same kind of moral perception, that had moved Justice Harlan more than a half-century earlier.[70]

Davis was so shattered by what he considered to be the sociological cast of the opinion that one of his partners was later to say that the decision had killed him. At the time the ruling came down, Davis tersely remarked to another partner that the opinion was simply "unworthy of the Supreme Court of the United States." Three days passed before he felt up to dictating a letter. Yet, in a sheer act of will, he congratulated Marshall over the telephone on the afternoon of the ruling. On the second day, Judge Proskauer found him alone in his office, his head cupped in his hands and his spirits as low as he had ever seen them. A week later, still brooding, Davis said to his partner, Ralph Carson, "You know, Ralph, I see the predicament of these whites in the South." Meanwhile, he praised Robert Figg for his services, saying that "no man or lawyer could have done more" than the South Carolinian had done. He added that he had "no stomach" for participation in the Court's effort to frame a decree: "I cannot think they would go so far (even as a legislative committee, which they are) as to pass some compulsory injunction redistributing black and white children." The

---

* As Blaustein and Ferguson conclude in *Desegregation and the Law* (136), "the facts of segregation . . . could have been recognized and applied by the Court under the doctrine of judicial notice without the help of the social scientists. The Court had in fact decided the Missouri Law School case without the benefit of any scientific testimony. Then, in *Sweatt v. Painter*, the Texas Law School case, the Court had ignored the voluminous data compiled by sociologists and based its decision on the knowledge the justices themselves, as lawyers, had about legal education."

state would have performed its "full duty" by making possible such freedom of movement.[71]

Davis' assessment of the decision's future impact varied with his mood and his correspondent. He sorrowfully predicted to his daughter, friends, and partners in New York that "turmoil" would ensue. He also wrote his old assistant, Judge William H. Timbers of the United States District Court in New Haven, that he echoed the sentiments of Andrew Jackson: "John Marshall has made his decision; now let him enforce it." For all his resentment of "the cavalier fashion" with which the Court had "treated history, precedent and sound political reason," however, he seems to have entered a subtle appeal to his Southern associates to accept the new law of the land. "I fancied," Davis wrote T. Justin Moore that fall, "that 90% of the Negroes would jubilate when compulsory segregation was abolished. I believe a similar percentage, when segregation becomes voluntary, would prefer to have their children go to school with those of their own kind." He further suggested that the South would reluctantly accept, and the courts willingly acquiesce in, *de jure* desegregation; that, as he carefully phrased it, the states would "repeal all statutes, rules and regulations that made segregation compulsory" but would not be forced by judicial order to "compel amalgamation." Finally, in what was surely the noblest but most painful statement of his fifty-nine years as a lawyer, he wrote Robert Figg that "looking at the matter philosophically, perhaps a unanimous opinion was better than a split Court." [72]

By 1956, when the White Citizen's Council movement was mobilizing in South Carolina with the endorsement of James F. Byrnes, and Harry F. Byrd and his lieutenants were secretly formulating a program of "massive resistance" to desegregation in Virginia, John W. Davis was dead.[73]

CHAPTER 29

The Last Years

Seldom can there have been a senior so beloved, a leadership so quietly effective. Facile princeps *Mr. Davis was in any company, but it was his choice that made him* primus inter pares.

GEORGE A. BROWNELL AND RALPH M. CARSON

« I »

Shortly before Davis' eightieth birthday in April 1953, John Dos Passos interviewed him in his office at 15 Broad Street. The novelist was struck by Davis' pink complexion and the level, steady gaze of his clear blue eyes—"a young man's eyes, except for a certain cool thoughtfulness that can only come from the experience, bitter and sweet, of a long, long life." Dos Passos was also taken by his soft mannerisms and colloquial turns of phrase. "As we used to say in West Virginia," Davis remarked, "I'm recuperated up." [1]

The talk drifted to political philosophy. "Jefferson remains the greatest political philosopher of all time," Davis said, pointing to the engraving on the wall behind his chair; "there he is, there's my idol." Dos Passos asked if Eisenhower's election and his own victory in the steel seizure case portended a trend against centralization. "It is always permitted to hope," Davis replied with a smile. "I speak as a Democrat in exile. . . . I have never been willing to concede defeat of the Jeffersonian principles." He added, with some vehemence, that the aim of government was to protect the individual's freedom of action, but that the "mental contagion" of statism was still gathering strength. Then, as though shocked by his own bitterness, the smile returned. He was reminded, he said, of a remark that Adam Smith had once made when someone had said a certain policy would ruin the nation: "There's a lot of ruin in every country." Nevertheless, it was heartbreaking to see the country militarized, even when it had to be. "We started with . . . Jefferson's principles. . . . We have an immense protection in our written constitution." [2]

"Of course," Davis added, "I don't tell my young men, because I don't want to discourage them, that with the present tax system they won't be able to put by enough to take care of their families and provide for their old age. An old age pension, that's a chilling prospect." He paused at length, a trace of anger in his eyes, then looked across his desk and said, "Why did you come to stir all these embers?" [3]

Late in the interview a young associate in a gray flannel suit appeared at the door. As Davis stood up, Dos Passos asked a final question about his practice. "It's a mixed bag," he replied, looking down at the papers on his desk with a wry smile. "Here's a broker suing for his fee. Here's a problem arising from the administration of a trust estate. Here are the government's proceedings against the oil companies under the Sherman Law. This one's a patent case. I never had a chance to specialize even if I had a taste for it. . . . A jackleg lawyer. I like that freedom." Putting his pipe in his mouth, he pulled out a drawer and picked up a statement he had copied from Trollope's autobiography:

> For what remains to me of my life, I trust for my happiness still chiefly to my work—hoping that when the power of work be over with me God may be pleased to take me from a world in which, according to my view, there can be no joy. [4]

Meanwhile, the honors and tributes poured in. He had not yet reached the point where he was insensible to them, Davis confessed, after reading a glowing account of his 1924 campaign for the presidency in Irving Stone's *They Also Ran*. He managed, nevertheless, to give most of them a light twist. As he remarked when the New York State Bar Association awarded him a gold medal in 1953 for distinguished service to the legal profession, "I can find no good reason for the action, but as Dr. Samuel Johnson said, when asked to comment on the King's appreciation of his dictionary: 'Who am I to bandy words with my sovereign?' " Three years earlier he had gone over to England for the last time, to receive an honorary degree from Oxford. Although the visit was a kind of triumphal tour, it had its poignant moments. He knew what Queen Mary meant, he observed, when she

sent for him with the message that she liked to see old friends because
they were becoming so few.[5]

By then most of his old intimates had been dead for years. Of the
four men who had originally attracted him to the firm, Allen Wardwell, George Gardiner, Lansing Reed, and Frank Polk, only Wardwell
still lived, and his death would precede Davis' by fifteen months. J. P.
Morgan had died in 1943, the same year as Nell, Davis' favorite sister,
Emma, and Polk. In Clarksburg only a handful of friends remained.
"The crowd you and I knew are rapidly passing away," he wrote in
1945. "A new generation has arisen which knew not Joseph nor John
W." To walk the streets was to reduce oneself to "melancholy." For a
while after Nell's death he had thought of selling Mattapan. But the
"spell of *vis inertia*," his reluctance to turn out his servants, and his
hope that Julia would spend an occasional summer with him made
him hold it. The decision hurt financially, for the place required more
servants than he needed and the upkeep was high. After 1946, the year
he reduced his percentage from the firm by a second full third, he was
forced almost annually to go into his capital for taxes.[6]

On April 13, 1953, the day Davis turned eighty, he was honored
from morning to night. The day began with an editorial salute by
The New York Times and ended with a surprise dinner at the Union
League Club. When John W. Davis speaks the word 'Constitution,'"
the *Times* declared, "there is a resonance in his voice that gives life
and power to plain, old-fashioned American words. . . . [His] is still
a voice that commands respect." On arriving at his office he found a
great spray of azaleas and roses and a note from his partners addressed
to "Our Beloved John W. Davis." At 10:30 Governor Byrnes presented
a scroll inscribed with the South Carolina legislature's resolution of
appreciation for his services in the segregation suit. After lunch the
British Consul General came in to notify him that Queen Elizabeth II
had awarded him the Honorary Knight Grand Cross of the Order of
the British Empire, the highest civilian distinction a foreigner could
receive. ("Are you sure the Queen won't change her mind before the
medallion arrives?" he said to the Consul.) Between the visits of
Byrnes and the British official, he gave an interview to a *New York
Times* reporter.[7]

Tilted back in his chair, his hands joined across his stomach below
his gold watch chain and his dark suit enlivened by a blue and white
bow tie, he presented a curious mixture of elegance and folksiness.
"The greatest changes I've seen in law," he said, "stem from the rela-

tionship between the citizen and his Government, with an ever-widen-
ing field of Government interference." The trend, he reflected, would
be difficult to arrest because of the rise of mass man and the durability
of government commissions and bureaus, "which once set up cling like
barnacles to a ship." [8]

And still the honors accumulated. In the spring of 1954, the Association of the Bar mounted Davis' bust, for which he had sat with some
hesitation, at the foot of the main stairwell of the Association's building. "We could not add to *his* honors," President Bethuel M. Webster
said in unveiling it. "His was a case for . . . giving ourselves, not him,
a portrait which could be placed with those of Evarts and Root and
Stimson in our Pantheon." (The bust was a reasonable likeness, but
the head was broader and heavier than it should have been and failed
to catch a certain light poise of the head on the neck which matched
Davis' facial expression.) Then, about three months before his death in
the spring of 1955, the Harrison County Bar Association placed a second casting of the bust in the county courthouse in Clarksburg. The
Association would have done better, Davis commented, to have "fixed
[it] on a pike in front of the county jail." But at heart he was deeply
moved. "I want to be identified with the bar of Harrison County and
West Virginia. I have never forgotten, and will not forget, the 'rock
from which I was hewn.' " [9]

As the years had begun to close in, Davis' thoughts had turned more
and more to the course of his career and his place in history. He said
time and again that he had never for a day regretted his choice of a
profession, but he also emphasized that "to plod again over the sequence of events, good and bad," would be quite unthinkable. Not
that he would have done everything the same. "No man is entirely
content as he nears the end of the road. The best any mortal can hope
for is that when the books are closed there must be a balance no matter how slight in one's favor." His own achievements, he said, in what
will probably be the judgment of history as well, were really quite
small. "I seem to have caught at the skirt of great events without really
influencing them." [10]

« II »

Davis never considered giving up practice. He liked to tell the story
of a West Virginia judge who opened an office on retiring from the
bench. "Judge," an old crony asked, on meeting him in the street, "I

understand you've hired an office. Are you going to practice?" The judge answered no. "Well, why did you hire the office?" "Because," he replied, "I want a place to go home from." [11]

In truth, Davis needed more than an office. "I never let him retire," his physician, Dr. Edward A. Lawrence, reported, "but I did stop him from going to active trial after his second argument in the segregation case in the fall of 1953." By then Davis was so unsteady on his feet that he accepted the decision without real protest. For several years, in fact, a male secretary or an associate had accompanied him whenever he left the office because of his unsteadiness. "Don't think," he wrote one of his fraternity brothers, "I shall take many, if any, more risks by going into Court. Indeed, if those birds at Washington would only decide my school segregation case favorably . . . I would be willing to take that as my swan song." Dr. Lawrence's solicitude probably sustained Davis' life a few extra months; but it also prevented him from rounding out his career by making a last trip to Washington to deliver the oral argument in the Oppenheimer hearings.[12]

« III »

Not until the last year or two of his life did Davis stop giving the graceful little ceremonial talks which were so much a part of his charm and contributed so much to his contemporary reputation. He began one "terrible" week in September 1951 by presiding at a dinner at the New York University Law School on a Saturday night. ("Very dull and stodgy and only mildly rewarded by an honorary degree.") On Monday morning he welcomed 4000 delegates to the American Bar Association meeting, and that night he attended a dinner for the Lord Mayor of London and the Lady Mayoress at the Union League Club. On Tuesday he again presided at a dinner. (That one, he conceded, "was a pretty good show," the Lady Mayoress being "not only very easy on the eyes," but a fine speaker.) On Wednesday he went to a function for Lord Chancellor Jowett, on Thursday, to the annual Bar Association dinner. The following day he gave a private luncheon for the Vice Chancellor of the British Exchequer. He was reminded, he said privately, of the army officer in charge of greeting visitors during the construction of the Panama Canal: "As one group of Congressmen came and [another] went he would stand on the pier and announce, 'The Lord giveth and the Lord taketh away.' " Nevertheless, the recognition, the elegance, and the sense of occasion all exerted an irresistible pull until he became too weak to go on.[13]

Of the half-dozen or so women Davis sometimes took to the theater, the opera, and musical comedies, Eleanor Belmont, the former Shavian actress and one of the most gracious, charming, and feminine women in New York, was his special favorite. He saw her often, usually at dinner parties at her apartment and frequently at the Metropolitan Opera, and he revealed himself to her as much as he did to anyone. "Last night," he wrote, after one of her parties, "was an evening to remember. . . . I am tempted to quote again—this time from Ecclesiasticus on the Apocrypha—that a 'faithful friend is medicine to the soul.'" And, in another note, "a lady socialite remarked to me on Saturday that she no longer went to the opera socially but *only* for the music, if she went at all. Could anything be more pathetic! Now *me,* I go both socially & musically, thanks to you!" Once he even dreamed that they had decided to marry, only to call off the wedding because of disagreement over who was to move into whose apartment with whose furniture. He also liked to tease Mrs. Belmont about her liberalism. "Entertaining as I do great concern for your economic and political soul . . . ," he began one letter. "Here is something which the leading advocate of the Beveridge Plan ought not to miss," he said in a note enclosing a satire on Lord Beveridge. "I didn't know until I looked at my March tax return how much money *your* dear Uncle Sam would leave me to contribute," he added in response to an appeal for one of her charities.[14]

Occasionally, Mrs. Belmont replied in kind. Once she signed a note with her full name, in order that he might know it was not "from the other Eleanor—Roosevelt." More commonly, she passed over his conservatism. "I idolized him," she said. "He was a lonely man, but a darling. There was something exciting about him. He had great wit, was charmingly simple, and was generous even in disagreement. The only instance of vanity I remember was when he sent me a print of the famous photograph of himself striding to the Supreme Court for the steel case. John was also a man of poetic mind—the most graceful user of the English language I have ever known. Women loved him. When Lady Reading came over for a visit shortly before his death she said to me, 'The only person I want to see is John Davis.'" [15]

The loneliness was also relieved a little by his daughter Julia's Spanish wards, Nena and Ramon Sender, who were in and out of Davis' apartment on vacations. He encouraged Ramon, with whom he often played chess, to pursue a career in music, and he gave him a practice keyboard on his graduation from the Children's Professional School. He also corresponded with him about poetry. "I know of no poet, unless it be Wordsworth, who is so uneven as Byron," he observed in response to one of Ramon's letters. "Some of his rhymes are terribly forced, some of his cantos are quite trivial, and every now and then he touches the heights." [16]

But it was Susannah, the only child of his manservant, Charles Hanson, who came closest to capturing Davis' heart. As a little girl in the 1940's she would stamp her feet waiting for him to come home to Mattapan on summer evenings and would then run out and throw herself into his arms. After dinner they often walked around the grounds together. When she was about ten, he took her to Sunday dinner at the Piping Rock Club. "She . . . could not have been more mannerly and courteous if she were going to Buckingham Palace," he reported to her grandfather in England.[17]

The bond between Davis and Hanson, always strong, grew even stronger as the years passed. "I looked at him from a long distance," Hanson reflected, "yet he was very close to me. He treated me always as a friend, always as a friend." Once, when Hanson's mother became ill, Davis sent him, his wife, and Susannah to Leicestershire for several weeks. In 1951, when Hanson himself was stricken, he arranged for and paid the noted surgeon Dr. Henry Cave to operate. Davis sat in the waiting room through the operation and afterwards visited the hospital every afternoon at four. He also had his own physician in South Carolina send Hanson a note of encouragement.[18]

Davis continued, as he had done for years, to watch over his relatives. On the death in 1950 of his nephew, Dr. Walter Preston of Cincinnati, he insisted on paying the college expenses of Preston's daughter. As always, moreover, he did so with consummate tact and grace. "Your letter," said her mother, "succeeded in making us both feel you really wanted to do it, and that it was not just a charitable duty." [19]

His own daughter filled more of the loneliness. Every morning of the last year or two of his life Julia came over from her near-by apartment to take breakfast with him, and they talked more freely than ever in the past. By then she was a successful professional writer, author of the best seller *Shenandoah* in the Rivers of America series. He often read her typewritten drafts, and he sometimes suggested editorial changes. He was hard pressed to contain his pride. "Did she tell you," he wrote a nephew, "that her book on the Lewis and Clark Expedition, *No Other White Men,* has sold over 74,000 copies in the paper-backed edition?" [20]

Julia's decision, in 1951, to take a third husband, Charles Pratt Healy, a Columbia University administrator, perturbed Davis deeply. Both of her previous marriages had been unhappy ones, and both had ended in divorce. ("They did not treat me any worse than I treated them," she said of her former husbands.) Davis felt that she had had "a hell of a time," and he feared that she would be no happier than before. "Julia, don't do it again." Gently but firmly, she insisted. He resigned himself to her decision, saying that he would always be available if necessary, and then gave her a lovely wedding in his apartment. Some time before his death he told her that Healy was the man she should have married in the beginning.[21]

« IV »

All through the last two years of his life Davis sensed that death was near. Dr. Lawrence put him on insulin in 1941, and from then until the end he took it regularly. Bursitis, lumbago, and influenza all plagued him at one time or another, and he had pneumonia at least four times in his last seven years. Stoically, he endured both the pain and the inconvenience. He would never tell Hanson, who was so solicitous that Davis called him "The Watchdog," that he was ill, and only once was he heard to cry out. "Oh God," he exclaimed, after collapsing from an insulin reaction one Easter morning, "be merciful to me." [22]

In bad weather Hanson would plant himself at the apartment door, overshoes in hand, and virtually force Davis to put them on; he would also slip up behind him, pills and water on a tray, and stand rigidly by his side until he had gulped them down. Davis loved fats too much to observe his diet strictly. "He would follow it for a while," Dr. Lawrence recalled, "then say 'the hell with it' and break it. If it hadn't been for Hanson, he would have eaten his head off." [23]

Davis never did stay at Yeamans Hall the two full months that Lawrence regularly prescribed. Neither would he send the physician, whom he addressed as "Boss," an informative report on how he felt while he was there. He showered him with ebullient notes about his golf game, the weather, and his performance at the bridge table, but little else. He had no apparent fear of death; and every time he was hospitalized he would look up at Lawrence and say, almost as though he were referring to someone else, "Boss, do you think you can pull the old carcass through again?" Then, as he began to recover, he would plead with him to dismiss the special nurses. He was so sensitive to appearances that he refused to let Lawrence accompany him to Washington for the steel seizure case in 1952, yet he was so fearful of collapsing in court that he was inwardly relieved by Lawrence's order to give up routine trial work.[24]

"Without question, Mr. Davis was my favorite patient," Dr. Lawrence said a few days after his death. "He was a lazy man physically, and he never really wanted to play more than three holes of golf. But he always had a sparkling eye, a kind word, a quip. His visits to my office were the bright spots of each week. I just literally loved the old man. He had his own way of doing things. He would argue, but he would do it. Toward the end, especially, he was a good patient despite his instinctive hostility to doctors." Davis also captivated Lawrence's nurse. The instant he entered the office, she said, the room would come alive. "He was a very sweet person. I loved him." Every Friday morning during his last year she gave him a shot in his apartment as he sat by a window overlooking Central Park. Sometimes he would ask her if his tie looked all right (he had taken to bright, bold patterns), and always he would invite her to have coffee afterward.[25]

Of the twenty-three Phi Psi's who had given him a silver loving cup at the time of his first marriage, Davis noted in 1949, only three were still alive. "How does this happen? No one of us survivors started with anything more than a good physical equipment. Certainly I didn't qualify in the athletic ranks, yet here we are." A fishing trip to the Gaspé in 1952 found him too weak to climb up and down the river banks. "One by one we lop off the things we used to do. The great point is to keep on doing what our strength permits and nothing more." Even at Mattapan his legs would be so swollen and painful by evening that he could not stroll through the gardens. Worse still, "I no longer carry my *licker* as well as I did." [26]

There were also many compensations. Felix Frankfurter wrote fairly often. "I shall always think of you as my leader—and a leader who symbolizes what is most honorable and civilized in our profession," he said in a typical note. "Bench and Bar have long felt the charm of your persuasive power, but only those of us who have been your juniors can bear testimony to the encouragement and generosity we always experienced at your hands." President Eisenhower thanked Davis for his "outstanding contribution to America as we know it today." Many others said as much or more. Among the gifts he received on his eightieth birthday was a calendar book with three hundred and sixty-five tributes from friends. "I'm not going to look at this with anybody watching me," he said. He took it to bed and "cried some" before finishing it at two o'clock.[27]

By February 1955 he realized that his time had come. "I plow along in my accustomed rut," he wrote Dr. Lawrence from Yeamans Hall, "not beset by fear nor greatly hoping . . . though at least the company is pleasant, barring a doctor or two." Early in March he came down with pneumonia and was removed to St. Francis Xavier Hospital in Charleston, where he lingered for three weeks. He regained enough strength to receive visitors for a while, and he passed many pleasant hours reminiscing with Sunderland, who spent a full week with him. "Actually, it was a happy experience," Sunderland recalled, tears glistening in his eyes. "He knew he was going to die, and he was reconciled to it." True to the forms to the last, Davis shaved himself in an oxygen tent before receiving Mrs. Sunderland. James F. Byrnes was in and out, and Julia and her husband were there all the while. Early in the third week he suffered a cardiac arrest, the first of his life. Just before going into a coma he turned to Julia and said, "you've been a very good daughter." She replied: "It is easy to be good when you love." On Thursday, March 24, he died. That evening, Byrnes went out to Yeamans Hall, put his arm around Hanson, who was borne down by grief, and took him for a walk down a long oak-lined lane.[28]

One thousand mourners, including Byrnes and his successor, Governor George Bell Timmerman, Jr., Arthur Vanderbilt, Judge Harold Medina, Admiral William F. Halsey, James A. Farley, Lloyd Paul Stryker, Thomas J. Watson, and Lady Astor attended the funeral service at the Brick Presbyterian Church on Monday morning, March 28, 1955. "For the dignity and integrity which he brought to the practice of law, the service of his country, the cause of international friendship and peace, and every relationship of life, we give Thee thanks," said his friend the Reverend Dr. Wolfe. He was buried beside Nell in Locust Valley.[29]

Among the most moving and perceptive commentaries was the editorial in the Washington *Post:*

He was a gentleman in the sense that Confucius used that much abused word—a superior man, with a courtliness that came from a fine intellect and a warm heart and a gentle manner. In whatever circle he moved, there was none other who seemed so fitted to be at the head of the table. To that place his fellows instinctively beckoned him. Nobody can say what kind of a President he would have made, but one can say with confidence that John W. Davis had a sense of statesmanship.[30]

CASES ARGUED ORALLY BY JOHN W. DAVIS BEFORE THE UNITED STATES SUPREME COURT

Between 1913 and 1954, John W. Davis orally argued one hundred and forty Supreme Court cases. At his death in 1955, no other twentieth-century lawyer had equaled this record. Only two nineteenth-century lawyers, Walter Jones and Daniel Webster, surpassed it. Maurice Baxter reports, in his *Daniel Webster and the Supreme Court* (Amherst, Mass., 1966), that Jones argued three hundred and seventeen cases from 1801 to 1850. Alfred S. Konefsky, who is currently editing Webster's papers, estimates that Webster argued between one hundred and eighty-five and two hundred cases.

Graham and the Title Guaranty and Surety Co. v. United States, 231 U.S. 474 (1913).

United States v. Carter, 231 U.S. 492 (1913).

United States v. Antikamnia Chemical Co., 231 U.S. 654 (1914).

United States v. Young, 232 U.S. 155 (1914).

Weeks v. United States, 232 U.S. 383 (1914).

United States v. Beatty, 232 U.S. 463 (1914).

United States v. Birdsall, 233 U.S. 223 (1914).

Diamond Coal and Coke Co. v. United States, 233 U.S. 236 (1914).

United States v. Axman, 234 U.S. 36 (1914).

Ocampo v. United States, 234 U.S. 91 (1914).

United States v. First National Bank of Detroit, 234 U.S. 245 (1914).

Stone, Sand and Gravel Co. v. United States, 234 U.S. 270 (1914).

The Pipe Line Cases, 234 U.S. 548 (1914).

Louisiana v. McAdoo, 234 U.S. 627 (1914).

Missouri, Kansas and Texas Ry. v. United States, 235 U.S. 37 (1914).

United States v. Mayer, 235 U.S. 55 (1914).

United States v. Reynolds, 235 U.S. 133 (1914).

Henry v. Henkel, 235 U.S. 219 (1914).

Burdick v. United States, 236 U.S. 79 (1915).

Curtin v. United States, 236 U.S. 96 (1915).

United States by McReynolds v. Louisville & Nashville Ry., 236 U.S. 318 (1915).

Pennsylvania Co. v. United States, 236 U.S. 351 (1915).

United States v. Midwest Oil Co., 236 U.S. 459 (1915).

United States v. United States Fidelity & Guaranty Co., 236 U.S. 512 (1915).

United States v. Hvoslef, 237 U.S. 1 (1915).

Thames and Mersey Marine Insurance Co. v. United States, 237 U.S. 19 (1915).

United States v. Emery, Bird, Thayer Realty Co., 237 U.S. 28 (1915).

Louisville & Nashville Ry. v. United States, 238 U.S. 1 (1915).

Guinn and Beal v. United States, 238 U.S. 347 (1915).

United States v. Mosley, 238 U.S. 383 (1915).

United States v. Delaware, Lackawanna and Western Ry., 238 U.S. 516 (1915).

Newman v. United States ex rel. Frizzell, 238 U.S. 537 (1915).

Gegiow v. Uhl, 239 U.S. 3 (1915).

United States v. Barnow, 239 U.S. 74 (1915).

United States v. New York and Porto Rico Steamship Co., 239 U.S. 88 (1915).

Lamar v. United States, 240 U.S. 60 (1916).

Tyee Realty Co. v. Anderson, 240 U.S. 115 (1916).

Dodge v. Osborn, 240 U.S. 118 (1916).

Dodge v. Brady, 240 U.S. 122 (1916).

Lamar v. United States, 241 U.S. 103 (1916).

United States v. Archer, 241 U.S. 119 (1916).

Lane v. United States ex rel. Mickadiet and Tiebault, 241 U.S. 201 (1916).

Cubbins v. Mississippi River Commission, 241 U.S. 351 (1916).

United States and Interstate Commerce Commission v. Pennsylvania Ry., 242 U.S. 208 (1916).

Yazoo & Mississippi Valley Ry. v. United States, 242 U.S. 621 (1917).

In the Matter of the Petition of Selling et al. v. Radford, 243 U.S. 46 (1917).

New Mexico v. Lane and Tallman, 243 U.S. 52 (1917).

The Five Per Cent. Discount Cases, 243 U.S. 97 (1917).

Wilson v. New, 243 U.S. 332 (1917).

Ewing v. United States ex rel. Fowler Car Co., 244 U.S. 1 (1917).

Mason v. United States, 244 U.S. 362 (1917).

Valdez v. United States, 244 U.S. 432 (1917).

Lee Wilson & Co. v. United States, 245 U.S. 24 (1917).

United States v. Chase, 245 U.S. 89 (1917).

United States v. Ness, 245 U.S. 319 (1917).

Selective Draft Law Cases, 245 U.S. 366 (1918).

Jones v. Perkins, 245 U.S. 390 (1918).

Towne v. Eisner, 245 U.S. 418 (1918).

Goldman et al. v. United States, 245 U.S. 474 (1918).

Kramer v. United States, 245 U.S. 478 (1918).

Ruthenberg v. United States, 245 U.S. 480 (1918).

Trogler v. United States, 245 U.S. 629 (1917).

Cox v. Wood, 247 U.S. 3 (1918).

United States v. Biwabik Mining Co., 247 U.S. 116 (1918).

Goldfield Consolidated Mines Co. v. Scott, 247 U.S. 126 (1918).

Doyle v. Mitchell Brothers Co., 247 U.S. 179 (1918).

United States v. Cleveland, Cincinnati, Chicago & St. Louis Ry., 247 U.S. 195 (1918).

Lynch v. Turrish, 247 U.S. 221 (1918).

Hammer v. Dagenhart, 247 U.S. 251 (1918).

Southern Pacific Co. v. Lowe, 247 U.S. 330 (1918).

Peabody v. Eisner, 247 U.S. 347 (1918).

Tempel v. United States, 248 U.S. 121 (1918).

United States v. United States Steel Corporation, 251 U.S. 417 (1920).

Pennsylvania Coal Co. v. Mahon, 260 U.S. 393 (1922).

City of New York v. New York Telephone Co., 261 U.S. 312 (1923).

Prendergast v. New York Telephone Co., 262 U.S. 43 (1923).

Pennsylvania v. West Virginia. Ohio v. West Virginia, 262 U.S. 553 (1923).

American Bank & Trust Co. v. Federal Reserve Bank of Atlanta, 262 U.S. 643 (1923).

Farmers and Merchants Bank of Monroe, North Carolina v. Federal Reserve Bank of Richmond, 262 U.S. 649 (1923).

National Association of Window Glass Manufacturers v. United States, 263 U.S. 403 (1923).

Cement Manufacturers Protective Association v. United States, 268 U.S. 588 (1925).

United States v. Anderson. United States v. Yale & Towne Manufacturing Co., 269 U.S. 422 (1926).

Independent Wireless Telegraph Co. v. Radio Corporation of America, 269 U.S. 459 (1926).

United States v. Zerbey, 271 U.S. 332 (1926).

United States v. Chemical Foundation, Inc., 272 U.S. 1 (1926).

Eastman Kodak Co. v. Southern Photo Materials Co., 273 U.S. 359 (1927).

Beech-Nut Packing Co. v. P. Lorillard Co., 273 U.S. 629 (1927).

James Duignan v. United States and Pall Mall Realty Co., 274 U.S. 195 (1927).

Hope Natural Gas Co. v. Hall and Lee, 274 U.S. 284 (1927).

Federal Trade Commission v. Eastman Kodak Co., 274 U.S. 619 (1927).

Heiner v. Colonial Trust Co. Lewellyn v. Colonial Trust Co., 275 U.S. 232 (1927).

Barber Asphalt Paving Co. v. Standard Asphalt & Rubber Co., 275 U.S. 372 (1928).

Emergency Fleet Corporation v. Western Union Telegraph Co., 275 U.S. 415 (1928).

Corona Cord Tire Co. v. Dovan Chemical Co., 276 U.S. 358 (1928).

Delaware, Lackawanna and Western Ry. v. Morristown, 276 U.S. 182 (1928).

City of New Brunswick v. United States, 276 U.S. 547 (1928).

Springer v. Government of the Philippine Islands, 277 U.S. 189 (1928).

Boston Sand and Gravel Co. v. United States, 278 U.S. 41 (1928).

Herkness v. Irion, 278 U.S. 92 (1928).

Williams v. Standard Oil Co. of Louisiana and the Texas Company, 278 U.S. 235 (1929).

United Fuel Gas Co. v. Railroad Commission of Kentucky, 278 U.S. 300 (1929).

United Fuel Gas Co. v. Public Service Commission of West Virginia, 278 U.S. 322 (1929).

Firemen's Insurance Co. v. Conway, 278 U.S. 580 (1929).

Brewster v. Gage, 280 U.S. 327 (1930).

Wisconsin v. Illinois. Michigan v. Illinois. New York v. Illinois, 281 U.S. 179 (1930).

Alexander Sprunt & Son, Inc. v. United States, 281 U.S. 249 (1930).

Paramount Famous Lasky Co. v. United States, 282 U.S. 30 (1930).

United States v. First National Pictures, Inc., 282 U.S. 44 (1930).

United States v. Chicago, Milwaukee, St. Paul and Pacific Ry., 282 U.S. 311 (1931).

International Paper Co. v. United States, 282 U.S. 399 (1931).

Merchants Warehouse Co. v. United States, 283 U.S. 501 (1931).

Smith v. Cahoon, 283 U.S. 553 (1931).

United States v. Macintosh, 283 U.S. 605 (1931).

United States v. Equitable Trust Company of New York, 283 U.S. 738 (1931).

United States v. George Otis Smith, 286 U.S. 6 (1932).

Page v. Arkansas Natural Gas Co., 286 U.S. 269 (1932).

Texas & Pacific Ry. v. United States, 286 U.S. 285 (1932).

Rogers v. Guaranty Trust Company of New York, 288 U.S. 123 (1933).

Heiner v. Diamond Alkali Co., 288 U.S. 502 (1933).

Johnson v. Manhattan Ry., 289 U.S. 479 (1933).

O'Donoghue v. United States, 289 U.S. 516 (1933).

Helvering v. Duke, 290 U.S. 591 (1933).

Louisville Joint Stock Land Bank v. Radford, 295 U.S. 555 (1935).

United States v. Halsey, Stuart & Co., 296 U.S. 451 (1935).

Radio Corporation of America v. Raytheon Manufacturing Co., 296 U.S. 459 (1935).

The Pep Boys, Manny, Moe & Jack of California v. Pyroil Sales Co., 299 U.S. 198 (1936).

Kvos, Inc. v. Associated Press, 299 U.S. 269 (1936).

Helvering v. Tex-Penn Oil Co., 300 U.S. 481 (1937).

Associated Press v. National Labor Relations Board, 301 U.S. 103 (1937).

Silas Mason Co. v. Tax Commission of Washington, 302 U.S. 186 (1937).

Guaranty Trust Co. v. United States, 304 U.S. 126 (1938).

Guaranty Trust Company of New York v. Berryman Henwood, 307 U.S. 247 (1939).

McGoldrick v. Berwind-White Coal Mining Co., 309 U.S. 33 (1940).

Sheldon v. Metro-Goldwyn Pictures Co., 309 U.S. 390 (1940).

United States v. Northern Pacific Ry. Northern Pacific Ry. v. United States, 311 U.S. 317 (1940).

Riggs v. Del Drago, 317 U.S. 95 (1942).

Guaranty Trust Co. v. York, 326 U.S. 99 (1945).

United States v. Paramount Pictures, Inc., 334 U.S. 131 (1948).

Youngstown Sheet & Tube Co. v. Sawyer, 343 U.S. 579 (1952).

Briggs v. Elliott, 347 U.S. 483 (1954). This was the South Carolina case in the suit known as Brown v. Board of Education of Topeka, 347 U.S. 483 (1954).

NOTES

All notations of letters and other communications to and from JWD refer to The Papers of John W. Davis in the Sterling Library of Yale University (cited as Davis Papers). All items from the thirty-five other manuscript collections and Department of Justice Files on which I have drawn are identified by collection as they occur. All my raw notes on primary sources have been deposited at Yale. These include the originals and transcripts of interviews, the numerous letters to me cited in the chapter notes, and the memoranda, or the pertinent passages of the memoranda, also cited in the chapter notes.

Interviews

Mr. Henry Alexander (December 1964)
Mrs. R. G. Altizer (June 1958)
Mr. Montgomery Angell (December 1958)
Mr. J. Howland Auchincloss (October 1959)
Miss Mary Elizabeth Barron (June 1962)
Miss Cornelia Bassell (June 1963)
Mr. James Beech (January 1960)
Mrs. Eleanor Belmont (December 1958)
Justice Hugo L. Black (April 1961)
Mr. Edwin F. Blair (April 1961)
Mr. George A. Brownell (December 1958–September 1972)
Senator Harry F. Byrd (June 1958)
Mr. William C. Cannon (December 1959)
Mr. Ralph M. Carson (December 1959–September 1972)
Mr. Porter R. Chandler (December 1959–August 1971)
Mr. William A. Delano (May 1958)
Mr. Reginald Dilli (January 1960)
Mr. Warren W. Eginton (August 1964)
Mr. Morris L. Ernst (August 1970)
Mr. Marion L. Fisher (August 1959)
Mr. Walter D. Fletcher (March 1958–June 1969)
Justice Felix Frankfurter (January 1960)
Mr. Lloyd K. Garrison (June 1961)

Mr. Grant Gilmore (*November 1960*)
Mr. Thurlow Gordon (*December 1959*)
Judge Learned Hand (*December 1958*)
Mr. Charles Hanson (*December 1958*)
Mrs. Julia Davis Healy (*March 1958–September 1972*)
Mr. Alger Hiss (*March 1973*)
Mr. Max Isenbergh (*May 1969*)
Mr. Charles B. Johnson (*June 1958*)
Mr. Theodore Kiendl (*May 1959*)
Mr. Peter H. Koblegard (*June 1958*)
Mr. Arthur Koontz (*June 1958*)
Mr. Arthur Krock (*April 1965*)
Dr. Edgar A. Lawrence (*June 1962*)
Mrs. Agnese Lockwood (*April 1973*)
Mr. William A. Lockwood (*May 1959*)
Mr. Martin Lyons (*December 1959*)
Mr. Stewart McReynolds (*June 1962*)
Justice Thurgood Marshall (*October 1966*)
Mr. John Lord O'Brian (*January 1960*)
Judge David A. Pine (*January 1960*)
Mrs. Frank L. Polk (*December 1958*)
Mr. Dorsey R. Potter (*June 1958*)
Mrs. John D. Preston (*June 1958*)
Mr. A. J. G. Priest (*1967–1970*)
Hon. Joseph M. Proskauer (*May 1959*)
Senator Jennings Randolph (*June 1962*)
Mr. Alfred Rathheim (*December 1959*)
Justice Stanley F. Reed (*June 1958*)
Mr. Frederick A. O. Schwarz (*August 1971*)
Mr. Edwin S. S. Sunderland (*December 1958*)
The Rev. Edwin S. S. Sunderland, Jr. (*January 1970*)
Mr. Osman E. Swartz (*June 1958*)
Mr. Robert Szold (*November 1959*)
Mrs. James A. Thomas (*November 1959*)
Mr. Huston Thompson (*January 1960*)
Judge William H. Timbers (*June–August 1964*)
Mrs. J. Carl Vance (*June 1958*)
Mr. Herbert Weschler (*September 1960*)
Mr. Frederick B. Wiener (*January 1960*)
Miss Anne Winslow (*April 1973*)

Notes to Chapter 1

1. Davis knew little of his forebears. JWD to Clarence J. Davis, Dec. 30, 1947. The most inclusive account is in the sketch of his father, John James Davis, in James M. Callahan, *A History of West Virginia, Old and New* (3 vols., New York, 1923), II, 284.

2. Henry Haymond, *History of Harrison County, West Virginia* (Morgantown, 1910), is the best source for the history of Clarksburg. The statement by the French visitor is quoted therein, 263. Also see "A Famous City in West Virginia," Clarksburg *Telegram*, June 24, 1898.

3. Haymond, *Harrison County*, 280–91; Clarksburg *Telegram*, June 24, 1898.

4. Callahan, *History of West Virginia*, II, 284; John Davis to John J. Davis, Nov. 25, 1854, The Papers of John J. Davis, Library of West Virginia University (hereafter cited as John J. Davis Papers).

5. Callahan, *History of West Virginia*, II, 284; Julia Davis, *Legacy of Love: A Memoir of Two American Families* (New York, 1961), 43–44.

6. Ollinger Crenshaw, *General Lee's College: The Rise and Growth of Washington and Lee University* (New York, 1969), 324–28.

7. John W. Brockenbrough, *Introductory Lecture* (pamphlet, Richmond, 1849). The Judge gave the same lecture, with minor variations, each year. I have used those delivered in 1849 and 1858, copies of which are in the Archives of Washington and Lee University. Also see Sallie E. Marshall Hardy, "Some Virginia Lawyers of the Past and Present," *The Green Bag*, X (Mar. 1898), 109–21.

8. Scattered comments by JWD in Davis Papers.

9. JWD to Julia McDonald, Apr. 29, 1900.

10. John J. Davis is vividly re-created in Davis, *Legacy of Love*. I have drawn on it heavily. There is also considerable material, some of it apocryphal, in Theodore A. Huntley, *The Life of John W. Davis* (New York, 1924).

11. JWD to Jacob Fisher, Feb. 1, 1946. In addition to Davis, *Legacy of Love*, I have drawn on a transcript of John W. Davis' Oral Memoir, transcribed for the Columbia University Oral History Project, 1954, copy in Davis Papers (hereafter cited as Davis, Oral Memoir); scattered allusions in Davis Papers; the long, full obituaries published in West Virginia newspapers on John J. Davis' death in 1916 (clippings of which are in John W. Davis' Congressional Scrapbook, Davis Papers); and interviews with the following: Harvey Horner, Charles B. Johnson, Peter Koblegard, Mrs. Michael L. McGraw, Stewart McReynolds, and Dorsey R. Potter.

12. Interviews cited above, n. 11; Davis, Oral Memoir, 18, 20; unidentified clipping, Davis Papers. The uses and misuses of the Jeffersonian heritage are

superbly analyzed in Merrill D. Peterson, *The Jefferson Image in the American Mind* (New York, 1960). Jefferson's concern for human freedom is abundantly documented in Dumas Malone's monumental biography, *Jefferson and his Times: Jefferson and the Rights of Man* (4 vols., Boston, 1948–70), II. For an analysis of Jefferson's hierarchy of values, see Malone's "The Relevance of Mr. Jefferson," *Virginia Quarterly Review*, XXXVII (Summer 1961), 332–49, wherein he concludes, among other things, that Jefferson would "not expect his academic heirs to pay much heed to specific things he once said about courses and regulations, but he would want them to apply to their life and learning *the final tests of value*." (Italics mine.)

13. The John J. Davis Papers at West Virginia University for this period have been skillfully annotated by F. Gerald Ham (ed.), "The Mind of a Copperhead: Letters of John J. Davis on the Secession Crisis and Statehood Politics in Western Virginia 1860–1862," *West Virginia History*, 24 (Jan. 1963), 93–109. Davis' call for a convention is printed in Granville D. Hall, *The Rending of Virginia* (Chicago, 1901), 144.

14. Ham (ed.), "The Mind of a Copperhead."

15. *Ibid.* Davis also figures fairly prominently in the excellent revisionist study, Richard Orr Curry, *A House Divided: A Study of Statehood Politics and the Copperhead Movement in West Virginia* (Pittsburgh, 1964). See esp. his summary statement, 109–15. Also see Charles H. Ambler, *Francis H. Pierpont: Union War Governor of Virginia and Father of West Virginia* (Chapel Hill, N.C., 1937), for occasional references to Davis.

16. Curry, *House Divided*, 109–15.

17. Forrest Talbott, "Some Legislative and Legal Aspects of the Negro Question in West Virginia During the Civil War and Reconstruction, Part III," *West Virginia History*, XXIV (Apr. 1963), 211–48; G. Wayne Smith, *Nathan Goff, Jr.: A Biography* (Charleston, W. Va., 1959), 84–85.

18. Smith, *Nathan Goff, Jr.*, 84–85.

19. *Congressional Globe*, 42nd Cong., 2nd sess., Appendix, 166–70.

20. *Congressional Record*, 43rd Cong., 1st sess., Appendix, 481.

21. Davis, Oral Memoir, 20.

22. Both the John J. Davis Papers at West Virginia and the Davis Papers at Yale contain the originals of many of John J. Davis' speeches.

23. Charles B. Johnson, "John William Davis: Lawyer and Statesman, 1873–1955," *West Virginia Bar Association* PROCEEDINGS, 13 (1955); *West Union Record*, Mar. 3, 1916; George W. Atkinson (ed.), *Bench and Bar of West Virginia* (Charleston, W. Va., 1919), 1–2; obituaries, Congressional Scrapbook; Walter Stuart to John J. Davis, Oct. 16, 1909, John J. Davis Papers.

24. Anna Kennedy Davis is richly delineated in Davis, *Legacy of Love.* Also see Huntley, *John W. Davis;* Davis, Oral Memoir, 24–27; and numerous passing comments in the Davis Papers.

Notes to Chapter 2

1. Childhood letters, report cards, and occasional remarks in other letters in Davis Papers; Davis, Oral Memoir; Huntley, *John W. Davis;* Davis, *Legacy of Love.* I have also drawn on incidents, related by Davis' friends, about his nomination for the presidency as reported in *New York Times,* July 11, 13, 15, 1924. The description of a typical Sunday is in JWD to Thomas Lamont, May 15, 1946.

2. JWD to Mabel Grouitch, Oct. 24, 1944.

3. For the first Lee's incumbency, see Douglas Southall Freeman, *R. E. Lee: A Biography* (4 vols., New York, 1934–35), IV, esp. 420–32. Custis Lee's tenure is well described in Ollinger Crenshaw, *General Lee's College: The Rise and Growth of Washington and Lee University* (New York, 1969). The volume is dedicated to Davis. For Wilson's inaugural address, see 244–45.

4. Crenshaw, *General Lee's College,* 241–42; Festus P. Summers, *William L. Wilson and Tariff Reform: A Biography* (New Brunswick, N.J., 1953), 257–58. Wilson was a Baptist. He created a chair in economics, which he supported partly out of his own salary. The first occupant was H. Parker Willis. Wilson died in 1900.

5. JWD to John N. Latane, Nov. 10, 1922, to E. L. Green, Sept. 10, 1945; Moreland statement, *New York Times,* July 12, 1924; Quarles to Clarksburg Board of Education, June 25, 1894, copy in Davis Papers.

6. See six-page statement by Davis, dated Aug. 19, 1941.

7. Numerous letters from JWD to his parents. The incident at the clergyman's house is in JWD to Fred A. Forsythe, Nov. 25, 1929. Davis described Dr. White and most of the other professors and administrators, including General Curtis Lee, in a long letter to M. W. Paxton, Oct. 29, 1924.

8. Davis, *Legacy of Love,* 3–7, 97ff; numerous letters from JWD to his parents. Especially valuable is a five-page reminiscence, JWD to Peerce McDonald, July 1, 1936.

9. JWD to Anna K. Davis, May 2, 1893; A. L. Nelson to JWD, Aug. 16, 1893.

10. Davis, Oral Memoir, 35.

11. James Bryce, *The American Commonwealth* (2 vols., London, 1888), II, 486; Harvey W. Harmer to JWD, Aug. 8, 1894.

12. Numerous letters to Davis at the time (1948) he was preparing to inaugurate the Tucker Lectures at Washington and Lee, all in Davis Papers; John W. Davis, "John Randolph Tucker: The Man and His Work," *The John Randolph Tucker Lectures* (Lexington, Va., 1952), 11–36; numerous letters, JWD to John J. Davis, 1894–95, and, esp., JWD to Fred M. Davis, Apr. 15, 1920; Davis, Oral Memoir, 30–32; sketch by R. T. Barton, 3 *Virginia Law Register* 1 (1897).

13. *Ibid.;* also JWD to John J. Davis, Apr. 28, 1895.

14. JWD to John J. Davis, Oct. 7, 1894, Apr. 28, 1895, to James Quarles, Oct. 19, 1939. Davis was especially impressed by Graves' use of "beautifully clear" diagrams in his course on real property. Also see long obituary, Charlottesville *Daily Progress,* Nov. 10, 1928. Graves helped found the *Virginia*

Law Register in 1895 and became professor of law at the University of Virginia in 1899.

15. Crenshaw, *General Lee's College,* 338; Davis, "John Randolph Tucker," 14; statement by Dwight in Robert Stevens, "Two Cheers for 1870: The American Law School," in Donald Fleming and Bernard Bailyn (eds.), *Perspectives in American History, V: Law in American History* (Cambridge, Mass., 1971), 443; Catalog of Washington and Lee University, 1895–96; Davis, Oral Memoir, 30–31. More generally, I have drawn from Stevens, "Two Cheers"; Brainerd Currie, "The Materials of Law Study," 3 *Journal of Legal Education* 331 at 375–76 (1951); *Report of the Commissioner of Education, 1893–94* (2 vols.; Washington, 1896), II, 1000; Alfred Z. Reed, *Training for the Public Profession of Law* (Carnegie Foundation for the Advancement of Teaching, *Bulletin* No. 15, 1921 [New York, 1921]), and Alfred Z. Reed, *Present Day Law Schools in the United States* (Carnegie Foundation for the Advancement of Teaching, *Bulletin* No. 21 [New York, 1928]); American Bar Association PROCEEDINGS (1895). I am also heavily indebted to James Willard Hurst, *The Growth of American Law: The Law Makers* (Boston, 1950). Both *Report of the Commissioner of Education, 1893–94,* Vol. I, and ABA PROC. (1895) contain comprehensive reviews of the teaching methods in vogue in the mid-1890's. According to the former, only three of sixty-seven schools used the case method exclusively, thirty-three relied mainly on lectures, and twenty-four depended basically on textbooks.

16. Bryce, *American Commonwealth,* II, 487–88; Arthur S. Link (ed.), *The Papers of Woodrow Wilson* (14 vols., Princeton, 1966–72), II, 357, VIII, 650. The point is that the kind of training law students received bore not only upon the practice of law in the United States, but also upon the governance of the nation. Lawyers constituted the overwhelming majority of judges and a disproportionately high percentage of legislators on all levels. They also held a disproportionate number of administrative positions in government. See Hurst, *The Law Makers,* 352–53. Davis himself spent ten years in public life. The problem is implicit in Davis' comment: "The function of the lawyer [by which he meant the practicing attorney] was hammered into us constantly, especially by Tucker. . . . I expected to go back and live the life of a country lawyer. . . . Lawyers did get into politics, but, personally, I never expected to divert from my practice for any public office." Davis, Oral Memoir, 32–34.

17. Newton D. Baker, "Academic Preparation for the Study of Law," *Southern Collegian* (May 1896), cited in Crenshaw, *General Lee's College,* 341; Richard W. Leopold, *Elihu Root and the Conservative Tradition* (Boston, 1954), 18. Also see the perceptive treatment of Root in Hurst, *Growth of American Law,* 368–70.

18. Kales, *A Comparative Study of the English and the Cook County Judicial Establishments,* 4 ILL. L. REV. 303, 319–20, cited in Hurst, *Growth of American Law,* 372–73; Bryce, *American Commonwealth,* II, 488; Davis, Oral Memoir, 34.

19. *Ibid.* 35.

20. *Ibid.* 32–33.

21. Forty-seven law schools required two years, thirteen required three years. *Report of the Commissioner of Education, 1893–94,* I, 987. The general and quoted statements about Davis' life at the time are extracted from numerous letters to his parents in Davis Papers.

22. John William Davis, "Law Class Oration," *The Southern Collegian,* XXVII (June 1895), 426–35.

Notes to Chapter 3

1. JWD to John J. Davis, n.d., (June 1895); JWD to Julia McDonald, July 21, 1895.

2. JWD to Julia McDonald, July 29, 1895.

3. *Ibid.* Aug. 4, 1895; Davis, Oral Memoir, 37–40.

4. JWD to Julia McDonald, Aug. 18, 1895; Davis, Oral Memoir, 41.

5. Davis, Oral Memoir, 42; JWD to Julia McDonald, Aug. 18, 1895.

6. Davis, Oral Memoir, 41–44.

7. *Ibid.* 44; Haymond, *History of Harrison County,* 234.

8. John L. Campbell, June 26, John R. Tucker, June 30, Charles A. Graves to JWD, June 30, 1896. Graves said, in part: "With good textbooks, and my notes and those of Mr. Tucker I think you could with careful preparation, do justice to yourself and to the students. . . . You would begin with Hutchinson on Carriers (an easy subject with an admirable textbook); then would come Clark on Contracts (an excellent book) with my notes; then Sales, with my Summary, of if you choose Tiffany on Sales. On Prof. Tucker's course you would take Negotiable Paper, with his notes; Corporations (perhaps); Agency, with an excellent textbook, Huffcut on Agency; and perhaps the Conflict of Laws. . . . On some subjects, cases might be used with Professor Tucker's notes instead of the textbook, if you would like to try that mode of teaching."

9. Rezin Davis to JWD, July 24, 1896.

10. Numerous letters to JWD, July, Aug., 1896.

11. JWD to Anna K. Davis, Sept. 13, to John J. Davis, Nov. 20, 1896; Diary of Oscar C. Huffman, Sept. 24, 1896, as quoted in Oscar B. Huffman to author, Apr. 2, 1962. Huffman became president of the Continental Can Company. His remark was actually made after Davis had been teaching for about ten days.

12. JWD to Anna K. Davis, Oct. 12, Nov. 8, Dec. 1, 1896, Feb. 21, 1897.

13. JWD to Anna K. Davis, Dec. 1, 1896; postscript in letter to same, Mar. 14, 1897; to Julia McDonald, Apr. 16, 1897.

14. J. R. Smith to JWD, May 14, 1924; JWD to John J. Davis, Apr. 16, 1897.

15. Copies of examinations, as well as Davis' gradebooks, are in Davis Papers. His grades ran high—in the upper 80's in some courses and in the low 90's in others—but he discriminated conscientiously within his scale.

16. Davis, "John Randolph Tucker," 23; JWD to Julia McDonald, Feb. 28, 1897.

17. JWD to John J. Davis, Jan. 2, Mar. 7, 1897, and numerous letters to

Julia McDonald and Anna K. Davis. William L. Wilson, the incoming president, reported in his diary, Mar. 10, 1897: "I had a long conversation with John Davis, who asked my counsel as to his continuing as instructor in the Law School. He is most highly spoken of by all, and the Univ. people are desirous for him to continue. But I told him he had reached, or nearly reached the time when he must decide, whether he meant to practice or teach law as his life work, if the former he must not delay much longer his life to the bar. . . ." Courtesy of Festus P. Summers, Professor of History Emeritus, West Virginia University, in letter to author, July 26, 1965.

18. JWD to John L. Stump, Apr. 10, 1924.

19. Davis Papers and Papers of Julia McDonald, Library of West Virginia University, contain literally hundreds of exchanges. Only those of special interest are cited.

20. Julia replied: "You don't know how your letter today grieved me dear. I know you didn't intend that it should & I am truly thankful that you speak your mind to me freely. . . . It is a great distress to me that the Episcopal Church in Clarksburg is ritualistic—I don't care for ritualism any more than you do. . . . I *love* the prayer book devotedly & never feel *at church* with any other form of worship." Julia McDonald to JWD, Dec. 20, 1898, Julia McDonald Papers.

21. Julia was content to wait until after marriage to build a house, but preferred to board out or rent rather than move in with John's parents. The elder Davises insisted that the young couple live with them, and John acquiesced, to Julia's disappointment. Among the many other letters on this theme, see Julia McDonald to JWD, Nov. 29, Dec. 16, 1898, Apr. 7, 1899, Julia McDonald Papers. "Can't we rent any old thing?" Julia wrote at one point. "The meaner the better, because we will not want to stay there & will push."

22. William L. Wilson to JWD, Apr. 7, 1899; JWD to Julia McDonald, Mar. 30, Apr. 21, Apr. 27, 1899.

23. Davis, *Legacy of Love,* 21–22; Virginia *Free Press,* June 21, 28, 1899.

24. This and the preceding paragraphs are based on Davis, *Legacy of Love,* 26–29, as supplemented by numerous letters in Davis Papers, including those of JWD to Mrs. Edward H. McDonald.

Notes *to Chapter 4*

1. Charles H. Ambler and Festus P. Summers, *West Virginia: the Mountain State* (Englewood Cliffs, N.J., 1958, 2nd ed.), 423ff.; Haymond, *History of Harrison County,* 275.

2. Davis, Oral Memoir, 10–15; economic review article, Clarksburg *Weekly Telegram,* Nov. 4, 1898, and random issues, 1897–1902.

3. William G. Brown, *History of Nicolas County,* quoted in Ambler and Summers, *West Virginia,* 438; Davis, Oral Memoir, 10–11. As Davis phrased it, it "was cash money in the farmer's hands, and very attractive."

4. Festus P. Summers, *Johnson Newlon Camden; A Study in Individualism* (New York, 1937), 561; Ambler and Summers, *West Virginia,* 309.

5. Arthur E. Suffern, *Conciliation and Arbitration in the Coal Industry of America* (Boston and New York, 1915), 72; Ambler and Summers, *West Virginia*, 306.

6. Davis, Oral Memoir, 15.

7. Evelyn L. K. Harris and Frank J. Krebs, *From Humble Beginnings: West Virginia State Federation of Labor, 1903–1957* (Charleston, W. Va., 1960), xvii.

8. Charles P. Anson, "A History of the Labor Movement in West Virginia" (unpublished Ph.D. dissertation, University of North Carolina, Chapel Hill, 1940), 198–99. Elsie Gluck, *John Mitchell: Miner* (New York, 1929), 45. John Brophy, *A Miner's Life* (Madison, Wis., 1964), 74.

9. West Virginia Labor Commission, *Report* (1898), 69; Anson, "History of the Labor Movement," 199–200.

10. Wheeling *Intelligencer*, Aug. 17, 18, 19, 1897; Clarksburg *Weekly Telegram*, Aug. 20, 1897.

11. Davis, Oral Memoir, 104. For authoritative historical accounts, by legal scholars, of the use and abuse of the injunction, see Felix Frankfurter and Nathan Greene, *The Labor Injunction* (New York, 1930), and Charles O. Gregory, *Labor and the Law* (New York, 1961, 2nd rev. ed.). Gregory (101) writes: "Unfortunately, such injunctions left little, if any, scope for even peaceful economic coercive activity on the part of unions. And the harm occasioned to unions by this summary suppression was not undone even when appellate courts, as they seldom but occasionally did, set aside or modified injunctions because they were against the weight of the evidence adduced or contrary to established law. By that time months had passed, the possible effect of the strike or boycott was long since neutralized, and the union's investment of time, effort and money to organize the pressure was lost."

12. Wheeling *Intelligencer*, Aug. 17, 18, 19, 1897; Clarksburg *Weekly Telegram*, Aug. 20, 1897.

13. *Ibid.* Davis' personal account is in a long letter to Julia McDonald, Aug. 22, 1897.

14. Wheeling *Intelligencer*, Aug. 21, 1897.

15. JWD to Julia McDonald, Aug. 22, 1897; Wheeling *Intelligencer*, Aug. 20, 21, 1897. The case is not included in the *Federal Reporter*. It is briefly summarized in Smith, *Nathan Goff, Jr.*, 256–60.

16. Judge Goff's opinion was published in full in the Clarksburg *Weekly Telegram*, Aug. 27, 1897. Goff had a point, technically; the strikers' silent demonstration was in fact a subtle form of intimidation. But in his wide-ranging *obiter dicta* he failed to add that the operators could legally exert much more powerful intimidation against the union than it could against them. They remained "free" to use spies, to fire union members at will, to force men to sign yellow-dog contracts under threat of dismissal, and to "intimidate" entire communities through their "right" to command private armies. They also remained free to purchase or coerce the press, the pulpit, and, through the property-consciousness of judges like Goff and Jackson, the judiciary. The miners were left "free" only to exert moral suasion through words uttered, and often not reported, away from the scene of action. Even

this right was repeatedly and forcibly denied them, sometimes at the cost of their lives, in company towns in the more remote parts of the state. In 1907, for example, Governor William M. O. Dawson, in a special message to the legislature, pointed out that guards often prevented organizers from gaining access to the miners. He added: "Many outrages have been committed by these guards, many of whom appear to be vicious and dare-devil men who seem to aim to add to their viciousness by bull-dozing and terrorizing people." Quoted in Ambler and Summers, *West Virginia*, 446. But see esp. U. S. Congress, Senate, *West Virginia Coal Fields*, S. Rep. 457, 67th Cong., 2nd sess. (1922).

17. JWD to Julia McDonald, Aug. 22, 1897.

18. See Chapter 6.

19. Numerous letters, JWD to Julia McDonald, 1897–99. Hurst's full statement is: "For better or for worse, the bar in the United States was middle class—in its outlook predominantly upper-middle class. That implied an unresolved mingling of the urge to get on, with an only partly articulate and partly practiced sense of social obligation such as men could afford to have who came from a point above the margin of subsistence." *The Growth of American Law*, 254. For Davis' deviations from this pattern, see my following paragraphs.

20. Numerous letters, JWD to Julia McDonald; Johnson, "John William Davis."

21. Numerous letters, JWD to Julia McDonald, esp. July 7, 1898.

22. JWD to Julia McDonald, Feb. 24, Apr. 3, 14, 1898.

23. JWD to Julia McDonald, Apr. 21, June 26, July 26, 1898.

24. Original in Davis Papers.

25. Numerous letters, JWD to Julia McDonald, 1897–99.

26. *Ibid.* The story about the Circuit Judge is in *Davis Polk Wardwell Sunderland & Kiendl: A Background with Figures* (New York, privately printed, 1965), 68 (hereafter cited as *Davis Polk History*).

27. Numerous letters, JWD to Julia McDonald, 1897–99. Generalization based on interviews with Osman E. Swartz, Potter, Horner, Johnson, Koblegard, and McReynolds (hereafter cited, except for specific statements, as composite interview, Clarksburg group). Swartz entered Davis and Davis in 1903. McReynolds became a member of the firm after Davis left it. Potter and Koblegard were businessmen. All except McReynolds were contemporaries of Davis'.

28. Numerous letters, JWD to Julia McDonald, 1897–99.

29. *Ibid.*; John W. Davis, "The Argument of An Appeal," address to Association of the Bar of the City of New York, Oct. 22, 1940 (privately printed).

30. Numerous letters, JWD to Julia McDonald, 1897–99.

31. *Ibid.*; composite interview, Clarksburg group; Huntley, *John W. Davis*, 74–75. Huntley must be used with extreme caution, for his biography was prepared for the 1924 campaign. Nevertheless, his interviews with Davis' old friends and acquaintances yielded numerous anecdotes of value.

32. JWD to Julia McDonald, Apr. 14, 1899.

33. Davis, "Argument of An Appeal"; JWD to Julia McDonald, Nov. 14, 1898.

34. Davis, Oral Memoir, 46–47; JWD to Julia McDonald, Mar. 4, Sept. 25, 1898, Aug. 17, 1899; JWD to Anna K. Davis, Aug. 17, 1899.

35. JWD to Julia McDonald, Jan. 22, 1898.

36. JWD to Julia McDonald, Jan. 17, 1898, Apr. 21, 1899, June 20, 1898.

37. JWD to Julia McDonald Davis, Apr. 18, 1900, to Julia McDonald, June 25, Sept. 16, 1898; Davis, Oral Memoir, 44. The senior Davis handled the murder trial, but John W. later handled a few himself. See Theodore Kiendl, "John W. Davis," W. Va. B. A. Proc. 100 (1935).

38. JWD to John C. Vance, Dec. 13, 1946.

39. This episode is described in great detail, almost week by week, in Clarksburg Weekly Telegram, May–Dec. 1897.

40. JWD to Julia McDonald, Nov. 19, 1897.

41. JWD to Julia McDonald, Nov. 14, 19, 20, 23, 1897; Clarksburg Weekly Telegram, Dec. 10, 1897.

42. JWD to Julia McDonald, Dec. 5, 1897; Clarksburg Weekly Telegram, Dec. 10, 1897. The point of my implied criticism in the text is not that Davis represented the Short Line. Nor is it that he stood on procedure or technicalities; obviously, it was his duty to do so. The point is that Davis was so rigidly committed to the letter of law, so totally identified with his client, so constrained to justify his own conduct, that he was unable to perceive privately that this was a clear instance wherein the public interest dictated a modification of the original authorization to the Short Line.

43. JWD to Julia McDonald, Jan. 12, 15, 1898.

44. Swartz and Potter interviews.

45. Numerous letters, JWD to Julia McDonald, 1897–99; composite interview, Clarksburg group.

Notes to Chapter 5

1. JWD to Julia McDonald, July 20, Aug. 31, 1898.

2. JWD to Julia McDonald, Aug. 26, 31, Sept. 23, 1898. For the bond case, see West Va. & Pa. R.R. v. Harrison County Court, 34 S.E. (W. Va.) 786 (1899).

3. JWD to Julia McDonald, Sept. 3, 15, 1898.

4. JWD to Julia McDonald, Oct. 7, 9, 22, 26, 30, Nov. 4, 6, 1898.

5. JWD to Julia McDonald, Oct. 26, Sept. 23, 1898; circular in Davis Papers.

6. JWD to Julia McDonald, Oct. 26, 1898; Clarksburg Weekly Telegram, Oct. 28, 1898; Huntley, John W. Davis, 60–61.

7. For occupational breakdown, see West Virginia Legislature, Journal of the House of Delegates of West Virginia (1899), v–vi (hereafter cited as Journal of the House). Most state legislatures had a far higher percentage of lawyers. Wheeling Register, Feb. 5, 1899; Charleston Herald, Nov. 27, 1898;

JWD to Julia McDonald, Nov. 26, 1898; Julia McDonald to JWD, Nov. 27, 1898, Julia McDonald Papers.

8. Wheeling *Register,* Jan. 12, 13, 1899; JWD to Julia McDonald, Jan. 11, 1899, Davis Papers; Huntley, *John W. Davis,* 62–63. The *Journal of the House* does not report remarks on the floor in detail.

9. JWD to Julia McDonald, Jan. 29, Feb. 8, 11, 1899.

10. Memorandum, Porter R. Chandler to Ralph M. Carson, June 29, 1971, courtesy of Ralph M. Carson.

11. JWD to Julia McDonald, Feb. 11, 1899; *Journal of the House,* 471.

12. *Journal of the House,* 73, 620, 466–67; JWD to Julia McDonald, Feb. 22, 1899.

13. JWD to Julia McDonald, Feb. 15, 1899; *Journal of the House,* 492, 414.

14. JWD to Julia McDonald, Feb. 22, 23, 1899; *Journal of the House,* 695–96.

15. JWD to John J. Davis, Feb. 8, 1899.

16. *Journal of the House,* 435, 677–81.

17. Clippings, Davis Papers; Holly G. Armstrong to John J. Davis, Feb. 24, 1899.

18. JWD to Julia McDonald, July 20, 1898; composite interview, Clarksburg group; Huntley, *John W. Davis,* 93–94.

19. Numerous comments in Davis' letters to his parents and to Julia McDonald, 1896–99; copy of speech, n. d. (delivered Oct. 1900), Davis Papers. For Bryan, see Louis W. Koenig, *Bryan: A Political Biography* (New York, 1971), and Paolo E. Coletta, *William Jennings Bryan,* I: *Political Evangelist, 1860–1908* (3 vols., Lincoln, Neb., 1964).

20. Quoted in Alpheus Thomas Mason, *Brandeis: A Free Man's Life* (New York, 1946), 101; composite interview, Clarksburg group, esp. Swartz; Davis, Oral Memoir, 47. Davis argued the power case in the Harrison County Circuit Court in May 1899. He was on the brief when it went to the West Virginia Supreme Court of Appeals. The plaintiff in error (Davis' adversary) appealed to the United States Supreme Court, but then moved for dismissal. Clarksburg Electric Light Co. v. City of Clarksburg, 46 L. Ed. (Sup. Ct.) 1267 (1902).

21. Davis, Oral Memoir, 47–48; JWD to Gilpin Robinson, Apr. 28, 1931.

22. *Ibid.*

23. *Ibid.;* also Smith, *Nathan Goff, Jr.,* 252–53.

24. U. S. v. Haggerty, 116 Fed. Rep. 510 (1902); Clarksburg *Telegram,* June 13, July 4, 1902; Wheeling *Register,* Nov. 3, 1910; Parkersburg *News,* Aug. 22, 1924.

25. *Ibid.*

26. *Ibid.;* Smith, *Nathan Goff, Jr.,* 255–56.

27. Composite interview, Clarksburg group; Johnson, "John William Davis."

28. JWD to E. G. Lockhard, statement, n. d. (c. 1937); John W. Davis, Foreword to Francis L. Wellman, *The Art of Cross-Examination* (New York, 1944, 4th ed., rev.), xiii; composite interview, Clarksburg group; JWD to

Julia McDonald, Jan. 7, Aug. 26, 28, 1898, to John C. Vance, Apr. 21, 1947.

29. Davis, Oral Memoir, 44–45.

30. Quoted in Huntley, *John W. Davis*, 74.

31. Davis described the fight and commented on it, usually at length, in four separate letters to Julia McDonald, May 13, 15, 16, and 18, 1898. Although the Clarksburg *Weekly Telegram*, May 20, 1898, gave no account, it did report that he was fined $25 and costs. The other two incidents are based on composite interview, Clarksburg group, esp. Swartz.

32. The senior Davis was twice offered, and twice declined, the presidency of the West Virginia Bar Association. Generalizations based on W. Va. B. A. PROC. 1888–1910. The organization seems to have been something more than the social club Hurst, *Growth of American Law*, 365, characterizes most local and state associations as being at that time. In most respects, however, it conformed to the pattern he ascribes (361–66) to the American Bar Association, i.e., neither truly progressive nor truly reactionary. For the revolution in due process, see Arnold M. Paul, *Conservative Crisis and the Rule of Law* (Ithaca, 1960), Robert Green McCloskey, *American Conservatism in the Age of Enterprise, 1865–1910* (Cambridge, 1951), and John P. Roche, "Entrepreneurial Liberty and the Fourteenth Amendment," *Labor History*, IV (Winter 1963), 3–31.

33. JWD to Edward H. McDonald, Feb. 2, 1907.

34. John J. Coniff, "Injunctions: What Legislation, if any, Is Needed in Regard to Them?" W. Va. B. A. PROC. (1902); Luther C. Anderson, "Workmen's Compensation," W. Va. B. A. PROC. 60 (1910).

35. Armistead C. Gordon, "The Citizen and the Republic," W. Va. B. A. PROC. 31 (1901); W. W. Brannon, "The Doctrine of Stare Decisis, As Understood and Misunderstood," W. Va. B. A. PROC. 89 (1904); T. R. Jacobs, remarks from floor, W. Va. B. A. PROC. 2 (1905).

36. John J. Jacob, "Presidential Address," W. Va. B. A. PROC. 81 (1888); Henry Brannon, "The Supreme Court of Appeals of West Virginia," W. Va. B. A. PROC. 108 (1909); D. C. Westenhaver, "The Mission of a Bar Association," W. Va. B. A. PROC. 21 (1890).

37. John W. Davis, "The Growth of the Commerce Clause," W. Va. B. A. PROC. 89 (1906). The address, which was delivered in December, missed many of the nuances of Marshall's, Taney's, and Waite's great opinions, as analyzed by Felix Frankfurter in *The Commerce Clause Under Marshall, Taney and Waite* (Chapel Hill, 1937).

38. Davis, "Growth of the Commerce Clause," 99–100.

39. Claude G. Bowers, *Beveridge and the Progressive Era* (New York, 1932), 252–55; Davis, "Growth of the Commerce Clause," 103.

40. For Roosevelt's views, see my *Power and Responsibility: The Life and Times of Theodore Roosevelt* (New York, 1961), 156; Davis, "Growth of the Commerce Clause," 110.

41. Composite interview, Clarksburg group; JWD to Anna K. Davis, July 26, 1910; handwritten statement, "Assets. Dec. 31, 1911"; copy of Income Tax Return, 1913.

42. Clipping from Greenbrier *Independent*, quoting also Parkersburg *Sen-*

tinel, n. d., Davis Papers; JWD to Walter Stuart, July 6, 1910, Walter Stuart Papers, Library of West Virginia University; Davis, Oral Memoir, 59; Huntley, *John W. Davis,* 65; clippings, Congressional Scrapbook.

43. JWD to Stuart, July 6, 1910, Stuart Papers; JWD to Anna K. Davis, July 5, 1910.

44. Huntley, *John W. Davis,* 67–69.

45. *Ibid.;* Davis, Oral Memoir, 60; Lucius Hoge to John J. Davis, July 23, 1910, John J. Davis Papers.

46. Charleston *Star,* July 31, 1910; Wheeling *Register,* Nov. 3, 1910.

47. Numerous clippings, Congressional Scrapbook, but see esp. Wheeling *Register,* Nov. 3, 1910.

48. Congressional Scrapbook.

Notes to Chapter 6

1. Clark's statement is in James C. McReynolds to JWD, Mar. 20, 1913.

2. Davis, Oral Memoir, 71; Huntley, *John W. Davis,* 84.

3. *Congressional Record,* 62nd Cong., 1st sess., 2138–43.

4. JWD to Anna K. Davis, Mar. 3, 1912; Frankfurter and Greene, *The Labor Injunction,* 154–59, 184–85.

5. JWD to Anna K. Davis, Mar. 3, 1912; U.S. Congress, House, *Regulation of Injunctions,* H. Rep. No. 612, 62nd Cong., 2nd sess. (1912).

6. JWD to John J. Davis, Apr. 12, 1912.

7. *Congressional Record,* 62nd Cong., 2nd sess., 6434–41.

8. *Ibid.* Davis cited *Farmers' Loan & Trust Co. v. Northern Pacific Railroad Co.*

9. Davis wrote his father that he wondered about the expedience of his "dig at the mighty Theodore," but added that he was "so thoroughly set against his third term and recall of judicial decisions, that I would as soon yield up my political life in that cause as in any that I know." It was his "duty to stand up where one can be seen and be counted." JWD to John J. Davis, May 21, 1912.

10. Frankfurter and Greene, *Labor Injunction,* 160; *Congressional Record,* 62nd Cong., 2nd sess., 6470–71; *New York Times,* May 15, 1912. For the subsequent history of the bill, see Arthur S. Link, *Wilson,* II: *The New Freedom* (Princeton, 1956), 427–33.

11. Cromwell Holmes Thomas, *Problems of Contempt of Court: A Study in Law and Public Policy* (Baltimore, 1934), 41–42.

12. U. S. Congress, House, *Procedure in Contempt Cases,* H. Rept. 613, Part 2 to accompany H.R. No. 22591, 62nd Cong., 2nd sess. (1912), 10, JWD to Anna K. Davis, June 11, 1912.

13. *Congressional Record,* 62nd Cong., 2nd sess., Appendix, 313–19; Frankfurter and Landis, *Power of Congress Over Procedure in Criminal Contempts in "Inferior" Federal Courts—A Study in Separation of Powers,* 37 Harv. L. Rev. 1010, at 1056 (1924).

14. Davis, Oral Memoir, 70–72; JWD to Anna K. Davis, Jan. 26, 1912.

15. JWD to John J. Davis, Feb. 10, 1912, to Anna K. Davis, July 11, 1911,

to John J. Davis, Jan. 21, 1913. Davis also arranged to have Carl Vance, his campaign manager, appointed postmaster of Clarksburg. See extensive file, "Clarksburg Post Office," in Davis Papers.

16. Davis, Oral Memoir, 75.

17. JWD to John J. Davis, Jan. 30, 1912.

18. Congressional Record, 62nd Cong., 1st sess., 4102.

19. Ibid.

20. Ibid. 2430. For a more detailed account, see Claude E. Barfield, Jr., "The Democratic Party in Congress, 1909–1913" (unpublished Ph.D. dissertation, Northwestern University, 1965), 370–79.

21. Congressional Record, 62nd Cong., 1st sess., 2433; ibid. 2nd sess., 6366. The comment on Root's and Sutherland's strategy is based on John B. Wiseman, "Racism in Democratic Politics, 1904–1912," Mid-America, LI (Jan. 1969), 38–58.

22. See the balanced account in James H. Timberlake, Prohibition and the Progressive Movement: 1900–1920 (Cambridge, Mass., 1963).

23. JWD to John J. Davis, Feb. 9, 1913; U.S. Congress, To Divest Liquors of Interstate Character in Certain Cases, H. Rept. No. 1461, Part 2, 62nd Cong., 3rd sess. (1913).

24. JWD to John J. Davis, Feb. 9, 1913.

25. Congressional Record, 62nd Cong., 3rd sess., 2818–22. Davis softened the speech a little for insertion in the Record.

26. Ibid. 2866–67.

27. JWD to John J. Davis, Feb. 9, to Anna K. Davis, Feb. 16, 1913; Congressional Record, 62nd Cong., 3rd sess., 4447.

28. For the origins of the fellow-servant rule, see the brilliant chapter in Leonard W. Levy, The Law of the Commonwealth and Chief Justice Shaw: The Evolution of American Law, 1830–1860 (Cambridge, Mass., 1957), 166–82. The developments leading to its abrogation are treated inclusively in Friedman and Ladinsky, Social Change and the Law of Industrial Accidents, 67 COLUM. L. REV. 50 (1967). Roy Lubove, The Struggle for Social Security: 1900–1935 (Cambridge, Mass., 1968), is especially informative on the movement in the states. I am also indebted to Charles T. Cullen, "A Common Law Conflict: Tort Law Versus Workmen's Compensation" (seminar paper, University of Virginia, 1968).

29. William H. Harbaugh (ed.), The Writings of Theodore Roosevelt (Indianapolis, 1967), 182–85; Congressional Record, 60th Cong., 1st sess., 6670.

30. E. H. Downey, Workmen's Compensation (New York, 1924), 6; Alice Hamilton, Exploring the Dangerous Trades (Boston, 1943), 9; Lubove, Struggle for Social Security, 46–47; Herman M. Somers and Anne R. Somers, Workmen's Compensation: Prevention, Insurance, and Rehabilitation of Occupational Disability (New York, 1954), 22; U.S., Congress Senate Document 338, Report of the Employers' Liability and Workmen's Compensation Commission. S. Doc. 338, 62nd Cong., 2nd sess. (1912). The report added: "The Constitution does not say that no person shall be deprived of his property, but that he shall not be so deprived without due process of law. . . . If this phrase could be now so construed as to prevent the adoption of a law, which

the almost universal sentiment of modern society regards as just and reasonable, it would amount to a bulwark against the advance of justice."

31. Davis, Oral Memoir, 46–47; JWD to Anna K. Davis, May 30, 1912, to John J. Davis, June 2, Aug. 5, 1912, Jan. 21, Feb. 2, 9, Mar. 8, 1913.

32. U.S., Congress, *Federal Accident Compensation Act,* H. Rept. No. 1441, 62nd Cong., 3rd sess. (1913), 56–59.

33. JWD to John J. Davis, Feb. 2, 1913; Arthur S. Link, *Wilson: Campaigns for Progressivism and Peace* (5 vols., Princeton, 1947–65), V, 56–59.

34. See, among many other works, Robert H. Wiebe, *The Search for Order: 1877–1920* (New York, 1967); Samuel P. Hays, *The Response to Industrialism: 1885–1914* (Chicago, 1957); George E. Mowry, *The Era of Theodore Roosevelt, 1900–1912* (New York, 1958); Richard Hofstadter, *The Age of Reform: From Bryan to F.D.R.* (New York, 1955); Arthur S. Link, *Woodrow Wilson and the Progressive Era, 1910–1917* (New York, 1954); Gabriel Kolko, *The Triumph of Conservatism: A Reinterpretation of American History, 1900–1916* (Glencoe, Ill., 1963); Horace Samuel Merrill and Marion Galbraith Merrill, *The Republican Command: 1897–1913* (Lexington, Ky., 1971).

35. JWD to John J. Davis, Aug. 5, 1912, and passing comments in several other letters; also, roll call votes on several bills.

36. Wheeling *Register,* July 19, 1912; Julia Davis to Mrs. Edward H. McDonald, Oct. 27, 1912; numerous clippings, Congressional Scrapbook.

37. Numerous clippings, Congressional Scrapbook.

38. *Ibid.*

39. *Ibid.*

40. JWD to Julia McDonald, Apr. 19, 1899, and several other letters. Bassell had read law under the senior Davis. A deep, underlying hostility developed between the two men. Bassell was cold, dispassionate, and meticulous, both as a lawyer and as a man. He was once asked, after losing a case to young John, if John was brighter than his father. "No," he replied, "but he's got more common sense." John W. respected Bassell. Composite interview, Clarksburg group, esp. Swartz. For a friendly, uncritical characterization of Bassell, see Atkinson, *Bench and Bar of West Virginia,* 33.

41. This and the following paragraphs draw heavily on Davis, *Legacy of Love.* JWD to Anna K. Davis, May 3, Apr. 19, 1911.

42. Davis, *Legacy of Love,* 136–37; Lillie Preston to Anna K. Davis, May 8, 1911.

43. JWD to Anna K. Davis, May 3, 1911.

44. Davis, *Legacy of Love,* 137–38; Anna K. Davis to Mrs. Edward H. McDonald, Jan. 3, 1912.

45. Ellen Bassell Davis to Anna K. Davis, Jan. 3, 1912; JWD to Anna K. Davis, Apr. 13, 1913.

46. Davis, *Legacy of Love,* 139–43.

47. *Ibid.* 141–42.

48. *Ibid.* 140.

49. John J. Davis' statement is in a letter, Ellen B. Davis to Cornelia Bassell, n.d., courtesy of Miss Bassell.

50. For a good summary account, see *The Literary Digest*, XLVI (Jan. 25, 1913), 169–70.

51. Joseph Borkin, *The Corrupt Judge: An Inquiry into Bribery and Other High Crimes and Misdemeanors in the Federal Courts* (New York, 1962). See esp. Appendix, "Federal Judges Whose Official Conduct Has Been The Subject of Congressional Inquiry." At the time Borkin wrote, there had been fifty inquiries and nine impeachments. Six judges had been found guilty and sixteen others had resigned after inquiries or hearings had begun. The letter quoted is A. Thompson to JWD, Jan. 14, 1913.

52. JWD to Anna K. Davis, May 12, 1912; Ellen B. Davis to Anna K. Davis, May 9, 1912.

53. JWD to Anna K. Davis, May 12, 1913. For a complete citation of all proceedings, see Borkin, *Corrupt Judge*, 221–22. Davis' interrogation of witnesses is in the *Congressional Record*, 62nd Cong., 3rd sess., 227–30, 264–67, 583–91. His questioning was fair, courteous, and pertinent.

54. JWD to John J. Davis, Dec. 29, 1912, Jan. 12, 1913.

55. *Congressional Record*, 62nd Cong., 3rd sess., 1266–69.

56. JWD to John J. Davis, Jan. 12, 1913; Davis, Oral Memoir, 83. Davis added that impeachment was "very cumbersome" and that he preferred "some system by which the Senate wouldn't have to sit day by day listening like a jury to witnesses before it."

57. U.S., Congress, *In the Case of Charles C. Glover for Assault upon Representative Thetus W. Sims*, H. Rept. No. 6, 63rd Cong., 1st sess., 1913.

58. *Congressional Record*, 63rd Cong., 1st sess., 500–503; enclosure, JWD to John J. Davis, Apr. 22, 1913.

59. *Congressional Record*, 63rd Cong., 1st sess., 1433.

60. *Ibid.;* see also Huntley, *John W. Davis*, 88–92.

61. Davis, Oral Memoir, 85; JWD to John J. Davis, Feb. 27, 1913.

62. Ellen B. Davis to Anna K. Davis, Feb. 24, 1913.

63. See folder, "Bid for Federal Judgeship," Davis Papers. Cox's statement is in James M. Cox, *Journey Through My Years* (New York, 1946), 330–31. A copy of judiciary committee's statement, signed by J. J. Speight, clerk of the committee, and dated Feb. 27, 1913, is in the Davis Papers.

64. Wilson's statement is reported in JWD to Nathan Goff, Apr. 3, 1913. Davis said that the quotation was close to verbatim. Davis, *Legacy of Love*, 142.

65. JWD to James M. Cox, Dec. 30, 1946; Davis, Oral Memoir, 86.

66. Davis, Oral Memoir, 63–64.

67. Copy of the agreement with Swartz and Templeman, dated Aug. 1, 1913, is in Davis Papers. Davis' appointment as Solicitor General was dated Aug. 30, 1913.

Notes to Chapter 7

NOTE: Oral arguments were not recorded, or the transcripts were not preserved, in those few instances when they were recorded, during this period. Newspaper reports varied in length with the importance of, or current interest in, the case. However, all of Davis' briefs as Solicitor General are available in his bound *Cases and Points* at Yale.

   1. JWD to John J. Davis, Jan. 5, 1914; "The United States As a Litigant," remarks to the Maryland Bar Association, July 9, 1915, copy in Davis Papers; Davis, Oral Memoir, 95 (the maxim was left in his office by Frederick William Lehmann, a predecessor); interview with Robert Szold.

   2. JWD to John J. Davis, Oct. 2, 1915; Davis, Oral Memoir, 89.

   3. *Ibid.* 90–92.

   4. Szold to author, Mar. 29, 1966; interview with Huston Thompson; Davis, Oral Memoir, 91.

   5. He was much happier when his client's interest allowed him to insist that the right remedy was legislation rather than judicial construction. This happened much more often afterwards, when he was in private practice.

   6. Davis, Oral Memoir, 93.

   7. The Pipe Line Cases, 234 U.S. 548 (1914).

   8. JWD to John J. Davis, Aug. 12, 1913; Davis, Oral Memoir, 89; interview with Thurlow Gordon; memoranda, Blackburn Esterline to Solicitor General, n. d., Aug. 20, 21, 22, Oct. 13, 1913, Solicitor General File, RG 60, Acc 1197, National Archives.

   9. Brief for United States at 52, Pipe Line Cases. For a sharp criticism of what he terms Davis' "unimaginative approach to argument" in this and several other commerce clause cases, see James R. Klonoski, "The Influence of Government Counsel on Supreme Court Decisions Involving the Commerce Power" (unpublished Ph.D. dissertation, University of Michigan, 1958). Klonoski's thesis is that little was added, consequently, to a broader conceptualization of Congress' power over commerce. Although I agree with this in the abstract, I stand on the conclusion that Davis probably went as far as it was feasible to go, given the composition and values of the Court at that time.

   10. JWD to Anna K. Davis, Sept. 14, to John J. Davis, Dec. 28, 1913.

   11. Szold interview; Brief for United States, Pipe Line Cases; Washington *Post*, Oct. 16, 1913.

   12. JWD to Anna K. Davis, Oct. 19, 1913.

   13. The Pipe Line Cases, 234 U.S. 548 (1914).

   14. JWD to Mark DeWolfe Howe, June 12, 1952; Felix Frankfurter to JWD, Oct. 8, 1948. For a fuller account, see *Felix Frankfurter Reminisces: Recorded in Talks with Dr. Harlan B. Philips* (New York, 1960), 294–99. Frankfurter's account differs slightly from Davis'. Although the oil companies resentfully divested themselves of their pipeline subsidiaries, the economic impact proved negligible. As the Jersey group's historians write, the company was technically out of the pipeline business, "yet everyone concerned . . . knew very well that Jersey Standard . . . remained heavily involved and keenly interested." George Sweet Gibb and Evelyn H. Knowlton, *History of the Standard Oil Company (New Jersey): The Resurgent Years* (New York, 1956), 166–78. For a dispassionate examination of the entire issue, see Arthur M. Johnson, *Petroleum Pipelines and Public Policy, 1906–1967* (Cambridge, Mass., 1967).

15. For general background, see Charles Flint Kellogg, *NAACP: A History of the National Association for the Advancement of Colored People*, I: *1909–1920* (Baltimore, 1967). Segregation under the Wilson administration is described in Link, *Wilson*, II: *The New Freedom*, 246–52.

16. Brief for the United States, Guinn and Beal v. United States, 238 U.S. 347 (1915). Giles v. Teasley, 193 U.S. 146 (1904), cited in Troy M. Stewart, Jr., "John W. Davis: Solicitor General of the United States, 1913–1918" (unpublished Ph.D. dissertation, West Virginia University, 1973). Professor Stewart graciously supplied me with a draft of this dissertation, so my several citations of it lack page references.

17. Certificate from the United States Circuit Court of Appeals for the Eighth Circuit, Guinn v. United States.

18. Ellen B. Davis to Anna K. Davis, Oct. 19, 1913, Davis Papers.

19. J. A. Fowler to Solicitor General, memorandum, July 30, 1913, Department of Justice File, 150719, National Archives; Brief for NAACP as *Amicus Curiae*, Guinn v. United States. William B. Hixon, Jr., *Moorfield Storey and the Abolitionist Tradition* (New York, 1972), 136–37, reports that Storey dropped the idea of relying on the Fourteenth Amendment. My reading of his brief indicates that he grounded it on both the Fourteenth and Fifteenth Amendments.

20. JWD to Anna K. Davis, Sept. 28, 1913; Brief for the United States at 23–24, Guinn v. United States.

21. Ellen B. Davis to Anna K. Davis, Oct. 19, 1913.

22. The fullest account of the oral argument is in the Washington *Star*, Oct. 18, 1913.

23. Guinn v. United States.

24. United States v. Mosley, 238 U.S. 383 (1915).

25. Brief for the United States at 14, 19, United States v. Mosley.

26. United States v. Mosley.

27. Andrew Salter to William H. Armbrecht, Jan. 20, 1911, Department of Justice File 155322, National Archives. For a brief general description, see Glenn U. Sisk, "Crime and Justice in the Alabama Black Belt, 1875–1917," *Mid-America*, XL (Apr. 1958), 106–13. A comprehensive study is James C. Daniel, "Peonage in the New South" (unpublished Ph.D. dissertation, University of Maryland, 1971).

28. See the voluminous correspondence on United States v. Reynolds; United States v. Broughton, 235 U.S. 133 (1914), Department of Justice File 155322, National Archives.

29. Brief for the United States at 11, United States v. Reynolds; United States v. Broughton.

30. Brief for the United States at 28.

31. United States v. Reynolds; United States v. Broughton, 235 U.S. 133 (1914).

32. JWD to John J. Davis, Feb. 4, 1914; United States v. Midwest Oil Company, 236 U.S. 459 (1915). For background, see J. Leonard Bates, "The Midwest Decision, 1915: A Landmark in Conservation History," *Pacific Northwest Quarterly*, LI (Jan. 1960), 26–34, and Bates, *The Origins of Tea-*

pot Dome: Progressives, Parties, and Petroleum, 1909–1921 (Urbana, Ill., 1963), 56–59.

33. Harbaugh, *Life and Times of Theodore Roosevelt*, 361; Bates, "Midwest Decision."

34. Bates, "Midwest Decision"; for the Western reaction, see Colby, *The New Public Land Policy with Special Reference to Oil Lands*, 3 CALIF. L. REV. 285 (1915).

35. JWD to John J. Davis, Dec. 7, 1913.

36. Brief for the United States.

37. JWD to Anna K. Davis, Jan. 12, to John J. Davis, Jan. 14, May 18, 1914; Bates, "Midwest Decision," 30.

38. United States v. Midwest Oil Company; Gregory statement is in Bates, *Origins of Teapot Dome*, 56. Justices Willis Van Devanter and Joseph McKenna concurred in Day's dissent. Van Devanter was from Wyoming, McKenna from California. Justice James C. McReynolds abstained. For additional comment, see Colby, *New Public Land Policy*, Note, 28 HARV. L. REV. 613 (1915); and "The President and the Public Lands," *Outlook*, CIX (Mar. 24, 1915), 657.

39. United States v. Midwest Oil Company, 236 U.S. 459 (1915) at 484–512 (Day, J., dissenting).

40. JWD to John J. Davis, Feb. 28, 1915.

41. Ellen B. Davis to Anna K. Davis, Nov. 7, 22, 1913; JWD to John J. Davis, Jan. 18, 1915, Apr. 10, 1914.

42. Interview with James Beech.

43. JWD to John J. Davis, n. d., and Oct. 14, 1914, Jan. 18, 1915.

44. Interviews with Huston Thompson, John Lord O'Brian, Robert Szold, and Thurlow Gordon; JWD to Anna K. Davis, Nov. 23, 1913.

45. JWD to John J. Davis, Apr. 2, 1915; Davis, Oral Memoir, 85; Lexington (Ky.) *Herald*, June 20, 1924.

46. Conclusion is based on examination of numerous memoranda on various cases in the Department of Justice File.

47. JWD to Anna K. Davis, Jan. 1, 1917, to John Lord O'Brian, Dec. 12, 1947.

48. See, for example, Esterline to Solicitor General, Mar. 13, 1914, Department of Justice File; Thompson interview.

49. JWD to Attorney General, Sept. 9, 1921; Gordon and Szold interviews; Szold to author, Aug. 15, 1966; JWD to Isidor Kresel, Apr. 8, 1929.

50. Thompson, Szold, Gordon, and O'Brian interviews; also, Szold to author, Mar. 29, July 28, Aug. 15, 1966. Szold's name appears on fourteen of Davis' briefs, but the case files indicate many other involvements. Szold himself made no estimate.

51. Szold and O'Brian interviews.

52. Davis, Oral Memoir, 87–95; numerous letters, JWD to John J. Davis, esp. Feb. 23, 1915. For a comprehensive survey of Davis' administrative duties, see Chapter III in Stewart, "John W. Davis: Solicitor General." Also see William E. Brigman, "The Office of the Solicitor General in the United

States" (unpublished Ph.D. dissertation, University of North Carolina, 1966), which emphasizes the recent past.

53. *Ibid.*

54. JWD to John J. Davis, to Anna K. Davis, n. d. and May 11, 1915.

55. Beech interview; occasional comments in Davis' letters; Davis' memorial remarks on McReynolds, copy in Davis Papers.

56. JWD to John J. Davis, Aug. 22, 1914; Davis, Oral Memoir, 94.

57. Davis, Oral Memoir, 96–97, 100–101; Davis' memorial remarks on Van Devanter, copy in Davis Papers. The fullest and fairest account of McReynnolds the man is in Stephen T. Early, "James Clark McReynolds and the Judicial Process," (unpublished Ph.D. dissertation, University of Virginia, 1954). Statement about Court's attitude toward Davis is by Edward G. Lowry as quoted in Clinton W. Gilbert, *You Takes Your Choice* (New York, 1924).

58. Davis, Oral Memoir, 101.

59. *Ibid.*

60. *Ibid.*

61. JWD to Otto E. Koegel, Apr. 25, 1950.

62. Davis, Oral Memoir, 98–100.

63. JWD to Herbert Brookes, Oct. 19, 1944.

Notes to Chapter 8

1. Quoted in Link, *Woodrow Wilson and the Progressive Era, 1910–1917*, 236; also see the fuller treatment in Link, *Wilson, V: Campaigns for Progressivism and Peace* (Princeton, 1965), 83–92.

2. Ray S. Baker and William E. Dodd (eds.), *The Public Papers of Woodrow Wilson* (6 vols., New York, 1925–27), *New Democracy*, II, 264–274.

3. See, in particular, the accounts in *The New York Times* and the New York *Sun*, Sept. 1–5, 1916.

4. Record at 49, Wilson v. New, 243 U.S. 332 (1917); JWD to Anna K. Davis, Dec. 8, 1916.

5. Characterization of Johnson is based on the laudatory treatment in Barnie F. Winkelman, *John G. Johnson: Lawyer and Art Collector 1841–1917* (Philadelphia, 1942), and the more critical observations in Benjamin R. Twiss, *Lawyers and the Constitution* (Princeton, 1942).

6. Memorandum, Szold to JWD, Jan. 2, 1917, Justice Department File, Wilson v. New. Szold's name was not on the brief, but he apparently figured importantly in its composition. Although the brief emphasized the hours-of-service argument, it also contended, as Davis did in oral argument, that the Act was constitutional, "even if only a wage law."

7. *The New York Times*, New York *Sun*, and Washington *Post*, Jan. 9, 10, 1917, all printed relatively lengthy excerpts from the oral arguments. I have used all three. The accounts square with the main points of all the briefs. Both the brief and Davis' oral argument seem to have misread, or at least excluded, that part of the debates in Congress and the testimony in the hearing which contradicted the hours-regulation thesis. See, for example, the statement of Elisha Lee for the railroads in U.S., Congress, Senate, Commit-

tee on Interstate Commerce. *Threatened Strike of Railway Employees*. *Hearing* before the Committee on Interstate Commerce, United States Senate, on bills in connection with legislation relative to the threatened strike of railway employees, S. Doc. No. 549, 64th Cong., 1st sess., 1916, 80–93.

8. *New York Times et al.*, Jan. 9, 1916.

9. *Ibid.* Jan. 10, 1916.

10. *Ibid.*

11. *Ibid.*

12. *Ibid.* "Speak it not aloud," Davis wrote of Hagerman's argument, "but it was an awful harangue." JWD to Anna K. Davis, Jan. 10, 1917.

13. James Hamilton Lewis to JWD, n. d.; JWD to Anna K. Davis, Jan. 8, 1917. *The New York Times*, Jan. 9, 1917, featured Davis in a subhead: "Davis Stirs Court in Eight-Hour Case."

14. Wilson v. New, 243 U.S. 332, 345, 359 (1917).

15. *Ibid.* (Day and Pitney, J. J., at 372, 380 dissenting). The case sparked a voluminous outpouring of articles in the law reviews. See, especially, the thoughtful analysis in Powell, *The Supreme Court and the Adamson Law*, 65 U. PENN. L. REV. 607 (1917). *Wilson v. New* proved ultimately to be an aberration rather than a landmark.

16. JWD to Anna K. Davis, n. d.; JWD to Wendell P. Barker, Dec. 22, 1938.

17. Davis' first oral argument in the *Harvester* case (it was argued a second time in 1917) is reported in *New York Times*, Apr. 9, 10, 1915. My account is from it. To Davis' disgust, Gregory insisted on opening for the government, thus forcing out Todd. Gregory merely read excerpts from the brief. JWD to John J. Davis, Apr. 11, 1915.

18. The consent decree is summarized in *Report of the Attorney General: 1918* (Washington, D.C., 1918), 61–62. For Davis' refusal to move to advance, see Henry C. Colton to R. V. Lindabury, May 2, 1916, Justice Department File 60–138, National Archives.

19. JWD to Anna K. Davis, Feb. 15, 22, 23, 26, 1917, Davis Papers. Szold worked steadily on the preparation for eight months with two stenographers. Szold to author, Aug. 15, 1966.

20. *New York Times*, Mar. 14, 1917.

21. *Ibid.* Mar. 15, 1917. For an uncritical view of Gary and his purported liberality, see Ida Tarbell, *The Life of Elbert H. Gary* (New York, 1925), 320. Gary's resistance to the elimination of the twelve-hour day is treated at some length in Robert H. Zeiger, *Republicans and Labor: 1919–1929* (Lexington, Ky., 1969), 100–106. Davis' outline of his oral argument was more detailed than usual in this case. See Justice Department File 60-138.

22. JWD to Anna K. Davis, Mar. 15, 1917.

23. United States v. United States Steel Corporation, 251 U.S. 417 (1920). Justices McReynolds and Brandeis did not participate.

24. *Ibid.* at 9, 10, 12, 13.

25. *Ibid.* (Day, J., at 3, 5, 6 dissenting). Also see Watkins, *The Change in Trust Policy*, 35-HARV. L. REV. 815 (1922).

26. JWD to William Wallace, Jr., Apr. 9, 1920.

27. See books by Link, cited above, n. 1, for Wilson's views and policies.

28. Stephen B. Wood, *Constitutional Politics in the Progressive Era: Child Labor and the Law* (Chicago, 1968), offers a full and often perceptive account of the case from its beginning to its end. Roscoe Pound to Thomas W. Gregory, Sept. 4, 1917, Justice Department File No. 92195; Szold interview; Louis F. Post to JWD, Nov. 12, 1917, Justice Department File 92195.

29. JWD to John J. D. Preston, Jan. 26, 1918; Szold interview. Wood, *Constitutional Politics*, 140, erroneously attributes the brief to Assistant Attorney General William Frierson. Davis rejected most of Frierson's draft for Szold's.

30. Roscoe Pound to JWD, March 23, 1918, Justice Department File No. 92195; Brief for Appellant, Hammer v. Dagenhart, 247 U.S. 251 (1918).

31. Brief for Appellant. See the excellent analysis of the briefs in Wood, *Constitutional Politics*, 142–51. But also see the sharp criticism in Klonoski, "The Influence of Government Counsel on Supreme Court Decisions." Much as I agree with Klonoski's analysis in the abstract, I must again stand on the proposition (confirmed by the negative decision) that the Davis-Szold brief was as broad as could be reasonably expected at that time.

32. *Washington Post*, Apr. 16, 17, 1918.

33. Hammer v. Dagenhart, 247 U.S. 251 (1918).

34. Szold to JWD, June 7, 1918; JWD to Thomas I. Parkinson, June 20, 1918, both in Justice Department File 92195.

35. JWD to Anna K. Davis, Mar. 8, 1914, to John J. Davis, Sept. 15, 1915.

36. For Social Darwinism and formalism in general, see Richard Hofstadter, *Social Darwinism in American Thought* (Philadelphia, 1944) and Morton White, *Social Thought in America: The Revolt Against Formalism* (New York, 1949).

37. JWD to John J. Davis, Nov. 1, 1915, Jan. 14, 1914.

38. *Ibid.* n.d. (early Jan. 1915). JWD replied on January 23. For a brief summary of Hatfield's administration, see Ambler and Summers, *West Virginia*, 383–85.

39. Davis, Oral Memoir, 118–21.

40. JWD to Anna K. Davis, Feb. 16, Nov. 3, 1916.

41. Szold to author, Mar. 29, 1966. Actually, the government confessed error three times in more than 350 cases, according to the Attorney General's annual reports. JWD to Herbert Brookes, Oct. 19, 1944, for the Holmes remark.

42. JWD to Anna K. Davis, Oct. 12, 1916; Philadelphia *Record*, Aug. 13, 1922.

43. JWD to Anna K. Davis, Mar. 31, 1917, Dec. 8, 1916.

44. JWD to John J. Davis, May 14, Aug. 22, 1914.

45. *Ibid.* July 28, Sept. 1, 1915; Edward M. House to Albert S. Burleson, July 25, 1915, Papers of Albert S. Burleson, Library of Congress. Lansing, so House reported, had "his heart set on Davis"; Gregory "feels that Davis cannot be spared."

46. JWD to John J. Davis, Jan. 6, 1916. Anticipating a vacancy in the summer of 1915, former President Taft expressed a preference for Davis over

Secretary of the Interior Franklin Lane and Secretary of War Lindley Garrison. Davis, he wrote, would make "a good judge" and was "quite as able a lawyer" as Lane. (Taft regarded Garrison as "bumptious and limited.") Taft to Gus Karger, June 11, 1915, Yale Letterbooks, v. 42, Papers of William Howard Taft, Library of Congress.

47. JWD to John J. Davis, Jan. 14, 1916; Link, *Wilson*, IV: *Confusions and Crises*, 324; JWD to Anna K. Davis, July 5, 1916.

48. JWD to Anna K. Davis, Mar. 31, 1917. The smaller firm of Rushmore, Bisbee & Stern offered Davis a minimum guarantee of $25,000 per year. He had also received a feeler two years earlier from the B. & O. to become general counsel for the line in West Virginia at a salary "not less" than that of the Solicitor General ($7500). JWD to John J. Davis, Jan. 10, 1915; to Charles E. Rushmore, Apr. 24, 1917, to Paul Cravath, May 12, 1917.

49. Interview with Cornelia Bassell; JWD to Anna K. Davis, Jan. 25, 1914, Nov. 11, 23, 1913.

50. JWD to John J. Davis, Oct. 11, 1915, to Anna K. Davis, Jan. 12, 1917.

51. Quoted in Nan Davis Richardson to Anna K. Davis, Jan. 5. 1914; Davis, *Legacy of Love*, 138–39; Szold interview; JWD to Anna K. Davis, Jan. 1, 1914.

52. JWD to Anna K. Davis, Apr. 17, 1916; Davis, *Legacy of Love*, 149–50.

53. JWD to John J. Davis, Oct. 14, 1914; Davis, "The United States As a Litigant"; numerous statements in Davis' letters to his parents, 1914–17; "Our New Ambassador to England is an Intellectual Prodigy," *Current Opinion*, LXV (Nov. 1918), 294; Charles Warren, "War Notes," Box 5, The Papers of Charles Warren, Library of Congress, quoted in Stewart, "John W. Davis: Solicitor General."

54. JWD to Anna K. Davis, Apr. 4, 1917. The basic case, of course, was Selective Draft Law Cases, 245 U.S. 366 (1918).

55. I am indebted to H. Joel Weintraub, "Religion, Conscientious Objection, and the Supreme Court" (honors thesis, University of Virginia, 1967), for a general analysis of these cases. Brief for Plaintiffs at 33–40, Goldman *et al.* v. United States, 245 U.S. 474 (1918).

56. Szold to author, Aug. 15, 1966; Brief for the United States at 82–83, Goldman *et al.* v. United States, 245 U.S. 474 (1918).

57. The background of the *Goldman* case is richly described in Richard Drinnon, *Rebel in Paradise: A Biography of Emma Goldman* (Chicago, 1961), 190–99. The excerpts from Davis' oral argument are from the Washington *Star*, Dec. 14, 1917, and the Washington *Post*, Dec. 15, 1917. For the harassment of Miss Goldman, see Drinnon, *Rebel in Paradise*, and the correspondence in Justice Department File 186233-13, Selective Service Cases.

58. Goldman *et al.* v. United States, 245 U.S. 474 (1918); see also Freeman, *The Constitutionality of Peacetime Conscription*, 31 VA. L. REV. 40 (1944) at 56.

59. JWD to Philip G. Auchampaugh, Dec. 21, 1936.

60. This section draws heavily on Stewart, "John W. Davis: Solicitor General," and Homer Cummings and Carl McFarland, *Federal Justice: Chapters*

in the History of Justice and the Federal Executive (New York, 1937), 413–27.

61. JWD to Gregory, Apr. 10, 1917, Solicitor General File, RG 60, Acc 186400, National Archives, cited in Stewart, "John W. Davis: Solicitor General." Davis, address to the Kentucky Bar Association, July 2, 1918, revised as *The Lawyer and the War*, 3 MARQUETTE L. REV. 14, at 23 (1918). For the *Abrams* case, see Zechariah Chaffee, Jr., *Freedom of Speech in the United States* (Cambridge, Mass., 1954), and Henry J. Abraham, *Freedom and the Court: Civil Rights and Liberties in the United States* (New York, 1967), 159–62.

62. Stewart, "John W. Davis: Solicitor General"; O'Brian, *New Encroachments on Individual Freedom*, 66 HARV. L. REV. 1, at 9 (1952); Cummings and McFarland, *Federal Justice*, 426; O. S. Hilton, "Public Opinion and Civil Liberties in War Time, 1917–1919," *Southwestern Social Science Quarterly*, XXVIII (Dec. 1947), 215; Harry N. Scheiber, *The Wilson Administration and Civil Liberties, 1917–1921* (Ithaca, N.Y., 1960), 42.

63. Stewart, "John W. Davis: Solicitor General"; Warren, *What Is Giving Aid and Comfort to the Enemy?*, 27 YALE L. J. 331 (1918); Wallace-Davis-Warren exchange is in Stewart, "John W. Davis: Solicitor General"; JWD to Warren, April [n. d.], and June 8, Warren Papers.

64. White's statement is in Richard R. McMahon to William Howard Taft, Jan. 26, Taft Papers, courtesy of Alexander Bickel; Hughes' statement is in the Brooklyn *Eagle*, May 11, 1924; Holmes' statement was made to Robert Szold, Szold interview. In 1948, after an exhaustive survey of Supreme Court records, Davis' firm printed privately a pamphlet, "In The Supreme Court of the United States, Matter of John W. Davis: An Amicus Brief," listing all the Supreme Court cases he had actually argued orally to that time. A summary statement on his record as Solicitor General reads as follows: "One hundred and sixty [cases] occurred during his term as Solicitor General; in 79 of these the court rendered written opinions, in four he appeared as *amicus curiae*, in 20 he appeared on the brief, and in 57, of which he argued only two, the Court gave *per curiam* decisions. Many in this last category were routine matters pertaining to the daily business of the Solicitor General's office."

Notes to Chapter 9

1. Davis, Oral Memoir, 128; Robert Lansing to JWD, Sept. 6, 1918, Ellen B. Davis to JWD, Sept. 6, 1918; copies in John W. Davis, Prisoners of War Conference Diary, Summary Letter, Sept. 6–Oct. 20, 1918. Also see Summary Entry, Dec. 18, 1918, in John W. Davis, Ambassadorial Diary. Both are in Davis Papers. Colonel Edward M. House suggested Davis to the President on Aug. 24. He preferred him over Frank Cobb, and called him "one of the best" and "perhaps the best" available man. The following day he suggested Vance McCormick, Bainbridge Colby, and Ellery Sedgwick. House to Wilson, Aug. 24, 25, 1918, Papers of Woodrow Wilson, Library of Congress.

2. JWD to Ellen B. Davis, Sept. 7, 1918.

3. Lansing to JWD, Dept. 9, 1918; Ellen B. Davis to JWD, Sept. 9, 1918; JWD to Ellen B. Davis, Sept. 8, 1918.

4. Prisoners of War Diary, Sept. 9, 1918.

5. JWD to Lansing, Sept. 11, 1918; Lansing to JWD, Sept. 14, 1918.

6. Davis, Oral Memoir, 131–32.

7. Undated clipping, Ambassadorial Scrapbook, Davis Papers.

8. Numerous clippings, Ambassadorial Scrapbook; Mark DeWolfe Howe (ed.), *The Holmes-Pollock Letters* (2 vols., Cambridge, Mass., 1941), I, 269; Samuel Halley to JWD, Sept. 20, 1918.

9. Raymond Stone, "The American-German Conference on Prisoners of War," *American Journal of International Law*, XIII (July 1919), 406–49; Frank L. Polk to Thomas W. Gregory, July 31, 1918; John Lord O'Brian to Gregory, Aug. 6, 1918; Robert Lansing to Gregory, Aug. 15, 1918, copies of all in the Davis Papers.

10. JWD to Julia Davis, Aug. 14, 1918; Prisoners of War Diary and Diary Letter, Sept. 16, 1918.

11. Stone, "American-German Conference," 411.

12. Prisoners of War Diary, Oct. 14, 28, 1918; JWD to Ellen B. Davis, n.d.

13. Stone, "American-German Conference," 417, 426.

14. *Ibid.* 419 and *passim.*

15. *Ibid.* 437.

16. *Ibid.* 414.

17. *Ibid.* 444–45; Prisoners of War Diary, Oct. 17, 1918.

18. Stone, "American-German Conference," 416–18. As Stone conceded, the Americans "were in large measure actuated by the knowlededge that Germany was much in need of trained submarine personnel."

19. *Ibid.* 416–29.

20. JWD to Thomas W. Gregory, Oct. 7, 1918; Stone, "American-German Conference," 438–39.

21. Davis, Oral Memoir, 124–25; Stone, "American-German Conference," 439.

22. Stone, "American-German Conference," 448.

23. Ralph M. Carson to author, memorandum, summer 1971.

24. JWD to Ellen B. Davis, Oct. 8, 1, Sept. 23, 1918.

25. JWD to Julia Davis, Dec. 3, 1918.

26. Summary Entry, Ambassadorial Diary, Dec. 18, 1918.

27. *Ibid.;* JWD to Secretary of State, Dec. 21, 1918, Box 1309, 123 D 296, National Archives.

28. Davis, Oral Memoir, 134.

29. Ambassadorial Diary, Dec. 17, 1919.

30. Julia D. Healy to author, memorandum, autumn 1971.

31. David Lloyd George, *Memoirs of the Peace Conference,* (2 vols., New Haven, 1939), I, 112.

32. Ambassadorial Diary, Dec. 27, 1918.

33. *Ibid.* Dec. 31, 1918.

34. Clipping, Ambassadorial Scrapbook.

Notes to Chapter 10

1. This chapter is based, essentially, on Davis' four-volume Ambassadorial Diary. The original is at Yale University, a microfilm is at Columbia University, and a xerox copy is at the University of Virginia. I am indebted to H. Maureen DeJure, "The Diary of a Diplomat: A Study of Anglo-American Relations, 1918–1921" (honors thesis, Bucknell University, 1966), for much of the preliminary work for this chapter. For a general account, see Seth P. Tillman, *Anglo-American Relations at the Paris Peace Conference in 1919* (Princeton, 1961).

2. Ambassadorial Diary, Jan. 22, 23, 25, 1919. Davis rejected Henry White's request that he edit the proposed Covenant of the League, although he made several informal suggestions on its wording.

3. *Ibid.* June 3, 1919.

4. Pierrepont B. Noyes, *While Europe Waits for Peace* (New York, 1921), 41–47; Ernst Fraenkel, *Military Occupation and the Rule of Law* (London, 1944), 74.

5. Noyes, *While Europe Waits*, 43; Ambassadorial Diary, May 29, 1919.

6. Ambassadorial Diary, May 31–June 10, 1919, inclusive.

7. Davis, Oral Memoir, 143–44; Fraenkel, *Military Occupation*, 77. JWD to Woodrow Wilson, June 10, 1919, Wilson Papers.

8. See Ambassadorial Diary, Feb. 22, 1920, for a summary review of these incidents.

9. Davis Oral Memoir, 133; JWD to Frank L. Polk, Jan. 4, 1919, and copies of numerous speeches in Davis Papers. Davis privately viewed Admiral Sims' statement, which was made to a Senate committee, as "reprehensible." Ambassadorial Diary, Jan. 19, 1920.

10. Ambassadorial Diary, Apr. 15, 1919; *Irish Freeman*, n.d.; *Jewish Guardian*, Jan. 30, 1920; London *Evening News*, Feb. 26, 1920; and many similar clippings, all in the Ambassadorial Scrapbook or in loose files in Davis Papers.

11. JWD to Charles Warren, Mar. 1, 1920, Papers of Charles Warren, Library of Congress.

12. Ambassadorial Diary, Nov. 30, 1919.

13. JWD to Henry D. Clayton, Sept. 23, 1919; Ambassadorial Diary, Feb. 26, Mar. 20, Sept. 16, Dec. 9, 1920.

14. *Ibid.* Jan. 9, Feb. 4, 1920.

15. *Ibid.* Dec. 3, 1919. The address was published by Oxford University Press under the title *The Treaty-Making Power of the United States*. Davis' statement on the two-thirds rule is in a letter to Charles Warren, Mar. 24, 1920, Warren Papers. Most English papers praised the address, although *The Spectator*, May 1, 1920, in rejecting Davis' defense of Wilson's failure to include a single Senator in the peace delegation, said that the Conference was "of such exceptionable importance" that technical or historical considerations were no real excuse for Wilson's action.

16. Ambassadorial Diary, Dec. 1, 1919.

17. *Ibid.*

18. Davis, *Legacy of Love*, 163–64; JWD to Thomas W. Gregory, Jan. 20, 1920; to Emma Davis, Jan. 17, 1919.

19. Julia Davis Healy to author, memorandum, summer 1971. See esp. Davis' long description of Holkam, Ambassadorial Diary, May 22, 1920.

20. Interview with Julia Davis Healy.

21. Interview with Montgomery Angell; JWD to Joseph P. Kennedy, Jan. 5, 1938, Davis Papers.

22. Julia D. Healy to author, memorandum, winter 1972.

23. *Ibid.*

24. *Ibid.;* Mrs. Godfrey R. Benson to Ellen Bassell Davis, July 6, 1922, courtesy of Cornelia Bassell.

25. H. C. F. Bell, *Woodrow Wilson and the People* (Garden City, N.Y. 1945), 238.

26. Davis, *Legacy of Love*, 159, 176.

27. *Ibid.* 198; Ambassadorial Diary, June 7, 1920; Julia D. Healy to author, memorandum, summer 1971; also, Ambassadorial Diary, July 29, 1919.

28. JWD to Henry D. Clayton, Sept. 23, 1919, to Robert Lansing, n. d. (fall 1919).

29. JWD to Samuel G. Graham, Oct. 1, 1919, *ibid.;* Ambassadorial Diary, Dec. 7, 31, 1920, May 19, 1919. Davis said that Midleton was "a man of high ideals, devoted to the old order & eager for the sake of his conscience to find arguments to defend it [the aristocracy], but not unaware of its shortcomings." Davis was bitterly criticized in labor circles, according to the Philadelphia *Public Ledger*, Oct. 10, 1919, for publicly praising "the eagerness for the reign of law and the determination to preserve order even if a fight had to be made for it." The *Public Ledger*'s correspondent reported that labor felt that it was in "a bitter struggle in which class hostility was imminent" and that the Ambassador's remarks put him, in effect, on the side of the Establishment. Davis dismissed the report as a reflection of the reporter's personal pique. Davis to Secretary of State, Nov. 5, 1919, State Department File, Box 1309-123 D 296, National Archives.

30. Davis, Oral Memoir, 133; Davis, *Legacy of Love*, 184; H. Montgomery Hyde, *Lord Reading* (New York, 1967), 314.

31. JWD to Julia Davis, Feb. 1, 1919.

32. Ambassadorial Diary, Feb. 11, 1920.

33. JWD to Lansing, Dec. 5, 1919, Davis Papers. Davis' frustration was intensified five days later by his attendance at a secret conference at 10 Downing Street, with Lloyd George, Clemenceau, the Italian Ambassador, and other British, French, and Italian officials, at which the Russian, Polish, Italian, and Turkish problems were discussed. As he explained, he was authorized neither to represent his government nor to express any opinion; and though he did serve as a sounding board, his chief function was that of a conduit. See four-page typescript, Memorandum of Conference, Ambassadorial Diary, Dec. 12, 1919.

34. JWD to Lansing, Feb. 15, 1920; Diary, Mar. 11, 1920, for King George's comment. For a full account, see Daniel M. Smith, "Robert Lansing

and the Wilson Interregnum, 1919–1920," *The Historian*, XXI (1959), 135–61.

35. JWD to Wilson, Feb. 18, 1920 (not sent). The one exception to Davis' scrupulous accuracy as a reporter was his life-long tendency to underestimate his income and financial prospects and to overestimate his taxes and expenses. In numerous letters during and immediately after his ambassadorship, he said that his service "had sorely depleted his modest savings"; later, he often wrote or said that he had come home "busted," or, "broke, not insolvent, but broke." He seems to have spent $45,000, perhaps $55,000, above his salary and allowances during his twenty-eight months as Ambassador. About one-half of this sum was drawn from dividends on earlier investments. The remainder came from the sale of securities. In 1920, for example, he realized a profit of $22,500 from the sale of certain stocks. His regular dividends in 1919 and 1920 were $10,776 and $13,329. His net worth on his resignation was probably between $50,000 and $80,000. Analysis is based on lists of assets in the Davis Papers and, especially, working copies of his income tax returns for 1919 and 1920. In August 1919, Davis said, "At this rate I shall spend at least $20,000 of my own funds this year." Ambassadorial Diary, Aug. 1, 1919.

36. See Chapter 11, "Reluctant Dark Horse."

37. Joseph P. Tumulty, *Woodrow Wilson As I Know Him* (Garden City, N.Y. 1921), 394–95. For a detailed account of the movement in Ireland, see Dorothy Macardle, *The Irish Republic* (New York, 1965). Aspects of the tension between the United States and Britain are well described in Tillman, *Anglo-American Relations*.

38. Ambassadorial Diary, Jan. 17, 18, 1919.

39. *Ibid.* Apr. 10, 1920; JWD to Andrew Peters, June 20, 1919.

40. Ambassadorial Diary, Dec. 17, 1919; JWD to Charles Warren, Mar. 4, 1920, Warren Papers.

41. Davis, Oral Memoir, 134; Ambassadorial Diary, Sept. 4, Mar. 17, 1919, Dec. 7, 1920; Cork *Examiner*, July 7, 1920, and a few other clippings in the Ambassadorial Scrapbook and in loose files in the Davis Papers.

42. Ambassadorial Diary, Dec. 7, 1920, Jan. 16, 1921.

43. *Ibid.* Dec. 11, 15, 1920, Jan. 2, 1921.

44. *Ibid.* Jan. 9, Feb. 9, Mar. 5, 1921.

45. *Ibid.* Jan. 21, Feb. 4, 1919.

46. *Ibid.* Sept. 27, Oct. 25, 1919. Davis' cable to the State Department reporting Churchill's request was subsequently leaked in full and reprinted in the American press.

47. *Ibid.* Sept. 27, Oct. 25, 1919.

48. Davis, *Legacy of Love*, 182.

49. JWD to Lansing, Nov. 25, Dec. 5, 1919.

50. Memorandum, Ambassadorial Diary, Feb. 6, 1920.

51. *Ibid.*

52. *Ibid.* Jan. 28, Aug. 13, 1920; JWD to Lansing, July 8, 9.

53. JWD to Lansing, July 8, 9, 1920.

54. Ambassadorial Diary, Aug. 11, 12, 18, 1919.

55. *Ibid.* Aug. 25, 1919.

56. Characterization based on various passing comments in Ambassadorial Diary; Davis, *Legacy of Love;* and Harold Nicolson, *Curzon: The Last Phase 1919–1925* (London, 1934).

57. Ambassadorial Diary, Aug. 11, 18, 1919.

58. *Ibid.* Aug. 20, 22, 26, 1919.

59. *Ibid.* Aug. 18, 1919.

60. *Ibid.* Aug. 26, Oct. 5, 1919.

61. *Ibid.* Oct. 17, 1919; Benjamin Shwadran, *The Middle East, Oil and the Great Powers* (New York, 1955), 27, for Curzon memorandum to the Cabinet; JWD to Lansing, Sept. 25, 1919, Davis Papers.

62. JWD to Lansing, Sept. 25, 1919.

63. Ambassadorial Diary, Oct. 2, 1919; Shwadran, *Middle East,* 30–31; Ambassadorial Diary, Oct. 7, 14, 1919.

64. Shwadran, *Middle East,* 28–31; Ambassadorial Diary, Apr. 14, 28, 29, 1920.

65. Ambassadorial Diary, May 12, 19, 1920.

66. *Ibid.* Aug. 5, 11, 1920; *Foreign Relations,* 1920, II, 663–67.

67. Ambassadorial Diary, Nov. 19, 21, 1920. Text of Colby's note is in *Foreign Relations,* 1920, II, 668–73. Laurence Evans, *United States Policy and the Partition of Turkey* (Baltimore, 1965), incorrectly reports that the note was not delivered until December 6. Davis reports that he dispatched it to the Foreign Office on November 22, 1920, as directed. Ambassadorial Diary, Nov. 22, 1920. Otherwise, Evans' account, 302–4, is full and accurate.

68. Ambassadorial Diary, Nov. 22, 1920.

69. *Ibid.* Nov. 25, Dec. 7, 1920.

70. JWD to Wilson, Dec. 23, 1920, Davis Papers; Ambassadorial Diary, Jan. 13, 1921, for texts of telegrams exchanged by Davis and Acting Secretary of State Norman Davis on the proposed resignation. Frank L. Polk, one of Davis' new partners, reported that the members of the firm were unanimous in the opinion "that it would look much better for you to stick it out a few weeks longer." Polk to JWD, Jan. 14, 1921.

71. Ambassadorial Diary, Nov. 11, 1920; *British Weekly,* Nov. 25, 1925; Ambassadorial Diary, Nov. 19, 1920, Jan. 10, 1921, Dec. 6, 1920. Text of speech in Davis Papers. Also see *The Daily Telegraph,* Jan. 18, 1921, and numerous clippings in the Davis Papers.

72. Ambassadorial Diary, Nov. 13, 14, 15, 1920. Entries include six single-spaced typescript pages of summary.

73. *Ibid.*

74. *Ibid.*

75. *Ibid.*

76. *Ibid.*

77. JWD to Lord Astor, Oct. 14, 1947, Davis Papers; Davis, Oral Memoir, 134, Davis later wrote that Thomas Jones' biography, *Lloyd George* (Cambridge, Mass., 1951), was "quite fair" on the whole, "although it does not shrink from criticism." JWD to Herbert Brookes, Nov. 23, 1951.

78. I am indebted to Julia Davis Healy for the description. Ambassadorial Diary, Jan. 8, 9, 1921.

79. *Ibid.*

80. *Ibid.*

81. *Ibid.*

82. *Ibid.*

83. Tillman, *Anglo-American Relations*, 277–78. Daniel M. Smith, *Aftermath of War: Bainbridge Colby and Wilsonian Diplomacy, 1920–1921* (Philadelphia, 1970), 89–92.

84. Colby's note is summarized by Davis in Ambassadorial Diary, Feb. 11, 1921.

85. *Ibid.* Feb. 15, 1921. Davis cabled the substance of Geddes' remarks to the State Department on February 16. Curzon also addressed his reply to Colby's earlier Mesopotamian note (the one that had been sent directly to himself) to Davis, rather than to Colby. See *Foreign Relations, 1921*, II, 80–84.

86. Ambassadorial Diary Feb. 26, 1920; clippings, Davis Papers, esp. the *Sunday Times*, Mar. 6, 1921. *The New York Times*, Mar. 22, 1921, praised the Pilgrims' speech unreservedly.

87. London *Observer*, Mar. 6, 1921; numerous clippings, Ambassadorial Scrapbook.

88. Ambassadorial Diary, Mar. 5, 1921.

89. *Ibid.*

90. *Ibid.*

91. *Ibid.* Mar. 4, 8, 9, 1921.

92. *Ibid.* Mar. 9, 1921.

Notes to Chapter 11

1. Ambassadorial Diary, Jan. 5, 1919; JWD to F. B. Byington, Feb. 24, 1919; to Lansing, June 12, 1919; Clayton, Aug. 13, 1919; J. W. Johnston, July 20, 1919; John J. Cornwell to JWD, July 11, 1919.

2. Ambassadorial Diary, July 27, Aug. 2, 1919.

3. JWD to Cornwell, Aug. 5, 1919, Ambassadorial Diary, Aug. 12, 1919, Sept. 12, 1919; JWD to C. F. Moore, Sept. 23, 1919.

4. David C. Reay to JWD, Dec. 1, 1919; Lansing to JWD, Jan. 9, 1920; JWD to John J. Cornwell, Feb. 6, 1920; to Charles Peddicord, Mar. 1, 1920; to William Wallace, Apr. 8, 1920.

5. John J. Cornwell to Clem Shaver, Mar. 9, 1920, Papers of John J. Cornwell, Library of West Virginia University; Ambassadorial Diary, Mar. 11, 12, 1919, for texts.

6. Lansing to JWD, Jan. 1, 1920. Lansing mistakenly assumed that Davis' wife would object: "Of course she wants another London season. Can't you dangle before her eyes White House possibilities. . . . From all I can learn

of her use of money I fear an appeal to a miserly instinct would get nowhere with her." Lansing also confessed that he was "a mighty queer sort of a Secretary of State" to urge Davis to resign. He asked that his advice be kept confidential, explaining that he was "more influenced by friendship and . . . [Davis'] own interests than by anything else." Lansing to JWD, Feb. 1, 1920.

7. Lansing to JWD, Mar. 30, 1920. For an understanding treatment of Palmer, a tragic figure, see Stanley Coben, *A. Mitchell Palmer: Politician* (New York, 1963). Lansing's views of the "red menace" are recounted on 210. Also see William Preston, Jr., *Aliens and Dissenters: Federal Suppression of Radicals, 1903–1933* (Cambridge, Mass., 1963), and Robert K. Murray, *Red Scare* (Minneapolis, 1955).

8. Lansing to JWD, Mar. 30, 1920.

9. Ambassadorial Diary, Apr. 5, 1920; JWD to Emma Davis, Apr. 5, 1920.

10. JWD to Clem L. Shaver, Apr. 24, 22, 1920; J. Carl Vance to JWD, Apr. 8, 1920.

11. *New York Times,* May 23, 1920.

12. JWD to Lansing, May 29, 1920.

13. John J. Cornwell to JWD, May 12, 1920; JWD to Cornwell, May 26, 1920, Cornwell Papers; JWD to Lansing, May 29, 1920.

14. *New York Times,* May 30, 1920. Among the papers that endorsed Davis were the Cleveland *Independent,* Chicago *Evening Post,* Atlanta *Journal,* Spartanburg (S.C.) *Journal,* Wheeling (W. Va.) *Record,* and numerous West Virginia weeklies and small-town dailies. Many others, including the Baltimore *Sun,* Indianapolis *Star,* Philadelphia *Record,* Springfield *Republican,* and Louisville *Times* praised him in editorials or special articles. For letters to the editor, see *New York Times,* May 26, 27, 28, 30, June 1, 3, 5, 24, 1920.

15. New York *Evening Post,* May 25, 1920; New York *World,* May 31, 1920.

16. Oswald Garrison Villard, "Ghosts at San Francisco," *The Nation,* CX (June 26, 1920), 845–46; Chicago *Evening Post,* May 25, 1920; *New York Times,* May 24, 1920; Chandler P. Anderson Diary, June 21, 1920, Papers of Chandler P. Anderson, Library of Congress.

17. For the reaction in London, see *New York Times,* May 26, 1920, and, in Ambassadorial Scrapbook, Belfast *Irish News,* July 7, 1920. The latter said: "Mr. Davis had been gleefully welcomed by more than one British Correspondent as a strong friend of the Anglo-American Alliance idea, the value of which in the opinion of the delegates may be judged from the fact that his largest poll was 76." JWD to Emma Davis, June 19, 1920; to Peerce McDonald, July 22, 1920.

18. *New York Times,* June 22, 1920.

19. Copy of Cummings memorandum in Papers of Ray Stannard Baker, Series 1A-Box 3, Library of Congress.

20. *New York Times,* June 24, 1920; JWD to Rose McDonald, July 13, 1920; Ambassadorial Diary, June 23, 1920, for text of cables to Watson.

21. *Ibid.* June 24, 1920; *New York Times,* June 24, 1920.

22. Ambassadorial Diary, June 25, 1920, for texts of exchange of cables.

23. *New York Times,* June 28, 1920; Ambassadorial Diary, week of June 28, for Watson's cables; *New York Times,* June 30, 1920. All of Davis' correspondents agreed that Cornwell made a superb nominating speech and that the seconding speeches were unusually effective.

24. For background, I have leaned heavily on the account of the convention in Wesley M. Bagby, *The Road to Normalcy* (Baltimore, 1962). There is also good material in David Burner, *The Politics of Provincialism: The Democratic Party in the 1920's* (New York, 1968), and Donald R. McCoy, "Election of 1920," in Arthur M. Schlesinger, Jr., and Fred L. Israel (eds.), *History of American Presidential Elections: 1789–1968* (4 vols., New York, 1971), III.

25. Arthur B. Koontz to JWD, July 16, 1920; *New York Times,* July 4, 1920; Raymond J. Hanks, "The Democratic Party in 1920: the Rupture of the Wilsonian Synthesis" (unpublished Ph.D. dissertation, University of Chicago, 1960), 278–79; Bagby, *Road to Normalcy,* 117. *The New York Times,* July 6, 1920, vigorously attacked the allegations that Davis was anti-Irish. "Has he ever shown an anti-Irish bias? No. . . . [Has] he in either his official duties or his private capacity done anything whatever to offend even the most delicate Irish sensibilities? It does not appear that he has, but he has been polite to the royal family and been on friendly terms with English Ministers, and that is said to be sufficient to damn him with Irish-Americans."

26. Clarence A. Watson, July 15; John J. Cornwell, July 12; James W. Ewing, July 17; Clem L. Shaver, July 10; W. H. Lamar, July 29, Franklin D. Roosevelt to JWD, July 24, 1920. Roosevelt wrote, "We nearly put you across . . . but it became apparent after the Sunday recess that the delegates were going to either McAdoo or Cox and the break came late Monday night." Lamar, a member of the Maryland delegation, wrote that the Marylanders were divided among Cox, McAdoo, and Davis. "All of this vote for McAdoo primarily preferred you, but Senator Watson thought it best to maintain this division until the occasion came for a break. Several of the voters for Cox were also primarily for you. . . . This condition was brought about largely by the fact that the business and professional men of Baltimore were opposed to McAdoo and took vigorous action to impress upon the delegation their preference for you. . . . The same may be said of Senator Wolcott and other delegates from Delaware, with the exception of ex-Senator Saulsbury who was primarily for the Vice President, you being his second choice. You also had many friends in the Pennsylvania delegation and in fact there is no doubt but if the McAdoo managers had not messed the situation you could have been nominated long before the break to Cox. These managers not only ignored the Postmaster General's [Albert Burleson's] advice with respect to the management of the McAdoo campaign, but made it impossible for him to direct those forces to you as was his desire in case of McAdoo's failure." Lamar added: ". . . barring Governor Cox you emerged from the San Francisco Convention the most prominent figure on the political horizon in the United States and with no enmities having been aroused against you in any quarter."

27. Arthur B. Koontz to JWD, July 16, 1920.

28. See numerous entries in Ambassadorial Diary, June 26–July 5, 1920.

29. JWD to Watson (cable), July 5, 1920; to John J. Cornwell, July 6, to Clem C. Shaver, July 9, to William Wallace, July 9, 1920, and to many others.

30. Ambassadorial Diary, Aug. 26–Oct. 10, 1920, numerous entries. Lansing agreed "reluctantly" to the proposal to withhold publication.

31. JWD to James M. Cox, Sept. 28, 1920. Wheeling *Register*, Oct. 13, 1920; *New York Times*, Oct. 15, 1920. Davis had been told to expect disorders at the meeting. Ambassadorial Diary, Oct. 14, 1920. Clarksburg *Exponent*, Oct. 19, 1920. Cleveland *Plain Dealer*, Oct. 29, 1920. The *Plain Dealer* gave Davis front page coverage. Root, who was for the League with reservations, had earlier labored manfully to hold the Republicans to that ground and to persuade Harding to move back onto it. See Leopold, *Elihu Root and the Conservative Tradition* (Boston, 1954), 130–50. But on Oct. 19, 1920, as Leopold writes, Root "went beyond the bounds of fairness in defining Cox's position and in construing what would be America's commitments under Article X." It was this speech that Davis attacked. The text of Davis' telegram to Harrison is in Ambassadorial Diary, Oct. 28, 1920.

Notes to Chapter 12

1. JWD to Julia Davis, May 12, 1921.

2. The minimum guarantee offered by several firms had risen from $25,-000 in 1917 to $50,000 in 1920. Lloyd C. Griscom to JWD, Jan. 21, 1920; JWD to Griscom, Feb. 11, 1920, Davis Papers. Griscom wrote that the two senior partners had earned $90,000 each in 1919. For the Sullivan & Cromwell offer see Ambassadorial Diary, Aug. 30, 1920. Sullivan & Cromwell's gross in the first eight months of 1920 was $950,000. Expenses were $250,000. William Wallace, Jr., to JWD, May 28, 1919, Feb. 10, 1920. Wallace seems to have assumed in his first letter that Davis would accept because of their earlier relations.

3. JWD to Swager Sherley, May 10, 1920; to Rees Turpin, May 28, 1934; Davis, Oral Memoir, 155.

4. *Davis Polk History*, 44; Brooklyn *Daily Eagle*, July 23, 1924; numerous interviews.

5. Allen Wardwell to JWD, Mar. 28, May 24, 1920.

6. JWD to Frank L. Polk, Apr. 19, 1920; Polk to JWD, Apr. 6, May 26, 1920.

7. *Davis Polk History*, 42–43.

8. Ambassadorial Diary, Aug. 28. In 1919 the firm had grossed $448,000. Thus the increase in 1920 was roughly 100 per cent. *Ibid.* Aug. 26, Sept. 18, 19, 1920. Davis was especially impressed by what he described as "the palatial home" of William D. Guthrie, Cravath's former partner.

9. *Ibid.* Sept. 20, 1920. The characterization of Cravath is formed from the mass of material in Robert T. Swaine, *The Cravath Firm* (2 vols., New York,

privately printed, 1946), and the brief sketch in Beryl Harold Levy, *Corporation Lawyer: Saint or Sinner?* (Philadelphia, 1961), 88–97.

10. Ambassadorial Diary, Sept. 20, 1920; Wardwell to JWD, Sept. 24, 1920, Davis Papers; Ambassadorial Diary, Sept. 28, 29, 1920. Wardwell also agreed to put Davis' name in the firm title as soon as he was admitted to the New York Bar. JWD to Paul D. Cravath, Sept. 28, 1920, to Henry P. Davison, Sept. 28, 1920.

11. Charles H. Russell wrote that "we always have been a very happy and united family." Russell, Oct. 3, 1920. Henry P. Davison, n. d.; Thomas W. Lamont to JWD Oct. 8, 1920, in which he reported Morgan's wire.

12. William Wallace, Oct. 2, 1920, Lansing to JWD, Oct. 1, 1920.

13. *Davis Polk History*, 22ff.

14. *Ibid*. 1–42. I have also found occasional references to Stetson in Herbert L. Satterlee's uncritical biography, *J. Pierpont Morgan: An Intimate Portrait* (New York, 1939), and Lewis Corey's sharply critical study, *The House of Morgan* (New York, 1930). The account of the bond episode in Allan Nevins, *Grover Cleveland: A Study in Courage* (New York, 1932), 649–76, is still unsurpassed. Also see Alexander Dana Noyes, *Forty Years of American Finance* (New York, 1907).

15. *Davis Polk History*, 11–42.

16. *Ibid.*; for Davis' comment, see Chapter 6, "The Ablest Lawyer in Congress."

17. Stetson and Gardiner did handle the $500,000,000 Anglo-French loan of 1915. *Davis Polk History*, 39.

18. *Ibid*. 96–100.

19. *Ibid*. for text of speech by Reed at a firm dinner in 1935.

20. Richmond *Times-Dispatch*, May 14, 1921.

21. Wardwell to Ralph M. Carson, *c*. 1950, courtesy of Carson; JWD to Peerce N. McDonald, Apr. 27, 1921; to Leland H. Littlefield, May 23, 1921; to J. Butler Wright, May 31, 1922; to William R. Vance, May 11, 1922.

22. JWD to William R. Vance, May 11, 1922.

23. Passing comments in Davis' letters.

24. JWD to Newton D. Baker, Sept. 13, 1922.

25. *New York Times*, Apr. 27, 1921; copy of speech on English bar, which was delivered to the Association of the Bar of the City of New York, May 4, 1921, in Davis Papers; JWD to Maxwell Pestcoe, Jan. 30, 1935.

26. Copy of letter, Charles B. Hilles to Warren G. Harding, Aug. 17, 1921, in Papers of Elihu Root, Box 228, Library of Congress. Also see *New York Times*, Aug. 17, 1921.

27. JWD to Lansing, Nov. 14, 1921; to Elliot H. Goodwin, Mar. 9, 1922; to Joseph T. Robinson, Mar. 16, 1922.

28. Ambassadorial Diary, Summary Entry, early Dec. 1919; *ibid*. June 1920; *ibid*. Oct. 9, 1920. The full entry on the McReynolds offer is as follows: "N. & I to dinner with McR. in his apartment. Makes proposition to resign on condition I succeed him—nonsense." For White's decision to hold his seat for Taft, see Alpheus Thomas Mason, *William Howard Taft: Chief Justice* (New York, 1964), 77.

29. See the penetrating article by Walter F. Murphy, "In His Own Image: Mr. Chief Justice Taft and Supreme Court Appointments," *The Supreme Court Review 1961.* The generalizations and some quotations about Taft come from it and from Mason, *Taft,* 163–71. I have also drawn from David J. Danelski's pioneering study, *A Supreme Court Justice Is Appointed* (New York, 1964), for the general background of the overture to Davis. I am further indebted to Alexander Bickel for leads into the Taft and Van Devanter Papers in the Library of Congress.

30. Quoted in Mason, *Taft,* 164.

31. Willis Van Devanter to Walter Sanborn, Oct. 11, 1922, Papers of Willis Van Devanter, Library of Congress; Taft to Max Pam, Oct. 28, 1922, Taft Papers.

32. Davis, Oral Memoir, 163; JWD to John H. Clarke, Sept. 5, 1922; to Samuel H. Halley, Jan. 30, 1923, wherein he writes that he turned down the appointment because he had come back from London "practically broke."

33. Mrs. Davis' attitude was reported by several of Davis' former partners in interviews. Charles C. Burlingham to Felix Frankfurter, Oct. 23, 1923, Papers of Felix Frankfurter, Box 64, Library of Congress. Supreme Court Justices were not taxed on their salaries at that time. Neither were they eligible for pensions. The salary was probably the equivalent of $60,000, before taxes, in 1970.

34. Thomas W. Shelton to Taft, Oct. 28, 1922, Taft Papers; Carter Glass to Shelton, Oct. 26, 1922, Papers of Carter Glass, University of Virginia; Van Devanter to JWD, Oct. 28, 1922. Glass wrote that Davis' appointment "would take out of the reckoning the ablest and best man for the Democratic nomination for the Presidency."

35. Thomas W. Shelton to JWD, Oct. 30, 1922.

36. JWD to Van Devanter, Oct. 31, 1922.

37. Van Devanter to JWD, Nov. 2, 1922; Taft to Van Devanter, Nov. 2, 1922, Taft Papers.

38. William H. Taft to C. C. Burlingham, Jan. 16, 1923, quoted in Henry F. Pringle, *The Life And Times Of William Howard Taft* (2 vols. New York, 1939), II, 1058.

39. JWD to Frank A. Nelson, Jan. 25, 1932, for "duty" statement, numerous other letters in Davis Papers for assertion that he would have accepted had the overture been made five years earlier or later. Davis-Harding incident is in JWD to Jerry A. Mathews, May 5, 1936. Statement by Davis on his love of advocacy is in Davis, Oral Memoir, 92.

Notes to Chapter 13

1. The activities of Davis supporters are described in dozens of incoming letters in Davis Papers. The columnist David Lawrence termed Davis "one of the most brilliant men ever suggested for the presidency." Atlanta *Journal,* July 10, 1923.

2. JWD to R. F. Dunlap, Feb. 14, 1922; to Rees Turpin, May 9, 1923; to John J. Cornwell, Aug. 22, 1923; to J. Horner Davis, Jan. 4, 1924; to F. J. Kearful, Jan. 16, 1924.

3. Pennsylvania Coal Company v. Mahon, 260 U.S. 393 (1922); Pennsylvania v. West Virginia, 262 U.S. 553 (1923); JWD to Harvey W. Harmer, June 7, 1923, for coal operators. Davis did not argue the first Coronado case. He was retained for the second, but presumably dropped out following his nomination for the presidency. His correspondence contains an unrevealing letter or two on the matter. For his effort to persuade Governor Smith to veto the tax on private bankers, see JWD to Charles F. Moore, May 22, 1923. The telephone rate increase is reported at some length in *New York Times*, May 2, 1924.

4. Speech in Clarksburg, W.Va. Nov. 4, 1922, copy in Davis Papers.

5. The address was delivered on August 29, 1923, in Minneapolis, copy in Davis Papers.

6. Clarksburg speech of Nov. 4, 1922, for League and soldiers' bonus; address to the American Bar Association for World Court. Davis' remarks on taxation were made to the Democratic Women's Club of Philadelphia on Jan. 24, 1924, copy in Davis Papers. For the Mellon Plan, see JWD to Matthew Neely, Dec. 27, 1923.

7. See Davis Papers for letters on Davis-for-President Clubs; *New York Times*, Jan. 27, 1924. The West Virginia State Federation of Labor, at its annual convention in 1923, denounced Davis as "the counsel for the favor-hunting, privilege-seeking, open-shop Wall Street gang that preys on the masses of the people, and oppresses those who toil." Papers of Calvin Coolidge, Series I, 2026 (Microfilm), cited in Carl S. Smith, "John W. Davis. Campaign for the Presidency," (seminar paper, Yale University, 1970).

8. Numerous letters in Davis Papers; JWD to E. G. Smith, Jan. 28, 1924; to D. C. Hodgkins, telegram and letter, Mar. 11, 1924; to Adolph S. Ochs, Jan. 31, 1924.

9. Unidentified clipping in Davis Papers; Theodore A. Huntley to JWD Feb. 20, 1923.

10. JWD to Samuel H. Halley, Jan. 30, 1923; to D. C. Hodgkins, May 17, 1923; to Rees Turpin, May 9, 1923.

11. David H. Stratton, "Splattered With Oil: William G. McAdoo and the 1924 Democratic Presidential Nomination," *Southwestern Social Sciences Quarterly*, XLIV (June 1963), 62–75.

12. JWD to Emma Davis, Feb. 12, 1924; to Jacob M. Dickinson, Feb. 19, 1924. At the time Davis wrote, it had not yet been revealed that McAdoo had also appeared before his own appointees in the Treasury Department, shortly after his resignation, as representative for Republic Iron & Steel in a huge tax refund matter.

13. Theodore Huntley to JWD Feb. 12, 20, 1924; JWD to Huntley, Mar. 4, 1924.

14. Huntley, *John W. Davis*, 135.

15. *Ibid.* Davis insisted that he had not written for publication. See JWD to Lansing, Apr. 5, 1924, to John J. Davis, Apr. 7, 1924. Probably he did not

do so consciously, for the letter's general phraseology is similar to that in several others. Yet it was carefully polished in a way the others were not.

16. Theodore Huntley to JWD, Mar. 31, 1924; clippings in Davis Papers; Nashville *Banner*, Apr. 13, 1924, for a survey of editorial reaction. Even *The Nation*, CXVIII (Apr. 9, 1924), 383, approved of Davis' "delightful candor."

17. See, among many other letters of commendation, those to Davis from George W. Wickersham, Apr. 1, William J. Hughes, Apr. 1, Otey B. Mitchell, Apr. 5, 1924.

18. William Ernest Hocking, "Leaders and Led," *The Yale Review*, XIII (July 1924), 637.

19. Phillips (ed.), *Felix Frankfurter Reminisces*, 194–95; "Abstemious Liberalism," *The New Republic*, CLIX (Aug. 6, 1924), 285–87. "There Comes a Time . . . ," *The New Republic*, CLIX (Aug. 3, 1968), 6–7, contains excerpts from the 1924 articles and confirms Frankfurter's authorship. For the effort to win amnesty for the prisoners, see Preston, *Aliens and Dissenters, Federal Suppression of Radicals, 1903–1933*, 257–63; Donald Johnson, *The Challenge to American Freedoms: World War I and the Rise of the American Civil Liberties Union* (Lexington, Ky., 1963), 176–93; and George Wharton Pepper, *Philadelphia Lawyer, An Autobiography* (Philadelphia, 1944), 194. Newton D. Baker served on the three-man commission that persuaded President Coolidge to release a number of prisoners in December 1923.

20. "Why Mr. Davis Shouldn't Run," *The New Republic*, XXXVIII (Apr. 16, 1924), 194–95.

21. *Ibid.* Frankfurter also wrote: "It is a mistake, as a general rule, to identify lawyers with their clients. But it is not a mistake when the lawyer does so himself. Mr. Davis, in his attitude and aspirations, has made this identification. He glories in his specialized practise for Big Business and identifies America with his clients."

22. For labor in general during the 1920's, see the exceptional, and often graphic, treatment in Irving Bernstein, *The Lean Years: A History of the American Worker 1920–1933* (Boston, 1960). There is a very brief account of the United States Steel Corporation's labor policies in Davis Brody, *Labor in Crisis: The Steel Strike of 1919* (Philadelphia, 1965). For the anthracite industry, in which the Erie Railroad was involved through subsidiaries, see Harold Kanarek, "Progressivism in Crisis: The United Mine Workers and the Anthracite Coal Industry During the 1920's" (unpublished Ph.D. dissertation, University of Virginia, 1972).

Notes to Chapter 14

1. William D. Bennett to Bainbridge Colby, Mar. 17, 1924, Papers of Bainbridge Colby, Box 4, Library of Congress; Thomas J. Walsh to William G. McAdoo, Apr. 3, 1924, Papers of Thomas J. Walsh, Library of Congress; T. R. Preston to Cordell Hull, n. d., Papers of Cordell Hull, Vol. 6, Series I Library of Congress. The most thoughtful and perceptive treatment of the

convention and Democratic politics during this period is David B. Burner, *The Politics of Provincialism: The Democratic Party in Transition, 1918–1932* (New York, 1968) and Burner's essay, "Election of 1924," in Schlesinger (ed.), *History of American Presidential Elections,* III 2459–81. Two honors theses at Harvard based on the Davis Papers also contain much useful information: Robert S. Leiter, "John W. Davis and His Campaign of Futility" (1958), and Frederick A. O. Schwarz, Jr., "The Political Career of John W. Davis" (1957). For the McAdoo phase of pre-convention and convention politics, I have also drawn on several other studies: J. Leonard Bates, "The Teapot Dome Scandal and the Election of 1924," *American Historical Review,* LX (Jan. 1955), 303–22; Stratton, "Splattered with Oil"; Lee N. Allen, "The McAdoo Campaign for the Presidential Nomination in 1924," *Journal of Southern History,* XXIX (May 1963), 211–28; Burl Noggle, *Teapot Dome: Oil and Politics in the 1920's* (Baton Rouge, La., 1952), 152–76.

2. *New York Times,* Mar. 16, 1923; F. D. Roosevelt to Irving Washburn, Aug. 13, 1923, Papers of Franklin D. Roosevelt, Franklin D. Roosevelt Library. F.D.R. had been urging Smith to speak out "on some national issue" for many months. The conclusion that Smith was merely a stalking horse at this time is implicit—and, in some cases, explicit—in most of the contemporary newspaper accounts and in much of the private correspondence I have examined.

3. Louis M. Howe to Thomas M. Osborne, Apr. 1, 1924, F. D. Roosevelt Papers; Robert W. Woolley to Edward M. House, June 15, 1924, Papers of Edward M. House, Yale University Library; Alfred E. Smith, *Up to Now, An Autobiography* (New York, 1929), 284; Henry F. Pringle, *Alfred E. Smith, A Critical Study* (New York, 1927), 307.

4. Lee N. Allen, "The Underwood Presidential Movement of 1924," *Alabama Review,* XV (Apr. 1962), 83–99; William Morton to F. D. Roosevelt, Jan. 2, 1924, F. D. Roosevelt Papers; Carter Glass to Henry C. Stuart, July 9, 1923, Glass Papers. F.D.R. replied to Morton (Jan. 17, 1924) that "Underwood is a delightful gentleman with a fine experience in the national legislature [but] . . . is distinctly representative of the conservative element and does not differ widely from many Republican leaders except on the matter of the tariff."

5. James E. Palmer, *Carter Glass: Unreconstructed Rebel,* (Roanoke, Va., 1938), and Rixey Smith and Norman Beasley, *Carter Glass* (New York, 1939), for background on Glass.

6. Carter Glass to Henry C. Stuart, July 9, 1923, to James P. Woods, Oct. 26, 1923, Glass Papers.

7. Sexson E. Humphreys, "The Nomination of the Democratic Candidate in 1924," *Indiana Magazine of History,* XXXI (Mar. 1935), 1–9; *New York Times,* June 6, July 1, 1924.

8. JWD to James W. Ewing, n. d., to Clyde B. Johnson, May 16, to Sveinbjorn Johnson, Apr. 23, 1924, and to many others; George Hurley to JWD, Apr. 19, 1924; John J. Davis to JWD, May 22, 1924. The results of the poll are in David Crutchfield to Frank L. Polk, Mar. 12, 1924, Papers of

Frank L. Polk, Yale University Library. The poll was taken between November 1923 and February 1924.

9. Diary of Edward M. House, Apr. 10, May 26, 1924, House Papers.

10. JWD to Clem Shaver, Mar. 18, 1924.

11. Copy of the pamphlet and Davis' memorandum are in Davis Papers.

12. Thomas M. Osborne to F. D. Roosevelt, Mar. 29, 1924, F. D. Roosevelt Papers.

13. See Burner, *The Politics of Provincialism*, and Burner, "Election of 1924," for background.

14. JWD to Theodore Huntley, May 15, to Lansing, June 16, 1924.

15. Walter Lippmann, "The Setting for John W. Davis," *Atlantic Monthly*, CXXXIV (Oct. 1924), 532–33.

16. William S. Coker, "Pat Harrison, Strategy for Victory," *Journal of Mississippi History*, XXVIII (Nov. 1966), 267–85; Daniel C. Roper, *Fifty Years of Public Life* (Durham, N.C. 1941), 224.

17. Quoted in Pringle, *Alfred E. Smith*, 306; *New York Times*, June 19, 1924.

18. *New York Times*, June 24, 1924; Robert W. Woolley to Edward M. House, June 24, 1924, Papers of Robert W. Woolley, Library of Congress. For a balanced and perceptive account of Bryan's role in the convention, see Lawrence W. Levine, *Defender of the Faith, William Jennings Bryan: The Last Decade, 1915–1925* (New York, 1965), esp. 299. The most recent biography, Louis W. Koenig, *Bryan: A Political Biography* (New York, 1971), confirms and amplifies Levine's treatment.

19. *New York Times*, June 20, 1924; *Christian Science Monitor*, June 26, 1924, which declared that the trend toward Davis was as "clear as a pike staff"; Robert W. Woolley to Edward M. House, June 24, 1924, Woolley Papers. Irish Free State v. Eamon de Valera, *et al.* 129 Misc. was a suit to prevent $2,500,000 remaining from two loans to the Irish Republic that had been raised in the United States from being turned over to de Valera and others.

20. JWD to Harold W. Kennedy, June 3, 1924; to J. Lionberger Davis, May 7, 1924; *New York Times*, May 7, 1924.

21. The account of the convention is taken largely from the day-by-day reports in *The New York Times*, the New York *World*, and the *Official Report of the Proceedings of the Democratic National Convention . . . 1924* (Indianapolis, 1925). I have also used Richard C. Bain, *Convention Decisions and Voting Records* (Washington, D.C., 1960), for statistical materials. The Davis Papers contain a handwritten list of Davis' callers for the period June 24–July 10.

22. *New York Times*, July 1, 1924.

23. *Ibid.* July 2, 1924.

24. Quoted in Levine, *Defender of the Faith*, 300.

25. Bain, *Convention Decisions*, 222–23.

26. *New York Times*, July 4–10, 1924; Burner, "Election of 1924"; McAdoo statement is in Claude G. Bowers, Oral Memoir (Columbia Univ.), 52.

27. James C. Prude, "William Gibbs McAdoo and the Democratic Na-

tional Convention of 1924," *The Journal of Southern History*, XXXVIII (Nov. 1972), 621–28. McAdoo finally made the proposal to substitute majority rule for the two-thirds rule after the seventy-third ballot. It was defeated. Bain, *Convention Decisions*, 223.

28. Jean Oliver McCauley, "The Candidate," (unpublished paper, Sept. 1924), Davis Papers. This three-page account of Davis' activities was written by a house guest of the Polks. JWD to G. Carroll Todd and to W. C. Houston, both July 7, 1924; to W. S. Goodwin, July 5, 1924.

29. JWD to D. E. French, July 4, 1924, Polk Papers.

30. Diary of Breckinridge Long, Oct. 17, 1924, Papers of Breckinridge Long, Library of Congress; Stratton, "Splattered with Oil," 74; Davis, Oral Memoir, 149.

31. Humphreys, "The Nomination of the Democratic Candidate," 7–8.

32. *Ibid.;* New York *World*, July 9, 1924. Frank Hague's brother later wrote Davis that the Mayor had "worked with might and main" to put Davis across. James T. Hague to JWD, July 15, 1924.

33. Carter Glass to Henry St. George Tucker, July 22, 1924, to Henry C. Stuart, July 22, 1924, Glass Papers. Both letters are full and explicit. Earlier, when McAdoo was beginning to reach his peak, Harry F. Byrd and John J. Cornwell persuaded Glass to withdraw a letter to the Virginia delegation directing it to switch to McAdoo. In return, Cornwell pledged that the West Virginia delegation would swing to Glass if Davis' name were later withdrawn. Cornwell to JWD, July 7, 1925, Davis Papers. McAdoo's charge of duplicity by Glass is in William G. McAdoo to Leslie C. Garnett, Nov. 15, 1924, Papers of William Gibbs McAdoo, Library of Congress.

34. Glass to Stuart, July 22, 1924, Glass Papers.

35. *New York Times,* July 10, 1924.

36. Glass to Stuart, July 22, 1924, Glass Papers.

37. *New York Times,* July 10, 1924. See esp. Elmer Davis' brilliant, sardonic story.

38. Bain, *Convention Decisions*, 225–26, reports that before the final switch near the end of the one hundred and third ballot, the correlation between the votes of those delegates who had supported the milder version of the KKK plan and the votes of those who voted for Davis was remarkably high (+.71). This analysis overlooks the tactics of the Eastern conservatives, as exemplified by New York's decision to withhold temporarily its vote for Davis. Prepared as they were to accept Glass, Underwood, or Davis, they deemed it desirable, for purposes of unity, that the West and Southwest take credit for the nomination. *New York Times,* July 10, 1924; New York *World,* July 10, 1924.

39. *New York Times,* July 10, 1924.

40. Davis, *Legacy of Love,* 216.

41. *New York Times,* July 10, 1924; Carter Glass to Mrs. Blair Banister, July 22, 1924, Glass Papers.

42. *New York Times,* July 10, 1924.

43. *Ibid.*

44. W. J. Bryan's first statement of support for Davis was made *before* his

brother was nominated. His second, and stronger, statement was made after Charles Bryan's nomination and after he himself had talked to Davis. *Ibid.* July 10, 11, 12, 1924. McAdoo's conference with Davis was arranged by Thomas L. Chadbourne, who pointed out that it would seem insincere for McAdoo to come out for Davis before conferring with him on his views. Memo of telephone conversation, July 10, 1924. McAdoo's statement is in *New York Times,* July 13, 1924.

45. Pringle, *Alfred E. Smith,* 311–14; *New York Times,* July 10, 1924.

46. Josephine O'Keane, *Thomas J. Walsh, A Senator from Montana* (Francestown, N.H., 1955), 159–60. Also see Burton K. Wheeler (with Paul F. Healy), *Yankee from the West* (Garden City, N.Y., 1962), 248–49. Wheeler urged Walsh not to accept.

47. JWD to [first name indecipherable] Meredith, July 10, 1924.

48. Diary of Charles Hamlin, Dec. 9, 1924, Papers of Charles Hamlin, Library of Congress. There had been some discussion of a Davis-Bryan ticket even before the convention. Among those suggesting it to Davis was Congressman Henry St. George Tucker of Virginia. Tucker to Davis, June 14, 1924, Tucker Family Papers, courtesy of Charles Cullen; Robert Woolley to John D. Edgerton, July 11, 1924, Woolley Papers.

49. Smith, *Up to Now,* 291; Glass to Mrs. Blair Banister, July 22, 1924, Glass Papers.

50. *New York Times,* July 11, 1924.

Notes to Chapter 15

1. Thompson interview; JWD to Albert Shaw, Nov. 13, 1945; Swartz interview.

2. Numerous incoming letters in Davis Papers; Robert W. Woolley to JWD, n. d.; A. Mitchell Palmer to JWD Sept. 30, 1924.

3. Robert W. Woolley to Edward M. House, Aug. 12, 1924, House Papers; Daniel C. Roper, *Fifty Years of Public Life* (Durham, N.C., 1941), 226; JWD to Cordell Hull, Aug. 17, 1924, Hull Papers, Vol. 7, Series I.

4. Carl Smith, "John W. Davis: Campaign for the Presidency," has a good account of the organizational aspects. David Burner, "Election of 1924," is the best account of the election as a whole. Kenneth C. MacKay, *The Progressive Movement of 1924* (New York, 1947), gives a detailed account of the La Follette side of the campaign, and Donald R. McCoy, *Calvin Coolidge: The Quiet President* (New York, 1967), 248–63, has a full account of the Republicans. The replies to Davis' circular letter are well summarized in Robert S. Leiter, "John W. Davis and His Campaign of Futility."

5. *New York Times,* July 25, 1924; Frank L. Polk to Walter Lippmann, July 28, 1924, Polk Papers.

6. Samuel P. Gompers, *Seventy Years of Life and Labor* (2 vols., New York, 1925), II, 537; Walsh and Tobin statements in Burner, "Election of 1924"; *New York Times,* Aug. 7, 8, 10, 1924, for texts of exchanges; Samuel P. Gompers to Frank Morison, Aug. 19, 1924, Papers of Samuel Gompers, Li-

brary of Congress. Robert Szold urged Davis to see Gompers. Frank Polk to Montgomery B. Angell, July 28, 1924, Polk Papers.

7. "Mr. Davis as a Friend of Labor," *Literary Digest*, LXXXII (Aug. 23, 1924), 11: JWD to William B. Wilson, Nov. 7, 1924.

8. Wheeler (with Healy), *Yankee from the West*, 251–66, gives an informative, if highly colored, account of Wheeler's part in the campaign.

9. The Davis Papers abound in complaints about Shaver's inefficiency. Burner, "Election of 1924"; Lansing to JWD, Nov. 6, 1924, Papers of Robert Lansing, Library of Congress.

10. Carl Smith, "John W. Davis: Campaign for the Presidency"; Claude Bowers to Josephus Daniels, Aug. 9, 1924, Papers of Josephus Daniels, Library of Congress; Robert W. Woolley to Edward M. House, Sept. 17, 1924, Woolley Papers. Key Pittman concluded that almost the entire campaign staff was "incompetent and inexperienced." See Burner, "Election of 1924." Taft remark is in Pringle, *Taft*, II, 1061.

11. JWD memorandum, n. d. (1928), in Davis Papers. Robert W. Woolley advised Davis against asking Smith to run. Woolley to Edward M. House, July 29, Aug. 5, 1924, House Papers.

12. Davis later contended that neither Smith or Tammany had "knifed" him.

13. For tributes to Davis, see Milton H. Plank to JWD, Nov. 6, 1924, and several other letters to the same effect; F. D. Roosevelt to Glenn Frank, Aug. 12, 1924, Group 16, Box 21, F. D. Roosevelt Papers; Robert W. Woolley to Edward M. House, Aug. 5, 1924, House Papers; Claude Bowers to Samuel M. Ralston, Aug. 21, 1924, cited in David Burner, "The Democratic Party in the Election of 1924," *Mid-America*, XLVI (Apr. 1964), 92–113; interview with Arthur Krock.

14. Clarksburg *Exponent*, Aug. 11, 12, 1924; *New York Times*, Aug. 10, 11, 12, 1924; text of speech in Davis Papers; *Literary Digest*, LXXXII (Aug. 23, 1924), 8–10; *The Nation*, CXIX (Aug. 20, 1924), 176; Johnson and Potter interviews.

15. Claude Bowers to Josephus Daniels, Aug. 9, 1924, Papers of Josephus Daniels, Library of Congress.

16. MacKay, *The Progressive Movement of 1924* 216–17. Belle Case La Follette and Fola La Follette, *Robert M. La Follette* (2 vols., New York, 1953), II, 1119, concede that La Follette's strength among farmers and labor groups made the issue "political dynamite," but do not describe the pressures that compelled La Follette to speak out.

17. Samuel Untermyer, July 15; James A. Farley, Aug. 11; Francis B. Hunter to JWD, Aug. 7, 1924, and many other letters to JWD.

18. Diary of Charles Hamlin, Sept. 16, 1924, Hamlin Papers; Davis, *Legacy of Love*, 218. The date of the Klan's offer is set the night before the speech by Cyrus R. Vance, whose father, Carl Vance, was in Davis' room when the offer was made. Ralph M. Carson, memorandum, summer 1971. Also see JWD to W. G. Peterkin, Nov. 12, 1924, wherein he mentions the incident but does not give a date. Text of speech is in Davis Papers. McCoy, *Calvin Coolidge*, 257, relates Coolidge's defense of his inaction.

19. William Nye to Frank Polk, n. d., Polk Papers.

20. David M. Chalmers, *Hooded Americans* (New York, 1965), 213. *New York Times,* Aug. 23, 1924, for Davis' Harlem speech.

21. Long Diary, Sept. 19, 1924; Bruce Clagett to George Fort Milton, Nov. 17, 1924, McAdoo Papers; J. W. Johnston to JWD, Nov. 6, 1924; MacKay, *The Progressive Movement of 1924,* 215.

22. *The Nation,* CXIX (Aug. 20, 1924), 176. For a scholarly analysis of this problem, especially as it involved the Republicans, see John L. Blair, "A Time for Parting: The Negro During the Coolidge Years," *Journal of American Studies,* III (Dec. 1969), 177–99.

23. JWD to George K. Kennedy, Nov. 18, 1924, to W. G. Peterkin, Nov. 12, 1924.

24. *The Nation,* CXIX (Sept. 10, 1924), 247. For a scholarly confirmation of *The Nation's* analysis, see Bernstein, *The Lean Years.*

25. Copy of list of cases in Davis Papers. The Cigar Makers' local boycotted the speech, and the union leader who introduced Davis explained that the invitation to speak had been issued because Davis was a native son. *New York Times,* Sept. 2, 1924. Presumably on Robert Szold's advice, Davis said nothing about La Follette's plan to limit the power of the courts. Szold to JWD, Aug. 29, 1924.

26. Thomas L. Chadbourne to JWD, Sept. 1, 1924. Chadbourne's implication was that the federal government would have to raise an umbrella over the organizing process, as the Wagner Act later did.

27. See David Brody, *Labor in Crisis: The Steel Strike of 1919;* Daniel Jordan, "The Mingo War of 1919–23," (seminar paper, University of Virginia, 1967); Frankfurter and Greene, *The Labor Injunction;* Bernstein, *The Lean Years;* La Follette and La Follette, *Robert M. La Follette,* II, 1138. Ickes statement is quoted in Richard T. Ruetten, "Senator Burton K. Wheeler and Insurgency in the 1920's," in Gene M. Gressley (ed.), *The American West: A Reorientation* (Laramie, Wyo., 1966), 118.

28. Charles Warren strongly urged Davis to avoid mentioning the Wilkerson Injunction. Warren to JWD, Aug. 23, 1924.

29. MacKay, *Progressive Movement,* 200; *The Nation* CXIX (Aug. 20, 1924), 173; "Mr. Davis As a Friend of Labor," *Literary Digest,* LXXII (Aug. 23, 1924), 11–12; Daniel J. Tobin, "Analyzing the Democratic Convention," *International Brotherhood of Teamsters, Chauffeurs, Stablemen and Helpers* (Aug. 1924); *New York Times,* Sept. 24, 1924.

30. *New York Times,* Sept. 25, 1924; McAdoo to George Fort Milton, Oct. 1, 1924, Hamlin Diary, Nov. 29, 1924.

31. Hamlin Diary, Sept. 30, Nov. 30, 1924.

32. William McKnight and R. P. Dunlap to William G. McAdoo, Oct. 17, 1924, McAdoo Papers; JWD to McAdoo, Oct. 4, 1924; McAdoo to Claude Swanson, Oct. 18, 1924, McAdoo Papers; Hamlin Diary, date indecipherable.

33. W. J. Bryan to JWD, Aug. 25, 1924; *New York Times,* Aug. 30, 1924; interview with JWD by Jerome I. Levinson, cited in Jerome I. Levinson, "John W. Davis, Conservative Democrat," (honors thesis, Harvard University, 1953), 71; W. J. Bryan to JWD, Aug. 28, 1924; W. J. Bryan to Clem Shaver, Nov. 17, 1924, Papers of William Jennings Bryan, Library of Congress.

34. E. G. Smith to JWD, Aug. 28, 1924; Levine, *Defender of the Faith*, 319–20.

35. Smith, "John W. Davis: Campaign for the Presidency."

36. Text in Davis Papers.

37. JWD to George D. Herron, May 11, 1925.

38. Acceptance Speech; "La Follette and the German-American," *New Republic*, XL (Oct. 1, 1924), 108–10; Hamlin Diary, Aug. 11, Sept. 30, Oct. 1, 20, 24, 28, 31, 1924. Hamilton Fish Armstrong, *Peace and Counter-Peace From Wilson to Hitler* (New York, 1971), 275.

39. Various speeches. Davis said nothing on Zionism, but in response to a query he had his secretary write Adolph L. Feuerlict, a Jewish publicist, that he was "completely in sympathy with the rebuilding of Palestine." (Sept. 24, 1924.)

40. *La Follette - Wheeler Text-Book*, 116–21.

41. Davis' correspondence on ethnic matters was considerable. He was especially solicitous of the Poles. See JWD to A. J. Sabbath, July 23, 1924.

42. "What Has the Campaign Accomplished?" *New Republic*, XL (Nov. 5, 1924), 238–39.

43. "What Was Wrong with the Democrats?" *Literary Digest*, LXXXIII (Nov. 22, 1924), 14–15; "Business Wins," *The Nation*, CXIX (Nov. 12, 1924), 510; George Henry Payne, "Great Conservative Victory," *Forum*, LXXII (Dec. 1924), 832–33; John H. Woods to JWD, Nov. 7, 1924.

44. Thomas Walker Page gave Davis a copy of the Nourse memorandum on which Coolidge also based his opposition to the McNary-Haugen bill. Theodore Saloutos and John D. Hicks, *Agricultural Discontent in the Middle West, 1900–1939* (Madison, Wis., 1951), 367–68, asserts that La Follette's program was "nothing more than an attempt to harness the prevailing sentiment of the western Middle West" and that there was considerable uncertainty "over what he was going to do for agriculture if elected."

45. Numerous speeches, especially one given in Albany on October 6.

46. C. H. Cramer, *Newton D. Baker: A Biography* (Cleveland, 1961), 223, for Pepper's statement; H. C. Pell to JWD, n. d.; Donald Day, *Will Rogers: A Biography* (New York, 1962), 157.

47. Davis, Oral Memoir, 150–51; numerous speeches.

48. McCoy, *Calvin Coolidge*, 255.

49. House Diary, Oct. 15, 1924; William Nye to Frank L. Polk, n. d., Polk Papers; House Diary, Oct. 15, 1924; Robert Woolley to JWD, Oct. 17, 1924, Woolley Papers.

50. Presidential Office Staff Note, n.d., Reel #162 - Series 1, Case File #2026, Papers of Calvin Coolidge (microfilm), courtesy of James Bridy.

51. Numerous articles in *The Nation* and, esp. in the *New Republic*, Sept.–Oct. 1924.

52. *Ibid.*

53. Newton D. Baker to Stephen A. Wise, Sept. 18, 1924, Papers of Newton D. Baker, Library of Congress.

54. Stephen A. Wise to Newton D. Baker, n. d., Newton D. Baker Papers. Also see Wise to Baker, July 22, 1924, wherein he writes that most of his "liberal friends seem to feel that there is little choice as between Coolidge and

Davis." Among those who also regarded Davis as a conservative, but finally supported him, was Raymond B. Fosdick. See Felix Frankfurter to Fosdick, Sept. 27, 1924, Frankfurter Papers, Box 64, Library of Congress.

55. Frankfurter to Stepehen A. Wise, Oct. 30, 1924, *ibid.*

56. Frankfurter to Charles Burlingham, Oct. 3, 1924, *ibid.*

57. Burlingham to Frankfurter, Oct. 23, 1924, *ibid.*

58. Walter Lippmann to Frankfurter, July 17, 1924; Frankfurter to Lippman, July 18, 1924, *ibid.*

59. Walter Lippmann, "Why I Shall Vote for Davis," *New Republic*, XL (Oct. 29, 1924), 218–19.

60. JWD to W. J. Bryan, Oct. 9, 1924, Bryan Papers; to Polk, Sept. 9, 1924, Polk Papers; to Lansing, Oct. 27, Lansing Papers; transcript of press conference at Indianapolis, Oct. 12, 1924, Davis Papers.

61. Charles Forbes to Stuart F. Douglas, n. d., F. D. Roosevelt Papers, Group 11, Box 2; "How 'Dangerous' Is La Follette?" *The Nation*, CXIX (Sept. 3, 1924), 229; Oswald Garrison Villard, "The Prairies Catching Fire," *The Nation*, CXIX (Oct. 15, 1924), 412–13; John Foster Dulles to JWD, July 18, 1924.

62. Bruce Clagett to George Fort Milton, Nov. 17, 1924, McAdoo Papers; William G. McAdoo to Gavin McNam, Oct. 1924. McAdoo Papers; Robert C. Bell, Aug. 12, 1924; C. C. Dill to JWD, July 18, 1924. W. J. Bryan also wrote from the West Coast that Davis had "no chance" there. Bryan to Davis, Sept. 29, 1924.

63. Quoted in Paul R. Leach, *That Man Dawes* (Chicago, 1930), 232–34.

64. *New York Times*, Sept. 28, 1924.

65. Newark *Evening News*, Oct. 25, 1924; Burner, "Election of 1924"; Malcolm Moos (ed.), *A Carnival of Buncombe* (Baltimore, 1956), 97.

66. See the running accounts of the campaign in McKay, *The Progressive Movement*, and in La Follette and La Follette, *Robert M. La Follette*, II. Also see James H. Shideler, "The La Follette Progressive Party Campaign of 1924," *Wisconsin Magazine of History*, XXXIII (Jan. 1950), 444–57; David A. Shannon, *The Socialist Party of America* (New York, 1955), 175–81; Burner, "Election of 1924"; and *New Republic*, XL (Nov. 12, 1924), 257–58.

67. Samuel W. Bedford to Key Pittman, Oct. 25, 1924, Papers of Key Pittman, Box 11, Library of Congress; Edward G. Dolan to F. D. Roosevelt, Oct. 27, 1924, F. D. Roosevelt Papers; George Fort Milton to William Gibbs McAdoo, Sept. 29, 1924, McAdoo Papers; Jesse Jones to Cordell Hull, Nov. 20, 1924, Hull Papers, Vol. 8, Series I; St. Louis *Post-Dispatch*, Nov. 6, 1924.

68. Numerous letters, Davis Papers; Joseph J. O'Brien to F. D. Roosevelt, Sept. 18, 1924, F. D. Roosevelt Papers; Beech interview.

69. Davis, Oral Memoir, 151–52.

70. JWD to Hale Houston, Oct. 31, 1924; Healy interview; JWD to Cordell Hull and to Jonathan Davis, both Nov. 12, 1924.

71. The most authoritative analysis of the results is David Burner, "The Election of 1924." I have supplemented it with Jack T. Camp, "The Election of 1924: A Voting Analysis" (unpublished M. A. thesis, University of Virginia, 1967), and Robert Allswang, *A House For All People* (Lexington, Ky., 1971).

72. Davis, *Legacy of Love*, 221.

73. In addition to the works by Burner, Camp, Allswang, MacKay, and McCoy already cited, see Bruce Martin Stave, "The 'La Follette Revolution' and the Pittsburgh Vote, 1924," *Mid-America*, XLIX (Oct. 1967), 244–51; Jerome M. Clubb and Howard W. Allen, "The Cities and the Election of 1928: Partisan Realignment?" *American Historical Review*, LXXIV (Apr. 1969), 1205–20; and Frederick T. Himmelein, "Scandinavian America—A Political Geography" (unpublished paper in the author's possession). The statement by F.D.R. is in Roosevelt to E. T. Meredith, Nov. 26, 1924, F. D. Roosevelt Papers.

74. Although many contemporary commentators, especially Davis' correspondents, thought the Klan figured large, almost all scholarly works contend the opposite, as did a good many of the post-election analyses in newspapers and periodicals.

75. Burner, "Election of 1924," 2477.

76. See the dozens upon dozens of incoming and outgoing letters in the Davis Papers.

77. JWD to George Olvaney, (date unclear, but Nov. 1924); to Albert Shaw, Dec. 6, 1946; to George Kennedy, Apr. 7, 1933.

78. Jouett Shouse to George Wolfskill, June 30, 1959, Papers of Jouett Shouse, University of Kentucky, courtesy of Donn Neal; JWD to Norman Davis, Nov. 15, 1924, Papers of Norman Davis, Library of Congress; to Lord Charnwood, Nov. 14, 1924.

79. Newton D. Baker, Nov. 7, 1924; Jesse H. Jones, Nov. 19, 1924; Robert W. Woolley, Nov. 8, 1924; Frances H. McAdoo, Nov. 21, 1924; Harold Hathaway to JWD, Nov. 21, 1924.

80. Cox, *Journey Through My Years*, 330–31; my statement on Davis' not changing the direction of the economy is implicit or explicit in most scholarly works on the period; Carson interview; JWD to Richard S. Arnold, Apr. 1, 1952; Davis, Oral Memoir, 149–50.

Notes to Chapter 16

1. Allen Wardwell, Oral Memoir (Columbia University), 42; Ferdinand Lundberg, "The Law Factories; Brains of the Status Quo," *Harper's Magazine*, CLXXIX (July 1939), 189.

2. Wardwell, Oral Memoir, 58.

3. *Davis Polk History*, 78–79.

4. Davis, Oral Memoir, 158–59.

5. *Davis Polk History*, 58; Davis, Oral Memoir, 159–60.

6. Ralph M. Carson, memorandum to author, summer 1971; numerous interviews; Davis, Oral Memoir, 161.

7. Quoted remark is by Edward Wardwell, cited in Allen Wardwell, Oral Memoir, 37.

8. Generalizations based on numerous interviews and especially on an analysis of biographies of the *Who's Who* variety which were assembled by Davis Polk and supplied to the author by George A. Brownell.

9. *Ibid.*

10. Spencer Klaw, "The Wall Street Lawyers," *Fortune,* LVII (Feb. 1958), 140–44ff., the accuracy of which was affirmed by Theodore Kiendl in an interview; Erwin O. Smigel, *The Wall Street Lawyer* (New York, 1964), esp. 176–77; Martin Mayer, *The Lawyers* (New York, 1966); Walter Fletcher, in *Virginia Law Weekly,* Oct. 26, 1967. Other materials supplied to author by Ralph M. Carson, memorandum, summer 1971.

11. Julia Healy to author, memorandum, summer 1971; JWD to Lord Shaw, Sept. 21, 1926; Proskauer to author, Apr. 25, 1958.

12. Statement by unnamed Davis Polk partner in Brooklyn *Eagle,* July 13, 1924.

13. Data and attitude of Davis supplied by Ralph M. Carson in various memoranda to author, summer 1971.

14. Numerous interviews with Davis Polk partners, fall 1958.

15. Interview with Edwin S. S. Sunderland, confirmed by numerous other interviews; JWD to Charles Warren, Dec. 3, 1925.

16. JWD to Lord Craigmyle, July 20, 1931; Ralph M. Carson to author, memorandum, summer 1971.

17. Paschall Davis, memorandum, summer 1971, courtesy of Ralph M. Carson; Kiendl incident, interview with Edwin F. Blair; golf story, interview with Alger Hiss.

18. Numerous interviews with Davis Polk partners; interview with Charles Hanson; interviews with several former associates of Davis Polk; Ralph M. Carson to author, various memoranda, summer 1972.

19. Copies of the recommendation to the Attorney General, which was for the appointment of Carroll C. Hincks to a judgeship on the Second Circuit, courtesy of Judge William H. Timbers.

20. Davis' financial records are not included in his papers at Yale. Statement based on figures shown to me by the firm. Various letters in Davis Papers refer to his assignment of securities to his daughter, investments to establish tax losses, and sale of stock the first few days of the Crash. See, in particular, JWD to Lynn S. Hornor, Apr. 24, 1923; Douglas Gibbons to Mrs. JWD, Feb. 15, 1932; C. M. G. to JWD, memorandum, June 16, 1939, in which reference is made to the purchase of a security in October 1929 in order to establish a tax loss; JWD to Lord Midleton, Feb. 8, 1930. It bears emphasizing that Davis' assertion in 1925 that the "super tax" should be reduced was accompanied by a statement that taxes should also be reduced on the lower levels. JWD to L. H. Barney, Jr., Dec. 7, 1925.

21. Charles C. Burlingham to Felix Frankfurter, Oct. 23, 1924, Box 64, Frankfurter Papers; JWD to Emma Davis, June 5, 1926; interview with Reginald Dilli; Davis, *Legacy of Love,* 229, confirmed in numerous letters; interview with Walter D. Fletcher.

22. Davis, *Legacy of Love,* 229; numerous letters in Davis Papers; JWD to Chester R. Ogden, Dec. 8, 1939. Davis' clubs were: Metropolitan, National Press, Lawyers (Washington, D.C.), Century Association, University, Recess, Down Town, Piping Rock Creek, and Links.

23. JWD to Allen Wardwell, Jan. 14, 1938, for an example of his attitude

toward fees; numerous interviews, all to the same point; figures supplied by Ralph M. Carson in letter to author, Aug. 28, 1971.

24. Montgomery Angell interview and numerous other interviews.

25. Numerous interviews with partners and acquaintances.

26. Generalization based on three or four interviews with associates who had left the firm, with two or three men who were associates at the time I talked to them, and with two partners.

27. I am indebted to Judge William H. Timbers for much of the information on the "West Virginia Calendar."

28. Interview with Arthur Koontz.

29. Numerous letters in the Davis Papers.

30. JWD to George S. Wallace, Apr. 21, 1930; interview with Edwin F. Blair.

31. Charles C. Burlingham to Felix Frankfurter, Oct. 23, 1924, Frankfurter Papers, Box 64; numerous interviews with Davis Polk partners; Ralph M. Carson to author, Oct. 5, 1972. All members of the firm have emphasized, in interviews, memoranda, and letters, Davis' insistence on preventive advice. Because of the privileged character of the lawyer-client relationship, they have been unable to supply me with specific examples.

32. Ralph M. Carson to author, memorandum, summer 1971.

33. Beech-Nut Packing Company v. P. Lorillard Company, 273 U.S. 629, 631 (1927).

34. "Matter of John W. Davis, An Amicus Brief," for list of cases; Rogers v. Guaranty Trust Company of New York et al., 288 U.S. 123 (1933). Davis won the suit on the ground that it should have been brought in the New Jersey, rather than the New York, courts. For comment, see Cooper, *Abuses of Employee Stock Purchase Plans by Management*, 21 Cal. L. Rev. 358 (1933).

35. JWD to Edward P. Hodges, Aug. 21, 1944, to John H. Amen, June 4, 1941, to Lansing, Aug. 29, 1925.

36. JWD to Thomas L. Chadbourne, Oct. 16, 1925.

37. O'Brian, Szold, and Thompson interviews.

38. Numerous interviews with Davis Polk partners.

39. Krock interview; Huston Thompson to Martha Jane Thompson, Mar. 1, 1941, Papers of Huston Thompson, Box 1, Library of Congress.

40. Generalization based on analysis of partners' biographies, n. 8 above; Davis statement on service is a paraphrase by George A. Brownell in letter to author, Sept. 15, 1971.

41. General review of the firm's contributions by the Legal Aid Society Development Office, Thomas P. Megan to George A. Brownell, July 29, 1971, copy in author's possession. Megan reported that the firm was one of fourteen qualifying as a "Class A" member when the Society's membership plan went into effect in 1925. He also reported that the firm contributed $146,700 to the Society between 1951 and 1971. For Brownell's own activities, I have relied on Ralph M. Carson to author, Oct. 5, 1972.

42. Ralph M. Carson to author, memorandum, summer 1971.

43. *Ibid.*

Notes to Chapter 17

1. JWD to Elijah Funkhouser, Sept. 9, 1926; to Samuel H. Halley, Nov. 16, 1928. This categorization of politicians was a recurring theme in earlier letters.

2. *New York Times*, Mar. 3, 1925; JWD to Theodore Huntley, Dec. 17, 1924; to William H. Lamar, Mar. 1, 1925; to Claude Meeker, June 11, 1925; to Lansing, Nov. 30, 1924, Davis Papers; JWD to Josephus Daniels, Nov. 11, 1924, Daniels Papers. For details on Roosevelt's proposal, see Frank Friedel, *Franklin D. Roosevelt: The Apprenticeship* (Boston, 1952), 201.

3. JWD to George D. Herron, May 11, to William H. Lamar, Mar. 1, 1925; *New York Times*, Apr. 24, Mar. 4, Dec. 14, 1925, Jan. 20, June 12, 1926; JWD to Ivy Lee, Feb. 23, 1926, to Newton D. Baker, Feb. 11, 1927.

4. Newton D. Baker to JWD, Feb. 7, 1927; JWD to Baker, Feb. 11, 1927.

5. JWD to Lord Shaw, Sept. 21, 1926.

6. JWD to Victor H. Hanson (date indecipherable, but sometime in December 1927); to Gilchrist B. Stockton, June 20, 1928; to Esther Lape, June 18, 1928; to Adelbert Moot, June 7, 1928; to Franklin D. Roosevelt, July 14, 1926.

7. Charles C. Marshall, "An Open Letter to The Honorable Alfred E. Smith," *The Atlantic Monthly*, CXXXIX (Apr. 1927), 540–49. Edmund A. Moore, *A Catholic Runs for President* (New York, 1956), 69.

8. Matthew and Hannah Josephson, *Al Smith: Hero of the Cities* (Boston, 1969), 358–61; Oscar Handlin, *Al Smith and His America* (Boston, 1958), 4; Moore, *A Catholic Runs for President*, 71–73; Alfred E. Smith, "Catholic and Patriot: Governor Smith Replies," *The Atlantic Monthly*, CXXXIX (May 1927), 721–28; JWD to Smith, Apr. 18, 1927.

9. John W. Davis, "Thomas Jefferson, Attorney-At-Law," 38 VA. B. A. REP. 316 (1926).

10. *Ibid.*

11. Undated clipping attached to letter, C. W. Osenton to JWD, Apr. 26, 1927.

12. JWD to William D. Guthrie, Jan. 18, 1928; *Congressional Record*, 70th Cong., 1st sess., 1654.

13. JWD to Emma K. Davis, Mar. 14, 1928.

14. *New York Times*, Jan. 25, 1928; JWD to J. W. Johnston, Jan. 23, 1928.

15. JWD to Thomas W. Gregory, Aug. 8, to Frank L. Polk, Aug. 29, 1928.

16. Lansing to JWD, July 21, Aug. 22, 1928; JWD to Alfred E. Smith, Aug. 23, 1928.

17. JWD to Thomas W. Gregory, Oct. 11, 1928; to Harry S. New, Oct. 4, 1928; New to JWD, Oct. 6, 1928. New enclosed a copy of a letter by Gregory as Attorney General to Postmaster General Albert S. Burleson, Nov. 9, 1914, in which Gregory said in part: "The modern doctrine . . . appears to be that the public has a right to discuss, in good faith, the public conduct and qualifications of a public man . . . with more freedom than they can take with a private matter. . . . Every subject has a right to comment on those acts of

public men which concern him as a subject of the realm, if he does not make his commentary a cloak for malice and slander."

18. Dallas *News*, Oct. 25, 1928; Jacob M. Dickinson, Jr., Oct. 18; J. Frank Norris to JWD, n.d.; JWD to Mrs. George Gordon Battle, Oct. 2, 1928.

19. JWD to C. E. Smith, Sept. 11, 1928. The total registration had increased by only 126,000, so Davis' point was well taken despite Smith's failure to campaign for him extensively. C. E. Smith to JWD, Sept. 13, 1928. The letter was also reprinted in the New York *World*, Sept. 23, 1928.

20. Walter L. Clements, Oct. 17, 1928; Clarence E. Martin, Sept. 26, 1928; M. F. Reddington to JWD, Sept. 25, 1928. Braden Vandeventer of Norfolk, Virginia, estimated that about one-half the Methodists and Baptists of Virginia disapproved of Bishop James Cannon, Jr.'s blatant anti-Catholicism. Vandeventer to James H. Corbitt, Oct. 1, 1928. For a thoughtful modification of these generalizations about the religious factor, see the chapter, "A Footnote to the Election of 1928," in Robert Moats Miller, *American Protestantism and Social Issues: 1919–1939* (Chapel Hill, N.C., 1958), 48–62.

21. Printed copy in Davis Papers. Some of Davis' research was done by Michael Williams, editor of *The Commonweal*. See Williams to JWD, Oct. 2, JWD to Williams, Oct. 4, 1928.

22. Finley Peter Dunne to JWD, Oct. 22, 1928.

23. Wheeling *Register*, Oct. 23, 1928; Memphis *Commercial Appeal*, Oct. 26, 1928. Davis also spoke on foreign policy and the tariff in Boston, where Republican leaders and manufacturers were warning workers that a Democratic tariff would close the plants. See H. L. Brown to JWD, Norman Hapgood to JWD, both Oct. 18, 1928.

24. "Politics and Bigotry," *America*, XL (Nov. 3, 1928), 77; "Religious Bigotry in the Campaign," *ibid.* (Nov. 10, 1928), 102; "The New Administration," *ibid.* (Nov. 17, 1928), 126. The public policy aspects of the campaign are well described in David Burner, *The Politics of Provincialism*, and in Lawrence H. Fuchs, "Election of 1928," in Schlesinger and Israel (eds.), *History of American Presidential Elections*, III, 2585–2704. Hoover was in some respects more progressive than Smith in his recommendations on economic policy. The most extended treatment of the religious issue is in Moore, *A Catholic Runs for President*.

25. Thomas Adams, Oct. 12; Annie Hugill, Oct. 11; J. J. Slechta, Oct. 16; William E. Sweet, Oct. 12; "A Listener-In" to JWD, Oct. 20, 1928. For favorable statements by prominent non-Catholics, see James F. Byrnes, Oct. 27; Charles Warren, Oct. 13, Henry D. Clayton to JWD, Oct. 27, 1928.

26. William D. Guthrie, Oct. 11; John P. McGoorty, Oct. 19; Mary B. Brennan to JWD, Oct. 17, 1928.

27. Providence *Visitor*, Nov. 16, 1928.

28. JWD to Nelson Phillips, Nov. 26, to William C. Adamson, Nov. 12, to David D. Reay, Nov. 7, 1928. Also, JWD to Marshall W. MacDonald, Mar. 19, 1929. For analyses of the vote, see Ruth C. Silva, *Rum, Religion and Votes: 1928 Re-Examined* (University Park, Pa., 1962), Burner, *The Politics of Provincialism*, Fuchs, "Election of 1928."

29. JWD to C. W. Johnson, Nov. 14, 1928.

Notes to Chapter 18

1. Dorothy Dunbar Bromley, "The Pacifist Bogey," *Harper's Magazine*, CLXI (Oct. 1930), 553–65, is an excellent journalistic account based partly on an examination of the briefs of this and related cases. I am also indebted to Joel Weintraub, "Religion, Conscientious Objection, and the Supreme Court" (honors thesis, University of Virginia, 1967).

2. My characterization of Macintosh is based on conversations with Yale professors and with Dr. Preston Warren, Jr., and Dr. Julian N. Hartt, both former students. Hartt succeeded Macintosh. Also see Jerome Davis, "If Not Dr. Macintosh, Who?" *The Christian Century*, L (March 8, 1933), 322–23.

3. Record, at 20, United States v. Macintosh, 283 U.S. 605 (1931).

4. *Ibid.;* Boston *Traveller,* May 26, 1931.

5. Record, United States v. Macintosh.

6. See the long historical exposition in the brief drafted by Poletti and submitted to the Circuit Court of Appeals for the Second District under Davis', Wardwell's, and Dean Clark's names. Irving Brant, in *James Madison: Father of the Constitution* (Indianapolis, 1950), 268–71, and *The Bill of Rights* (Indianapolis, 1965), 66–67, supports the view that the phrase "rights of conscience" was struck for purposes of brevity and that it was meant to be implied. Mansfield, "Conscientious Objection—1964 Term," *Religion and Public Order* I (1965), 59–60, suggests that the Framers did not intend to mandate conscientious objection.

7. Joseph Story, *Commentaries on the Constitution* (Boston, 1833), II, Section 1876; Davis v. Beason, 133 U.S. 333, 342 (1890). Davis had argued in the *Selective Draft Law* cases that the exemption from combatant service of members of "well-recognized religious sects" amply upheld the constitutional guarantee of religious freedom.

8. Hazard, *"Attachment to the Principles of the Constitution" as Judicially Construed,* 23 AM. J. INT. L. 783 (1929); Bromley, "The Pacifist Bogey," 554.

9. Bromley, "The Pacifist Bogey," 563–64.

10. "To Fight or Not to Fight," *The Literary Digest,* CII (July 13, 1929), 12.

11. Forrest Bailey to Douglas C. Macintosh, June 12, 1929; Roger Baldwin to Macintosh, June 25, 1929; Baldwin to Harry Ward, June 28, 1929, all in Vol. 372, American Civil Liberties Union Files, Princeton University.

12. United States v. Schwimmer, 279 U.S. 644 (1929); Bromley, "The Pacifist Bogey," 555.

13. Bland v. United States, 42 F. 2d 842 (2d cir. 1930). Miss Bland's case lacked the intellectual drama of *Macintosh* because she based her qualification of the oath on pacifism rather than on possible objection to a particular war.

14. Roger Baldwin to Harry Ward, June 28, 1929; Ward to Baldwin, July 12, 1929, Vol. 372, ACLU files.

15. Jerome Davis to Allen Wardwell, June 24, 28, 1929; Wardwell to Jerome Davis, July 15; to JWD, July 15; to Douglas C. Macintosh, July 19, 1929, copies in Davis Papers.

16. JWD to Mrs. Hilary G. Richardson, May 21, 1930; statement of John W. Davis, Hearings on S. 3275. Before the Senate Committee on Immigration, 72nd Cong., 1st sess., (1932).

17. Ralph M. Carson to author, memorandum, summer 1971; Porter R. Chandler to author, memorandum, summer 1971; Chandler to Charles E. Clark, May 9, 1946, copy in Davis Papers.

18. Allen Wardwell to Jerome Davis, July 24, 1929, copy in Davis Papers. Macintosh had earlier issued a public statement at the instance of Roger Baldwin. At this time, the ACLU was pressing for a united front on the *Bland* and *Macintosh* appeals. Baldwin later conceded the wisdom of John W. Davis' insistence that the cases be handled separately. In fact, when Emily Marx, counsel for Miss Bland, insisted on arguing *Bland* on the heels of *Macintosh*, the ACLU withdrew its support. Forrest Bailey to Marie A. Bland, May 14, 1930, copy in Davis Papers.

19. Brief for Appellant, United States v. Macintosh, 42 F. 2d 845 (2d. Cir. 1930).

20. Copy of statement in Davis Papers; remark on Kellogg-Briand Pact is in Davis' testimony before the subcommittee of Senate Committee on Immigration, 72nd Cong. 1st sess., 8; Brief for Appellant, United States v. Macintosh, 42 F. 2d 845 (2d Cir. 1930).

21. Roger Baldwin to Charles Poletti, May 5, 1930; Charles H. Clark to Allen Wardwell, May 1, 1930, to Poletti, May 5, 1930, copies in Davis Papers.

22. Charles Poletti to Felix Frankfurter, May 6, 1930, copy in Davis Papers. Poletti added: "Despite all this, I would appreciate your writing me whatever suggestions you may have. We can always use them in oral argument. . . ."

23. Charles Poletti to Douglas C. Macintosh, May 9, 16, 1930, copies in Davis Papers; *New York Times,* May 20, 1930.

24. *New York Times,* May 20, 21, 1930; Porter R. Chandler to Charles H. Clark, May 9, 1946; George H. Cohen to Poletti, May 21, 1930; Poletti to Clark, May 21, 1930, copies in Davis Papers.

25. United States v. Macintosh, 42 F. 2d 845 (2d Cir. 1930).

26. James R. Sheffield to JWD, July 2, 1930; JWD to Sheffield, same date.

27. Roger Baldwin to Charles Poletti, July 2, 1930; Charles Howland to Allen Wardwell, July 17, 1930, copies in the Davis Papers; "Citizenship for Conscientious Objectors?" *The Literary Digest,* CVI (July 12, 1930), 7. Also see the symposium by J. H. Wigmore, K. C. Sears, Ernest Freund, Frederick Gree, and R. W. Hale in 26 ILL. L. REV. 375 and 681 (1931).

28. *New York Times,* Apr. 28, 1931; Poletti to Baldwin, July 3, 1930, copy in the Davis Papers. The brief writers did change the order of their arguments and make revisions designed to meet the contentions in the government's briefs. At Porter Chandler's instance, they also included much footnote material on the historical attitudes of various religious groups toward military service. Porter R. Chandler to JWD, Apr. 25, 1931; to John La-Farge, Apr. 24, 1931. Father LaFarge, who was editor of *America,* the Jesuit weekly, was supporting Macintosh's position editorially.

29. JWD to William A. Bell, May 28, 1931; *New York Times,* Apr. 28, 1931; Dilli interview; JWD to Warren, Apr. 28, 1931.

30. United States v. Macintosh, 283 U.S. 625, 622; "Conscience versus Citizenship," *The Literary Digest,* CIX (June 6, 1931), 7; *New York Times,* May 26, 1931; New York *Herald Tribune,* May 26, 1931. In addition to the symposium by Wigmore *et al.,* cited above, see Macgill, *Selective Conscientious Objection: Divine Will and Legislative Grace,* 54 VA. L. REV. 1355 (1968).

31. JWD to Douglas C. Macintosh, May 26, to William A. Bell, May 28, 1931.

32. Boston *Traveller,* May 27, 1931.

33. JWD to Harold Evans, June 19, 1931; Porter R. Chandler to John La-Farge, June 16, to E. M. Pickman, June 1, 1931; Charles Poletti to Roger Baldwin, June 1, 1931, copies in Davis Papers. "I do hope," Poletti wrote Baldwin, "that your organization . . . will drive home to the public the serious implications of the decision of the majority. Justice Sutherland's opinion really staggers me." United States v. Macintosh, 283 U.S. 605, 634–35 (1931) (Hughes, C. J., dissenting).

34. Charles H. Clark to Allen Wardwell, June 13, 1931, copy in Davis Papers. On the other hand, Justice Roberts was later reported to have told a friend that Hughes had tried hard to get him to switch, but that he still thought he was right. This came in after the decision to file had been made. Allen S. Olmsted II to JWD, July 2, 1931.

35. "Dr. Macintosh Asks a Rehearing," *The Christian Century,* XLVIII (July 22, 1931), 942–43. Three weeks earlier, an editorial had censured the Baptists because only one denominational newspaper and a few ministers had spoken out on the case and because the Northern Baptist Convention had buried a resolution on the matter. Where, the editorial asked, was the Baptist doctrine of "soul liberty"? "Have Baptists Lost Their Courage?" *ibid.* (July 1, 1931), 862–63. In general, however, organized Protestantism was deeply concerned. Miller, *American Protestantism and Social Issues,* 336–37.

36. New York *World Telegram,* June 27, 1931.

37. Charles Poletti to Harold Evans, Sept. 28, 1931, copy in Davis Papers.

38. Poletti to Jerome Davis, Jan. 21, 1932, copy in Davis Papers; John Haynes Holmes, Mar. 23, 1932; Roger Baldwin to JWD, Mar. 24, 1932; ACLU Newsletter, Mar. 23, 1932; Hearings on S. 3275.

39. Frederick Bernays Wiener, *Effective Appellate Advocacy* (New York, 1950), 110–11, 184; Macgill, *Selective Conscientious Objection.*

40. Girouard v. United States, 328 U.S. 61 (1946).

41. Julien Cornwell to JWD, Feb. 14, 1946; Brief for American Civil Liberties Union as *Amicus Curiae,* Girouard v. United States, 328 U.S. 61 (1946).

42. Girouard v. United States, 328 U.S. 61, 68 (1946).

43. Allen Wardwell to Douglas C. Macintosh, May 28, 1931, copy in Davis Papers.

44. Mrs. Douglas C. Macintosh to Porter R. Chandler, May 7, 1946, copy in Davis Papers. Dr. Macintosh commented briefly on the case in one of his books, *Social Religion* (New York, 1939), 285–96.

Notes to Chapter 19

1. U.S. Congress, House, *Charges Against Hon. Grover M. Moscowitz*, H. Rept. No. 1106, 71st Cong., 2nd sess., 1–4, (1930). *Congressional Record*, 70th Cong., 2nd sess., 4610–13.

2. Grover M. Moscowitz to George S. Graham, Feb. 25, 1929. This letter was released to the press. STETSON (code name for firm) to JWD, Feb: 27, 1929.

3. JWD to STETSON, Feb. 28, 1929; Moscowitz statement to press, Mar. 1, 1929, copy in Davis Papers.

4. *Congressional Record*, 70th Cong., 2nd sess., 4611–12. Also see *New York Times*, June 20, 1929, for a summary statement which fills in some of the details.

5. *Congressional Record*, 70th Cong., 2nd sess., 4611–12. House Report, No. 1106, 1–3.

6. Theodore Kiendl to Earl C. Michener, Mar. 4, 1929, copy in Davis Papers; Michener to JWD, Mar. 29; JWD to Howard C. Dickinson, May 2, to Michener, Mar. 11, 1929; *New York Times*, Apr. 12, 1929.

7. *Brooklyn Eagle*, Apr. 27, 1929; JWD to Andrew L. Somers, May 2, 1929; Somers to JWD, May 6, 1929.

8. New York *World*, June 5, 1929; New York *Evening Post*, June 5, 1929; Lansing P. Reed to Julian N. Mason, June 14, 1929, copy in Davis Papers.

9. *New York Times*, June 21, 1929.

10. Andrew L. Somers to JWD and all members of the subcommittee, June 21, 1929. The original of Davis' speech is in U.S., Congress, Senate, *Trial of Impeachment of Robert W. Archbald*, S. Doc., 1140, 62nd Cong., 3rd sess., 1480–81, (1913).

11. House Report, No. 1106, 1–4.

12. Statement, n.d.

13. Moscowitz to JWD, Sept. 12, 1930; also see Moscowitz to JWD, Dec. 31, 1937, Dec. 30, 1941, and many others.

14. JWD to Lord Craigmyle, June 10, 1932; O'Brian interview.

15. The Marcus-Singer trial is well described in Martin Mayer, *Emory Buckner* (New York, 1968), 269–77.

16. Kresel's career is reviewed in *New York Times*, Nov. 16, 1933. See Herbert Mitgang, *The Man Who Rode the Tiger: The Life and Times of Judge Samuel Seabury* (Philadelphia, 1963), 172–75, 180–83, 181–91, *passim*, for Seabury's statement and other information about Kresel.

17. Characterization of Steuer is based on Richard O. Boyer's romantic yet realistic biographical fragment, *Max Steuer: Magician of the Law* (New York, 1932); also on materials in Mitgang, *Man Who Rode the Tiger*.

18. See the accounts of the Marcus-Singer trial in both Boyer, *Steuer*, and Mitgang, *Man Who Rode the Tiger;* JWD to Lord Craigmyle, June 10, 1932.

19. Anna Johansson to JWD, May 24, 1932; Medina statement in Mayer, *Buckner*, 271.

20. Blair interview; *New York Times*, June 1, 1932.

21. *New York Times*, June 9, 10, 15, 1932; Mayer, *Buckner*, 275; Boyer, *Steuer*, 210–13.

22. *New York Times*, June 16, 1932; Ralph M. Carson to author, memorandum, summer 1972.

23. *New York Times*, June 22, 1932.

24. *New York Times*, June 23, 1932, for full text.

25. *Newsweek*, II (Nov. 25, 1933), 30; *New York Times*, Aug. 4, 1932, Mar. 15, 1933.

26. Direct quotations and summaries taken from record, People v. Kresel, 243 App. Div. 137, 277 N.Y.S. 168 (1935), color from running account in *New York Times* and Blair interview.

27. Record, 2983.

28. *Ibid.* 3754–3868.

29. *Ibid.* 3868–4095.

30. *Ibid.*

31. *Ibid.* 4118–4281.

32. *New York Times*, Nov. 15, 1933, Apr. 14, 1934; Blair interview; Kiendl, "John W. Davis," W. VA. B. A. PROC. 106 (1954).

33. Kiendl, "Davis," 106; Isador J. Kresel to JWD, Nov. 23, 1933.

34. William D. Guthrie to JWD, Nov. 16, 1933; Blair interview; also see Frederick R. Coudert to JWD, Jan. 19, 1934, and several other letters.

35. *New York Times*, Nov. 22, 1934, contains liberal extracts from Davis' oral argument.

36. Kiendl, "Davis," 107; Blair interview; Life Assur. Soc., 266 N.Y. 71, 193 N.E. 897 (1934).

37. People v. Kresel. The text of the opinion is also in *New York Times*, Jan. 7, 1935. As Mayer notes, in *Buckner*, 277, the court also emphasized that Kresel had not been an officer or director of (or the lawyer of) the safe-deposit company, the funds of which Marcus and Singer had actually misapplied.

38. *New York Times*, Jan. 17, 1935.

39. *Ibid.*

40. Confidential interview with one of Kresel's former partners, Dec. 8, 1959; numerous exchanges between Davis and Kresel in Davis Papers.

41. *New York Times*, Jan. 18, 1935; JWD to George Wallace, Jan. 23, 1935.

42. Joseph Borkin, *Corrupt Judge* (New York, 1962), 25–82, is the authority on the Manton case.

43. William Howard Taft to George W. Wickersham, Sept. 18, 1922, Taft Papers; Borkin, *Corrupt Judge*, 44; Charles C. Burlingham to JWD, June 8, 1939.

44. Blair interview; New York *Herald Tribune*, June 1, 1939.

45. Charles Burlingham to JWD, June 6, 1939; JWD to Burlingham, June 7, 1939.

46. Burlingham to JWD, June 8, 1939.

47. For a general account of the Levy matter, see Borkin, *Corrupt Judge*,

82–93; also see *Time,* XXIV (Nov. 27, 1939), 15; *New York Times,* Aug. 5, 8, 1939; and In re Levy, 30 F. Supp. 317 (S.D. N.Y. 1939).

48. *New York Times,* Aug. 5, 1939.

49. *Ibid.*

50. Blair interview; Lloyd Paul Stryker to JWD, Aug. 8, 1939.

51. In re Levy, 30 F. Supp. 317, 328–29 (S.D. N.Y. 1939).

52. JWD to Frank L. Polk, Aug. 8, 1939.

53. See, for example, the scathing indictment of bar associations in general for their failure to move against unethical practitioners in "Ethics in the Legal Profession," *Christian Century,* LVI (Nov. 29, 1939), 1461; Hugh P. Macmillan, "The Ethics of Advocacy," *Jurisprudence in Action: A Pleader's Anthology,* Legal Essays Selected by the Association of the Bar of the City of New York (New York, 1953), 307–31; Frankfurter to JWD, June 13, 1953.

Notes to Chapter 20

1. McCoy, *Calvin Coolidge,* 319; Herbert Hoover to Arch W. Shaw, Feb. 17, 1933, in Hoover's *Addresses Upon the American Road, 1933–1938* (New York, 1938), 20–25; William Starr Myers and Walter H. Newton, *The Hoover Administration, A Documented Narrative* (New York, 1936), 505, 193, 189; Vincent P. Carosso, *Investment Banking in America, A History* (Cambridge, Mass., 1970), 322–23.

2. Carosso, *Investment Banking,* 323–27; *New York Times,* Mar. 2, July 20, 1932, Jan. 1, Feb. 7, 1933. Also see Arthur M. Schlesinger, Jr., *The Age of Roosevelt: The Coming of the New Deal* (3 vols., Boston, 1957–60), II, 434–39.

3. Banton, *Ferdinand Pecora,* 67 U.S. L. REV. 302 (1933); editorial, *ibid.* at 537; *New York Times,* May 21, 1933.

4. *New York Times,* May 21, 1933.

5. For Pecora's general philosophy, see Ferdinand Pecora, *Wall Street Under Oath* (New York, 1939).

6. Carosso, *Investment Banking,* 328–35.

7. *Ibid.* 335; *New York Times,* Mar. 14, 16, 1933.

8. JWD to Arthur Krock, Apr. 22, 1924. Four years later, Davis asserted that although the Teapot Dome investigation had had "good results," Congress had "wasted a great deal of valuable time" in investigations over the preceding ten years. JWD to C. Burgess Taylor, Dec. 8, 1928. For statements on Hoover and socialism and on the Democrats and individualism, see the articles by Davis in *New York Times,* Oct. 30, 1932, and Mar. 5, 1933, entitled "Why I Am a Democrat" and "The Torch Democracy Keeps Alive."

9. JWD, memorandum, Mar. 22, 1933.

10. *Ibid.* Mar. 24, 1933; JWD to Duncan U. Fletcher, Mar. 30, 1933.

11. JWD to Duncan U. Fletcher, Mar. 30, 1933; JWD, memorandum, Mar. 27, 1933; *New York Times,* Mar. 31, 1933; New York *Herald Tribune,* Apr. 1, 1933.

12. Pecora to JWD, Apr. 3, 1933.

13. JWD, memorandum of telephone conversation with Pecora, Apr. 10, 1933; JWD to Pecora, Apr. 17, May 2, 1933; JWD memorandum of telephone conversation, May 2, 1933; Pecora to JWD, May 8, 1933; JWD to Pecora, May 10, 1933; New York *World-Telegram*, Apr. 20, 1933. For Lamont's statement to F. D. R., see Carosso, *Investment Banking*, 336.

14. Characterization of Morgan drawn from *New York Times*, May 23, 24, 25, 1933, and sketches in the periodical press, esp. *The Literary Digest*, *Newsweek*, *Time*, *The Nation*, *New Republic*, and *Business Week*.

15. Davis, *Legacy of Love*, 224.

16. Hearings on S. Res. 84 and S. Res. 46 before the Senate Banking and Currency Committee, *Stock Exchange Practices:* Hearings, 73d Cong., 1 sess. (1933), pt. 1, 3–6; *New York Times*, May 24, 1933; Pecora, *Wall Street Under Oath*, 5.

17. *New York Times*, May 24, 1933; *Stock Exchange Practices:* Hearings, pt. 1, 96.

18. *New York Times*, May 24, 25, 30, 1933, and numerous accounts in periodicals cited above, n. 15.

19. Paul Y. Anderson, "The Great Stampede," *The Nation*, CXXXVI (June 21, 1933), 693–94; *New York Times*, May 26, 1933; "What Will Happen to the House of Morgan?" *The Literary Digest*, CXV (June 10, 1933), 3; Henry Morrow Hyde Ms. Diary, June 13, 1933, quoted in William E. Leuchtenburg, *Franklin D. Roosevelt and the New Deal* (New York, 1963), 59.

20. *Stock Exchange Practices:* Hearings, pt. 1, 9. Also see Carosso, *Investment Banking*, 338–39, for additional comments by Pecora.

21. Carter Glass to Fred W. Scott, Apr. 15, 1933, copy in Davis Papers; *Stock Exchange Practices:* Hearings, pt. 1, 335–38, pt. 2, 335ff; Birmingham *News*, May 30, 1933.

22. Paul Mallon in Birmingham *News*, May 30, 1933; "Morgan & Co." *Business Week* (June 7, 1933), 5.

23. Pecora, *Wall Street Under Oath*, 20, 5.

24. *Stock Exchange Practices:* Hearings, pt. 1, 42–44, 53, 70ff; *New York Times*, May 24, 1933.

25. *Stock Exchange Practices:* Hearings, pt. 2, 879–81; quoted in "Where Morgan's Income-Tax Exemption Points," *The Literary Digest*, CXV (June 3, 1933), 5; "Morgan & Co.," *Business Week* (June 7, 1933), 5.

26. *Stock Exchange Practices:* Hearings, pt. 1, 80, 87.

27. For disposition of the Lamont tax cases, see *New York Times*, Oct. 26, 1933, May 26, Oct. 24, 1934.

28. *Stock Exchange Practices:* Hearings, pt. 2, 558–61.

29. *Ibid.* 779–80; *Congressional Record*, 73d Cong., 1 sess. (1933), 5066–67; *New York Times*, June 8, 1933.

30. *Stock Exchange Practices:* Hearings, pt. 2, 779–80.

31. *Ibid.* 782–801.

32. *Ibid.* 800–801.

33. *New York Times*, May 26, 1934; U.S., Congress, Senate, *Stock Exchange Practices*, S. Rept. 1455, 73rd Cong., 2nd sess., 4, (1934).

34. "No Banking is Private," *Business Week* (June 7, 1933), 32.

35. *Stock Exchange Practices:* Report, 101–6; Hearings, pt. 2, 370–72; Pecora, *Wall Street Under Oath*, 206–23.

36. *Stock Exchange Practices:* Hearings, pt. 2, 399, 885–99.

37. *New York Times*, May 27, 1933.

38. JWD to Adolph S. Ochs, May 27, 1933.

39. John N. Brooks, *Once in Golconda* (New York, 1969), 190. Carosso, *Investment Banking*, 340–42, though moderate in its treatment, seems to lean more toward Pecora's interpretation. The construction of Davis and the Morgan partners was eventually sustained decisively in a stockholders' suit, Litwin v. Allen, 25 NYS 2d 667 (1940).

40. For details, see Lansing P. Reed to JWD, memorandum, May 31, 1933.

41. Pecora, *Wall Street Under Oath*, 5–6; *Stock Exchange Practices:* Hearings, pt. 2, 904–46; Report, 389.

42. "No Banking is Private," *Business Week* (June 7, 1933), 32.

43. *Stock Exchange Practices:* Hearings, pt. 1, 66, 96; JWD to Theodore L. Bailey, June 14, 1933; "Effect of the Morgan Disclosures," *The Literary Digest*, CXV (June 24, 1933), 6; (June 10, 1933), 4.

44. JWD to George B. Case, June 13, to Herbert L. Satterlee, June 14, to Theodore L. Bailey, June 14, 1933.

45. JWD to Herbert Brookes, Dec. 7, 1933; Wardell, Oral Memoir.

46. *Business Week* (June 7, 1933), 32; Lippmann, quoted in "What Will Happen to the House of Morgan?" *The Literary Digest*, CXV (June 10, 1933), 4; William E. Dodd to JWD, Aug. 8, 1933; JWD to Dodd, Aug. 24, 1933.

47. JWD to Carter Glass, June 13, 1933, Glass Papers; Morgan Partners to JWD, June 12, 1933.

Notes to Chapter 21

1. JWD to William H. King, mid-Feb. 1925. This was in a letter urging Senator King to support the Ransdell bill to establish a National Institute of Health. Davis made the request, reluctantly, at the instance of his daughter, who had been engaged for some time in social work. To my knowledge, it was the only paternalist measure he supported from 1925 to his death.

2. JWD to Walter Lippman, June 24, 1935. Davis' reference, of course, was to Lippmann's famous article, "The Permanent New Deal," *Yale Review*, XXIV (June 1935), 649–67. In his reply, Lippmann insisted that "responsibility for the successful operation of a nation's economy is now just as much a function of government as is the national defense." Lippmann to JWD, July 1, 1935.

3. Frank Sheldon, Nov. 28, 1932; James M. Beck, Apr. 7, 1932; Oscar M. Voorhees, Sept. 5, 1932; Izzetta J. Miller to JWD, June 6, 1932.

4. JWD to Charles MacVeagh, Oct. 21, 1931.

5. JWD to Emma Davis, n. d., to John J. Davis, Nov. 25, 1935, to J. K. Breedin, Jan. 5, 1932, to David C. Reay, Oct. 2, 1932. The Davis Papers con-

tain many similar letters. Davis added to his sister, "almost with shame," that he turned down most requests. As nearly as I can ascertain, he contributed $250 to a relief committee for lawyers and sent two $1000 checks to the Emergency Unemployment Relief Committee for New York.

6. *New York Times,* Jan. 9, 1932. By April Smith was assailing F. D. R., who was calling for government spending for unemployment relief on a vast scale and for "bold, persistent experimentation." See Matthew and Hannah Josephson, *Al Smith: Hero of the Cities* (New York, 1969), 437, for analysis of Smith's reversion to conservatism.

7. *New York Times,* Jan. 9, 1932. Cox's speech, though not as well written as Davis', differed little in substance.

8. Schwarz, "The Political Career of John W. Davis," 85–86.

9. Swartz interview; JWD to Albert Ritchie, July 11, to Mrs. John A. Preston, July 8, to George R. Kennedy, May 3, 1932.

10. *New York Times,* Oct. 10, 1932; JWD to Stephen T. Tierney, Sept. 12, 1932.

11. JWD to T. K. Helm, Sept. 30, to J. Arthur Barrett, Oct. 21, to John J. Davis, Nov. 23, to Samuel J. Graham, Dec. 8, 1932.

12. JWD to Daniel C. Roper, Feb. 10, 1933, to Hatton W. Summers, Feb. 28, 1933. For an extended account of F.D.R.'s campaign, one that captures all its contradictions, ambiguities, and occasional creative thrusts, see Frank Friedel, *Franklin D. Roosevelt: The Triumph* (Boston, 1956).

13. JWD to Herbert Brookes, Dec. 7, 1933.

14. *Ibid.; New York Times,* Aug. 14, 1933.

15. JWD to John E. Nevin, Aug. 18, 1933. See Peterson, *The Jeffersonian Image,* 355–76, for a thoughtful analysis of the New Dealers' effort to identify the New Deal with the essential moral base of Jeffersonianism and the anti-New Dealers' insistence on regarding Jeffersonianism as a closed system.

16. JWD to Desha Breckinridge, Nov. 8, 1933; *New York Times,* Feb. 28, 1934.

17. JWD to Reynolds Vance, Feb. 26, to Lorenzo W. Chance, July 29, to Rees Turpin, July 31, 1934.

18. John W. Davis, "The Old Order" (privately printed, 1934).

19. See full scrapbook of editorial comments in Davis Papers.

20. George Wolfskill, *The Revolt of the Conservatives* (Boston, 1962), 22–25. I have drawn heavily on this informative study. I have also drawn on John Michael Ray, "The American Liberty League" (seminar paper, University of Connecticut, 1960).

21. Wolfskill, *Revolt of the Conservatives,* 27–28, 35; Donald Day, *Franklin D. Roosevelt's Own Story* (Boston, 1951), 221–22; Samuel Rosenman (ed.), *The Public Papers and Addresses of Franklin D. Roosevelt* (13 vols., New York, 1938–50), III, 422.

22. *New York Times,* Aug. 29, 1934.

23. Wolfskill, *Revolt of the Conservatives,* 65–66.

24. For example, JWD to Ernest M. Hopkins, Oct. 24, to Daniel Willard, Oct. 30, 1934. Also see Schwarz, "The Political Career of John W. Davis," for summary account. Cramer, *Newton D. Baker,* 265–66, reports that Baker felt

that the League was really a political organization and that he preferred to work within the Democratic party.

25. Charles A. Richmond, Aug. 24; Daniel Willard to JWD, Oct. 25, Nov. 1, 1934.

26. John H. Clarke to JWD, Nov. 9, 1934.

27. William L. Clayton to JWD, Nov. 14, 1934.

28. "Liberty for Millionaires," *New Republic*, LXXX (Sept. 5, 1934), 89; *Congressional Record*, 74th Cong., 2nd sess., 1196–98.

29. C. E. Berridge to JWD, Aug. 24, 1934.

30. JWD to C. E. Berridge, Sept. 13, 1934.

31. Twiss, *Lawyers and the Constitution*, 244.

32. JWD to Charles A. Richmond, Feb. 1, 1935; Carson interview, JWD to Horace Bowker, Jan. 7, to S. H. Dent, Oct. 9, 1935, to Bennett Champ Clark, Mar. 16, 1936.

33. JWD to Horace Bowker, Jan. 7, 1935, to John J. Davis, May 1, 1936.

34. Original in Davis Papers.

35. Wolfskill, *Revolt of the Conservatives*, 71–72.

36. *Ibid.* National Lawyers Committee of the American Liberty League, "Report on the Constitutionality of the National Labor Relations Act" (Pittsburgh, Sept. 5, 1935). For additional analysis, see Twiss, *Lawyers and the Constitution*, 243ff. Twiss concludes: "The lawyers . . . were trying to square the circle, to settle a conflict of political economic interests with a legal argument which should have final, absolute, certain authority."

37. Wolfskill, *Revolt of the Conservatives*, 72–73; *New York Times*, Sept. 20, 1935; "A Conspiracy by Lawyers," *The Nation*, CXLI (Oct. 2, 1935), 369; *New York Times*, Oct. 2, 1935.

38. Johnson, *The Fifty-Eight Lawyers*, 70 U.S. L. REV. 22 (1936).

39. George Roberts to JWD, Oct. 22, 1935.

40. Thomas Reed Powell, "Fifty-eight Lawyers Report," *New Republic*, LXXXV (Dec. 11, 1935), 119–22.

41. JWD to Thomas G. Haight, n. d. (fall 1935).

42. *Ibid.*, copy of bill enclosed.

43. Thomas G. Haight, Aug. 27, Sept. 25, 1935; Jouett Shouse to JWD, Sept. 28, 1935; JWD to Haight, Oct. 8, 1935; *New York Times*, Oct. 17, Nov. 2, 1935.

44. JWD to Haight, June 4, 1936, to George H. Gardiner, Nov. 1, 1935, to James R. Sheffield, Dec. 4, 1935. Davis' Oral Memoir does not mention the Liberty League.

45. *New York Times*, Feb. 2, 1936.

46. Speech, "The Redistribution of Power," copy in Davis Papers.

47. Quoted in *New York Times*, Feb. 2, 1936.

48. JWD to John Preston, Sept. 29, 1936.

49. Raoul Desvernine to JWD, Oct. 5, 1936; *New York Times*, Oct. 22, 1936; Alfred E. Smith, Oct. 21; Walter Lippmann, Oct. 21; Henry L. Stimson to JWD, Oct. 22, 1936.

50. JWD to Frank O. Lowden, Oct. 23, to J. P. Morgan, Oct. 21, 1936; *New York Times*, Oct. 27, 1936.

51. McReynolds interview; Marion W. Rippy, Oct. 19, 1936; W. Guy Merritt, Oct. 13, 1936; C. D. Barksdale to JWD, Nov. 4, 1936.

52. JWD to Barksdale, Nov. 6, 1936; to William Stanley, Oct. 31, 1936.

53. Francis Pickens Miller, *The Blessings of Liberty* (Chapel Hill, N.C., 1936), 29–30; memorandum, William Diebold to Bayless Manning, Jan. 28, 1972, Council on Foreign Relations Files, courtesy of Hamilton Fish Armstrong.

Notes to Chapter 22

1. For a general account, see Schlesinger, *The Age of Roosevelt*. Vols. II and III: *The Coming of the New Deal* and *The Politics of Upheaval;* Freidel, *Franklin D. Roosevelt: The Triumph*. The Frazier-Lemke Act was radical only in means. Its purpose, the preservation of individual property ownership, was patently conservative. In 1930, 44 per cent of total mortgage indebtedness was on tenant-operated farms. Even in Iowa, 47.3 per cent of farms were operated by tenants. See U.S., Congress, House. *The Farm Debt Problem*. H. Doc. 9, 73d. Cong., 1st sess., (1933); and Senate. *To Create the Farmers' Home Corporation*. Rep. 446, 74th Cong., 1st sess., (1935).

2. Charles Warren, *Bankruptcy in United States History* (Cambridge, 1935), Foreword, and 152.

3. JWD to John J. Parker, Sept. 10, 1934; Paschall Davis to George A. Brownell, July 10, 1972, copy, courtesy of Mr. Brownell. This seven-page, single-spaced letter describes the cases treated in this chapter from the point of view of one of Davis' main assistants at the time.

4. Edward C. Blackorby, *Prairie Rebel: The Public Life of William Lemke* (Lincoln, Neb., 1963); Russel B. Nye, *Midwestern Progressive Politics* (New York, 1959), 291 for Townley quotation.

5. Theodore Saloutos and John D. Hicks, *Twentieth Century Populism: Agricultural Discontent in the Middle West, 1900–1939* (Lincoln, Neb., 1951) 448–49.

6. Blackorby, *Prairie Rebel*, 195–201; Schlesinger, *The Coming of the New Deal*, 65; *New York Times*, Apr. 11, June 14, 19, 20, July 1, 1934; T. Harry Williams, *Huey Long* (New York, 1970), 709–11.

7. *New York Times*, July 1, 1935. For a survey of the accomplishments of the Farm Credit Administration and other New Deal measures, see Saloutos and Hicks, *Twentieth Century Populism*, 498–500.

8. Louisville Joint Stock Land Bank v. Radford, 74 F. 2d 576 (1935) is the most detailed account of the origins of the case; Louisville Joint Stock Land Bank v. Radford, 8 F. Supp. 489 (1935).

9. Paschall Davis to George A. Brownell, July 10, 1972; Mark Edelman, "The Minnesota Moritorium Case" (seminar paper, University of Virginia, 1971).

10. JWD to Charles Warren, Feb. 21, 1935; Warren to JWD, Feb. 23, 1935; 74 F. 2d 576.

11. Paschall Davis to George A. Brownell, July 10, 1972; JWD to William

Marshall Bullitt, Feb. 15, 1935; *New York Times,* June 14, 1939 for report on fee. Bullitt's firm also received $30,000.

12. Memorandum by Edwin F. Blair, Mar. 4, 1935, copy in Davis Papers; John E. Tarrant to JWD, Mar. 7, 1935, enclosing suggestions of Leon Leighton, who urged Tarrant to emphasize the Tenth Amendment; Paschall Davis to George A. Brownell, July 10, 1972; Brief for Petitioner, Louisville v. Radford, 295 U.S. 555 (1935).

13. *Ibid.*

14. See the summary of the two briefs at 562–572, Louisville v. Radford, 295 U.S. 555.

15. See, in particular, the brief signed by Radford's principal counsel, Edwin A. Krauthoff, at 13 and 10.

16. Continental Illinois National Bank and Trust Co. of Chicago v. Chicago, Rock Island, & Pacific Ry Company, 294 U.S. 648 (1935); *New York Times,* April 2, 1935; Bradford v. Fahey, 76 F. 2d 628 (1935).

17. *New York Times,* Apr. 3, 1935; Campbell v. Alleghany, 75 F. 2d. 947 (4th Cir. 1935); Newton D. Baker to JWD, Apr. 8, 1935; Additional Brief for Respondent, Louisville v. Radford, 295 U.S. 555.

18. Louisville v. Radford, 295 U.S. 555, 588 (1935); JWD to Reginald C. Dilli, May 31, 1935, to William Marshall Bullitt, n. d. The Davis brief said at 18: "the sale is invariably made so as to obtain the highest possible price for the property. No court would authorize a sale at a price less than that which the lien creditor himself offered to pay in cash for the property." Brandeis substituted the word *always* for *invariably* and put the second statement in the past tense. 295 U.S. at 584.

19. New York *Sun,* New York *Post, New York Times,* May 28, 1935; Blackorby, *Prairie Rebel,* 217.

20. *New York Times,* May 29, 1935.

21. JWD to Edward C. Martz, Nov. 13, 1935.

22. Warren, *Bankruptcy,* 156–59.

23. Ray Tucker, "National Whirligig," in the Beckley (West Virginia) *Post,* Oct. 8, 1935; T.R.B., "Funny Business in Baltimore," *New Republic,* LXXXV (Nov. 20, 1935), 35–37; *New York Times,* Mar. 31, 1936.

24. See the superb chapters in Schlesinger, *The Politics of Upheaval,* 302–24, and in E. W. Hawley, *The New Deal and the Problem of Monopoly* (Princeton, 1966), 325–43. But see especially the eighty-four volumes published by the FTC, *Utility Corporations* (S. Doc. 92, 70th Cong., 1st sess. [1929–36]); the six volumes published by the House Interstate and Foreign Commerce Committee, *Relation of Holding Companies to Operating Companies in Power and Gas Affecting Control,* H. Rept., 827, 73rd Cong., 2nd sess., (1934); and the *Report of the National Power Policy Committee on Public-Utility Holding Companies,* H. Doc. 137, 74th cong., 1st sess., (1935).

25. Quoted in Schlesinger, *Politics of Upheaval,* 308; A. J. G. Priest, *Principles of Public Utility Regulation* (2 vols., Charlottesville, Va., 1969), II, 507–8.

26. "Message from the President," H. Doc. 137, 74th Cong., 1st sess., (1935); Schlesinger, *Politics of Upheaval,* 311.

27. Harry S Truman, *Memoirs by Harry S Truman: Year of Decisions* (2 vols., New York, 1955–56), I, 151; Schlesinger, *Politics of Upheaval*, 313, 323–324.

28. Hawley, *The New Deal*, 335–37; Priest, *Principles of Public Utility Regulation*, 507, 519; interview with A. J. G. Priest.

29. JWD to Newton D. Baker, June 11, to W. R. Vance, Sept. 19, 1935.

30. Krock, "In Washington," *New York Times*, Mar. 31, 1936. Excerpts and summaries of the testimony on charges of collusion, the hearing on constitutionality, the oral arguments and briefs, and the opinion are in *New York Times*, Sept. 17, 28, 29, Oct. 4, 25, 26, and Nov. 8, 1936; T.R.B., "Funny Business in Baltimore," and Edison Electric Institute *Bulletin*, III (Oct. 1935), 380–82, 406 (Nov. 1935), 414. Also see In re American States Public Service Co., 12 F. Supp. 667 (D.C. Md. 1935).

31. See the brief sketch of Judge Coleman in *New York Times*, Nov. 8, 1935.

32. *Ibid.* Sept. 13, 1935.

33. *Ibid.*; Paschall Davis to George A. Brownell, July 10, 1972.

34. Baltimore *Sun*, Sept. 29, 1935; editorial in Washington *Post*, Sept. 29, 1935, on Corcoran's protest; Krock, "In Washington," *New York Times*, Mar. 31, 1936, in which he summarized the history of the case.

35. In re American States Public Service Co., 12 F. Supp. 667 (D.C. Md. 1935).

36. *New York Times*, Sept. 29, Oct. 4, 1936.

37. *New York Times*, Sept. 28, 29, Oct. 25, 26, 1936.

38. The opinion ran 20,000 words and 97 typewritten pages. The letter is in *New York Times*, Nov. 12, 1935; the reaction of utility executives is *ibid.*, Nov. 8, 1935.

39. Unidentified clipping, Davis Papers; Opinion in Burco, Inc. v. Whitworth, 81 F. 2d 721 (4th Cir. 1936), at 740. For an analysis which supports the Holding Company Act as a whole but which gives some credence to Davis' charge that the Act was "an attempt to regulate not the mails but the conduct of those who use them," see the extended comment, *Federal Regulation of Holding Companies: The Public Utility Act of 1935*, 45 YALE L.J. 468 (1936). Attorneys for the utilities pressed the same point in the ultimate case, Electric Bond and Share Co. v. SEC, 303 U.S. 419 (1938), but Chief Justice Hughes dismissed it summarily in his majority opinion: "We think that the imposition of such a penalty does not transgress any constitutional provision." 303 U.S. at 442–43. A. J. G. Priest, the number two man on the utility side in the preparation of that case, later concluded that Hughes was right. "One reaches for things when one is fighting a case," he said. Priest interview.

40. Burco, Inc. v. Whitworth, *cert. denied*, 297 U.S. 724 (1936); Reed's statement is in *New York Times*, Mar. 31, 1936.

41. Krock, "In Washington," *New York Times*, Mar. 31, 1936.

42. Paschall Davis to George A. Brownell, July 10, 1972; JWD to Arthur Krock, Dec. 3, 1935; Krock to JWD, Dec. 5, 1935.

43. I am indebted to Phyllis McClure, "The Associated Press and the

Wagner Act" (seminar paper, University of Connecticut, 1960), for initial leads.

44. JWD to John H. Buffham, June 30, 1937; to William G. Davisson, June 3, 1946; to Herbert Brookes, Nov. 27, 1946.

45. Jerold S. Auerbach, *Labor and Liberty: The La Follette Committee and the New Deal* (Indianapolis, 1966), 113, for GM, and *passim* for the story as a whole; William Green to JWD, Feb. 14, 1928; JWD to James Quarles, Mar. 29, 1949; to Herbert Brookes, Dec. 7, 1933. See Daniel J. Leab, *A Union of Individuals: the Formation of the American Newspaper Guild, 1933–1936* (New York, 1970), for the story of the Guild.

46. *Fortune*, XV (Feb. 1937), 88.

47. Phyllis McClure, "The Associated Press and the Wagner Act," (seminar paper, University of Connecticut, 1960); Oliver Gramling, *AP: The Story of News* (New York, 1940), 423–40; report of finding of Charles E. Clark, trial examiner for the National Labor Relations Board, *New York Times*, Apr. 25, 1936.

48. *Ibid.*; Heywood Broun to Kent Cooper, Oct. 17, 1935; Cooper to Broun, October 22, 1935, copies in Davis Papers.

49. William Cannon, memorandum, Nov. 19, 1935, copy in Davis Papers.

50. *New York Times*, Jan. 18, 1936.

51. *Ibid.*

52. *Ibid.*

53. Heywood Broun to William Bondy, Feb. 27, 1936, copy in Davis Papers. The letter was approved by the general membership of the Guild in a meeting on February 26.

54. JWD to Cannon, Feb. 29, 1936; *New York Times*, Apr. 25, 1936.

55. Frank B. Noyes to JWD, Dec. 10, 1935; Cooper to Noyes, Dec. 13, 1935; Weymouth Kirkland to Robert McCormick, Sept. 21, 1936, copies of last two in Davis Papers.

56. *Editor and Publisher*, LXVI (Apr. 14, 1934), 5, 46; New York *Evening Post*, July 25, 1936; quoted in Ferdinand Lundberg, *Imperial Hearst* (New York, 1936), 351; quoted in George Seldes, *Freedom of the Press* (Indianapolis, 1935), 191–92.

57. Paschall Davis to George A. Brownell, July 10, 1972; Cannon to Lloyd Stratton, Feb. 3, 1936.

58. Paschall Davis to George A. Brownell, July 10, 1972.

59. *Time*, XXXII (June 29, 1936), 32–33. For decision, National Labor Relations Board v. Associated Press see 85 F. 2d 56 (2d. Cir. 1936).

60. Kent Cooper to Harold W. Bissell, June 11; JWD to Cooper, June 12; Bissell to JWD, July 17; Cooper to Lansing P. Reed, July 30; JWD to Bissell, July 29, 1936.

61. Cooper to JWD, June 13; Stratton to Cannon, Sept. 11; John M. Polk to Stratton, Sept. 12, 1936, copies in Davis Papers. See the AP story of Davis' petition to the Supreme Court, *New York Times*, Sept. 15, 1936; also the vicious denunciation of the Guild by the publisher's spokesman, Marlen Pew, in *Editor & Publisher*, LXIX (Sept. 19, 1936), 59. Colonel McCormick's attorney, Weymouth Kirkland, told the Colonel that "we heartily concur" in

Davis' refusal to make a First Amendment argument. Kirkland to McCormick, Sept. 21, 1936, copy in Davis Papers. The briefs are extensively analyzed in Richard C. Cortner, *The Wagner Act Cases* (Knoxville, Tenn., 1964), 157–69.

62. Paschall Davis to George A. Brownell, July 10, 1972. Another associate, Edwin F. Blair, said flatly that pressure from the AP was the decisive factor in Davis' emphasis on the First Amendment. Blair interview.

63. *Ibid.*

64. The oral arguments are printed verbatim in Associated Press v. National Labor Relations Board, 301 U.S. 103 (1937), (appendix at 719). For color and other incidentals, see *New York Times*, Feb. 10, 1937.

65. *Ibid.*

66. Heywood Broun, "Mr. Davis Comes in Second," *The Nation*, CXLIV (Feb. 27, 1937), 241; AP v. NLRB (appendix at 734); *Editor & Publisher*, LXX (Feb. 13, 1937) 3–4. Although Davis consented to Morris Ernst's request that he make an argument as *amicus curiae*, Solicitor General Stanley Reed refused. See the extensive correspondence in Department of Justice File 134-51-1, National Archives.

67. AP v. NLRB, at 133 (Sutherland, J. dissenting).

68. JWD to Harry H. Byrer, Dec. 14; to Walter C. Preston, Apr. 13, 1937. Davis' statement is in *New York Times*, Apr. 14, 1937.

69. JWD to Thomas N. Bell, Mar. 22, to James Quarles, Mar. 4; Edward R. Murrow to JWD, Feb. 16; JWD to C. Burgess Taylor, May 18, 1937.

70. JWD to Clarence J. Shearn, Mar. 18, 23, 1937; copy of statement in Davis Papers; JWD to Lippmann, Mar. 16, 1937; to George, Mar. 18, 22, to Pettengill, May 4, 1937; copies of memoranda in Davis Papers. Davis had Finlay's article printed and distributed to every member of Congress.

71. JWD to Pettengill, May 4, 1937.

72. JWD to Walter C. Preston, Apr. 13, 1937.

73. JWD to James C. McReynolds, Apr. 13, 1937.

Notes to Chapter 23

1. William A. Lockwood to JWD, July 5, 1953; Helen Healy to Julia D. Healy, Dec. 25, 1971, courtesy of Julia D. Healy.

2. Davis, *Legacy of Love*, 212ff.; JWD to Emma Davis, Apr. 8, 1923; to Mrs. George E. Brower, Oct. 30, 1946.

3. "Yeamans Hall Club" (pamphlet, privately printed, 1923).

4. Davis, *Legacy of Love*, 213, 227; Charles Hanson and Edwin S. S. Sunderland, Jr., interviews.

5. JWD to James W. Ewing, Apr. 19, 1938; Henry Alexander interview.

6. Davis, *Legacy of Love*, 213; William Lockwood interview.

7. JWD to Hale Houston, Feb. 27, 1934; to Herbert Brookes, Aug. 26, 1935; to Walter C. Preston, Sept. 23, 1929; to Emma Davis, Aug. 19, 1927; to John H. Buffhan, Dec. 29, 1936.

8. Numerous interviews; William A. Lockwood to JWD, July 5, 1953.

There is also considerable miscellaneous correspondence on the Round Table in the Davis Papers.

9. Numerous interviews.

10. Davis, *Legacy of Love*, 211, 228–30; JWD to John J. D. Preston, Oct. 5, 1943; *New York Times*, July 14, 16, 1943.

11. Davis, *Legacy of Love*, 228–29; Emma Davis to JWD, Sept. 24, 1938; various letters.

12. Julia D. Healy to author, July 5, 1972; JWD to Katerine Halley, Sept. 13, 1946.

13. Davis, *Legacy of Love*, 212–13; Edwin S. S. Sunderland, Sr., interview.

14. Numerous interviews; JWD to Walter Lippmann, Oct. 18, 1937; *New York Times*, Apr. 13, 1954; JWD to D. L. Chambers, Apr. 13, 1925.

15. JWD to Mrs. John J. Davis, Mar. 3, 1912; to A. W. Paull, Nov. 7, 1935; to John J. Davis, Jan. 18, 1915.

16. Samuel Halley to JWD, Dec. 29, 1931; JWD to A. W. Paull, Nov. 7, 1935; JWD to Rush Sloan, Dec. 5, 1944.

17. JWD to Thomas W. Lamont, May 15, 1946; to Randolph T. Shields, Aug. 28, 1947.

18. JWD to John Godfrey Saxe, Aug. 24, 1933; to John Foster Dulles, June 2, 1941; Chandler interview; JWD to Herbert Brookes, Nov. 27, 1946.

19. Numerous interviews; many letters by JWD to Paul A. Wolfe and others; Porter R. Chandler to author, memorandum and several enclosures, Aug. 4, 19, 1971.

20. JWD to Francis P. Gaines, Aug. 6, 1945; Harrington Waddell to JWD, Feb. 26, 1926, JWD to Waddell, Mar. 4, 1926; to W. P. Williams, Sept. 12, 1927.

21. Copy of proposed deed in Davis Papers; JWD to George W. St. Clair, Feb. 16, 1931.

22. JWD to George W. St. Clair, Nov. 26, 1927.

23. James N. Veech to JWD, Mar. 26; Newton D. Baker to Veech, Mar. 29, 1935, copy in Davis Papers.

24. Francis P. Gaines to JWD, Apr. 2, 1935.

25. JWD to James N. Veech, Apr. 5, 1935.

26. JWD to Gaines, Apr. 17, 1935. Newton D. Baker felt as Davis did. See Baker to JWD, June 7, 1935. Crenshaw, *General Lee's College*, does not relate the incident.

27. Henry Louis Smith to JWD, May 5, 12, 1930.

28. JWD to George W. St. Clair, Oct. 25, 1929.

29. JWD to Francis P. Gaines, Feb. 3, 1936; to Rees Turpin, May 10, 1935; quoted in Robert S. Keefe, "Davis: 'The country lawyer,'" *The Alumni Magazine of Washington and Lee*, XLVIII (Apr. 1973), 4.

30. JWD to W. H. Moreland, Jan. 19, 1932.

31. Copy of address in Davis Papers.

32. JWD to George W. St. Clair, Nov. 26, 1937; Francis P. Gaines, Dec. 3, 1937; W. H. Moreland to JWD, Dec. 4, 1937. (Moreland, who was dean of the Law School, wrote in part: "I have always felt the Law School had in you a devoted and influential friend, able to understand our problems and

willing to do all in your power to help us.") JWD to Gaines, May 17, 1949.
For the Davis Prize, see Denis O'L. Cohalan to Gaines, Mar. 5, and Gaines
to Cohalan, Mar. 20, 1946, copies in Davis Papers.

Notes to Chapter 24

1. JWD to Frederick W. Scott, Dec. 20, 1932; to Louis Fitz Henry, Mar.
17, 1930. Among the other institutions seriously interested in Davis at one
point or another were the University of Georgia and West Virginia University.

2. JWD to Frank Du Moulin, May 11, 1937.

3. Interviews with Max Isenbergh, Felix Frankfurter, Robert Szold, and
Mrs. Eleanor Belmont.

4. JWD to Harry E. Stone, Apr. 23, 1928; Sunderland interview. Dec. 6,
1958. Also see JWD to Arthur T. Vanderbilt, Mar. 12, 1950.

5. The paper was privately printed, and has since been included in several
anthologies. All quotations are from the original text.

6. George A. Brownell and Ralph M. Carson in *Memorial Volume,* (Association of the Bar of the City of New York, 1935). Interviews with Herbert
Wechsler, A. J. G. Priest, and Grant Gilmore.

7. Brownell and Carson, *Memorial Volume;* interviews with Learned
Hand, Felix Frankfurter, and David Pine.

8. Pine interview; Beryl H. Levy, *Corporation Lawyer: Saint or Sinner?*
(Philadelphia, 1961), 81; Ralph M. Carson to author, memorandum, Sept. 8,
1971.

9. Isenbergh interview; Joseph M. Proskauer in "Letters from Readers,"
Commentary, XLIX (Jan. 1970), 4; Arthur R. Charpentier (ed.), *Counsel on
Appeal* (New York, 1968), 211; Arthur Krock to author, Mar. 26, 1965.

10. Angell interview; Phillips (ed.), *Felix Frankfurter Reminisces,* 267.

11. Interviews with Priest, Pine, Hand, and Krock.

12. *Davis Polk History,* 52; Blair interview.

13. Wayne C. Williams, "Equal Justice Under Law," Denver Bar Association REP, 39 (1948).

14. Davis, "The Case for the Case Lawyer," A.B.A. PROC. 757 (1916); Frederick Bernays Wiener, *Effective Appellate Advocacy, How to Brief and
Argue Cases on Appeal—Including Examples of Winning Briefs and Oral
Arguments* (New York, 1950), 137–38.

15. Frankfurter interview; R. Horr to JWD, June 1, 1938, for Baker's comment on Davis; Cramer, *Newton D. Baker,* repeats the comment in less detail (222) but also reports (186) that Holmes was once heard to say that
Baker was the outstanding lawyer of his generation.

16. Interviews with Morris Ernst and Frederick B. Wiener; *Cross-Examination,* 32 MISS. L. J. 243, (1961) 245; William Howard Taft to Robert A. Taft,
Jan. 28, 1928, Taft Papers.

17. Interview with Stanley F. Reed; CBS News Special, "Justice Black and
the Bill of Rights," Dec. 3, 1968. Justice Black added in a letter to the author, Dec. 9, 1969, "I could have said much more about him [Davis] because

he was one of the ablest advocates that ever appeared before our Court." Merlo J. Pusey, *Charles Evans Hughes* (2 vols., New York, 1951), contains no value judgments on or substantive references to Davis by Hughes. Nor could I find any in a cursory examination of the Hughes Papers in the Library of Congress.

18. JWD to Samuel Halley, May 19, 1931; *Our New President* 8 A.B.A.J. 552 (1922).

19. JWD to Samuel Seabury, May 14, 1925; George Martin, *Causes and Conflicts: The Centennial History of the Association of the Bar of the City of New York 1870–1970* (Boston, 1970), 237–38.

20. George Martin to author, Jan. 1, Apr. 6, 1970.

21. *Ibid.* Martin added that other members of the Association echoed De Witt's and Tweed's judgment.

22. Conversation with Mrs. Wright Abbot, Aug. 1970; Paul L. Wilson to author, Jan. 22, 1973; numerous interviews; Stryker, *John W. Davis—A Tribute,* 1 N.Y.L. FORUM 206 (1955) 207.

23. JWD to W. R. Vance, Feb. 17, 1922; George Martin to author, Apr. 6, 1970; JWD to Frank L. Crawford, Jan. 4, 1934; Address to the New York State Bar Association, Jan. 18, 1930.

24. *Ibid.;* copy of verse, undated, in Davis Papers.

25. Radio Speech on Legal Aid, Oct. 5, 1938; Address to the New York State Bar Association, Jan. 18, 1930; "My Vocation," in Earl G. Lockhart, *My Vocation by Eminent Americans* (New York, 1938); Address on the 75th Anniversary of the Association of the Bar of the City of New York, Mar. 16, 1946, originals of all in Davis Papers.

26. JWD to Frederick Roe, Feb. 8, 1924; John W. Davis, *The Lawyers of Louis XVI* (privately printed, New York, 1941).

27. JWD to Perry Belmont, Sept. 10, 1941; to M. S. Sherman, June 12, 1942; to George A. Solter, June 10, 1941; to Hartwell Cabell, Oct. 3, 1946.

28. New York State Bar Association REP. 482 (1948); Ralph M. Carson to author, memorandum, summer, 1971.

29. Quoted in Link, (ed.), *The Papers of Woodrow Wilson,* II, 351–52.

30. Carson and Sunderland interviews. Carson observed that Davis' scholarly allusions were frequently beyond the scope of his associates. Davis, *The Lawyers of Louis XVI.*

31. Ernst interview.

32. Statement appears in several letters and was often quoted to me in interviews.

33. JWD to Frank O. Salisbury, Aug. 21, 1944; to Ralph Dawson, Apr. 8, 1941, to Joseph H. Willits, Dec. 24, 1945; to Eustace Seligman, Nov. 30, 1949; to Chase Mellen, Jr., Dec. 8, 1949. In addition to Purcell, for legal realism, see Wilfrid E. Rumble, Jr., *American Legal Realism: Skepticism, Reform, and the Judicial Process* (Ithaca, 1968); Eugene V. Rostow, *The Sovereign Prerogative: The Supreme Court and the Quest for Law* (New Haven, 1962); and especially, Woodard, *The Limits of Legal Realism: An Historical Perspective,* 54 VA. L. REV. 689 (1968).

34. Pound, *Mechanical Jurisprudence,* 8 COLUM. L. REV. 605 (1908); JWD

to Edward S. Dore, Mar. 28, 1946; to Frank A. Nelson, Jan. 11, 1936; Charles Evans Hughes, *The Supreme Court of the United States* (New York, 1928), 68.

35. Original of McReynolds eulogy in Davis Papers; JWD to M. S. Sherman, June 12, 1942; Joseph Guttman, "The Evolution of the Concept of Stare Decisis in the Papers of the State Bar Associations: 1884–1930 (seminar paper, University of Virginia, 1969). Davis' views were close to the extreme right, as compared, for example, to those of Henry U. Sims of Alabama, president of the ABA in 1929. Sims warned: "We must not fall back into the error that the courts do not make law, nor into the error of approving the doctrine of *stare decisis,* that courts must not correct the law when decisions of courts have previously made it wrong. *Stare decisis* is the death knell of the judicial process; and without the judicial process, the law will show very slow improvement upon what it now is." Henry U. Sims, "The Problem of Stare Decisis in the Reform of the Law," Pennsylvania Bar Association, REP. 170, at 187–88 (1930).

36. Original of Supreme Court speech in Davis Papers; see also remarks by Davis in New York State Bar Association REP. 85 (1937).

37. JWD to Courtenay Dinwiddie, Nov. 28, 1933; to William D. Mitchell, Apr. 26, 1949; to W. R. Vance, July 12, 1926.

38. JWD to John J. Parker, Nov. 12, 1940.

39. JWD to Edward H. Warren, Oct. 7, 1942.

40. Rostow, *The Sovereign Prerogative,* 20.

41. JWD to Rees Turpin, May 10, 1935; to Walter H. Buck, Apr. 3, 1950; to Charles Warren, Oct. 19, 1942.

42. Wardwell, Oral Memoir, 36, 123. Wardwell added: "It's pretty hard for lawyers to devise schemes that their own clients don't want. The lawyers in New York dealing with businessmen sympathize with their clients, but I think they're less conservative than their business clients as a rule."

43. JWD to Rees Turpin, May 10, 1935; to Julian S. Gravely, Feb. 25, 1935; to John D. Sweeney, Mar. 19, 1940. Sometimes Davis added Cornell, Vanderbilt, and Tulane to the list of schools he considered superior.

44. JWD to Jacob Becheisen, Nov. 25, 1936; to Fred M. Blaich, Jr., Oct. 27, 1950.

45. JWD to Leslie J. Tompkins, Dec. 30, 1925; *New York Times,* June 9, 1926; JWD, for the Committee on Legal Education and Admission to the Bar, to the New York State Bar Association, transmitting a resolution of the Joint Conference on Legal Education of June 28–29, 1926; JWD to Arthur T. Vanderbilt, Oct. 31, 1941; Jerold S. Auerbach, "Enmity and Amity: Law Teachers and Practitioners, 1900–1922," in Donald Fleming and Bernard Bailyn (eds.), *Perspectives in American History,* (Cambridge, 1971), 351–604. Davis' papers do not indicate that he was in any sense moved by the anti-Semitism that caused Elihu Root and several other members of the ABA committee to come in with the two-year recommendation in 1922.

46. Jerome Frank's remark is in Ralph M. Carson to author, memorandum, summer 1971.

Notes to Chapter 25

1. *New York Times,* April 14, 1945.

2. JWD to Robert L. Owen, June 19, 1926; to Joseph T. Robinson, Apr. 29, 1935; to Eugene Meyer, Nov. 19, 1935; copy of statement by J. P. Morgan, Jan. 7, 1936, in Davis Papers.

3. JWD to Thomas Amory Lee, Aug. 24, 1925, to Joseph T. Robinson, Jan. 21, 1926, and Nov. 6, 1930.

4. Hamilton Fish Armstrong to author, June 27, 1972. Also see John W. Davis, "Anglo-American Relations and Sea Power," *Foreign Affairs,* VII (Apr. 1929), 345-55, and "The Permanent Bases of American Foreign Policy," *Foreign Affairs,* X (Oct. 1931), 1-12.

5. JWD to Lord Cecil, Feb. 20, 1939. The remark quoted was made before the invasions of Albania and Czechoslovakia, but it faithfully represents Davis' attitude toward these events.

6. JWD to Dorothy Thompson, Nov. 15, 1938; to Charles Robbins, Feb. 3, 1938; to John H. Buffham, Dec. 12, 1935; Lord Midleton to JWD, Oct. 15, 1938; JWD to Buffham, June 30, 1939. Davis' daughter asserts that he opposed the Munich settlement; his correspondence is unrevealing.

7. JWD to Lord Midleton, Apr. [?], 1940.

8. JWD to Lord Lee, Jan. 11, 1941; to the Marchioness of Reading, Dec. 12, 1940; to the Countess of Midleton, Jan. 6, 1941.

9. Copy of speech in Davis Papers; JWD to W. A. White, May 24, 1940; to Ben E. Hulse, Oct. 4, 1940, and many other letters; *New York Times,* May 29, 1941.

10. JWD to Grenville Clark, Apr. 2, 1941; *New York Times,* May 29, 1941; JWD to George S. Wallace, Oct. 30, 1941.

11. JWD to Arthur Cole, Dec. 15, 1942; to Charles Warren, Nov. 16, 1943; to Hale Houston, Jan. 25, 1943; and numerous letters to Lawrence Bunker, Porter Chandler, and others.

12. JWD to Ben E. Hulse, Oct. 4, 1940; to Jonathan M. Davis, May 13, 1943; to Wendell Willkie, Apr. 7, 1944; to Herbert Brookes, Oct. 19, 1944.

13. JWD to D. M. Ogden, Jan. 30, 1945. (Actually, he did complain, though not as often as he had in the past. See, for example, JWD to Paul West, Dec. 2, 1943, and JWD to Hamilton Fish Armstrong, Feb. 24, 1942.)

14. JWD to Bertrand W. Gearhard, Apr. 16, 1945; to John Foster Dulles, Dec. 17, 1943. Copy of resolution in Davis Papers.

15. JWD to Goldthwaite H. Dorr, July 12, Aug. 8, 1945.

16. *Ibid.*

17. Charles Warren to JWD, Feb. 12, 1944; JWD to Warren, Feb. 14, 1944.

18. JWD to Herbert Brookes, July 18, 1946. For authoritative analysis of the substance of the Nuremberg indictments, see William J. Bosch, *Judgment on Nuremberg* (Chapel Hill, 1970), and Telford Taylor, *Nuremberg and Vietnam: an American Tragedy* (Chicago, 1970).

19. JWD to John Foster Dulles, Apr. 6, 1944. For an account of Dulles' in-

ternationalist views at this time, see Louis L. Gerson, *John Foster Dulles* (New York, 1967).

20. *New York Times,* Nov. 5, 1944.

21. *Ibid.* Dec. 10, 29, 1944, Feb. 18, 1945.

22. *Ibid.* Feb. 5, 1945; A. Willis Robertson to JWD, Feb. 6, 1945; JWD to Robertson, Feb. 9, 1945; to Lorenzo W. Chance, May 8, 1947.

23. JWD to George W. Maxey, Oct. 29, 1947; to Will Clayton, May 3, 1949; also many other letters, especially during the war years.

24. JWD to Lord Queensborough, Sept. 10, 1945; to Herbert Brookes, July 18, 1946; to Rees Turpin, Nov. 8, 1946; to Brookes, Mar. 12, 1948.

25. JWD to Rees Turpin, Nov. 30, 1948; to Herbert Brookes, Dec. 4, 1948; interview with William Meagher.

26. Statement of the Citizens' Political Committee, Mar. 21, 1950, in Davis Papers; J. Harvie Williams to JWD, June 12, Nov. 22, 1950; Williams to Albert W. Hawkes, June 14, 1950, copy in Davis Papers; JWD to Harry F. Byrd, n. d.

27. JWD to Claude Bowers, Aug. 24, 1950; to Herbert Brookes, July 18, 1946.

28. JWD to James W. Gerard, Apr. 14, 1947; to Hamilton Fish Armstrong, July 8, 1947; to Rees Turpin, Dec. 11, 1947; to Walter Mitchell, May 2, 1950. David Rockefeller was so disturbed by Davis' acceptance of Hazlitt's contentions that he sent him a refutation prepared by the economic adviser of the Bank for International Settlements. Rockefeller to JWD, Jan. 13, 1948.

29. JWD to Herbert Brookes, Dec. 13, 1945; to James F. Byrnes (telegrams) Nov. 28, Dec. 5, 1945; to Brookes, Mar. 12, 1948.

30. JWD to Earl G. Harrison, Jan. 15, 1947; to E. T. Coman, May 16, 1947.

31. JWD to James W. Gerard, Oct. 14, 1947.

32. JWD to Herbert Brookes, June 17, 1952, Dec. 4, 1948; to William Roy Vallance, Mar. 28, 1950.

33. JWD to Lord Astor, Jan. 6, 1950. The Truman statement, published the same day as Davis' letter, in effect dismissed the defense of Formosa, though it promised to continue economic aid. See text in *New York Times,* Jan. 6, 1950.

34. Julia D. Healy to author, memorandum, summer 1972 (Mrs. Healy was at Cliveden at the time); JWD to Lewis Douglas, July 17, 1950; to Claude Bowers, Aug. 17, 1950; to Lord Astor, Sept. 5, 1950.

35. JWD to John J. Cornwell, June 19, 1951; to Francis P. Gaines, Nov. 21, 1951; Joseph Proskauer to JWD, Dec. 21, 27, 1950; JWD to Proskauer, Dec. 28, 1950. Influenced by the letters of his former secretary, Colonel Lawrence Bunker, who had been on General MacArthur's staff and returned with the General, Davis took a surprisingly tolerant view of MacArthur. On November 23, 1951, for example, following a conversation with Bunker, Davis wrote that MacArthur "had a truer grasp of the Korean situation than did his critics." He was pleased, however, when MacArthur's speech to the Republican Convention in July 1952 failed to prompt a stampede for his

nomination. JWD to Mrs. August Belmont, July 8, 1952, courtesy of Mrs. Belmont.

36. JWD to Mrs. August Belmont, July 8, 1954.

37. JWD to Herbert Brookes, Nov. 23, 1951.

38. *Ibid.;* JWD to Brookes, June 14, 1952.

39. JWD to Brookes, Nov. 23, 1951.

40. JWD to James M. Thomson, Aug. 12, 1952; to James F. Byrnes, Sept. 25, 1952; *New York Times,* Oct. 23, 1952.

41. For Dulles' reasoning, see Louis L. Gerson, *John Foster Dulles* (New York, 1967). For the long-range effect of the emasculation of the Far Eastern Division, see David Halberstam, *The Best and the Brightest* (New York, 1972).

42. There is no scholarly monograph on the Bricker amendment. I have pieced my account together from contemporary newspaper accounts and from brief treatments in Gerson, *Dulles;* Emmet John Hughes, *The Ordeal of Power: A Political Memoir of the Eisenhower Years* (New York, 1963); Robert J. Donovan, *Eisenhower: The Inside Story* (New York, 1956); Dwight D. Eisenhower, *Mandate for Change* (New York, 1963); the angry polemic, Frank E. Holman, *Story of the "Bricker" Amendment* (New York, 1954); and, especially, Herbert S. Parmet, *Eisenhower and the American Crusades* (New York, 1972), 306–12.

43. *New York Times,* June 25, 27, 1953.

44. Martin, *Causes and Conflicts: The Centennial History of the Association of the Bar of the City of New York,* 287–90; Eisenhower, *Mandate for Change,* 283–84.

45. Hughes, *Ordeal of Power,* 144–45.

46. Dwight D. Eisenhower to John J. McCloy, Jan. 13, 1954, copy in Davis Papers.

47. JWD to Eisenhower, Jan. 12, 1954.

48. Eisenhower, *Mandate for Change,* 284.

Notes to Chapter 26

1. JWD to Paul Windels, May 9, 1939.

2. Windels to JWD, Feb. 6, 1939; JWD to Windels, Jan. 25, Feb. 20, 1939. Copies of the memoranda are in Davis Papers.

3. *New York Times,* Jan. 4, 5, Feb. 3, 9, 16, 1939. Also see Article I, section 12, of the New York State Constitution. The memorandum in this instance was written by former Attorney General William D. Mitchell, also a member of the committee, under the date Mar. 5, 1939. Windels to JWD, Apr. 3, 1939; JWD to Windels, Apr. 4, 1939.

4. Draft letter, Charles Burlingham to Lewis B. Schwellenbach, William H. King, and Warren R. Austin, July 19, 1940 (also signed by JWD and Thomas D. Thacher); JWD to Burlingham, July 19, 1940; Schwellenbach to JWD, Aug. 27, 1940; JWD to Schwellenbach, Sept. 6, 1940. Also see Thomas D. Thacher to Schwellenbach, Sept. 4, 1940, for a somewhat more thoughtful

analysis than Davis'. Schwellenbach, who succeeded in burying the bill, did not need to be convinced. His own statement, incorporated in U.S., Congress. Senate. *Investigation of the Alien Harry Bridges*, in S. Rep. 2031, 76th Cong. 3d sess. (1940) was both compelling and inclusive. In Tiaco v. Forbes, 228 U.S. 529 (1913), the alien received a fair hearing before deportation.

5. Corliss Lamont, Memo to the A.C.L.U. Sedition Cases Committee, Dec. 1, 1942, copy in Davis Papers; JWD to Arthur Garfield Hays, Oct. 19, 1942; to Lamont, June 7, 1943; to Hays, Apr. 21, 1943.

6. JWD's letter to Mundt is reprinted in part in *Congressional Record*, 79th Cong., 2nd sess., 5216–17.

7. *Ibid.*

8. Corliss Lamont to JWD, July 1, 1946.

9. JWD to Corliss Lamont, July 9, 1946; confidential interview.

10. JWD to John Lord O'Brian, June 4, 1948; JWD to Howard Mumford Jones, Sept. 27, 1951.

11. Hays to JWD, Dec. 27, 1948; JWD to Hays, Jan. 3, 1949.

12. Burlingham to JWD, Oct. 17, 1949, copy of the Holmes statement enclosed; JWD to Burlingham, Oct. 18, 1949; Burlingham to JWD, Nov. 6, 1950; JWD to Burlingham, Nov. 6, 1950. For a perceptive analysis of Medina's ruling and Hand's opinion, see Milton R. Konvitz, *Expanding Liberties: Freedom's Gains in Postwar America* (New York, 1966), 117ff.

13. Osmand K. Fraenkel to JWD, Oct. 27, 1949, copy of proposed *amicus* brief enclosed.

14. JWD to Fraenkel, Oct. 28, 1949; Sacher v. United States, 343 U.S. 1, 35 (1952). Black said, in part: "I cannot reconcile this summary blasting of legal careers with a fair system of justice. Such a procedure constitutes an overhanging menace to the security of every courtroom advocate in America. The menace is most ominous for lawyers who are obscure, unpopular or defenders of unpopular persons or unorthodox cases." *Ibid.* at 18. Douglas also dissented. Again, see Konvitz, *Expanding Liberties*, 130–32, for analysis.

15. Burlingham to JWD, Feb. 8, 1950; JWD to Burlingham, Feb. 9, 1950; Burlingham to JWD, Feb. 14, 1950; *New York Times*, 1950–1951.

16. Francis Biddle to JWD, Aug. 28, 1950; Fred J. Cook, *The Nightmare Decade: The Life and Times of Senator Joe McCarthy* (New York, 1971), 193.

17. Gus Hall to JWD, Aug. 31, 1950; JWD to Hall, Sept. 6, 1950; *New York Times*, Nov. 18, 1950.

18. "A Publisher Looks at the Law," *The Record*, Vol. 7, No. 1 (Jan. 1952), 14–28, quoted in Martin, *Causes and Conflict*, 275–77.

19. *Ibid.* 277.

20. George Martin to author, Dec. 18, 1969, Jan. 1, Apr. 6, 1970.

21. Martin, *Causes and Conflict*, 279–81.

22. U.S. Congress, House. Select Committee to Investigate Tax-Exempt Foundations. *Hearings*, Dec. 10, 1952. Testimony of John W. Davis, 569ff. Statement prepared for the Carnegie Endowment by John Foster Dulles, Dec. 27, 1948, copy in Davis Papers; Richard D. Challener, "New Light on a

Turning Point in U.S. History," *University: A Princeton Quarterly,* LVI (Spring 1973), 1–3, 28–33.

23. *Ibid.*

24. Alger Hiss to author, Feb. 13, 1973; interview with Alger Hiss.

25. Alistair Cooke, *A Generation on Trial: U.S.A. v. Alger Hiss* (New York, 1950), 55–90; Alger Hiss, *In the Court of Public Opinion* (New York, 1957); Richard M. Nixon, *Six Crises* (New York, 1962, Giant Cardinal Edition) 22–23; Earl Mazo, *Richard Nixon: A Political and Personal Portrait* (New York, 1960 edition), 57. For sympathetic treatments of Dulles' dismissal of Vincent and Davies, see Gerson, *Dulles,* 112, and Michael A. Guhin, *John Foster Dulles: A Statesman and His Times* (New York, 1972), 198–200.

26. Hiss to author, Feb. 13, 1973; Hiss interview.

27. Cooke, *Generation on Trial,* 238–40; Dulles statement, Dec. 27, 1948; Hiss to author, Feb. 13, 1973; Hiss interview; telephone interviews with Miss Anne Winslow and Mrs. Agnese Lockwood; Challener, "New Light," 31.

28. JWD to William L. Marbury, Oct. 6, to David P. Barrows, Nov. 22, 1948; Hiss to author, Feb. 13, 1973; Hiss interview.

29. Hiss to author, Feb. 13, 1973; Hiss interview.

30. Hiss interview; Henry R. Wriston to author, Apr. 9, 1970.

31. Wriston to author, Apr. 9, 1970.

32. *Ibid.;* testimony of Henry R. Wriston, *Hearings,* 184, Dec. 10, 1952; William M. Bullitt to JWD, Dec. 16, 1948.

33. JWD to Bullitt, Dec. 22, and to Earl G. Harrison, Dec. 22, 1948; Philadelphia *Inquirer,* Dec. 17, 1948; *Hearings,* Dec. 10, 1952, 571.

34. JWD to Herbert Brookes, May 29, 1950. Davis also said in a letter to Myron C. Taylor (n. d.): "I am still unconvinced of the guilt of Hiss. I have a profound feeling that the whole story has never been told."

35. *New York Times,* Aug. 5, 10, 19, Sept. 20, 21, 24, Oct. 14, 15, 1952.

36. *Ibid.* Oct. 18, 22, 25, 1952; Rodney Siever, "Adlai Stevenson: an Intellectual Biography" (unpublished Ph.D. dissertation, University of Virginia, 1971).

37. *New York Times,* Oct. 25, 1952; Wriston to author, Apr. 9, 1970; Hiss interview.

38. JWD to Dulles, Dec. 30, 1948; Wriston to author, Apr. 9, 1970; *Hearings,* Dec. 10, 1952, 570.

39. Interview with Lloyd K. Garrison.

40. Most statements and incidents drawn from Philip M. Stern (with the collaboration of Harold P. Green), *The Oppenheimer Case: Security on Trial* (New York, 1970). For Truman, see his *Year of Decisions,* 418.

41. Stern, *Oppenheimer Case.* Compare Stern's close examination of the relationship between Strauss and Oppenheimer with the gloss in Lewis L. Strauss, *Men and Decisions* (New York, Popular Library Edition, 1963), Chapter XIV.

42. Eisenhower, *Mandate For Change,* 310–14; Stern, *Oppenheimer Case,* 191.

43. Cited in Stern, *Oppenheimer Case*, 111.

44. Stern, *Oppenheimer Case*, 43–45, *passim*.

45. *In the Matter of J. Robert Oppenheimer, Texts of Principal Documents and Letters of Personnel Security Board, General Manager, Commissioners, May 27, 1954* (Washington, D.C., 1954), 22, 65.

46. *Ibid.* 837–38, for text of Borden letter; Eisenhower, *Mandate For Change*, 311.

47. Stern, *Oppenheimer Case*, 231–32; *In the Matter of J. Robert Oppenheimer—Transcript of Hearing before Personnel Security Board* (Washington, 1954), 7–20, for Nichols' letter. Stern reports that after the meeting with Strauss, Oppenheimer went to the law offices of Joseph Volpe on K Street, N.W., and there discussed the charges with Volpe and Harry Marks, an attorney who was to perform yeoman service for him. The office had been bugged by the government, presumably some time before, and the entire conversation was recorded. As Stern also notes, in 1967 the Supreme Court ordered a new trial in another case in which the government had eavesdropped on a lawyer-client discussion.

48. Stern, *Oppenheimer Case*, 241, 508. See, in particular, the section, "Responses by Lloyd K. Garrison to Various Questions Asked by Philip M. Stern." 504–46.

49. *Ibid.* 507.

50. *Ibid.* 508–9; Garrison interview.

51. Stern, *Oppenheimer Case*, 255, 273, for McCarthy; *Transcript*, 990, for Garrison.

52. *Texts of Principal Documents*, 19.

53. Letter (name withheld by me) to JWD, June 14, 1954; text of Garrison-Davis letter to Nichols in *Texts of Principal Documents*, 31–36; Garrison to JWD, July 19, 1949; Nichols reply, *ibid.* 39–40. Nichols wrote that the "procedures make no provision for submission of a brief, or for oral argument, when the case then comes to the General Manager for final determination." He added that the Commission would give the brief "very careful consideration," but that it did not "feel that it can accede to your suggestion that there be oral argument as well."

54. Garrison to JWD, May 31, June 10, 1954; Garrison interview; Stern, *Oppenheimer Case*, 519–20; *New York Times*, June 16, 1954, for text of main portion of Garrison brief, which Davis signed as "of counsel."

55. *Texts and Principal Documents*, 41–48.

56. *Ibid.* 51–63, for majority and concurring opinions, 63–67, for Dr. Smyth's dissent; Parmet, *Eisenhower and the American Crusade*, 344.

57. JWD to John S. Stover, July 7, to Ferdinand I. Haber, Oct. 11, 1954.

58. Stern, *Oppenheimer Case*, 455–56. Also see Stern's account, 441–46, of the Senate's vote against confirmation of Strauss for Secretary of Commerce in June and, especially, of the conflicts in his testimony. As Stern writes, the minority report of the commerce committee was remarkably similar to the statements Strauss and his three colleagues on the AEC had made about Oppenheimer: "Lacking in the sincerity and the tolerance required for confirmation . . . guilty of an outright misrepresentation . . . resorted to unneces-

sary untruths . . . has shown a willingness to fit the facts to his preconceived notions . . . lacking in the degree of integrity and competence essential to proper performance of the duties of the office to which he has been nominated."

Notes to Chapter 27

1. *New York Times*, New York *Herald Tribune*, May 13, 14, 1952.

2. For informative summary accounts, see A. H. Raskin in *New York Times*, Apr. 6, 1952, and Mary K. Hammond, "The Steel Strike of 1952," *Current History*, XXIII (Nov. 1952), 285–90. The most comprehensive account of the strike from all points of view is Grant McConnell, *The Steel Seizure of 1952* [The Inter-University Case Program # 52], (Indianapolis, 1960). I have drawn heavily on it, as well as on Alan F. Westin, *The Anatomy of a Constitutional Law Case: Youngstown Sheet and Tube Co. v. Sawyer* (New York, 1959). More specifically, I have used "Basic Steel Industry," in 18 Labor Arbitration Reports at 132, and the statement of Ellis Arnall before the Senate Committee on Labor and Public Welfare, Apr. 16, 1952, reprinted as *Statement on Steel*, S. Doc. 118, 82nd Cong., 2d sess. (1952).

3. McConnell, *Steel Seizure*, 14–15.

4. *Ibid.* 16.

5. *Ibid.* 17; *New York Times*, Apr. 5, 1952; Hammond, "Steel Strike of 1952," 290.

6. Harry S Truman, *Years of Trial and Hope* (New York, 1956), II, 467; McConnell, *Steel Seizure*, 9, 16.

7. JWD to Mrs. August Belmont, July 8, 1952, courtesy of Mrs. Belmont; *Congressionl Record*, 82d Cong., 2nd sess., Apr. 16, 1952, 4014–16.

8. JWD to Republic Steel Corporation, Oct. 27, 1949, copy, courtesy of the Republic Steel Corporation.

9. *Ibid.*

10. *Ibid.*

11. See *The New York Times* during this period for highlights of the testimony; also McConnell, *Steel Seizure*.

12. *Ibid.*

13. McConnell, *Steel Seizure*, 24–26; "Basic Steel Industry: Recommendations of Wage Stabilization Board," 18 L.A. 112 (1952); "Charles E. Wilson's Own Story of Break with Truman," *U.S. News & World Report*, XXXII (May 2, 1952), 11–14; Truman, *Years of Trial and Hope*, 469: text of Truman-Wilson exchange in *New York Times*, Mar. 31, 1952.

14. *New York Times*, Mar. 22, 28, 30, 1952.

15. McConnell, *Steel Seizure*, 31.

16. JWD to Republic Steel Corporation, Mar. 31, 1952, copy, courtesy of Republic Steel Corporation.

17. McConnell, *Steel Seizure*, 31–34.

18. Truman, *Years of Trial and Hope*, II, 469–70; McConnell, *Steel Seizure*, 32.

19. Charles Sawyer, *Concerns of A Conservative Democrat* (Carbondale,

Ill., 1968), 258. See esp. informative notes, 372–81, prepared by Eugene P. Trani.

20. *Public Papers of the Presidents—Harry S. Truman—1952–53,* (Washington, D.C. 1966), 246–50.

21. *Ibid.*

22. Clarence B. Randall, *Over My Shoulder* (Boston, 1956), 215–16.

23. *New York Times,* Apr. 10, 1952.

24. *Ibid.* Randall refused to retract or apologize, but did concede later that the public members had been paid by both sides. *Ibid.* Apr. 26, 1952.

25. See the excellent survey in Westin, *Anatomy,* 44–52. I have supplemented it with statements from *The New York Times* and the *Congressional Record.*

26. *Public Papers,* 250–51; *New York Times,* June 11, 27, 1952. The vote in the House was 228–164.

27. Westin, *Anatomy,* 53–55. For a laudatory article on Pine and Kiendl, see Beverly Smith, "What a Spanking He Gave Truman!" *Saturday Evening Post,* CCXXV (Aug. 2, 1952), 27ff; also see the brief sketch, "Judge Pine—the Man who Said 'No' to the President," *U.S. News & World Report,* XXXII (May 9, 1952), 73.

28. Sawyer, *Concerns,* 261. The transcript is neatly condensed in Westin, *Anatomy,* 56–65. I have used the full record as printed in U.S. Congress, House, *The Steel Seizure Case,* H. Doc. 534, pt. 1, 82nd Cong., 2nd sess., (1952).

29. *Ibid.* 313–16.

30. Freund, *The Supreme Court, 1951 Term,* 66 HARV. L. REV. 89 (1952).

31. *The Steel Seizure Case,* at 371–72.

32. *Ibid.* 378ff.

33. "The President's News Conference of April 24, 1952," *Public Papers,* 290–96; Westin, *Anatomy,* 66–68; *New York Times,* Apr. 28, 1952, for texts of Jones-Truman letters.

34. Youngstown Sheet & Tube Co. v. Sawyer, 103 F. Supp. 509 (D. C. 1952).

35. *Ibid.; New York Herald Tribune,* Apr. 30, 1952.

36. *New York Journal American,* Apr. 30, 1952; Westin, *Anatomy,* 73–74; Sawyer, *Concerns,* 262–63; ACLU Weekly Bulletin #1542, May 19, 1952.

37. McConnell, *Anatomy,* 43.

38. JWD to Herbert R. O'Conor, Apr. 24, to Herbert Brookes, June 12, 1952.

39. E. S. S. Sunderland to JWD, May 9, 1952.

40. Chandler interview; brief reprinted in *The Steel Seizure Case,* 82nd Cong., 2nd Sess., House Doc. No. 534, pt. 2.

41. Interview with Chandler and with various clerks in the Davis Polk offices, fall 1959; Sunderland interview.

42. *New York Herald Tribune,* May 4, 1952.

43. Account of arguments is drawn from *New York Times,* New York *Herald Tribune,* and Washington *Post,* May 13, 14, 1952.

44. *Ibid.*

45. *Ibid.*

46. Washington *Post,* Dec. 7, 1952.

47. *Ibid.* May 13, 1952; Chapter IX, above. Also see Arthur Krock, "In The Nation," *New York Times,* May 13, 1952, for an interesting analysis of the arguments and, especially, the residual power issue.

48. *New York Times,* New York *Herald Tribune,* and Washington *Post,* May 13, 1952.

49. *Ibid.*

50. *Ibid.*

51. JWD to John L. Hall, May 20, 1953.

52. *New York Times,* New York *Herald Tribune,* Washington *Post,* May 13, 1952.

53. *Ibid.*

54. Youngstown Sheet & Tube Co. v. Sawyer, 343 U.S. 579 (1952); *New York Times,* June 3, 1952, for color.

55. Youngstown Sheet & Tube Co. v. Sawyer, 343 U.S. 579 (1952).

56. *Ibid.*

57. *Ibid.*

58. *Ibid.* I have drawn for analysis in considerable part from the superb treatment of the constitutional background and development of the case in John P. Roche, "Executive Power and Domestic Emergency: The Quest for Prerogative," *The Western Political Quarterly,* V (Dec. 1952), 592–618.

59. Youngstown Sheet & Tube Co. v. Sawyer, 343 U.S. 579 (1952).

60. Corwin, *The Steel Seizure Case: A Judicial Brick Without Straw,* 53 COLUM L. REV. 53 (1953); Freund, *The Supreme Court, 1951 Term,* 66 HARV. L. REV. 89 (1952); Glendon A. Schubert, Jr., *The Presidency in the Courts* (Minneapolis, 1957), 25, 326.

61. "The American Lesson," *Time,* LIX (June 9, 1952), 17–18; Freund, *Supreme Court.*

62. JWD to John L. Hall, May 20, 1952, to Thomas B. Sweeney, June 20, 1952.

63. Charles Burlingham, May 16, 1952; John L. Hall, May 19, 1952; Learned Hand to JWD, May 13, 1952.

64. Reproduced in a letter to Scotland G. Highland, sender unknown, Aug. 14, 1952, copy in Davis Papers; JWD to George S. Wallace, May 19, 1952, to Charles G. Middleton, Oct. 9, 1952.

65. JWD to Mrs. August Belmont, July 8, 1952, courtesy of Mrs. Belmont.

Notes to Chapter 28

1. James F. Byrnes, *All In One Lifetime* (New York, 1958), 412; Howard H. Quint, *Profile in Black and White: A Frank Portrait of South Carolina* (Washington, D.C., 1958), 16; James F. Byrnes to author, July 20, 1965; interview with Harry F. Byrd.

2. Numerous interviews; Davis, *Legacy of Love,* 232; Meagher interview. For example, Porter Chandler, a strong integrationist and later chairman of

the New York City Board of Higher Education, which instituted "open admissions," helped his wife found the Catholic Interracial Council of Washington, D.C. in 1944.

3. All quotations drawn from the informative and balanced work, Robert Lewis Terry, "J. Waties Waring: Spokesman For Racial Justice In The New South," (unpublished Ph.D. dissertation, University of Utah, 1970). Also see "Mrs. Waring Meets the Press," *American Mercury*, LXX (May 1950), 562–69; and *New York Times*, Nov. 1, 1968.

4. Quint, *Profile in Black and White*, 13; Harry S. Ashmore, *The Negro and The Schools* (Chapel Hill, 1954), 156ff., for much other statistical data.

5. Terry, "J. Waties Waring," 191–93.

6. Byrnes, *All In One Lifetime*, 407–08; Quint, *Profile in Black and White*, 16–17.

7. "Mr. Justice Parker," *New Republic*, LXII (Apr. 2, 1930), 177–78.

8. Richard L. Watson, Jr., "The Defeat of Judge Parker: A Study in Pressure Groups and Politics," *Mississippi Valley Historical Review*, L (Sept. 1963), 213–34; *John J. Parker: Senior Circuit Judge: Fourth Circuit*, 32 A.B.A.J. 856 (1946); Lowitt, *Norris: The Persistence of a Progressive*, 438–39; Terry, "J. Waties Waring," 70.

9. *The New York Times*, May 29, 30, 1951, has a reasonably long account of the oral arguments.

10. Briggs *et al.* v. Elliott *et al.*, 98 F. Supp. 529 (E.D.S.C. 1951).

11. *Ibid.*

12. Briggs *et al.* v. Elliott *et al.*, 103 F. Supp. 920 (E.D.S.C. 1952), describes the equalization program; Briggs v. Elliott, 342 U.S. 350 (1952); also, Albert P. Blaustein and Clarence Clyde Ferguson, Jr., *Desegregation and The Law: The Meaning and Effect of the School Segregation Cases* (New York, 1962, 2d ed. rev.), 47; interview with Thurgood Marshall.

13. *New York Times*, Jan. 18, 1968.

14. Sunderland and Meagher interviews; JWD to Mrs. J. M. Proskauer, Oct. 23, 1951, courtesy of Judge Proskauer.

15. See JWD to Mrs. Mary C. Collins, Dec. 18, 1952, wherein he wrote that "voluntary association" is "certainly a fundamental right." After his second oral argument, Davis encircled the exerpt from the *Plessy* opinion as quoted above on a clipping of an article, "The Fading Line," from *Time*, LXII (Dec. 21, 1953), 15.

16. Pine interview; JWD to Hale Houston, Nov. 17, 1927; Sunderland interview; L. Hollingsworth Wood to JWD, July 28, 1941; Davis, *Legacy of Love*, 232; Chandler interview.

17. See, for example, JWD to Charles Warren, Nov. 16, 1943, in which he supported poll taxes.

18. William H. Lewis to JWD, Dec. 16, 1929; JWD to Walter White, Feb. 4, 1930.

19. Roger Baldwin, Nov. 15, 1933; Sam S. Leibowitz to JWD, Oct. 24, 1934; JWD to Leibowitz, Nov. 1, 1934; to Norman S. Burdett, Jan. 20, 1936; Dan T. Carter, *Scottsboro: A Tragedy of the American South* (Baton Rouge, 1969), 316–22. Leibowitz won the appeal, with Hughes making a significant

expansion of judicial power. See *Norris v. Alabama*, 294 U.S. 587 at 589–90 (1935).

20. JWD to Walter White, Jan. 22, 1935; *New York Times,* Feb. 28, 1945; to Matthew P. Andrews, July 19, 1945; Finletter *et al.* to JWD, Apr. 6, 1948.

21. Alice N. Proskauer to JWD, Oct. 21, 1951.

22. JWD to Alice N. Proskauer, Oct. 23, 1951.

23. JWD to Robert McC. Figg, Sept. 24, 1951.

24. JWD to James F. Byrnes, Dec. 23, 1952.

25. *Ibid.*

26. The standard work on the Fourteenth Amendment is Joseph B. James, *The Framing of the Fourteenth Amendment* (Urbana, Ill., 1956). Also see: Graham, *The Fourteenth Amendment and School Segregation,* 3 BUFF. L. REV. 1 (1953); Bickel, *The Original Understanding and the Segregation Decision,* 69 HARV. L. REV. 1 (1955); and Robert J. Harris, *The Quest for Equality* (Baton Rouge, 1960). For Sumner's efforts to enact school legislation see Alfred H. Kelly, "The Congressional Controversy over School Segregation, 1867–1875," *American Historical Review,* LXIV (Apr. 1959), 537–63, and David Donald, *Charles Sumner and The Rights of Man* (New York, 1970). Hughes' statement was made in Home Building and Loan Association v. Blaisdell, 290 U.S. 398, 443 (1934), Marshall's in McCulloch v. Maryland, 4 Wheat. 316, 407 (1819). I have been guided generally by the admirable study by Blaustein and Ferguson, *Desegregation;* also by Alexander Bickel's perceptive treatment of legislative intent in his *The Least Dangerous Branch* (Indianapolis, 1962), 55–57. See also Harper v. Va. State Bd. of Elections, 383 U.S. 663 at 670 (1966) (Black, J., dissenting).

27. See Blaustein and Ferguson, *Desegregation,* 100–102; also, "The Vinson Court Prepares for the Warren Court," in Milton R. Konvitz, *Expanding Liberties: Freedom's Gains in Postwar America* (New York, 1966), 245–55.

28. Plessy v. Ferguson, 163 U.S. 537 (1896).

29. Konvitz, *Expanding Liberties;* Alfred H. Kelly and Winfred A. Harbison, *The American Constitution* (New York, 1963, 3rd ed.), 928; Shelley v. Kraemer, 334 U.S. 1 (1948); Clark, *Book Review,* 36 CHIC. L. REV. 239, 241 (1968); JWD to Farris R. Russell, Oct. 18, 1951.

30. Franklin B. Lord, Oct. 17, 1951, and Frederick D. Bolles to JWD, same date; Herbert Brookes to JWD, May 5, 1954.

31. *E.g.,* JWD to Frederick D. Bolles and to Franklin B. Lord, Oct. 17, 1951, to John P. Zebley, Nov. 24, 1952, to Walter White, Dec. 23, 1952.

32. JWD to Robert McC. Figg, Sept. 29, 1952; Brief for Appellants, No. 2, in Brown v. Board of Education, 347 U.S. 483 (1954); Cahn, *Jurisprudence,* 30 N.Y.U. L. REV. 150 at 157–58, 167 (1955). For further discussion of the quality of the experts' testimony, see Clark, *The Desegregation Cases: Criticism of the Social Scientist's Role,* 5 VILL. L. REV. 224 (1959), and Van Den Haag, *Social Science Testimony in the Desegregation Cases—A Reply to Professor Kenneth Clark,* 6 VILL. L. REV. 69 (1960). For a commentary on social science and the race question generally, see the revised edition of I. A. Newby, *Challenge to the Court: Social Scientists and the Defense of Segregation* (Baton Rouge, 1969).

33. JWD to Robert McC. Figg, July 11, Sept. 3, 1952; Brief for Appellees, No. 2, at 6, 17, 18; Brief for Appellants, No. 2, at 42, 28, 13. Marshall's brief further contended that the desirability of maintaining public peace was no rationale for the deprivation of constitutional rights (43).

34. JWD to Figg, Sept. 3, 1952; Brief for Appellees, No. 2, at 19, 20–23, 34. Compare Kenneth B. Clark and Mamie P. Clark, "Racial Identification and Preference in Negro Children," in Eleanor Maccaby, Theodore M. Newcomb, and Eugene L. Hartley (eds.), Readings in Social Psychology (New York, 1958, 3rd. ed.), 602–11, with his testimony in the lower court.

35. Du Bois' statement is in "Does the Negro Need Separate Schools?" Journal of Negro Education, IV (July 1935) 328, 330. For a sensitive treatment of Du Bois' move to separatism, see Elliott M. Rudwick, W. E. B. Du-Bois, Propagandist of the Negro Protest (New York, Atheneum Ed., 1968), 272–85.

36. James F. Byrnes to JWD, Sept. 8, 1952.

37. T. Justin Moore to JWD, July 25; JWD to Moore, July 28, 1952; Paul L. Wilson to author, Jan. 22, 1973.

38. JWD to Figg, Oct. 16, 1952; JWD to Alice Proskauer, Oct. 3, 1952; Alice Proskauer to JWD, n. d., JWD to Figg, Oct. 9, 1952; Davis finally concluded that someone had simply decided that it would be wise to "avoid agitating" the matter during the presidential campaign. JWD to P. F. Henderson, Oct. 16, 1952.

39. "The Segregation Issue," Time, LX (Dec. 22, 1952), 12–13; Quint, Profile in Black and White, 16–17.

40. The best characterization and brief biography is John P. MacKenzie, "Thurgood Marshall," in Leon Friedman and Fred L. Israel (eds.), The Justices of the United States Supreme Court 1789–1969: Their Lives and Major Opinions (4 vols., New York, 1969), IV, 3063–89.

41. Ibid.; Leon Friedman (ed.), Argument: The Oral Argument Before The Supreme Court in Brown v. Board of Education of Topeka, 1952–55 (New York, 1969) contains the full transcript of the oral arguments in all the suits.

42. MacKenzie, "Thurgood Marshall," as supplemented by numerous contemporary newspaper characterizations.

43. Marshall interview; "The Segregation Issue," Time, LX (Dec. 22, 1952), 12–13.

44. Paul L. Wilson to author, Jan. 22, 1973.

45. Ibid.; Friedman (ed.), Argument, 26–33.

46. Friedman (ed.), Argument, 36–51.

47. Ibid., 51–61; Paul L. Wilson to author, Jan. 22, 1973. Also see, in the Introduction to Friedman (ed.), Argument, the thoughtful analysis of Marshall's and Davis' arguments by Yale Kamizar.

48. Paul L. Wilson to author, Jan. 22, 1973.

49. JWD to Arthur Cole, Dec. 16; to John J. Cornwell, Dec. 17, 1952.

50. S. Sidney Ulmer, "Earl Warren and the Brown Decision," Journal of Politics, XXXII (Aug. 1971), 689–702. This article is based exclusively on

the recently opened Papers and Diary of the late Justice Burton in the Library of Congress.

51. Brown v. Board of Education, 345 U.S. 972 (1953).

52. Time figure supplied by Davis Polk; James F. Byrnes to author, July 20, 1965; Byrnes, *All in One Lifetime*, 412.

53. JWD to James F. Byrnes, July 6; Byrnes to JWD June 20; JWD to Byrnes, July 6, 1953.

54. Memorandum on Meeting of June 17, 1953, prepared by T. Justin Moore, copy in the Davis Papers.

55. Memorandum, Taggart Whipple, June 3, 1971, courtesy of Ralph M. Carson. Brief for Appellees, No. 2, at 3–4, 77, *infra* and appendices. Davis Polk was slow to complete its assignment, so the Virginia group also undertook research on the origins of the Fourteenth Amendment. See Thomas P. Gay, *The Hunton Williams Firm and Its Predecessors: 1877–1954* (Richmond, Va., 1971), I, 314.

56. Brief for Appellees, No. 2; speech by Alfred H. Kelly at the annual meeting of the American Historical Association, Dec. 28, 1961, copy, courtesy of Dr. Kelly. Also see Carleton Putnam, *Race and Reality: A Search for Solutions* (Washington, D.C., 1967), 71–72.

57. Kelly, speech, AHA.

58. *Ibid.* Also see Alfred H. Kelly, "The School Segregation Case," in John A. Garraty (ed.), *Quarrels That Have Shaped the Constitution* (New York, 1966), 243–68.

59. U.S. Congress, Senate, Committee on the Judiciary. *Hearings on the Nomination of Thurgood Marshall, of New York, to be an Associate Justice of the Supreme Court of the United States,* July 13, 14, 18, 19, and 24, 1967. Statement by Alfred H. Kelly, 184–86.

60. Arthur Larson, *Eisenhower: The President Nobody Knew* (New York, 1968), 124. For Eisenhower's curious rationalization of—really, a simple statement on—his failure to give moral leadership, see Eisenhower, *Mandate for Change*, 229–230; for a thoughtful analysis of Congress' intent, see the long appendix in Alexander M. Bickel, *Politics and the Warren Court* (New York, 1965). The first government brief, prepared in 1952 under the direction of then Attorney General James P. McGranery, stood strongly on the *McLaurin* and *Sweatt* decisions and declared that " 'separate but equal' is wrong as a matter of constitutional law, history, and policy."

61. JWD to James F. Byrnes, June (n. d.), Sept. 8; to T. Justin Moore, Dec. 2, 1953.

62. *New York Times*, Dec. 8, 1953; "May it Please the Court . . . ," *Time*, LXII (Dec. 21, 1953), 15–19.

63. *Ibid.* Also see the full sketch by Anthony Lewis in Friedman and Israel (eds.), *Justice of the . . . Supreme Court*, IV, 2721–46.

64. I have drawn on contemporary press accounts for color, on Friedman (ed.), *Argument*, for the actual texts of the oral arguments.

65. Friedman (ed.), *Argument*, 194–206 and 233–40, for Marshall's argument and rebuttal.

66. Davis, *Legacy of Love,* 232; "May it Please the Court . . . ," 18–19.

67. Friedman (ed.), *Argument,* 206–17, reprints Davis' argument in full. He did not make a rebuttal.

68. Interviews with Thurgood Marshall and Stanley Reed; Bickel, *The Least Dangerous Branch,* 249.

69. Ulmer, "Earl Warren and the Brown Decision." I have checked the entries in Burton's diary in the Library of Congress against Ulmer's account. Ulmer is full and accurate.

70. Brown v. Board of Education, 347 U.S. 483 (1954).

71. Putnam, *Race and Reality,* 70; Julia D. Healy, Meagher, Marshall, Proskauer, and Carson interviews; JWD to Robert Figg, May 20, 24, 1954.

72. Numerous interviews; JWD to William H. Timbers, June 2, 1954; to Robert Figg, May 20, 1954; to T. Justin Moore Oct. 25, 1954.

73. Quint, *Profile in Black and White,* 50; J. Harvie Wilkinson III, *Harry Byrd and the Changing Face of Virginia Politics: 1945–1966* (Charlottesville, Va., 1968), 113.

Notes to Chapter 29

1. John Dos Passos, "Old Jeffersonian," New York *Herald Tribune,* Dec. 7, 1952.

2. *Ibid.*

3. *Ibid.*

4. *Ibid.*

5. JWD to Walter C. Preston, Mar. 14, 1947; to Samuel J. Harris, Dec. 24, 1952; to George S. Wallace, Nov. 24, 1950.

6. JWD to A. Judson Findley, Mar. 27, 1955; to Hale Houston, Dec. 9, 1943. His average annual income from 1946 through 1954 was $147,000. Figures supplied by firm.

7. *New York Times,* Apr. 13, 14, 1953.

8. *Ibid.* Apr. 14, 1953.

9. Copy of Webster's statement in Davis Papers; George A. Brownell and Ralph M. Carson, "John W. Davis," Association of the Bar *Yearbook* (1955), 28–29; copy of Davis' response, Dec. 20, 1954, Davis Papers.

10. JWD to Emma Davis, Apr. 16, 1927; to Daniel M. Ogden, Apr. 11, 1947; to Arthur C. Murray, Mar. 6, 1945; to Michael Benedum, July 11, 1949; to Kenneth McKellar, Dec. 5, 1941; to Viscount Simon, May 1, 1953.

11. Cannon interview; JWD to Cornelia Bassel, Aug. 24, 1950.

12. Interview with Edgar A. Lawrence; JWD to Randolph Shields, May 1, 1954, courtesy of Shields family.

13. JWD to Cornelia Bassel, Sept. 20, 1951.

14. JWD to Eleanor Belmont, Dec. 29, 1951, Nov. 11, 1947, Dec. 12, 1944, Aug. 29, 1944, Mar. 13, 1951, all courtesy of Mrs. Belmont. The story about Davis' dream was related to me by half a dozen different people.

15. Interview with Mrs. Eleanor Belmont.

16. JWD to Mrs. John Preston, Aug. 6, 1952; to Ramon Sender, Oct. 24,

1952; Ramon Sender to JWD, n. d., in which he also thanks him "for the innumerable things that you have done for me through the years."

17. Hanson interview; JWD to Alfred Hanson, Dec. 26, 1951.

18. Hanson interview; JWD to William H. Frampton, Apr. 24, 1951.

19. Mrs. Walter Preston to JWD, n. d.; Anne Custis Preston to JWD, n. d.; JWD to John J. D. Preston, Nov. 13, 1950.

20. JWD to John J. D. Preston, Nov. 13, 1950.

21. Lawrence, Dorsey Potter, and Mrs. Frank L. Polk interviews and several confidential sources; Julia Davis, June 18, 1951; Charles P. Healy to JWD, June 21, 1951; JWD to Randolph Shields, Sept. 16, 1951, courtesy of Shields family; Julia D. Healy to author, June 28, 1971.

22. Lawrence and Hanson interviews.

23. *Ibid.*

24. Numerous notes and postcards in Davis' medical file, courtesy of Dr. Lawrence; Lawrence interview.

25. Lawrence interview; interview with Mary Elizabeth Barron.

26. JWD to Frank A. Nelson, Sept. 7, 1949; to Dorsey Potter, July 16, 1962; to Randolph Shields, Sept. 16, 1951, courtesy of Shields family.

27. Felix Frankfurter to JWD, Dec. 6, 1948, Frankfurter Papers Box 10; Dwight D. Eisenhower to JWD, Apr. 15, 1953; Davis, *Legacy of Love*, 234.

28. JWD to Edgar A. Lawrence, Feb. 4, 1955, medical file; Sunderland, Healy, and Hanson interviews.

29. *New York Times*, Mar. 29, 1955. Davis left the bulk of his estate, which came to a little over a million dollars, to his daughter. Of this, about half went to taxes. He left $31,500 to charities, including $25,000 to Washington and Lee and $2500 to the Clarksburg Public Library. All his servants received six months' pay and housing, *ibid.* Mar. 31, 1955.

30. Washington *Post,* Mar. 29, 1955.

INDEX